Fighting Heart Disease and Stroke

THE NEW AMERICAN HEART ASSOCIATION COOKBOOK

Sixth Edition

Published by Clarkson Potter/Publisher, New York, New York. Member of the Crown Publishing Group, a division of Random House, Inc.

www.randomhouse.com

Originally published in hardcover by Clarkson Potter/Publishers in 1998.

Earlier editions of this work were published in 1973, 1975, 1979, 1984, 1991, and 1998.

Your contribution to the American Heart Association supports research that helps make publications like this possible. For more information, call 1-800-AHA-USA1 (1-800-242-8721) or contact us online at www.americanheart.org.

Printed in the United States of America

Art direction by Naomi Osnos
Book design by Maura Fadden Rosenthal

Library of Congress Cataloging-in-Publication data
The New American Heart Association cookbook/American Heart Association—25th anniversary ed.
p. cm.
1. Heart—Diseases—Diet therapy—Recipes. I. American Heart Association.
RC684.D5 A44 2001
641.5'6311—dc21

2001133029

ISBN: 0-609-80890-7

10 9 8 7 6 5

Sixth Edition

Front cover: Grilled Lemon-Sage Chicken (page 200)

PREFACE

A lot has changed in the quarter century since the *American Heart Association Cookbook* first appeared. Within that 25-year span, American lifestyles and attitudes have undergone many dramatic shifts. Perhaps no changes are more far reaching than those in our approach to nutrition and health.

In 1973, the American Heart Association published the first edition of this cookbook. At that time, researchers were just beginning to establish cause-and-effect links between high fat consumption and high blood cholesterol, a major risk factor for heart disease. Now we know beyond a shadow of a doubt that too much dietary fat raises the blood cholesterol and increases heart attack risk. This is especially true of saturated fat. As a result, tens of millions of Americans have adopted more-healthful eating patterns and permanently changed the way they buy and prepare food.

Seven years have passed since we published the fifth edition of this cookbook. The rate of change in Americans' food choices has accelerated tremendously during that time. Thousands of new fat-free and low-fat foods unheard-of in 1991 are easy to find in today's marketplace. That means it's easier than ever before for us to enjoy our favorite dishes and still follow a heart-healthy diet. Another factor is that Congress has enacted a law that requires all retail food product labels to give essential nutrition information. This allows us to tell at a glance how many calories and how much total fat, saturated fat, cholesterol, fiber, and sodium the food product contains. These labels reduce the guesswork and uncertainty that plagued so many grocery shoppers in the past. In response to these developments, we have designed this sixth edition of the *American Heart Association Cookbook* to be a completely new resource, one that can help you take maximum advantage of the new foods now widely available.

We have reevaluated every recipe that appeared in the fifth edition. We kept our favorites (and yours, too, we hope) and updated many of them. (We also renamed a number of recipes to describe more accurately what the dishes contain. If you have trouble finding an old favorite, try looking in the index for a recipe title that describes the dish.) In addition, we've added more than 150 totally new recipes. Many of these are bound to become your favorites. We've added several time-savers, including microwave and bread machine instructions. Also, we list how much of a produce item you need to buy to yield enough for the recipe.

AHA scientists now agree that dietary fiber can help lower blood cholesterol. To assist you with your menu selection, we now give the fiber analysis of recipes, along with the analysis of other nutrients.

We also updated the text to help you stay abreast of the latest research findings relating to nutrition and health. Medical researchers are closer than ever to understanding how cholesterol and fats in the blood contribute to the development of heart disease and stroke. They are also learning more about how various vitamins in the diet help prevent disease. Furthermore, researchers are unlocking new secrets about the role of heredity and how it interacts with lifestyle and environment to produce health or disease. We can't control heredity, of course. We can, however, make lifestyle choices that promote good health and help stave off illness. We can be physically active. We can quit smoking or, better yet, never start. We can avoid eating or drinking too much. We can make every effort to keep our blood pressure and weight under control. And we can make sure that the foods we eat help protect our health instead of increasing our risk of disease.

Since 1973, when the first edition of this cookbook was published, we have dramatically changed how we eat. Many of these changes have resulted from the AHA's efforts in public education and advocacy. However, today's AHA dietary recommendations aren't all that different from the ones we published in 1973—a sign that research has been on the right track for at least that long. The AHA still emphasizes the need to eat a wide variety of foods and to limit saturated fat, cholesterol, and sodium. In this sixth edition of the cookbook, we use the new Healthy Heart Food Pyramid to simplify our nutrition guidelines.

We updated information on shopping, cooking, how to adapt recipes, quick and easy foods, menus for special occasions, and science related to cholesterol. You'll find all this in the appendixes that follow the recipes—the heart of the book. Along with its hundreds of great recipes, this book brings a positive, upbeat message—we can follow a health-building, nutritionally sound diet without sacrificing any of the enjoyment of good food. We can treat ourselves and our loved ones to delicious meals without worrying or feeling guilty about hidden health risks that might be lurking among the goodies. This is the whole purpose of the sixth edition. It's a cookbook for everyone who loves the art of good cooking, the pleasure of good eating, and the good times that go along with them.

ACKNOWLEDGMENTS

AHA Senior Science Consultant: Mary Winston, Ed.D., R.D.

AHA Nutrition Science Consultant: Terry Bazzarre, Ph.D.

AHA Managing Editor: Jane Anneken Ruehl

AHA Senior Editor: Janice Roth Moss

AHA Editor: Ann Melugin Williams

Recipe Developers: Claire Criscuolo
Sarah Fritschner
FRP
Nancy S. Hughes
Carol Ritchie
Marjorie Steenson
Linda Foley Woodrum

Recipe Consultant: Carol Ritchie

Writer: Bill Sloan

Nutrient Analyses: FRP

Scores of individuals have contributed their skills and devoted service to producing the six editions of the *American Heart Association Cookbook* compiled and published over the past 25 years. These people include amateur and professional cooks, secretaries, typists, proofreaders, writers, editors, and some of this country's most outstanding authorities on health and nutrition. Along the way, each has contributed something special in the evolution and development of one of the world's most popular and widely used cookbooks.

When the idea for such a cookbook was first conceived in the early 1970s, no one was more supportive or provided more initial resources than the members of the AHA's Nutrition Committee and the Subcommittee of Dietitians and Nutritionists. Singled out for special thanks in the cookbook's first edition were committee chairpersons René Bine, Jr., M.D.; John Mueller, M.D.; Eleanor Williams, Ph.D.; and Virginia Stucky.

In 1972 the public was beginning to get the AHA's message that eating less fat and less cholesterol could reduce heart disease risk. However, there were almost no cookbooks to help the home cook prepare healthful meals. Campbell Moses, M.D., AHA's medical director at that time, saw this as an opportunity for the organization to help consumers make the dietary changes it was promoting. For a health organization run by volunteers, it was a long journey from the vision to the published book. Without the leadership and guidance of Dr. Moses, that first volume might never have seen the light of day.

Dedicated American Heart Association volunteers and staff gathered tasty, healthful recipes from kitchens across the nation to form the nucleus of the AHA's first book.

Mary Winston, Ed.D., R.D., acted as nutrition consultant for the first edition and has left her mark on every one of the six editions of this cookbook. Her exceptional knowledge of nutrition, her call for realism, and her dedication to quality and readability are evidenced throughout the cookbook's history.

Ruthe Eshleman, Ph.D., also exerted a long-time positive influence on the cookbook, serving as an editor for the first four editions. She recently retired as associate professor of nutrition and dietetics at the University of Rhode Island.

The two most recent editions of the cookbook testify to the awe-inspiring organizational skills of AHA Managing Editor Jane Anneken Ruehl. She always manages to keep "the big picture" in front of recipe developers, freelancers, and staff.

Over the years, crucial support has come from past and present senior staff members and advisors in the AHA national headquarters, including Richard Hurley, M.D.; Wallace G. Frasher, Jr., M.D.; Dudley H. Hafner; M. Cass Wheeler; Sam Inman; and Rodman D. Starke, M.D.

To those who had the original vision and to all who have played a part in the success of our "Big Red Cookbook" during the past quarter-century, hats off and many thanks!

CONTENTS

RECIPES

APPENDIXES

INTRODUCTION

"Eat your meat and potatoes, or you can't have any dessert."

"Drink all your milk, or you'll never be big and strong."

"Clean your plate. You shouldn't let food go to waste."

Few of us made it through childhood and adolescence without hearing these and other mealtime admonitions repeated over and over again. Now that we're adults, these sayings often linger in our subconscious. They still lead us to associate certain foods with fun and enjoyment and others with an unpleasant chore. Consequently, many of us draw a huge mental distinction between foods we identify as "fun stuff" and those with the unsavory reputation of being "good for us."

Vast recent increases in our knowledge about nutrition—especially its relationship to health and disease—have revealed the fallacy of many of those old "truisms" about the food we eat. For example, if the meat on your plate is deep-fried and the potatoes are drenched in gravy, it may be wise to skip them and go straight to a dessert of fat-free frozen yogurt. Likewise, if your glass holds fat-laden whole milk instead of fat-free milk, it may raise your blood cholesterol level even as it's making you "big and strong."

NEW FOODS, NEW RULES

The rules have changed, and so have the kinds of food available. This cookbook has two main functions. One is to prove that healthful food can also be zestful food. The other is to help you choose foods and create meals that are both deliciously appealing and healthful. In addition to the wonderful recipes, the appendixes also will help you. For instance, you'll find tips on shopping for low-fat foods (see appendix A) and cooking with your heart in mind (see appendix B).

However, even with the convenience of new fat-free and low-fat foods, one thing *hasn't* changed. No one can force you to cut down on the saturated fat in your diet today. No one can make you consume enough fiber, complex carbohydrates, or vitamins and minerals to get the health benefits they can provide. You alone have the power to decide whether you want to eat healthfully. If you can do this without spending any more time, effort, or money, and without sacrificing any taste, enjoyment, or convenience, why not? That's what this cookbook is all about.

DIET AND DISEASE

We've known for a long time that nutrition and health are closely related. Just 40 or 50 years ago, our main dietary concerns involved diseases, such as pellagra, scurvy, rickets, goiter, and anemia, caused by nutritional deficiencies.

Today, most of these diseases are rare to nonexistent in North America. Now we're more concerned with chronic, life-threatening disorders that we can set in motion through nutritional excess. These disorders include coronary heart disease, stroke, cancer, and diabetes. Eating too many rich, fatty foods can increase the risk of coronary heart disease, cancer, and obesity. In addition, obesity can lead to the development of diabetes in people with a family history of the disorder. Eating too much salt has been linked to high blood pressure, a major risk factor for both heart disease and stroke. Scientific research has shown an indisputable relationship between diet and these diseases. It also has shown a secondary link between diet and stroke, since both heart disease and high blood pressure are major risk factors for stroke. (For a detailed discussion of heart disease and atherosclerosis, see appendix F or go to the AHA's website, www.americanheart.org.)

DIET AND RISK FACTORS

High blood cholesterol is a major risk factor for heart disease. Reducing dietary cholesterol and saturated fat can decrease blood cholesterol to a desirable level.

Diet can also alter other risk factors. Obesity, caused by overeating and too little physical activity, can lead to the development of diabetes in someone with the genetic tendency toward the disease. Obesity and diabetes are major risk factors for heart disease. Losing weight often results in lowered blood pressure, blood sugar, and blood cholesterol levels.

Our recipes can be used with a weight-loss or weight-maintenance eating plan. In addition to being low in total fat, saturated fat, and cholesterol and moderate in sodium, most of them have been modified to decrease total calories. The high-calorie recipes are intended only for special occasions.

A diet high in sodium is often implicated as a contributor to high blood pressure, another important risk factor for heart disease and stroke. Although the relationship hasn't been proved, compelling evidence suggests that it's wise to avoid too much salt in your diet.

In the nutrient analysis with each recipe, we've included the sodium content. We've tried to keep salt and other high-sodium items to a minimum in the recipes. New products, such as very low sodium Worcestershire sauce, make that easier. You can find more low-salt recipes in the *American Heart Association Low-Salt Cookbook, Second Edition.*

If you have high blood pressure, congestive heart failure, or edema, your doctor can help you determine how much sodium is safe for you.

AMERICAN HEART ASSOCIATION'S SEVEN STEPS TO GOOD NUTRITION

1. Eat at least five servings of fruits and vegetables daily.
2. Eat at least six servings of grain products daily.
3. Eat no more than 6 ounces (cooked weight) of lean meat, fish, or skinless poultry per day. Have at least two servings of fish per week.
4. Balance food intake with physical activity to achieve and maintain a healthy weight.
5. Choose a diet low in saturated fat, trans fat, and cholesterol and moderate in salt (sodium) and sugar. Eat less than 10 percent of your calories as saturated fat. Limit yourself to less than 300 milligrams (mg) of cholesterol and less than 2,400 mg of sodium daily. (If you have had a heart attack or have coronary heart disease, the limits are lower. Your saturated fat intake should be less than 7 percent of your total calories, and your cholesterol intake should be less than 200 milligrams per day.)
6. Include fat-free and low-fat dairy products, legumes, poultry and lean meats in your eating plan.
7. If you drink, limit yourself to one drink per day if you are a woman and two drinks per day if you are a man.

FATS

We're still learning about the composition of fats and the effects that various types of fat have on blood cholesterol. It's a complex subject, but it helps to understand a few basics.

- Foods from all animal sources contain dietary cholesterol. Plants don't contain cholesterol.
- Foods from animals also contain saturated fat. So do a few vegetable fats, such as coconut and palm oil.

- Chicken, turkey, and seafood contain less saturated fat than does red meat.
- Most fat in plants is polyunsaturated and monounsaturated.

Most fat-bearing foods contain some of all three types of fat—saturated, polyunsaturated, and monounsaturated. Although their effect on cholesterol is similar to that of polyunsaturated fats, monounsaturated fats may have some advantages. A high intake of polyunsaturated fats may promote cancer and/or gallstones, recent research indicates. Monounsaturated fats don't have this liability. Also, "monos" aren't as susceptible to chemical changes that make it easier for cholesterol to build up in the arteries.

SODIUM

For the general public, a daily limit of 6 grams of sodium chloride—or 2,400 milligrams of sodium—is recommended. That's 1 teaspoon of table salt per day. This includes salt in prepared foods, not just the salt you add to food in cooking or at the table.

Thanks to the new nutrition labels now required on all packaged foods, there's no longer any guesswork about how much saturated fat, cholesterol, and sodium each product contains. One quick look at the label can tell you how—or whether—a certain food fits into a healthful diet.

THE HEALTHY HEART FOOD PYRAMID

Eating a variety of foods in balanced amounts is the only sure way to get the nutrients required for good health. Sometimes, though, it may seem a little complicated. In our hurried, fast-paced world, it's easy to get stuck in a doughnuts-and-coffee, burgers-and-fries rut. It's tempting even to skip some meals. The AHA has an illustration to help you visualize and remember what you need for good nutrition. It's called the Healthy Heart Food Pyramid, and it looks like this:

Healthy Heart Food Pyramid

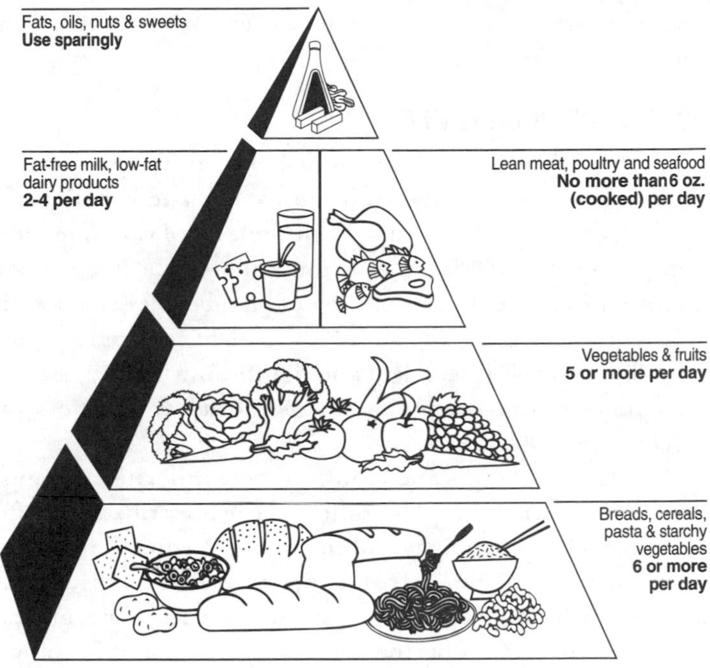

The Food Pyramid's foundation consists of breads, cereals, pasta, and starchy vegetables. These bulky, satisfying foods are high in complex carbohydrates and low in fat. The next-largest section is made up of vegetables and fruits that are rich in fiber, vitamins, and minerals. They're virtually fat free. Then comes a smaller section, one side of which is occupied by fat-free milk and nonfat and low-fat dairy products. The other side has lean meat, poultry, and seafood. These are the foods that supply vital protein and calcium, but they also contain fat. That's why they occupy a smaller portion of the pyramid. Finally, at the very top of the pyramid are the foods that rank at the bottom of our nutritional needs. These are discretionary "now-and-then" foods, such as fats, oils, nuts, and sweets. They contain mostly fat and sugar and are high in calories. They should be eaten very sparingly.

Think about what kinds of food you eat on an average day. How do they stack up when compared with this pyramid? Are the sections in the right order? If not, beware. Too much of those top-of-the-pyramid foods can mean a bulging waistline, soaring cholesterol level, and sharply increased odds of serious disease.

One of the easiest ways to stay within the AHA's dietary guidelines is to base your eating patterns on the Food Pyramid. By following its deceptively simple outline, you'll automatically be adhering to the AHA's recommendations.

A DIET FOR OLD AND YOUNG ALIKE

Since 1983, the AHA has recommended the same type of diet for all healthy persons over the age of two. It's just as safe and beneficial for children and teenagers as it is for adults. High cholesterol isn't something people should wait until their 40s or 50s to think about. The Food Pyramid diet may help reduce or prevent the rapid rise of blood cholesterol seen in many 20- and 30-year-olds in our country. If overweight children are put on this diet, they will most likely lose weight and significantly reduce associated risk factors. Feeding children wisely at home should at least promote good eating habits for their adult years.

Some people, both adults and children, have inherited metabolic patterns that require special diets. These diets can be prescribed only after studies of the person's body chemistry. All children who come from families with a history of high blood cholesterol or premature heart disease or stroke should have their blood fats and lipoproteins measured periodically.

As you use this book to apply the principles of the Food Pyramid to your daily meals, you'll find that it offers the variety and appeal of other major cookbooks. In addition, every recipe in the following pages has been carefully analyzed for use in an overall plan of healthful eating.

BALANCE AND VARIETY

Another feature of this book is that, except for a few of the "now-and-then" foods, its recipes avoid adding the kind of "empty" calories that provide no real nutritional benefit. Many foods readily available today provide a lot of calories but offer little or no nutritive value other than energy.

Scientists have identified more than 50 nutritional elements. We need each in varying amounts as part of a complete, health-building, illness-fighting diet. Research continues to reveal more and more about these nutrients and how they work within the body. Just recently, for example, studies have shown that high blood levels of an amino acid called homocysteine may be another key risk factor for heart disease. For most people, though, a diet adequate in vitamin B_{12} and folic acid, another of the B vitamins, can help keep homocysteine at a safe level.

rich natural sources of folic acid and other B vitamins. These same foods also contain fiber. Foods rich in fiber also tend to be rich in complex carbohydrates. Wheat bran is a main source of insoluble fiber, which helps keep the digestive tract healthy. Soluble fiber, which may play a role in lowering blood cholesterol, is found in whole-grain oats, corn, rice, dried peas and beans, and many fruits and vegetables. Those are the same foods, by and large, that make up the two bottom sections of the Food Pyramid.

The more research uncovers about nutrition, the more it confirms the wisdom of the AHA's emphasis on variety in diet and on fruits, vegetables, grains, and fat-free and low-fat dairy products.

For instance, the National Heart, Lung, and Blood Institute's 1997 guidelines for high blood pressure say that the U.S. population should adopt the DASH (Dietary Approaches to Stop Hypertension) diet to prevent—or even treat—high blood pressure. The DASH study found that eating a diet rich in fruits, vegetables, and low-fat dairy foods with reduced saturated and total fats significantly lowers blood pressure. This diet is similar to the AHA diet, but with more servings of fruits and vegetables.

USING COMMON SENSE

Fat has increasingly become a "dirty word" in our society, but small amounts of fat are still essential to good nutrition and overall health. Besides, stamping out fat completely from your diet would be impossible, since fat occurs naturally in many grains, vegetables, and fruits. The idea is to keep fat within limits and not eat too much of any one type.

Eggs also have had a lot of bad press because of the high amount of cholesterol in their yolks. A typical egg yolk contains 213 to 220 milligrams of cholesterol. This means a couple of scrambled eggs for breakfast will put you well over the AHA-recommended daily limit of 300 milligrams of cholesterol. Consequently, we've limited the use of egg yolks in our recipes, but eggs aren't forbidden. Egg whites are cholesterol free and can be substituted for whole eggs. Commercial egg substitutes also are readily available.

Complex carbohydrates, or starches, have gotten a bad name for being high in calories and therefore fattening. Actually, potatoes, breads, pastas, and other complex carbohydrates are relatively low in calories, considering the vital nutrients they carry. Also, the bulk they provide helps satisfy hunger. The excess calories come from the butter, margarine, gravy, and rich sauces often added to starchy foods.

By the way, don't confuse complex carbohydrates with the simple carbohydrates found in sugar, corn syrup, honey, and molasses. These sugars supply only empty calories. Use them in moderation for flavor. Increasing complex carbohydrates is a good way to replace some of the fat you're cutting out. Chances are, you'll be surprised at how little you miss it.

NUTRIENT ANALYSIS OF THESE RECIPES

To help you in meal planning, we analyzed the recipes in this cookbook for various nutrients. Each computer analysis is based on a single serving unless otherwise indicated. You'll find the amount of calories, protein, carbohydrate, total fat, saturated fat, polyunsaturated fat, monounsaturated fat, cholesterol, fiber, and sodium.

You'll find a fairly large variation in the amount of each nutrient from one recipe to another. If you're on a restricted diet, read the analyses and choose your recipes carefully. For example, if you're on a low-sodium diet, concentrate on recipes with less sodium. If you're trying to lose weight, select recipes lower in calories.

You may notice that sometimes the values for saturated, monounsaturated, and polyunsaturated fats don't add up to the total amount of fat in the recipe. That's because the total fat includes the fatty acids we list, other fatty substances, and glycerol. Also, we've rounded the values listed in the analyses to whole numbers. For a few recipes, the nutrient analysis shows a dash instead of a number for polyunsaturated fat and monounsaturated fat. That means these values were not available for at least one ingredient in the recipe.

INGREDIENTS USED IN ANALYSIS

In most cases, each analysis includes all the ingredients listed in the recipe. There are a few exceptions, however. Optional ingredients and foods suggested as accompaniments aren't analyzed. Neither are garnishes, such as parsley sprigs or lemon wedges, that may not be consumed.

When the recipe calls for "acceptable vegetable oil," we used corn oil for the analysis. When the recipe calls for a specific oil, the calculation is, of course, based on that oil. You may use any oil with no more than 2 grams of saturated fat per tablespoon—corn, canola, olive, safflower, sunflower, soybean, walnut, or almond. For a flavor change, you can occasionally use peanut oil.

When selecting an "acceptable margarine," remember to choose one that lists liquid vegetable oil as the first ingredient. It should contain no more than 2 grams of saturated fat per tablespoon. We used corn oil margarine for the analysis. When possible, we used light margarine.

If meat, poultry, or seafood is marinated, we used U.S. Department of Agriculture data and calculated only the amount of marinade absorbed. No such data exist for marinated vegetables, so we calculated the total amount of the marinade in our analyses. We did the same for liquids used for basting or dipping.

After you brown ground beef or ground poultry without seasonings, you can wash some of the fat out by rinsing the food under hot running water. Our recipes tell you to do this when it's practical, and this is how the beef or poultry was analyzed. We used 91 percent fat-free ground beef in our analyses.

The specific ingredients listed in each recipe were analyzed. For instance, we used both nonfat and low-fat cream cheese in this collection of recipes, depending on the taste and texture desired. In each case, the type listed was used for both the recipe itself and the nutrient analysis. If you prefer a different variety, use it. Of course, the fat values will change with such substitutions. Other nutrient values, such as sodium, may change as well.

On the other hand, if you want to substitute reconstituted lemon juice for fresh, or white onions for yellow, the substitutions won't change the ingredient analyses enough to matter.

When ingredient options, such as ½ cup nonfat or low-fat cream cheese, appear in a recipe, we used the first one for the analysis.

Ingredients with a range—for example, a 2½- to 3-pound chicken—were analyzed using the average amount.

When no quantity is listed for an ingredient in a recipe, that ingredient cannot be figured into the analysis. For example, we don't list a quantity for the small amount of flour used to prepare a surface for kneading dough. Therefore, we don't include it in the analysis.

In the bread machine recipes, the analysis is for one serving of the 1½-pound loaf. The 1- and 2-pound loaves will be quite similar.

SHOPPING EQUIVALENTS

The specific amounts of the ingredients listed, not the amounts sometimes shown in parentheses, were analyzed. The amounts in parentheses are guidelines to help you decide how much of an ingredient you need when you go to the store or the refrigerator. For example, when a recipe calls for 3 tablespoons lime juice (2 medium limes), we analyzed the 3 tablespoons of juice, not the 2 limes. (You may use only 1½ limes, but you'll need to buy 2 or take 2 from the refrigerator.) The parenthetical amounts are, of course, estimates, based on the best information we have.

Generally, we don't list a shopping equivalent if the recipe needs only one of an item. You can assume that you need at least one. For example, 1 medium onion yields about ½ cup chopped onion. If the recipe calls for ½ cup chopped onion or less, we don't list 1 medium onion.

SODIUM

Because many people today are watching their sodium intake, we keep the sodium values low in most recipes, and we use salt sparingly. For canned or frozen foods, we use a no-salt-added or low-sodium variety if it is readily available. If you are used to saltier food, you may wish to add a little salt to the recipes until your taste buds adjust to the change. The small amount of salt you add will not raise the sodium level as much as using a prepared food product processed with salt.

Some canned items are not available (or are hard to find) without added salt. In this case, the recipes may call for the product to be rinsed and drained. Some canned items frequently rinsed are capers, clams, chiles, and beans.

TEMPERATURE VARIATIONS

Our microwave instructions are written for a 600- to 650-watt oven. If your microwave is different, please adjust the times accordingly. Other cooking times and temperatures depend on your oven and stovetop. We give these as a guide, but, as in all cooking, you need to adapt them to your kitchen.

HERE'S THE FUN PART

Knowing what foods to eat for a healthy heart is an important first step in any diet. But then comes the fun—cooking and eating! In this cookbook, you'll find a dazzling collection of dishes that will show you how delicious low-fat, low-cholesterol eating can be.

Concentrate on the new foods you can try, not on the foods you think you can't have. Look on this as an adventure. Every week, try at least one new recipe, experiment with one new spice or herb, and sample a new fruit or vegetable. By concentrating on new foods and new recipes, you won't focus on what you're reducing or omitting.

Recipes

APPETIZERS, SNACKS, AND BEVERAGES

Mexican Bean Dip

Creamy Chick-Pea Dip

Smoked Salmon Party Dip

Curry Yogurt Dip

Cucumber and Yogurt Dip

Artichoke Dip

Spinach Dip

Apricot Dip

Fire-and-Ice
Cream Cheese Spread

Herb Cream Cheese Spread

Mock Boursin Cheese Spread

Torta with Chèvre Cheese
and Sun-Dried Tomatoes

Yogurt Cheese

Plum Tomatoes with Blue Cheese

Sweet-and-Sour Spring Rolls

Carrot, Parsnip,
and Potato Pancakes

Crumb-Crusted Mushrooms
with Lemon

Stuffed Mushrooms

Cold Veggie Pizza Snacks

Spinach Pinwheels

Basil Pesto Squares

Fiesta Black Bean Nachos

Tortilla Stacks
with Cumin Sour Cream

Roasted-Pepper Hummus

Roasted-Pepper Fondue

Skewered Chicken Strips
with Soy-Peanut Marinade

Meatballs in Beer Sauce

Pita Crisps

Nibbles

Sparkling Cranberry Cooler

Berry Good Smoothie

Frozen Fruit Slush

Mexican Bean Dip

Serves 16; 2 tablespoons per serving

A colorful array of garnishes, such as cilantro, radishes, tomatoes, green and red onions, and jalapeño peppers, would be perfect with this creamy dip.

2 teaspoons low-sodium beef bouillon granules
¼ cup hot water
15.25-ounce can no-salt-added kidney beans, drained
½ cup no-salt-added tomato sauce
½ cup chopped yellow onion
¼ cup chopped green bell pepper
2 medium cloves garlic, minced, or 1 teaspoon bottled minced garlic
2 tablespoons plus 1½ teaspoons fresh lime juice (2 medium limes)
¼ teaspoon cayenne, or to taste
1 tablespoon extra-virgin olive oil

Put bouillon granules in a cup or small bowl. Pour water over granules, stirring to dissolve. Pour into a food processor or blender. Add remaining ingredients except oil; puree.

To serve at room temperature, stir in olive oil (don't process it). To serve warm, put dip in a small saucepan and heat over medium heat for 5 to 6 minutes, stirring frequently. Remove from heat and stir in olive oil.

Cook's Tip

Try strips of green bell pepper for dipping, or top rounds of crookneck squash with 1 teaspoon of dip and a sprinkling of assorted garnishes.

Cook's Tip on Veggie Bowls

When entertaining, halve butternut and acorn squash lengthwise and remove seeds. Put a different garnish in each squash half. For the dip, cut the top off a large acorn squash and remove seeds, or use a decorative bowl. Arrange garnish-filled squash halves around the dip.

Calories 36
Protein 2 g
Carbohydrates 5 g
Cholesterol 0 mg
Total Fat 1 g
Saturated 0 g
Polyunsaturated 0 g
Monounsaturated 1 g
Fiber 2 g
Sodium 5 mg

Creamy Chick-Pea Dip

Serves 16; 2 tablespoons per serving

This dip is really quick to make. You can serve it immediately or cover and refrigerate it for later use.

20-ounce can no-salt-added chick-peas (garbanzo beans), drained
½ cup nonfat or low-fat cottage cheese
⅓ cup fresh lemon juice (1 to 2 medium lemons)
3 tablespoons fat-free milk
2 medium cloves garlic, minced, or 1 teaspoon bottled minced garlic
1 tablespoon sesame seeds, dry-roasted
1 tablespoon olive oil
⅛ teaspoon salt
Dash of red hot-pepper sauce
1 tablespoon finely snipped fresh parsley

In a food processor or blender, puree all ingredients except parsley.

Pour dip into a small bowl and sprinkle with parsley.

Calories 52
Protein 3 g
Carbohydrates 6 g
Cholesterol 0 mg
Total Fat 2 g
Saturated 0 g
Polyunsaturated 0 g
Monounsaturated 1 g
Fiber 1 g
Sodium 44 mg

Smoked Salmon Party Dip

Serves 20; 2 tablespoons per serving

A hollowed-out red cabbage bowl makes a striking container for this dip, especially when you surround it with the brilliant colors of bell peppers. What a great way to lure your guests to take a heart-healthy dip!

DIP

1 cup nonfat or low-fat cottage cheese

1 cup nonfat or light sour cream

4 ounces smoked salmon, chopped (½ cup)

4 green onions (white and green parts), finely chopped (about ½ cup)

2 teaspoons fresh lemon juice

¼ teaspoon garlic powder

1 medium red cabbage (optional)

8 leaves curly leaf lettuce (optional)

¼ teaspoon paprika

2 medium green bell peppers, cut into 1-inch strips

2 medium red bell peppers, cut into 1-inch strips

2 medium yellow bell peppers, cut into 1-inch strips

Put cottage cheese in a food processor or blender. Puree for 30 seconds, or until smooth. Scrape into a medium bowl.

Stir in remaining dip ingredients. Cover and refrigerate.

To make a cabbage bowl, trim core end of cabbage so cabbage will sit flat. Starting at top of cabbage, hollow out inside with a sharp knife and spoon. (A grapefruit knife and grapefruit spoon work well for this.)

To assemble, line a large platter with lettuce leaves. Place cabbage in center. Pour dip into cabbage and sprinkle with paprika. Arrange bell pepper strips around cabbage. Cover with plastic wrap and refrigerate until serving time.

Calories 37
Protein 4 g
Carbohydrates 5 g
Cholesterol 2 mg
Total Fat 0 g
Saturated 0 g
Polyunsaturated 0 g
Monounsaturated 0 g
Fiber 1 g
Sodium 98 mg

Curry Yogurt Dip

Serves 8; 2 tablespoons per serving

This is a delightful dip for raw vegetables or apple slices.

Calories 28
Protein 2 g
Carbohydrates 5 g
Cholesterol 1 mg
Total Fat 0 g
Saturated 0 g
Polyunsaturated 0 g
Monounsaturated 0 g
Fiber 0 g
Sodium 77 mg

1 cup Yogurt Cheese (see page 16)

3 tablespoons fat-free, cholesterol-free or light, reduced-calorie mayonnaise dressing

2 teaspoons curry powder

In a small bowl, whisk together all ingredients. Cover and refrigerate until serving time.

Cucumber and Yogurt Dip

Serves 11; 2 tablespoons per serving

In addition to being a tasty dip, this dish is an excellent sauce for chilled poached or grilled salmon.

1 cup seeded and diced cucumber, unpeeled

½ cup finely chopped green onions (about 4 or 5)

2 medium cloves garlic, minced, or 1 teaspoon bottled minced garlic

½ cup plain nonfat or low-fat yogurt

⅓ cup fat-free, cholesterol-free or light, reduced-calorie mayonnaise dressing

¼ cup grated Parmesan cheese

1 teaspoon white wine Worcestershire sauce

In a medium bowl, combine all ingredients, stirring well.

Cover and refrigerate for at least 1 hour to allow flavors to blend.

Calories 23
Protein 2 g
Carbohydrates 3 g
Cholesterol 2 mg
Total Fat 1 g
Saturated 0 g
Polyunsaturated 0 g
Monounsaturated 0 g
Fiber 0 g
Sodium 106 mg

Artichoke Dip

Serves 14; 2 tablespoons per serving

Surround a bowl of this dip with Pita Crisps (see page 32) or baked chips.

9-ounce package frozen no-salt-added artichoke hearts, thawed and drained
4 ounces fat-free or low-fat cream cheese, room temperature
½ cup plain nonfat or low-fat yogurt
¼ cup thinly sliced green onions (green part only)
1½ teaspoons cream sherry
1 teaspoon salt-free Italian herb seasoning
⅛ teaspoon garlic powder
⅛ teaspoon salt

Blot artichokes dry on paper towels. Chop into small pieces.

In a medium bowl, whisk together remaining ingredients, blending well. Stir in artichokes.

Cover and refrigerate for at least 1 hour to allow flavors to blend. Stir before serving.

Calories 20
Protein 2 g
Carbohydrates 3 g
Cholesterol 1 mg
Total Fat 0 g
Saturated 0 g
Polyunsaturated 0 g
Monounsaturated 0 g
Fiber 1 g
Sodium 79 mg

Spinach Dip

Serves 12; 2 tablespoons per serving

Use a variety of fresh vegetables as dippers for this peppery appetizer.

10-ounce package frozen no-salt-added chopped spinach

5 green onions (green and white parts), coarsely chopped

½ cup watercress, stems removed, or arugula

¼ cup fresh parsley, stems removed

8 ounces plain nonfat or low-fat yogurt

1 medium avocado, peeled and chopped

1¼ teaspoons salt-free garlic seasoning

⅛ teaspoon pepper

⅛ teaspoon salt (optional)

⅛ teaspoon red hot-pepper sauce, or to taste

Cook spinach using package directions, omitting salt and margarine. Drain; squeeze out all liquid.

Finely chop spinach, onions, watercress, and parsley in a food processor, or chop with a knife and transfer to a blender. Process just until blended; mixture should be coarse. Transfer to colander to drain excess liquid.

Puree remaining ingredients in processor or blender.

In a medium bowl, combine the two mixtures, stirring well. Cover and refrigerate for at least 1 hour to allow flavors to blend.

Calories 41
Protein 2 g
Carbohydrates 4 g
Cholesterol 0 mg
Total Fat 3 g
  Saturated 0 g
  Polyunsaturated 0 g
  Monounsaturated 2 g
Fiber 2 g
Sodium 31 mg

Cook's Tip

For chunkier avocado in this dip, mash it with a fork instead of pureeing it. Stir the avocado in with the vegetables and yogurt mixture.

Apricot Dip

Serves 16; 2 tablespoons per serving

Is this dish better as a dip for fresh fruits, such as strawberries, bananas, and apple slices, or as a sauce over angel food cake? Try it both ways and decide for yourself.

1 cup fresh orange juice (about 3 medium oranges)
½ cup finely chopped dried apricots (3 to 4 ounces)
½ cup unsweetened applesauce
¼ teaspoon ground cinnamon
2 dashes ground nutmeg
8 ounces nonfat or low-fat vanilla yogurt

In a small nonaluminum saucepan, combine orange juice and apricots. Bring to a boil over medium-high heat, then reduce heat to low, stirring frequently. As apricots become tender, mash them slightly with back of wooden spoon. Cook for about 20 minutes, or until all juice is absorbed. Transfer to a medium bowl and stir well.

Stir in applesauce, cinnamon, and nutmeg. Cover bowl and let cool.

Stir in yogurt.

Cover and refrigerate for at least 1 hour.

Cook's Tip on Cutting Sticky Foods

To cut dried apricots or other sticky foods easily, use kitchen shears lightly sprayed with vegetable oil spray.

Calories 30
Protein 1 g
Carbohydrates 7 g
Cholesterol 0 mg
Total Fat 0 g
Saturated 0 g
Polyunsaturated 0 g
Monounsaturated 0 g
Fiber 0 g
Sodium 10 mg

Fire-and-Ice Cream Cheese Spread

Serves 4; 3 tablespoons per serving

Easy but elegant, this cream cheese spread is spiced with hot red pepper and cooled with the sweet taste of apricots. Serve with fat-free cracked-pepper crackers and fresh pear slices arranged decoratively around the apricot-domed cream cheese mixture.

¼ cup fat-free cream cheese (in tub)

¼ cup nonfat or light sour cream

¼ cup apricot all-fruit spread

¼ teaspoon crushed red pepper flakes

2 tablespoons finely chopped red bell pepper

In a small mixing bowl, beat cream cheese and sour cream with an electric mixer until well blended. Spoon into a small bowl lined with plastic wrap or a 6-ounce ramekin. Press mixture slightly to get rid of any air pockets; smooth evenly with rubber scraper.

Refrigerate for at least 30 minutes to firm slightly.

Meanwhile, in a small saucepan, heat fruit spread and red pepper flakes over medium heat until spread just begins to melt, about 3 minutes, stirring occasionally. Remove from heat and stir in bell pepper. Let cool to room temperature.

To serve, if using bowl, invert mixture onto a serving plate, remove plastic wrap, and spoon apricot mixture on top. If using ramekin, top cream cheese mixture with apricot mixture.

Cook's Tip on Pears

Brush lemon juice or pineapple juice on pear slices to prevent discoloration.

Calories 72
Protein 3 g
Carbohydrates 14 g
Cholesterol 1 mg
Total Fat 0 g
Saturated 0 g
Polyunsaturated 0 g
Monounsaturated 0 g
Fiber 0 g
Sodium 91 mg

Herb Cream Cheese Spread

Serves 8; 2 tablespoons per serving

Serve this incredibly easy to make spread with fresh vegetables or fat-free, low-sodium crackers.

8 ounces fat-free or reduced-fat cream cheese
2 sprigs of fresh parsley, snipped
1 medium clove garlic, mashed, or ½ teaspoon bottled minced garlic
½ teaspoon pepper
¼ teaspoon dried thyme, crumbled
¼ teaspoon dried chervil, crumbled

In a food processor or blender, process all ingredients for 10 seconds.

Transfer to a glass bowl, cover, and refrigerate for at least 1 hour to allow flavors to blend.

Cook's Tip on Chervil

An herb of the parsley family, chervil is available fresh and dried. It has a delicate aniselike taste that may be reduced when cooked. Chervil gives color and a lightly zesty touch to sauces for vegetables and when sprinkled on salads, soups, lamb, veal, and pork.

Calories 28
Protein 4 g
Carbohydrates 2 g
Cholesterol 2 mg
Total Fat 0 g
- Saturated 0 g
- Polyunsaturated 0 g
- Monounsaturated 0 g

Fiber 0 g
Sodium 155 mg

Mock Boursin Cheese Spread

Serves 8; 2 tablespoons per serving

Traditionally a triple-cream cheese, boursin can be part of a healthful eating plan if you use this easy recipe.

¾ cup Yogurt Cheese (see page 16)
¼ cup nonfat or light sour cream
2 teaspoons minced fresh parsley
½ teaspoon dried basil, crumbled
¼ teaspoon dried rosemary, crushed
¼ teaspoon dried thyme, crumbled
¼ teaspoon dried tarragon, crumbled
¼ teaspoon dried sage, crumbled
¼ teaspoon sugar
½ small clove garlic, crushed; ¼ teaspoon bottled minced garlic; or ⅛ teaspoon garlic powder
1 teaspoon pepper, or to taste

In a small bowl, whisk together Yogurt Cheese and sour cream.

Whisk in remaining ingredients except pepper.

Pour into a serving bowl. Sprinkle generously with pepper. Cover bowl and refrigerate for at least 8 hours to allow flavors to blend.

Cook's Tip

Don't limit yourself to black peppercorns. Try white, red, pink, and green, separately or mixed.

Calories 27
Protein 2 g
Carbohydrates 4 g
Cholesterol 1 mg
Total Fat 0 g
Saturated 0 g
Polyunsaturated 0 g
Monounsaturated 0 g
Fiber 0 g
Sodium 34 mg

Torta with Chèvre Cheese and Sun-Dried Tomatoes

Serves 12; 2 tablespoons per serving

Chèvre (SHEHV-ruh), *or goat cheese, lends its unique tart flavor to this spread.*

1 cup water

½ cup dry-packed sun-dried tomatoes (about 1 ounce)

1 teaspoon dried oregano, crumbled

1 medium clove garlic, minced, or ½ teaspoon bottled minced garlic

¼ teaspoon dried basil, crumbled

⅛ teaspoon pepper

4 ounces nonfat or low-fat cream cheese, softened

4 ounces goat cheese (½ cup)

¼ cup snipped fresh parsley

¼ teaspoon paprika

1 tablespoon pine nuts

Bring water to a boil in a small saucepan. Add tomatoes, turn off heat, and let soak 10 to 15 minutes. Using a slotted spoon, transfer tomatoes to a bowl. Let cool 5 minutes. Chop coarsely, squeezing out excess liquid.

In a food processor or blender, process tomatoes, oregano, garlic, basil, and pepper for 20 to 30 seconds, or until desired consistency (mixture can be slightly chunky or smooth).

In a medium mixing bowl, beat cream cheese until smooth, about 1 minute. Add goat cheese and beat until smooth, 20 to 30 seconds.

Line a 1½-cup round container with plastic wrap. Spread one fourth of cheese mixture on bottom of container. Top with one third of tomato mixture. Alternate cheese and tomato layers, ending with cheese. Cover with plastic wrap and refrigerate for at least 30 minutes.

To serve, uncover and invert onto a plate. Remove plastic. Press parsley on sides of torta. Sprinkle top with paprika and pine nuts.

Calories 63
Protein 5 g
Carbohydrates 2 g
Cholesterol 11 mg
Total Fat 4 g
Saturated 2 g
Polyunsaturated 0 g
Monounsaturated 1 g
Fiber 0 g
Sodium 127 mg

Yogurt Cheese

Makes 1 cup

You'll be amazed at how easy it is to make your own yogurt cheese. The texture is similar to that of thick sour cream.

16-ounce container plain nonfat or low-fat yogurt without gelatin

Put a double-thick layer of fine-mesh cheesecloth or paper coffee filters in a rustproof colander. Put colander in a deep bowl. (Colander must not touch bottom of bowl.) Pour yogurt into colander and cover with plastic wrap. Refrigerate for at least 8 hours.

Put yogurt in a small bowl. Cover and refrigerate for up to a week. Drain off any whey that separates.

Cook's Tip on Yogurt Cheese and Whey

When you drain yogurt, you get about half yogurt cheese and half whey, or liquid. The yogurt cheese can replace sour cream or cream cheese in most recipes. You can use the whey in place of water, fat-free or low-fat milk, or buttermilk in cooking. The whey not only is rich in protein, vitamins, and minerals, but also reacts well with baking soda, helping baked goods rise beautifully and have a light texture. Why should you start with yogurt without gelatin? Gelatin holds in the whey, so you won't get the consistency you need.

(FOR 1 CUP)
Calories 180
Protein 16 g
Carbohydrates 28 g
Cholesterol 10 mg
Total Fat 0 g
Saturated 0 g
Polyunsaturated 0 g
Monounsaturated 0 g
Fiber 0 g
Sodium 300 mg

Plum Tomatoes with Blue Cheese

Serves 8; 3 pieces per serving

This recipe tops colorful tomatoes with a spicy blue cheese mixture and chopped green onions.

1½ ounces blue cheese

1 tablespoon plus 2 teaspoons fat-free milk

¼ teaspoon red hot-pepper sauce

12 medium Italian plum tomatoes

2 tablespoons finely chopped green onions (2 medium)

Put cheese, milk, and hot-pepper sauce into a medium mixing bowl (to reduce splattering). Using an electric mixer, blend completely, scraping sides of bowl with a rubber scraper. Transfer to a small container, cover, and refrigerate for at least 30 minutes (up to 24 hours) to let flavors blend and mixture set slightly.

Cut tomatoes in half lengthwise. Top each half with cheese mixture, and sprinkle with green onions. Serve at room temperature or cover and refrigerate for up to 1 hour.

Tomatoes with Feta Cheese

Substitute 2 ounces feta cheese for blue cheese and plain nonfat or low-fat yogurt for milk. (calories 40; protein 2 g; carbohydrates 5 g; cholesterol 6 mg; total fat 2 g; saturated 1 g; polyunsaturated 0 g; monounsaturated 0 g; fiber 1 g; sodium 94 mg)

Red Potatoes with Cheese and Basil

Cut eight 1½-ounce red potatoes in half lengthwise. Steam for 10 minutes, plunge in a bowl of ice water for 2 minutes, and drain well on paper towels. Top each piece with feta cheese mixture. Sprinkle with 2 tablespoons finely chopped fresh basil leaves or green onions. (calories 58; protein 2 g; carbohydrates 9 g; cholesterol 6 mg; total fat 2 g; saturated 1 g; polyunsaturated 0 g; monounsaturated 0 g; fiber 1 g; sodium 88 mg)

Calories 40
Protein 2 g
Carbohydrates 5 g
Cholesterol 4 mg
Total Fat 2 g
Saturated 1 g
Polyunsaturated 0 g
Monounsaturated 0 g
Fiber 1 g
Sodium 88 mg

Sweet-and-Sour Spring Rolls

Serves 4; 3 spring rolls per serving

These vegetarian spring rolls are pan-fried, then glazed with a sweet-and-sour sauce.

Vegetable oil spray
½ teaspoon acceptable vegetable oil
1½ cups shredded cabbage
4 medium cloves garlic, minced, or 2 teaspoons bottled minced garlic
½ cup chopped green onions (green and white parts) (4 to 5 medium)
8-ounce can bamboo shoots, drained
2 teaspoons light soy sauce
⅛ teaspoon pepper
3 sheets frozen phyllo, thawed
Vegetable oil spray
½ teaspoon acceptable vegetable oil
1 tablespoon plus 1 teaspoon bottled sweet-and-sour sauce

Spray a large nonstick skillet with vegetable oil spray. Pour ½ teaspoon oil into skillet, swirling to coat bottom. Heat over medium-high heat for 1 minute. Sauté cabbage and garlic for 3 minutes, stirring constantly.

Add green onions and bamboo shoots. Cook for 30 seconds, stirring constantly. Remove from heat. Stir in soy sauce and pepper.

Keeping unused phyllo covered with a damp dish towel to prevent drying, lightly spray 1 sheet of dough with vegetable oil spray. Working quickly, cut dough into fourths. Put three of the quarter sheets under the towel. On the fourth piece, put 1 rounded tablespoon cabbage mixture 2 to 3 inches from one end. Fold that end over filling, then fold in sides and roll tightly. Set aside, seam side down. Repeat with remaining phyllo and filling.

Spray and oil skillet again. Heat over medium-high heat for 1 minute. Cook spring rolls in skillet for 6 minutes, turning occasionally. Brush with sweet-and-sour sauce and serve.

Calories 94
Protein 3 g
Carbohydrates 16 g
Cholesterol 0 mg
Total Fat 2 g
Saturated 0 g
Polyunsaturated 1 g
Monounsaturated 0 g
Fiber 5 g
Sodium 194 mg

Carrot, Parsnip, and Potato Pancakes

Serves 12; 2 pancakes per serving

Enjoy these wholesome pancakes with a mug of hot apple cider.

2 medium carrots, peeled
1 medium parsnip, peeled
3 medium potatoes (about 1 pound), peeled
Egg substitute equivalent to 5 eggs
1 small yellow onion, minced
3 tablespoons snipped fresh chives or green onions (green part only)
2 tablespoons all-purpose flour
2 tablespoons plain dry bread crumbs
¼ teaspoon salt
Pepper to taste
Vegetable oil spray, Asian flavored or plain
1 cup nonfat or light sour cream (optional)
Unsweetened applesauce (optional)

Coarsely grate carrots, parsnip, and potatoes using large holes of a four-sided grater. Put vegetables in a colander set in a large bowl.

Press down on vegetables, squeezing out as much liquid as you can. Discard liquid and return vegetables to bowl.

Stir in egg substitute, onion, chives, flour, bread crumbs, salt, and pepper.

Heat a large nonstick skillet over medium heat. Spray with vegetable oil spray. Drop heaping tablespoons of batter onto skillet, using a spoon to flatten pancakes slightly. Cook for 3 to 4 minutes, or until bottom is golden brown. Turn over each pancake and cook for about 3 minutes, or until golden brown. Transfer to a serving platter. Cook remaining batter, stirring to combine and spraying skillet between batches as needed.

Serve pancakes hot or at room temperature by themselves or with nonfat or low-fat sour cream or applesauce.

Calories 79
Protein 4 g
Carbohydrates 13 g
Cholesterol 0 mg
Total Fat 1 g
Saturated 0 g
Polyunsaturated 0 g
Monounsaturated 0 g
Fiber 2 g
Sodium 116 mg

Crumb-Crusted Mushrooms with Lemon

Serves 4

Coat whole mushrooms with yogurt and a crust of seasoned bread crumbs, bake them for a few minutes, and watch them disappear!

Vegetable oil spray
2 slices bread
Vegetable oil spray
2 teaspoons acceptable margarine
4 medium cloves garlic, minced, or 2 teaspoons bottled minced garlic
1 teaspoon salt-free dried Italian seasoning, crumbled
⅛ teaspoon salt-free lemon pepper (optional)
1 tablespoon grated lemon zest (1 to 2 medium lemons)
8 ounces whole small mushrooms (3 to 3½ cups)
⅓ cup nonfat or low-fat plain yogurt
Paprika
Lemon wedges

Preheat oven to 450° F. Spray a baking sheet with vegetable oil spray and set aside.

Tear bread into pieces and put in a food processor or blender. Process until consistency of commercial bread crumbs.

Spray a large nonstick skillet with vegetable oil spray. Melt margarine over medium-high heat. Cook garlic, Italian seasoning, lemon pepper, and bread crumbs for 6 minutes, or until golden brown, stirring frequently.

Remove from heat and stir in lemon zest.

In a large bowl, combine mushrooms and yogurt, stirring gently to coat completely. Arrange a single layer of mushrooms about ¼ inch apart on baking sheet.

Sprinkle mushrooms with bread crumbs, then with paprika.

Bake for 5 minutes. Gently place mushrooms on a serving platter and sprinkle with bread crumbs from baking sheet. Serve immediately with lemon wedges and wooden toothpicks.

Calories 86
Protein 3 g
Carbohydrates 13 g
Cholesterol 1 mg
Total Fat 3 g
- Saturated 1 g
- Polyunsaturated 1 g
- Monounsaturated 1 g

Fiber 2 g
Sodium 117 mg

Crumb-Crusted Tomato Slices

Spray a 9-inch square baking pan with vegetable oil spray. Cut 2 tomatoes (about 8 ounces each) into 4 slices each and place in pan. Spoon yogurt over each slice and top with crumb topping. Bake at 450° F for 20 minutes, or until soft. (calories 91; protein 3 g; carbohydrates 14 g; cholesterol 1 mg; total fat 3 g; saturated 1 g; polyunsaturated 1 g; monounsaturated 1 g; fiber 1 g; sodium 123 mg)

Stuffed Mushrooms

Serves 6; 3 mushrooms per serving

Fill plump mushrooms with a mixture of bell peppers and bread crumbs. Then savor them as an appetizer or jazz up your next spaghetti dinner by placing them on top of your plate of spaghetti and sauce.

18 medium mushrooms (about 1 pound)
1 tablespoon olive oil
3 medium cloves garlic, minced, or 1½ teaspoons bottled minced garlic
¼ cup diced red bell pepper
¼ cup diced yellow bell pepper
¼ cup sliced green onions
¾ cup fresh whole-wheat bread crumbs (1½ slices bread)
Egg substitute equivalent to 1 egg or 1 egg, slightly beaten
2 tablespoons grated Parmesan cheese
½ teaspoon salt-free Italian herb seasoning

Preheat oven to 425° F.

Remove and mince mushroom stems. Put caps in a 13 × 9 × 2-inch baking dish and set aside.

Heat oil in a medium nonstick skillet over medium heat. Swirl to coat bottom. Sauté mushroom stems and garlic for 5 minutes.

Stir in bell peppers and cook until soft, 2 to 3 minutes.

Add green onion and cook for 2 minutes.

Remove pan from heat and stir in remaining ingredients. Stuff filling into mushroom caps.

Bake, uncovered, for 25 minutes.

Calories 72
Protein 4 g
Carbohydrates 7 g
Cholesterol 2 mg
Total Fat 4 g
- Saturated 1 g
- Polyunsaturated 1 g
- Monounsaturated 2 g

Fiber 2 g
Sodium 90 mg

Cold Veggie Pizza Snacks

Serves 20; 1 piece per serving

Need a new way to entice the kids to eat their veggies? This dish may be the answer!

Vegetable oil spray

10-ounce package refrigerated pizza dough

8 ounces fat-free or low-fat cream cheese, softened

½ cup nonfat or light sour cream

2 tablespoons fat-free or low-fat ranch salad dressing

4 cups chopped or finely sliced fresh vegetables (broccoli, carrots, radishes, mushrooms, cucumbers, seeded and drained cherry tomatoes, celery, red onion, or any combination)

Preheat oven using package directions on dough. Spray a 13 × 9 × 2-inch baking pan or a baking sheet with vegetable oil spray.

Pat dough over bottom of pan or pat into a 13 × 9-inch rectangle on baking sheet.

Bake dough using package directions. Let stand until cool, 10 to 15 minutes.

In a small bowl, beat cream cheese and sour cream until smooth. Stir in salad dressing. Spread over crust.

Arrange vegetables on top. Cover with plastic wrap and refrigerate until serving time.

To serve, cut into 20 squares.

Apple Dessert Pizza Snacks

Replace the salad dressing with a mixture of ½ cup firmly packed light brown sugar and ½ teaspoon vanilla extract, and replace the vegetables with 2 medium unpeeled chopped apples mixed with 1 tablespoon fresh lemon juice. (calories 78; protein 3 g; carbohydrates 15 g; cholesterol 1 mg; total fat 0 g; saturated 0 g; polyunsaturated 0 g; monounsaturated 0 g; fiber 1 g; sodium 133 mg)

Calories 57
Protein 4 g
Carbohydrates 10 g
Cholesterol 1 mg
Total Fat 1 g
Saturated 0 g
Polyunsaturated 0 g
Monounsaturated 0 g
Fiber 1 g
Sodium 151 mg

Spinach Pinwheels

Serves 24; 1 slice per serving

These eye-catching pinwheels will wow your guests.

1 teaspoon light margarine
½ cup finely chopped onion
10-ounce package frozen no-salt-added chopped spinach, thawed
½ cup nonfat or part-skim ricotta cheese
1 tablespoon fresh lemon juice
Dash of nutmeg
Dash of cayenne
10-ounce package refrigerated pizza dough
Vegetable oil spray
White of 1 egg, slightly beaten
1 tablespoon sesame seeds

In a small nonstick skillet, heat margarine over medium-high heat. Swirl to cover bottom. Sauté onion until translucent, 2 to 3 minutes.

In a medium bowl, combine onion, spinach, ricotta, lemon juice, nutmeg, and cayenne. Blend well.

Press dough into a 12 × 14-inch rectangle. Cut in half, forming two 7 × 12-inch rectangles.

With a rubber scraper, spread half the spinach mixture on each piece of dough. Roll up, starting from a 12-inch side. Pinch each end of rolled dough. Cover and refrigerate for 30 minutes.

Preheat oven to 425° F. Lightly spray a baking sheet with vegetable oil spray.

With a sharp knife, cut each roll into 12 slices. Put pieces on baking sheet. Brush with egg white and sprinkle with sesame seeds.

Bake for 15 to 18 minutes, or until light golden brown.

Calories 37
Protein 2 g
Carbohydrates 6 g
Cholesterol 0 mg
Total Fat 1 g
Saturated 0 g
Polyunsaturated 0 g
Monounsaturated 0 g
Fiber 1 g
Sodium 78 mg

Basil Pesto Squares

Serves 8; 2 squares per serving

Try dipping these luscious little squares into warmed marinara sauce (low fat and low sodium, of course).

Olive oil spray
1 cup fat-free milk
Egg substitute equivalent to 3 eggs
½ cup fresh basil leaves
1 tablespoon grated Parmesan cheese
1 tablespoon extra-virgin olive oil
1 large clove garlic, quartered
2½ cups all-purpose flour
1 tablespoon baking powder
¼ teaspoon pepper
⅛ teaspoon salt

Preheat oven to 375° F. Spray an 8-inch square baking pan with olive oil spray. Set aside.

Put milk, egg substitute, basil, Parmesan, oil, and garlic in a food processor or blender and puree.

In a large bowl, whisk together remaining ingredients.

Pour milk mixture over flour mixture all at once. Whisk to mix well.

Pour batter into baking pan, using a rubber scraper to smooth top.

Bake for 30 to 40 minutes, or until cake tester or toothpick inserted in center comes out clean. Turn onto serving plate. Cut into 16 squares.

Calories 202
Protein 9 g
Carbohydrates 34 g
Cholesterol 1 mg
Total Fat 3 g
  Saturated 1 g
  Polyunsaturated 1 g
  Monounsaturated 2 g
Fiber 2 g
Sodium 294 mg

Fiesta Black Bean Nachos

Serves 4

Show off your creativity with these decorative nachos. Try them as an appetizer or as an entrée for a meatless lunch or dinner.

Vegetable oil spray

4 cups no-salt-added baked tortilla chips (4 ounces)

1 cup dried black beans, sorted for stones, rinsed, and cooked (see Cook's Tip on Black Beans below), or 15-ounce can, rinsed and drained

½ small red onion, diced (3 tablespoons)

½ medium yellow bell pepper, diced (½ cup)

16 cherry tomatoes, cut in half

1 cup shredded fat-free or low-fat Cheddar cheese

¼ cup nonfat or light sour cream

Preheat oven to 350° F.

Lightly spray a baking sheet with vegetable oil spray. Spread chips in a single layer on baking sheet.

Sprinkle chips with beans, onion, bell pepper, tomatoes, and cheese.

Bake for 10 to 12 minutes, or until mixture is warmed through and cheese has melted. Top with sour cream and serve warm.

Cook's Tip on Black Beans

Follow the package directions for cooking dried beans, but after soaking the beans and discarding the liquid, add 4 cups fresh water to a large saucepan along with the beans, ½ teaspoon salt, ½ teaspoon crushed red pepper flakes, ½ teaspoon black pepper, and ½ teaspoon liquid smoke (optional). Bring to a boil over high heat, then reduce heat to low and cook, covered, for 1½ to 2 hours, or until beans are tender. Drain; if desired, use liquid in other recipes, such as vegetable soup or stew.

Calories 356
Protein 22 g
Carbohydrates 61 g
Cholesterol 6 mg
Total Fat 4 g
- Saturated 1 g
- Polyunsaturated 0 g
- Monounsaturated 1 g

Fiber 13 g
Sodium 193 mg

Tortilla Stacks with Cumin Sour Cream

Serves 4; 3 wedges per serving

Pile seasoned sour cream, tomatoes, black olives, and cilantro on crispy tortilla wedges for a tasty treat.

2 8-inch nonfat or low-fat flour tortillas
½ teaspoon chili powder
¼ cup nonfat or light sour cream
1 teaspoon ground cumin
¼ to ½ teaspoon red hot-pepper sauce
⅓ cup seeded and finely chopped tomato
9 medium black olives, each cut into 4 slices
¼ cup snipped fresh cilantro or parsley

Preheat oven to 475° F.

Cut each tortilla into 6 triangles. Sprinkle tortillas with chili powder and put on a baking sheet. Bake for 3 minutes, or until edges of tortillas begin to brown. Set aside.

In a small bowl, combine sour cream, cumin, and hot-pepper sauce, stirring well. Spread over each tortilla wedge.

Sprinkle wedges with tomato, olives, and cilantro. Serve immediately.

Cook's Tip

You can make the sour cream mixture up to 24 hours in advance. Cover and store it in the refrigerator. Don't worry if the tortillas puff up while baking. They'll give your tortilla stacks an extra bit of character.

Cook's Tip on Flour Tortillas

Nonfat and low-fat flour tortillas can be high in sodium. When shopping, select the ones with the lowest sodium value or substitute corn tortillas.

Calories 70
Protein 3 g
Carbohydrates 13 g
Cholesterol 0 mg
Total Fat 1 g
  Saturated 0 g
  Polyunsaturated 0 g
  Monounsaturated 1 g
Fiber 2 g
Sodium 202 mg

Roasted-Pepper Hummus

Serves 16; 2 tablespoons per serving

Roasted bell pepper not only boosts the flavor of this creamy chick-pea spread but adds color as well. Serve with heart-healthy crackers, toasted pita bread pieces, or vegetable dippers, such as cauliflower florets, baby carrots, and celery sticks.

Vegetable oil spray
1 medium red bell pepper or ½ cup roasted red bell pepper in a jar, rinsed and drained
2 tablespoons sesame seeds
15- or 16-ounce can chick-peas, rinsed and drained
¼ cup water
2 tablespoons fresh lime juice (1 to 2 medium limes)
1 medium clove garlic, minced, or ½ teaspoon bottled minced garlic
¼ teaspoon salt
⅛ teaspoon pepper

Preheat broiler on high.

Spray a broiling pan and rack with vegetable oil spray. Broil bell pepper 3 to 4 inches from heat on broiling rack for 2 to 3 minutes on each side, or until charred. Seal bell pepper in an airtight plastic bag or put in a bowl and cover with plastic wrap. Let cool for 5 to 10 minutes, or until cool enough to handle. Peel with fingers or a sharp paring knife. Remove and discard stem, ribs, and seeds. Blot bell pepper with paper towel. Dice bell pepper.

While bell pepper cools, dry-roast sesame seeds in a small nonstick skillet over medium heat for 3 to 4 minutes, shaking pan occasionally. Put sesame seeds in a food processor or blender and process for 30 seconds.

Add bell pepper and remaining ingredients and puree. Serve at room temperature or refrigerate in an airtight container for up to 5 days and serve chilled.

Calories 42
Protein 2 g
Carbohydrates 7 g
Cholesterol 0 mg
Total Fat 1 g
Saturated 0 g
Polyunsaturated 0 g
Monounsaturated 0 g
Fiber 1 g
Sodium 86 mg

Roasted-Pepper Fondue

Serves 6; ¼ cup per serving

Fondue makes a comeback with this creamy roasted red bell pepper version. Try it with broccoli and cauliflower florets and toasted pita triangles. Folklore suggests that a person who loses a piece of food in the fondue pot must be kissed, so make sure you serve this to your favorite guests!

Vegetable oil spray

1 medium red bell pepper or ½ cup diced roasted red bell pepper in a jar, rinsed and drained

1 cup fat-free evaporated milk

1 tablespoon cornstarch

1 ounce fat-free Swiss cheese, diced

2 green onions, thinly sliced (about ¼ cup)

⅛ teaspoon pepper

⅛ teaspoon cayenne

Preheat broiler on high.

Spray a broiler pan and rack with vegetable oil spray. Broil bell pepper about 4 inches from heat for 2 to 3 minutes on each side, or until charred. Put bell pepper in an airtight plastic bag or put in a bowl and cover with plastic wrap. Let cool for 5 to 10 minutes, or until cool enough to handle. Peel with fingers or a sharp paring knife. Remove and discard stem, ribs, and seeds. Blot bell pepper with paper towel. Coarsely chop bell pepper, then puree in a food processor or blender.

In a medium saucepan, whisk together milk and cornstarch. Bring to a boil over medium-high heat, stirring occasionally. When mixture starts to thicken, reduce heat to medium and cook for 1 to 2 minutes, stirring occasionally.

Reduce heat to low and add bell pepper, cheese, green onions, pepper, and cayenne. Cook for 1 to 2 minutes, or until mixture is warmed through, stirring occasionally.

To serve, transfer mixture to a fondue pot or chafing dish set on low.

Calories 50
Protein 5 g
Carbohydrates 8 g
Cholesterol 2 mg
Total Fat 0 g
Saturated 0 g
Polyunsaturated 0 g
Monounsaturated 0 g
Fiber 0 g
Sodium 112 mg

Skewered Chicken Strips with Soy-Peanut Marinade

Serves 16; 2 skewers per serving

This flavorful chicken strip appetizer will be the talk of your next party. (See Cook's Tip on Skewered Food on page 199 for how to make a festive presentation.) Try this recipe for dinner, using unsliced chicken breast halves.

4 boneless, skinless chicken breast halves (about 4 ounces each), all visible fat removed

SOY-PEANUT MARINADE

2 tablespoons fresh lime juice (1 to 2 medium limes)

1 tablespoon light soy sauce

1 tablespoon reduced-fat peanut butter

1 tablespoon rice vinegar

2 medium cloves garlic, minced, or 1 teaspoon bottled minced garlic

½ teaspoon toasted sesame oil

½ teaspoon ground cumin

¼ teaspoon pepper

Rinse chicken and pat dry with paper towels. Put chicken smooth side up between two sheets of plastic wrap. Using a tortilla press or smooth side of a meat mallet, lightly flatten chicken. Cut each piece lengthwise into 8 long strips.

In a small nonmetallic bowl, whisk together marinade ingredients. Put marinade and chicken in an airtight plastic bag and turn bag to coat. Seal and refrigerate for 30 minutes to 8 hours, turning bag occasionally.

Meanwhile, soak 32 wooden skewers in cold water for at least 10 minutes.

Preheat grill on medium-high.

Thread 1 strip of chicken on each skewer. Grill for 2 to 3 minutes on each side, or until chicken is cooked through. Serve hot or cover and refrigerate to serve chilled.

Calories 30
Protein 6 g
Carbohydrates 0 g
Cholesterol 16 mg
Total Fat 1 g
  Saturated 0 g
  Polyunsaturated 0 g
  Monounsaturated 0 g
Fiber 0 g
Sodium 51 mg

Meatballs in Beer Sauce

Serves 16; 2 meatballs per serving

You can make the sauce while these easy meatballs bake.

Vegetable oil spray

MEATBALLS

2 slices whole-wheat bread, cut into cubes

4 ounces light beer or nonalcoholic beer

1 pound lean ground beef

½ cup shredded nonfat or part-skim mozzarella cheese (about 2 ounces)

½ teaspoon pepper, or to taste

SAUCE

1 teaspoon light margarine

½ cup chopped onion

1 tablespoon all-purpose flour

8 ounces light beer or nonalcoholic beer

2 tablespoons light brown sugar

2 tablespoons cider vinegar

2 tablespoons Beef Broth (see page 39 or use commercial low-sodium variety)

Preheat oven to 350° F. Lightly spray a baking sheet with vegetable oil spray.

For meatballs, in a medium bowl, soak bread cubes in beer for 2 to 3 minutes. Add remaining meatball ingredients, blending well.

Form mixture into 32 meatballs. Arrange on baking sheet.

Bake for 15 minutes.

Meanwhile, for sauce, melt margarine in a small skillet over medium-high heat. Swirl to coat bottom. Sauté onion until translucent, 2 to 3 minutes.

Add flour and cook for 1 to 2 minutes, stirring constantly.

Stir in remaining sauce ingredients. Reduce heat and simmer for 10 minutes.

When meatballs are done, drain on paper towels and pat to remove fat. Add meatballs to sauce and simmer for 20 minutes.

Calories 72
Protein 8 g
Carbohydrates 4 g
Cholesterol 12 mg
Total Fat 2 g
  Saturated 1 g
  Polyunsaturated 0 g
  Monounsaturated 0 g
Fiber 0 g
Sodium 71 mg

Pita Crisps

Serves 18; 2 wedges per serving

Excellent as snacks, these herb-flecked bread wedges also complement soups and salads.

3 6-inch whole-wheat pita breads
¼ cup very finely snipped fresh parsley
2 green onions, finely chopped
1 teaspoon olive oil
¾ teaspoon dried basil, crumbled
½ teaspoon dried rosemary, crushed
1 medium clove garlic, minced, or ½ teaspoon bottled minced garlic
Olive oil spray
2 tablespoons grated Parmesan cheese

Preheat oven to 350° F.

Separate each pita bread into 2 round single layers.

In a small bowl, combine parsley, green onions, olive oil, basil, rosemary, and garlic. Stir well. Spread mixture evenly over pita breads.

Lightly spray tops with olive oil spray, then sprinkle with Parmesan. Cut each pita bread half into 6 wedges.

Bake on ungreased baking sheet for 12 minutes, or until crisp. Serve warm.

Cook's Tip

Store any leftovers in an airtight container for up to a week.

Calories 27
Protein 1 g
Carbohydrates 5 g
Cholesterol 1 mg
Total Fat 1 g
  Saturated 0 g
  Polyunsaturated 0 g
  Monounsaturated 0 g
Fiber 1 g
Sodium 42 mg

Nibbles

Serves 16; ½ cup per serving

Serve this snack warm, or cool it thoroughly and store it in an airtight container.

5 cups dry cereal (such as rice squares, wheat squares, oat circles, and puffed corn, or a combination)

2 cups unsalted pretzel sticks, broken in half

¼ cup fat-free margarine

2 teaspoons very low sodium or low-sodium Worcestershire sauce

1 teaspoon celery flakes

1 teaspoon onion powder

½ teaspoon garlic powder

½ cup raw peanuts or unsalted dry-roasted nuts

Preheat oven to 275° F.

In a large bowl, combine cereal and pretzel sticks.

In a small saucepan, melt margarine over low heat. Add remaining ingredients except nuts, stirring well. Stir into cereal mixture.

Add nuts and stir to combine. Transfer mixture to a shallow roasting pan.

Bake for 1 hour, stirring every 10 minutes.

Southwestern Nibbles

Add ½ teaspoon ground cumin, ½ teaspoon chili powder, and ⅛ teaspoon red hot-pepper sauce to melted margarine with the other seasonings.

Cook's Tip on Dry-Roasting Nuts

One way to dry-roast nuts is to put them in a shallow baking pan and roast them in a 350° F oven for 10 to 15 minutes, stirring occasionally. If you prefer, heat them in an ungreased skillet over medium heat for 1 to 5 minutes, stirring frequently.

Calories 89
Protein 2 g
Carbohydrates 14 g
Cholesterol 0 mg
Total Fat 2 g
Saturated 0 g
Polyunsaturated 1 g
Monounsaturated 1 g
Fiber 1 g
Sodium 121 mg

Sparkling Cranberry Cooler

Serves 4

Chill your prettiest glasses for serving this festive drink.

1½ cups cranberry juice (not cranberry drink)

1 cup purple grape juice

½ cup burgundy, other dry red wine, or nonalcoholic red wine

2 teaspoons fresh lime juice

1½ cups lemon-lime soda

Calories 149
Protein 0 g
Carbohydrates 33 g
Cholesterol 0 mg
Total Fat 0 g
Saturated 0 g
Polyunsaturated 0 g
Monounsaturated 0 g
Fiber 0 g
Sodium 22 mg

In a glass pitcher, combine all ingredients except soda, stirring to mix. Refrigerate for at least 1 hour, or until well chilled.

To serve, stir in soda and add ice, if desired. Serve immediately.

Sparkling Orange Juice Cooler

Replace cranberry juice with orange juice, purple grape juice with white grape juice, and burgundy with dry white wine or nonalcoholic white wine. (calories 136; protein 1 g; carbohydrates 20 g; cholesterol 0 mg; total fat 0 g; saturated 0 g; polyunsaturated 0 g; monounsaturated 0 g; fiber 0 g; sodium 16 mg)

Berry Good Smoothie

Serves 2

Drink your dessert and get more fresh fruit into your diet at the same time.

1 cup fresh strawberries, hulled and halved, or raspberries

1 medium banana, cut into large pieces

1 cup fresh orange juice (3 medium oranges)

In a food processor or blender, puree all ingredients.

Cook's Tip

If your food processor or blender can crush ice, add ½ to 2 cups ice to make a sherbetlike dessert.

Calories 132
Protein 2 g
Carbohydrates 32 g
Cholesterol 0 mg
Total Fat 1 g
  Saturated 0 g
  Polyunsaturated 0 g
  Monounsaturated 0 g
Fiber 3 g
Sodium 3 mg

Frozen Fruit Slush

Serves 6

No matter your age, you never outgrow the love of frozen fruit concoctions on a stick. These treats will bring back sweet childhood memories.

½ cup water
¼ cup frozen limeade concentrate
½ 16-ounce bag unsweetened frozen mixed fruit, slightly thawed
1 tablespoon plus 1 teaspoon sugar
12 ice cubes (about 2 cups)

Put half of each ingredient in a blender and process until smooth. Pour into three ⅓-cup molds. Repeat with remaining ingredients.

Freeze until firm, about 4 hours.

Calories 50
Protein 0 g
Carbohydrates 12 g
Cholesterol 0 mg
Total Fat 1 g
  Saturated 0 g
  Polyunsaturated 0 g
  Monounsaturated 0 g
Fiber 1 g
Sodium 2 mg

SOUPS

Beef Broth

Chicken Broth

Vegetable Broth

Greek Egg and Lemon Soup

Creamy Asparagus Soup

Chilled Asparagus Soup

Broccoli Yogurt Soup

Cucumber Watercress Soup

Fresh Mushroom Soup

Onion Soup

Spinach Pasta Soup

Summer Squash Soup

Flavorful Tomato Bouillon

Tomato Corn Soup

Gazpacho

Vegetable Soup

Minestrone

Five-Minute Soup

Any-Season Fruit Soup

Yogurt Fruit Soup

Minted Cantaloupe Soup with Fresh Lime

Black Bean Soup

European Cabbage and White Bean Soup

Spicy Chick-Pea and Chayote Soup

Lentil Soup

Lentil Chili Soup

Split Pea Soup

New England Fish Chowder

Shrimp Gumbo

Chile-Chicken Tortilla Soup

Chicken, Greens, and Potato Soup

Beef Barley Soup

Beef Broth

Makes 3½ quarts

Roasting the bones is the key to making this beef broth so flavorful.

Vegetable oil spray
6 pounds beef bones (or beef and veal combination)
1 teaspoon acceptable vegetable oil
2 large carrots, sliced
2 large leeks (white and green parts), sliced
2 ribs celery, including leaves, coarsely chopped
1 large onion, quartered
5 quarts water
8 whole peppercorns
3 sprigs of fresh thyme
6 to 8 sprigs of fresh parsley

Preheat oven to 400° F. Lightly spray a large baking pan with vegetable oil spray.

Arrange beef bones in baking pan and brown in oven for 40 minutes to 1 hour.

Meanwhile, pour oil into a large stockpot over medium-high heat. Sauté carrots, leeks, celery, and onion for 6 minutes, stirring occasionally. Cook, covered, for 15 to 20 minutes, or until leeks are limp.

Add remaining ingredients, including browned bones. Bring to a boil over high heat. Reduce heat and simmer, covered, for 4 to 5 hours. Strain broth and discard solids. Cover broth and refrigerate for 6 to 8 hours. Remove congealed fat from surface and discard.

(FOR 1 CUP)
Calories 3
Protein 0 g
Carbohydrates 0 g
Cholesterol 0 mg
Total Fat 0 g
Saturated 0 g
Polyunsaturated 0 g
Monounsaturated 0 g
Fiber 0 g
Sodium 10 mg

Cook's Tip on Freezing Broth

Freeze broth for future use in covered plastic containers or clean waxed containers, such as milk cartons. For smaller amounts, freeze broth in a muffin tin or ice cube trays, then store it in an airtight plastic freezer bag. Thaw broth for several hours in the refrigerator or by heating in the microwave.

Chicken Broth

Makes 4 quarts

Homemade broth is so much more flavorful—and so much lower in sodium—than canned that it really is worth taking the time to make your own. You can skip the roasting bones, but the roasting definitely adds flavor. (See the Cook's Tip on Freezing Broth, page 39, for how to always have a supply of homemade broth on hand.)

Vegetable oil spray
4 pounds chicken bones
1 teaspoon acceptable vegetable oil
2 medium carrots, sliced
2 medium leeks (white and green parts), sliced
1 rib celery, including leaves, coarsely chopped
1 large onion, quartered
2 cups dry white wine (regular or nonalcoholic)
5 quarts water
8 whole peppercorns
1 bay leaf
3 sprigs of fresh thyme
6 to 8 sprigs of fresh parsley

Preheat oven to 400° F. Lightly spray a large baking pan with vegetable oil spray.

Arrange chicken bones in baking pan and brown in oven for 1 hour. (If you prefer a lighter-colored broth, brown bones for only 30 to 40 minutes.)

Meanwhile, pour the oil into a large stockpot over medium-high heat. Sauté carrots, leeks, celery, and onion for 5 minutes, stirring occasionally. Cook, covered, for 10 minutes.

Add wine and boil, uncovered, for 5 to 10 minutes, or until wine evaporates.

Add remaining ingredients, including browned bones. Bring to a boil over high heat. Reduce heat and simmer, covered, for about 5 hours. Strain broth and discard solids. Cover broth and refrigerate for about 8 hours. Remove congealed fat from surface and discard.

(FOR 1 CUP)
Calories 23
Protein 0 g
Carbohydrates 0 g
Cholesterol 0 mg
Total Fat 0 g
Saturated 0 g
Polyunsaturated 0 g
Monounsaturated 0 g
Fiber 0 g
Sodium 11 mg

Vegetable Broth

Makes 1¾ quarts

Aromatic vegetables are the base for this versatile broth. Use it in other soups and in vegetarian dishes. It's great for moistening corn bread dressing and as a substitute for water when cooking rice. *(See the Cook's Tip on Freezing Broth, page 39, for how to always have a supply of homemade broth on hand.)*

1 teaspoon acceptable vegetable oil
2 medium onions, quartered
2 large leeks (white and green parts), sliced
9 to 10 cups water
2 medium carrots, sliced
3 ribs celery, including leaves, coarsely chopped
3 large sprigs of fresh parsley
3 or 4 sprigs of fresh thyme
12 whole peppercorns
1 bay leaf

In a heavy stockpot, heat oil over medium-high heat for about 30 seconds, swirling to coat bottom of pot. Sauté onions and leeks for 4 to 5 minutes, stirring occasionally.

Add remaining ingredients. Bring to a boil over high heat. Reduce heat and simmer for 1¼ to 1½ hours, or until reduced to 8 cups. Strain broth and discard solids. Cover broth and refrigerate. Remove congealed fat from surface, if necessary, and discard.

Vegetable Bouillon

Simmer cooked broth until reduced by half, 20 to 30 minutes. Use when recipe calls for canned bouillon. (For 1 cup: calories 7; protein 0 g; carbohydrates 0 g; cholesterol 0 mg; total fat 1 g; saturated 0 g; polyunsaturated 0 g; monounsaturated 0 g; fiber 0 g; sodium 10 mg)

(FOR 1 CUP)
Calories 7
Protein 0 g
Carbohydrates 0 g
Cholesterol 0 mg
Total Fat 1 g
Saturated 0 g
Polyunsaturated 0 g
Monounsaturated 0 g
Fiber 0 g
Sodium 10 mg

Greek Egg and Lemon Soup

Serves 4

Avgolemono (ahv-goh-LEH-moh-noh) *is the Greek name for this simply delicious soup. It's fun to stir in the egg–lemon mixture and watch it create an interesting texture and appearance.*

1 quart Chicken Broth (see page 40 or use commercial low-sodium variety)

¼ cup uncooked rice

Egg substitute equivalent to 3 eggs, room temperature

¼ cup fresh lemon juice (1 to 2 medium lemons)

Pour broth into a large stockpot and bring to a boil over medium-high heat.

Stir in rice. Reduce heat and simmer, covered, until rice is tender, 15 to 20 minutes. Remove from heat.

In a medium bowl, whisk together egg substitute and lemon juice. Whisk half the broth, a little at a time, into egg mixture. Pour egg mixture back into remaining broth, whisking well.

Reduce heat to low and cook just until soup has thickened, 4 to 5 minutes, stirring constantly. Don't let soup boil.

(FOR 1 CUP)
Calories 109
Protein 7 g
Carbohydrates 12 g
Cholesterol 0 mg
Total Fat 2 g
Saturated 0 g
Polyunsaturated 1 g
Monounsaturated 0 g
Fiber 0 g
Sodium 86 mg

Creamy Asparagus Soup

Serves 4

Pureed rice adds creaminess to this simple-to-make soup.

1 tablespoon Chicken Broth (see page 40 or use commercial low-sodium variety)

½ cup chopped onion (1 medium)

½ cup chopped celery (1 medium rib)

4 cups Chicken Broth (see page 40 or use commercial low-sodium variety)

10-ounce package frozen no-salt-added asparagus spears, thawed

¼ cup uncooked rice

Dash of ground white pepper

Dash of ground nutmeg

In a large saucepan, heat 1 tablespoon broth over medium-high heat. Sauté onion and celery for 2 to 3 minutes, or until onion is translucent, stirring occasionally.

Add 4 cups broth and bring to a boil.

Meanwhile, trim tips off asparagus and reserve. Cut stalks into 1-inch pieces.

When broth is boiling, stir in asparagus pieces (not tips) and rice. Reduce heat and simmer, covered, for 15 minutes, or until rice is tender.

In a food processor or blender, process broth mixture until completely smooth. Return to pan.

Add asparagus tips, pepper, and nutmeg; reheat.

Calories 94
Protein 3 g
Carbohydrates 15 g
Cholesterol 0 mg
Total Fat 1 g
 Saturated 0 g
 Polyunsaturated 0 g
 Monounsaturated 0 g
Fiber 2 g
Sodium 26 mg

Chilled Asparagus Soup

Serves 3

In spring and summer, when fresh asparagus is plentiful, try this refreshing make-ahead soup.

2 cups fresh asparagus, cut into ¾-inch pieces (about 8 ounces)
1½ cups Chicken Broth (see page 40 or use commercial low-sodium variety)
½ cup chopped onion (1 medium)
1 to 2 teaspoons grated gingerroot
1 tablespoon cornstarch
½ cup Chicken Broth (see page 40 or use commercial low-sodium variety)
¼ teaspoon salt
⅓ cup nonfat or light sour cream

In a medium saucepan, combine asparagus, 1½ cups broth, onion, and gingerroot. Bring to a boil over medium-high heat. Reduce heat and simmer, covered, for about 5 minutes, or until vegetables are tender.

Carefully pour about half the hot mixture into a food processor or blender; puree. Return mixture to saucepan.

Put cornstarch in a small bowl. Add remaining broth, stirring to dissolve. Add cornstarch mixture and salt to vegetable mixture. Cook until slightly thickened and bubbly, about 2 minutes, whisking constantly. Continue to cook for 2 minutes, whisking constantly.

Pour soup into a large bowl. Cover and refrigerate until chilled, about 2 hours.

To serve, whisk in sour cream.

Calories 81
Protein 4 g
Carbohydrates 13 g
Cholesterol 0 mg
Total Fat 0 g
  Saturated 0 g
  Polyunsaturated 0 g
  Monounsaturated 0 g
Fiber 2 g
Sodium 231 mg

Cook's Tip on Asparagus

An asparagus spear has a natural bending point where the tough stem ends. Holding a spear of asparagus at the top and the bottom, bend the spear; snap at the bending point. Discard the tough part, or save it to use in making broths and other soups.

Broccoli Yogurt Soup

Serves 6

This flavorful soup does double duty—serve it either hot or cold.

1½ pounds fresh broccoli

1 tablespoon Chicken Broth (see page 40 or use commercial low-sodium variety)

1 cup diced onion (about 2 medium)

5 cups water or Chicken Broth (see page 40 or use commercial low-sodium variety)

1½ teaspoons curry powder

16-ounce container plain nonfat or low-fat yogurt

½ teaspoon pepper, or to taste

⅛ teaspoon ground nutmeg

Trim broccoli, cutting florets so they have a 1-inch stem. Peel stalks and cut into 1-inch pieces.

Pour 1 tablespoon broth into a small skillet over medium-high heat. Sauté onions for 2 to 3 minutes, or until translucent.

In a large saucepan over high heat, bring water or broth to a boil. Add broccoli and boil gently for 6 to 7 minutes, or until just tender.

Stir in onion and curry powder. Reduce heat and simmer, partially covered, for 10 to 15 minutes.

In a food processor or blender, puree vegetables and broth in batches.

To serve hot, return pureed mixture to saucepan and add remaining ingredients. Blend well. Heat, but do not boil.

To serve cold, cover and refrigerate pureed mixture. Remove from refrigerator and blend in remaining ingredients just before serving.

Calories 70
Protein 6 g
Carbohydrates 12 g
Cholesterol 2 mg
Total Fat 1 g
Saturated 0 g
Polyunsaturated 0 g
Monounsaturated 0 g
Fiber 4 g
Sodium 85 mg

Cucumber Watercress Soup

Serves 6

Dainty cucumber and watercress sandwiches are popular at high tea. Why not serve this soup for a change? It combines the same mellow cucumber and peppery watercress. Serve it hot or chilled at everything from tea to picnics.

1 large cucumber, unpeeled

1 tablespoon Chicken Broth (see page 40 or use commercial low-sodium variety)

1 cup finely chopped onion (about 2 medium)

4 cups Chicken Broth (see page 40 or use commercial low-sodium variety)

1 large bunch watercress, leaves only (about 2 cups, packed)

2 tablespoons uncooked rice

¼ teaspoon white pepper

1 tablespoon finely snipped fresh dillweed or 1 teaspoon dried, crumbled

¼ cup plain nonfat or low-fat yogurt

1 Italian plum tomato, thinly sliced (optional)

Cut cucumber in half lengthwise. Scoop out seeds with a spoon; discard seeds. Dice cucumber.

Pour 1 tablespoon broth into a large saucepan over medium-high heat. Sauté onions for 2 to 3 minutes, or until translucent.

Reduce heat to medium. Stir in cucumber, 4 cups broth, watercress, rice, and pepper. Cook for 15 to 20 minutes, or until rice is tender.

Add dillweed and cook for 2 minutes.

In a food processor or blender, puree mixture in batches.

To serve hot, return mixture to saucepan and whisk in yogurt. Heat, but do not boil. Garnish with tomato slices.

To serve cold, cover and refrigerate pureed mixture. Just before serving, whisk in yogurt and garnish with tomato slices.

Calories 54
Protein 2 g
Carbohydrates 8 g
Cholesterol 0 mg
Total Fat 0 g
Saturated 0 g
Polyunsaturated 0 g
Monounsaturated 0 g
Fiber 1 g
Sodium 192 mg

Fresh Mushroom Soup

Serves 4

Try a variety of mushrooms to make your soup exotic. Among the choices are shiitake, portobello, oyster, golden Italian, and, of course, button.

1 teaspoon light margarine
4 ounces fresh mushrooms, finely chopped (1 to 1¼ cups)
4 ounces fresh mushrooms, sliced (1 to 1¼ cups)
1 cup chopped onion (about 2 medium)
2 medium cloves garlic, minced, or 1 teaspoon bottled minced garlic
3½ cups Chicken Broth (see page 40 or use commercial low-sodium variety)
5-ounce can fat-free evaporated milk
⅓ cup all-purpose flour
1½ tablespoons finely snipped fresh parsley
1 tablespoon dry sherry
½ teaspoon grated lemon zest
1 teaspoon fresh lemon juice
¼ teaspoon salt
⅛ teaspoon white pepper

In a large saucepan, heat margarine over medium heat, swirling to coat bottom of pan. Cook mushrooms, onions, and garlic, covered, for 8 to 10 minutes, stirring occasionally. Increase heat to high and cook, uncovered, for 2 to 3 minutes, allowing moisture to evaporate.

In a medium bowl, whisk together broth, milk, and flour. Immediately whisk broth mixture into mushroom mixture. Bring to a boil over medium-high heat, stirring occasionally. Cook for 3 to 5 minutes, or until thickened, stirring occasionally.

Stir in remaining ingredients.

Cook's Tip

If you can't immediately add the broth mixture to the mushroom mixture, stir the broth mixture to keep the flour from settling to the bottom of the bowl.

Calories 117
Protein 5 g
Carbohydrates 18 g
Cholesterol 1 mg
Total Fat 1 g
  Saturated 0 g
  Polyunsaturated 0 g
  Monounsaturated 0 g
Fiber 2 g
Sodium 204 mg

Onion Soup

Serves 6

Caramelized onions give this soup its rich flavor. Once you master the technique, you can use caramelized onions to enhance the flavor of other dishes. For starters, try them in casseroles, in quiches, and on pizzas.

12 slices French bread (baguette) (about ⅓ ounce each)

4 tablespoons grated Parmesan cheese

1 teaspoon light margarine

1 teaspoon acceptable vegetable oil

3 cups thinly sliced onions (about 3 medium)

½ teaspoon sugar

¼ teaspoon salt

6 cups Beef Broth (see page 39 or use commercial low-sodium variety)

½ cup dry white wine (regular or nonalcoholic)

1 bay leaf

¼ teaspoon dried thyme, crumbled

¼ teaspoon pepper, or to taste

⅛ teaspoon ground nutmeg

Calories 120
Protein 4 g
Carbohydrates 16 g
Cholesterol 3 mg
Total Fat 3 g
Saturated 1 g
Polyunsaturated 1 g
Monounsaturated 1 g
Fiber 1 g
Sodium 306 mg

Preheat oven to 350° F.

Put bread slices on a baking sheet and bake for 10 minutes, or until toasted. Sprinkle with Parmesan and bake for 1 to 2 minutes, or until cheese melts. Set aside.

Heat margarine and oil in a large saucepan over medium-high heat, swirling to coat bottom of pan. Sauté onions for 2 minutes. Reduce heat to low and cook, covered, until translucent, about 5 minutes.

Add sugar and salt. Increase heat to medium-high and cook, uncovered, until onions are golden brown, 15 to 20 minutes, stirring occasionally. After the first 10 minutes, stir more often to prevent onions from sticking and burning.

Stir in remaining ingredients and bring to a boil. Simmer, partially covered, for 15 minutes.

To serve, ladle soup into bowls. Put 2 toasted bread slices in each bowl.

Spinach Pasta Soup

Serves 4

Very easy to make and attractive as well, this soup will fast become a favorite.

4 cups Chicken Broth (see page 40 or use commercial low-sodium variety)
½ cup water
¼ cup plus 1 tablespoon no-salt-added tomato paste
½ teaspoon grated lemon zest (optional)
¼ cup orzo or pastina
6 cups chopped fresh spinach, leaves only, patted dry (about 8 ounces), or ½ of 10-ounce package frozen chopped spinach, thawed and well drained
¼ cup sliced green onions (about 2)
¼ teaspoon pepper
¼ teaspoon salt

In a medium saucepan over medium-high heat, combine broth, water, tomato paste, and lemon zest. Whisk until smooth. Bring to a boil.

Stir in pasta. Reduce heat to medium and cook for 5 to 7 minutes, or until pasta is tender.

Stir in spinach and green onions and cook for 2 to 3 minutes.

To serve, stir in pepper and salt.

Cook's Tip on Orzo

Orzo looks like, and is a good substitute for, rice. Actually, it's very small pasta, so look for it in your supermarket's pasta section.

Cook's Tip on Pastina

Pastina, or tiny pasta, is frequently used in soups. If you cannot find pastina, crush any type of macaroni.

Calories 95
Protein 4 g
Carbohydrates 15 g
Cholesterol 0 mg
Total Fat 1 g
Saturated 0 g
Polyunsaturated 0 g
Monounsaturated 0 g
Fiber 3 g
Sodium 222 mg

Summer Squash Soup

Serves 5

With summer squash available all year round, you can enjoy this comforting thyme-flavored soup anytime.

1 cup chopped onion (about 2 medium)

1 teaspoon light margarine

2 medium crookneck squash, zucchini, or a combination, diced (10 to 12 ounces)

2 cups Chicken Broth (see page 40 or use commercial low-sodium variety)

2 tablespoons uncooked rice

1 teaspoon dried thyme, crumbled

2 cups Chicken Broth (see page 40 or use commercial low-sodium variety)

½ cup grated peeled carrots

½ cup plain nonfat or low-fat yogurt

Calories 76
Protein 2 g
Carbohydrates 12 g
Cholesterol 1 mg
Total Fat 1 g
Saturated 0 g
Polyunsaturated 0 g
Monounsaturated 0 g
Fiber 2 g
Sodium 36 mg

In a medium saucepan over medium-high heat, sauté onions in margarine until translucent, 2 to 3 minutes.

Add squash and cook for 5 minutes. Remove 1 cup of the mixture and set aside.

Add 2 cups broth, rice, and thyme to pan. Cook over medium heat for 20 minutes, or until rice is tender. In a food processor or blender, carefully process (in batches if necessary) until pureed.

Return pureed mixture to pan. Add 2 cups broth and carrots. Cook over medium-high heat for 5 minutes, stirring occasionally. Reduce heat to low and add reserved squash mixture. Cook for 1 to 2 minutes, stirring occasionally.

Stir in yogurt and cook for 1 to 2 minutes, or until warmed through.

Cook's Tip

Don't rinse the extra starch off the rice. It will help thicken the soup.

Flavorful Tomato Bouillon

Serves 6

A wide variety of herbs and spices transforms basic tomato juice and beef broth into a soothing bouillon. Serve some today and freeze the rest for other uses, such as flavoring vegetables, poached fish, and pasta.

46-ounce can no-salt-added tomato juice

2 cups Beef Broth (see page 39 or use commercial low-sodium variety)

2 to 3 tablespoons snipped fresh dillweed or 2 teaspoons dried, crumbled

2 bay leaves

6 whole cloves

½ teaspoon dried basil, crumbled

½ teaspoon dried marjoram, crumbled

½ teaspoon dried oregano, crumbled

½ teaspoon sugar

¼ to ½ teaspoon pepper

6 thin slices lemon (optional)

Whisk together tomato juice and broth in a large glass bowl or jar.

Add remaining ingredients except lemon and stir to blend.

Pour soup into a medium-size heavy saucepan and bring to a boil over medium-high heat. Reduce heat and simmer for 30 minutes. Remove cloves and bay leaves.

Ladle soup into soup bowls or mugs and top each serving with a slice of lemon.

Microwave Method

Put all ingredients except lemon in a 3-quart microwave-safe baking dish. Cover and bring to a boil on 100 percent (high). Reduce power to 50 percent (medium), and cook for 7 to 8 minutes. Let soup rest for 5 minutes, then serve topped with slices of lemon.

Calories 41
Protein 2 g
Carbohydrates 10 g
Cholesterol 0 mg
Total Fat 0 g
Saturated 0 g
Polyunsaturated 0 g
Monounsaturated 0 g
Fiber 2 g
Sodium 26 mg

Tomato Corn Soup

Serves 5

You can put this comforting soup together quickly with ingredients you usually have on hand.

1 teaspoon olive oil
½ cup chopped onion (about 1 medium)
14.5-ounce can no-salt-added whole tomatoes, crushed
17-ounce can no-salt-added cream-style corn
2 cups fat-free milk
½ teaspoon bouquet garni (optional)
½ teaspoon salt-free all-purpose seasoning
¼ teaspoon salt (optional)

Heat a large, heavy saucepan over medium heat. Add oil and swirl to coat bottom of skillet. When oil is hot, sauté onion for 5 minutes, stirring occasionally.

In a food processor or blender, puree onion and tomatoes. Pour mixture back into saucepan.

Puree corn and pour into tomato mixture.

Increase heat to medium-high and bring tomato mixture to a boil. Reduce heat and simmer for 20 minutes.

Stir in remaining ingredients. Increase heat to medium-high and bring mixture just to boiling point.

Cook's Tip on Bouquet Garni

Traditionally, a bouquet garni (French for "garnished bouquet") consists of parsley, thyme, and a bay leaf, tied together by their stems or tied in cheesecloth and cooked in soups or stews. Make your own bouquet garni or buy it—with different herbs—in a jar at the supermarket.

Calories 131
Protein 6 g
Carbohydrates 27 g
Cholesterol 2 mg
Total Fat 2 g
 Saturated 0 g
 Polyunsaturated 0 g
 Monounsaturated 1 g
Fiber 3 g
Sodium 62 mg

Gazpacho

Serves 7

This cold soup is versatile as well as refreshing. Make it part of a late-night supper with a sandwich or low-fat cheese and crackers, or serve a small portion as a palate cleanser between courses. It's also a great salsa for dipping baked chips or for topping grilled chicken or fish.

6 cups peeled and chopped tomatoes (8 to 9 medium) or canned no-salt-added Italian plum tomatoes
1 medium onion, coarsely chopped (about ½ cup)
½ cup coarsely chopped green bell pepper
½ cup coarsely chopped cucumber (peeled if outer skin is tough)
1 medium clove garlic, minced, or ½ teaspoon bottled minced garlic
2 cups no-salt-added tomato juice
¼ cup red wine vinegar
½ teaspoon sugar
½ teaspoon ground cumin (optional)
⅛ to ¼ teaspoon pepper
Garlic croutons (optional)
1 cup finely chopped tomato (optional) (about 2 medium)
½ cup finely chopped onion (optional)
½ cup finely chopped green bell pepper (optional)
½ cup finely chopped cucumber (optional)

In a food processor or blender, puree 6 cups tomatoes, medium onion, ½ cup bell pepper, ½ cup cucumber, and garlic in batches. Pour each batch into a large bowl.

Add tomato juice, vinegar, sugar, cumin, and pepper, stirring well. Cover and refrigerate for at least 30 minutes.

Ladle into individual serving bowls. Sprinkle with croutons. Put remaining ingredients in individual dishes for use as garnishes.

Calories 59
Protein 2 g
Carbohydrates 13 g
Cholesterol 0 mg
Total Fat 1 g
Saturated 0 g
Polyunsaturated 0 g
Monounsaturated 0 g
Fiber 3 g
Sodium 22 mg

Vegetable Soup

Serves 9

Pureeing part of the vegetables gives this soup body and thickness. Add or substitute other vegetables, such as squash or leeks, to vary the flavor.

6 cups Beef Broth (see page 39 or use commercial low-sodium variety)

2 cups peeled, diced potatoes (2 to 3 medium)

2 cups diced carrots (about 2 large)

1 cup green beans (about 4 ounces fresh)

1 cup diced celery (about 2 medium ribs)

1 cup chopped onion (about 2 medium)

1 cup shredded cabbage

6-ounce can no-salt-added tomato paste

1 teaspoon dried thyme, crumbled

¼ teaspoon pepper

¼ teaspoon salt

⅓ cup finely snipped fresh parsley

Combine all ingredients except parsley in a large stockpot and bring to a boil over medium-high heat. Reduce heat and simmer for 20 minutes, or until vegetables are tender.

Remove 3 cups vegetables and broth, and puree in a food processor or blender. Return puree to pot, add parsley, and reheat.

Calories 75
Protein 2 g
Carbohydrates 17 g
Cholesterol 0 mg
Total Fat 1 g
 Saturated 0 g
 Polyunsaturated 0 g
 Monounsaturated 0 g
Fiber 3 g
Sodium 122 mg

Minestrone

Serves 10

One of the best things about a recipe like this is that almost anything works. The combination of vegetables can be different each time you make the soup.

1 cup dried navy beans, sorted for stones and rinsed (about 8 ounces), or 15-ounce can

2 teaspoons olive oil

1 medium onion, chopped (about ½ cup)

2 medium carrots, chopped (about 1½ cups)

2 ribs celery, including leaves, chopped (about 1 cup)

2 medium cloves garlic, chopped, or 1 teaspoon bottled minced garlic

8 cups water

2 medium potatoes, peeled and cubed (about 2 cups)

4 medium tomatoes, peeled and cubed, or 15-ounce can no-salt-added diced tomatoes

1 small zucchini, cubed

1 teaspoon pepper, or to taste

½ pound fresh green beans, sliced (about 2 cups)

½ cup whole-wheat dried pasta (shells or elbow macaroni)

1 tablespoon dried basil, crumbled

1 medium clove garlic, whole, or ½ teaspoon bottled minced garlic

1 to 2 cups water (optional)

2 tablespoons grated Parmesan cheese

Cook navy beans using package instructions. Drain. Or drain and rinse canned beans.

Heat stockpot over medium-high heat. Add oil and swirl to coat bottom of pot. When oil is hot, add onion, carrots, celery, and 2 cloves garlic. Sauté for 2 to 3 minutes, or until onion is translucent, stirring occasionally.

Add water, potatoes, tomatoes, zucchini, and pepper. Reduce heat and simmer for 30 minutes.

Add navy beans, green beans, pasta, basil, and 1 clove garlic. Add 1 to 2 cups water if soup is too thick. Heat through.

Slightly mash soup ingredients with a potato masher to help thicken soup. Simmer for 15 minutes.

To serve, sprinkle each serving with Parmesan.

Calories 158
Protein 7 g
Carbohydrates 30 g
Cholesterol 1 mg
Total Fat 2 g
Saturated 1 g
Polyunsaturated 0 g
Monounsaturated 1 g
Fiber 6 g
Sodium 51 mg

Five-Minute Soup

Serves 6

Serve this quick-cooking soup immediately, while the vegetables are fresh and colorful.

4 cups Chicken Broth (see page 40 or use commercial low-sodium variety), heated

½ medium cucumber or 1 medium zucchini, sliced very thin

4 fresh medium mushrooms, sliced

2 cups shredded fresh spinach, lettuce, or cabbage

1 medium tomato, cubed

½ cup cooked chicken or lean meat, shredded

Calories 53
Protein 4 g
Carbohydrates 3 g
Cholesterol 10 mg
Total Fat 1 g
Saturated 0 g
Polyunsaturated 0 g
Monounsaturated 0 g
Fiber 1 g
Sodium 30 mg

Put all ingredients in a large saucepan. Bring to a boil over medium-high heat. Reduce heat and simmer for 5 minutes.

Any-Season Fruit Soup

Serves 8

Because it's made with dried fruit, you can enjoy this fruit soup any time of the year.

2 quarts water

1 cup pitted prunes (about 8 ounces)

1 cup small dried apricot halves (4 to 5 ounces)

1 cup golden or dark raisins (about 5 ounces)

1 stick cinnamon

2 tablespoons cornstarch

¼ cup cold water

In a large saucepan, combine water, prunes, apricots, raisins, and cinnamon stick. Bring mixture to a boil over medium-high heat. Reduce heat and simmer, covered, until fruit is tender but not falling apart, about 15 minutes. Remove cinnamon stick.

In a cup or small bowl, dissolve cornstarch in water. Add to fruit and cook until thickened, 2 to 3 minutes, stirring constantly.

Serve hot or cover and refrigerate to serve cold.

Calories 113
Protein 1 g
Carbohydrates 29 g
Cholesterol 0 mg
Total Fat 0 g
  Saturated 0 g
  Polyunsaturated 0 g
  Monounsaturated 0 g
Fiber 4 g
Sodium 11 mg

Yogurt Fruit Soup

Serves 4

Chilled soup is a wonderful way to begin a brunch or luncheon.

2 cups peeled and cubed fresh peaches (about 4 medium)
16-ounce container plain nonfat or low-fat yogurt
1 cup fresh strawberries, hulled (about ½ pint)
½ cup fresh orange juice
½ cup water
1 tablespoon honey
Sprigs of fresh mint (optional)

Put all ingredients except mint leaves in a food processor or blender. Process until well blended and desired consistency.

Pour into a glass bowl, cover, and refrigerate for at least 3 hours.

To serve, garnish with mint leaves.

Variation

Try a wide variety of fruits in place of peaches and strawberries. Substitute unsweetened frozen peaches, blueberries, or mixed fruit for fresh peaches (defrost fruit before using), or use 1 or 2 medium bananas in place of strawberries.

Calories 137
Protein 5 g
Carbohydrates 30 g
Cholesterol 3 mg
Total Fat 0 g
  Saturated 0 g
  Polyunsaturated 0 g
  Monounsaturated 0 g
Fiber 3 g
Sodium 77 mg

Minted Cantaloupe Soup with Fresh Lime

Serves 4

Delicately sweetened melon blended with vanilla, mint, and lime—what a refreshing treat on a hot summer day!

8-ounce container nonfat or low-fat vanilla yogurt
4 cups diced cantaloupe
1 tablespoon plus 1 teaspoon sugar
¼ cup chopped fresh mint leaves
1½ to 2 tablespoons fresh lime juice
Sprigs of fresh mint (optional)

Put yogurt, cantaloupe, sugar, and ¼ cup mint, in order listed, in a food processor or blender. Process until smooth.

Pour into a large stainless steel or glass bowl, cover with plastic wrap, and refrigerate until well chilled, at least 1 hour.

To serve, stir in lime juice. Pour soup into individual bowls, garnish with mint leaves, and serve immediately.

Time-Saver: To chill the soup quickly, put it in the freezer for 20 to 25 minutes, or until *very* cold, occasionally stirring at the edges with a rubber scraper. Chill the soup bowls at the same time.

Variation

For a taste of the Caribbean, add 1 teaspoon grated fresh gingerroot and 3 tablespoons frozen orange-pineapple concentrate to the food processor or blender and process with the yogurt mixture.

Calories 126
Protein 4 g
Carbohydrates 28 g
Cholesterol 1 mg
Total Fat 1 g
  Saturated 0 g
  Polyunsaturated 0 g
  Monounsaturated 0 g
Fiber 1 g
Sodium 53 mg

Black Bean Soup

Serves 8

Use an assortment of small bowls for the optional garnishes suggested for this soup. They'll perk up your table setting and let each person select his or her favorite toppings.

1 pound dried black beans, sorted for stones and rinsed
1 medium onion
2 whole cloves
1 bay leaf
1 sprig of fresh parsley
1 medium onion
1 medium green bell pepper
1 teaspoon olive oil
2 medium cloves garlic, minced, or 1 teaspoon bottled minced garlic
8-ounce can no-salt-added tomato sauce
¼ cup dry sherry
1 teaspoon dried oregano, crumbled
1 teaspoon dried thyme, crumbled
1 teaspoon white vinegar
Chopped onion, chopped parsley, snipped chives, chopped cucumber, or peeled and seeded orange sections (optional)

Put black beans in a large bowl. Add enough water to cover. Let sit for at least 6 hours. Drain water from beans and put them in a stockpot.

Peel onion; stick cloves into onion. Add onion, bay leaf, and parsley to pot. Cook using bean package directions.

Meanwhile, chop remaining onion and bell pepper. Put with oil and garlic in a small skillet over medium-high heat. Cook until vegetables are soft, 3 to 4 minutes, stirring occasionally. Add to cooked beans.

Stir in tomato sauce, sherry, oregano, thyme, and vinegar.

For a smooth soup, puree in a food processor or blender. For a thick soup, mash some of the beans right in the pot.

Ladle soup into serving bowls and let each person choose a garnish or two.

Calories 213
Protein 13 g
Carbohydrates 38 g
Cholesterol 0 mg
Total Fat 1 g
- Saturated 0 g
- Polyunsaturated 0 g
- Monounsaturated 0 g

Fiber 13 g
Sodium 8 mg

European Cabbage and White Bean Soup

Serves 8

Be sure to have plenty of hard-crusted bread on hand for dunking!

1 tablespoon extra-virgin olive oil

3 medium leeks (white and pale green parts), coarsely chopped (about 2 cups)

1 large sweet onion, such as Texas Sweet, coarsely chopped (about ¾ cup)

1 pound dried cannellini or Great Northern beans, sorted for stones and rinsed

4 quarts water

2 bay leaves

3 dried juniper berries, crushed with mortar and pestle

6 to 8 green beans, cut into 1-inch pieces

4 ribs celery, including leaves, cut into ½-inch pieces

1 large head green cabbage, coarsely chopped

1 cup coarsely chopped fresh Italian (flat-leaf) parsley

2 tablespoons fresh whole basil leaves

1 tablespoon finely chopped fresh thyme or 1 teaspoon dried, crumbled

1 tablespoon fresh rosemary or 1 teaspoon dried, crushed

½ teaspoon salt

½ teaspoon pepper, or to taste

1 cup fresh basil

Heat a stockpot over medium-low heat. Add oil and swirl to coat bottom; add leeks and onion. Cover and cook for 15 minutes, stirring occasionally.

Add beans, water, bay leaves, and juniper berries. Cover; bring to a boil. Simmer, covered, for 1½ hours. Add hot water if needed.

Stir in remaining ingredients except 1 cup basil. Simmer, covered, for about 45 minutes, or until beans are soft and celery is tender, stirring occasionally.

Ladle 1½ to 2 cups of soup into a food processor or blender. Add basil and puree. Pour pureed mixture into soup. Stir well.

Calories 241
Protein 14 g
Carbohydrates 42 g
Cholesterol 0 mg
Total Fat 3 g
Saturated 1 g
Polyunsaturated 1 g
Monounsaturated 1 g
Fiber 15 g
Sodium 199 mg

Spicy Chick-Pea and Chayote Soup

Serves 4

This soup highlights plump chick-peas, also known as garbanzo beans, and tender cubes of chayote (ky-OH-tay) squash in a zesty tomato broth. Serve it with a mixed green or fresh fruit salad and Pita Crisps (see page 32).

1 chayote squash, peeled, seeded, and diced (about 8 ounces)

18 ounces no-salt-added tomato juice

3 tablespoons no-salt-added tomato paste

2 medium cloves garlic, minced, or 1 teaspoon bottled minced garlic

¼ to ½ teaspoon red hot-pepper sauce, or to taste

15-ounce can no-salt-added chick-peas, drained

¾ cup cubed cooked chicken or turkey

½ teaspoon dried oregano, crumbled

¼ teaspoon salt

¼ teaspoon white pepper

2 tablespoons snipped fresh cilantro or parsley

Put squash in a small saucepan with water to cover by 1 inch. Bring to a boil over high heat. Cook for 8 to 10 minutes, or until tender. Drain.

Meanwhile, in a large saucepan, heat tomato juice, tomato paste, garlic, and hot-pepper sauce over medium-high heat for 4 to 5 minutes, stirring to mix well.

Add squash, chick-peas, and chicken to tomato mixture.

Reduce heat to medium-low. Stir in remaining ingredients except cilantro. Simmer, partially covered, for 5 minutes.

To serve, sprinkle with cilantro.

Calories 195
Protein 15 g
Carbohydrates 27 g
Cholesterol 23 mg
Total Fat 4 g
Saturated 1 g
Polyunsaturated 1 g
Monounsaturated 1 g
Fiber 7 g
Sodium 203 mg

Lentil Soup

Serves 8

For a change of pace, you can puree the cooked soup until it's smooth and creamy.

1 tablespoon Chicken Broth (see page 40 or use commercial low-sodium variety)

1 medium onion, chopped

2 medium cloves garlic, finely chopped, or 1 teaspoon bottled minced garlic

7 cups water

1 cup dried lentils, sorted for stones and rinsed (8 ounces)

1½ teaspoons ground cumin

¼ teaspoon ground ginger

¼ teaspoon ground cloves

⅛ teaspoon cayenne

⅛ teaspoon ground cinnamon

Pepper to taste

In a large stockpot, heat broth over medium-high heat. Cook onion and garlic for 2 to 3 minutes, or until onion is translucent.

Add remaining ingredients. Bring to a boil, reduce heat, and simmer, partially covered, for 35 to 40 minutes, or until lentils are tender.

Calories 81
Protein 6 g
Carbohydrates 14 g
Cholesterol 0 mg
Total Fat 0 g
Saturated 0 g
Polyunsaturated 0 g
Monounsaturated 0 g
Fiber 6 g
Sodium 8 mg

Lentil Chili Soup

Serves 7

Incorporate more lentils into your diet with this robust soup. It gets its full-bodied flavor from beer, chicken broth, and a variety of seasonings.

1 teaspoon acceptable vegetable oil
2 medium onions, chopped (about 1 cup)
1 medium green bell pepper, finely chopped (about 1 cup)
3 medium cloves garlic, minced, or 1½ teaspoons bottled minced garlic
3½ cups Chicken Broth (see page 40 or use commercial low-sodium variety)
12-ounce can light beer or 1½ cups water
1¼ cups water
1½ cups dried lentils, sorted for stones and rinsed (12 ounces)
6-ounce can no-salt-added tomato paste
2½ to 3 tablespoons chili powder
1½ teaspoons ground cumin
1 teaspoon salt-free all-purpose seasoning
1 teaspoon sugar
¼ teaspoon cayenne
6 green onions, finely chopped (about ⅔ cup)
2 ounces grated nonfat or low-fat Cheddar cheese (about ½ cup)

In a heavy stockpot, heat oil over medium-high heat, swirling to coat bottom of pot. Sauté onions, bell pepper, and garlic for 8 to 10 minutes.

Add broth, beer, 1¼ cups water, lentils, tomato paste, chili powder, cumin, all-purpose seasoning, sugar, and cayenne. Bring to a boil. Reduce heat and simmer, partially covered, for 35 to 40 minutes, or until lentils are tender. Stir occasionally and add water if necessary.

To serve, ladle into soup bowls and sprinkle with green onions and Cheddar.

Calories 222
Protein 15 g
Carbohydrates 35 g
Cholesterol 1 mg
Total Fat 2 g
Saturated 0 g
Polyunsaturated 1 g
Monounsaturated 0 g
Fiber 13 g
Sodium 126 mg

Split Pea Soup

Serves 4

Easy to prepare, homemade split pea soup is lower in sodium than its canned cousins. Our version is flavorful even without the usual ham.

1 cup dried split peas, sorted for stones and rinsed (about 8 ounces)
1 teaspoon light margarine
½ cup chopped onion (about 1 medium)
4 cups cold water
3 ribs celery, including leaves, chopped
1 medium carrot, chopped
½ cup snipped fresh parsley
1 teaspoon pepper, or to taste
½ teaspoon dried marjoram
½ teaspoon dried thyme, crumbled
½ teaspoon dried basil, crumbled
½ teaspoon celery seeds
1 bay leaf

Calories 172
Protein 11 g
Carbohydrates 31 g
Cholesterol 0 mg
Total Fat 1 g
Saturated 0 g
Polyunsaturated 0 g
Monounsaturated 0 g
Fiber 12 g
Sodium 56 mg

Soak split peas using package directions.

In a large saucepan, melt margarine over medium-high heat. Swirl to coat bottom of pan. Sauté onion until lightly browned, about 5 minutes.

Add remaining ingredients, including peas. Reduce heat and simmer, covered, 1 to 1½ hours, or until peas are tender, stirring occasionally.

Cook's Tip

If you like soup with lots of texture, serve as is. For a little less texture, use a potato masher for blending the ingredients. For an even smoother texture, process soup in batches in a food processor or blender until desired consistency.

New England Fish Chowder

Serves 6

Chunks of potato and firm-fleshed fish join dainty peas in a creamy chowder that will disappear quickly from the soup pot.

4 cups fat-free milk

2 cups peeled and diced potatoes (2 to 3 medium)

½ teaspoon salt

1 pound fresh cod or haddock

1 teaspoon light margarine

1 cup sliced leeks (white part only) or chopped onion

1 cup frozen baby green peas

2 tablespoons finely snipped fresh parsley

1 tablespoon fresh lemon juice

⅛ teaspoon white pepper

In a large saucepan, bring milk, potatoes, and salt to a simmer over medium heat. Reduce heat to low and cook, covered, for 25 to 30 minutes.

Meanwhile, rinse fish and pat dry with paper towels. Cut into 1-inch pieces.

In a small nonstick skillet, melt margarine over medium-low heat. Swirl to coat bottom of skillet. Add leeks and sauté for 2 to 3 minutes, or until limp.

Remove about 1 cup potatoes and 1 cup liquid from saucepan. Put in a food processor or blender and process until smooth. Return mixture to saucepan.

Add fish and remaining ingredients. Increase heat to medium-high and bring to a boil. Reduce heat and simmer for 10 minutes, or until fish flakes easily when tested with a fork.

Calories 196
Protein 23 g
Carbohydrates 23 g
Cholesterol 39 mg
Total Fat 1 g
Saturated 0 g
Polyunsaturated 0 g
Monounsaturated 0 g
Fiber 2 g
Sodium 347 mg

Shrimp Gumbo

Serves 4

For a great winter meal, try this thick gumbo with a touch of hot-pepper sauce to warm up your taste buds.

¼ cup all-purpose flour
1 teaspoon acceptable vegetable oil
2 cups sliced fresh okra (about 1 pound) or 10-ounce package frozen no-salt-added sliced okra
1 cup chopped onion (about 2 medium)
½ cup chopped green bell pepper
½ cup chopped celery
3 medium cloves garlic, minced, or 1½ teaspoons bottled minced garlic
½ teaspoon pepper, or to taste
2 cups Chicken Broth (see page 40 or use commercial low-sodium variety)
14½-ounce can no-salt-added diced tomatoes, undrained
1 bay leaf
1 cup uncooked rice
1 pound fresh medium shrimp, peeled and deveined
¼ teaspoon salt
6 drops red hot-pepper sauce

In a medium nonstick skillet over medium heat, cook flour for 8 to 10 minutes, or until light brown, stirring occasionally. Set aside.

Heat oil in a large nonstick stockpot over medium-high heat, swirling to coat bottom of pot. When oil is hot, sauté okra for 10 minutes.

Add onions, bell pepper, celery, garlic, and pepper. Cook for 3 to 5 minutes.

Add flour, broth, tomatoes, and bay leaf. Reduce heat and simmer, covered, for 20 minutes.

Meanwhile, cook rice using package directions, omitting salt and margarine. Set aside.

Add shrimp to okra mixture. Cook, covered, for 3 to 5 minutes, or until shrimp is done (it turns pink and opaque). Don't overcook, or shrimp will become rubbery.

Remove bay leaf. Stir in salt and hot-pepper sauce. Put ½ cup cooked rice in each soup bowl. Ladle gumbo over rice.

Calories 358
Protein 22 g
Carbohydrates 59 g
Cholesterol 135 mg
Total Fat 3 g
- Saturated 1 g
- Polyunsaturated 1 g
- Monounsaturated 1 g

Fiber 4 g
Sodium 335 mg

Chile-Chicken Tortilla Soup

Serves 8

This is a terrific soup for using up leftover chicken or turkey.

1 teaspoon acceptable vegetable oil
½ cup chopped onion
2 medium cloves garlic, minced, or 1 teaspoon bottled minced garlic
4 cups Chicken Broth (see page 40 or use commercial low-sodium variety)
15-ounce can no-salt-added pinto beans, drained
14½-ounce can no-salt-added whole tomatoes, crushed
1 cup cooked chicken or turkey, cubed
2 fresh Anaheim chile peppers, diced (about 2 ounces) (see Cook's Tip, page 115)
1 teaspoon ground cumin
1 teaspoon chili powder
½ teaspoon dried oregano, crumbled
¼ teaspoon salt
⅛ teaspoon pepper
Vegetable oil spray
8 5½- or 6-inch corn tortillas
Vegetable oil spray
½ teaspoon chili powder
2 green onions, thinly sliced

In a large nonstick saucepan, heat oil over medium heat, swirling to coat bottom of pan. Sauté onion and garlic for 2 to 3 minutes, or until onion is translucent, stirring occasionally.

Add broth, beans, tomatoes, chicken, peppers, cumin, 1 teaspoon chili powder, oregano, salt, and pepper. Bring to a boil over medium-high heat. Reduce heat and simmer, covered, for 20 to 25 minutes, stirring occasionally.

Meanwhile, preheat oven to 350° F. Lightly spray a baking sheet with vegetable oil spray.

Cut tortillas in half, then into ¼-inch strips. Place in one layer on baking sheet. Lightly spray with vegetable oil spray. Sprinkle with ½ teaspoon chili powder. Bake 10 minutes, or until crisp.

To serve, ladle soup into bowls, sprinkle with tortilla strips, and garnish with green onions.

Calories 168
Protein 10 g
Carbohydrates 24 g
Cholesterol 16 mg
Total Fat 3 g
  Saturated 1 g
  Polyunsaturated 1 g
  Monounsaturated 1 g
Fiber 5 g
Sodium 150 mg

Chicken, Greens, and Potato Soup

Serves 4

Adding chicken and mustard greens or spinach turns potato soup into a main dish. Leeks, dillweed, and thyme make a good thing even better.

3 medium potatoes, peeled and cut into ½-inch pieces (about 3 cups)

2½ cups Chicken Broth (see page 40 or use commercial low-sodium variety)

Vegetable oil spray

1 medium leek, sliced (white part only) (about 1 cup), or 9 green onions, sliced (about 1 cup)

4 medium cloves garlic, minced, or 2 teaspoons bottled minced garlic

10 ounces boneless, skinless chicken or turkey breasts, cut into bite-size pieces

12-ounce can fat-free evaporated milk

½ 10-ounce package no-salt-added frozen mustard greens or chopped spinach, thawed and drained

1 teaspoon snipped fresh dillweed or ¼ teaspoon dried, crumbled

1 teaspoon chopped fresh thyme or ¼ teaspoon dried, crumbled

¼ teaspoon salt

⅛ teaspoon pepper

In a Dutch oven, combine potatoes and broth. Bring to a boil over medium-high heat. Reduce heat and simmer, covered, for 20 minutes, or until tender. Don't drain. Let cool slightly, then puree in a food processor or blender. Set aside.

Wipe Dutch oven with paper towels. Spray with vegetable oil spray. Sauté leek over medium heat for 5 minutes, stirring occasionally.

Add garlic and cook for 1 minute, stirring occasionally.

Add chicken. Cook for 5 minutes, or until chicken is tender and no longer pink, stirring often.

Stir potato mixture and remaining ingredients into Dutch oven. Cook over low heat for 2 to 3 minutes, or until heated through, stirring occasionally.

Calories 265
Protein 24 g
Carbohydrates 35 g
Cholesterol 42 mg
Total Fat 2 g
Saturated 1 g
Polyunsaturated 1 g
Monounsaturated 1 g
Fiber 3 g
Sodium 302 mg

Beef Barley Soup

Serves 12

With a crisp salad with Ranch-Style Herb Dressing (see page 123) and Whole-Wheat Muffins (see page 510), this filling soup makes a meal that will help drive away the winter chill.

Vegetable oil spray

1 pound eye-of-round roast, cut into 1-inch cubes, all visible fat removed

6 cups water

2 cups Beef Broth (see page 39 or use commercial low-sodium variety)

1 medium onion, quartered

1 bay leaf

1 teaspoon salt

¼ teaspoon pepper

3 cups peeled and diced potatoes (about 3 medium)

1¼ cups peeled and thickly sliced carrots

1 cup thickly sliced celery

3 tablespoons uncooked pearl barley

2 teaspoons dried thyme, crumbled

1 teaspoon salt

Heat a Dutch oven over medium-high heat for 2 to 3 minutes. Remove from heat. Lightly spray with vegetable oil spray. Replace on heat. Brown meat for 10 to 12 minutes, stirring occasionally.

Add water, broth, onion, bay leaf, 1 teaspoon salt, and pepper. Bring to a boil over high heat. Reduce heat and simmer, covered, for 1 hour, or until meat is tender.

Put remaining ingredients in pot and bring to a boil over medium-high heat. Reduce heat and simmer, partially covered, for 20 to 25 minutes, or until vegetables are tender.

Remove bay leaf before serving soup.

Calories 103
Protein 9 g
Carbohydrates 13 g
Cholesterol 20 mg
Total Fat 1 g
Saturated 1 g
Polyunsaturated 0 g
Monounsaturated 1 g
Fiber 2 g
Sodium 424 mg

SALADS AND SALAD DRESSINGS

Hot and Spicy Watercress and Romaine Salad

Spinach Salad with Kiwifruit and Raspberries

Mandarin Spinach Salad with Sesame-Garlic Topping

Spinach-Chayote Salad with Orange Vinaigrette

Dijon-Marinated Vegetable Medley

Sicilian Vegetable Salad with Feta and Lemon Dressing

Garden Vegetable Salad with Herb Marinade

Tossed Vegetables in Creamy Vinaigrette

Marinated Asparagus, Tomato, and Hearts of Palm Salad

Tomato-Basil Salad with Balsamic Dressing

Roasted Beet and Orange Salad

Tangy Cucumbers

Asian Coleslaw

Confetti Coleslaw

Waldorf Salad

Parsnip Salad with Jícama and Apple

Carrot Salad with Jícama and Pineapple

Chilled Melon Slices with Citrus Marinade

Fresh Fruit Salad Romanoff

Cranberry Orange Salad

Zesty Corn Relish

Parsley Potato Salad

Tabbouleh

Marinated White Beans and Cucumbers with Basil

Sixteen-Bean Salad

Curried Quinoa Salad with Cranberries and Almonds

Marinated Pasta Salad

Greek Pasta Salad

Vegetable Rice Salad

Curried Rice and Bean Salad

Italian Rice Salad with Artichokes

Fresh Salmon Salad

Tuna and Rotini Salad

Salade Niçoise

Curried Tuna Salad

Picante Shrimp with Broccoli and Snow Peas

Mexican Shrimp Salad

Curried Chicken Salad

Chicken Vegetable Salad

Cajun Chicken Salad

Asian Chicken and Rice Salad

Island Chicken Salad with Fresh Mint

Grilled Flank Steak Salad with Sweet-and-Sour Sesame Dressing

Southwestern Pork Salad

Warm Orzo Salad with Black Beans and Ham

Zesty Tomato Dressing

Apple Juice Dressing

Creamy Cottage Cheese Dressing

Creamy Chef's Dressing

Chunky Cucumber and Garlic Dressing

Ranch-Style Herb Dressing

Yogurt Dressing

Minted Lime Dressing

Poppy Seed Dressing with Kiwifruit

Hot and Spicy Watercress and Romaine Salad

Serves 4

This salad combines jícama, also called Mexican potato, with peppery watercress, crunchy romaine, and several staples of Asian cooking. The result? Greens with an attitude.

DRESSING

1½ tablespoons light soy sauce

2½ teaspoons toasted sesame oil

1 tablespoon white wine vinegar

1½ teaspoons sugar

1 teaspoon chili oil

SALAD

1 head romaine, torn into pieces

2 bunches watercress, stems removed, torn into pieces

6 medium radishes, thinly sliced

½ cup matchstick-size jícama strips

4 green onions, thinly sliced (about ½ cup)

In a small bowl, whisk together dressing ingredients.

In a large bowl, combine salad ingredients. Pour dressing over salad and toss lightly. Serve immediately.

Calories 68
Protein 2 g
Carbohydrates 6 g
Cholesterol 0 mg
Total Fat 4 g
Saturated 1 g
Polyunsaturated 2 g
Monounsaturated 1 g
Fiber 2 g
Sodium 201 mg

Spinach Salad with Kiwifruit and Raspberries

Serves 4

The raspberries contrast beautifully with the dark green spinach leaves in this easy, festive salad.

1 tablespoon all-fruit raspberry jam
1½ tablespoons white wine vinegar
1½ tablespoons acceptable vegetable oil
4 cups torn fresh spinach leaves
2 kiwifruit, peeled and sliced
½ cup fresh raspberries

Put jam and vinegar in a food processor or blender. Add oil in a stream, processing constantly until mixed.

Combine spinach, half the kiwifruit, and half the raspberries in a salad bowl. Add vinegar mixture and toss well.

To serve, place salad on plates. Top with remaining kiwifruit and raspberries.

Calories 91
Protein 1 g
Carbohydrates 10 g
Cholesterol 0 mg
Total Fat 5 g
Saturated 1 g
Polyunsaturated 3 g
Monounsaturated 1 g
Fiber 3 g
Sodium 27 mg

Mandarin Spinach Salad with Sesame-Garlic Topping

Serves 4

This Asian-inspired salad uses seasoned cereal to provide a new twist to croutons.

SESAME-GARLIC TOPPING

1 tablespoon peanut oil

1 tablespoon light soy sauce

2 teaspoons sesame seeds

¼ teaspoon minced garlic

⅛ teaspoon ground ginger

1 cup rice squares cereal

DRESSING

¼ cup fresh orange juice

1 tablespoon honey

1 teaspoon light soy sauce

SALAD

6 cups torn fresh spinach leaves

11-ounce can mandarin oranges in light syrup, drained

8-ounce can sliced water chestnuts, drained

In a large skillet, combine topping ingredients except cereal, stirring well. Bring to a boil over medium-high heat.

Add cereal and stir until coated. Reduce heat to medium and cook for 2 minutes, stirring constantly. Drain on paper towels; let cool.

Meanwhile, in a small bowl, whisk together dressing ingredients.

For salad, place one layer each of spinach, oranges, and water chestnuts in a large salad bowl. Pour dressing over salad and toss well.

Add cereal croutons and toss again. Serve immediately.

Calories 218
Protein 4 g
Carbohydrates 42 g
Cholesterol 0 mg
Total Fat 5 g
Saturated 1 g
Polyunsaturated 2 g
Monounsaturated 2 g
Fiber 4 g
Sodium 287 mg

Spinach-Chayote Salad with Orange Vinaigrette

Serves 10

If you've wondered how to use the pale-green, pear-shaped chayote, this no-cook salad is the answer.

DRESSING

½ teaspoon grated orange zest

½ cup fresh orange juice (1 to 2 medium oranges)

3 tablespoons acceptable vegetable oil

2 tablespoons sugar

2 tablespoons white wine vinegar

1 tablespoon fresh lemon juice

SALAD

1 chayote (about 8 ounces), peeled, seeded, and thinly sliced

6 cups fresh spinach or other greens, stems removed, leaves torn into bite-size pieces (6 to 8 ounces)

11-ounce can mandarin oranges in light syrup, drained

1 small cucumber, thinly sliced (1 cup)

2 tablespoons sliced green onion

Combine dressing ingredients in a jar with a tight-fitting lid. Shake until thoroughly blended.

Put squash in a large bowl and stir in 2 tablespoons dressing. Let sit for 5 to 10 minutes.

Add remaining salad ingredients. Toss to mix well.

Pour remaining dressing over salad and toss lightly.

Calories 85
Protein 1 g
Carbohydrates 12 g
Cholesterol 0 mg
Total Fat 4 g
Saturated 1 g
Polyunsaturated 3 g
Monounsaturated 1 g
Fiber 2 g
Sodium 18 mg

Cook's Tip on Chayote

The chayote (*ky-OH-tay*) is a mild-flavored squash, also called mirliton. A vegetable peeler works well to remove the skin except at the puckered end. You'll need a sharp knife for that. Then cut the squash in half lengthwise to remove its one seed. Use chayote raw in salads, cook it like summer squash, or stuff and bake it like acorn squash.

Dijon-Marinated Vegetable Medley

Serves 4

Picnic-perfect, this easy-to-make salad offers a rainbow of color to brighten any lunch or dinner.

SALAD

3/4 cup frozen no-salt-added whole-kernel corn

3/4 cup frozen no-salt-added cut green beans

3/4 cup canned black beans

2 cups chopped, seeded tomatoes (3 to 4 medium)

1/2 cup chopped red onion

DRESSING

1/4 to 1/2 cup balsamic vinegar plus water to make 3/4 cup

2 tablespoons Dijon mustard

2 tablespoons chopped fresh basil or 2 teaspoons dried, crumbled

1 tablespoon extra-virgin olive oil

1 teaspoon sugar

1 tablespoon chopped fresh thyme

2 medium cloves garlic, minced, or 1 teaspoon bottled minced garlic

1/4 teaspoon white pepper

4 lettuce leaves

Rinse corn, green beans, and black beans in a colander; drain well. Put in a large bowl.

Add tomatoes and onion to corn mixture, stirring gently.

In a medium bowl, whisk together dressing ingredients. Pour dressing over salad and toss gently.

Cover and refrigerate for 4 to 8 hours, stirring occasionally; drain.

To serve, line four plates with lettuce and spoon on vegetable mixture.

Calories 167
Protein 6 g
Carbohydrates 28 g
Cholesterol 0 mg
Total Fat 5 g
Saturated 1 g
Polyunsaturated 1 g
Monounsaturated 3 g
Fiber 6 g
Sodium 299 mg

Sicilian Vegetable Salad with Feta and Lemon Dressing

Serves 4

This salad, with its bounty of vegetables, is as beautiful as it is tasty.

1½ cups fresh or frozen no-salt-added cut green beans (about 8 ounces)

1½ cups chopped tomatoes (2 medium)

½ cup canned chick-peas, rinsed and drained

¼ cup Lemon Dressing (see recipe below)

2 tablespoons crumbled feta cheese, rinsed

Vegetable oil spray

1-pound eggplant, peeled, cut into 8 slices

¾ cup Lemon Dressing (see recipe below)

8-ounce zucchini, cut lengthwise into 4 slices

1 small fennel bulb, thinly sliced (8 ounces)

4 red bell pepper rings

4 green bell pepper rings

3 cups mixed salad greens

1 cup unseasoned toasted croutons

Steam green beans until tender-crisp, 3 to 4 minutes. Plunge beans into ice water immediately to stop cooking process; drain.

In a large bowl, combine green beans, tomatoes, chick-peas, ¼ cup dressing, and feta cheese, stirring well. Set aside.

Preheat broiler.

Spray a baking sheet with vegetable oil spray. Put eggplant on baking sheet and brush with some of the remaining dressing.

Broil 4 to 5 inches from heat for 5 minutes, or until brown; turn.

Put zucchini, fennel, and bell peppers on baking sheet. Brush with some of the remaining dressing.

Broil for 3 minutes, or until vegetables are desired crispness. Remove from baking sheet and let cool.

Calories 231
Protein 7 g
Carbohydrates 41 g
Cholesterol 4 mg
Total Fat 6 g
- Saturated 1 g
- Polyunsaturated 1 g
- Monounsaturated 3 g

Fiber 8 g
Sodium 300 mg

For each serving, place ¾ cup salad greens on a plate. Arrange 2 eggplant slices, 1 zucchini slice, one fourth of the fennel slices, 1 red pepper ring, and 1 green pepper ring on each plate. Top each with 1 cup tomato mixture. Sprinkle with croutons. Drizzle with remaining dressing.

LEMON DRESSING

½ cup fresh lemon juice (3 medium lemons)

2 tablespoons water

1 tablespoon snipped fresh parsley

1 tablespoon chopped fresh oregano

1 tablespoon extra-virgin olive oil

1 tablespoon honey

1 tablespoon Dijon mustard

2 medium cloves garlic, minced, or 1 teaspoon bottled minced garlic

½ teaspoon fennel seeds, crushed

In a small bowl, whisk together all ingredients.

Cook's Tip on Fennel

Known primarily as an Italian herb and spice, fennel has a *delicate* anise flavor. The two main kinds of fennel have feathery leaves and celerylike stems. Garden, or common, fennel produces the fennel seed that is used as a spice. Fennel seeds resemble caraway seeds and are usually ground before using. Florence fennel, or *finocchio,* is prized for the thickened leaf stalks that form a bulb at the base. The bulb and stems of both kinds can be used like a vegetable, raw or cooked, much as celery is used. The leaves can be snipped and used for flavoring. Add to cooked dishes at the last minute so the flavor doesn't dissipate.

Garden Vegetable Salad with Herb Marinade

Serves 8

The herb marinade adds a unique taste to the variety of vegetables in this salad.

VEGETABLE MIXTURE

¼ pound fresh green beans, sliced (1 cup)

¼ pound fresh shelled green peas (¼ cup)

¼ pound fresh mushrooms, sliced (1¼ cups)

1 medium green bell pepper, sliced (1 cup)

1 medium cucumber, peeled and sliced (1½ cups)

1 medium zucchini or crookneck squash, cubed (1 cup)

1 medium carrot, shredded (¾ cup)

1 cup fresh alfalfa sprouts

¼ cup sliced ripe olives

2 green onions, sliced

2 tablespoons salt-free pumpkin seeds (optional)

MARINADE

¼ cup fat-free or low-fat Italian salad dressing

3 tablespoons fresh lemon juice

1½ teaspoons chopped fresh mint or ½ teaspoon dried, crumbled

1 teaspoon sugar

1½ teaspoons chopped fresh basil or ½ teaspoon dried, crumbled

1½ teaspoons chopped fresh thyme or ½ teaspoon dried, crumbled

1 medium clove garlic, minced, or ½ teaspoon bottled minced garlic

⅛ teaspoon pepper, or to taste

SALAD GREENS

½ pound fresh spinach

1 head romaine

1 bunch leaf lettuce

Put green beans in a small saucepan with water to cover. Bring to a boil over medium-high heat. Reduce heat and simmer, covered, for 4 to 5 minutes, or until almost tender.

Stir in peas and simmer for about 1 minute, or until beans and peas are tender. Drain well, then put in a large salad bowl with remaining vegetable mixture ingredients.

In a medium bowl, whisk together marinade ingredients. Pour over vegetable mixture. Cover and refrigerate for at least 30 minutes.

Calories 64
Protein 4 g
Carbohydrates 12 g
Cholesterol 0 mg
Total Fat 1 g
Saturated 0 g
Polyunsaturated 0 g
Monounsaturated 0 g
Fiber 5 g
Sodium 151 mg

Meanwhile, remove stems from spinach and tear salad greens into bite-size pieces. Cover and chill.

To serve, toss marinated vegetables with salad greens.

Cook's Tip on Whisks

Available in several sizes, whisks are handy for combining ingredients, such as in the marinade here. They're also excellent for whipping eggs and other foods to incorporate air into them. A small whisk is perfect for dissolving a small amount of cornstarch in a cold liquid.

Tossed Vegetables in Creamy Vinaigrette

Serves 8

Take this dish on a picnic or enjoy it at home on a hot summer day.

DRESSING

¼ cup nonfat or low-fat plain yogurt

2 tablespoons white wine vinegar

1 tablespoon Dijon mustard

1 teaspoon sugar

1 teaspoon acceptable vegetable oil

½ teaspoon coarsely ground pepper

¼ teaspoon salt

2 cups sliced carrots (2 large)

8 ounces fresh green beans, trimmed and cut into 1½-inch pieces (1½ cups)

4 ounces fresh medium mushrooms, cut into quarters (1¼ cups)

2 medium tomatoes, each cut into 8 wedges

⅓ cup thinly sliced green onions (green part only) (3 to 4 medium)

For dressing, whisk together all ingredients in a medium bowl.

Steam carrots and green beans for 3 to 4 minutes, or until tender-crisp. Remove from heat and plunge into bowl of ice water to stop cooking. Drain, pat dry with paper towels, and put in a shallow glass bowl.

Add mushrooms, tomatoes, and green onions.

Pour dressing over all and toss gently. Cover and refrigerate for at least 30 minutes or up to 4 hours.

Calories 46
Protein 2 g
Carbohydrates 8 g
Cholesterol 0 mg
Total Fat 1 g
- Saturated 0 g
- Polyunsaturated 1 g
- Monounsaturated 0 g

Fiber 2 g
Sodium 148 mg

Marinated Asparagus, Tomato, and Hearts of Palm Salad

Serves 6

This colorful and inviting salad is popular at any dinner party or buffet.

8 ounces fresh asparagus, trimmed and cut into 2-inch pieces (about 2 cups)

1 pound Italian plum tomatoes, cut into ¼-inch slices

14-ounce can hearts of palm, rinsed and drained

¼ cup thinly sliced yellow onion

DRESSING

¼ cup red wine vinegar

2 tablespoons dry red wine (regular or nonalcoholic)

2 teaspoons sugar

¼ teaspoon pepper

Steam asparagus for 3 minutes, or until tender-crisp. Immediately put asparagus in a shallow glass baking dish.

Add a layer of tomatoes, then one of hearts of palm, and one of onion.

In a small bowl, whisk together dressing ingredients until sugar has dissolved. Pour over vegetables.

Cover dish and refrigerate for 30 minutes, stirring occasionally.

Cook's Tip

You can make this salad up to 24 hours in advance, but *don't* add hearts of palm until about 30 minutes before serving. They become discolored from the wine if added sooner.

Cook's Tip on Hearts of Palm

Hearts of palm, which really do come from palm trees, taste somewhat like artichokes. Sometimes, the outer stem of the larger pieces is a bit tough. Make a small slit in the tough layer and peel it off before using the tender part.

Calories 57
Protein 3 g
Carbohydrates 10 g
Cholesterol 0 mg
Total Fat 1 g
Saturated 0 g
Polyunsaturated 0 g
Monounsaturated 0 g
Fiber 3 g
Sodium 181 mg

Tomato-Basil Salad with Balsamic Dressing

Serves 6

Serve as a complement to Pasta Primavera (see page 306) or Spaghetti with Perfect Pesto (see page 309).

SALAD

4 medium tomatoes, sliced

2 tablespoons chopped fresh basil or 2 teaspoons dried, crumbled

DRESSING

2 tablespoons balsamic vinegar

1 tablespoon olive oil

½ teaspoon sugar

¼ teaspoon pepper

2 tablespoons shredded fat-free mozzarella cheese

2 teaspoons grated Parmesan cheese

For salad, arrange tomato slices on a large, flat plate. Sprinkle with basil.

In a small bowl, whisk together dressing ingredients. Pour over tomatoes.

Sprinkle with mozzarella and Parmesan. Cover and refrigerate until serving time.

Cook's Tip on Slicing Tomatoes

If you slice tomatoes vertically instead of horizontally, they'll lose less of their juice.

Calories 50
Protein 2 g
Carbohydrates 5 g
Cholesterol 1 mg
Total Fat 3 g
Saturated 0 g
Polyunsaturated 0 g
Monounsaturated 2 g
Fiber 1 g
Sodium 45 mg

Roasted Beet and Orange Salad

Serves 4

The sweet-savory flavor of roasted beets meets the tang of oranges and lime in this attractive salad.

2 pounds fresh beets
Vegetable oil spray

DRESSING
3 tablespoons white wine vinegar
1 tablespoon salad oil
1 tablespoon fresh orange juice or water
2 teaspoons maple syrup or honey
1 teaspoon grated lime zest

4 lettuce leaves
11-ounce can mandarin oranges in light syrup
¼ cup slivered almonds, dry-roasted
Sprigs of fresh mint (optional)

Preheat oven to 350° F. Spray a shallow baking pan with vegetable oil spray.

Cut off all but 1 to 2 inches of stems from beets. Put beets in a single layer on baking pan. Lightly spray beets with vegetable oil spray.

Roast beets for about 1 hour, or until they can be pierced easily with a knife. Let cool slightly, then remove skins. Coarsely chop beets (you should have about 3 cups); put in a bowl with a lid.

In a jar with a tight-fitting lid, combine dressing ingredients. Cover and shake until well combined. Pour over beets, tossing gently to coat. Cover and marinate in the refrigerator for 2 to 24 hours.

To serve, place a lettuce leaf on each salad plate. Rinse and drain oranges. Gently stir into beet mixture. Using a slotted spoon, transfer beet mixture onto lettuce leaves. Sprinkle each serving with almonds and garnish with mint.

Time-Saver: Fresh roasted beets give this salad a delicious concentrated beet flavor. However, if you don't have time to roast fresh beets, you can use two 16-ounce cans or jars of diced beets, rinsed and drained, instead.

Calories 226
Protein 5 g
Carbohydrates 38 g
Cholesterol 0 mg
Total Fat 7 g
Saturated 1 g
Polyunsaturated 3 g
Monounsaturated 3 g
Fiber 6 g
Sodium 169 mg

Tangy Cucumbers

Serves 4

These sweet-and-sour cucumbers are equally good with or without the yogurt sauce. Try them with Baked Catfish (see page 142).

MARINADE

½ cup cider vinegar

4 green onions, chopped (½ cup)

¼ cup sugar

¼ cup snipped fresh parsley

½ teaspoon pepper

3 medium cucumbers

1 medium red onion, sliced (1 cup)

YOGURT SAUCE (OPTIONAL)

½ cup plain nonfat or low-fat yogurt

1 teaspoon sugar

1 teaspoon fresh lemon juice

½ teaspoon dry mustard

For marinade, whisk together all ingredients in a large bowl. Cover and refrigerate.

Peel cucumbers if desired. Cut in half lengthwise and scrape out seeds. Cut cucumbers crosswise into thin slices.

Stir cucumbers and red onion into marinade. Cover and refrigerate for 1 to 2 hours.

If using sauce, whisk together all ingredients in a small bowl.

Drain vegetables and serve plain or mixed with sauce. (Prepared with yogurt sauce: calories 116; protein 3 g; carbohydrates 27 g; cholesterol 1 mg; total fat 1 g; saturated 0 g; polyunsaturated 0 g; monounsaturated 0 g; fiber 3 g; sodium 29 mg)

(WITHOUT YOGURT SAUCE)

Calories 98

Protein 2 g

Carbohydrates 24 g

Cholesterol 0 mg

Total Fat 0 g

Saturated 0 g

Polyunsaturated 0 g

Monounsaturated 0 g

Fiber 3 g

Sodium 10 mg

Cook's Tip on Seeding Cucumbers

A grapefruit spoon is a good tool for seeding cucumbers. It's sharper than a regular spoon, so the job goes more quickly.

Asian Coleslaw

Serves 6

You can make this salad a day ahead, and there's no mayonnaise to worry about—perfect picnic fare.

SLAW

1 small head napa cabbage, thinly sliced (about 2 pounds)

1 medium carrot, peeled and coarsely grated (about 3/4 cup)

2 green onions (white and pale green parts), thinly sliced on diagonal (about 1/4 cup)

1 medium red bell pepper, thinly sliced

1 medium clove garlic, finely chopped, or 1/2 teaspoon bottled minced garlic

DRESSING

2 tablespoons light soy sauce

2 tablespoons rice vinegar

1 tablespoon finely grated fresh gingerroot (about 1 inch) or 1 teaspoon ground ginger

2 teaspoons toasted sesame oil or acceptable vegetable oil

1/4 teaspoon crushed red pepper flakes

In a large bowl, combine slaw ingredients, tossing well.

In a small bowl, whisk together dressing ingredients. Pour over slaw. Toss well.

Serve at room temperature or chilled, tossing again just before serving. If refrigerated, this salad keeps well for a day.

Cook's Tip on Napa Cabbage

Napa, or Chinese, cabbage has long, crinkly, cream-colored leaves with pale green tips. It's delicious in salads, soups, and stir-fries. You can store napa cabbage in the vegetable bin of your refrigerator for up to 5 days.

Calories 56
Protein 3 g
Carbohydrates 9 g
Cholesterol 0 mg
Total Fat 2 g
Saturated 0 g
Polyunsaturated 1 g
Monounsaturated 1 g
Fiber 6 g
Sodium 188 mg

Confetti Coleslaw

Serves 12

Bursting with color and flavor, this tangy coleslaw is excellent for a barbecue.

DRESSING

1/3 cup white wine vinegar

1/4 cup sugar

1 tablespoon honey

1 tablespoon acceptable vegetable oil

1/4 teaspoon salt

1/4 teaspoon coarsely ground pepper

3/4 pound green cabbage, shredded (about 4 cups)

1/2 pound red cabbage, shredded (about 3 cups)

1/2 cup thinly sliced green onions (4 to 5 medium)

1/2 cup diced red bell pepper (1/2 medium)

1/2 cup diced green bell pepper (1/2 medium)

Calories 49
Protein 1 g
Carbohydrates 9 g
Cholesterol 0 mg
Total Fat 1 g
  Saturated 0 g
  Polyunsaturated 1 g
  Monounsaturated 0 g
Fiber 1 g
Sodium 56 mg

For dressing, whisk together all ingredients in a large bowl.

Add remaining ingredients. Toss to coat evenly. Cover and refrigerate for at least 30 minutes.

Waldorf Salad

Serves 6

This is a very easy, traditional salad for the holidays. With some leftover turkey or chicken tossed in, you'll have an entrée salad.

2 cups diced unpeeled apples (2 to 3 medium)

1 cup diced celery (2 ribs)

1/2 cup Yogurt Cheese (see page 16) or fat-free, cholesterol-free or light, reduced-calorie mayonnaise dressing

1/2 cup raisins or halved seedless grapes

1/4 cup coarsely chopped dry-roasted walnuts or pecans

1 teaspoon fresh lemon juice

In a large bowl, combine all ingredients. Cover and refrigerate.

Cook's Tip

Turn this old favorite into the unexpected by adding ¼ teaspoon curry powder.

Calories 108
Protein 3 g
Carbohydrates 19 g
Cholesterol 1 mg
Total Fat 3 g
- Saturated 0 g
- Polyunsaturated 2 g
- Monounsaturated 1 g

Fiber 2 g
Sodium 44 mg

Parsnip Salad with Jícama and Apple

Serves 4

Jícama contributes a nutty flavor but no fat to this unusual slawlike salad.

⅓ cup fat-free or light sour cream
Juice of ½ medium lemon (1½ tablespoons)
1 tablespoon snipped fresh parsley
¾ teaspoon sugar
3 medium parsnips, peeled and shredded
1 cup matchstick-size jícama strips
1 tablespoon finely chopped onion
1 unpeeled medium apple (Delicious preferred)
⅓ cup golden raisins (optional)

In a large bowl, whisk together sour cream, lemon juice, parsley, and sugar.

Stir in parsnips, jícama, and onion. Cover and refrigerate for 2 hours.

To serve, chop apple, then stir it and raisins into salad. Serve immediately.

Calories 153
Protein 3 g
Carbohydrates 36 g
Cholesterol 0 mg
Total Fat 1 g
- Saturated 0 g
- Polyunsaturated 0 g
- Monounsaturated 0 g

Fiber 9 g
Sodium 29 mg

Carrot Salad with Jícama and Pineapple

Serves 6

A longtime favorite gets an update with the refreshing crunch of jícama.

2 cups shredded carrots (2 large)
½ cup diced jícama
½ cup drained pineapple tidbits canned in their own juice
¼ cup golden raisins

DRESSING
¼ cup plain nonfat or low-fat yogurt
2 tablespoons fat-free, cholesterol-free or light, reduced-calorie mayonnaise dressing
2 tablespoons fresh lemon juice
1 teaspoon sugar

In a large bowl, combine carrots, jícama, pineapple, and raisins, stirring well.

In a small bowl, whisk together dressing ingredients. Pour over carrot mixture and stir well.

Cook's Tip on Jícama

A Mexican vegetable, jícama (*HEE-kah-mah*) looks like a turnip in a potato skin. Peeled and sliced or diced, it looks and tastes something like apple, although not so sweet, and something like potato, although not so bland, and even something like cucumber. Either raw or cooked, jícama adds a nice crunchy texture. For an easy appetizer, cut jícama into sticks and sprinkle with fresh lime juice and cayenne.

Calories 62
Protein 1 g
Carbohydrates 15 g
Cholesterol 0 mg
Total Fat 0 g
- Saturated 0 g
- Polyunsaturated 0 g
- Monounsaturated 0 g

Fiber 2 g
Sodium 56 mg

Chilled Melon Slices with Citrus Marinade

Serves 4

For a colorful presentation, leave space in the center of the serving platter for some Bing cherries with stems or a few clusters of seedless red grapes. Add them just before serving time.

1 medium cantaloupe, cut into 16 vertical slices, rind removed

½ cup frozen pineapple, orange, and banana juice concentrate, slightly thawed

2 tablespoons fresh lemon juice

2 tablespoons fresh lime juice (1 to 2 medium limes)

Arrange melon on a platter.

In a small bowl, combine remaining ingredients, stirring until blended. Spoon over melon. Refrigerate for 30 minutes.

Cook's Tip on Cantaloupe

When buying cantaloupe, use your nose as well as your eyes. Smell the melon. If it smells sweet, it's probably ripe. Cantaloupes are better when they have ripened on the vine. That's why you want to be sure the indentation at the stem end is smooth. If it has a piece of stem, the cantaloupe was green when picked. Also, look for a close pattern of thick veins on the rind. If the melon isn't quite ripe when you buy it, put it in a brown paper bag for a day at room temperature.

Calories 116
Protein 2 g
Carbohydrates 28 g
Cholesterol 0 mg
Total Fat 0 g
Saturated 0 g
Polyunsaturated 0 g
Monounsaturated 0 g
Fiber 1 g
Sodium 22 mg

Fresh Fruit Salad Romanoff

Serves 4

Serve this delectable salad as a side dish or for dessert. It's especially good when served in chilled bowls.

FRUIT SALAD

2 peaches, peeled and chopped (1 cup)

1 cup honeydew melon cubes or balls

½ cup blueberries

½ cup sliced strawberries

20 red grapes, cut into halves

TOPPING

3 tablespoons fresh orange juice

2 tablespoons light brown sugar

½ cup fat-free or light sour cream or plain nonfat or low-fat yogurt

2 tablespoons light brown sugar

In a large bowl, gently combine the fruit salad ingredients.

For topping, in a small bowl, combine orange juice and 2 tablespoons brown sugar. Sprinkle over fruit and toss well. Cover and refrigerate for about 2 hours, or until thoroughly chilled.

To serve, stir together sour cream and 2 tablespoons brown sugar in a small bowl. Spoon fruit into glass dessert bowls. Top with sour cream mixture.

Calories 137
Protein 3 g
Carbohydrates 32 g
Cholesterol 0 mg
Total Fat 0 g
Saturated 0 g
Polyunsaturated 0 g
Monounsaturated 0 g
Fiber 2 g
Sodium 32 mg

Cranberry Orange Salad

Serves 8

Get out your prettiest glass serving plate, line it with dark green romaine, and serve this salad on it for a holiday buffet.

3-ounce package lemon gelatin
1 cup boiling water
1 cup fresh orange juice (3 medium oranges)
12- or 16-ounce container cranberry-orange relish
1 unpeeled apple, chopped (3/4 cup)
1/4 cup plus 2 tablespoons chopped pecans
Vegetable oil spray

Put gelatin in a medium bowl. Pour in water and stir constantly until gelatin has dissolved.

Stir in orange juice. Cover and refrigerate until almost jelled, about 30 minutes.

In a small bowl, combine remaining ingredients except vegetable oil spray, stirring well. Fold into gelatin mixture. Spray a 1-quart mold with vegetable oil spray. Pour mixture into mold. Cover and refrigerate until firm, about 1 hour.

Cook's Tip on Unmolding Gelatin

Insert a spatula or knife between the mold and the gelatin in several places. Set the mold in hot water up to 1/4 inch from the top. Leave the mold in the water for only a couple of seconds, remove the mold from the water, and dry it. Rinse a serving plate in cold water; dry the plate. Center the plate over the mold and invert both together. The salad should drop out. If it doesn't, shake the mold. Still no luck? Repeat the process. Whatever you do, don't leave the mold in the hot water for long or your salad may start to melt.

Calories 188
Protein 2 g
Carbohydrates 39 g
Cholesterol 0 mg
Total Fat 4 g
- Saturated 0 g
- Polyunsaturated 1 g
- Monounsaturated 2 g

Fiber 2 g
Sodium 53 mg

Zesty Corn Relish

Serves 8; ½ cup per serving

Serve this corn and bell pepper combination on leaf lettuce as a salad, or use about one fourth as much as a relish with ham or turkey. Although cilantro and coriander usually are not interchangeable, you can use either in this particular dish.

1 tablespoon olive oil

3 cups fresh corn kernels (6 large ears) or 16- or 20-ounce package frozen no-salt-added whole-kernel corn, thawed

1 medium red bell pepper, finely diced (1 cup)

¼ cup minced red onion

½ fresh jalapeño pepper, seeded and minced (see Cook's Tip, page 115)

2 tablespoons dry white wine (regular or nonalcoholic) (optional)

2 teaspoons fresh lime juice

6 medium fresh basil leaves, finely chopped, or ½ teaspoon dried, crumbled

3 or 4 sprigs of cilantro, coarsely chopped, or ⅛ teaspoon dried coriander seeds, crushed

3 sprigs of fresh thyme, stems removed, or ½ to 1 teaspoon dried, crumbled

1 small clove garlic, crushed, or ¼ teaspoon bottled minced garlic

¼ teaspoon salt

¼ teaspoon pepper, or to taste

Heat oil in a large skillet over medium heat. Swirl to coat bottom of skillet. Sauté corn, bell pepper, onion, and jalapeño until tender, 2 to 3 minutes. Remove skillet from heat and allow mixture to cool, about 10 minutes.

Stir in remaining ingredients. Transfer to a glass dish. Cover and refrigerate for at least 30 minutes or up to 2 days.

Calories 87
Protein 2 g
Carbohydrates 17 g
Cholesterol 0 mg
Total Fat 3 g
Saturated 0 g
Polyunsaturated 1 g
Monounsaturated 1 g
Fiber 2 g
Sodium 84 mg

Parsley Potato Salad

Serves 6

Great flavor, crunch, and color—this salad has them all!

2 cups diced cooked red potatoes (2 to 3 medium)
½ cup diced celery (1 rib)
2 tablespoons snipped fresh parsley
1 tablespoon chopped onion
1 tablespoon chopped red bell pepper
1½ teaspoons cider vinegar
1 teaspoon dry mustard
½ teaspoon celery seeds
¼ teaspoon salt
⅛ teaspoon pepper
¼ cup fat-free, cholesterol-free or light, reduced-calorie mayonnaise dressing
Lettuce (optional)
Pimiento or red bell pepper strips (optional)

In a large bowl, combine potatoes, celery, parsley, onion, bell pepper, vinegar, mustard, celery seeds, salt, and pepper, tossing lightly.

Stir in mayonnaise, mixing well. Cover and refrigerate for several hours.

Serve in lettuce cups and garnish with pimiento.

Mustard Potato Salad

Reduce salt to ⅛ teaspoon, and substitute 2 tablespoons mustard for half the mayonnaise.(calories 70; protein 2 g; carbohydrates 15 g; cholesterol 0 mg; total fat 0 g; saturated 0 g; polyunsaturated 0 g; monounsaturated 0 g; fiber 2 g; sodium 181 mg)

Calories 71
Protein 2 g
Carbohydrates 15 g
Cholesterol 0 mg
Total Fat 1 g
Saturated 0 g
Polyunsaturated 0 g
Monounsaturated 0 g
Fiber 2 g
Sodium 211 mg

Tabbouleh

Serves 8

This very refreshing summer salad is good with lamb or grilled Turkey Fillets with Fresh Herbs *(see page 226).*

SALAD

½ cup fine bulgur

2 bunches of fresh parsley

1 cup diced red bell pepper (1 medium)

1 medium cucumber, peeled, seeded, and cubed (1½ cups)

½ cup finely chopped green onions (4 to 5)

⅓ cup chopped fresh mint

½ teaspoon pepper

¼ teaspoon salt

DRESSING

Juice of 2 medium lemons (about ⅜ cup)

2 tablespoons olive oil

1 to 2 medium cloves garlic, pressed or minced, or ½ to 1 teaspoon bottled minced garlic

18 cherry tomatoes, quartered

Lettuce leaves (optional)

For salad, put bulgur in a large bowl. Add hot water to cover. Let sit for about 30 minutes. Drain and squeeze dry. Return to bowl and fluff with a fork.

Meanwhile, snip enough parsley for 2 cups. Add to prepared bulgur and stir in remaining salad ingredients.

In a small bowl, whisk together dressing ingredients. Pour over salad and toss. Cover and refrigerate for 3 to 4 hours.

To serve, stir in tomatoes and spoon onto lettuce leaves.

Calories 95
Protein 3 g
Carbohydrates 15 g
Cholesterol 0 mg
Total Fat 4 g
Saturated 1 g
Polyunsaturated 0 g
Monounsaturated 3 g
Fiber 4 g
Sodium 89 mg

Cook's Tip on Bulgur

Bulgur, also known as bulgur wheat or wheat bulgur, consists of cooked wheat kernels that are dried and coarsely broken or ground into grain. It lends a delicious nutty flavor and texture to food.

Marinated White Beans and Cucumbers with Basil

Serves 4 as an entrée

This filling salad will become a favorite entrée in the summertime, when tomatoes, cucumbers, and basil are plentiful and bursting with flavor.

SALAD

19-ounce can cannellini beans, rinsed and drained

4 medium tomatoes, chopped (3 cups)

2 cups chopped peeled cucumbers (2 medium)

1/3 cup chopped red onion

MARINADE

3 tablespoons white wine vinegar

2 tablespoons finely chopped fresh basil

1 1/2 tablespoons extra-virgin olive oil

1 medium clove garlic, crushed, or 1/2 teaspoon bottled minced garlic

1/4 teaspoon salt

Pepper to taste

4 lettuce leaves (optional)

In a large bowl, combine salad ingredients and toss well.

In a small bowl, whisk together marinade ingredients. Pour over salad. Cover and refrigerate for 1 to 2 hours, stirring occasionally.

To serve, place 1 lettuce leaf on each salad plate. Spoon bean mixture evenly over lettuce.

VARIATION

Instead of chopping the tomatoes, make tomato cups to hold the salad. Slice the top off each tomato; discard tops. Scoop out and discard pulp. Spoon one fourth of the bean mixture into each cup.

Calories 193
Protein 7 g
Carbohydrates 28 g
Cholesterol 0 mg
Total Fat 6 g
- Saturated 1 g
- Polyunsaturated 1 g
- Monounsaturated 4 g

Fiber 7 g
Sodium 327 mg

Sixteen-Bean Salad

Serves 4

Here's one way to eat your soup with a fork! Using soup mix provides real variety with a minimum of effort.

1 cup 16-bean soup mix, sorted for stones and shriveled beans and rinsed
½ cup peeled, seeded, and chopped tomato
⅓ cup chopped red bell pepper
⅓ cup chopped yellow bell pepper
⅓ cup thinly sliced green onions (3 medium)
¼ cup Salsa Cruda (see page 449 or use commercial variety)
1 tablespoon snipped fresh cilantro
⅛ teaspoon pepper
4 cups torn mixed salad greens

Discard seasoning packet from soup mix. Cook beans until just tender using package directions, omitting salt. Drain and let cool to room temperature, about 30 minutes.

In a large bowl, combine beans with remaining ingredients except salad greens, tossing gently. Cover and refrigerate for 4 hours, stirring occasionally.

To serve, place 1 cup salad greens on each plate. Spoon bean mixture evenly over salad greens.

Cook's Tip

For a really quick lunch, wrap some of the leftovers in a nonfat flour tortilla (look for the lowest sodium available) and zap it in the microwave until it's warm.

Cook's Tip on Salsa

Salsa can be high in sodium. When shopping, select a salsa that contains no fat and has the lowest sodium value.

Calories 421
Protein 34 g
Carbohydrates 87 g
Cholesterol 0 mg
Total Fat 0 g
Saturated 0 g
Polyunsaturated 0 g
Monounsaturated 0 g
Fiber 43 g
Sodium 68 mg

Curried Quinoa Salad with Cranberries and Almonds

Serves 4

Toss quinoa (KEEN-wah) *with a sweet soy and curry sauce, then top it with toasted almonds for this entrée salad.*

2 cups water
1 cup uncooked quinoa
2 tablespoons light soy sauce
1 tablespoon cider vinegar
1 tablespoon honey
½ teaspoon curry powder
¼ teaspoon crushed red pepper flakes, or to taste
½ cup chopped green bell pepper
½ cup finely chopped celery
8-ounce can sliced water chestnuts, drained
½ cup dried cranberries or mixed dried fruit
½ teaspoon grated orange zest
¼ cup sliced almonds, dry-roasted

In a medium saucepan, bring water to a boil over high heat. Stir in quinoa. Reduce heat and simmer, uncovered, for 15 minutes, or until water is absorbed. Remove from heat and let cool.

Meanwhile, in a small bowl, combine soy sauce, vinegar, honey, curry powder, and red pepper flakes, stirring until completely blended.

In a large bowl, combine remaining ingredients except almonds.

Gently stir in cooled quinoa, then soy sauce mixture.

To serve, sprinkle with almonds.

Time-Saver: A quick way to cool cooked quinoa is to spread it in a thin layer on a baking sheet. Put the baking sheet on a cooling rack and let the quinoa cool for 10 minutes.

Cook's Tip on Quinoa

Serve quinoa hot or cold, press it into molds to serve as timbales, make it into a curry, or add vegetables and herbs to give it a Mediterranean or all-American flavor. Serve it for breakfast, lunch, or dinner.

Calories 332
Protein 9 g
Carbohydrates 62 g
Cholesterol 0 mg
Total Fat 6 g
 Saturated 1 g
 Polyunsaturated 2 g
 Monounsaturated 3 g
Fiber 7 g
Sodium 288 mg

Marinated Pasta Salad

Serves 8

This is a wonderful make-ahead dish to take to potluck gatherings.

8 ounces dried pasta, such as rotini, farfalle, or ziti (3 to 4 cups)

½ pound fresh asparagus (6 to 10 spears) or 10-ounce package no-salt-added frozen asparagus, thawed

½ cup very thinly sliced red bell pepper (½ medium)

½ cup very thinly sliced zucchini

½ cup finely chopped red onion (1 medium)

½ cup thinly sliced celery (1 medium rib)

¼ cup nonfat or low-fat Italian salad dressing

3 tablespoons white wine vinegar

2 tablespoons finely snipped fresh parsley

¼ teaspoon salt

¼ teaspoon dried bouquet garni

⅛ teaspoon coarsely ground pepper

Several dashes of crushed red pepper flakes or red hot-pepper sauce

Cook pasta using package directions, omitting salt and oil. Drain, rinse, and let cool. Put in a large bowl.

Meanwhile, cut asparagus into 1-inch pieces. Steam for 5 minutes, then plunge into ice water to stop cooking. Drain.

Add asparagus and remaining ingredients to pasta. Toss well. Cover and refrigerate for several hours or overnight.

Calories 108
Protein 4 g
Carbohydrates 21 g
Cholesterol 0 mg
Total Fat 1 g
  Saturated 0 g
  Polyunsaturated 0 g
  Monounsaturated 0 g
Fiber 2 g
Sodium 159 mg

Greek Pasta Salad

Serves 8

Enhanced with feta cheese and fresh dillweed, this winning pasta-vegetable combination is sure to bring compliments.

SALAD

12-ounce package dried tricolor rotini (4½ to 6 cups)

1¼ cups frozen baby peas, thawed

1 cup diced red bell pepper (1 medium)

⅔ cup unpeeled seeded and diced cucumber (½ medium)

½ cup thinly sliced green onions (4 to 5 medium)

4 ounces crumbled feta cheese, rinsed

DRESSING

½ cup nonfat or low-fat cottage cheese

½ cup plain nonfat or low-fat yogurt

¼ cup fat-free, cholesterol-free or light, reduced-calorie mayonnaise dressing

¼ cup thinly sliced green onions (green part only) (3 to 4 medium)

1 to 2 tablespoons finely snipped fresh dillweed

¼ teaspoon pepper

For salad, cook pasta using package directions, omitting salt and oil. Drain and put in a large bowl.

Stir in remaining salad ingredients. Set aside.

In a food processor or blender, puree cottage cheese, yogurt, mayonnaise, and green onions.

Stir in dillweed and pepper, then combine with pasta mixture. Cover and refrigerate until chilled, about 30 minutes.

Calories 224
Protein 11 g
Carbohydrates 36 g
Cholesterol 14 mg
Total Fat 4 g
Saturated 2 g
Polyunsaturated 0 g
Monounsaturated 1 g
Fiber 3 g
Sodium 271 mg

Cook's Tip on Dillweed

Formerly used in charms against witchcraft, dillweed now leads a less exotic existence. It's used primarily to flavor pickles, sauces, and soups. Because its leaves are feathery and fragrant, dillweed also makes a pretty garnish.

Vegetable Rice Salad

Serves 6

You can keep this dish in the refrigerator for up to four days, so it's perfect for carefree entertaining.

SALAD

2 cups thinly sliced crookneck squash (2 medium)

3 cups cooked brown rice (1 cup uncooked)

½ cup diced red bell pepper

⅓ cup diced red onion

1 tablespoon dry-roasted unsalted sunflower seeds

DRESSING

2 tablespoons Dijon mustard

2 tablespoons vinegar

2 tablespoons fat-free, cholesterol-free or light, reduced-calorie mayonnaise dressing

1 tablespoon olive oil

¼ teaspoon salt

Freshly ground pepper to taste

3 tablespoons finely snipped fresh parsley

For salad, steam squash until tender-crisp, 4 to 5 minutes. Drain, put in a large bowl, and stir in remaining salad ingredients.

In a medium bowl, whisk together all dressing ingredients except parsley. Pour over vegetable mixture, add parsley, and stir well. Cover and refrigerate for at least 30 minutes to allow flavors to blend.

Calories 161
Protein 4 g
Carbohydrates 27 g
Cholesterol 0 mg
Total Fat 5 g
  Saturated 1 g
  Polyunsaturated 1 g
  Monounsaturated 2 g
Fiber 3 g
Sodium 265 mg

Curried Rice and Bean Salad

Serves 6

Make this your entrée, accompanied by Easy Refrigerator Rolls (see page 500) and fresh tomato and cucumber slices.

SALAD

3 cups cooked brown rice (1 cup uncooked)

1½ cups canned no-salt-added kidney beans, drained (12 ounces)

2 ribs celery, diced (1 cup)

4 green onions, chopped (½ cup)

½ medium green bell pepper, diced (½ cup)

¼ cup snipped fresh parsley

DRESSING

¼ cup fat-free, cholesterol-free or light, reduced-calorie mayonnaise dressing

¼ cup plain nonfat or low-fat yogurt

2 teaspoons curry powder

Dash of pepper

For salad, combine ingredients in a large bowl, stirring well.

In a small bowl, whisk together dressing ingredients. Pour over salad and stir well.

Cook's Tip on Brown Rice

Brown rice is whole-grain rice. Its bran covering provides color, fiber, and an extra helping of vitamins and minerals, compared with white rice. The bran also doubles the cooking time. White rice, also called polished rice, has had the bran removed.

Calories 179
Protein 7 g
Carbohydrates 36 g
Cholesterol 0 mg
Total Fat 1 g
  Saturated 0 g
  Polyunsaturated 0 g
  Monounsaturated 0 g
Fiber 8 g
Sodium 104 mg

Italian Rice Salad with Artichokes

Serves 6

This salad reflects the red, white, and green of the Italian flag.

SALAD

8 ounces uncooked arborio rice (1¼ cups)

9-ounce package frozen no-salt-added artichoke hearts, thawed

4 medium Italian plum tomatoes

1 cup frozen peas, thawed (5 ounces)

¼ cup diced red onion

DRESSING

2 tablespoons grated Parmesan cheese

2 tablespoons fresh lemon juice

1 tablespoon chopped fresh basil

1 tablespoon olive oil

1 medium clove garlic, minced, or ½ teaspoon bottled minced garlic

½ teaspoon sugar

¼ teaspoon salt

⅛ teaspoon pepper

Cook rice using package directions, omitting salt and margarine. Let cool to room temperature.

Meanwhile, blot artichoke hearts dry with paper towels. Cut each heart in half. Put in a large bowl. Cut tomatoes in half lengthwise, then in thin slices. Add tomatoes, rice, peas, and onion to artichokes. Stir well.

For dressing, combine ingredients in a food processor or blender. Process for 20 seconds. Pour over salad and gently stir with a rubber scraper. Cover and refrigerate for several hours to allow flavors to blend.

Calories 213
Protein 6 g
Carbohydrates 40 g
Cholesterol 2 mg
Total Fat 3 g
- Saturated 1 g
- Polyunsaturated 0 g
- Monounsaturated 2 g

Fiber 3 g
Sodium 187 mg

Cook's Tip on Arborio Rice

Arborio rice absorbs more flavor than other rice. It is also what gives this dish its creaminess. Look for it in supermarkets, Italian markets, and health food stores. If you don't find it, you can substitute medium-grain rice.

Fresh Salmon Salad

Serves 6

When served on dark, crisp greens, this salad is especially attractive. You can grill the salmon instead of baking it if you prefer.

Vegetable oil spray (olive oil flavor preferred)
1½ pounds fresh salmon steaks, ¾ to 1 inch thick
2 tablespoons fresh lemon juice
Vegetable oil spray (olive oil flavor preferred)
½ teaspoon dried thyme, crumbled
¼ teaspoon pepper, or to taste
2 ribs celery, diced (1 cup)
½ cup diced red bell pepper (½ medium)
½ cup finely diced onion (1 medium)
½ cup fat-free, cholesterol-free or light, reduced-calorie mayonnaise dressing
10 small black olives, thinly sliced (optional)
Juice of 1 medium lemon (3 tablespoons)
2 tablespoons finely snipped fresh parsley
¼ teaspoon red hot-pepper sauce, or to taste

Preheat oven to 450° F. Spray an ovenproof 13 × 9 × 2-inch glass baking dish with vegetable oil spray.

Rinse salmon and pat dry with paper towels. Pour 2 tablespoons lemon juice over salmon. Lightly spray one side of salmon with vegetable oil spray. Sprinkle with thyme and pepper. Put salmon in baking dish.

Bake for 10 minutes, or until salmon flakes easily when tested with a fork.

Carefully remove all skin and bones from salmon. Put salmon in a medium bowl and flake with a fork.

Add remaining ingredients and stir well. Cover and refrigerate for several hours before serving.

Calories 197
Protein 22 g
Carbohydrates 6 g
Cholesterol 68 mg
Total Fat 9 g
Saturated 2 g
Polyunsaturated 2 g
Monounsaturated 4 g
Fiber 1 g
Sodium 210 mg

Tuna and Rotini Salad

Serves 4

Much like Salade Niçoise (see page 107) with pasta added, this dish can be served hot or cold.

3 cups dried tricolor rotini

8 small red potatoes, quartered (about 8 ounces)

1½ cups fresh green beans, cut into 1-inch pieces (about 8 ounces)

1 tablespoon acceptable vegetable oil

2 tablespoons chopped green onion

3 medium cloves garlic, minced, or 1½ teaspoons bottled minced garlic

2 tablespoons minced fresh tarragon or 2 teaspoons dried, crumbled

1½ tablespoons coarse-grain mustard

1 tablespoon acceptable vegetable oil

1 tablespoon white wine vinegar

2 6-ounce cans chunk tuna, packed in distilled or spring water, drained

Pepper to taste

Prepare pasta using package directions, omitting salt and oil. Drain well and cover to keep warm.

Meanwhile, put potatoes in a medium saucepan with enough water to cover. Bring to a boil over high heat. Reduce heat and simmer, uncovered, for 7 minutes.

Add green beans to potatoes and cook for 3 minutes, or until green beans are tender-crisp; drain.

In a large saucepan, heat 1 tablespoon oil over medium heat, swirling to coat bottom of pan. Sauté green onion for 3 minutes.

Add potato mixture and garlic to green onion. Cook for 3 minutes, stirring occasionally.

In a small bowl, combine tarragon, mustard, 1 tablespoon oil, and vinegar, stirring well.

To serve, combine pasta, potato mixture, and tuna in a large bowl and toss well. Drizzle with mustard mixture, add pepper, and toss to coat.

Calories 482
Protein 32 g
Carbohydrates 68 g
Cholesterol 38 mg
Total Fat 9 g
Saturated 1 g
Polyunsaturated 5 g
Monounsaturated 2 g
Fiber 5 g
Sodium 135 mg

Salade Niçoise

Serves 12

Toss this traditional French salad in our flavorful vinaigrette. With crusty French bread on the side and fresh fruit salad, you have a splendid meal.

DRESSING

¼ cup white wine vinegar

2 tablespoons Dijon mustard

2 tablespoons Chicken Broth (see page 40 or use commercial low-sodium variety)

1 tablespoon olive oil

2 teaspoons chopped fresh thyme or 1 teaspoon dried, crumbled

3 medium cloves garlic, minced, or 1½ teaspoons bottled minced garlic

1 teaspoon sugar

½ teaspoon pepper, or to taste

SALAD

2 pounds fresh green beans, cut into 1-inch pieces (5 to 6 cups)

4 ribs celery, thickly sliced (2 cups)

3 6-ounce cans white tuna, packed in distilled or spring water, drained and flaked

5 medium red potatoes, cooked and sliced (about 5 cups)

1 green bell pepper, cut into rings

1 red bell pepper, cut into rings

1 pint cherry tomatoes

10 large black olives, sliced

10 stuffed green olives, sliced

1 large red onion, sliced and separated into rings

⅓ cup snipped fresh parsley

¼ cup finely chopped green onions (2 to 3 medium)

2 tablespoons chopped fresh basil or 2 teaspoons dried, crumbled

In a small bowl, whisk together dressing ingredients. Cover and refrigerate.

Steam green beans until tender-crisp, 6 to 8 minutes. Drain and put in a large bowl.

Cook celery in boiling water for 15 seconds. Remove and rinse in cold water. Add celery and remaining salad ingredients to beans. Stir well.

Pour dressing on salad and toss to mix well.

Calories 168
Protein 14 g
Carbohydrates 23 g
Cholesterol 19 mg
Total Fat 3 g
Saturated 0 g
Polyunsaturated 0 g
Monounsaturated 2 g
Fiber 5 g
Sodium 213 mg

Curried Tuna Salad

Serves 4

A quick lunch for four, this salad features a mild tuna mixture seasoned with a sweet curry mayonnaise and crunchy celery, water chestnuts, and red bell peppers. Complete the meal with sliced pineapple and clusters of seedless red grapes.

TUNA SALAD

5/8 cup fat-free, cholesterol-free or light, reduced-calorie mayonnaise dressing

1 tablespoon sugar (plus 1 teaspoon if using light mayonnaise)

2 teaspoons curry powder

1/8 teaspoon cayenne

2 6-ounce cans white tuna, packed in distilled or spring water, drained and flaked

8-ounce can sliced water chestnuts, drained

1 cup chopped red bell pepper

3/4 cup chopped celery (1 to 2 medium ribs)

8 red leaf lettuce leaves

4 slices pineapple, fresh or canned in its own juice (optional)

1/4 cup pecan pieces, dry-roasted (1 ounce)

4 small clusters seedless red grapes (optional)

In a medium mixing bowl, whisk together mayonnaise, sugar, curry powder, and cayenne.

Stir in remaining tuna salad ingredients.

To serve, line plates with lettuce. Place pineapple on lettuce and top each pineapple slice with a scoop of tuna salad. Sprinkle with pecans. Place a grape cluster on each plate.

Calories 168
Protein 14 g
Carbohydrates 23 g
Cholesterol 19 mg
Total Fat 3 g
Saturated 0 g
Polyunsaturated 0 g
Monounsaturated 2 g
Fiber 5 g
Sodium 213 mg

Picante Shrimp with Broccoli and Snow Peas

Serves 4

Sit back and enjoy the rave reviews when you serve this dish at your next luncheon.

SALAD

2 cups broccoli florets

1 cup snow peas, cut into halves

12 ounces frozen cooked and peeled shrimp, thawed

½ cup red bell pepper strips

DRESSING

¼ cup picante sauce

¼ cup fat-free or low-fat Italian salad dressing

¾ teaspoon grated fresh gingerroot

¾ teaspoon light soy sauce

4 romaine leaves

½ cup cucumber sticks

Bring water to a boil in a vegetable steamer over high heat. Steam broccoli for 2 minutes. Stir in snow peas and steam for 5 minutes, or until vegetables are tender-crisp. Drain in a colander and rinse with cold water to stop cooking process.

Put broccoli and snow peas in a large bowl. Stir in shrimp and bell pepper strips.

In a small bowl, whisk together dressing ingredients. Pour over salad.

Cover and refrigerate for 2 hours, stirring occasionally.

To serve, line 4 salad plates with lettuce. Stir cucumber strips into salad and spoon onto plates.

Calories 133
Protein 21 g
Carbohydrates 8 g
Cholesterol 166 mg
Total Fat 1 g
Saturated 0 g
Polyunsaturated 1 g
Monounsaturated 0 g
Fiber 3 g
Sodium 459 mg

Cook's Tip on Steaming Vegetables

If you don't own a vegetable steamer, you can use a spaghetti cooker or set a metal colander or sieve in a saucepan. The boiling water shouldn't touch the vegetables.

Mexican Shrimp Salad

Serves 5

Spicy shrimp and a bed of jícama and raw spinach are the stars of this salad. Try it with crisp crackers and chilled Cucumber Watercress Soup (see page 46).

2½ quarts water

1½ pounds raw medium-size shrimp, shells on

2 teaspoons liquid crab-and-shrimp boil

½ cup sliced green onions (4 to 5 medium)

⅓ cup fat-free, cholesterol-free or light, reduced-calorie mayonnaise dressing

⅓ cup plain nonfat or low-fat yogurt

2 tablespoons chili sauce

1 tablespoon chopped fresh cilantro (optional)

2 teaspoons prepared horseradish

1 teaspoon chili powder

½ teaspoon grated lime zest

Red hot-pepper sauce to taste

3 cups coarsely chopped fresh spinach (6 to 8 ounces)

½ medium jícama (about 12 ounces)

Pour water into a large saucepan and bring to a boil over high heat. Add shrimp and crab-and-shrimp boil. Return to boil, remove from heat, and set aside for 5 minutes, or until shrimp turn pink. Drain shrimp in colander and run under cool water. Peel, devein, and cut shrimp in half lengthwise to retain *C* shape.

In a large bowl, combine green onions, mayonnaise, yogurt, chili sauce, cilantro, horseradish, chili powder, lime zest, and hot-pepper sauce. Add shrimp and stir well. Cover and refrigerate for at least 2 hours to allow flavors to blend.

To serve, toss together spinach and jícama in a large bowl. Place on plates and spoon shrimp mixture on top.

Calories 140
Protein 19 g
Carbohydrates 12 g
Cholesterol 162 mg
Total Fat 1 g
Saturated 0 g
Polyunsaturated 1 g
Monounsaturated 0 g
Fiber 4 g
Sodium 441 mg

Curried Chicken Salad

Serves 6

Serve this flavorful dish cold on a bed of lettuce or heat it gently and present it over cooked rice or noodles. This salad will keep for up to four days in the refrigerator.

DRESSING

½ cup fat-free, cholesterol-free or light, reduced-calorie mayonnaise dressing

1 tablespoon fresh lemon juice

2 teaspoons rice vinegar or white vinegar

½ teaspoon curry powder

¼ teaspoon salt

⅛ teaspoon pepper

⅛ teaspoon cayenne

CHICKEN SALAD

4 cups cubed, cooked chicken, white meat only, skin and all visible fat removed (1½ pounds boneless, skinless breasts)

4 ribs celery, chopped (2 cups)

8 thin strips green bell pepper (optional)

In a large bowl, whisk together dressing ingredients.

Stir in chicken and celery. Cover and refrigerate for at least 30 minutes.

To serve, garnish with bell pepper.

Cook's Tip on Rice Vinegar

Used in Chinese and Japanese cooking, rice vinegar is slightly milder than most North American vinegars. Unless a recipe specifies black rice vinegar, use white or red rice vinegar. The black has a distinctive, heavier flavor; the red and white are interchangeable.

Calories 202
Protein 27 g
Carbohydrates 5 g
Cholesterol 83 mg
Total Fat 7 g
Saturated 2 g
Polyunsaturated 2 g
Monounsaturated 3 g
Fiber 1 g
Sodium 342 mg

Chicken Vegetable Salad

Serves 6

Whether you serve this crunchy mixture over crisp salad greens or use it as the filling for a pita bread wrap, you're sure to love it.

2 cups diced cooked chicken or turkey, white meat only, skin and all visible fat removed (about ¾ pound boneless, skinless chicken breasts)
½ medium cucumber, peeled and diced (½ cup)
½ cup diced celery
½ cup sliced water chestnuts, drained
¼ cup diced green bell pepper
¼ cup chopped pimiento, drained
¼ cup sliced green onions (2 to 3 medium)
¼ cup fat-free, cholesterol-free or light, reduced-calorie mayonnaise dressing
2 tablespoons capers, rinsed
¼ teaspoon paprika

Calories 104
Protein 15 g
Carbohydrates 5 g
Cholesterol 40 mg
Total Fat 2 g
Saturated 1 g
Polyunsaturated 1 g
Monounsaturated 1 g
Fiber 1 g
Sodium 182 mg

In a large bowl, combine chicken, cucumber, celery, water chestnuts, bell pepper, pimiento, green onion, and mayonnaise. Toss to mix well.

Sprinkle with capers and paprika.

Tuna Vegetable Salad

Substitute two 6-ounce cans water-packed white chunk tuna (distilled or spring water), drained and flaked, for chicken. (calories 84; protein 15 g; carbohydrates 5 g; cholesterol 25 mg; total fat 1 g; saturated 0 g; polyunsaturated 0 g; monounsaturated 0 g; fiber 1 g; sodium 181 mg)

Cook's Tip on Cucumbers

When you make salad ahead of time, add the cucumber just before serving so it won't "weep" and make the salad watery.

Cajun Chicken Salad

Serves 4

Need a little spice in your life? Try this bed of mixed greens piled high with roasted red bell peppers, mushrooms, strips of Triple-Pepper Chicken (see page 203), and feta cheese.

DRESSING

6 tablespoons cider vinegar

1 tablespoon extra-virgin olive oil

3 medium cloves garlic, minced, or 1½ teaspoons bottled minced garlic

1½ teaspoons sugar

½ teaspoon red hot-pepper sauce

8 ounces fresh mushrooms, sliced (2½ to 3 cups)

7.2-ounce jar roasted red bell peppers, drained and thinly sliced, or 1 large red bell pepper, roasted and thinly sliced

⅓ cup chopped green onions (3 medium)

6 cups torn mixed greens

4 cooked Triple-Pepper Chicken breast halves (see page 203)

2 ounces feta cheese, crumbled

In a small bowl, whisk together dressing ingredients until well blended.

In a large, shallow glass baking dish, combine mushrooms, peppers, and green onions. Pour dressing over all, stirring to coat completely. Let stand for 20 minutes.

Arrange 1½ cups mixed greens on each dinner plate.

Cut chicken into thin strips and stir into mushroom mixture. Spoon over mixed greens and sprinkle with feta.

Cook's Tip

You can make the mushroom mixture up to 8 hours in advance. Cover and refrigerate it until serving time.

Calories 272
Protein 29 g
Carbohydrates 14 g
Cholesterol 75 mg
Total Fat 12 g
- Saturated 4 g
- Polyunsaturated 2 g
- Monounsaturated 5 g

Fiber 3 g
Sodium 397 mg

Asian Chicken and Rice Salad

Serves 8

Made in a ring mold, this salad is a worthy centerpiece for a luncheon. Or serve it in edible bowls—hollowed tomatoes or bell pepper halves.

SALAD

3 cups cooked rice (1 cup long-grain)

10-ounce package frozen green peas, thawed (2 cups)

1½ pounds cooked chicken, white meat only, skin and all visible fat removed, diced (about 2 pounds boneless, skinless breasts)

4 green onions, sliced (½ cup)

1 rib celery, diced (½ cup)

2 tablespoons diced green bell pepper

DRESSING

¼ cup rice vinegar

2 tablespoons acceptable vegetable oil

2 tablespoons dry sherry

1 tablespoon light soy sauce

1 tablespoon Dijon mustard

¼ teaspoon hot-pepper oil (optional)

⅛ teaspoon ground ginger

Vegetable oil spray (optional)

Sprigs of fresh cilantro (optional)

Fresh bean sprouts (optional)

In a large bowl, combine salad ingredients, stirring well.

For dressing, put ingredients in a jar with a tight-fitting lid. Shake to combine thoroughly. Pour over rice mixture, stirring well.

Cover bowl or spray a ring mold with vegetable oil spray, spoon salad in, packing firmly, and cover with plastic wrap. Refrigerate for at least 30 minutes.

If using a ring mold, turn salad out onto serving platter. Place cilantro and/or bean sprouts in center. If serving as individual salads, garnish each serving with cilantro and bean sprouts.

Calories 293
Protein 30 g
Carbohydrates 23 g
Cholesterol 72 mg
Total Fat 8 g
- Saturated 2 g
- Polyunsaturated 3 g
- Monounsaturated 2 g

Fiber 2 g
Sodium 184 mg

Island Chicken Salad with Fresh Mint

Serves 4

Light and utterly refreshing, this salad begins with Sweet-Spice Glazed Chicken on a bed of mixed greens. Mango and kiwifruit with a bit of jalapeño heat surround it, and a cooling sweet citrus dressing and fresh mint top it.

DRESSING
3/8 to 1/2 cup fresh lime juice (4 medium limes)
3 tablespoons sugar
2 teaspoons acceptable vegetable oil

4 cups torn mixed greens
4 cooked Sweet-Spice Glazed Chicken breast halves, cut into thin strips **(see page 201)**
1 1/2 to 2 cups diced mango (2 to 3 medium)
3 kiwifruit, peeled and diced
1 to 2 fresh jalapeños, seeded and finely chopped (optional)
1/4 cup chopped fresh mint leaves

In a small mixing bowl, whisk together dressing ingredients until sugar has dissolved.

To assemble, place 1 cup mixed greens on each plate, and top with chicken. Arrange mango and kiwifruit around chicken. Sprinkle jalapeño over fruit. Drizzle lime mixture over salad, then sprinkle with mint. Serve immediately.

Cook's Tip on Hot Chile Peppers

Wear rubber gloves when handling hot peppers, or wash your hands thoroughly after handling. Your skin, especially around your eyes, is sensitive to oil from peppers. The hottest part of a chile pepper is the ribs, so remove them to cut back on the heat. Removing the seeds also helps. So does slitting a fresh or dried pepper and adding it during cooking. Taste as the dish cooks and remove the pepper when the dish is hot enough. Another way to get chile pepper flavor without a lot of "burn" is to add a chopped pepper, fresh or dried, near the end of cooking.

Calories 400
Protein 25 g
Carbohydrates 54 g
Cholesterol 63 mg
Total Fat 8 g
  Saturated 1 g
  Polyunsaturated 4 g
  Monounsaturated 2 g
Fiber 20 g
Sodium 257 mg

Grilled Flank Steak Salad with Sweet-and-Sour Sesame Dressing

Serves 4

Leftover steak is a rare occurrence. If you plan ahead, however, you'll have some Grilled Lemongrass Flank Steak (see page 247) to use in this salad of colorful vegetables, earthy wild rice, and crisp napa cabbage. A sweet-and-sour dressing melds the varied flavors and textures.

SWEET-AND-SOUR SESAME DRESSING

1 tablespoon sesame seeds

½ teaspoon grated lemon zest

2 tablespoons fresh lemon juice

2 tablespoons rice vinegar

1 tablespoon light brown sugar

1 tablespoon Chinese plum sauce

4 cups shredded napa cabbage (12 to 16 ounces)

2 cups cooked wild rice, chilled

4 ounces asparagus, cooked (3 to 5 spears)

8 cherry tomatoes (gold preferred)

½ medium cucumber, thinly sliced

½ medium red bell pepper, thinly sliced

½ medium red onion, thinly sliced

½ cup alfalfa sprouts

6 to 8 ounces grilled flank steak, thinly sliced across grain, warm or chilled

Calories 257
Protein 20 g
Carbohydrates 30 g
Cholesterol 33 mg
Total Fat 7 g
Saturated 3 g
Polyunsaturated 1 g
Monounsaturated 3 g
Fiber 6 g
Sodium 112 mg

Heat a small skillet over medium heat. Toast sesame seeds for 1 to 2 minutes, or until golden, stirring occasionally. Transfer to a medium bowl and let cool for 5 minutes.

Add remaining dressing ingredients and whisk together.

To serve, arrange cabbage on a large platter. Mound rice in center of cabbage. Decoratively arrange asparagus, tomatoes, cucumber, bell pepper, red onion, and alfalfa sprouts on cabbage. Lay beef slices on rice. Drizzle dressing over all.

Southwestern Pork Salad

Serves 6

From the tangy vinaigrette to the hearty black beans, this is a delicious portable salad. Try it at your next picnic, or take it to a potluck dinner. The orange and grape garnish makes a nice contrast to the salad, which will keep in the refrigerator for up to four days.

2 cups pork tenderloin, roasted, all visible fat removed, cut into small cubes (about 1 pound)

1 cup Cuban Black Beans (see page 326) or canned black beans (about half of 16- to 17-ounce can), rinsed and drained

½ cup finely chopped green onions (4 to 5 medium)

½ cup chopped green or red bell pepper (½ medium)

1 small clove garlic, minced, or ½ teaspoon bottled minced garlic

DRESSING

¼ cup snipped fresh parsley

¼ cup cider vinegar

2 tablespoons Chicken Broth (see page 40 or use commercial low-sodium variety)

1½ tablespoons sugar

2 teaspoons olive oil

½ teaspoon dried oregano, crumbled

½ teaspoon dry mustard

1 cup cherry tomatoes, cut into quarters

6 black olives, chopped (optional)

3 cups crisp salad greens

Fresh orange slices (optional)

Fresh green grapes (optional)

In a large bowl, combine pork, Cuban Black Beans, green onions, bell pepper, and garlic.

For dressing, combine ingredients in a jar with a tight-fitting lid. Shake well. Pour over pork mixture, tossing to coat evenly. Cover and refrigerate for at least 30 minutes before serving, stirring occasionally.

Immediately before serving, gently stir in tomatoes and olives. Spoon over salad greens, and garnish with orange slices and grapes.

Calories 227
Protein 26 g
Carbohydrates 18 g
Cholesterol 60 mg
Total Fat 6 g
Saturated 2 g
Polyunsaturated 1 g
Monounsaturated 3 g
Fiber 5 g
Sodium 58 mg

Warm Orzo Salad with Black Beans and Ham

Serves 4

Bright yellow noodles, dark black beans, and colorful bell peppers make this currylike salad beautiful. It's a great one-dish meal to take on a picnic or pack for brown bag lunches.

Vegetable oil spray

1 medium onion, diced (½ cup)

1 medium clove garlic, minced, or ½ teaspoon bottled minced garlic

2 large red or yellow bell peppers or combination, seeded and diced (2½ cups)

½ cup dry white wine (regular or nonalcoholic) or Chicken Broth (see page 40 or use commercial low-sodium variety)

½ to 1 cup frozen no-salt-added whole-kernel corn

1 cup dried orzo, tiny dried pasta shells, or other dried noodles

2 tablespoons red wine vinegar

2 teaspoons olive oil

1 teaspoon ground cumin

½ teaspoon powdered turmeric

⅛ to ¼ teaspoon crushed red pepper flakes

15-ounce can black beans, rinsed and drained

1 cup minced baked ham or turkey ham (about 4½ ounces)

Spray a large nonstick skillet with vegetable oil spray. Add onion and garlic; cook over medium-high heat for about 3 minutes, stirring occasionally.

Reduce heat to medium. Stir in bell peppers and cook for 2 to 3 minutes. Add wine and cook until peppers are very soft and most of the wine has evaporated, about 5 minutes. Stir in corn and cook just to heat through, 1 to 2 minutes.

Prepare orzo using package directions, omitting salt and oil. Drain well.

In a large bowl, combine vinegar, oil, cumin, turmeric, and red pepper flakes. Stir in beans, ham, bell pepper mixture, and orzo.

Serve warm or at room temperature.

Calories 336
Protein 17 g
Carbohydrates 50 g
Cholesterol 14 mg
Total Fat 5 g
- Saturated 1 g
- Polyunsaturated 1 g
- Monounsaturated 2 g

Fiber 9 g
Sodium 457 mg

Zesty Tomato Dressing

Serves 10; 2 tablespoons per serving

You'll enjoy this refreshing recipe so much as a dressing that you'll also want to use it as a dip.

1 cup no-salt-added tomato juice
2 green onions (green and white parts), thinly sliced (¼ cup)
2 tablespoons fresh lemon juice
2 tablespoons red wine vinegar
1 teaspoon dried parsley, crumbled
1 teaspoon sugar
½ teaspoon dried oregano, crumbled
½ teaspoon dry mustard
½ teaspoon light soy sauce
¼ teaspoon pepper

Put all ingredients in a jar with a tight-fitting lid. Shake vigorously until mixed thoroughly. Cover and refrigerate.

Calories 10
Protein 0 g
Carbohydrates 2 g
Cholesterol 0 mg
Total Fat 0 g
Saturated 0 g
Polyunsaturated 0 g
Monounsaturated 0 g
Fiber 0 g
Sodium 12 mg

Apple Juice Dressing

Serves 4; 2 tablespoons per serving

This dressing is delightful on either a green salad or fresh fruit.

¼ cup unsweetened apple juice
3 tablespoons snipped fresh parsley
2½ tablespoons apple cider vinegar
2 tablespoons minced sweet onion or 1 large shallot, minced
2 teaspoons Dijon mustard
1 teaspoon dried tarragon, crumbled
Generous amount of pepper

Put all ingredients in a food processor or blender. Process until smooth. Cover and refrigerate for several hours.

Calories 19
Protein 0 g
Carbohydrates 4 g
Cholesterol 0 mg
Total Fat 0 g
Saturated 0 g
Polyunsaturated 0 g
Monounsaturated 0 g
Fiber 0 g
Sodium 66 mg

Creamy Cottage Cheese Dressing

Serves 10; 2 tablespoons per serving

For variety, make this versatile dressing eight different ways.

1 cup nonfat or low-fat cottage cheese

⅓ cup nonfat or low-fat buttermilk (plus more as needed)

Put ingredients in a food processor or blender. Process until smooth and creamy. For a thinner consistency, add more buttermilk. Cover and refrigerate.

For each variation below, add the suggested ingredients to the basic recipe before processing.

Creamy Blue Cheese Dressing

1 tablespoon blue cheese and pepper to taste. (calories 23; protein 3 g; carbohydrates 1 g; cholesterol 3 mg; total fat 0 g; saturated 0 g; polyunsaturated 0 g; monounsaturated 0 g; fiber 0 g; sodium 99 mg)

Creamy French Dressing

1 teaspoon paprika, 1 teaspoon dry mustard, 1 teaspoon onion powder, 1 teaspoon garlic powder (or to taste), 1 teaspoon no-salt-added tomato juice, and 1 teaspoon very low sodium or low-sodium Worcestershire sauce. (calories 24; protein 3 g; carbohydrates 2 g; cholesterol 2 mg; total fat 0 g; saturated 0 g; polyunsaturated 0 g; monounsaturated 0 g; fiber 0 g; sodium 88 mg)

Creamy Green Goddess Dressing

3 anchovies, 1 tablespoon snipped fresh parsley, 1 teaspoon chopped green onion, and chopped fresh tarragon or dried tarragon, crumbled, to taste. (calories 22; protein 4 g; carbohydrates 1 g; cholesterol 3 mg; total fat 0 g; saturated 0 g; polyunsaturated 0 g; monounsaturated 0 g; fiber 0 g; sodium 132 mg)

Calories 20
Protein 3 g
Carbohydrates 1 g
Cholesterol 2 mg
Total Fat 0 g
Saturated 0 g
Polyunsaturated 0 g
Monounsaturated 0 g
Fiber 0 g
Sodium 87 mg

Creamy Italian Dressing

½ teaspoon dried oregano, crumbled; ½ teaspoon garlic powder; and ½ teaspoon dehydrated onion flakes, or to taste. (calories 21; protein 3 g; carbohydrates 1 g; cholesterol 2 mg; total fat 0 g; saturated 0 g; polyunsaturated 0 g; monounsaturated 0 g; fiber 0 g; sodium 87 mg)

Creamy Horseradish Dressing

1 to 2 tablespoons fresh grated or prepared horseradish. (calories 21; protein 3 g; carbohydrates 2 g; cholesterol 2 mg; total fat 0 g; saturated 0 g; polyunsaturated 0 g; monounsaturated 0 g; fiber 0 g; sodium 88 mg)

Creamy Thousand Island Dressing

2 tablespoons sweet pickle relish, 1 to 2 tablespoons chili sauce, and dry mustard to taste (optional). (calories 24; protein 3 g; carbohydrates 2 g; cholesterol 2 mg; total fat 0 g; saturated 0 g; polyunsaturated 0 g; monounsaturated 0 g; fiber 0 g; sodium 112 mg)

Creamy Dill Dressing

1 tablespoon snipped fresh dillweed or ½ to 1 teaspoon dried, crumbled. (calories 20; protein 3 g; carbohydrates 1 g; cholesterol 2 mg; total fat 0 g; saturated 0 g; polyunsaturated 0 g; monounsaturated 0 g; fiber 0 g; sodium 87 mg)

Creamy Chef's Dressing

Serves 8; 2 tablespoons per serving

Rich buttermilk and cottage cheese provide a creamy base for this zesty dressing. Serve it over a combination of crisp lettuces with a sprinkle of shredded red cabbage.

¾ cup nonfat or low-fat buttermilk
¼ cup nonfat or low-fat cottage cheese
½ small white onion, minced (⅛ cup)
1 tablespoon finely snipped fresh parsley
½ tablespoon minced green onion
¼ teaspoon prepared mustard
Dash of red hot-pepper sauce

Calories 18
Protein 2 g
Carbohydrates 2 g
Cholesterol 2 mg
Total Fat 0 g
Saturated 0 g
Polyunsaturated 0 g
Monounsaturated 0 g
Fiber 0 g
Sodium 65 mg

Puree all ingredients in a food processor or blender. Cover and refrigerate.

Chunky Cucumber and Garlic Dressing

Serves 6; 2 tablespoons per serving

Be as cool as a cucumber on a hot summer day and serve this dressing on your favorite salad or a grilled chicken, pork, or beef pita sandwich.

½ cup plain nonfat or low-fat yogurt
½ medium cucumber, peeled and chopped (¾ cup)
1 tablespoon sugar
1 tablespoon acceptable vegetable oil
½ teaspoon dehydrated onion flakes
¼ teaspoon garlic powder
¼ teaspoon pepper
1 tablespoon red wine vinegar

In a small bowl, whisk yogurt until smooth.

Whisk in remaining ingredients except vinegar.

Gradually whisk in vinegar until smooth. Cover and refrigerate for at least 4 hours to allow flavors to blend.

Calories 39
Protein 1 g
Carbohydrates 4 g
Cholesterol 0 mg
Total Fat 2 g
  Saturated 0 g
  Polyunsaturated 1 g
  Monounsaturated 1 g
Fiber 0 g
Sodium 13 mg

Ranch-Style Herb Dressing

Serves 8; 2 tablespoons per serving

Freshly made ranch-style dressing is delightful on a salad or baked potato or as a dip for vegetables.

¾ cup nonfat or low-fat cottage cheese
⅓ cup nonfat or low-fat buttermilk
1½ tablespoons finely chopped onion
2 tablespoons fat-free, cholesterol-free or light, reduced-calorie mayonnaise dressing
2 tablespoons finely snipped fresh parsley
1 teaspoon dried dillweed, crumbled
1 teaspoon dried basil, crumbled
½ teaspoon dried oregano, crumbled
¼ teaspoon garlic powder
⅛ teaspoon salt
Dash of red hot-pepper sauce

In a food processor or blender, puree cottage cheese, buttermilk, onion, and mayonnaise.

Add remaining ingredients and process for 10 seconds. Cover and refrigerate for at least 1 hour to allow flavors to blend.

Calories 25
Protein 3 g
Carbohydrates 2 g
Cholesterol 2 mg
Total Fat 0 g
  Saturated 0 g
  Polyunsaturated 0 g
  Monounsaturated 0 g
Fiber 0 g
Sodium 151 mg

Cook's Tip

For a richer flavor—but a dressing with a higher calorie count—increase the amount of mayonnaise and reduce the amount of cottage cheese.

Yogurt Dressing

Serves 5; 2 tablespoons per serving

A few simple additions change plain yogurt into salad dressing that's fit for almost any lettuce or vegetable salad.

Calories 34
Protein 1 g
Carbohydrates 2 g
Cholesterol 1 mg
Total Fat 3 g
Saturated 0 g
Polyunsaturated 2 g
Monounsaturated 1 g
Fiber 0 g
Sodium 18 mg

½ cup plain nonfat or low-fat yogurt
1 tablespoon acceptable vegetable oil
2 teaspoons fresh lemon juice
½ teaspoon paprika
⅛ teaspoon garlic powder (optional)
Dash of red hot-pepper sauce

Combine all ingredients in a food processor or blender and process for 5 seconds. Cover and refrigerate.

Minted Lime Dressing

Serves 14; 2 tablespoons per serving

Fruit salads shine when topped with this dressing.

½ cup nonfat or low-fat vanilla yogurt
½ cup nonfat or low-fat cottage cheese
⅓ cup acceptable vegetable oil
¼ cup fresh lime juice (2 to 3 medium limes)
1 tablespoon grated or finely chopped onion
1 tablespoon honey
¼ teaspoon salt
Dash of white pepper
2 tablespoons finely chopped fresh mint

Calories 66
Protein 2 g
Carbohydrates 4 g
Cholesterol 1 mg
Total Fat 5 g
Saturated 1 g
Polyunsaturated 3 g
Monounsaturated 1 g
Fiber 0 g
Sodium 74 mg

Puree all ingredients except mint in a food processor or blender.

Stir in mint. Cover and refrigerate for several hours to allow flavors to blend.

Poppy Seed Dressing with Kiwifruit

Serves 8; 2 tablespoons per serving

Serve this delicately sweet dressing over a crisp lettuce and jícama salad, seasonal fresh fruit, or nonfat or low-fat cottage cheese or frozen yogurt.

¾ cup pineapple juice
1 tablespoon cornstarch
2 kiwifruit
2 tablespoons honey
1 tablespoon fresh lime juice
1 teaspoon poppy seeds

In a small saucepan, whisk together pineapple juice and cornstarch. Bring to a boil over medium-high heat, whisking occasionally until mixture thickens, 3 to 4 minutes. Spoon into a small bowl and let cool at room temperature for 5 minutes. Cover and refrigerate until cold, at least 15 minutes.

Meanwhile, peel and dice kiwifruit.

Spoon cold pineapple mixture into a food processor or blender. Add kiwifruit, honey, and lime juice. Process until smooth.

Pour dressing into a bowl and stir in poppy seeds. Serve immediately or cover and refrigerate for up to 5 days.

Cook's Tip on Kiwifruit

Choose kiwifruit that yields to gentle pressure (it should not be soft or mushy). If kiwifruit is extremely firm, let it sit on the counter for a few days to ripen. Although the fuzzy skin is almost always removed, it is edible, as are the tiny black seeds.

Calories 47
Protein 0 g
Carbohydrates 12 g
Cholesterol 0 mg
Total Fat 0 g
Saturated 0 g
Polyunsaturated 0 g
Monounsaturated 0 g
Fiber 1 g
Sodium 2 mg

SEAFOOD

Ginger Broiled Fish

Broiled Fish Roll-Ups

Broiled Marinated Fish Steaks

Poached Fish

Mushroom-Stuffed Fish Rolls

Confetti Fish Fillets

Fish Fillets with Asparagus

French-Style Braised Fish Fillets

Mediterranean Fish

Fish Fillets in Foil

Baked Catfish

Crispy Cajun Catfish Nibbles with Red Sauce

Cod Baked with Vegetables

Haddock with Tomatoes and Ginger

Orange Roughy with Tomatoes and Spinach

Teriyaki Halibut

Red Snapper à l'Orange

Salmon with Cucumber-Dill Sauce

Grilled Salmon Oriental

Salmon Cakes

Salmon Alfredo

Crispy Baked Fillet of Sole

Sole Baked with Mushrooms

Sole with Walnuts and White Wine

Sole with Parsley and Mint

Grilled Tuna with Pineapple-Nectarine Salsa

Tuna Chili

Tuna Salad Pitas

Crabmeat Maryland

Linguine with White Clam Sauce

Scallops and Asparagus in Wine Sauce

Oven-Fried Scallops with Cilantro and Lime

Cioppino

Ginger Broiled Fish

Serves 8

Fresh ginger and wine are a winning combination in this simple fish dish.

Vegetable oil spray
2 pounds fresh or frozen fish fillets or steaks, about ¾ inch thick
¾ cup dry white wine (regular or nonalcoholic)
2 green onions (green and white parts), chopped
1 tablespoon light soy sauce
2 teaspoons grated fresh gingerroot
2 teaspoons prepared horseradish, drained
1 teaspoon acceptable vegetable oil

Preheat broiler. Lightly spray a broilerproof baking dish with vegetable oil spray. Put dish under broiler for 1 to 2 minutes.

Rinse fish and pat dry with paper towels. Cut fish into 8 equal portions. Arrange in a single layer in preheated dish.

In a small bowl, combine remaining ingredients, stirring well. Pour over fish.

Broil fish about 2 inches from heat for 5 to 6 minutes. Turn carefully and broil for 5 to 6 minutes, or until fish flakes easily when tested with a fork.

Cook's Tip on Gingerroot

You can find gingerroot in the produce section. Choose a root with smooth skin. To keep it from drying out, peel just as much as you need to grate, keeping a "handle" with the peeling left on. Keep leftover unpeeled gingerroot wrapped in a paper towel and refrigerate it in an airtight plastic bag for up to 3 weeks. For longer storage, put peeled gingerroot in a small jar with a tight-fitting lid and cover the ginger with dry sherry. Refrigerate for up to 3 months. Both the ginger and the ginger-flavored sherry will be great for cooking.

Calories 115
Protein 19 g
Carbohydrates 1 g
Cholesterol 53 mg
Total Fat 2 g
  Saturated 0 g
  Polyunsaturated 1 g
  Monounsaturated 0 g
Fiber 0 g
Sodium 148 mg

Broiled Fish Roll-Ups

Serves 6

Pearly white fillets are rolled up with a moist, colorful stuffing, then broiled to perfection.

Vegetable oil spray

1½ pounds thin fish fillets, such as flounder, sole, or tilapia

STUFFING

½ cup chopped celery

3 tablespoons water (plus more as needed)

2 tablespoons chopped onion

3 slices bread, lightly toasted and coarsely crumbled

¼ cup chopped cooked spinach (4 to 6 ounces fresh)

½ teaspoon dried thyme, crumbled

Pepper to taste

COATING

White of 1 large egg, lightly beaten

¼ cup fat-free milk

½ cup finely crushed cracker crumbs (about 14 fat-free, low-sodium saltines)

2 tablespoons all-purpose flour

1 teaspoon snipped fresh parsley

Preheat broiler. Soak six wooden toothpicks in cold water for about 10 minutes. Lightly spray broiler pan and rack with vegetable oil spray. Rinse fish and pat dry with paper towels. Set aside.

For stuffing, combine celery, water, and onion in a medium saucepan. Bring to a boil over medium-high heat. Reduce heat and simmer, covered, for 3 to 4 minutes, or until vegetables are tender. Remove from heat.

Add bread crumbs, spinach, thyme, and pepper to celery mixture. Stir well, adding water to moisten if necessary.

Place an equal amount of mixture down the middle of each fillet. Starting from a short side, roll up jelly-roll style and secure with wooden toothpicks.

For coating, in a small, shallow bowl, whisk together egg white and milk. On a plate, combine cracker crumbs and flour. Roll stuffed fillets in egg

Calories 203
Protein 23 g
Carbohydrates 21 g
Cholesterol 54 mg
Total Fat 2 g
  Saturated 1 g
  Polyunsaturated 1 g
  Monounsaturated 1 g
Fiber 1 g
Sodium 275 mg

white mixture, then in cracker crumb mixture. Place fillets on broiler rack.

Broil 4 to 5 inches from heat for 5 to 7 minutes. Turn carefully and broil for about 5 minutes, or until fish flakes easily when tested with a fork.

To serve, remove toothpicks and sprinkle fish with parsley.

Time-Saver on Cracker Crumbs: When you have a few fat-free or low-fat crackers left in the box, crush them in a food processor or blender or with a rolling pin. Freeze the crumbs in an airtight plastic freezer bag for future use. This tip not only saves time but also gives you a flavorful mixture of various types of cracker.

Broiled Marinated Fish Steaks

Serves 6

The assertiveness of tarragon vinegar boosts the flavor of mild fish. Serve these steaks with French-cut green beans and Spinach Salad with Kiwifruit and Raspberries (see page 74).

1½ pounds fish steaks, such as orange roughy, swordfish, or Atlantic or Pacific halibut, about 1 inch thick

⅓ cup tarragon vinegar

2 tablespoons snipped fresh parsley

2 teaspoons pepper, or to taste

2 teaspoons acceptable vegetable oil

1 teaspoon very low sodium or low-sodium Worcestershire sauce

1 bay leaf

Vegetable oil spray

Rinse fish and pat dry with paper towels.

In an airtight plastic bag, combine remaining ingredients except vegetable oil spray. Add fish steaks, turning bag to coat fish. Seal and refrigerate for at least 30 minutes, turning occasionally.

Preheat broiler. Lightly spray a broiler pan and rack with vegetable oil spray.

Remove steaks from marinade and arrange on rack. Broil about 3 inches from heat for about 5 minutes. Turn carefully and broil for about 5 minutes, or until fish flakes easily when tested with a fork.

Cook's Tip on Halibut

Atlantic and Pacific halibut, with 2 grams of fat per 3 ounces raw, are much lower in fat than Greenland halibut, with 12 grams per 3 ounces.

Calories 81
Protein 17 g
Carbohydrates 0 g
Cholesterol 24 mg
Total Fat 1 g
  Saturated 0 g
  Polyunsaturated 0 g
  Monounsaturated 1 g
Fiber 0 g
Sodium 76 mg

Poached Fish

Serves 8

Poaching is a great way to cook lean fish because the technique keeps the fish moist. Serve with one of our sauces, such as Lemon Parsley Sauce (see page 446).

2 pounds fish fillets, such as cod, sea bass, salmon, or tilapia, skinned
1 teaspoon acceptable vegetable oil
1 small onion, chopped
¼ cup chopped celery
1 cup hot water or dry white wine (regular or nonalcoholic)
2 tablespoons fresh lemon juice
1 bay leaf
Pepper to taste
Sprigs of fresh parsley (optional)

Rinse fish and pat dry with paper towels.

Heat oil in a large nonstick skillet over medium-high heat, swirling to coat bottom. When oil is hot, sauté onion and celery for 2 to 3 minutes, or until tender.

Place fillets flat on top of vegetables, or roll each fillet, securing it with a toothpick, and place rolls on vegetables. Add remaining ingredients except parsley. Bring to a simmer over medium-high heat. Reduce heat and simmer, covered, for about 8 minutes, or until fish flakes easily when tested with a fork.

Carefully transfer fillets to a serving platter. Remove toothpicks, and garnish fillets with parsley.

Time-Saver on Chopped Onions: Buy frozen chopped onions or freeze your own in an airtight plastic freezer bag. You don't even need to thaw them to use them. A bonus: Because of the extra moisture, you can reduce or eliminate the amount of oil or margarine needed for sautéing in most recipes.

Cook's Tip on Freezing Lemon Juice

Pour fresh lemon juice into the compartments of a plastic ice tray—each compartment holds about 1 tablespoon of juice—and freeze it. Remove the cubes and store them in an airtight plastic bag in the freezer. They'll be ready whenever you need them.

Calories 92
Protein 18 g
Carbohydrates 1 g
Cholesterol 37 mg
Total Fat 1 g
Saturated 0 g
Polyunsaturated 1 g
Monounsaturated 0 g
Fiber 0 g
Sodium 75 mg

Mushroom-Stuffed Fish Rolls

Serves 6

You can prepare these elegant fish rolls quickly. To save even more time, try our easy microwave method.

Vegetable oil spray
6 thin mild fish fillets, such as sole or orange roughy (about 4 ounces each)
1 teaspoon light margarine
¾ pound fresh mushrooms, finely diced (3 to 3¾ cups)
8 green onions, thinly sliced
½ cup diced red bell pepper
2 tablespoons minced fresh parsley
¼ teaspoon salt
¼ teaspoon pepper
2 to 3 tablespoons fresh lemon juice
½ cup dry white wine (regular or nonalcoholic)
2 tablespoons all-purpose flour
2 tablespoons cold water
¾ teaspoon paprika
2 tablespoons minced fresh parsley

Preheat oven to 350° F. Lightly spray a 9-inch round or square casserole dish with vegetable oil spray. Rinse fish and pat dry with paper towels.

Heat margarine in a heavy nonstick skillet, swirling to coat bottom. Sauté mushrooms, green onions, bell pepper, and 2 tablespoons parsley for 3 to 5 minutes, or until tender.

Sprinkle salt and pepper on fillets, then spoon mushroom mixture evenly down center of each.

Starting at a short side, roll up jelly-roll style, and secure with wooden toothpicks.

Put fillets in casserole dish. Sprinkle with lemon juice, then pour wine over all.

Cover with aluminum foil and bake for 25 to 35 minutes, or until fish flakes easily when tested with a fork.

Use a slotted spoon to transfer cooked fish to a serving plate. Remove toothpicks and cover platter with aluminum foil to keep fish warm. Pour cooking liquid into a small saucepan.

In a small bowl, whisk together flour, water, and paprika. Add to liquid in saucepan. Cook over

Calories 140
Protein 21 g
Carbohydrates 7 g
Cholesterol 53 mg
Total Fat 2 g
- Saturated 0 g
- Polyunsaturated 1 g
- Monounsaturated 0 g

Fiber 2 g
Sodium 189 mg

medium heat until thickened, 2 to 3 minutes, stirring constantly.

To serve, spoon sauce over fish and sprinkle with parsley.

Microwave Method

Put margarine, mushrooms, green onions, bell pepper, and 2 tablespoons parsley in a microwave-safe bowl. Cook at 100 percent power (high) for 1½ to 2 minutes, or until just tender. Sprinkle fillets with salt and pepper. Spoon mushroom mixture evenly down center of each fillet and roll as directed above. Secure with toothpicks. Place in prepared casserole dish and cook, covered, at 100 percent power (high) for 6 to 8 minutes. Remove and let fish rest for 5 to 10 minutes, or until it flakes easily when tested with a fork. Proceed as directed above.

Confetti Fish Fillets

Serves 6

Bright red bell pepper and vivid green onions and parsley add color to this dish. The flavor combination works well with any firm white fish. This is a dish worth celebrating!

Vegetable oil spray
1½ teaspoons acceptable vegetable oil
½ cup finely chopped onion
¼ cup diced red bell pepper
2 tablespoons snipped fresh chives or minced green onion (green part only)
1 tablespoon snipped fresh parsley
1½ slices (3 ounces) white bread
1 teaspoon grated lemon zest
1½ pounds firm white fish fillets, such as mahimahi or catfish
1 tablespoon fresh lemon juice
¼ teaspoon salt
White pepper to taste

Calories 133
Protein 18 g
Carbohydrates 9 g
Cholesterol 67 mg
Total Fat 2 g
Saturated 0 g
Polyunsaturated 1 g
Monounsaturated 1 g
Fiber 1 g
Sodium 248 mg

Preheat oven to 400° F. Spray a 13 × 9 × 2-inch baking dish with vegetable oil spray.

Heat oil in a small nonstick skillet over medium-high heat, swirling to coat bottom. Add onion and bell pepper. Sauté for 2 to 3 minutes, or until onion is translucent.

Stir in chives and parsley. Remove from heat and set aside.

Using a food processor or blender, process bread into fine crumbs. Add crumbs and lemon zest to onion mixture. Stir thoroughly.

Rinse fish and pat dry with paper towels. Arrange fish in baking dish. Sprinkle with remaining ingredients, then spread vegetable mixture evenly over fish.

Bake until fish flakes easily when tested with a fork, about 10 minutes per inch of thickness at the thickest point.

Fish Fillets with Asparagus

Serves 4

Fish and asparagus always pair up well. Crown them with a puffy, rich-tasting topping and you have a special treat.

Vegetable oil spray
4 mild fish fillets, such as haddock or cod (about 4 ounces each)
1 tablespoon fresh lemon juice
½ teaspoon pepper
Vegetable oil spray
12 stalks cooked asparagus

TOPPING

⅓ cup nonfat or light sour cream
⅓ cup plain nonfat or low-fat yogurt
2 teaspoons snipped fresh chives or minced green onion (green part only)
2 teaspoons prepared horseradish, drained
½ teaspoon dried dillweed, crumbled
White of 1 large egg (see Cook's Tip, page 345)
2 tablespoons snipped fresh parsley

Preheat broiler. Lightly spray a broiler pan and rack with vegetable oil spray. Rinse fish and pat dry with paper towels.

Pour lemon juice over fish, sprinkle with pepper, and spray with vegetable oil spray. Broil on rack about 6 inches from heat for 4 minutes. Turn fish and broil for about 4 minutes, or until fish almost flakes when tested with a fork. Remove from broiler and top each fillet with 3 stalks of asparagus.

In a small bowl, whisk together all topping ingredients except egg white.

In another small bowl, beat egg white until stiff peaks form; fold into sour cream mixture. Spread over each fillet to cover fish and asparagus.

Broil about 6 inches from heat for 1 to 2 minutes, or until golden brown. Sprinkle with parsley.

Calories 146
Protein 25 g
Carbohydrates 8 g
Cholesterol 66 mg
Total Fat 1 g
Saturated 0 g
Polyunsaturated 0 g
Monounsaturated 0 g
Fiber 1 g
Sodium 140 mg

French-Style Braised Fish Fillets

Serves 4

This classic dish from France is simple to prepare in American kitchens.

1 pound mackerel, trout, sole, or orange roughy fillets
6 sprigs of fresh thyme
4 sprigs of fresh parsley
1 bay leaf

MARINADE
1 cup dry white wine (regular or nonalcoholic) or water
1 small onion, thinly sliced (¾ cup)
1 medium carrot, thinly sliced (¾ cup)
1 tablespoon fresh lemon juice
1 shallot, thinly sliced
1 teaspoon olive oil
1 medium clove garlic, minced, or ½ teaspoon bottled minced garlic
¼ teaspoon salt
⅛ teaspoon pepper

Lemon slices (optional)
Sprigs of fresh thyme (optional)

Rinse fish and pat dry with paper towels. Put in an airtight plastic bag.

Using kitchen twine, tie 6 sprigs of thyme, parsley, and bay leaf in a bunch. Add to fish.

Add marinade ingredients and turn bag to coat. Seal and refrigerate for 30 minutes to 1 hour, turning bag occasionally.

Transfer fish and marinade to a shallow pan. Bring to a simmer. Reduce heat to low and cook, covered, for 10 to 12 minutes, or until fish flakes easily when tested with a fork. Remove fish with a slotted spoon and discard liquid. To serve, garnish fish with lemon and thyme.

Calories 131
Protein 25 g
Carbohydrates 0 g
Cholesterol 66 mg
Total Fat 3 g
- Saturated 1 g
- Polyunsaturated 1 g
- Monounsaturated 1 g

Fiber 0 g
Sodium 359 mg

Mediterranean Fish

Serves 6

The aroma of these elegant fish fillets baking will attract a hungry crowd to your kitchen.

Vegetable oil spray

1½ pounds fish fillets, such as Atlantic or Pacific halibut

1 medium onion, thinly sliced

2 large fresh tomatoes or 14.5-ounce can no-salt-added tomatoes, sliced

1½ cups sliced fresh mushrooms (about 6 ounces)

½ medium green bell pepper, sliced

¼ cup snipped fresh parsley

½ cup dry white wine (regular or nonalcoholic), or Chicken Broth (see page 40 or use commercial low-sodium variety)

2 tablespoons fresh lemon juice

1 teaspoon fresh dillweed or ¼ teaspoon dried, crumbled

Pepper to taste

½ cup plain dry bread crumbs

1 tablespoon olive oil

½ teaspoon dried basil, crumbled

Preheat oven to 350° F. Lightly spray a 13 × 9 × 2-inch baking dish with vegetable oil spray. Rinse fish and pat dry with paper towels.

Arrange onion slices in baking dish. Top with fish.

In a medium bowl, combine tomatoes, mushrooms, bell pepper, and parsley. Spoon evenly over fish.

In a measuring cup, combine wine, lemon juice, dillweed, and pepper. Pour over fish.

Bake fish, covered, for 20 to 25 minutes.

In a small bowl, combine remaining ingredients. Sprinkle over fish and vegetables. Bake, uncovered, for 5 to 10 minutes, or until fish flakes easily when tested with a fork.

Calories 224
Protein 27 g
Carbohydrates 13 g
Cholesterol 37 mg
Total Fat 6 g
  Saturated 1 g
  Polyunsaturated 2 g
  Monounsaturated 3 g
Fiber 1 g
Sodium 149 mg

Cook's Tip

For ½-inch-thick fillets, such as sole or orange roughy, cook for 15 to 20 minutes, covered, and 5 minutes, uncovered.

Fish Fillets in Foil

Serves 4

Cooking fish in aluminum foil packets keeps the filling and the fillets moist. Custom-design your dinner with one of the variations below.

Vegetable oil spray
4 thin fish fillets, such as flounder (about 4 ounces each)
½ teaspoon pepper

MUSHROOM SAUCE
Vegetable oil spray
1 teaspoon light margarine
1 tablespoon chopped shallots or green onions
½ pound fresh mushrooms, chopped (2 to 2½ cups)
3 tablespoons dry white wine (regular or nonalcoholic)
1 tablespoon snipped fresh parsley
1 tablespoon fresh lemon juice

Preheat oven to 400° F. Lightly spray four 8-inch square pieces of heavy-duty aluminum foil with vegetable oil spray. Rinse fish and pat dry with paper towels. Place a fillet on each piece of foil; season with pepper. Set aside.

For mushroom sauce, lightly spray a medium nonstick skillet with vegetable oil spray. Put skillet over medium-high heat. Melt margarine, then sauté shallots for 2 to 3 minutes, or until soft.

Add mushrooms and cook for 5 minutes, stirring occasionally.

Stir in remaining sauce ingredients and cook until most liquid evaporates, 2 to 3 minutes. Spoon mushroom sauce evenly over fish. Seal foil tightly.

Bake for 20 minutes, or until fish flakes easily when tested with a fork. Serve in foil.

Calories 118
Protein 20 g
Carbohydrates 3 g
Cholesterol 53 mg
Total Fat 2 g
Saturated 0 g
Polyunsaturated 1 g
Monounsaturated 0 g
Fiber 1 g
Sodium 90 mg

Variations

In place of mushroom sauce, use any of the combinations listed below. Amounts of all ingredients except margarine may be varied to suit individual taste. Use the margarine to dot each serving.

- Spinach, fresh or no-salt-added frozen, thawed and squeezed to remove excess moisture
  Fresh lemon juice
  Ground nutmeg
  1 teaspoon light margarine
- Tomato, thinly sliced or chopped
  Green onions, thinly sliced
  Basil, fresh or dried and crumbled
  Fresh lemon juice
  1 teaspoon light margarine
- Cucumber, thinly sliced
  Fresh lemon juice
  Fresh dillweed and/or parsley, snipped
  1 teaspoon light margarine
- Celery, thinly sliced
  Fresh lemon juice
  Thyme, fresh or dried and crumbled
  1 teaspoon light margarine
- Green onions, thinly sliced
  Carrots, very thinly sliced
  Curry powder
  Green bell pepper, thinly sliced
  1 teaspoon light margarine

Baked Catfish

Serves 6

Crisp on the outside and moist on the inside, these fish fillets go well with mashed potatoes.

Vegetable oil spray

6 catfish fillets (about 4 ounces each)

3/4 cup nonfat or low-fat buttermilk

1/4 teaspoon salt

1/4 teaspoon red hot-pepper sauce

3 ounces fat-free, low-sodium whole-wheat crackers, crushed (about 30)

1 tablespoon light margarine, melted

Vegetable oil spray

2 tablespoons snipped fresh parsley

6 lemon wedges (optional)

Preheat oven to 400° F. Lightly spray a 13 × 9 × 2-inch baking dish with vegetable oil spray. Rinse fish and pat dry with paper towels.

Combine buttermilk, salt, and hot-pepper sauce in a small, shallow dish. Put cracker crumbs on a plate.

Dip fillets in buttermilk mixture, then in crumbs, coating fish evenly.

Put fillets in baking dish. Drizzle with margarine and lightly spray with vegetable oil spray.

Bake, uncovered, for 15 to 20 minutes, or until fish flakes easily when tested with a fork.

To serve, sprinkle fish with parsley and garnish with lemon wedges.

Calories 215
Protein 19 g
Carbohydrates 14 g
Cholesterol 59 mg
Total Fat 9 g
Saturated 2 g
Polyunsaturated 2 g
Monounsaturated 4 g
Fiber 1 g
Sodium 379 mg

Crispy Cajun Catfish Nibbles with Red Sauce

Serves 4

Do you like fried popcorn shrimp? Then you'll love these crisp bites of catfish. They're served with a zesty sauce similar to cocktail sauce.

Vegetable oil spray

COATING
3 tablespoons cornmeal
½ teaspoon chili powder
½ teaspoon ground cumin
¼ teaspoon salt
¼ teaspoon garlic powder
⅛ teaspoon pepper

1 pound catfish fillets, cut into ½-inch pieces
Egg substitute equivalent to 1 egg, or 1 egg
½ cup cornflake crumbs
Vegetable oil spray

RED SAUCE
¼ cup low-sodium ketchup
2 tablespoons white wine vinegar
2 tablespoons fresh lemon juice
1 tablespoon honey
1 tablespoon bottled horseradish

Preheat oven to 400° F. Lightly spray a baking sheet with vegetable oil spray. Set aside.

Combine coating ingredients in a large airtight plastic bag.

Add fish pieces, turning bag to coat evenly.

Pour egg substitute into bag and shake gently to coat.

Put cornflake crumbs in a shallow bowl. Using a slotted spoon, add fish to cornflake crumbs, turning gently with spoon to coat. Spread fish in a single layer on baking sheet. Lightly spray fish with vegetable oil spray.

Bake for 7 to 8 minutes, or until fish flakes easily when tested with a fork.

Meanwhile, in a small bowl, whisk together sauce ingredients. Serve with fish.

Calories 261
Protein 21 g
Carbohydrates 26 g
Cholesterol 58 mg
Total Fat 8 g
- Saturated 2 g
- Polyunsaturated 2 g
- Monounsaturated 4 g

Fiber 1 g
Sodium 431 mg

Cod Baked with Vegetables

Serves 6

This one-dish comfort meal preserves the mildness of cod yet is full of flavor.

Vegetable oil spray

2 cups cubed red potatoes, unpeeled (10 to 12 ounces)

1 cup sliced carrots

2 tablespoons light margarine, melted

2 tablespoons fresh lemon juice

¼ teaspoon salt

¼ teaspoon pepper

1½ pounds cod

¼ teaspoon salt

¼ teaspoon pepper

½ cup sliced green onions (4 to 5 medium)

2 tablespoons snipped fresh parsley or 2 teaspoons dried, crumbled

1 tablespoon finely snipped fresh dillweed or 1 teaspoon dried, crumbled

Preheat oven to 400° F. Spray a 13 × 9 × 2-inch baking dish with vegetable oil spray.

Put potatoes and carrots in baking dish.

In a small bowl, combine margarine, lemon juice, ¼ teaspoon salt, and ¼ teaspoon pepper. Pour over vegetables.

Bake, covered, for 25 minutes.

Rinse fish and pat dry with paper towels. Cut fish into 2-inch pieces. Sprinkle with ¼ teaspoon salt, ¼ teaspoon pepper, and green onions.

Stir fish mixture into cooked vegetables. Sprinkle with parsley and dillweed.

Bake, covered, for 15 to 20 minutes, or until fish flakes easily when tested with a fork.

Microwave Method

Prepare vegetables and margarine mixture as directed. Cover baking dish with vented plastic wrap and microwave at 100 percent power (high) for 8 to 10 minutes. Add remaining ingredients and microwave, covered and vented, at 100 percent power (high) for 5 to 7 minutes.

Calories 133
Protein 14 g
Carbohydrates 15 g
Cholesterol 30 mg
Total Fat 2 g
  Saturated 0 g
  Polyunsaturated 1 g
  Monounsaturated 0 g
Fiber 2 g
Sodium 282 mg

Haddock with Tomatoes and Ginger

Serves 6

A citrusy tomato sauce with an Asian flair tops mild haddock fillets. Serve with brown rice.

Vegetable oil spray
1½ pounds haddock fillets
3 tablespoons all-purpose flour
Dash of pepper
1 tablespoon acceptable vegetable oil
1 tablespoon grated fresh gingerroot
2 medium cloves garlic, minced, or 1 teaspoon bottled minced garlic
2 cups seeded, chopped tomatoes (about 4 medium)
⅓ cup sliced green onions (about 3 medium)
1 cup fresh orange juice (about 3 medium oranges)
½ cup dry white wine (regular or nonalcoholic)
1½ tablespoons cornstarch
1 tablespoon light soy sauce
1 tablespoon snipped fresh parsley

Preheat oven to 350° F. Spray a 13 × 9 × 2-inch baking dish with vegetable oil spray. Rinse fish and pat dry with paper towels.

Combine flour and pepper on a plate or in a shallow bowl. Coat fillets one at a time. Shake off excess flour.

Heat oil in a nonstick skillet over medium high heat, swirling to coat bottom. Brown fillets for 1 minute. Turn over and brown for 1 minute. Transfer fillets to baking dish.

Bake for 10 to 15 minutes, or until fish flakes easily when tested with a fork.

Meanwhile, sauté gingerroot and garlic in the residual oil in skillet over medium heat for 10 to 15 minutes. Stir in tomatoes and green onions. Simmer for 3 to 4 minutes.

In a small bowl, whisk together remaining ingredients except parsley. Add mixture to skillet and cook over medium-high heat until thickened, 2 to 3 minutes, whisking constantly. Stir in parsley.

To serve, spoon sauce over fish.

Calories 201
Protein 23 g
Carbohydrates 15 g
Cholesterol 65 mg
Total Fat 4 g
Saturated 1 g
Polyunsaturated 2 g
Monounsaturated 1 g
Fiber 1 g
Sodium 173 mg

Orange Roughy with Tomatoes and Spinach

Serves 6

While this aromatic dish bakes, slice some crusty French bread and fresh strawberries to serve with it.

6 orange roughy fillets (about 4 ounces each)

1 teaspoon olive oil

1 cup finely chopped onion (about 2 medium)

3 medium cloves garlic, minced, or 1½ teaspoons bottled minced garlic

3 tablespoons water

28-ounce can no-salt-added Italian plum tomatoes

½ cup dry white wine (regular or nonalcoholic)

10-ounce package fresh spinach, stems removed, coarsely torn

2 tablespoons finely snipped fresh dillweed

2 tablespoons snipped fresh parsley

2 tablespoons fresh lemon juice

Vegetable oil spray

½ teaspoon pepper

2 tablespoons cornstarch (optional)

2 tablespoons water (optional)

Calories 146
Protein 20 g
Carbohydrates 10 g
Cholesterol 24 mg
Total Fat 2 g
Saturated 0 g
Polyunsaturated 0 g
Monounsaturated 1 g
Fiber 3 g
Sodium 115 mg

Preheat oven to 400° F. Rinse fish and pat dry with paper towels. Set aside.

Heat a large nonstick skillet over medium-high heat. Add oil and swirl to coat bottom. Sauté onions and garlic for 2 minutes. Add water and cook until it evaporates, stirring constantly.

Stir in undrained tomatoes and wine; crush tomatoes with a wooden spoon. Cook, uncovered, over medium-high heat for 7 to 8 minutes, or until liquid is reduced slightly.

Stir in spinach. Cook, covered, for 3 to 5 minutes, or until spinach is wilted.

Remove spinach mixture from heat and add dillweed, parsley, and lemon juice.

Lightly spray an oblong, nonaluminum baking dish with vegetable oil spray. Pour half of sauce into dish. Place fillets on sauce and sprinkle with pepper. Fold each fillet in half and pour remaining sauce over all. Cover dish with aluminum foil.

Bake for 15 to 18 minutes, or until fish flakes easily when tested with a fork.

If a thicker sauce is desired, place fillets on platter. Cover platter with aluminum foil to keep fish warm. Pour sauce into a nonstick skillet. Put cornstarch in a cup or small bowl. Add water, whisking to dissolve. Stir cornstarch mixture into sauce. Bring to a boil over medium-high heat. Cook until desired consistency, stirring constantly.

To serve, pour sauce over fish.

Cook's Tip on Cooking Wine

Avoid wine bottled and labeled as cooking wine. It's loaded with sodium. It won't do your dish—or your body—any good.

Teriyaki Halibut

Serves 8

Steam some rice and bright green snow peas to complement this dish.

MARINADE

½ cup dry white wine (regular or nonalcoholic)

3 tablespoons light soy sauce

1 tablespoon light brown sugar

1 teaspoon all-purpose flour

1 teaspoon acceptable vegetable oil

½ teaspoon dry mustard

2 pounds Atlantic or Pacific halibut fillets

Vegetable oil spray

8 slices pineapple, canned in their own juice

In a small saucepan, combine marinade ingredients. Bring to a boil over medium-high heat. Reduce heat and simmer for 3 minutes. Pour into a small bowl, cover, and refrigerate for 30 to 60 minutes.

Rinse fish and pat dry with paper towels. Put fish in an airtight plastic bag, add marinade, and turn bag to coat fish. Seal and refrigerate for 15 minutes.

Preheat broiler. Lightly spray a broiler pan and rack with vegetable oil spray.

Remove fish from marinade and put on rack.

In a small saucepan, bring marinade to a boil over medium-high heat. Boil for 5 minutes. Brush fish with hot marinade.

Broil fish 5 to 6 inches from heat for 5 minutes. Turn over and top with pineapple. Broil for about 5 minutes or until fish flakes easily when tested with a fork.

Cook's Tip

Seafood doesn't need to marinate for long. Too much marinating time can cause it to become rubbery.

Calories 182
Protein 25 g
Carbohydrates 10 g
Cholesterol 37 mg
Total Fat 3 g
  Saturated 1 g
  Polyunsaturated 1 g
  Monounsaturated 1 g
Fiber 0 g
Sodium 254 mg

Red Snapper à l'Orange

Serves 6

Cooking an elegant fish dish is as easy as 1-2-3 when all you need to do is (1) put the fish in a casserole dish, (2) pour the sauce over the fish, and (3) bake the whole thing.

Vegetable oil spray
1½ pounds red snapper fillets, cut into 6 pieces
1 teaspoon grated orange zest
2 tablespoons fresh orange juice
1 teaspoon acceptable vegetable oil
Pepper to taste
⅛ teaspoon ground nutmeg

Preheat oven to 350° F. Spray a 13 × 9 × 2-inch baking dish with vegetable oil spray. Rinse fish and pat dry with paper towels. Arrange fish pieces in a single layer in the baking dish.

Combine remaining ingredients except nutmeg in a small bowl. Pour over fish. Sprinkle with nutmeg.

Bake for 20 to 30 minutes, or until fish flakes easily when tested with a fork.

Calories 86
Protein 16 g
Carbohydrates 1 g
Cholesterol 28 mg
Total Fat 2 g
Saturated 0 g
Polyunsaturated 1 g
Monounsaturated 0 g
Fiber 0 g
Sodium 34 mg

Salmon with Cucumber-Dill Sauce

Serves 4

Serve this light, elegant entrée warm, at room temperature, or chilled.

1-pound fresh salmon fillet

1 cup dry white wine (regular or nonalcoholic)

2 bay leaves

2 tablespoons finely snipped fresh dillweed or 2 teaspoons dried, crumbled

Pepper to taste

CUCUMBER-DILL SAUCE

2 medium cucumbers, peeled, seeded, and cut into ½-inch slices (3 cups)

1 rib celery, including leaves, cut into ½-inch slices (½ cup)

3 tablespoons snipped fresh dillweed or 1 tablespoon dried, crumbled

1 teaspoon extra-virgin olive oil

¼ teaspoon salt

Pepper to taste

Time-Saver: Get a head start on another meal by cooking extra salmon to combine with pasta, fat-free Italian dressing, diced tomato, finely chopped red onion, and steamed green peas or other favorite vegetables.

Preheat oven to 350° F.

Rinse salmon and pat dry with paper towels. Put salmon in a glass baking dish just large enough to hold it and the wine.

Pour wine over salmon, add bay leaves, and sprinkle with dillweed and pepper. Cover tightly with aluminum foil.

Bake salmon for 10 minutes per inch of thickness, or until it flakes easily when tested with a fork. Remove from oven and keep covered.

For sauce, put ingredients in a large saucepan with enough water to barely cover vegetables. Boil, covered, over high heat for about 30 minutes, or until celery is soft, stirring occasionally.

Carefully ladle mixture into a food processor or blender and puree.

To serve, spoon half the sauce onto a large serving platter. Place salmon on sauce. Spoon remaining sauce over salmon or serve on side.

Calories 194
Protein 22 g
Carbohydrates 3 g
Cholesterol 68 mg
Total Fat 10 g
Saturated 2 g
Polyunsaturated 2 g
Monounsaturated 5 g
Fiber 1 g
Sodium 212 mg

Grilled Salmon Oriental

Serves 6

Summertime and the grilling is easy. Let the salmon soak up the pineapple-lime marinade flavors, then grill it in almost no time. Serve with jasmine rice and pineapple slices.

1½ pounds fresh salmon steaks or fillets

MARINADE

6 ounces pineapple juice

½ cup finely chopped onion

½ teaspoon grated lime zest

2 tablespoons fresh lime juice (1 to 2 medium limes)

1 tablespoon grated fresh gingerroot

1 tablespoon light soy sauce

2 medium cloves garlic, minced, or 1 teaspoon bottled minced garlic

1 teaspoon hot-pepper oil (optional)

1 teaspoon acceptable vegetable oil

Vegetable oil spray

Rinse fish and pat dry with paper towels. Put fish in an airtight plastic bag.

Combine marinade ingredients and pour over fish, turning bag to coat fish evenly. Seal and refrigerate for 15 minutes to 1 hour, turning bag occasionally.

Preheat grill on medium-high or preheat broiler. Lightly spray grill or broiler pan and rack with vegetable oil spray.

Remove fish from marinade. Grill fish or broil it 4 to 5 inches from heat. Cook for 5 to 7 minutes, turn, and cook for 5 to 7 minutes, or until fish flakes easily when tested with a fork.

Cook's Tip on Hot-Pepper Oil

Also called chili oil, this is vegetable oil flavored with hot red chiles. Commonly used in Chinese cuisine, it can be *very* hot. Treat it with respect. You can make your own by steeping crushed red pepper flakes in an acceptable vegetable oil.

Calories 169
Protein 21 g
Carbohydrates 0 g
Cholesterol 68 mg
Total Fat 9 g
 Saturated 2 g
 Polyunsaturated 2 g
 Monounsaturated 4 g
Fiber 0 g
Sodium 137 mg

Salmon Cakes

Serves 8

Remember salmon croquettes? Here's a distant cousin. Serve with steamed asparagus and corn on the cob.

1 pound fresh salmon fillets
Whites of 2 large eggs
½ cup finely chopped green onions (4 to 5)
10 fat-free, low-sodium whole-wheat crackers, finely crushed
Egg substitute equivalent to 1 egg, or 1 egg, slightly beaten
2 to 3 tablespoons fresh lime juice (2 medium limes)
1½ tablespoons capers, rinsed and chopped
1 tablespoon snipped fresh parsley or 1 teaspoon dried, crumbled
1 tablespoon snipped fresh dillweed or 1 teaspoon dried, crumbled
½ teaspoon paprika
¼ teaspoon pepper
¼ teaspoon dry mustard
⅛ teaspoon cayenne, or to taste
1 tablespoon acceptable vegetable oil

Rinse fish and pat dry with paper towels. Steam fish for 6 to 8 minutes, or until it flakes easily when tested with a fork. Cover and refrigerate until cool. Remove skin.

Flake fish, checking to be sure all bones have been removed.

In a medium bowl, beat egg whites until frothy. Add remaining ingredients except oil, stirring to combine.

Add salmon and stir gently. Divide into 8 patties.

In a large nonstick skillet, heat oil over medium-high heat, swirling to coat bottom. Sauté patties for 3 to 4 minutes, turn, and sauté for 3 to 4 minutes.

Calories 126
Protein 13 g
Carbohydrates 3 g
Cholesterol 34 mg
Total Fat 6 g
Saturated 1 g
Polyunsaturated 2 g
Monounsaturated 3 g
Fiber 0 g
Sodium 134 mg

Salmon Alfredo

Serves 4

The sauce in this high-protein dish is as rich-tasting as conventional Alfredo.

⅔ cup frozen green peas
8 ounces fresh salmon fillets
8 ounces dried plain or spinach fettuccine or spaghetti
Vegetable oil spray
3 medium cloves garlic, minced, or 1½ teaspoons bottled minced garlic
10.5-ounce package reduced-fat silken tofu
⅔ cup fat-free milk
2 ounces low-fat cream cheese
¼ to ½ teaspoon white pepper
⅛ teaspoon ground nutmeg
1 tablespoon grated Parmesan cheese
1 tablespoon fresh lemon juice

Set out peas to thaw.

Rinse fish and pat dry with paper towels. Steam or poach fish for 6 to 8 minutes, or until it flakes easily when tested with a fork.

Meanwhile, cook pasta using package directions, omitting salt and oil. Drain. Cover and keep warm.

While pasta cooks, spray a large saucepan with vegetable oil spray. Sauté garlic over medium-high heat for about 30 seconds.

In a food processor or blender, process tofu and milk until smooth. Add tofu mixture, cream cheese, pepper, and nutmeg to saucepan. Cook over medium-high heat until cheese is melted and mixture is smooth, 2 to 3 minutes, whisking constantly.

Stir in peas, Parmesan, and lemon juice; cook for 1 minute.

Remove skin from salmon. Flake salmon into saucepan; stir. Heat through, about 1 minute.

Serve sauce over pasta.

Calories 368
Protein 26 g
Carbohydrates 45 g
Cholesterol 44 mg
Total Fat 9 g
- Saturated 3 g
- Polyunsaturated 1 g
- Monounsaturated 3 g

Fiber 6 g
Sodium 206 mg

Crispy Baked Fillet of Sole

Serves 6

Asian-flavored fillets are coated with an aromatic crumb coating, then baked for crispness. Steamed baby carrots and Fresh Green Beans with Water Chestnuts (see page 357) complete the meal.

MARINADE

¾ cup finely chopped onion (about 2 medium)

2 teaspoons grated lime zest

¼ cup fresh lime juice (2 to 3 medium limes)

1 tablespoon grated fresh gingerroot

1 tablespoon acceptable vegetable oil

1 tablespoon light soy sauce

¼ teaspoon salt

¼ teaspoon pepper

1½ pounds sole or other thin fish fillets

Vegetable oil spray

1¼ cups plain dry bread crumbs

2 tablespoons snipped fresh parsley

2 tablespoons finely chopped green onion

Combine marinade ingredients in an airtight plastic bag.

Rinse fish and pat dry with paper towels. Add to marinade, turning bag to coat fish. Seal and refrigerate for 15 minutes to 1 hour.

Preheat oven to 450° F. Spray a 9 × 13 × 2-inch baking dish with vegetable oil spray.

Combine remaining ingredients on a plate. Remove fillets from marinade and coat with crumb mixture, shaking off excess. Put fillets in baking dish.

Bake, uncovered, for 15 to 18 minutes, or until fish flakes easily when tested with a fork.

Calories 182
Protein 22 g
Carbohydrates 17 g
Cholesterol 53 mg
Total Fat 2 g
- Saturated 1 g
- Polyunsaturated 1 g
- Monounsaturated 1 g

Fiber 1 g
Sodium 463 mg

Sole Baked with Mushrooms

Serves 6

Try this dish with a variety of exotic mushrooms—shiitake, oyster, portobello, golden Italian, or whatever looks fresh and appealing.

Vegetable oil spray

1½ pounds sole or other thin fish fillets

1 teaspoon light margarine

12 ounces fresh mushrooms, sliced (3 to 3¾ cups)

¼ cup snipped fresh parsley

1 tablespoon finely chopped onion

½ teaspoon pepper

¼ cup dry white wine (regular or nonalcoholic)

1 tablespoon light margarine

½ cup fat-free milk

1 tablespoon all-purpose flour

2 tablespoons snipped fresh parsley

¼ teaspoon paprika

Preheat oven to 350° F. Spray a 13 × 9 × 2-inch baking dish with vegetable oil spray. Rinse fish and pat dry with paper towels.

Heat 1 teaspoon margarine in a medium nonstick skillet over medium-high heat. Sauté mushrooms, ¼ cup parsley, and onion for 2 to 3 minutes, or until onion is translucent, stirring frequently.

Place half the fish in the baking dish and sprinkle with half the pepper. Spread mushroom mixture over fish. Top with remaining fish and sprinkle with remaining pepper. Pour wine over all and dot with 1 tablespoon margarine.

Bake, uncovered, for 15 minutes. Using a slotted spatula, put fish and mushrooms on a platter; reserve liquid.

In a small saucepan, whisk together milk and flour. Add reserved pan liquid and cook over medium-high heat for 2 to 3 minutes, or until thickened, stirring constantly.

Place fish back in baking dish. Pour sauce over fish. Bake, uncovered, for 5 minutes. To serve, sprinkle with 2 tablespoons parsley and paprika.

Calories 134
Protein 21 g
Carbohydrates 5 g
Cholesterol 53 mg
Total Fat 2 g
  Saturated 1 g
  Polyunsaturated 1 g
  Monounsaturated 1 g
Fiber 1 g
Sodium 112 mg

Sole with Walnuts and White Wine

Serves 4

White sauce with walnuts makes this dish something special. You can whip up the sauce as the fish bakes. Serve with sugar snap peas and fresh peach slices.

Vegetable oil spray

1 pound sole or other thin fish fillets

½ cup dry white wine (regular or nonalcoholic)

½ cup Chicken Broth (see page 40), commercial low-sodium chicken broth, fish stock, or clam juice

Dash of cayenne

SAUCE

2 tablespoons light margarine

2 tablespoons all-purpose flour

½ cup Chicken Broth (see page 40), commercial low-sodium chicken broth, fish stock, or clam juice

½ cup dry white wine (regular or nonalcoholic)

¼ cup fat-free milk

Dash of white pepper

¼ cup chopped dry-roasted walnuts (about 1 ounce)

Sprigs of fresh parsley (optional)

Calories 228
Protein 21 g
Carbohydrates 7 g
Cholesterol 53 mg
Total Fat 8 g
Saturated 1 g
Polyunsaturated 5 g
Monounsaturated 2 g
Fiber 1 g
Sodium 132 mg

Preheat oven to 350° F. Spray a 9-inch round or square baking dish with vegetable oil spray.

Rinse fish and pat dry with paper towels. Put fillets in baking dish and add wine, broth, and cayenne. Cover dish with aluminum foil.

Bake for 20 minutes, or until fish flakes easily when tested with a fork.

Meanwhile, for the sauce, melt margarine in a small saucepan over low heat. Whisk in flour and cook for about 1 minute, stirring occasionally. (Don't let flour brown.)

Increase heat to medium-high. Whisk in broth, wine, milk, and white pepper. Cook for 3 to 4 minutes, or until mixture thickens, stirring constantly. Reduce heat. Add walnuts and simmer for 1 minute.

To serve, arrange fish on a platter. Pour sauce over fish and garnish with parsley.

Sole with Parsley and Mint

Serves 4

Serve this dish with or without the sauce—either way is easy and unusual.

Vegetable oil spray

1 pound sole or other thin fish fillets

2 tablespoons minced fresh parsley

1 tablespoon chopped fresh mint

2 teaspoons acceptable vegetable oil

1 medium clove garlic, chopped, or ½ teaspoon bottled minced garlic

SAUCE (OPTIONAL)

1 teaspoon light margarine

1 green onion, chopped

½ cup dry white wine (regular or nonalcoholic)

¼ cup water

¼ teaspoon white pepper

Preheat broiler. Lightly spray a broiler pan and rack with vegetable oil spray. Rinse fish and pat dry with paper towels. Put fish on rack.

In a small bowl, combine parsley, mint, oil, and garlic. Rub pastelike mixture on fish.

Broil 4 inches from heat for 5 to 8 minutes, or until fish flakes easily with a fork.

For sauce, heat margarine in a nonstick skillet over medium-high heat, swirling to coat bottom. Sauté green onion for 1 to 2 minutes; add pan juices from fish and remaining sauce ingredients. Heat thoroughly. Pour over fish. (Prepared with sauce: calories 139; protein 19 g; carbohydrates 1 g; cholesterol 53 mg; total fat 4 g; saturated 1 g; polyunsaturated 2 g; monounsaturated 1 g; fiber 0 g; sodium 92 mg)

Cook's Tip on White Pepper

Milder in flavor than black pepper, white pepper is often used because its color blends in with a white or light-colored sauce. You can buy whole peppercorns or ground pepper.

(WITHOUT SAUCE)
Calories 114
Protein 19 g
Carbohydrates 0 g
Cholesterol 53 mg
Total Fat 3 g
Saturated 1 g
Polyunsaturated 2 g
Monounsaturated 1 g
Fiber 0 g
Sodium 83 mg

Grilled Tuna with Pineapple-Nectarine Salsa

Serves 4

Citrus-marinated tuna sizzles on the grill, then is topped with a cool, refreshing fruit salsa. Try this recipe with other firm-fleshed fish, such as halibut, too.

MARINADE

1 teaspoon grated lime zest

2 tablespoons fresh lime juice (1 to 2 medium limes)

2 tablespoons fresh orange juice

1 tablespoon snipped fresh cilantro

1 teaspoon acceptable vegetable oil

¼ teaspoon salt

⅛ teaspoon pepper

1 pound tuna, cut into 4 serving pieces

PINEAPPLE-NECTARINE SALSA

1 medium nectarine, diced (¾ to 1 cup)

8-ounce can pineapple tidbits in their own juice

1 kiwifruit, peeled and diced

2 tablespoons diced red onion

1 tablespoon snipped fresh cilantro

1 teaspoon fresh lemon juice

Combine marinade ingredients in an airtight plastic bag.

Add fish and turn bag to coat. Seal and refrigerate for 15 minutes to 1 hour, turning bag occasionally.

Meanwhile, combine salsa ingredients in a medium bowl. Cover and refrigerate.

Preheat grill on medium-high.

Grill fish for 5 to 7 minutes on each side, or until fish is cooked through and flakes easily when tested with a fork.

To serve, place fish on dinner plates. Top with salsa.

Calories 191
Protein 28 g
Carbohydrates 16 g
Cholesterol 53 mg
Total Fat 1 g
Saturated 0 g
Polyunsaturated 0 g
Monounsaturated 0 g
Fiber 2 g
Sodium 190 mg

Cook's Tip on Using Leftover Cilantro

Here are four quick ideas for using up a large bunch of cilantro:

1. Add 2 tablespoons chopped fresh cilantro to low-fat meat loaf recipe (try Turkey Loaf on page 234).
2. Top healthful homemade chicken soup—broth, broth-based, or cream—or canned low-fat, low-sodium soup with chopped fresh cilantro.
3. Combine 2 chopped medium tomatoes; ½ chopped medium onion; 1 fresh jalapeño pepper, seeded and diced (see Cook's Tip, page 115); 2 tablespoons chopped fresh cilantro; and 1 tablespoon fresh lime juice for a quick pico de gallo (a spicy relish) to serve over grilled chicken or seafood.
4. Serve roasted pork tenderloin and roasted vegetables on a bed of cilantro leaves.

Tuna Chili

Serves 4

Here's an easy way to work more seafood into your diet—a warming bowl of chili with tuna instead of beef.

2 tablespoons olive oil
1 medium onion, chopped (½ cup)
1 medium green bell pepper, chopped (1 cup)
2 medium cloves garlic, minced, or 1 teaspoon bottled minced garlic
4 medium tomatoes, chopped (3 cups)
1½ cups cooked pinto beans, drained (cooked without salt)
2 6-ounce cans white chunk tuna, packed in distilled or spring water, drained
⅔ cup Salsa Cruda (see page 449) or picante sauce
1½ teaspoons chili powder
1 teaspoon ground cumin
1 tablespoon plus 1 teaspoon shredded nonfat or reduced-fat Cheddar cheese
1 tablespoon plus 1 teaspoon sliced green onion (green and white parts)

In a large saucepan, combine olive oil, onion, bell pepper, and garlic. Cook over medium-high heat until onion begins to brown, 4 to 5 minutes, stirring occasionally.

Add tomatoes, beans, tuna, Salsa Cruda, chili powder, and cumin, stirring well. Simmer, covered, for 20 to 30 minutes, or until vegetables are tender and mixture is heated through.

To serve, ladle chili into bowls. Top each serving with cheese and green onion.

Calories 309
Protein 30 g
Carbohydrates 31 g
Cholesterol 38 mg
Total Fat 9 g
Saturated 1 g
Polyunsaturated 1 g
Monounsaturated 5 g
Fiber 8 g
Sodium 155 mg

Cook's Tip on Canned Beans

If you use canned beans instead of dried beans cooked without salt, be sure to rinse them. That will remove some of the sodium. Even so, the canned beans will have more sodium than the home-cooked beans.

Tuna Salad Pitas

Serves 5

Cilantro and lemon liven up tuna salad in this easy recipe.

TUNA SALAD

9 ounces white chunk tuna packed in distilled or spring water, drained and flaked

½ cup diced seeded tomato

½ cup diced seeded cucumber, unpeeled

¼ cup plus 2 tablespoons fat-free, cholesterol-free or light, reduced-calorie mayonnaise dressing

¼ cup sliced green onions

¼ cup plain nonfat or low-fat yogurt

1 tablespoon finely snipped fresh cilantro

½ teaspoon grated lemon zest

Dash of red hot-pepper sauce

5 6½-inch whole-wheat pita breads

5 small pieces of leaf lettuce

In a medium bowl, combine tuna salad ingredients. Cover and refrigerate until thoroughly chilled, at least 30 minutes.

Split each pita carefully around top edge, about one third of the circumference of the bread. Put lettuce leaf and about ½ cup tuna mixture in each pita.

Calories 225
Protein 18 g
Carbohydrates 36 g
Cholesterol 21 mg
Total Fat 2 g
Saturated 0 g
Polyunsaturated 1 g
Monounsaturated 0 g
Fiber 5 g
Sodium 472 mg

Crabmeat Maryland

Serves 8

Each diner gets an individual casserole, which adds a special touch.

3 cups flaked crabmeat, rinsed (fresh, frozen, or canned) (1 pound fresh)

Vegetable oil spray

2 tablespoons minced onion

2 cups fat-free milk

3 tablespoons all-purpose flour

1 rib celery, finely chopped; 1 teaspoon celery flakes; or 1/4 teaspoon celery seeds

2-ounce jar diced pimientos, drained (about 1/4 cup)

2 tablespoons minced green bell pepper

1 tablespoon snipped fresh parsley

Dash of red hot-pepper sauce

2 tablespoons dry sherry

Egg substitute equivalent to 1 egg, or 1 egg, beaten

1/4 teaspoon pepper, or to taste

2 slices bread, lightly toasted and crumbled

Vegetable oil spray

Thaw crabmeat if frozen or drain if canned. Remove any shells or cartilage from fresh or frozen crabmeat. Set crabmeat aside.

Preheat oven to 350° F. Spray eight individual casserole dishes with vegetable oil spray. Set aside.

Heat a large nonstick skillet over medium-high heat. Remove from heat and spray with vegetable oil spray. Return skillet to heat and sauté onion until transparent, 2 to 3 minutes, stirring occasionally.

In a medium bowl, whisk milk and flour together. Add to skillet and cook for 3 to 5 minutes, or until thickened, stirring occasionally.

Stir in celery, pimientos, bell pepper, parsley, and hot-pepper sauce.

Remove skillet from heat and stir in sherry.

Whisk a little sauce into egg substitute; slowly pour egg mixture into sauce, whisking constantly.

Calories 119
Protein 14 g
Carbohydrates 11 g
Cholesterol 35 mg
Total Fat 1 g
Saturated 0 g
Polyunsaturated 0 g
Monounsaturated 0 g
Fiber 1 g
Sodium 195 mg

Stir in pepper and crabmeat. Spoon into casserole dishes and sprinkle with bread crumbs. Spray crumbs lightly with vegetable oil spray.

Bake, uncovered, for 15 to 20 minutes, or until lightly browned.

Linguine with White Clam Sauce

Serves 4

We suggest fresh green beans and Spinach-Chayote Salad with Orange Vinaigrette (see page 76) to go with this longtime favorite.

8-ounce bottle clam juice

½ cup dry white wine (regular or nonalcoholic)

8 ounces dried linguine

1 teaspoon olive oil

½ cup finely chopped onion

4 medium cloves garlic, minced, or 2 teaspoons bottled minced garlic

2 tablespoons all-purpose flour

2 6½-ounce cans minced clams, rinsed and drained

2 tablespoons finely snipped fresh parsley

2 tablespoons grated Parmesan cheese

In a small saucepan, combine clam juice and wine. Bring to a boil over high heat; boil, uncovered, until mixture is reduced to 1¼ cups, about 5 minutes. Set aside.

Cook linguine using package directions, omitting salt and oil. Drain.

Meanwhile, heat a small nonstick skillet over medium-high heat. Add olive oil, swirling to coat bottom. Sauté onion until translucent, 2 to 3 minutes, then add garlic and sauté for 2 minutes.

Stir in flour and cook for 1 minute.

Add hot clam juice mixture and stir until thickened, 2 to 3 minutes.

Stir in clams and parsley. Cook for 2 minutes, or until clams are thoroughly heated, stirring constantly.

To serve, spoon sauce over pasta and sprinkle with Parmesan.

Calories 429
Protein 34 g
Carbohydrates 55 g
Cholesterol 64 mg
Total Fat 5 g
- Saturated 1 g
- Polyunsaturated 1 g
- Monounsaturated 2 g

Fiber 5 g
Sodium 247 mg

Scallops and Asparagus in Wine Sauce

Serves 4

Scallops are surrounded with a velvety sauce, delicate shallots, and tender asparagus. Serve with your favorite pasta.

1 pound fresh or frozen scallops, thawed

8-ounce bottle clam juice

½ cup dry white wine (regular or nonalcoholic)

3 tablespoons all-purpose flour

¼ teaspoon pepper

6 ounces fresh asparagus, trimmed, or 4 ounces frozen asparagus, thawed

1 teaspoon light margarine

¼ cup minced shallots (about 4 large)

3 tablespoons finely snipped fresh parsley

1 tablespoon fresh lemon juice

Rinse scallops and pat dry with paper towels. Cut in quarters if large. Set aside.

In a large saucepan, whisk together clam juice, wine, flour, and pepper. Bring to a boil over medium-high heat; boil for 4 to 5 minutes, or until mixture is thickened, stirring occasionally. Set aside.

Cut asparagus diagonally into 1-inch pieces. Steam fresh asparagus until tender-crisp, about 2 minutes, and set aside (don't cook frozen asparagus).

In a small nonstick skillet, heat margarine over medium-high heat, swirling to coat bottom. Sauté shallots until translucent, 2 to 3 minutes.

Stir shallots and scallops into clam sauce. Reduce heat to medium and cook for 5 minutes, stirring frequently. Don't let the mixture come to a boil. Add asparagus, parsley, and lemon juice. Cook for 2 to 3 minutes, or until scallops are opaque and mixture is heated. Be careful not to overcook.

Calories 121
Protein 11 g
Carbohydrates 9 g
Cholesterol 18 mg
Total Fat 2 g
Saturated 0 g
Polyunsaturated 1 g
Monounsaturated 1 g
Fiber 1 g
Sodium 367 mg

Oven-Fried Scallops with Cilantro and Lime

Serves 4

Tender, moist scallops soak in a fresh cilantro–buttermilk marinade with the bright taste of lime. Then they're coated in crumbs and baked.

Vegetable oil spray

1 pound fresh or frozen scallops, thawed

½ cup nonfat or low-fat buttermilk

2 tablespoons snipped fresh cilantro

2 tablespoons fresh lime juice (1 to 2 medium limes)

⅛ teaspoon salt

¼ teaspoon pepper

½ cup plain dry bread crumbs

Dash of paprika

Vegetable oil spray

2 tablespoons fresh cilantro leaves (optional)

4 lime wedges (optional)

Preheat oven to 400° F. Lightly spray a 9-inch round or square baking dish with vegetable oil spray.

Rinse scallops and pat dry with paper towels.

Whisk together buttermilk, snipped cilantro, lime juice, salt, and pepper in a small, shallow bowl. Soak scallops for 10 minutes.

Put bread crumbs on a plate or in a shallow bowl. Roll scallops in crumbs. Shake off excess.

Arrange scallops in a single layer in the baking dish. Sprinkle with paprika. Lightly spray scallops with vegetable oil spray.

Bake for 10 to 13 minutes, or until scallops are opaque.

To serve, sprinkle scallops with cilantro leaves and garnish with lime wedges.

Calories 129
Protein 12 g
Carbohydrates 13 g
Cholesterol 19 mg
Total Fat 3 g
Saturated 1 g
Polyunsaturated 1 g
Monounsaturated 1 g
Fiber 0 g
Sodium 454 mg

Cioppino

Serves 10

Pronounced chuh-PEE-noh, *this fish stew will be pronounced delicious by all who taste it.*

1½ pounds red snapper or other firm white fish fillets, skinned

1½ teaspoons olive oil

1½ cups chopped onion (about 3 medium)

1 cup coarsely chopped green bell pepper

3 medium cloves garlic, minced, or 1½ teaspoons bottled minced garlic

4 cups chopped tomatoes (5 to 6 medium)

¼ cup dry red wine (regular or non-alcoholic)

¼ cup clam juice

2 tablespoons snipped fresh parsley

2 bay leaves

¾ teaspoon dried basil, crumbled

¼ teaspoon pepper

3 to 4 dashes of red hot-pepper sauce

½ pound medium shrimp, peeled and deveined (13 to 15)

½ teaspoon salt

Juice of 1 medium lemon

Rinse fish and pat dry with paper towels. Cut into 2-inch cubes and set aside.

Heat a heavy stockpot over medium heat. Add oil and swirl to coat bottom. Sauté onions, bell pepper, and garlic for about 5 minutes.

Add tomatoes, wine, clam juice, parsley, bay leaves, basil, pepper, and hot-pepper sauce. Simmer for 15 minutes.

Add fish and cook over low heat for 25 minutes, stirring occasionally.

Add shrimp and simmer for 8 minutes, stirring occasionally.

Stir in salt and lemon juice.

Time-Saver on Chopped Bell Peppers: Like chopped onions, chopped green bell peppers are available in the frozen food section of your supermarket. You can also seed and chop them yourself, then freeze them in an airtight plastic freezer bag.

Calories 108
Protein 14 g
Carbohydrates 9 g
Cholesterol 44 mg
Total Fat 2 g
Saturated 0 g
Polyunsaturated 1 g
Monounsaturated 1 g
Fiber 1 g
Sodium 198 mg

POULTRY

Lemon-Herb Roast Chicken

Chicken with Apricot Glaze

Chicken with Orange Sauce

Sesame Chicken

Sweet-and-Sour Baked Chicken

Chicken Casserole with Dilled Sherry Sauce

Rosemary Chicken

Chicken Jambalaya

Crispy Baked Chicken

Lemongrass-Lime Baked Chicken

Chicken Philippine Style

Chicken and Snow Pea Stir-Fry

Chicken and Mushroom Stir-Fry

Rosé Chicken with Artichoke Hearts and Mushrooms

Chicken Columbo

Chicken Creole

Chicken Southwestern

Chicken Chili

Burgundy Chicken with Mushrooms

Chicken in White Wine and Tarragon

Italian Chicken Roll-Ups

Baked Chicken Parmesan

Broiled Chicken with Hoisin-Barbecue Sauce

Grilled Lemon-Sage Chicken

Sweet-Spice Glazed Chicken

Spicy Grilled Chicken

Triple-Pepper Chicken

Savory Microwave Chicken

Chicken-Spinach Manicotti

Chipotle Chicken Wraps

Lemon-Cayenne Chicken

Chicken and Broccoli in Mushroom Sauce

Dill Chicken Enchiladas

Chicken Fajitas

Chicken Stew with Cornmeal Dumplings

Chicken à la King

Spicy Chicken and Grits

Down South Chicken Hash and Corn Cakes

Mexican Chicken and Vegetables with Chipotle Peppers

Chicken Curry in a Hurry

Caribbean Grilled Chicken Thighs

Slow-Cooker White Chili

Roasted Garlic-Lemon Turkey Breast

Turkey Fillets with Fresh Herbs

Turkey on a Bed of Sliced Tomatoes

Turkey Rolls with Garden Pesto

Southwestern Turkey Wraps

Swiss Garden Wraps

Turkey Sausage Patties

Turkey Lasagna

Turkey Loaf

Porcupine Meatballs

Stuffed Cornish Hens with Orange-Brandy Sauce

Cornish Hens Provence Style

Lemon-Herb Roast Chicken

Serves 6

Try this juicy, delicately flavored roast chicken for a Sunday dinner treat.

Vegetable oil spray
1½ teaspoons dried thyme, crumbled
½ teaspoon dried basil, crumbled
½ teaspoon pepper
¼ teaspoon salt
4- to 4½-pound roasting chicken
2 medium cloves garlic, minced, or 1 teaspoon bottled minced garlic
1 lemon, cut into wedges
1 bay leaf
½ medium onion
½ cup dry white wine (regular or nonalcoholic)
Vegetable oil spray

Preheat oven to 350° F. Spray roasting pan and rack with vegetable oil spray.

Combine thyme, basil, pepper, and salt.

Remove giblets and neck from chicken and save for other use or discard. Rinse chicken and pat dry with paper towels. Rub outside of chicken with herb mixture. Put chicken breast side up on rack in roasting pan.

Put garlic, lemon, bay leaf, and onion in chicken, then pour in wine.

Lightly spray outside of chicken with vegetable oil spray.

Roast for about 20 minutes per pound, or until juices run clear when you pierce a thigh with a sharp skewer or a meat thermometer registers 180° F when you insert it in thigh. Remove from oven and let rest for 15 minutes before carving. Remove skin before serving chicken.

Time-Saver: Make a double recipe and have extra chicken to use during the week in other recipes, such as Chicken and Broccoli in Mushroom Sauce (see page 210).

Calories 241
Protein 34 g
Carbohydrates 1 g
Cholesterol 102 mg
Total Fat 9 g
Saturated 2 g
Polyunsaturated 2 g
Monounsaturated 4 g
Fiber 0 g
Sodium 200 mg

Cook's Tip on Chicken Yields

A 4-pound chicken, cooked, yields about the following:

Breast meat: 12 oz
Leg meat: 4 oz
Thigh meat: 6 oz
Wing meat: 1½ oz
Back meat: 2 oz
Total: 25½ oz

Chicken with Apricot Glaze

Serves 4

Layers of flavor await your palate.

2 pounds chicken pieces, skinned, all visible fat removed

¼ cup all-purpose flour

⅛ teaspoon white pepper

1 tablespoon acceptable vegetable oil

Vegetable oil spray

½ cup all-fruit apricot preserves

16-ounce can apricot halves in natural juices

⅔ cup pineapple juice

1 tablespoon dry sherry

2 teaspoons light soy sauce

1 teaspoon dried marjoram, crumbled

1 teaspoon grated fresh gingerroot

1 teaspoon grated lemon zest

⅛ teaspoon red hot-pepper sauce

1 cup diced green bell pepper (1 medium)

Rinse chicken and pat dry with paper towels.

Combine flour and pepper in a paper or plastic bag. Add chicken one piece at a time and shake bag to coat chicken evenly. Shake off excess flour.

Put oil in a large nonstick skillet over medium-high heat. Lightly spray meatier side of chicken pieces with vegetable oil spray. Put meatier side down in skillet and brown for 5 to 6 minutes.

Remove skillet from heat. Lightly spray top side of chicken pieces with vegetable oil spray. Spread apricot preserves on chicken. Set aside.

Drain liquid from apricots; pour liquid into a small bowl. Cut apricots in half and set aside.

Add remaining ingredients except bell pepper to apricot liquid. Stir.

Return skillet with chicken to heat. Add juice mixture. Simmer, covered, for 50 to 60 minutes, or until chicken is tender.

Stir in bell pepper. Cook for 7 to 8 minutes.

To serve, transfer chicken to a serving platter. Spoon apricots and sauce over all.

Calories 389
Protein 26 g
Carbohydrates 48 g
Cholesterol 72 mg
Total Fat 10 g
Saturated 2 g
Polyunsaturated 4 g
Monounsaturated 3 g
Fiber 3 g
Sodium 166 mg

Chicken with Orange Sauce

Serves 4

Orange juice tenderizes and adds flavor to this dish. Serve the chicken warm over yolk-free noodles or chill it to take on a picnic.

Vegetable oil spray

2½- to 3-pound chicken, cut into serving pieces, skinned, all visible fat removed

½ teaspoon paprika

1 medium onion, sliced (1 cup)

½ cup frozen orange juice concentrate

⅓ cup water

2 tablespoons brown sugar

2 tablespoons snipped fresh parsley

1 teaspoon light soy sauce

1 teaspoon dry sherry

½ teaspoon ground ginger

Preheat broiler. Lightly spray a baking sheet with vegetable oil spray.

Rinse chicken and pat dry with paper towels. Sprinkle with paprika and put on baking sheet.

Broil about 6 inches from heat until lightly browned on all sides, 4 to 5 minutes. Transfer chicken to a Dutch oven or large, deep skillet and top with onion slices.

In a small bowl, whisk together remaining ingredients. Pour over chicken and onions.

Bring sauce to a boil over medium-high heat. Reduce heat and simmer, covered, for 55 to 60 minutes, or until chicken is tender.

Time-Saver: Prepare a double recipe so you'll have chicken to fill a pita bread for an unusual sandwich or to top either a green salad or an Asian noodle salad using soba or rice noodles.

Optional Cooking Method

Put browned chicken and onion slices in a casserole dish. Pour orange juice mixture over all and bake, covered, in a preheated 350° F oven for 55 to 60 minutes, or until chicken is tender.

Calories 288
Protein 30 g
Carbohydrates 23 g
Cholesterol 89 mg
Total Fat 8 g
Saturated 2 g
Polyunsaturated 2 g
Monounsaturated 3 g
Fiber 1 g
Sodium 135 mg

Sesame Chicken

Serves 4

Lemon juice and wine flavor meaty chicken pieces, and a light crust of sesame seeds keeps them moist. Serve with bok choy and have Claret-Spiced Oranges (see page 607) for dessert.

Vegetable oil spray

⅓ cup all-purpose flour

¼ teaspoon pepper

2½- to 3-pound chicken, cut into serving pieces, skinned, all visible fat removed

Vegetable oil spray

1 tablespoon fresh lemon juice

¼ cup sesame seeds, divided use

3 tablespoons minced green onions (1 to 2 medium)

½ cup dry white wine (regular or nonalcoholic) (plus more as needed)

Preheat oven to 375° F. Spray a 13 × 9 × 2-inch baking pan with vegetable oil spray. Set aside.

Put flour in a shallow bowl and stir in pepper.

Rinse chicken and pat dry with paper towels. Dredge chicken pieces in flour, shaking off excess.

Lightly spray meatier side of each chicken piece with vegetable oil spray. Arrange meatier side down in baking pan so pieces don't touch.

Lightly spray top side of chicken pieces. Sprinkle with lemon juice and half the sesame seeds.

Bake for 30 minutes, or until lightly browned. Turn chicken over and sprinkle with remaining sesame seeds and green onions. Pour wine around chicken.

Bake for 30 to 45 minutes, basting occasionally, until done.

Calories 335
Protein 37 g
Carbohydrates 10 g
Cholesterol 99 mg
Total Fat 14 g
 Saturated 3 g
 Polyunsaturated 4 g
 Monounsaturated 5 g
Fiber 1 g
Sodium 105 mg

Sweet-and-Sour Baked Chicken

Serves 4

Serve this dish on a bed of fluffy rice so you don't miss a single drop of the fantastic sauce.

1 pound boneless, skinless chicken breast halves, all visible fat removed, cut into ½-inch strips

8½-ounce can pineapple chunks in their own juice

½ cup jellied cranberry sauce

2 tablespoons light brown sugar

2 tablespoons rice vinegar or cider vinegar

2 tablespoons frozen orange juice concentrate

1 tablespoon dry sherry

1 teaspoon reduced-sodium soy sauce

¼ teaspoon ground ginger

2 tablespoons cornstarch

2 tablespoons water

1 medium green bell pepper, cut into thin strips (1 cup)

Preheat oven to 350° F.

Rinse chicken and pat dry with paper towels. Put in an 8-inch square nonstick baking pan and set aside.

Drain juice from pineapple into a small saucepan and set pineapple aside. Put pan over medium heat and whisk in cranberry sauce, brown sugar, vinegar, orange juice concentrate, sherry, soy sauce, and ginger.

Put cornstarch in a cup or small bowl. Add water, whisking to dissolve. Whisk into juice mixture.

Increase heat to medium-high and cook for 3 to 4 minutes, or until thickened, stirring occasionally.

Add pineapple chunks and pour over chicken.

Bake, covered, for 35 minutes. Add bell pepper, and baste chicken with sauce. Bake, uncovered, for 5 minutes.

Calories 266
Protein 24 g
Carbohydrates 36 g
Cholesterol 63 mg
Total Fat 3 g
- Saturated 1 g
- Polyunsaturated 1 g
- Monounsaturated 1 g

Fiber 1 g
Sodium 111 mg

Chicken Casserole with Dilled Sherry Sauce

Serves 4

With its creamy dill sauce, this quick casserole is elegant enough to serve to company.

Vegetable oil spray
2 medium potatoes, peeled and quartered
2 large carrots, cut into 2-inch pieces
2 medium onions, quartered
4 whole cloves garlic, peeled
4 chicken breast halves (about 2 pounds), skinned, all visible fat removed
½ cup dry sherry
½ teaspoon pepper
½ teaspoon dried dillweed, crumbled
1⅓ cups Chicken Broth (see page 40 or use commercial low-sodium variety)
¼ cup all-purpose flour
¼ cup water
2 tablespoons finely chopped green onion

Preheat oven to 350° F. Lightly spray a deep baking pan or ovenproof earthenware pot with vegetable oil spray.

Put potatoes, carrots, onions, and garlic in baking pan.

Rinse chicken and pat dry with paper towels. Arrange chicken over vegetable mixture.

Pour sherry over all, then sprinkle with pepper and dill.

Bake, covered, for 50 to 55 minutes.

Transfer chicken and vegetables to a serving platter, reserving ⅔ cup pan juice. Cover platter with aluminum foil and set aside.

Whisk together reserved pan juice and broth in a small saucepan.

In a small bowl, combine flour and water; whisk into pan juice mixture. Bring to a boil over medium-high heat, stirring constantly.

Stir in green onion.

To serve, pour sauce over chicken and vegetables.

Calories 346
Protein 37 g
Carbohydrates 33 g
Cholesterol 90 mg
Total Fat 4 g
Saturated 1 g
Polyunsaturated 1 g
Monounsaturated 1 g
Fiber 3 g
Sodium 114 mg

Rosemary Chicken

Serves 8

While the chicken bakes, make the sauce, a salad, and a vegetable. Sit down and enjoy.

Vegetable oil spray

8 chicken breast halves (about 4 pounds), skinned, all visible fat removed

2 tablespoons chopped fresh rosemary or 2 teaspoons dried, crushed

Vegetable oil spray

3 tablespoons all-purpose flour

½ cup Chicken Broth (see page 40 or use commercial low-sodium variety)

¾ cup plain nonfat or low-fat yogurt

¼ cup dry white wine (regular or nonalcoholic)

1 tablespoon light margarine

1 teaspoon grated lemon zest

Pepper to taste

1 cup sliced fresh mushrooms (4 ounces)

Lemon twist (optional)

Sprig of parsley (optional)

Preheat oven to 350° F. Spray a 13 × 9 × 2-inch baking pan with vegetable oil spray. Set aside.

Rinse chicken and pat dry with paper towels. Rub rosemary on chicken. Spray with vegetable oil spray. Put meaty side down in baking pan.

Bake, covered, for 30 minutes.

Meanwhile, put flour in a medium saucepan and whisk in broth. Cook over medium-high heat for 2 to 3 minutes, stirring occasionally.

Reduce heat to low. Whisk in yogurt, wine, margarine, lemon zest, and pepper.

Remove pan from oven. Drain. Turn each chicken breast. Cover with mushrooms. Pour sauce over all. Bake, uncovered, for 30 to 45 minutes, or until tender. Garnish with lemon or parsley.

Time Saver: Proceed as above, but use eight 4-ounce boneless, skinless chicken breast halves. Bake, covered, for 20 minutes, add mushrooms and sauce, then bake, uncovered, for 20 minutes.

Calories 210
Protein 34 g
Carbohydrates 4 g
Cholesterol 91 mg
Total Fat 4 g
Saturated 1 g
Polyunsaturated 1 g
Monounsaturated 1 g
Fiber 0 g
Sodium 103 mg

Chicken Jambalaya

Serves 6

Capture the flavors of Louisiana with this casserole. Your family will love the taste—and you'll love the simple preparation.

Vegetable oil spray
6 chicken breast halves (about 3 pounds), skinned, all visible fat removed
1 cup Chicken Broth (see page 40 or use commercial low-sodium variety)
1 cup dry white wine (regular or nonalcoholic)
½ cup chopped onion
¼ cup chopped green bell pepper
¼ cup snipped fresh parsley
½ teaspoon dried basil, crumbled
½ teaspoon dried thyme, crumbled
1 small bay leaf
1 cup uncooked rice
1 cup canned no-salt-added tomatoes, drained
½ cup cubed low-fat, low-sodium ham

Preheat oven to 350° F. Lightly spray a 13 × 9 × 2-inch or 1½-quart casserole dish with vegetable oil spray.

Rinse chicken pieces and pat dry with paper towels. Put chicken in casserole dish.

In a medium saucepan, combine broth, wine, onion, bell pepper, parsley, basil, thyme, and bay leaf. Bring to a boil over medium-high heat, stirring constantly. Remove from heat.

Add remaining ingredients to casserole dish. Pour broth mixture over all.

Bake, covered, for 55 to 60 minutes, or until chicken and rice are tender.

Calories 356
Protein 38 g
Carbohydrates 31 g
Cholesterol 95 mg
Total Fat 5 g
Saturated 1 g
Polyunsaturated 1 g
Monounsaturated 2 g
Fiber 1 g
Sodium 186 mg

Crispy Baked Chicken

Serves 4

Remember when you didn't want to fry chicken because it was such a mess to clean up? Now you have two good reasons to cook this chicken—no pan to wash and a really moist low-fat "fried" chicken!

Vegetable oil spray
1 cup fat-free milk
1 cup cornflake crumbs (3 cups cornflakes)
1 teaspoon dried rosemary, crushed
½ teaspoon pepper
4 boneless, skinless chicken breast halves (about 4 ounces each) or 2½- to 3-pound chicken, cut into serving pieces, skinned, all visible fat removed

Preheat oven to 400° F. Line a 13 × 9 × 2-inch baking pan with aluminum foil; lightly spray foil with vegetable oil spray.

Pour milk into a shallow bowl. Combine cornflake crumbs, rosemary, and pepper in another shallow bowl.

Rinse chicken and pat dry with paper towels. Dip chicken pieces into milk, then into crumb mixture. Allow to stand for 5 to 10 minutes so coating will adhere. Arrange chicken in baking pan so that pieces don't touch.

Bake boneless breasts for about 30 minutes, chicken pieces for 55 to 60 minutes, or until done and crumbs form a crisp "skin."

Calories 245
Protein 27 g
Carbohydrates 27 g
Cholesterol 64 mg
Total Fat 3 g
  Saturated 1 g
  Polyunsaturated 1 g
  Monounsaturated 1 g
Fiber 1 g
Sodium 376 mg

Lemongrass-Lime Baked Chicken

Serves 4

Are you ready for a flavor adventure? See the Cook's Tip on Lemongrass that accompanies this recipe to learn how to handle lemongrass, then prepare this delicious dish.

Vegetable oil spray
1 tablespoon fresh lemon juice
1 tablespoon fresh lime juice
1 teaspoon acceptable vegetable oil or acceptable margarine, melted
1 medium clove garlic, minced, or ½ teaspoon bottled minced garlic
¼ teaspoon pepper
2 stalks lemongrass or 1 tablespoon grated lemon zest
4 boneless, skinless chicken breast halves (about 4 ounces each) or 2½- to 3-pound chicken, cut into serving pieces, skinned, all visible fat removed

Preheat oven to 350° F. Lightly spray a 9-inch square baking pan or 1-quart casserole dish with vegetable oil spray.

In a small bowl, combine lemon juice, lime juice, oil, garlic, and pepper. Set aside.

Remove outer leaf of lemongrass. Slice bottom 6 to 8 inches of lemongrass crosswise into ½-inch pieces. Add to lemon juice mixture.

Rinse chicken and pat dry with paper towels. Put chicken in baking pan. Add juice mixture.

Bake boneless breasts, covered, for 30 minutes, or pieces for 40 minutes, or until tender, basting occasionally; uncover and bake for 10 minutes, or until brown. Remove and discard lemongrass.

Calories 135
Protein 23 g
Carbohydrates 1 g
Cholesterol 63 mg
Total Fat 4 g
Saturated 1 g
Polyunsaturated 1 g
Monounsaturated 1 g
Fiber 0 g
Sodium 55 mg

Cook's Tip on Lemongrass

Look in the produce section of your grocery for lemongrass. Because it is tough and fibrous, lemongrass is not eaten; use the bottom 6 to 8 inches to impart the characteristic perfume and sour lemon flavor.

Chicken Philippine Style

Serves 4

Easy to make, this interesting dish has a sour tang suggestive of the Philippine adobo seasoning. You will love the fact that there is only a skillet to wash. Serve hot or cold with Gingered Carrots (see page 374) and a green vegetable for contrast.

MARINADE

1/3 to 1/2 cup white wine vinegar, to taste

1/3 cup pineapple juice

2 tablespoons light soy sauce

1 medium clove garlic, minced, or 1/2 teaspoon bottled minced garlic

1/8 teaspoon pepper

4 boneless, skinless chicken breast halves (about 4 ounces each) or 2 1/2- to 3-pound chicken, cut into pieces, skinned, all visible fat removed

Combine marinade ingredients in a large skillet.

Add chicken to skillet. Cover and marinate in the refrigerator for about 30 minutes, turning once.

Put skillet over medium-high heat; heat until marinade comes to a boil. Reduce heat and simmer breast halves, covered, for 20 minutes, chicken pieces for 40 minutes, or until chicken is tender, turning once.

Calories 150
Protein 24 g
Carbohydrates 4 g
Cholesterol 63 mg
Total Fat 3 g
Saturated 1 g
Polyunsaturated 1 g
Monounsaturated 1 g
Fiber 0 g
Sodium 309 mg

Chicken and Snow Pea Stir-Fry

Serves 6

This stir-fry highlights crunch from a combination of water chestnuts, celery, and snow peas.

4 boneless, skinless chicken breast halves (about 4 ounces each), all visible fat removed

1 cup uncooked rice

¼ cup Chicken Broth (see page 40 or use commercial low-sodium variety)

1 tablespoon dry sherry

1 tablespoon light soy sauce

1 teaspoon freshly grated gingerroot

1 medium clove garlic, minced, or ½ teaspoon bottled minced garlic

⅛ teaspoon hot-pepper oil (optional)

Vegetable oil spray

1 small onion, thinly sliced (¾ cup)

½ cup thinly sliced celery (1 medium rib)

10-ounce package frozen no-salt-added snow pea pods

8-ounce can sliced water chestnuts, rinsed and drained (1 cup)

8-ounce can bamboo shoots, rinsed and drained

1 tablespoon cornstarch

1 teaspoon sugar

¼ cup cold water

2 tablespoons dry-roasted almond slivers

Rinse chicken and pat dry with paper towels. Cut into thin slices. Set aside.

Cook rice using package directions, omitting salt and margarine.

Meanwhile, in a small bowl, whisk together broth, sherry, soy sauce, gingerroot, garlic, and hot-pepper oil. Set aside.

Heat a wok or large, heavy skillet over high heat. Remove from heat and lightly spray with vegetable oil spray. Put back on heat. Sauté chicken for 3 to 4 minutes, stirring occasionally.

Add onion and celery. Sauté for 3 minutes, stirring occasionally.

Add snow peas, water chestnuts, bamboo shoots, and broth mixture. Reduce heat to medium. Cook, covered, for 5 minutes.

Put cornstarch and sugar in a cup or small bowl. Add water, whisking to dissolve. Pour over chicken

Calories 283
Protein 21 g
Carbohydrates 40 g
Cholesterol 42 mg
Total Fat 4 g
Saturated 1 g
Polyunsaturated 1 g
Monounsaturated 1 g
Fiber 5 g
Sodium 140 mg

and cook over medium-high heat for 2 minutes, or until thick, stirring occasionally.

To serve, spoon chicken mixture over rice and sprinkle with almonds.

Cook's Tip on Chicken

Semifrozen chicken is easier to slice. Put the chicken in the freezer for about 30 minutes before cutting.

Chicken and Mushroom Stir-Fry

Serves 6

This colorful blend of vegetables and chicken is delicious over rice or pasta.

4 boneless, skinless chicken breast halves (about 4 ounces each), all visible fat removed

1 tablespoon grated fresh gingerroot

1 tablespoon hot-pepper oil

3 medium cloves garlic, minced, or 1½ teaspoons bottled minced garlic

1 teaspoon toasted sesame oil

2 tablespoons light brown sugar

2 tablespoons Chicken Broth (see page 40 or use commercial low-sodium variety)

2 tablespoons dry sherry

1 tablespoon light soy sauce

1 tablespoon rice vinegar

1 tablespoon cornstarch

Vegetable oil spray

8 ounces fresh mushrooms, sliced (2½ to 3 cups)

1 cup diced red bell pepper (1 medium)

1 medium zucchini, diced (1 cup)

½ medium onion, sliced (½ cup)

8 cherry tomatoes, halved

Rinse chicken and pat dry with paper towels. Cut into 1-inch cubes and put in a large bowl.

Add gingerroot, hot-pepper oil, garlic, and sesame oil to bowl. Marinate for 15 minutes in refrigerator.

Meanwhile, in a small bowl, combine brown sugar, broth, sherry, soy sauce, vinegar, and cornstarch. Set aside.

Heat a large nonstick skillet or wok over high heat. Remove from heat and spray with vegetable oil spray. Put back on heat. Stir-fry chicken with marinade for 3 to 4 minutes, or until chicken is lightly browned.

Stir in mushrooms, bell pepper, zucchini, and onion. Reduce heat to medium-high and cook, covered, for 5 minutes, stirring occasionally.

Add chicken broth mixture and cherry tomatoes. Cook until sauce is thick, 3 to 4 minutes, stirring occasionally.

Calories 157
Protein 17 g
Carbohydrates 10 g
Cholesterol 42 mg
Total Fat 5 g
  Saturated 1 g
  Polyunsaturated —
  Monounsaturated —
Fiber 2 g
Sodium 127 mg

Beef-Vegetable Stir-Fry

Substitute 1 pound thinly sliced sirloin or round steak, all visible fat removed, for chicken. (calories 178; protein 15 g; carbohydrates 10 g; cholesterol 40 mg; total fat 9 g; saturated 3 g; polyunsaturated —; monounsaturated —; fiber 2 g; sodium 119 mg)

Cook's Tip on *Mise en Place*

The French call it *mise en place (meez ahn plahs)*—it means having all your ingredients ready (measured, sliced, melted, etc.) before you start cooking. This advance preparation probably is never more important than in stir-frying, in which the cooking steps must move very quickly.

Rosé Chicken with Artichoke Hearts and Mushrooms

Serves 4

Delicious as is, this one-skillet dish is also great over penne pasta.

4 boneless, skinless chicken breast halves (about 4 ounces each), all visible fat removed

¼ cup all-purpose flour

½ teaspoon olive oil

8 ounces fresh mushrooms, quartered (2½ to 3 cups)

2 medium cloves garlic, minced, or 1 teaspoon bottled minced garlic

½ teaspoon olive oil

9-ounce package frozen no-salt-added artichoke hearts, thawed and halved

14.5-ounce can no-salt-added diced tomatoes, undrained

¼ cup Chicken Broth (see page 40 or use commercial low-sodium variety)

¼ cup rosé wine, dry white wine (regular or nonalcoholic), or dry vermouth

1 tablespoon fresh lemon juice

1 teaspoon dried oregano, crumbled

¼ teaspoon salt

½ cup thinly sliced green onions (4 to 5 medium)

Rinse chicken and pat dry with paper towels. Coat chicken lightly with flour. Shake off excess.

Set a large nonstick skillet over medium heat and add ½ teaspoon olive oil. Brown chicken for 4 minutes on each side. Remove from skillet and set aside.

Stir in mushrooms, garlic, and ½ teaspoon olive oil. Cook, covered, for 7 to 10 minutes.

Add artichoke hearts and cook, uncovered, for 1 to 2 minutes, or until juices evaporate.

Add chicken and remaining ingredients except green onions. Cook over medium heat for 10 minutes, or until chicken is cooked through.

Stir in green onions; cook for 1 minute.

Calories 235
Protein 28 g
Carbohydrates 20 g
Cholesterol 63 mg
Total Fat 5 g
Saturated 1 g
Polyunsaturated 1 g
Monounsaturated 2 g
Fiber 5 g
Sodium 245 mg

Chicken Columbo

Serves 8

Seasoned wheat germ coats the chicken and gives it an interesting crunch. Shell pasta is a good accompaniment—it helps soak up the savory sauce.

½ cup fat-free milk

⅓ cup wheat germ or plain dry bread crumbs

1 teaspoon dried oregano, crumbled

¼ teaspoon garlic powder

¼ teaspoon onion powder

Pepper to taste

8 boneless, skinless chicken breast halves (about 4 ounces each), all visible fat removed

Vegetable oil spray

1 tablespoon light margarine

½ pound fresh mushrooms, sliced (2½ to 3 cups)

¼ cup marsala or dry sherry

3 tablespoons no-salt-added tomato paste

2 tablespoons snipped fresh parsley

Pour milk into a shallow bowl. Combine wheat germ, oregano, garlic powder, onion powder, and pepper on a plate. Rinse chicken and pat dry with paper towels. Dip into milk, then into wheat germ mixture, coating pieces well.

Spray a large nonstick skillet with vegetable oil spray. Melt margarine over medium-high heat and sauté chicken until golden, 3 to 4 minutes per side.

Combine remaining ingredients except parsley in a medium bowl; pour over chicken. Reduce heat and simmer for 10 minutes.

To serve, sprinkle with parsley.

Cook's Tip on Wheat Germ

Wheat germ is a good source of vitamin E and protein. Eat wheat germ as a cereal or sprinkle it over other cereals to add a nutty flavor, crunch, and nutrients. Store it, tightly covered, in the refrigerator.

Calories 167
Protein 25 g
Carbohydrates 7 g
Cholesterol 63 mg
Total Fat 3 g
Saturated 1 g
Polyunsaturated 1 g
Monounsaturated 1 g
Fiber 1 g
Sodium 78 mg

Chicken Creole

Serves 8

In typical Creole fashion, this dish features tomatoes, onion, celery, and garlic. Serve it over rice, with melon slices on the side.

8 boneless, skinless chicken breast halves (about 4 ounces each), all visible fat removed

Vegetable oil spray

1 teaspoon acceptable vegetable oil

1 cup thinly sliced onion (1 medium)

2 cups thinly sliced fresh mushrooms (6 to 8 ounces)

1 cup chopped celery (2 medium ribs)

2 tablespoons minced garlic

1 tablespoon chopped fresh oregano or 1 teaspoon dried, crumbled

1 tablespoon chopped fresh basil or 1 teaspoon dried, crumbled

2 cups sliced green bell pepper (2 medium)

2 cups peeled, diced tomatoes (3 medium)

½ cup dry white wine (regular or nonalcoholic)

2 tablespoons fresh lemon juice

½ teaspoon crushed red pepper flakes

Vegetable oil spray

½ teaspoon pepper, or to taste

2 tablespoons finely snipped fresh parsley

Rinse chicken and pat dry with paper towels. Cut into ½-inch cubes and set aside.

Spray a large skillet with vegetable oil spray. Add oil to skillet and heat over medium-high heat. Sauté onion until translucent, 2 to 3 minutes.

Add mushrooms and cook over medium-high heat until liquid evaporates, 3 to 4 minutes.

Add celery, garlic, oregano, and basil and cook for 1 minute.

Add bell pepper and cook for 2 minutes.

Add tomatoes and cook for 5 minutes.

Stir in wine, lemon juice, and red pepper flakes. Set aside.

Spray a large nonstick skillet with vegetable oil spray. Heat over high heat. Add half the chicken and sprinkle with about half the pepper. Cook until pieces are cooked evenly throughout and are lightly

Calories 179
Protein 25 g
Carbohydrates 10 g
Cholesterol 63 mg
Total Fat 4 g
Saturated 1 g
Polyunsaturated 1 g
Monounsaturated 1 g
Fiber 2 g
Sodium 75 mg

browned, 5 to 6 minutes, stirring occasionally. Don't overcook. Transfer chicken to a plate.

Respray skillet and repeat procedure, then return first batch of chicken to skillet.

Pour sauce over all and stir gently to blend. Simmer for 5 to 10 minutes.

To serve, sprinkle with parsley.

Cook's Tip on Fresh Parsley

You can snip enough fresh parsley at one time to last all week. Wash the parsley and let it air-dry completely. Break off the tops from the stems (they're good for flavoring soups). Using kitchen shears, snip the tops, put them in an airtight plastic bag, and refrigerate them for up to a week.

Chicken Southwestern

Serves 6

Serve this spicy dish with warm corn tortillas and wedges of ice-cold watermelon. You can adjust the heat level by cutting back on the jalapeño (see Cook's Tip on Hot Chile Peppers, *page 115)* *and chili powder.*

Vegetable oil spray

1½ cups orange, red, or yellow bell pepper strips or combination (1½ medium)

2 teaspoons seeded and minced fresh jalapeño pepper

½ cup diagonally sliced green onions (4 to 5 medium)

6 boneless, skinless chicken breast halves (about 4 ounces each), all visible fat removed

⅓ cup all-purpose flour

1½ teaspoons chili powder

¼ teaspoon pepper

¼ teaspoon salt

2 teaspoons acceptable vegetable oil, divided use

28-ounce can no-salt-added whole tomatoes

1 teaspoon chili powder

¼ teaspoon pepper

1 teaspoon grated lime zest

Calories 202
Protein 25 g
Carbohydrates 15 g
Cholesterol 63 mg
Total Fat 5 g
Saturated 1 g
Polyunsaturated 2 g
Monounsaturated 1 g
Fiber 3 g
Sodium 177 mg

Heat a large nonstick skillet over medium-high heat. Remove skillet from heat and lightly spray with vegetable oil spray.

Return skillet to heat. Sauté bell pepper and jalapeño for 4 to 5 minutes, stirring occasionally.

Add green onions and sauté for 1 minute. Transfer vegetables to a plate and set aside.

Rinse chicken and pat dry with paper towels. Put chicken smooth side up between two sheets of plastic wrap. Using a tortilla press or the smooth side of a meat mallet, flatten chicken to ½-inch thickness.

Combine flour, 1½ teaspoons chili powder, ¼ teaspoon pepper, and salt in a paper or plastic bag. Add chicken one piece at a time and shake to coat with flour mixture. Shake off excess flour.

In a large nonstick skillet, heat 1 teaspoon oil over medium-high heat. Add half the chicken pieces and lightly brown on both sides, 3 to 4 minutes per side. Repeat process with remaining oil and chicken. Transfer to plate containing vegetables.

Add undrained tomatoes to skillet, breaking up whole tomatoes with a wooden spoon.

Stir in 1 teaspoon chili powder and ¼ teaspoon pepper. Reduce heat and simmer for 3 to 4 minutes.

Add lime zest, vegetables, and chicken. Heat over medium heat for 5 to 6 minutes, or until heated throughout and chicken is no longer pink in the center.

Chicken Chili

Serves 8

Learn how to cook dried beans in the microwave with this recipe. Corn and red bell pepper add a touch of color to this satisfying dish.

11 ounces dried pinto beans, sorted for stones and rinsed (about 1½ cups), or 2 15-ounce cans no-salt-added pinto beans

2⅔ cups water

½ teaspoon salt

6 to 8 sprigs of fresh parsley

3 sprigs of fresh thyme

1 bay leaf

2½ pounds boneless, skinless chicken breast halves, all visible fat removed

1 teaspoon acceptable vegetable oil

1 cup finely chopped onion (2 medium)

4 medium cloves garlic, minced, or 2 teaspoons bottled minced garlic

1 cup dry white wine (regular or nonalcoholic)

8 ounces fresh mushrooms, thinly sliced (2½ to 3 cups)

1½ cups frozen no-salt-added whole-kernel corn

1 cup diced red bell pepper (1 medium)

4-ounce can diced green chiles, rinsed and drained

1½ teaspoons ground cumin

1½ teaspoons dried oregano, crumbled

½ teaspoon red hot-pepper sauce, or to taste

½ teaspoon salt

½ cup finely snipped fresh parsley

Calories 350
Protein 38 g
Carbohydrates 35 g
Cholesterol 78 mg
Total Fat 5 g
Saturated 1 g
Polyunsaturated 1 g
Monounsaturated 1 g
Fiber 10 g
Sodium 478 mg

Put beans, water, and salt in a microwave-safe 1½-quart casserole dish.

Tie parsley, thyme, and bay leaf together with kitchen twine. Add to bean mixture.

Cover and microwave on 100 percent power (high) for 30 minutes. Microwave on 50 percent power (medium) for 1 hour, stirring after 30 minutes, adding water if necessary.

Meanwhile, rinse chicken and pat dry with paper towels. Cut into 1½-inch cubes.

Pour oil into a large stockpot. Sauté onions over medium-high heat for 2 to 3 minutes, or until translucent; add garlic and sauté for 1 minute.

Stir in chicken, wine, and mushrooms. Reduce heat to medium and cook, covered, for 5 minutes.

Remove casserole containing beans from the microwave. Remove tied herbs.

Drain beans and stir half into chicken mixture; mash remaining beans and add to pot.

Stir in remaining ingredients except parsley. Simmer for 20 minutes to allow flavors to blend.

To serve, stir in parsley.

Cook's Tip

If you don't have a microwave, soak and cook beans according to package instructions, using amount of water specified on package. Add tied herbs and salt to cooking liquid. Proceed as directed.

Burgundy Chicken with Mushrooms

Serves 4

Company really goes for this—chicken smothered in mushrooms and a hint of burgundy, then sprinkled with fresh parsley and drizzled with olive oil. A bonus is that you can do most of the cooking before your guests arrive.

4 boneless, skinless chicken breast halves (about 4 ounces each), all visible fat removed

Olive oil spray

8 ounces fresh mushrooms, sliced (2½ to 3 cups)

¼ cup finely chopped yellow onion

2 medium cloves garlic, minced, or 1 teaspoon bottled minced garlic

2 tablespoons burgundy, other dry red wine, or nonalcoholic red wine

¼ teaspoon salt

2 tablespoons finely chopped fresh parsley

2 teaspoons extra-virgin olive oil

Rinse chicken and pat dry with paper towels. Spray a large nonstick skillet with olive oil spray. Heat over medium-high heat for 1 minute. Add chicken and cook for 5 minutes; turn pieces over and cook for 4 to 5 minutes, or until beginning to brown on outside and no longer pink in center. Put chicken on a plate.

Add mushrooms, onion, garlic, and burgundy to any pan residue. Cook for 2 minutes.

Add chicken and its juices. Cook for 5 minutes, or until mushrooms just begin to brown slightly.

To serve, place chicken on a platter. Spoon mushroom mixture on top. Sprinkle with salt, then with parsley. Drizzle with oil. Serve immediately.

Calories 163
Protein 24 g
Carbohydrates 3 g
Cholesterol 63 mg
Total Fat 5 g
- Saturated 1 g
- Polyunsaturated 1 g
- Monounsaturated 3 g

Fiber 1 g
Sodium 203 mg

Chicken in White Wine and Tarragon

Serves 4

Make a double batch of this fragrant chicken so you can pair it with angel hair pasta one night and still have enough for sandwiches later in the week.

4 boneless, skinless chicken breast halves (about 4 ounces each) or 2½- to 3-pound chicken, quartered and skinned, all visible fat removed

1 cup dry white wine (regular or nonalcoholic)

1 tablespoon dried tarragon, crumbled

4 medium cloves garlic, minced, or 2 teaspoons bottled minced garlic

1 teaspoon dry mustard

¼ teaspoon pepper

Preheat oven to 350° F.

Rinse chicken and pat dry with paper towels. Arrange chicken in a shallow broilerproof pan.

Pour wine over chicken.

Combine remaining ingredients in a small bowl. Rub on chicken. Cover pan with aluminum foil.

Bake for 35 minutes (45 minutes for chicken quarters). Remove foil and turn oven setting to broil. Broil chicken about 5 inches from heat for 2 to 3 minutes, or until lightly browned.

Calories 173
Protein 23 g
Carbohydrates 2 g
Cholesterol 63 mg
Total Fat 3 g
Saturated 1 g
Polyunsaturated 1 g
Monounsaturated 1 g
Fiber 0 g
Sodium 59 mg

Italian Chicken Roll-Ups

Serves 4

Serve these attractive chicken rolls with a simple salad of red onion slices, yellow and red tomatoes (cherry tomatoes if they're available), and baby spinach leaves. Dish up some Sunny Mango Sorbet (see page 618) for dessert.

1 cup water
6-ounce can no-salt-added tomato paste
1 medium clove garlic, minced, or ½ teaspoon bottled minced garlic
¾ teaspoon dried oregano, crumbled
¾ teaspoon dried basil, crumbled
½ teaspoon dried marjoram, crumbled
¼ teaspoon pepper, or to taste
4 boneless, skinless chicken breast halves (about 4 ounces each), all visible fat removed
4 ounces nonfat or low-fat cottage cheese, drained (½ cup)
2 ounces grated nonfat or part-skim mozzarella cheese (½ cup)

Calories 202
Protein 32 g
Carbohydrates 11 g
Cholesterol 66 mg
Total Fat 3 g
Saturated 1 g
Polyunsaturated 1 g
Monounsaturated 1 g
Fiber 2 g
Sodium 312 mg

Preheat oven to 350° F.

In a small saucepan, whisk together water, tomato paste, and garlic.

In a small bowl, combine oregano, basil, marjoram, and pepper. Add three fourths of mixture to saucepan. Bring to a boil over medium-high heat. Reduce heat and simmer for 10 minutes, stirring occasionally.

Meanwhile, rinse chicken and pat dry with paper towels. Put chicken smooth side up between two sheets of plastic wrap. Using a tortilla press or the smooth side of a meat mallet, lightly flatten chicken to ¼-inch thickness.

In a small bowl, combine remaining herb mixture with cottage cheese. Leaving a ½-inch edge all around, spoon onto chicken. From narrow end, roll each breast jelly-roll style.

Spoon half the tomato sauce into a 10 × 6-inch baking pan. Arrange chicken rolls seam side down on sauce. Spoon remaining tomato sauce over chicken rolls, then sprinkle with mozzarella.

Bake for 45 minutes, or until chicken is tender.

Baked Chicken Parmesan

Serves 6

Chicken pieces take a double dip (in buttermilk and in seasoned bread crumbs), then bake on a rack so they stay crispy all over.

Vegetable oil spray
4 slices whole-wheat bread
1/4 cup plus 2 tablespoons grated Parmesan cheese (1 1/2 ounces)
1 1/2 tablespoons finely snipped fresh parsley
1 1/2 teaspoons paprika
3/4 teaspoon garlic powder
1/2 teaspoon dried thyme, crumbled
1/2 cup nonfat or low-fat buttermilk
6 boneless, skinless chicken breast halves (about 4 ounces each), all visible fat removed
Vegetable oil spray

Preheat oven to 450° F. Lightly spray a rectangular baking sheet and slightly smaller cooling rack with vegetable oil spray. Put rack on baking sheet. Set aside.

In a food processor or blender, process bread into fine crumbs. Pour into a shallow bowl.

Stir Parmesan, parsley, paprika, garlic powder, and thyme into crumbs.

Pour buttermilk into a shallow bowl.

Rinse chicken and pat dry with paper towels. Dip chicken into buttermilk, shake off excess liquid, dredge in crumbs, and shake off excess crumbs. Put chicken on cooling rack. Spray each breast with vegetable oil spray.

Bake for 15 minutes, turn chicken, and bake for 10 minutes, or until done.

Calories 209
Protein 28 g
Carbohydrates 11 g
Cholesterol 68 mg
Total Fat 6 g
Saturated 2 g
Polyunsaturated 1 g
Monounsaturated 2 g
Fiber 1 g
Sodium 303 mg

Broiled Chicken with Hoisin-Barbecue Sauce

Serves 4

Chicken broiled in a red hoisin sauce with a hint of ginger is served on yellow rice that's been tossed with green peas.

Vegetable oil spray (optional)
1 cup uncooked rice
½ teaspoon powdered turmeric

HOISIN-BARBECUE SAUCE
¼ cup hoisin sauce
⅛ cup barbecue sauce
1 teaspoon sugar
1 teaspoon cider vinegar
¾ teaspoon very low sodium or low-sodium Worcestershire sauce
½ teaspoon grated fresh gingerroot
⅛ teaspoon cayenne

1 pound boneless, skinless chicken breast halves
1 cup frozen green peas, thawed and drained
¼ cup finely snipped fresh cilantro or parsley

If using long metal skewers, spray eight skewers with vegetable oil spray. If using bamboo skewers, soak eight skewers in cold water for at least 10 minutes.

Preheat broiler. Line broiler pan with aluminum foil. Spray broiler rack with vegetable oil spray and put in pan.

Prepare rice using package directions, omitting salt and margarine but adding turmeric.

Meanwhile, in a small bowl, whisk together sauce ingredients.

Rinse chicken and pat dry with paper towels. Cut chicken into 1-inch cubes and thread onto skewers. Put on broiler rack.

Broil 2 to 3 inches from heat for 3 minutes. Turn skewers and spoon sauce evenly over all. Broil for 3 minutes, or until chicken is cooked through.

To serve, stir peas into rice and place on a serving platter. Arrange skewers on rice and sprinkle with cilantro.

Calories 382
Protein 29 g
Carbohydrates 55 g
Cholesterol 63 mg
Total Fat 4 g
Saturated 1 g
Polyunsaturated 1 g
Monounsaturated 1 g
Fiber 3 g
Sodium 420 mg

Curried Sweet-and-Sour Chicken

Substitute 3/8 cup sweet-and-sour sauce for hoisin and barbecue sauces, and substitute 1 teaspoon curry powder for gingerroot. (calories 402; protein 29 g; carbohydrates 61 g; cholesterol 63 mg; total fat 4 g; saturated 1 g; polyunsaturated 1 g; monounsaturated 1 g; fiber 15 g; sodium 233 mg)

Cook's Tip on Skewered Food

Poke skewered items into a large, heavy vegetable. Try butternut squash, eggplant, or red cabbage. Slice a thin piece off the bottom so it will sit flat. Surround the vegetable with parsley sprigs or other fresh herbs. If you're serving fruit kebabs, stick them into a pineapple.

Grilled Lemon-Sage Chicken

Serves 6

Fresh sage and rosemary impart a different flavor to grilled chicken. Tomato halves and corn on the cob can grill along with the chicken.

MARINADE

1 teaspoon olive oil

1 teaspoon grated lemon zest

¼ cup fresh lemon juice (1 to 2 medium lemons)

¼ cup chopped fresh sage leaves

1 tablespoon chopped fresh rosemary, or 1 teaspoon dried, crushed

2 or 3 medium cloves garlic, minced, or 1 to 1½ teaspoons bottled minced garlic

1 teaspoon whole black peppercorns, cracked

½ teaspoon salt

6 boneless, skinless chicken breast halves (about 4 ounces each), all visible fat removed

6 lemon slices, cut in half (optional)

Fresh sage leaves (optional)

Time-Saver: Prepare a recipe and a half of Grilled Lemon-Sage Chicken to have extra chicken for Chicken-Spinach Manicotti (see page 206).

In an airtight plastic bag, combine marinade ingredients.

Rinse chicken and pat dry with paper towels.

Put chicken smooth side up between two sheets of plastic wrap. Using a tortilla press or the smooth side of a meat mallet, lightly flatten chicken to ⅛-inch thickness. Add to marinade and turn to coat evenly. Seal and refrigerate for at least 30 minutes or overnight, turning bag occasionally. Discard marinade.

Preheat grill to medium-high.

Grill chicken for 6 to 7 minutes on each side, or until done.

To serve, garnish with lemon and sage.

Calories 122
Protein 23 g
Carbohydrates 0 g
Cholesterol 63 mg
Total Fat 3 g
  Saturated 1 g
  Polyunsaturated 1 g
  Monounsaturated 1 g
Fiber 0 g
Sodium 241 mg

Sweet-Spice Glazed Chicken

Serves 4

Allspice, cloves, sweet-and-sour sauce, and a hint of bourbon sumptuously flavor the glaze in this recipe. The extra chicken you cook is the main ingredient in Island Chicken Salad with Fresh Mint (see page 115), an easy dinner for later in the week.

Vegetable oil spray

GLAZE

1 cup sweet-and-sour sauce

¼ cup bourbon

1 tablespoon plus 1 teaspoon very low sodium or low-sodium Worcestershire sauce

1 tablespoon plus 1 teaspoon acceptable vegetable oil

1 tablespoon cider vinegar

½ teaspoon crushed red pepper flakes

½ teaspoon ground allspice

½ teaspoon ground cloves

8 boneless, skinless chicken breast halves (about 4 ounces each), all visible fat removed

Preheat broiler. Spray broiler pan and rack with vegetable oil spray.

In a small bowl, whisk together glaze ingredients. Divide in half.

Rinse chicken and pat dry with paper towels. Put chicken smooth side down on broiler rack and brush lightly with glaze. Broil 2 to 3 inches from heat for 4 minutes. Turn chicken and broil for 3 minutes. Using a pastry brush, brush half the glaze over chicken. Broil for 2 to 3 minutes, or until chicken is no longer pink in center and begins to brown.

Meanwhile, wash pastry brush with hot, soapy water, rinse, and dry with paper towels.

Remove chicken from broiler and brush with remaining glaze. Serve 4 breasts. Refrigerate remaining breasts in an airtight container to use in Island Chicken Salad with Fresh Mint.

Calories 243
Protein 23 g
Carbohydrates 19 g
Cholesterol 63 mg
Total Fat 5 g
- Saturated 1 g
- Polyunsaturated 2 g
- Monounsaturated 1 g

Fiber 16 g
Sodium 238 mg

Spicy Grilled Chicken

Serves 4

This recipe will give you the basis for two easy dinners: grilled chicken for tonight and extra for whenever you want Chicken Fajitas (see page 213) and a south-of-the-border fiesta.

MARINADE

1 small onion, finely chopped (3/8 cup)

2 to 3 tablespoons fresh lime juice (1 to 2 medium limes)

2 tablespoons olive oil

1 to 2 tablespoons finely chopped fresh cilantro

1 small clove garlic, crushed, or 1/4 teaspoon bottled minced garlic

1/2 teaspoon chili powder

Pepper to taste

7 boneless, skinless chicken breast halves (about 4 ounces each), all visible fat removed

In an airtight plastic bag, combine all marinade ingredients.

Rinse chicken and pat dry with paper towels. Add to marinade and turn to coat. Seal and refrigerate for 2 to 3 hours, turning occasionally.

Preheat grill to medium-high or preheat broiler.

Grill chicken or broil it about 6 inches from heat for 6 to 7 minutes on each side, or until no longer pink in center. Reserve 3 breasts for Chicken Fajitas.

Calories 122
Protein 23 g
Carbohydrates 0 g
Cholesterol 63 mg
Total Fat 3 g
- Saturated 1 g
- Polyunsaturated 1 g
- Monounsaturated 1 g

Fiber 0 g
Sodium 57 mg

Triple-Pepper Chicken

Serves 4

Turn up the heat with a spicy paste of cayenne, lemon pepper, and black pepper! This recipe makes enough for two meals.

8 boneless, skinless chicken breast halves (about 4 ounces each), all visible fat removed

SPICE RUB

1 tablespoon chili powder

2 teaspoons fresh lime juice

1½ teaspoons dried oregano, crumbled

2 medium cloves garlic, minced, or 1 teaspoon bottled minced garlic

½ teaspoon salt-free lemon pepper

½ teaspoon black pepper

½ teaspoon onion powder

½ teaspoon ground cumin

½ teaspoon very low sodium or low-sodium Worcestershire sauce

½ teaspoon liquid smoke

¼ teaspoon cayenne

Vegetable oil spray

1 tablespoon plus 1 teaspoon acceptable margarine

Rinse chicken and pat dry with paper towels. Put chicken in a 12 × 8-inch glass baking dish.

In a small bowl, whisk together spice rub ingredients. Apply a thin paste to chicken. Cover with plastic wrap and refrigerate for 4 hours.

Spray a large nonstick skillet with vegetable oil spray. Add half the margarine and heat over high heat until medium brown. Add half the chicken, immediately reduce heat to medium, and cook for 4 minutes. Turn chicken and cook for 3 to 4 minutes, or until no longer pink in center. Place on a plate; cover with aluminum foil.

Respray skillet. Increase heat to high and melt remaining margarine. Repeat process.

Serve 4 breasts immediately, refrigerating remaining chicken in an airtight container for use in Cajun Chicken Salad (see page 113).

Time-Saver: You can refrigerate the chicken with rub for as little as 30 minutes. The flavor intensifies with the longer marinating, however.

Calories 145
Protein 23 g
Carbohydrates 1 g
Cholesterol 63 mg
Total Fat 5 g
Saturated 1 g
Polyunsaturated 1 g
Monounsaturated 2 g
Fiber 0 g
Sodium 87 mg

Savory Microwave Chicken

Serves 6

Take advantage of the speedy microwave and prepare this chicken dish—complete with vegetables—in a snap.

6 boneless, skinless chicken breast halves (about 4 ounces each), all visible fat removed
2 cups Chicken Broth (see page 40 or use commercial low-sodium variety)
1 teaspoon light margarine
2 cups small broccoli florets
1 cup finely chopped onion (2 medium)
1 cup sliced carrots (1 large)
1 cup Chicken Broth (see page 40 or use commercial low-sodium variety)
1 teaspoon grated orange zest
1 cup fresh orange juice (3 medium oranges)
2 tablespoons cornstarch
2 tablespoons dry sherry
1 tablespoon light soy sauce
½ teaspoon garlic powder
¼ teaspoon salt
⅓ cup slivered almonds (1 to 1½ ounces)

Calories 221
Protein 26 g
Carbohydrates 14 g
Cholesterol 63 mg
Total Fat 6 g
Saturated 1 g
Polyunsaturated 1 g
Monounsaturated 3 g
Fiber 2 g
Sodium 262 mg

Rinse chicken and pat dry with paper towels. Cut chicken into 1-inch cubes.

Put 2 cups broth and chicken in a microwave-safe casserole dish. Cook, covered, on 50 percent power (medium) for 5 minutes. Stir; cook for 5 minutes.

Drain chicken and discard broth or save for another use. Transfer chicken to a plate and set aside.

In the same casserole dish, melt margarine on 100 percent power (high) for 20 seconds. Add broccoli, onions, and carrots. Cook, covered, on 100 percent power (high) for 7 minutes. Remove from microwave and add chicken pieces. Set aside.

In a microwave-safe bowl, combine remaining ingredients except almonds. Cook on 100 percent power (high) for 5 minutes. Stir into chicken mixture.

Cook, covered, on 50 percent power (medium) for 3 minutes, or until all ingredients are evenly heated.

To serve, sprinkle with almonds.

Chicken-Spinach Manicotti

Serves 6; 2 shells per person

This recipe is a great way to use leftover chicken. The Grilled Lemon-Sage Chicken *(see page 200)**, for instance, would give deep flavor to the filling.*

Vegetable oil spray

1 package manicotti shells (12 shells)

FILLING

2 cups diced cooked chicken (about ¾ pound boneless, skinless breasts)

1½ cups nonfat or low-fat cottage cheese (12 ounces)

10-ounce package frozen no-salt-added spinach, thawed and squeezed dry

Egg substitute equivalent to 3 eggs

⅓ cup grated Parmesan cheese (1½ ounces)

2 teaspoons dried basil, crumbled

Pepper to taste

SAUCE

1 teaspoon olive oil

1 cup chopped onion (2 medium)

3 medium cloves garlic, minced, or 1½ teaspoons bottled minced garlic

14½-ounce can diced no-salt-added tomatoes, undrained

1 cup water

6-ounce can no-salt-added tomato paste

1 teaspoon salt-free Italian herb seasoning

1 teaspoon dried basil, crumbled

3 tablespoons grated Parmesan cheese

Calories 394
Protein 34 g
Carbohydrates 46 g
Cholesterol 46 mg
Total Fat 8 g
  Saturated 3 g
  Polyunsaturated 2 g
  Monounsaturated 3 g
Fiber 5 g
Sodium 474 mg

Lightly spray a 13 × 9 × 2-inch pan with vegetable oil spray. Set aside.

Cook pasta using package directions, omitting salt and oil. Drain and set aside.

Meanwhile, in a large bowl, combine all filling ingredients. Set aside.

For sauce, heat olive oil in a medium saucepan over medium-high heat. Sauté onions until translucent, 2 to 3 minutes.

Add garlic and sauté for 1 minute.

Stir in remaining sauce ingredients. Crush tomatoes slightly with wooden spoon. Reduce heat and simmer for 8 to 10 minutes. Spread 1 cup sauce in pan.

Preheat oven to 375° F.

Stuff shells with filling and arrange them on sauce. Spoon remaining sauce over shells, then sprinkle with 3 tablespoons Parmesan.

Bake for 30 minutes, or until thoroughly heated.

Microwave Method

Combine olive oil, onion, and garlic in a 1-quart microwave-safe bowl. Microwave on 100 percent power (high) for 3 minutes. Add remaining sauce ingredients and cook on 50 percent power (medium) for 10 minutes. Put half the sauce in a microwave-safe baking dish. Fill shells as directed and arrange on sauce. Cover with remaining sauce. Top with 3 tablespoons Parmesan. Cover with vented plastic wrap and microwave on 50 percent power (medium) for 25 minutes. Let stand, covered, for 5 minutes.

Chipotle Chicken Wraps

Serves 4

Smoky chicken saved from Mexican Chicken and Vegetables with Chipotle Peppers (see page 220) is rolled in flour tortillas with sour cream, cilantro, red onion, black olives, and freshly squeezed lime juice. It's yummy!

Reserved Mexican Chicken and Vegetables with Chipotle Peppers (see page 220)

8 8-inch nonfat or low-fat flour tortillas, warmed (see Cook's Tip, page 230)

½ cup nonfat or light sour cream

½ cup finely chopped red onion

¼ cup chopped cilantro leaves (optional)

16 medium black olives, quartered

Pepper to taste

Fresh lime juice to taste

In a small saucepan, warm reserved chicken mixture over medium heat until heated through, about 10 minutes, stirring occasionally.

To assemble, layer as follows down center of a tortilla: ¼ cup chicken mixture (use a slotted spoon), 1 tablespoon sour cream, 1 tablespoon onion, 1½ teaspoons cilantro, 8 olive quarters, pepper, and lime juice. Fold right third of tortilla to center. Fold bottom half up to top. Roll bottom edge up to top. Repeat with remaining ingredients.

Calories 268
Protein 22 g
Carbohydrates 35 g
Cholesterol 45 mg
Total Fat 5 g
  Saturated 1 g
  Polyunsaturated 1 g
  Monounsaturated 2 g
Fiber 4 g
Sodium 264 mg

Lemon-Cayenne Chicken

Serves 4

Cayenne and a tart lemon sauce provide the zip for these breaded chicken breasts.

4 boneless, skinless chicken breast halves (about 4 ounces each), all visible fat removed
½ cup all-purpose flour
¾ teaspoon paprika
½ teaspoon salt
¼ teaspoon cayenne
⅛ teaspoon black pepper
Vegetable oil spray
1 tablespoon extra-virgin olive oil
3 tablespoons water
1 tablespoon light margarine
1 teaspoon fresh lemon juice
2 tablespoons finely chopped fresh parsley

Rinse chicken and pat dry with paper towels. Put chicken smooth side up between two sheets of plastic wrap. Using a tortilla press or smooth side of a meat mallet, lightly flatten chicken to ¼-inch thickness, being careful not to tear meat.

In a shallow bowl, combine flour, paprika, salt, cayenne, and black pepper. Coat chicken, shaking off excess.

Spray a large nonstick skillet with vegetable oil spray. Add oil and put over medium-high heat for 1 minute, or until hot. Cook chicken for 8 minutes. Turn and cook for 7 to 8 minutes, or until golden brown. Place chicken on a serving platter.

To pan residue, add water, margarine, and lemon juice. Scrape any browned bits from skillet. Bring mixture to a boil. Boil for about 30 seconds, or until sauce is slightly thickened.

To serve, drizzle sauce over chicken and sprinkle with parsley.

Calories 222
Protein 25 g
Carbohydrates 13 g
Cholesterol 63 mg
Total Fat 7 g
  Saturated 2 g
  Polyunsaturated 2 g
  Monounsaturated 4 g
Fiber 1 g
Sodium 365 mg

Chicken and Broccoli in Mushroom Sauce

Serves 6

Earthy mushrooms, bright-green broccoli, and creamy sauce form a succulent team in this casserole. If you're a cook on the run, see our Time-Saver below.

Vegetable oil spray

10 ounces fresh broccoli spears or 10-ounce package no-salt-added frozen broccoli spears

2 cups diced cooked chicken

SAUCE

1 teaspoon light margarine

8 ounces fresh mushrooms, sliced (2½ to 3 cups)

1⅓ cups Chicken Broth (see page 40 or use commercial low-sodium variety)

5-ounce can fat-free evaporated milk (⅔ cup)

¼ cup all-purpose flour

¼ cup sliced green onions (2 medium)

3 tablespoons grated Parmesan cheese

Dash of nutmeg

TOPPING

¼ cup fresh bread crumbs (½ slice bread)

2 tablespoons finely snipped fresh parsley

1 teaspoon grated lemon zest

Calories 165
Protein 18 g
Carbohydrates 12 g
Cholesterol 38 mg
Total Fat 5 g
  Saturated 2 g
  Polyunsaturated 1 g
  Monounsaturated 2 g
Fiber 2 g
Sodium 150 mg

Lightly spray a 9-inch square baking pan with vegetable oil spray.

Steam broccoli spears until tender-crisp, then plunge into ice water to stop cooking. Drain and blot dry on paper towels. Arrange in baking pan.

Evenly place chicken over broccoli. Set aside.

For sauce, heat margarine in a medium nonstick skillet over medium heat. Swirl to coat bottom. Cook mushrooms, covered, for 7 to 9 minutes, or until they've released their juices. Increase heat to high and cook, uncovered, for 1 to 2 minutes to allow liquid to evaporate. Set aside.

Preheat oven to 375° F.

Pour broth and milk into a medium saucepan. Whisk in flour. Bring to a boil over medium-high heat; cook until thickened, 3 to 4 minutes, stirring occasionally.

Stir in green onions, Parmesan, nutmeg, and mushrooms. Pour over chicken in baking pan.

In a small bowl, combine topping ingredients. Sprinkle over casserole.

Bake for 25 minutes.

Time-Saver: Substitute 1 can low-fat, low-sodium cream of chicken soup mixed with 1/2 cup low-sodium chicken broth for the broth-milk-flour sauce (no heating required). Add cooked mushrooms, green onions, Parmesan, and nutmeg and proceed as directed.

Dill Chicken Enchiladas

Serves 9, 2 enchiladas per person

Dill and yogurt flavor this full-of-vegetables casserole. Serve it with Mexican Fried Rice (see page 407) or even wild rice.

Vegetable oil spray
½ pound fresh broccoli, chopped (1 cup)
½ pound fresh mushrooms, sliced (2½ to 3 cups)
18 5½- or 6-inch corn tortillas
2 cups finely chopped cooked chicken
1 cup plain nonfat or low-fat yogurt
¼ cup chopped onion
2 tablespoons snipped fresh dillweed or ¼ teaspoon dried, crumbled
1 tablespoon snipped fresh parsley
1 cup plain nonfat or low-fat yogurt
1 tablespoon snipped fresh parsley

Preheat oven to 350° F. Lightly spray a 13 × 9 × 2-inch baking dish with vegetable oil spray.

Steam broccoli and mushrooms until tender, 3 to 4 minutes. Set aside.

Wrap tortillas in foil and bake for 5 minutes to soften. Set aside.

In a medium bowl, combine chicken, 1 cup yogurt, onion, dillweed, and 1 tablespoon parsley, stirring well. Add broccoli and mushrooms and stir gently.

Put 3 tablespoons chicken filling on each tortilla. Roll up jelly-roll style and place seam side down in baking dish.

Spoon 1 cup yogurt over enchiladas and sprinkle with 1 tablespoon parsley. Cover dish with aluminum foil.

Bake for 20 minutes.

Calories 201
Protein 14 g
Carbohydrates 30 g
Cholesterol 24 mg
Total Fat 4 g
Saturated 1 g
Polyunsaturated 1 g
Monounsaturated 1 g
Fiber 4 g
Sodium 148 mg

Chicken Fajitas

Serves 4

Spicy Grilled Chicken (see page 202) saved from another meal is the base for this super-speedy entrée.

1 teaspoon acceptable margarine

1 large white onion, thinly sliced (1¼ cups)

1 large green bell pepper, thinly sliced (1¼ cups)

3 cooked chicken breast halves from Spicy Grilled Chicken, thinly sliced

6 6-inch nonfat or low-fat flour tortillas (see Cook's Tip, page 27) or 3 pita breads, halved

⅓ cup Salsa Cruda (see page 449) or low-sodium commercial salsa (see Cook's Tip, page 98)

Preheat oven to 325° F.

In a large nonstick skillet, melt margarine over medium-high heat. Sauté onion and bell pepper for about 5 minutes, or until onion is slightly brown, stirring constantly.

Add chicken and cook for 2 to 3 minutes, or until warmed through.

Meanwhile, wrap tortillas or pita breads in aluminum foil; warm in oven for 6 to 8 minutes.

To serve, place chicken strips down center of tortillas. Top with onions, peppers, and salsa. Roll up.

Calories 257
Protein 23 g
Carbohydrates 34 g
Cholesterol 47 mg
Total Fat 4 g
Saturated 1 g
Polyunsaturated 1 g
Monounsaturated 1 g
Fiber 4 g
Sodium 415 mg

Chicken Stew with Cornmeal Dumplings

Serves 6

Chicken and dumplings is a family-style dish found on many southern dinner tables. This creamy version is full of lean chicken and vegetables, topped with fluffy cornmeal dumplings.

STEW

4 chicken breasts (about 2½ pounds), skinned and all visible fat removed

4½ cups water

1 bay leaf

1 teaspoon dried basil, crumbled

1 teaspoon dried oregano, crumbled

¼ teaspoon salt

¼ teaspoon ground sage

¼ teaspoon pepper

CORNMEAL DUMPLINGS

½ cup all-purpose flour

⅓ cup cornmeal

¼ cup snipped fresh parsley

1½ teaspoons baking powder

¼ teaspoon salt

⅛ teaspoon white pepper

Egg substitute equivalent to 1 egg, or 1 egg

¼ cup fat-free milk

1 tablespoon acceptable vegetable oil

1 medium zucchini, halved lengthwise and sliced

1 medium crookneck squash, halved lengthwise and sliced

1 cup fat-free milk

½ cup all-purpose flour

Calories 306
Protein 34 g
Carbohydrates 27 g
Cholesterol 76 mg
Total Fat 6 g
Saturated 1 g
Polyunsaturated 2 g
Monounsaturated 2 g
Fiber 2 g
Sodium 437 mg

In a Dutch oven, combine stew ingredients. Bring to a boil over medium-high heat. Reduce heat and simmer, covered, for 45 minutes, or until chicken is tender and no longer pink in center.

Meanwhile, for dumplings, combine flour, cornmeal, parsley, baking powder, salt, and white pepper in a small bowl.

Whisk together remaining dumpling ingredients. Add to flour mixture, whisking just until moistened. Set aside.

Add zucchini and crookneck squash to stew mixture.

Remove bay leaf from stew and discard. Remove cooked chicken from stew. When chicken is cool enough to handle, remove meat from bones; cut chicken into bite-size pieces (you should have 2½ to 3 cups). Set aside.

In a jar with a tight-fitting lid, combine milk and flour. Cover and shake well. Add to stew mixture. Cook over medium to medium-high heat until thickened and bubbly, about 5 minutes, stirring constantly. Stir in chicken.

Using a spoon, drop dumpling batter in 6 mounds on simmering stew. Reduce heat and simmer, covered, for 10 to 12 minutes, or until a cake tester or toothpick inserted in one of the dumplings comes out clean. (Don't peek at dumplings while they cook.) Ladle into bowls.

Chicken à la King

Serves 6

An old standby gets a contemporary flavor with fragrant jasmine rice and oyster mushrooms. Feel free to substitute other mushrooms, such as shiitake or portobello.

1 cup uncooked jasmine or long-grain rice
1 teaspoon light margarine
½ pound fresh oyster mushrooms, sliced (2½ to 3 cups)
¼ cup diced green bell pepper
2 cups Chicken Broth (see page 40 or use commercial low-sodium variety)
5-ounce can fat-free evaporated milk (⅔ cup)
¼ teaspoon salt
¼ teaspoon white pepper
⅓ cup all-purpose flour
⅓ cup water
2 cups diced cooked chicken
7-ounce jar pimientos, drained and chopped
2 tablespoons dry sherry (optional)
2 or 3 drops red hot-pepper sauce
1 tablespoon snipped fresh parsley

Cook rice using package directions, omitting salt and margarine.

Meanwhile, in a large, heavy saucepan over medium-high heat, melt margarine. Reduce heat to medium-low and sauté mushrooms and bell pepper for 2 to 3 minutes, or until tender, stirring occasionally.

Whisk in broth, milk, salt, and pepper.

In a small bowl, whisk together flour and water. Whisk into mushroom mixture. Bring to a boil over medium-high heat, stirring occasionally. Reduce heat to medium-low and cook for 2 to 3 minutes, or until thickened, stirring occasionally.

Stir in chicken and pimientos. Heat thoroughly.

Stir in sherry and hot-pepper sauce.

To serve, spoon chicken mixture over rice and sprinkle with parsley.

Calories 229
Protein 18 g
Carbohydrates 28 g
Cholesterol 36 mg
Total Fat 4 g
  Saturated 1 g
  Polyunsaturated 1 g
  Monounsaturated 1 g
Fiber 2 g
Sodium 185 mg

Spicy Chicken and Grits

Serves 4

Cooks who watch both their time and their fat intake love boneless, skinless chicken breasts—they're fast and easy to prepare and are low in fat. This recipe uses a spice rub for lots of flavor, adds soothing grits, and keeps everything savory and moist with a chicken broth sauce.

1 cup quick-cooking grits
4 cups Chicken Broth (see page 40 or use commercial low-sodium variety)
4 boneless, skinless chicken breast halves (about 4 ounces each), all visible fat removed
1 teaspoon paprika
1 teaspoon sugar
½ teaspoon black pepper
½ teaspoon cayenne
1 small onion
½ medium green bell pepper
1 medium clove garlic
1 tablespoon olive oil
2 cups Chicken Broth (see page 40 or use commercial low-sodium variety)

Prepare grits using package directions, substituting 4 cups broth for water and omitting salt and margarine. Cover and set aside.

Meanwhile, rinse chicken and pat dry with paper towels. In a small bowl, combine paprika, sugar, black pepper, and cayenne. Rub on chicken to coat completely. Set aside.

Mince onion, bell pepper, and garlic. Heat a large nonstick skillet over medium heat. Add oil and swirl to coat bottom. When oil is hot, sauté vegetables for 10 minutes, or until softened, stirring occasionally.

Meanwhile, cut chicken into thin slivers across grain. Add to vegetables and cook over high heat for about 3 minutes, stirring often. Scrape contents of skillet onto a platter.

Add 2 cups broth to skillet and boil rapidly to reduce broth to ¾ cup, about 5 minutes.

Return chicken mixture to skillet and cook for 2 minutes, or until heated through. Serve chicken and broth over grits.

Calories 358
Protein 27 g
Carbohydrates 38 g
Cholesterol 63 mg
Total Fat 7 g
Saturated 1 g
Polyunsaturated 1 g
Monounsaturated 4 g
Fiber 1 g
Sodium 72 mg

Down South Chicken Hash and Corn Cakes

Serves 4

Southerners turn chicken or turkey hash into a great brunch dish by adding corn cakes, which are pancakes made with corn bread batter—quick, easy, and delicious. This makes a great dinner, too, with roasted brussels sprouts and Basil Roasted Peppers (see page 396).

CHICKEN HASH

1 teaspoon acceptable vegetable oil

1 medium onion, minced

8 ounces fresh mushrooms, thinly sliced (2½ to 3 cups)

1½ pounds potatoes, cooked and peeled (4 to 5 medium)

3 boneless, skinless chicken breast halves (about 4 ounces each), all visible fat removed, cut into ½-inch cubes

1 teaspoon dried thyme, crumbled

½ to 1 teaspoon pepper

1 cup Chicken Broth (see page 40 or use commercial low-sodium variety)

1 tablespoon all-purpose flour

2 medium fresh tomatoes, peeled, seeded, and finely chopped (optional) (1 cup)

CORN CAKES (OPTIONAL)

1 cup white or yellow cornmeal

2 tablespoons all-purpose flour

1 teaspoon baking powder

½ teaspoon salt

½ teaspoon baking soda

⅛ teaspoon pepper

1 cup nonfat or low-fat buttermilk

Egg substitute equivalent to 1 egg, or 1 egg

1 tablespoon acceptable vegetable oil

Vegetable oil spray

½ cup minced fresh parsley (optional)

Calories 458
Protein 28 g
Carbohydrates 66 g
Cholesterol 49 mg
Total Fat 9 g
Saturated 2 g
Polyunsaturated 4 g
Monounsaturated 2 g
Fiber 6 g
Sodium 434 mg

Preheat oven to 140° F.

For hash, in a Dutch oven, heat vegetable oil over medium-high heat, swirling to coat. Sauté onion for about 1 minute, stirring occasionally.

Increase heat to high and add mushrooms. Cook until slightly brown, 3 to 4 minutes, stirring occasionally.

Reduce heat to medium. Add potatoes and cook for 4 to 5 minutes, stirring occasionally.

Add chicken, thyme, and pepper, and cook for about 5 minutes, stirring occasionally.

In a small bowl, whisk together broth and flour until smooth. Stir into chicken mixture and bring to a boil. Cook until gravy thickens and barely coats hash ingredients.

Stir in tomatoes, then spoon hash into an ovenproof casserole dish. Cover and keep warm in oven while preparing corn cakes.

For corn cakes, combine cornmeal, flour, baking powder, salt, baking soda, and pepper on a piece of wax paper.

In a medium bowl, beat buttermilk and egg substitute; beat in oil.

Add cornmeal mixture and blend with a few swift strokes.

Lightly spray a large nonstick griddle or skillet with vegetable oil spray. Heat over medium-high heat until drops of water sizzle on surface. Pour about ¼ cup batter for each corn cake onto hot griddle. Cook until surface is bubbly, 2 to 3 minutes. Turn and cook other side for about 2 minutes. If corn cakes seem to be browning too quickly, reduce heat. Put cooked corn cakes in an ovenproof dish and keep warm in oven while cooking remaining corn cakes.

To serve, sprinkle hash with parsley. Serve corn cakes on the side. (Prepared without corn cakes: calories 264; protein 21 g; carbohydrates 36 g; cholesterol 47 mg; total fat 4 g; saturated 1 g; polyunsaturated 1 g; monounsaturated 1 g; fiber 4 g; sodium 51 mg)

Cook's Tip

Don't skimp on the pepper—it adds lots of flavor. So do the parsley and the tomatoes. Though they're optional, we highly recommend them.

Mexican Chicken and Vegetables with Chipotle Peppers

Serves 4

Chicken simmered with bell peppers and tomatoes, richly seasoned with chipotle peppers (smoked jalapeño peppers), and served over yellow rice—a low-fat dish that will satisfy the most demanding Mexican-food enthusiast.

1½ cups water
4 dried chipotle peppers (see Cook's Tip, page 339)
2 pounds chicken breast halves, skinned, all visible fat removed
Olive oil spray
2 cups chopped yellow onion (4 medium)
4 medium cloves garlic, minced, or 2 teaspoons bottled minced garlic
14.5-ounce can no-salt-added diced tomatoes
1 cup chopped green bell pepper
1½ teaspoons dried oregano, crumbled
1 cup uncooked rice
½ teaspoon powdered turmeric
½ teaspoon salt
1 to 2 teaspoons extra-virgin olive oil (optional)

Calories 318
Protein 22 g
Carbohydrates 50 g
Cholesterol 45 mg
Total Fat 3 g
Saturated 1 g
Polyunsaturated 1 g
Monounsaturated 1 g
Fiber 2 g
Sodium 344 mg

Pour water into a small saucepan and bring to a boil over high heat. Remove from heat. Add chipotle peppers and let stand for 30 minutes.

Meanwhile, rinse chicken and pat dry with paper towels. Spray a Dutch oven with olive oil spray. Put over medium-high heat for 1 minute. Add half the chicken, meaty side down, and brown for 5 minutes. Turn chicken and cook for 3 minutes. Transfer to a plate and set aside. Repeat with remaining chicken.

Add onion and garlic to any pan residue and cook for 5 to 7 minutes, or until golden brown, stirring occasionally. Remove from heat.

Drain chipotle peppers, reserving water. Remove and discard stems, seeds, and membranes from peppers. Put peppers and water in a food processor or blender and process until smooth.

Add pepper mixture, chicken and its juices, undrained tomatoes, bell pepper, and oregano to onion mixture. Bring to a boil over medium heat. Reduce heat and simmer, covered, for 20 minutes. Remove from heat. Put chicken on a plate and let cool slightly.

Meanwhile, prepare rice using package directions, omitting salt and margarine but adding turmeric.

When chicken is cool enough to handle, debone. Chop or shred chicken.

Put half the chicken and 1 cup tomato mixture in an airtight container. Refrigerate and reserve for Chipotle Chicken Wraps (see page 208).

Return remaining chicken to Dutch oven. Stir in salt. If necessary, reheat chicken, covered, over medium heat until heated through, stirring frequently. Remove from heat and stir in oil. Serve over rice.

Cook's Tip

This stew is even better if refrigerated overnight. It's a good dish to make on the weekend for a quick dinner (two if you also make the Chipotle Chicken Wraps) during the week. Just reheat the stew, add the oil, and serve over rice.

Chicken Curry in a Hurry

Serves 4

Serve this quick and easy hit over steamed rice or Rice Pilaf (see page 408). Offer small bowls of toppings such as sliced green onions or Cranberry Chutney (see page 428).

1 teaspoon acceptable vegetable oil

2 cups diced cooked chicken or turkey

½ pound fresh mushrooms, thinly sliced (2½ to 3 cups)

⅓ cup chopped onion

3 tablespoons all-purpose flour

1 cup water

1 cup finely chopped apple (Granny Smith preferred) (about 1 medium)

1 cup homemade Chicken Broth (see page 40 or use commercial low-sodium variety)

¾ cup fat-free milk

¼ cup snipped fresh parsley

1½ teaspoons curry powder

Heat oil in a large nonstick skillet over medium-high heat. Swirl to coat bottom. Sauté chicken, mushrooms, and onion until chicken is warm and vegetables are tender, 4 to 5 minutes. Transfer to a medium saucepan.

Put flour in a small jar with a tight-fitting lid. Add water and shake well to combine. Pour mixture into saucepan.

Stir in remaining ingredients. Bring to a boil over medium-high heat, stirring constantly. Reduce heat and simmer for 3 minutes, or until apple pieces are tender-crisp, stirring constantly.

Calories 207
Protein 21 g
Carbohydrates 15 g
Cholesterol 53 mg
Total Fat 6 g
- Saturated 2 g
- Polyunsaturated 2 g
- Monounsaturated 2 g

Fiber 2 g
Sodium 84 mg

Cook's Tip on Curry Powder

Make your own curry powder by mixing a half teaspoon each of cardamom, cinnamon, cloves, and turmeric, which gives curry powder its characteristic yellow color. Other spices commonly used are chiles, coriander, cumin, fennel seed, fenugreek, mace, nutmeg, red and black pepper, poppy and sesame seeds, saffron, and tamarind.

Caribbean Grilled Chicken Thighs

Serves 4

An important part of this delicious blend of flavors, bananas are easier to handle on the grill if they're slightly underripe.

MARINADE

⅔ cup pineapple juice

2 tablespoons minced onion

2 tablespoons fresh lime juice (1 to 2 medium limes)

1 tablespoon curry powder

1 tablespoon honey

¼ teaspoon salt

¼ teaspoon pepper

¼ teaspoon red hot-pepper sauce

4 skinless chicken thighs (about 6 ounces each), all visible fat removed

2 bananas, halved lengthwise and crosswise (8 pieces)

For marinade, combine all ingredients in a large airtight plastic bag.

Rinse thighs and pat dry with paper towels. Add thighs to bag. Seal and refrigerate for 2 to 12 hours, turning occasionally.

Preheat grill on medium.

Meanwhile, remove chicken from marinade. Pour marinade into a small saucepan and bring to a boil over high heat. Boil for 5 minutes; set aside.

Grill chicken on covered grill for about 20 minutes, turning occasionally.

Brush bananas generously with marinade; place on grill. Grill chicken and bananas for 10 to 15 minutes, or until chicken is tender, turning bananas once. Brush chicken and bananas with marinade before serving.

Calories 275
Protein 23 g
Carbohydrates 26 g
Cholesterol 79 mg
Total Fat 10 g
 Saturated 3 g
 Polyunsaturated 2 g
 Monounsaturated 4 g
Fiber 2 g
Sodium 228 mg

Slow-Cooker White Chili

Serves 6

Using bone-in chicken adds a savory quality to this cook-while-you-work dish. You can easily stretch the chili to serve more people by ladling it over rice.

CHILI

1 pound skinless chicken thighs, all visible fat removed

1 pound dried navy or Great Northern beans, sorted for stones or shriveled beans and rinsed (about 2¼ cups)

6 cups Chicken Broth (see page 40 or use commercial low-sodium variety)

2 4-ounce cans chopped green chiles, drained and rinsed

1 medium onion, chopped (½ cup)

4 medium cloves garlic, minced, or 2 teaspoons bottled minced garlic

1 fresh jalapeño, seeded (if desired) and minced (see Cook's Tip, page 115)

2 teaspoons ground cumin

2 teaspoons dried oregano, crumbled

⅛ to ¼ teaspoon ground cloves

¼ teaspoon cayenne

Salsa Cruda (see page 449 or use commercial low-sodium salsa) (optional)

Nonfat or light sour cream (optional)

Rinse chicken and pat dry with paper towels.

Put beans in a slow cooker and add chicken and remaining chili ingredients. Cook on high for 10 hours, or until beans and chicken are tender.

Remove and discard bones from chicken; return chicken to chili.

To serve, ladle chili into bowls and top with salsa and sour cream.

Calories 370
Protein 26 g
Carbohydrates 51 g
Cholesterol 35 mg
Total Fat 6 g
Saturated 1 g
Polyunsaturated 2 g
Monounsaturated 2 g
Fiber 12 g
Sodium 312 mg

Roasted Garlic-Lemon Turkey Breast

Serves 8

A highly aromatic marinade of garlic, lemon, rosemary, thyme, and parsley flavors this roasted turkey breast. Save half the cooked turkey to use in Turkey on a Bed of Sliced Tomatoes (see page 227).

3½-pound frozen half turkey breast with skin (ask butcher to cut)
Vegetable oil spray
2 tablespoons grated lemon zest (2 to 3 medium lemons)
¼ cup fresh lemon juice
3 tablespoons extra-virgin olive oil
6 medium cloves garlic, minced, or 1 tablespoon bottled minced garlic
1½ teaspoons Dijon mustard
¾ teaspoon dried rosemary, crushed
½ teaspoon dried thyme, crumbled
½ teaspoon salt
½ cup snipped fresh parsley

Thaw turkey breast half; rinse and pat dry with paper towels. Spray a large glass baking dish with vegetable oil spray. Put turkey in baking dish.

In a small bowl, whisk together remaining ingredients except parsley. Stir in parsley.

Gently loosen but don't remove turkey skin, creating a pocket. Being careful to not break skin, spoon parsley mixture as evenly as possible under skin. Gently pull skin over any exposed meat. Cover tightly with plastic wrap and refrigerate for 8 to 12 hours.

Preheat oven to 325° F.

Remove plastic wrap and bake turkey for about 1¾ hours, or until cooked through and juices run clear. Let stand on cooling rack for 15 minutes for easy carving. Remove and discard skin. Thinly slice turkey. Remove any remaining pieces of meat from rib.

Calories 238
Protein 41 g
Carbohydrates 2 g
Cholesterol 113 mg
Total Fat 6 g
Saturated 1 g
Polyunsaturated 1 g
Monounsaturated 4 g
Fiber 0 g
Sodium 243 mg

Turkey Fillets with Fresh Herbs

Serves 6

No more dry turkey! The buttermilk tenderizes the fillets and keeps them moist as they cook. Refrigerate any leftovers and serve slices of chilled turkey over your favorite salad greens.

1½ pounds skinless turkey fillets, about ¾ inch thick, all visible fat removed

MARINADE

2 cups nonfat or low-fat buttermilk

1 cup finely chopped onion (2 medium)

1 tablespoon finely chopped fresh dill

1 tablespoon finely chopped fresh tarragon

1 tablespoon finely chopped fresh cilantro

1 tablespoon finely chopped fresh rosemary

1 tablespoon acceptable vegetable oil

1 teaspoon pepper

¼ teaspoon salt

Rinse turkey fillets and pat dry.

In an airtight plastic bag, combine marinade ingredients.

Add turkey to marinade, turning to coat evenly. Seal and refrigerate for at least 1 to 12 hours, turning bag several times.

Preheat grill or broiler.

Remove turkey from marinade; discard marinade. Grill over medium-high heat for 4 to 5 minutes. Turn and grill for 4 to 5 minutes. Or broil about 6 inches from heat for 5 to 7 minutes. Turn and broil for 5 to 7 minutes. Turkey should be cooked through and no longer pink in center.

Calories 139
Protein 24 g
Carbohydrates 0 g
Cholesterol 62 mg
Total Fat 4 g
Saturated 1 g
Polyunsaturated 1 g
Monounsaturated 1 g
Fiber 0 g
Sodium 243 mg

Cook's Tip on Herbs

In most recipes, such as this one, you can substitute dried herbs for fresh, though the flavor won't be quite as good. The ratio is 1 teaspoon of dried herbs for 1 tablespoon of fresh herbs.

Turkey on a Bed of Sliced Tomatoes

Serves 4

Serve cooked turkey in a refreshingly simple salad of mixed greens and sweet red onions, tossed with a vinaigrette and prettily arranged on slices of vine-ripened tomatoes.

4 cups torn mixed greens or romaine

12 ounces oven-roasted turkey breast, cut into 1-inch pieces

⅓ cup thinly sliced red onion

2 teaspoons capers, rinsed and drained

DRESSING

3 tablespoons cider vinegar

2 tablespoons extra-virgin olive oil

1 medium clove garlic, minced, or ½ teaspoon bottled minced garlic

¼ teaspoon pepper

12 slices tomato

Pepper to taste

In a large bowl, combine greens, turkey, onion, and capers. In a small bowl, whisk together dressing ingredients until well blended. Stir into salad mixture.

To serve, arrange 3 tomato slices on each dinner plate, spoon salad on top, and sprinkle with pepper.

Cook's Tip on Capers

Capers are the flavorful flower buds of a prickly bush native to the Mediterranean and Asia. Found with the pickles and olives at the supermarket, capers most often are packed in brine. Always rinse them to remove excess salt before using. Cut larger capers in half if you wish.

Calories 203
Protein 27 g
Carbohydrates 6 g
Cholesterol 71 mg
Total Fat 8 g
Saturated 1 g
Polyunsaturated 1 g
Monounsaturated 5 g
Fiber 2 g
Sodium 96 mg

Turkey Rolls with Garden Pesto

Serves 4

If you have any turkey rolls left over, slice them for great sandwiches.

GARDEN PESTO

½ cup packed fresh basil leaves

1 small tomato, peeled, seeded, and chopped (⅓ cup)

1 tablespoon pine nuts, dry-roasted

1 large clove garlic, minced, or ¾ teaspoon bottled minced garlic

2 tablespoons grated Parmesan cheese

2 8-ounce turkey tenderloins, halved lengthwise

Vegetable oil spray

1 tablespoon honey

1 tablespoon very low sodium or low-sodium soy sauce

Preheat oven to 350° F.

For pesto, combine all ingredients except Parmesan in a food processor or blender. Process until nearly smooth. Stir in Parmesan.

Rinse turkey and pat dry with paper towels.

Spread 1 rounded tablespoon pesto mixture on a piece of turkey. Roll up from one short end. Repeat with remaining turkey. Set aside any remaining pesto.

Spray an 8-inch square baking pan with vegetable oil spray. Place turkey rolls seam side down in pan.

In a cup or small bowl, combine honey and soy sauce; brush on turkey rolls.

Bake 40 to 45 minutes, or until cooked through. Top turkey rolls with remaining pesto.

Calories 240
Protein 31 g
Carbohydrates 14 g
Cholesterol 65 mg
Total Fat 7 g
  Saturated 2 g
  Polyunsaturated 2 g
  Monounsaturated 2 g
Fiber 6 g
Sodium 251 mg

Cook's Tip on Peeling and Seeding Tomatoes

Plunge tomatoes into boiling water for 10 to 15 seconds, then into ice water for 1 minute. The skin will come off easily. Remove the cores and cut the tomatoes in half horizontally. With your fingers or a spoon, remove the seeds.

Southwestern Turkey Wraps

Serves 4

These wraps get their kick from salsa and Dijon mustard and give you an easy way to use leftover turkey.

3 ounces fat-free or light cream cheese, softened

2 tablespoons Salsa Cruda (see page 449) or low-sodium commercial salsa (see Cook's Tip, page 98)

2 tablespoons sliced green onion

1 teaspoon Dijon mustard

4 8-inch nonfat or low-fat flour tortillas (see Cook's Tip, page 27)

1⅓ cups shredded lettuce

6 ounces very thinly sliced or finely chopped roasted turkey breast, skin and all visible fat removed

¼ cup shredded nonfat or reduced-fat Cheddar cheese

4 strips red bell pepper, about ¼ inch wide

In a small bowl, combine cream cheese, salsa, green onion, and mustard, stirring well.

To assemble, spread 2 tablespoons mixture over each tortilla. Layer ⅓ cup lettuce, one fourth of the turkey, 1 tablespoon Cheddar, and 1 red pepper strip over cream cheese mixture. Roll to enclose filling.

Wrap tightly in plastic wrap and refrigerate for several hours or until serving time. To serve as appetizers, cut each tortilla roll into fourths.

Calories 177
Protein 22 g
Carbohydrates 20 g
Cholesterol 38 mg
Total Fat 1 g
Saturated 0 g
Polyunsaturated 0 g
Monounsaturated 0 g
Fiber 3 g
Sodium 445 mg

Swiss Garden Wraps

Serves 4

Wrap warm tortillas around leftover turkey and a salad for a new kind of sandwich.

2 tablespoons plain nonfat or low-fat yogurt

2½ teaspoons prepared mustard

¼ teaspoon honey

¼ teaspoon pepper

4 8-inch nonfat or low-fat flour tortillas, warmed (see Cook's Tip, page 27)

4 red leaf lettuce leaves

4 ounces thinly sliced roasted turkey breast, skin and all visible fat removed

4 1-ounce slices nonfat or reduced-fat Swiss cheese

½ cup finely chopped red onion

¼ medium peeled cucumber, cut into 8 thin slices and halved

2 medium Italian plum tomatoes, each cut lengthwise into 8 slices

Pepper to taste (optional)

In a small bowl, combine yogurt, mustard, honey, and pepper.

To assemble wraps, spread mixture evenly over tortillas. Top each with 1 lettuce leaf, 1 ounce turkey, 1 slice cheese, 2 tablespoons onion, 4 slices cucumber, and 4 slices tomato. Sprinkle with pepper. Fold sides of each tortilla to center, overlapping slightly; place seam side down on plate.

Cook's Tip on Tortillas

Warming tortillas makes them pliable and brings out the flavors. Wrap the tortillas in damp paper towels and microwave on 100 percent power (high) for 30 to 60 seconds. Or wrap them in aluminum foil and heat in a 325° F oven for 6 to 8 minutes.

Calories 193
Protein 21 g
Carbohydrates 23 g
Cholesterol 34 mg
Total Fat 2 g
- Saturated 1 g
- Polyunsaturated 0 g
- Monounsaturated 1 g

Fiber 3 g
Sodium 359 mg

Turkey Sausage Patties

Serves 8

For brunch, serve this tasty, low-fat meat with Drop Biscuits (see page 504) and Cranberry Chutney (see page 428). After you find out how good it is, you'll want to try it in sandwiches and even as a dinner entrée.

1 pound lean ground turkey breast, skin removed before grinding
¼ cup plain fine bread crumbs
1 tablespoon salt-free Italian herb seasoning
1¼ teaspoons dried coriander
1 teaspoon paprika
½ to ¾ teaspoon cayenne
½ teaspoon ground cumin
½ teaspoon garlic powder
¼ teaspoon pepper
¼ teaspoon salt
½ cup Chicken Broth (see page 40 or use commercial low-sodium variety)

In a large bowl, combine all ingredients except broth, stirring well.

Add chicken broth and stir again. Let stand for 15 minutes.

Form into 8 patties, about ¾ inch thick.

Heat a large nonstick skillet over medium heat. Cook patties for 7 to 8 minutes on each side, or until done.

Cook's Tip on Ground Turkey Breast

Select a piece of skinless turkey breast and ask the butcher to grind it. The ground turkey already in the meat case often contains skin.

Calories 84
Protein 15 g
Carbohydrates 3 g
Cholesterol 41 mg
Total Fat 1 g
Saturated 0 g
Polyunsaturated 0 g
Monounsaturated 0 g
Fiber 0 g
Sodium 129 mg

Turkey Lasagna

Serves 9

You won't need to worry about what to take to potluck dinners with this recipe in your repertoire. Your friends will love the taste and will be happy that you brought something healthful.

Vegetable oil spray
8-ounce package lasagna noodles
1 pound lean ground turkey breast, skin removed before grinding
8 ounces fresh mushrooms, sliced (2½ to 3 cups)
½ cup chopped onion (1 medium)
3 medium cloves garlic, minced, or 1½ teaspoons bottled minced garlic
3 cups no-salt-added tomato sauce
2 teaspoons dried basil, crumbled
½ teaspoon dried oregano, crumbled
Pepper to taste
10-ounce package frozen no-salt-added chopped spinach, thawed and squeezed dry
16 ounces nonfat or low-fat cottage cheese (2 cups)
Dash of nutmeg
8 ounces part-skim mozzarella cheese, grated (2 cups)

Calories 287
Protein 32 g
Carbohydrates 28 g
Cholesterol 54 mg
Total Fat 5 g
Saturated 3 g
Polyunsaturated 0 g
Monounsaturated 1 g
Fiber 3 g
Sodium 342 mg

Preheat oven to 375° F. Lightly spray a 13 × 9 × 2-inch baking dish with vegetable oil spray.

Cook noodles using package directions, omitting salt and oil.

Meanwhile, in a large nonstick skillet over medium-high heat, combine turkey, mushrooms, onion, and garlic. Sauté until turkey is no longer pink, 8 to 10 minutes, stirring occasionally.

Cover skillet and cook over low heat until mushrooms have released their juices, 3 to 4 minutes. Uncover and cook over high heat until juices evaporate, 2 to 3 minutes.

Stir in tomato sauce, basil, oregano, and pepper. Reduce heat to low and heat through, 5 to 6 minutes.

In a large bowl, combine spinach, cottage cheese, and nutmeg, stirring well.

Arrange one third of cooked noodles in baking dish; add one half of spinach mixture, one third of turkey mixture, and one third of mozzarella. Repeat layers. Finish with remaining noodles, turkey mixture, and mozzarella. Cover dish with aluminum foil.

Bake for 35 to 40 minutes, or until casserole is thoroughly heated and mozzarella has melted.

Turkey Loaf

Serves 8

This meat loaf substitute is so moist that you'll gobble it up! Try it with Spinach-Chayote Salad with Orange Vinaigrette (see page 76).

Vegetable oil spray (optional)
4 slices whole-wheat bread
¼ cup fat-free milk
2 pounds lean ground turkey breast, skin removed before grinding
1 cup grated or finely chopped onion (2 medium onions)
1 cup canned no-salt-added stewed tomatoes, crushed
½ cup diced celery (1 medium rib)
½ cup chopped red bell pepper
Egg substitute equivalent to 2 eggs, or 2 eggs
¼ cup minced fresh parsley
1 teaspoon seeded and finely minced fresh jalapeño pepper, or to taste (see Cook's Tip, page 115)
¼ teaspoon salt
¼ teaspoon pepper
2 tablespoons no-salt-added ketchup

Preheat oven to 350° F. Lightly spray a 10½ × 5½ × 2½-inch loaf pan with vegetable oil spray, or use a nonstick loaf pan.

Put bread in a food processor or blender and process into fine crumbs.

In a shallow bowl, combine bread crumbs and milk. Let crumbs soak for 5 minutes.

In a large bowl, combine remaining ingredients except ketchup. Stir lightly.

Drain bread and squeeze out any excess milk to form a paste. Add to turkey mixture and blend well. Spoon into loaf pan and spread ketchup over loaf.

Bake, uncovered, for about 1½ hours. Let stand 5 to 10 minutes before serving.

Calories 204
Protein 34 g
Carbohydrates 12 g
Cholesterol 82 mg
Total Fat 2 g
  Saturated 0 g
  Polyunsaturated 1 g
  Monounsaturated 1 g
Fiber 2 g
Sodium 244 mg

Porcupine Meatballs

Serves 5

Use ground turkey and brown rice to update this longtime favorite.

Vegetable oil spray

1 pound lean ground turkey breast, skin removed before grinding

1 cup cooked brown rice (¼ to ⅓ cup uncooked)

¼ cup chopped onion

1 teaspoon salt-free Italian herb seasoning

1 teaspoon acceptable vegetable oil

¼ teaspoon pepper

2 cups no-salt-added tomato juice or mixed-vegetable juice

½ cup chopped green bell pepper

½ teaspoon chili powder

Preheat broiler. Lightly spray broiler pan and rack with vegetable oil spray.

In a large bowl, combine turkey, rice, onion, Italian herb seasoning, oil, and pepper, stirring well. Shape into fifteen 1-inch balls and put on broiler rack.

Broil about 6 inches from heat, turning meatballs occasionally until browned evenly on all sides, 6 to 8 minutes.

In a medium saucepan, combine remaining ingredients. Bring to a boil over medium-high heat.

Add meatballs. Reduce heat and simmer, covered, for 20 minutes, stirring occasionally.

Cook's Tip on Shaping Meatballs

To help make your meatballs uniform in size and shape, use the large end of a melon baller. Scoop out balls of mixture, using your other hand to round the tops.

Calories 180
Protein 26 g
Carbohydrates 14 g
Cholesterol 66 mg
Total Fat 2 g
- Saturated 0 g
- Polyunsaturated 1 g
- Monounsaturated 0 g

Fiber 2 g
Sodium 56 mg

Stuffed Cornish Hens with Orange-Brandy Sauce

Serves 12

Petite Cornish hens get four-star treatment with rice stuffing and brandied orange sections.

Vegetable oil spray

STUFFING

1⅓ cups uncooked long grain and wild rice combination or 1 package wild rice mix, uncooked

1 teaspoon light margarine

1 medium onion, chopped (½ cup)

1 teaspoon dried sage, thyme, savory, or tarragon, crumbled

6 Cornish hens (about 14 ounces each), all visible fat, tails, and giblets removed

Vegetable oil spray

½ cup Chicken Broth (see page 40 or use commercial low-sodium variety)

SAUCE

½ cup water

1 cup orange sections (1 to 2 medium)

¼ cup brandy

Calories 248
Protein 28 g
Carbohydrates 19 g
Cholesterol 117 mg
Total Fat 5 g
Saturated 1 g
Polyunsaturated 1 g
Monounsaturated 1 g
Fiber 1 g
Sodium 74 mg

Preheat oven to 350° F. Lightly spray roasting pan and cooking rack(s) with vegetable oil spray.

For stuffing, cook rice until still slightly firm, using package directions, omitting salt, margarine, and seasoning packet.

In a large skillet over medium-high heat, melt margarine. Sauté onion until lightly browned, 3 to 4 minutes.

Stir in rice and sage. Remove from heat.

Rinse hens and pat dry with paper towels. Stuff lightly with rice mixture. Skewer or sew cavities closed.

Spray hens with vegetable oil spray and put breast side up on rack in roasting pan.

Roast, uncovered, basting occasionally with broth, for about 1 hour, or until hens are done.

Remove hens from pan. Cut in half (kitchen scissors work well), remove skin, and place hens on serving platter.

For sauce, heat roasting pan, with juices, over medium-high heat. Add water to drippings, stirring to dislodge browned particles from pan.

Add orange sections and brandy. Cook for 2 minutes, stirring constantly. Serve sauce over hens or on the side.

Cook's Tip on Savory

Native to the Mediterranean area, savory is an herb belonging to the mint family. Among the varieties are summer savory and winter savory, which is more pungent. Look for dried savory with the spices in the supermarket. To buy fresh savory, you may have to go to a specialty produce market. Use savory in poultry stuffings and dressings, in soups, and with ground beef and vegetables.

Cook's Tip on Sewing Poultry

Keep stuffing moist in any kind of poultry by skewering or sewing the cavity. Pull it closed and weave a sharp, thin metal or wooden skewer into the skin at the sides of the cavity. (If using wooden skewers, be sure to soak them in cold water for at least 10 minutes first.) If you prefer, buy a large-eyed sewing needle at a craft or carpet store and thread it with thin kitchen twine. Sew the cavity closed.

Cornish Hens Provence Style

Serves 4

You'll be amazed at how moist and tender a clay cooker keeps these hens. No clay cooker? You can use a roaster instead.

2 Cornish game hens (about 14 ounces each), all visible fat, tails, and giblets removed
½ teaspoon dried basil, crumbled
½ teaspoon dried thyme, crumbled
½ teaspoon salt
½ teaspoon pepper
½ pound boiling onions
8 medium cloves garlic, unpeeled
4 large sprigs of parsley
½ pound small red potatoes, cut in half
1 medium onion, sliced and separated into rings
¼ teaspoon salt-free all-purpose seasoning
½ teaspoon pepper
¼ teaspoon dried herbes de Provence or other dried herbs (see Cook's Tip on Herbes de Provence, page 244), crumbled
1 cup dry white wine (regular or nonalcoholic)

Soak a clay cooker in cold water for 15 minutes.

Meanwhile, rinse hens and pat dry with paper towels. Season inside and out with basil, thyme, salt, and ½ teaspoon pepper.

Stuff hens with boiling onions, garlic, and parsley. Put in clay cooker.

Put potatoes and onion rings around hens.

Sprinkle all-purpose seasoning, ½ teaspoon pepper, and herbes de Provence over hens and vegetables.

Pour wine into clay cooker.

If using an electric oven, put clay cooker in cold oven and set temperature to 450° F. Bake for 1¼ hours, or until done. Hens are done when juices from pierced thigh run clear.

If using a gas oven, put clay cooker in cold oven and set temperature to 300° F. Increase temperature 50 degrees every 10 minutes until temperature reaches 450° F. Cook for 1½ hours, or until done.

Calories 250
Protein 27 g
Carbohydrates 15 g
Cholesterol 117 mg
Total Fat 4 g
Saturated 1 g
Polyunsaturated 1 g
Monounsaturated 1 g
Fiber 2 g
Sodium 368 mg

Discard stuffing. Cut hens in half (kitchen scissors work well), remove skin, and serve hens with vegetables.

Optional Cooking Method

Instead of using a clay cooker, you can cook hens, covered, in a heavy roaster at 350° F for 45 to 50 minutes. Uncover and cook for 5 to 10 minutes longer to brown.

MEATS

Pot Roast Ratatouille and Pasta
Fillet of Beef with Herbes de Provence
Pepper-Coated Steak
Rosemary-Sage Steak
Grilled Lemongrass Flank Steak
Steak Marinated in Beer and Green Onions
Smothered Steak with Sangría Sauce
Beef Stroganoff
Portobello Mushrooms and Sirloin Strips over Spinach Pasta
Beef Skillet Oriental
Sukiyaki
Braised Sirloin Tips
Italian Beef Kebabs
Savory Beef Stew
Shredded Beef Soft Tacos
Philadelphia-Style Cheese Steak Wrap
Salisbury Steaks with Mushroom Sauce
Beef Bourguignon
Beef and Pasta Skillet
Glazed Meatballs on Water Chestnut and Bell Pepper Rice
Shepherd's Pie
Tamale Pie
Spaghetti with Meat Sauce
Beef Tostadas
Chili
Bowl of Red
Crustless Ham and Spinach Tart
New Orleans Muffaletta Wrap
Ham Roll-Ups
Bayou Red Beans and Rice
Savory Black-Eyed Peas and Pasta
Ham and Rice Croquettes
Herb-Rubbed Pork Tenderloin with Dijon-Apricot Mop Sauce
Marinated Pork Tenderloin
Orange Pork Medallions
Pork with Spiced Sauerkraut
Sweet-and-Sour Pork
Scaloppine al Limone
Veal Stufino
Osso Buco
Veal with Bell Peppers and Mushrooms
Venison Stew
Lamb Chops Dijon
Lamb Kebabs
Armenian Lamb Casserole
Lamb Stew

Pot Roast Ratatouille and Pasta

Serves 8

You still can serve beef worthy of a special occasion and do your health a favor, as this dish proves. Choose any pasta variety—from angel hair to shells to penne—for this excellent dish.

1½ pounds eye-of-round roast, all visible fat removed

½ teaspoon salt-free all-purpose seasoning

¼ teaspoon pepper

Olive oil spray

2 cups chopped eggplant (about 10 ounces)

2 cups sliced zucchini (2 medium)

5 medium Italian plum tomatoes, chopped

10¾-ounce can no-salt-added tomato puree

1 cup chopped onion (Spanish preferred) (2 medium)

1 cup sliced celery (2 medium ribs)

1 teaspoon dried oregano or salt-free dried Italian seasoning, crumbled

1 medium clove garlic, minced, or ½ teaspoon bottled minced garlic

1 bay leaf

¼ teaspoon dried basil, crumbled

8 ounces dried pasta

Preheat oven to 350° F.

Sprinkle meat with all-purpose seasoning and pepper.

Spray a Dutch oven with olive oil spray. Cook roast over medium-high heat for 10 minutes, or until brown on all sides.

Add remaining ingredients except pasta, stirring well.

Bake, covered, for 2½ hours, or until roast is very tender.

Prepare pasta using package directions, omitting salt and oil; drain well.

Meanwhile, remove roast from sauce. Slice thinly across grain, then slice into thin strips. Remove and discard bay leaf from sauce.

To serve, put roast on pasta and top with sauce.

Calories 277
Protein 27 g
Carbohydrates 34 g
Cholesterol 45 mg
Total Fat 4 g
  Saturated 1 g
  Polyunsaturated 0 g
  Monounsaturated 2 g
Fiber 4 g
Sodium 76 mg

Fillet of Beef with Herbes de Provence

Serves 6

Freshly ground black pepper, herbes de Provence, and a good measure of garlic flavor this tender cut of beef. Very easy and elegant—excellent for company.

1½ pounds beef tenderloin, all visible fat removed

3 medium cloves garlic, minced, or 1½ teaspoons bottled minced garlic

2 teaspoons dried herbes de Provence or mixed dried herbs, crumbled (see Cook's Tip on Herbes de Provence, below)

1 teaspoon pepper, or to taste

Olive oil spray

2 medium carrots, finely diced

1 medium onion, sliced

¼ teaspoon salt

Sprigs of fresh parsley (optional)

Calories 177
Protein 19 g
Carbohydrates 5 g
Cholesterol 57 mg
Total Fat 9 g
Saturated 4 g
Polyunsaturated 0 g
Monounsaturated 4 g
Fiber 1 g
Sodium 154 mg

Preheat oven to 400° F.

Tie meat in three or four places with kitchen twine. Rub garlic all over meat, then sprinkle with herbes de Provence and pepper. Put in a heavy nonstick roasting pan. Spray roast with olive oil spray.

Scatter carrots and onions around meat.

Cook, uncovered, for 25 to 30 minutes per pound for medium-rare. Remove from oven and sprinkle with salt.

Cover with aluminum foil and let stand for 10 to 15 minutes. Slice and garnish with parsley.

Cook's Tip on Herbes de Provence

Herbes de Provence is a combination of herbs used quite frequently in southern France: basil, thyme, rosemary, marjoram, sage, and lavender. If you don't have herbes de Provence, use a combination of at least two of these, blended in equal amounts.

Pepper-Coated Steak

Serves 4

In France, where it's called boeuf au poivre, *this steak is typically served with skillet-fried potatoes. For a more healthful option, choose one of the potato dishes you'll find in this cookbook (see pages 397–400) and Hot and Spicy Watercress and Romaine Salad (see page 73).*

4 small beef tenderloin steaks (about 1 pound), all visible fat removed
2 teaspoons coarsely cracked black pepper
Vegetable oil spray
¼ cup brandy or unsweetened apple juice
5-ounce can fat-free evaporated milk

Sprinkle both sides of meat with pepper, pressing it into meat's surface.

Spray a large skillet with vegetable oil spray. Heat over medium-high heat. Cook meat for 5 minutes. Turn and cook for 3 to 5 minutes, or until desired doneness. Remove meat from skillet; cover with aluminum foil to keep warm. Remove pan from heat and let cool for 1 minute.

Reduce heat to low. Gradually pour brandy into skillet. Cook for 1 minute, stirring to scrape up browned bits.

Stir in milk. Bring to a boil over high heat. Reduce heat and simmer for 2 to 3 minutes, or until thickened, stirring frequently. Pour over steaks.

Cook's Tip on Peppercorns

If you don't have a pepper mill, you can buy pepper already coarsely ground or use a mortar and pestle to crack whole peppercorns.

Calories 220
Protein 21 g
Carbohydrates 5 g
Cholesterol 58 mg
Total Fat 9 g
  Saturated 4 g
  Polyunsaturated 0 g
  Monounsaturated 5 g
Fiber 0 g
Sodium 83 mg

Rosemary-Sage Steak

Serves 8

Have a meat-and-potatoes dinner with this herb-flavored steak, Rustic Potato Patties (see page 399), and tossed salad.

2 pounds boneless top sirloin steak, all visible fat removed

MARINADE

½ cup chopped onion (1 medium)

¼ cup fresh lemon juice (1 to 2 medium lemons)

3 tablespoons dry white wine (regular or nonalcoholic)

2 tablespoons finely chopped fresh rosemary or 2 teaspoons dried, crushed

2 tablespoons finely chopped fresh sage or 2 teaspoons dried

1 tablespoon Dijon mustard

3 medium cloves garlic, minced, or 1½ teaspoons bottled minced garlic

1 teaspoon olive oil

½ teaspoon pepper

¼ teaspoon salt

Put steak in an airtight plastic bag.

In a small bowl, combine marinade ingredients. Pour over steak and turn to coat evenly. Seal and refrigerate for 1 to 24 hours, turning occasionally.

Preheat grill on medium-high.

Drain steak, then grill for 8 to 12 minutes per side, or until desired doneness.

Calories 164
Protein 25 g
Carbohydrates 0 g
Cholesterol 75 mg
Total Fat 6 g
Saturated 3 g
Polyunsaturated 0 g
Monounsaturated 3 g
Fiber 0 g
Sodium 176 mg

Cook's Tip on Fresh Rosemary

For a real taste treat, save woody, more mature rosemary stems to use as skewers. Strip the leaves to use in recipes such as this one. With a sharp object—a wooden or thin metal skewer works well—poke a hole through the foods you'll use for your kebabs. Thread the rosemary stem through the foods and grill or broil as usual. Try this tip soon with Italian Beef Kebabs or Lamb Kebabs (see pages 257 and 299).

Grilled Lemongrass Flank Steak

Serves 4

Flank steak is marinated in a fragrant lemongrass mixture that also spotlights delicate rice vinegar and zesty chili garlic sauce. Serve four people tonight and refrigerate the extra two servings to use in Grilled Flank Steak Salad with Sweet-and-Sour Sesame Dressing *(see page 116)* *later in the week.*

MARINADE

3 stalks lemongrass (see Cook's Tip, page 180)

⅓ cup rice vinegar

3 medium cloves garlic, minced, or 1½ teaspoons bottled minced garlic

1 teaspoon chili garlic sauce

1 teaspoon light soy sauce

1 teaspoon acceptable vegetable oil

1½ pounds beef flank steak, all visible fat removed

Remove outer leaf of lemongrass. With a sharp knife, slice bottom 6 to 8 inches of lemongrass crosswise into ¼-inch pieces. Put sliced lemongrass and remaining marinade ingredients in an airtight plastic bag.

Add meat, turning to coat. Seal and refrigerate for 2 to 12 hours, turning occasionally.

Preheat grill on medium-high.

Remove meat from marinade; discard marinade. Grill for 8 to 9 minutes on each side for medium-rare. Let stand for 5 minutes, then thinly slice across grain. Refrigerate 6 to 8 ounces of meat in an airtight plastic bag for another use.

Cook's Tip on Chili Garlic Sauce

Not surprisingly, chili garlic sauce is made of pureed chiles and garlic. Look for it in the Asian section of the grocery store and in Asian markets. This sauce heightens the flavor of such dishes as soups, stir-fries, and dipping sauces.

Calories 181
Protein 24 g
Carbohydrates 0 g
Cholesterol 59 mg
Total Fat 9 g
- Saturated 4 g
- Polyunsaturated 0 g
- Monounsaturated 4 g

Fiber 0 g
Sodium 136 mg

Steak Marinated in Beer and Green Onions

Serves 8

Many Asian hosts serve beer rather than wine for special meals. It's no wonder then that beer is often used in recipes, too. You'll savor each juicy bite of this Asian-flavored steak.

2 pounds boneless top sirloin steak, all visible fat removed

MARINADE

1½ cups light beer (regular or nonalcoholic) (12 ounces)

4 green onions, minced

2 tablespoons light brown sugar

2 tablespoons dry sherry

1 tablespoon grated fresh gingerroot

1 tablespoon light soy sauce

2 medium cloves garlic, minced, or 1 teaspoon bottled minced garlic

1 teaspoon crushed red pepper flakes

1 teaspoon acceptable vegetable oil

Dash of red hot-pepper oil

Put steak in an airtight plastic bag.

In a medium bowl, combine marinade ingredients. Pour over steak and turn to coat evenly. Seal and refrigerate for 1 to 24 hours, turning occasionally.

Preheat grill on medium-high.

Drain steak, then grill for 8 to 12 minutes per side, or until desired doneness.

Calories 164
Protein 25 g
Carbohydrates 0 g
Cholesterol 75 mg
Total Fat 6 g
Saturated 3 g
Polyunsaturated 0 g
Monounsaturated 3 g
Fiber 0 g
Sodium 121 mg

Smothered Steak with Sangría Sauce

Serves 4

Different and easy, this dish is great for company. Serve it over rice or pasta so you can enjoy all the sauce.

SANGRÍA SAUCE
1 cup sangría (white preferred)
1 medium tomato, chopped (¾ cup)
¾ cup chopped green bell pepper
¼ cup golden raisins
¼ cup dried apricots
1 large bay leaf
1 teaspoon dried basil, crumbled
½ teaspoon dried thyme, crumbled
Pepper to taste

Vegetable oil spray
4 wafer-thin slices boneless round steak (about 4 ounces each), all visible fat removed

In a medium bowl, combine sauce ingredients, stirring well.

Spray a large nonstick skillet with vegetable oil spray. Heat skillet over medium-high heat. Brown meat for 2 to 3 minutes per side.

Pour sauce into skillet. Reduce heat and simmer, covered, for 40 minutes, or until meat is tender. Discard bay leaf.

Time-Saver: Use cube steaks instead of round steak and reduce simmering time to 20 to 25 minutes.

Calories 284
Protein 32 g
Carbohydrates 23 g
Cholesterol 76 mg
Total Fat 4 g
Saturated 2 g
Polyunsaturated 0 g
Monounsaturated 2 g
Fiber 1 g
Sodium 47 mg

Beef Stroganoff

Serves 6

Serve this old favorite over noodles or rice. Fresh Green Beans with Water Chestnuts (see page 357) offers a nice crunch and a color contrast to complete the meal.

1 pound beef tenderloin, boneless round steak, or boneless sirloin, all visible fat removed

½ teaspoon pepper, or to taste

1 teaspoon acceptable vegetable oil

½ pound fresh mushrooms, sliced (2½ to 3 cups)

1 medium onion, sliced

2 tablespoons all-purpose flour

2 cups Beef Broth (see page 39 or use commercial low-sodium variety)

2 tablespoons no-salt-added tomato paste

2 tablespoons dry sherry

1 teaspoon dry mustard

¼ teaspoon dried oregano, crumbled

¼ teaspoon dried dillweed, crumbled

⅓ cup nonfat or light sour cream

Put meat in freezer for 30 minutes for easier slicing. Slice meat into thin strips about 2 inches long. Sprinkle with pepper.

Heat oil in a large, heavy skillet over medium-high heat, swirling to coat bottom. Sauté mushrooms until tender, 2 to 3 minutes. Transfer to a plate.

Sauté onion in same skillet until brown, 3 to 4 minutes. Add to mushrooms.

Add meat to skillet and brown quickly on all sides until rare, 2 to 3 minutes for tenderloin, 3 to 5 minutes for round steak or sirloin. Add to mushrooms.

Add flour to skillet. Gradually pour in broth, whisking constantly. Cook over medium-high heat for 2 to 3 minutes, or until thickened, whisking constantly. Reduce heat to low.

Whisk in remaining ingredients except sour cream.

Stir in mushrooms, onions, and meat. Cook for 15 minutes.

Calories 162
Protein 14 g
Carbohydrates 9 g
Cholesterol 38 mg
Total Fat 7 g
- Saturated 3 g
- Polyunsaturated 1 g
- Monounsaturated 3 g

Fiber 1 g
Sodium 47 mg

Put sour cream in a small bowl. Stir in a small amount of meat mixture. Add sour cream mixture to skillet and cook for 5 minutes, or until heated through, stirring occasionally.

Cook's Tip on Reducing the Sodium in Canned Broth

If you don't want to make your own broth and can't find the canned low-sodium variety, replace a little more than half the low-sodium broth called for with regular broth and use water for the rest.

Portobello Mushrooms and Sirloin Strips over Spinach Pasta

Serves 4

Beef and robust, beefy-tasting portobello mushrooms, both marinated in red wine and seasonings, make a terrific combination.

MARINADE

⅓ cup burgundy, other dry red wine, or nonalcoholic red wine

3 tablespoons light soy sauce

3 tablespoons very low sodium or low-sodium Worcestershire sauce

6 medium cloves garlic, minced, or 1 tablespoon bottled minced garlic

2 teaspoons extra-virgin olive oil

1½ teaspoons dried oregano, crumbled

12 ounces portobello mushrooms, sliced

12 ounces top sirloin, all visible fat removed, cut into thin strips

8 ounces dried spinach fettuccine

Olive oil spray

Calories 378
Protein 30 g
Carbohydrates 45 g
Cholesterol 57 mg
Total Fat 8 g
Saturated 2 g
Polyunsaturated 1 g
Monounsaturated 4 g
Fiber 8 g
Sodium 468 mg

Combine marinade ingredients in an airtight plastic bag. Add mushrooms and beef and turn to coat thoroughly. Seal and refrigerate for 30 minutes, turning bag frequently.

Cook pasta using package directions, omitting salt and oil.

Spray a large nonstick skillet with olive oil spray. Heat over medium-high heat for 1 minute. Using a slotted spoon, transfer half the beef mixture to skillet. Cook for 4 minutes, or until meat is no longer pink, stirring frequently. Put on a plate and set aside. Repeat with remaining beef mixture, reserving all marinade and leaving beef mixture in skillet.

Return reserved beef mixture with juices to skillet and add marinade. Increase heat to high and cook for 1 minute, stirring gently. Remove from heat. To serve, spoon beef mixture and sauce over pasta.

Beef Skillet Oriental

Serves 8

A bed of white rice contrasts nicely with the dark beef and green snow peas in this dish.

1 pound flank steak, all visible fat removed

Vegetable oil spray

1 teaspoon acceptable vegetable oil

½ cup chopped onion (1 medium)

3 medium cloves garlic, minced, or 1½ teaspoons bottled minced garlic

4 cups small fresh cauliflower florets (about 1 medium head)

2 cups Beef Broth (see page 39 or use commercial low-sodium variety)

1¾ cups diced red bell pepper (about 2 medium)

6 ounces fresh snow peas, trimmed

¼ cup cold water

¼ cup dry sherry

2 tablespoons cornstarch

2 tablespoons light soy sauce

1 tablespoon grated fresh gingerroot

¼ teaspoon red hot-pepper sauce

Put flank steak in freezer for 30 minutes for easier slicing. Slice across grain into strips 2 to 3 inches long and ½ to 1 inch wide.

Heat a nonstick electric skillet to 400° F. Spray skillet with vegetable oil spray. Or spray a large nonstick skillet with vegetable oil spray and heat over medium-high heat.

Add half the beef and stir-fry just until browned, 3 to 4 minutes. Remove and set aside. Repeat with remaining beef.

Heat oil in skillet, swirling to coat bottom. Sauté onion and garlic until onion is translucent, 2 to 3 minutes.

Add cauliflower and broth. Cook for 2 minutes, stirring occasionally. Add bell pepper and snow peas. Cook for 1 minute.

In a small bowl, whisk together remaining ingredients. Pour into skillet.

Add beef and cook for 2 to 3 minutes, or until sauce thickens.

Calories 135
Protein 12 g
Carbohydrates 9 g
Cholesterol 24 mg
Total Fat 5 g
Saturated 2 g
Polyunsaturated 1 g
Monounsaturated 2 g
Fiber 2 g
Sodium 167 mg

Sukiyaki

Serves 10

For a fun meal, cook this Japanese dish at the table. Traditional preparation keeps each vegetable separate as you cook it. For full flavor, coat each vegetable mound with broth while cooking.

2 pounds beef tenderloin or boneless sirloin steak, all visible fat removed

2 cups uncooked rice

½ cup Beef Broth (see page 39 or use commercial low-sodium variety)

½ cup dry sherry

2 tablespoons light brown sugar

2 tablespoons light soy sauce

2 teaspoons grated fresh gingerroot

1 teaspoon hot-pepper oil

½ teaspoon pepper

1 cup diagonally sliced green onions (about 9)

1 cup diagonally sliced celery (about 2 ribs)

8-ounce can water chestnuts, drained and thinly sliced

1 cup thinly sliced fresh mushrooms, any variety (about 4 ounces)

8-ounce can bamboo shoots, drained and slivered

1 pound fresh bean sprouts (3 to 4 cups)

4 cups fresh spinach leaves, stems removed (6 to 7 ounces)

1 teaspoon acceptable vegetable oil

Calories 361
Protein 22 g
Carbohydrates 46 g
Cholesterol 46 mg
Total Fat 9 g
Saturated 3 g
Polyunsaturated 1 g
Monounsaturated 4 g
Fiber 4 g
Sodium 212 mg

Put meat in freezer for 30 minutes for easier slicing. Slice across grain into strips 2 to 3 inches long and ½ to 1 inch wide. Set aside.

Cook rice using package directions, omitting salt and margarine.

Meanwhile, in a small bowl, whisk together broth, sherry, brown sugar, soy sauce, gingerroot, hot-pepper oil, and pepper. Put bowl on large platter or tray.

Arrange remaining ingredients except oil in separate piles on platter.

Heat a large nonstick electric skillet to 350° F, or heat a large nonstick skillet over medium-high heat. Heat vegetable oil, then sauté meat for 3 to 4 minutes, or until browned.

Add broth mixture and stir to coat meat. Push meat to side of pan.

When sauce begins to bubble, add green onions and celery in separate piles. If using stovetop, increase heat to high. Stir each pile gently for about 1 minute, then push each aside.

Add water chestnuts and mushrooms in separate piles. Cook, stirring each constantly, for 1 minute, or just until heated. Push each pile aside.

Add bamboo shoots, bean sprouts, and spinach in separate piles. Cook, stirring each gently, for 2 minutes, or just until thoroughly heated. If skillet becomes too crowded, transfer some piles of cooked food to a plate; return them to skillet before serving.

Serve immediately with rice.

Cook's Tip on Stir-Frying

The trick in stir-frying is to have all the ingredients ready before you start to cook. You'll need to move quickly and won't have time to stop and measure an ingredient.

Cook's Tip on Fresh Bean Sprouts

Choose bean sprouts, grown from green mung peas, that are crisp and fresh. They should feel dry to the touch, not slimy. Store them in a plastic bag in the refrigerator for up to 3 days. Rinse, drain, and pat dry just before using. If cooking bean sprouts, remember that they'll lose their crispness if heated for more than a minute.

Braised Sirloin Tips

Serves 8

For a real treat, try this dish with Rice Pilaf (see page 408) or Wild Rice with Mushrooms (see page 409).

Vegetable oil spray

2 pounds sirloin tip, all visible fat removed, cubed

¼ teaspoon pepper

½ cup finely chopped onion (1 medium)

2 medium cloves garlic, minced, or 1 teaspoon bottled minced garlic

1¼ cups Beef Broth (see page 39 or use commercial low-sodium variety)

⅓ cup dry red wine (regular or nonalcoholic)

1 tablespoon light soy sauce

2 tablespoons cornstarch

¼ cup cold water

¼ cup snipped fresh parsley

Spray a large nonstick skillet with vegetable oil spray. Heat over medium-high heat.

Sprinkle meat with pepper. Cook meat until well browned, on all sides, 8 to 10 minutes, turning often.

Add onion and garlic and cook until onion is translucent, 2 to 3 minutes.

Add broth, wine, and soy sauce and heat to boiling. Reduce heat and simmer, covered, for 1½ hours, or until meat is tender.

Put cornstarch in a cup or small bowl. Add water, stirring to dissolve. Slowly pour mixture into skillet, stirring constantly. Increase heat to medium-high. Cook until gravy thickens, 2 to 3 minutes, stirring constantly.

Sprinkle with parsley.

Calories 175
Protein 20 g
Carbohydrates 3 g
Cholesterol 60 mg
Total Fat 8 g
Saturated 3 g
Polyunsaturated 0 g
Monounsaturated 4 g
Fiber 0 g
Sodium 110 mg

Italian Beef Kebabs

Serves 8

Get your guests in on the fun by letting them thread their own skewers.

MARINADE

1 medium onion, finely chopped (about ½ cup)

¾ cup dry red wine (regular or nonalcoholic)

2 tablespoons fat-free or low-fat Italian salad dressing

¼ cup very low sodium or low-sodium Worcestershire sauce

2 tablespoons light soy sauce

1 teaspoon dried thyme, crumbled

1 teaspoon dried rosemary, crushed

1 teaspoon acceptable vegetable oil

½ teaspoon pepper

1½ pounds sirloin tip, all visible fat removed, cut into 16 cubes

1 quart water

8 red potatoes (about 2-inch diameter), cut in half

8 boiling onions (about 1-inch diameter), outer skin removed

16 medium fresh mushrooms

16 large cherry tomatoes

1 large green bell pepper, cut into 16 squares

2 tablespoons fat-free or low-fat Italian salad dressing

Pour marinade ingredients into an airtight plastic bag. Add beef and turn to coat. Refrigerate for about 8 hours. Drain and discard marinade.

Soak 8 wooden skewers in cold water for at least 10 minutes before using.

In a medium saucepan, bring water to a boil over high heat. Parboil potatoes for 3 minutes.

Add onions and cook for 1½ minutes. Rinse vegetables under cold water. Cut onions in half.

Preheat grill on medium-high or preheat broiler.

On each skewer, thread in order meat cube, potato half, onion, mushroom, cherry tomato, meat cube, potato half, bell pepper square, mushroom, and cherry tomato.

Grill or broil 3 to 4 inches from heat for 12 to 15 minutes. Turn and baste often.

Calories 245
Protein 18 g
Carbohydrates 35 g
Cholesterol 41 mg
Total Fat 4 g
Saturated 2 g
Polyunsaturated 0 g
Monounsaturated 2 g
Fiber 4 g
Sodium 226 mg

Savory Beef Stew

Serves 12

This exciting array of seasonings makes for an interesting stew. Try Drop Biscuits (see page 504) with it.

Vegetable oil spray

2½ pounds eye-of-round roast, all visible fat removed, cut into bite-size pieces

Vegetable oil spray

1 teaspoon olive oil

1 cup finely chopped onion (about 2 medium)

5½ cups Beef Broth (see page 39 or use commercial low-sodium variety)

1 teaspoon dried thyme, crumbled

1 teaspoon dried marjoram, crumbled

1 bay leaf, broken in half

1 pound red potatoes, unpeeled (about 3 medium)

2 large carrots

8 ounces fresh mushrooms (3 to 3½ cups)

1 cup diced red bell pepper (1 medium)

½ cup thinly sliced green onion (green and white parts) (4 to 5)

2 cups homemade Beef Broth (see page 39 or use commercial low-sodium variety)

¼ cup plus 2 tablespoons cornstarch

¼ cup no-salt-added tomato paste

1 teaspoon dried thyme, crumbled

1 teaspoon salt-free Italian herb seasoning

¾ teaspoon pepper

½ teaspoon salt

Calories 173
Protein 18 g
Carbohydrates 17 g
Cholesterol 38 mg
Total Fat 4 g
Saturated 1 g
Polyunsaturated 0 g
Monounsaturated 2 g
Fiber 2 g
Sodium 156 mg

Preheat broiler.

Lightly spray a broiler pan and rack with vegetable oil spray. Broil meat about 6 inches from heat for 15 to 20 minutes, or until meat is brown on all sides, turning occasionally.

Spray a stockpot with vegetable oil spray and heat over medium-high heat. Add oil and swirl to coat bottom of pot. Sauté onions until translucent.

Add meat, any pan juices, 5½ cups broth, thyme, marjoram, and bay leaf. Bring to a boil over high heat. Reduce heat and simmer, covered, for 1½ hours, or until meat is tender.

Meanwhile, cut potatoes into chunks, slice carrots, and quarter mushrooms. Add to pot. Simmer, covered, for 30 minutes.

Add bell pepper and green onion.

In a medium bowl, whisk together remaining ingredicnts. Pour into stew. Bring to a boil over high heat, stirring constantly. Reduce heat to low. Cook for 5 minutes, or until thickened, stirring constantly. Remove bay leaf before serving stew.

Cook's Tip on No-Salt-Added Tomato Paste

Sometimes you can save money by reading nutrition labels. For instance, a can of tomato paste labeled "No salt added" may cost more than certain brands of "regular" tomato paste with the same sodium content—about 20 milligrams per serving.

Cook's Tip on Red Bell Peppers

Buy red bell peppers when they're on sale and broil them for later use. Freeze them in airtight bags for up to 4 months.

Shredded Beef Soft Tacos

Serves 8

Let your slow cooker fix dinner while you're at work. Then give your family a Mexican feast of sirloin, onions, and bell peppers with cumin, all wrapped in warm tortillas. Serve with plenty of napkins!

1½ pounds top sirloin steak or sirloin tip roast, all visible fat removed

3 cups chopped yellow onion (6 medium)

1 cup chopped green bell pepper

¼ cup dry red wine (regular or nonalcoholic)

½ cup low-sodium ketchup

2 tablespoons cider vinegar

6 medium cloves garlic, minced, or 1 tablespoon bottled minced garlic

2 teaspoons low-sodium beef bouillon granules

2 bay leaves

¾ teaspoon liquid smoke

½ teaspoon ground cumin

½ teaspoon red hot-pepper sauce

¼ teaspoon pepper

½ teaspoon ground cumin

1 teaspoon dark brown, light brown, or white sugar

8 8-inch nonfat or low-fat flour tortillas (see Cook's Tip, page 27)

Put meat in slow cooker. Add onions and bell pepper.

In a medium bowl, whisk together wine, ketchup, vinegar, garlic, bouillon granules, bay leaves, liquid smoke, ½ teaspoon cumin, hot-pepper sauce, and pepper.

Pour wine mixture into slow cooker, cover tightly, and cook on low setting for 9 hours, or until meat is tender.

Shred meat using two forks, and return it to slow cooker. Remove and discard bay leaves.

Add ½ teaspoon cumin and sugar and let mixture stand for 1 hour to allow flavors to blend.

Preheat oven to 325° F.

Wrap tortillas in aluminum foil and warm for 6 to 8 minutes. Spoon meat mixture down center of a tortilla. Fold one end and each side of tortilla toward center. Repeat with remaining tortillas.

Calories 225
Protein 19 g
Carbohydrates 28 g
Cholesterol 45 mg
Total Fat 4 g
Saturated 2 g
Polyunsaturated 0 g
Monounsaturated 2 g
Fiber 3 g
Sodium 268 mg

Variation

Before folding tortillas over the filling, add chopped tomatoes, shredded lettuce, and nonfat or low-fat Cheddar cheese. Or try salsa, nonfat or light sour cream, and nonfat or low-fat Cheddar.

Cook's Tip

If you can't find low-sodium ketchup, use ¼ cup ketchup and 2 tablespoons water.

Philadelphia-Style Cheese Steak Wrap

Serves 6

When you wrap marinated beef, onions, and bell peppers in a tortilla with a bit of cheese, you have a modern twist on a classic.

MARINADE

1 tablespoon balsamic vinegar or red wine vinegar

2 teaspoons very low sodium or low-sodium Worcestershire sauce

1 teaspoon sugar

1 teaspoon dried oregano, crumbled

1 teaspoon olive oil

2 medium cloves garlic, minced, or 1 teaspoon bottled minced garlic

¼ teaspoon pepper

12 ounces eye-of-round roast, all visible fat removed

1 small onion

1 medium green bell pepper

2 slices fat-free processed sharp Cheddar cheese slices (2 ounces)

Vegetable oil spray

6 6-inch nonfat or reduced-fat flour tortillas (see Cook's Tip, page 27)

Calories 164
Protein 16 g
Carbohydrates 19 g
Cholesterol 29 mg
Total Fat 3 g
Saturated 1 g
Polyunsaturated 0 g
Monounsaturated 1 g
Fiber 2 g
Sodium 302 mg

Combine marinade ingredients in an airtight plastic bag or small nonmetallic bowl.

With a sharp knife, cut meat across grain into very thin slices, about ⅛ inch thick. Add to marinade and turn to coat. Seal bag or cover bowl with plastic wrap. Marinate at room temperature for 10 minutes or refrigerate for up to 8 hours, turning occasionally.

Meanwhile, thinly slice onion and bell pepper. Cut each piece of cheese into 3 slices. Set aside.

Preheat oven to 350° F if using.

Preheat a nonstick griddle over medium-high heat. Remove griddle from heat and lightly spray surface with vegetable oil spray. Brown meat for 3 to 5 minutes, or until no longer pink, stirring occasionally. Put meat in a bowl and cover with aluminum foil to keep warm.

Wipe griddle with paper towel. Lightly spray griddle with vegetable oil spray. Cook onion and bell pepper for 5 to 6 minutes, or until tender, stirring occasionally.

To assemble, spoon meat down center of each tortilla. Top with onion mixture and cheese. To microwave, place 2 tortillas with filling on microwave-safe plate. Microwave on 100 percent power (high) for 30 seconds. Roll tortillas jelly-roll style over filling; secure with toothpick if desired. Repeat with remaining tortillas and filling. For oven, place tortillas with filling in a large, shallow baking pan. Cover with aluminum foil and heat for 4 to 5 minutes. Roll up tortillas as directed.

Salisbury Steaks with Mushroom Sauce

Serves 8

Use the soaking liquid from dried mushrooms in the sauce for this dressed-up hamburger patty. Complete the meal with Baked Fries with Creole Seasoning (see page 400) and sliced tomatoes.

MEAT PATTIES

1½ pounds lean ground beef

1 medium onion, grated or minced

3 tablespoons all-purpose flour

1 tablespoon very low sodium or low-sodium Worcestershire sauce

¾ teaspoon salt-free all-purpose seasoning

½ teaspoon dried thyme, crumbled

⅛ teaspoon pepper

¼ cup fat-free milk

MUSHROOM SAUCE

¾ ounce dried mushrooms, any variety

1 cup hot water

½ cup (about) Beef Broth (see page 39 or use commercial low-sodium variety)

½ cup dry red wine (regular or nonalcoholic)

¼ cup grated carrots

2 to 3 tablespoons snipped fresh parsley

In a large bowl, thoroughly combine all meat patty ingredients except milk.

Add milk and stir again.

Shape into 8 patties. Cover and refrigerate.

Meanwhile, for sauce, put mushrooms in a small bowl. Cover mushrooms with hot water and let soak for 20 to 30 minutes. Drain mushrooms, reserving liquid. Chop mushrooms and set aside.

Strain liquid through a coffee filter or paper towel into a liquid measuring cup. (This will remove any dirt.) Add enough broth to strained liquid to make 1 cup.

Stir in wine. Set aside.

Heat a heavy nonstick skillet over medium-high heat. Add beef patties and brown for 5 to 6 minutes per side, or until no longer pink in center. Remove from skillet and drain on paper towels.

Calories 167
Protein 20 g
Carbohydrates 6 g
Cholesterol 34 mg
Total Fat 6 g
  Saturated 3 g
  Polyunsaturated —
  Monounsaturated —
Fiber 1 g
Sodium 60 mg

Pour off any liquid left in skillet and return skillet to heat. Add mushrooms, wine mixture, and carrots to skillet. Bring to a boil over high heat and reduce liquid by one third, 2 to 3 minutes.

Add beef patties. Reduce heat and simmer for 10 minutes. Sprinkle with parsley.

Beef Bourguignon

Serves 8

Like other stews, Beef Bourguignon tastes best when made ahead so the flavors have time to mingle. Serve it on rice or noodles.

Vegetable oil spray
1 teaspoon olive oil
5 medium onions, sliced (5 cups)
2 pounds lean top sirloin roast (or other lean cut), all visible fat removed, cut into 1-inch cubes
1½ tablespoons all-purpose flour
¼ teaspoon dried marjoram, crumbled
¼ teaspoon dried thyme, crumbled
½ teaspoon pepper, or to taste
1 cup dry red wine (regular or nonalcoholic) (plus more as needed)
½ cup Beef Broth (see page 39 or use commercial low-sodium variety) (plus more as needed)
½ pound fresh mushrooms (3 to 3½ cups)

Lightly spray a large, heavy skillet with vegetable oil spray. Add oil and heat over medium-high heat. Sauté onions until translucent, 2 to 3 minutes. Remove onions and set aside.

Sauté beef cubes until browned on all sides, 10 to 12 minutes. Sprinkle with flour, marjoram, thyme, and pepper. Stir to mix well.

Stir in wine and broth. Reduce heat and simmer, covered, for 1½ to 2 hours, or until almost tender. Add more wine and broth (2 parts wine to 1 part broth) as necessary to keep beef barely covered.

Meanwhile, slice mushrooms.

Return onions to skillet and add mushrooms. Cook, covered, for 30 minutes, stirring occasionally. Add more wine and broth if necessary. Sauce should be thick and dark brown.

Calories 217
Protein 21 g
Carbohydrates 9 g
Cholesterol 60 mg
Total Fat 9 g
Saturated 4 g
Polyunsaturated 0 g
Monounsaturated 4 g
Fiber 1 g
Sodium 47 mg

Cook's Tip on Marjoram

Available fresh as well as dried, marjoram tastes much like oregano. It is especially good with meats and vegetables.

Beef and Pasta Skillet

Serves 6

Serve this family-pleasing dish with steamed zucchini and a dessert of Fresh Fruit Salad Romanoff (see page 92).

8 ounces dried tricolor rotini pasta (about 3 to 4 cups)

8 ounces fresh mushrooms, sliced (about 2½ to 3 cups)

½ pound lean ground beef

1 cup chopped onion (about 2 medium)

3 medium cloves garlic, minced, or 1½ teaspoons bottled minced garlic

1½ teaspoons salt-free Italian herb seasoning

1½ teaspoons dried basil, crumbled

1 cup water

6-ounce can no-salt-added tomato paste

2 tablespoons grated Parmesan cheese

2 tablespoons finely snipped fresh parsley

1 teaspoon very low sodium or low-sodium Worcestershire sauce

¼ teaspoon salt

Cook pasta using package directions, omitting salt and oil. Set aside.

Put mushrooms, beef, onions, garlic, herb seasoning, and basil in a large skillet. Cook, covered, over medium-high heat for 8 to 10 minutes, or until mushrooms have released their juices and are fully cooked, stirring occasionally.

In a small bowl, whisk together remaining ingredients and add them and pasta to skillet. Heat thoroughly.

Calories 230
Protein 16 g
Carbohydrates 34 g
Cholesterol 17 mg
Total Fat 4 g
Saturated 2 g
Polyunsaturated —
Monounsaturated —
Fiber 3 g
Sodium 186 mg

Glazed Meatballs on Water Chestnut and Bell Pepper Rice

Serves 4

Yellow rice tossed with water chestnuts and bell peppers makes a bed for flavor-packed meatballs in this dish. The rice combination is equally good in Vegetarian Stir-Fry *(see page* 311*).*

MEATBALLS

12 ounces lean ground beef

3/4 cup finely chopped red or green bell pepper or combination

1/3 cup uncooked quick-cooking oatmeal

Whites of 2 large eggs

2 1/2 teaspoons light soy sauce

2 teaspoons cornstarch

2 teaspoons orange zest

1/4 to 1/2 teaspoon crushed red pepper flakes

WATER CHESTNUT AND BELL PEPPER RICE

3 cups water

1 1/2 cups uncooked rice

1/2 teaspoon powdered turmeric

1 cup finely chopped red or green bell pepper or combination

8-ounce can sliced water chestnuts, drained

Vegetable oil spray

GLAZE

3 tablespoons grape jelly

2 tablespoons low-sodium ketchup

1 tablespoon plus 2 1/2 teaspoons light soy sauce

1 teaspoon sugar

1 teaspoon very low sodium or low-sodium Worcestershire sauce

Calories 453
Protein 28 g
Carbohydrates 70 g
Cholesterol 34 mg
Total Fat 7 g
  Saturated 3 g
  Polyunsaturated —
  Monounsaturated —
Fiber 3 g
Sodium 452 mg

In a large bowl, combine meatball ingredients. Shape into 24 meatballs and set aside.

For rice, in a medium saucepan, bring water to a boil over high heat. Add rice and turmeric; stir. Return to a boil. Reduce heat and simmer, covered, for 20 minutes. Stir in bell pepper and water chestnuts.

Meanwhile, spray a large nonstick skillet with vegetable oil spray. Heat over medium-high heat for

1 minute. Add meatballs and cook for 12 minutes, or until cooked through and browned (reduce heat to medium if necessary). Turn meatballs frequently (using two spoons works well). Drain meatballs on paper towels. Wipe skillet. Return meatballs to skillet.

In a small bowl, whisk together glaze ingredients. Pour into skillet. Using a rubber scraper, gently coat meatballs. Cook over medium-high heat for about 2 minutes, stirring constantly until meatballs are well glazed. Remove from heat.

Reserve 3 cups of rice mixture in an airtight container and refrigerate for use in Vegetarian Stir-Fry. Place remaining rice mixture on a serving platter and top with meatballs.

Shepherd's Pie

Serves 6

While pleasing the meat and potato lovers in your family, this one-dish meal gives them some veggies, too.

1 pound lean ground beef

1 cup Beef Broth (see page 39 or use commercial low-sodium variety)

1 teaspoon pepper

2 bay leaves

2 whole cloves

Dash of dried thyme, crumbled

1 cup sliced carrots (1 large)

1 cup sliced onions (about 2 medium)

1 cup sliced fresh mushrooms (about 4 ounces)

1 cup diced celery (about 2 medium ribs)

1 cup canned no-salt-added whole-kernel corn

Vegetable oil spray

1 tablespoon plus ¾ teaspoon all-purpose flour

½ cup Beef Broth (see page 39 or use commercial low-sodium variety)

1 pound potatoes, peeled, cooked, and diced (about 3 medium)

½ cup fat-free milk

1 tablespoon light margarine

1 tablespoon snipped chives or green onions (green part only)

4 ounces nonfat or part-skim mozzarella cheese, shredded (about 1 cup)

Calories 276
Protein 26 g
Carbohydrates 30 g
Cholesterol 32 mg
Total Fat 3 g
Saturated 1 g
Polyunsaturated —
Monounsaturated —
Fiber 4 g
Sodium 285 mg

Brown beef in a large skillet over medium-high heat. Put beef in a colander and rinse under hot water. Wipe skillet with paper towels. Return beef to skillet. Stir in broth, pepper, bay leaves, cloves, and thyme. Reduce heat and simmer, covered, for 30 minutes.

Add carrots, onions, mushrooms, celery, and corn. Simmer, covered, until vegetables are tender, 4 to 5 minutes.

Preheat oven to 375° F. Lightly spray a casserole dish with vegetable oil spray.

Put flour in a small bowl and gradually add broth, whisking constantly to form a smooth paste. Add to beef mixture. Simmer for 5 minutes, or until slightly thickened. Remove bay leaves and cloves. Transfer beef mixture to casserole dish.

Mash potatoes with milk, margarine, and chives. Spread evenly over meat, then sprinkle with mozzarella.

Bake for 10 minutes.

Tamale Pie

Serves 8

This hearty one-dish meal is sure to be a hit at your next family gathering or potluck dinner.

Vegetable oil spray

CRUST

1 cup yellow cornmeal

2½ cups Beef Broth (see page 39 or use commercial low-sodium variety), divided use

1 teaspoon baking powder

FILLING

1 teaspoon acceptable vegetable oil

¼ cup chopped onion

1 teaspoon minced garlic

1 pound lean ground beef

14½-ounce can no-salt-added tomatoes, crushed

¼ cup no-salt-added tomato paste (plus more as needed)

1 tablespoon chili powder

1 teaspoon dried oregano, crumbled

½ teaspoon ground cumin

15¼-ounce can no-salt-added whole-kernel corn

½ cup sliced fresh mushrooms (about 2 ounces)

4-ounce can chopped green chiles, rinsed and drained

2 tablespoons grated nonfat or low-fat Cheddar cheese

Calories 210
Protein 17 g
Carbohydrates 26 g
Cholesterol 23 mg
Total Fat 3 g
Saturated 1 g
Polyunsaturated 1 g
Monounsaturated 0 g
Fiber 4 g
Sodium 242 mg

Preheat oven to 350° F. Lightly spray a 2½-quart casserole dish with vegetable oil spray.

For crust, combine cornmeal and ½ cup beef broth in a large saucepan.

In a small saucepan, bring remaining broth to a boil. Stir into cornmeal mixture. Cook, covered, over medium heat until mixture thickens, 3 to 5 minutes, stirring occasionally.

Stir in baking powder. Set aside and let cool.

For filling, heat oil in a large skillet over medium-high heat, swirling to coat bottom. Lightly sauté onion and garlic for 1 to 2 minutes.

Add beef in small portions and cook until brown, stirring occasionally.

Pour beef mixture into a colander and rinse under hot water. Wipe skillet with paper towel.

Put undrained tomatoes, tomato paste, chili powder, oregano, and cumin in skillet. Bring to a simmer over medium heat; simmer for 5 minutes. If sauce is too thin, add more tomato paste.

Add beef mixture and remaining ingredients except Cheddar. Stir gently and remove from heat.

Pour cornmeal mixture into casserole dish. Spread over bottom and up side. Spoon in filling and sprinkle with Cheddar.

Bake for 30 minutes.

Cook's Tip

For a bit more bite, substitute 2 Anaheim peppers, stemmed, seeded, and chopped, for the canned chiles. Just be sure to wear rubber gloves or wash your hands in warm, soapy water immediately after handling the hot peppers.

Spaghetti with Meat Sauce

Serves 8

Savory and traditional, this meat sauce is heavy on the vegetables. Serve it with fruit for dessert and help the kids get their five a day.

MEAT SAUCE

Vegetable oil spray

1½ pounds lean ground beef

2 cups chopped onions (about 4 medium)

2 cups chopped celery (about 4 ribs)

1 cup chopped green bell pepper (1 medium)

28-ounce can no-salt-added Italian plum tomatoes

6-ounce can no-salt-added tomato paste

1 tablespoon very low sodium or low-sodium Worcestershire sauce

1 teaspoon pepper

1 teaspoon dried oregano, crumbled

1 teaspoon dried basil, crumbled

1 teaspoon garlic powder

2 bay leaves

16 ounces dried spaghetti (about 4 cups)

½ cup grated Parmesan cheese (about 2 ounces)

Time-Saver: If you're in a hurry, you can reduce the simmering time for the sauce to 30 minutes. The flavor won't be quite as rich and blended, but the sauce will still be good.

For sauce, spray a stockpot with vegetable oil spray. Sauté beef over medium-high heat until no longer pink, 10 to 12 minutes, stirring frequently. Put beef in a colander and rinse under hot water. Wipe pot with paper towels. Return beef to pot.

Add onions and sauté over medium-high heat until slightly brown, 3 to 4 minutes.

Add celery and bell pepper and sauté for about 2 minutes.

Add remaining sauce ingredients. Reduce heat and simmer, covered, for 2 hours, stirring occasionally.

Meanwhile, cook spaghetti using package directions, omitting salt and oil.

To serve, drain spaghetti and top with sauce and Parmesan.

Calories 436
Protein 32 g
Carbohydrates 58 g
Cholesterol 39 mg
Total Fat 5 g
- Saturated 2 g
- Polyunsaturated —
- Monounsaturated —

Fiber 7 g
Sodium 221 mg

Beef Tostadas

Serves 6

Almost as fast as fast food and much better for you.

6 5½- or 6-inch corn tortillas

Vegetable oil spray

FILLING

1 pound lean ground beef

½ cup finely chopped onion (1 medium)

1½ to 2 teaspoons chili powder

½ teaspoon ground cumin

½ teaspoon dried oregano, crumbled

½ teaspoon garlic powder

¼ teaspoon salt

Dash red hot-pepper sauce

2 cups shredded lettuce

2 medium Italian plum tomatoes or 1 large regular tomato, chopped

¾ cup Salsa Cruda (see page 449 or use nonfat, low-sodium commercial salsa)

¾ cup shredded nonfat or low-fat Cheddar cheese (about 3 ounces)

Preheat oven to 450° F.

Put tortillas on a heavy baking sheet. Lightly spray tortillas with vegetable oil spray. Bake for 8 to 10 minutes, or until crisp.

Meanwhile, in a large nonstick skillet over medium-high heat, combine beef and onion. Sauté until meat is browned, 8 to 10 minutes, stirring occasionally.

Pour meat mixture into a colander and rinse under hot water. Wipe skillet with paper towel; return meat to skillet.

Stir remaining filling ingredients into meat mixture.

For each tostada, spread about ⅓ cup meat mixture over crisped tortilla. Layer remaining ingredients over meat.

Calories 214
Protein 24 g
Carbohydrates 17 g
Cholesterol 31 mg
Total Fat 3 g
  Saturated 1 g
  Polyunsaturated —
  Monounsaturated —
Fiber 3 g
Sodium 346 mg

Chili

Serves 8

When you get the first hint that Jack Frost is on the way, it's time to make chili.

1 cup dried pinto or kidney beans, sorted for stones and rinsed (about 6 ounces), or 15-ounce can no-salt-added pinto or kidney beans, rinsed and drained

Vegetable oil spray

1 teaspoon acceptable vegetable oil

2 cups chopped onions (about 4 medium)

1 medium green bell pepper, chopped (1 cup)

1 pound lean ground beef

2 cups chopped tomatoes (2 to 3 medium)

6-ounce can no-salt-added tomato paste

¾ cup water

2 to 3 tablespoons chili powder

1 tablespoon cider vinegar

1 bay leaf

1 to 2 teaspoons minced garlic

1 teaspoon dried oregano, crumbled

1 teaspoon ground cumin

½ teaspoon pepper

Time-Saver: If you're in a hurry, you can reduce the simmering time in the final step of the recipe to 30 minutes. The flavor won't be quite as rich and blended, but the chili will still be good.

Calories 228
Protein 20 g
Carbohydrates 28 g
Cholesterol 23 mg
Total Fat 3 g
Saturated 1 g
Polyunsaturated 1 g
Monounsaturated 0 g
Fiber 8 g
Sodium 85 mg

Prepare dried beans using package directions. Drain and set aside. Or use canned beans.

Spray a Dutch oven or large, deep skillet with vegetable oil spray. Add oil and heat over medium-high heat. Cook onions and bell pepper until onions are translucent, 2 to 3 minutes.

Add meat and brown. Pour into a colander and rinse under hot water. Wipe skillet with paper towel. Return meat to skillet.

Add beans and remaining ingredients. Bring to a boil over medium-high heat. Reduce heat and simmer, covered, for 1½ hours, stirring occasionally. Remove and discard bay leaf.

Vegetarian Chili

For a vegetarian entrée or side dish, omit meat. (calories 144; protein 7 g; carbohydrates 28 g; cholesterol 0 mg; total fat 2 g; saturated 0 g; polyunsaturated 1 g; monounsaturated 0 g; fiber 8 g; sodium 55 mg)

Bowl of Red

Serves 6

Texans love to eat chili almost as much as they love to argue over which version is the best. This one has cubed beef and skips the beans.

Vegetable oil spray

CHILI

2 pounds boneless beef top round steak, all visible fat removed, cut into ½-inch cubes

2 cups water

16 ounces dark or regular beer or nonalcoholic beer

8-ounce can no-salt-added tomato sauce

1 medium onion, chopped (about ½ cup)

6 ancho peppers, seeded and chopped

2 fresh jalapeño or serrano peppers, seeded and chopped (see Cook's Tip, page 115)

4 medium cloves garlic, minced, or 2 teaspoons bottled minced garlic

2 tablespoons chili powder

2 tablespoons ground cumin

1 teaspoon ground coriander

1 teaspoon dried oregano, crumbled

½ teaspoon salt

¼ teaspoon pepper

¼ teaspoon cayenne

¼ cup plus 2 tablespoons nonfat or light sour cream (optional)

Fresh cilantro, snipped (optional)

Spray a Dutch oven with vegetable oil spray. Put over medium-high heat. Brown half the meat on all sides. Remove with a slotted spoon. Brown remaining meat.

Return beef to Dutch oven. Add remaining chili ingredients and stir. Bring to a boil over medium-high heat. Reduce heat and simmer, covered, for 1 hour, stirring occasionally. Uncover and simmer for 15 to 30 minutes, or until desired consistency, stirring occasionally.

To serve, add a dollop of sour cream to each serving and sprinkle with cilantro.

Calories 269
Protein 35 g
Carbohydrates 16 g
Cholesterol 80 mg
Total Fat 5 g
Saturated 2 g
Polyunsaturated 1 g
Monounsaturated 2 g
Fiber 3 g
Sodium 277 mg

Crustless Ham and Spinach Tart

Serves 6

This is a great brunch dish. Serve with Southern Raised Biscuits (see page 504) and Claret-Spiced Oranges (see page 607).

Vegetable oil spray

1½ tablespoons grated Parmesan cheese

1 teaspoon olive oil

1 cup finely chopped onions (about 2 medium)

2 medium cloves garlic, minced, or 1 teaspoon bottled minced garlic

10-ounce package frozen no-salt-added chopped spinach, thawed and squeezed dry

3 slices (½ ounce each) low-fat, cracked-black-pepper ham, cut into strips

1¼ cups fat-free milk

Egg substitute equivalent to 3 eggs

4½ tablespoons grated Parmesan cheese (about 1 ounce)

1½ tablespoons all-purpose flour

1 tablespoon finely chopped fresh basil or 1 to 2 teaspoons dried, crumbled

½ teaspoon pepper

Dash of nutmeg

Preheat oven to 350° F. Lightly spray a 9-inch glass pie pan with vegetable oil spray. Dust with 1½ tablespoons Parmesan.

Heat a medium nonstick skillet over medium-high heat. Add oil and swirl to coat bottom of skillet. Sauté onions until translucent, 2 to 3 minutes, stirring occasionally.

Add garlic and sauté for 1 minute.

Stir in spinach and ham, mixing well. Spread mixture evenly in pie pan.

In a medium bowl, combine remaining ingredients. Pour over spinach mixture.

Bake for 50 to 55 minutes, or until knife inserted in center comes out clean.

Calories 115
Protein 11 g
Carbohydrates 8 g
Cholesterol 8 mg
Total Fat 4 g
  Saturated 2 g
  Polyunsaturated 1 g
  Monounsaturated 2 g
Fiber 2 g
Sodium 308 mg

New Orleans Muffaletta Wrap

Serves 6

For a combination of Louisiana and Mexico, the traditional stuffing ingredients of the popular New Orleans muffaletta—olive salad, meat, and cheese—are wrapped in a flour tortilla. You might even try making your own flavored tortillas (see page 519).

1 medium carrot, peeled and diced (3/4 cup)

1 rib celery, diced (1/2 cup)

1/2 medium red bell pepper, diced (1/2 cup)

2 ounces low-fat, low-sodium ham, diced (1/2 cup)

1 green onion, thinly sliced (2 tablespoons)

1/4 cup shredded fat-free or part-skim mozzarella cheese

4 medium pimiento-stuffed green olives, chopped (1 tablespoon)

4 medium black olives, chopped (1 tablespoon)

1 tablespoon olive oil

1 tablespoon red wine vinegar

1 medium clove garlic, minced, or 1/2 teaspoon bottled minced garlic

1/4 teaspoon dried oregano, crumbled

1/4 teaspoon pepper

1/4 teaspoon sugar

6 6-inch nonfat or low-fat flour tortillas (see Cook's Tip, page 27)

In a medium bowl, combine all ingredients except tortillas, stirring well.

To assemble, put a tortilla on a microwave-safe plate. Spoon 1/3 cup mixture down middle of tortilla. Microwave on 100 percent power (high) for 30 seconds. Roll tortilla jelly-roll style over filling, securing with a toothpick if desired. Repeat with remaining ingredients.

Calories 135
Protein 6 g
Carbohydrates 20 g
Cholesterol 4 mg
Total Fat 4 g
Saturated 1 g
Polyunsaturated 0 g
Monounsaturated 2 g
Fiber 3 g
Sodium 433 mg

Ham Roll-Ups

Serves 8

Even young children will have fun helping you prepare dinner with this recipe. They can stack the ingredients on the bread, then roll up their sandwiches for you to broil.

DRESSING

1 tablespoon light margarine

3 tablespoons plain nonfat or low-fat yogurt

2 teaspoons finely chopped fresh basil

2 teaspoons finely snipped fresh dillweed

1 teaspoon Dijon mustard

8 slices thinly sliced white bread (must be fresh)

4 ounces Muenster cheese, sliced into 8 thin pieces

8 thin slices low-fat, low-sodium ham (½ ounce per slice)

16 fresh asparagus spears, cooked until tender-crisp, or frozen no-salt-added asparagus spears, thawed

Soak eight wooden toothpicks in cold water for at least 10 minutes.

For dressing, whisk together all ingredients in a small bowl.

Preheat broiler.

Slightly flatten bread slices with palm of hand.

To assemble, spread about 1 teaspoon dressing on each side of bread slices. Stack 1 slice each of cheese and ham on each slice of bread. Arrange 2 asparagus spears on each so one tip points left and the other points right. Roll up each piece of bread and secure with a toothpick. Place on broiler pan.

Broil about 6 inches from heat for 2½ to 3 minutes, or until cheese is bubbly.

Calories 169
Protein 9 g
Carbohydrates 15 g
Cholesterol 21 mg
Total Fat 7 g
Saturated 3 g
Polyunsaturated 0 g
Monounsaturated 2 g
Fiber 1 g
Sodium 393 mg

Bayou Red Beans and Rice

Serves 8

This recipe will show you how easy it is to prepare Louisiana's most popular comfort food.

1 pound dried red kidney beans (2½ cups), sorted for stones and rinsed

2 cups Chicken Broth (see page 40 or use commercial low-sodium variety)

1 ham bone

1 cup chopped low-fat, low-sodium ham

1 large onion, chopped (1¼ cups)

2 ribs celery with leaves, chopped (1 cup)

2 teaspoons red hot-pepper sauce

1⅓ cups uncooked white rice

Prepare beans using package directions but substituting broth for 2 cups water for cooking. Add water as necessary so beans don't become dry. Water should barely cover beans at end of cooking time.

Add remaining ingredients except rice. Simmer, covered, for 1 hour, or until vegetables are tender, stirring occasionally.

Prepare rice using package directions, omitting salt and margarine.

Meanwhile, remove ham bone from bean mixture. Set aside.

Using a potato masher, mash about one fourth of the bean mixture while it is in the pot. Stir mixture. Cook over low heat until thick, about 10 minutes.

Cut ham from bone and return meat to beans.

To serve, put rice in individual bowls and top with bean mixture.

Time-Saver: Use three 15-ounce cans no-salt-added kidney beans instead of dried. Drain and rinse. Cover with broth and proceed as with cooked beans above. Also, cook 2 cups instant rice instead of regular rice. Using canned beans in this dish won't give you the "old-fashioned" taste, but you may be willing to compromise some flavor to save time.

Calories 338
Protein 19 g
Carbohydrates 60 g
Cholesterol 10 mg
Total Fat 2 g
  Saturated 1 g
  Polyunsaturated 1 g
  Monounsaturated 1 g
Fiber 9 g
Sodium 255 mg

Savory Black-Eyed Peas and Pasta

Serves 4

Here's what you can do with a little bit of ham left over from your holiday dinner.

Vegetable oil spray
½ cup minced baked ham
1 medium carrot, peeled and finely chopped (¾ cup)
1 small onion, finely chopped (⅓ cup)
¼ cup minced fresh parsley
1 medium clove garlic, minced, or ½ teaspoon bottled minced garlic
15.5-ounce can black-eyed peas, rinsed and drained
2 cups Chicken Broth (see page 40 or use commercial low-sodium variety) or water
½ teaspoon dried thyme, crumbled
½ teaspoon dried basil, crumbled
½ teaspoon dried oregano, crumbled
½ teaspoon pepper
Dash of cayenne, or to taste
4 quarts water
8 ounces dried small shell pasta

Spray a large nonstick skillet with vegetable oil spray. Add ham, carrot, onion, parsley, and garlic. Cook over medium-high heat for 15 minutes, stirring occasionally.

Add peas, broth, thyme, basil, oregano, pepper, and cayenne. Bring to a boil over medium-high heat. Reduce heat and simmer, uncovered, for about 15 minutes.

Meanwhile, in a stockpot, bring water to a boil over high heat. Prepare pasta using package directions, omitting salt and oil; cook until barely tender. Drain well and combine with bean mixture.

Calories 370
Protein 17 g
Carbohydrates 66 g
Cholesterol 9 mg
Total Fat 3 g
Saturated 1 g
Polyunsaturated 1 g
Monounsaturated 1 g
Fiber 7 g
Sodium 387 mg

Vegetarian Savory Black-Eyed Peas and Pasta

Omit ham, substitute water for chicken broth, and sprinkle with 1 tablespoon plus 1 teaspoon minced black or green olives. (calories 336; protein 14 g; carbohydrates 65 g; cholesterol 0 mg; total fat 2 g; saturated 0 g; polyunsaturated 1 g; monounsaturated 0 g; fiber 7 g; sodium 240 mg)

Ham and Rice Croquettes

Serves 4

A great candidate for a quick meal, this comforting main dish features leftover ham and rice. You'll need only one mixing bowl and a skillet to make it.

CROQUETTES

2 cups cooked rice

1 small zucchini, shredded (1 cup)

½ cup diced low-fat, low-sodium ham (2 ounces)

½ cup diced red bell pepper

Egg substitute equivalent to 2 eggs, or 2 eggs

¼ cup plain dry bread crumbs

2 tablespoons grated Parmesan cheese

2 green onions, thinly sliced (about ¼ cup)

1 tablespoon Dijon mustard

⅛ teaspoon salt

⅛ teaspoon pepper

2 teaspoons acceptable vegetable oil, divided use

Vegetable oil spray

In a medium bowl, combine croquette ingredients, stirring well.

Heat a large nonstick skillet over medium heat. Add 1 teaspoon vegetable oil and swirl to coat bottom. With a measuring cup, scoop up ¼ cup of mixture. Carefully mound it in skillet, then flatten slightly with spatula. Repeat with 7 more ¼-cup mounds, using half the mixture.

Lightly spray tops of croquettes with vegetable oil spray. Cook over medium heat for 4 to 5 minutes, or until browned on bottom. Turn over and cook for 4 to 5 minutes, or until browned. Repeat with remaining oil and croquette mixture.

Calories 221
Protein 11 g
Carbohydrates 31 g
Cholesterol 9 mg
Total Fat 6 g
Saturated 2 g
Polyunsaturated 2 g
Monounsaturated 2 g
Fiber 1 g
Sodium 462 mg

Cook's Tip

To reheat in the microwave, put 4 croquettes on a microwave-safe plate. Microwave on 100 percent power (high) for 1 to 2 minutes, or until warmed through.

Herb-Rubbed Pork Tenderloin with Dijon-Apricot Mop Sauce

Serves 8

A dry herb rub flavors the pork and makes a nice crust. You may want to stop right there, or you can go one step further and add the tangy mop sauce.

HERB RUB

1 tablespoon dried rosemary, crushed

1 tablespoon dried thyme, crumbled

1 tablespoon ground cumin

2 teaspoons coarsely ground pepper

2 teaspoons paprika

2 teaspoons celery seeds

2 1-pound pork tenderloins, all visible fat removed

DIJON-APRICOT MOP SAUCE

1 teaspoon acceptable vegetable oil

1 small onion, finely chopped (3/8 cup)

1/2 cup cider vinegar

1/4 cup honey

1/4 cup all-fruit apricot preserves

2 tablespoons Dijon mustard

1 teaspoon grated lemon zest

1 tablespoon fresh lemon juice

Vegetable oil spray

Calories 151
Protein 24 g
Carbohydrates 2 g
Cholesterol 67 mg
Total Fat 5 g
Saturated 2 g
Polyunsaturated 0 g
Monounsaturated 2 g
Fiber 1 g
Sodium 49 mg

In a small bowl, combine rub ingredients. Using your hands or a spoon, rub mixture evenly over pork. Set aside.

Preheat oven to 350° F or preheat grill on medium-high.

For mop sauce, heat oil in a small saucepan over medium-high heat, swirling to coat. Sauté onion for 2 to 3 minutes, or until translucent, stirring occasionally.

Stir in remaining sauce ingredients. Bring to a boil. Reduce heat and simmer for 5 minutes, stirring occasionally. (You may wish to reserve 1/2 cup sauce to use as a dipping sauce for cooked pork.)

Lightly spray a broiling pan and rack with vegetable oil spray. Put tenderloins on rack in pan. Bake for 30 minutes. Using a pastry brush or basting mop (a small dishwashing mop can be used—new and clean, of course!), baste on all sides. Bake for 10 minutes, then baste again. Bake for 10 to 15 minutes, or until pork is no longer pink in center or registers 165° F on meat thermometer. Or grill tenderloins for 10 minutes per side (40 minutes total), then baste with mop sauce and cook for 2 to 3 minutes per side, or until pork is cooked through. (Sauce: calories 218; protein 25 g; carbohydrates 18 g; cholesterol 67 mg; total fat 5 g; saturated 2 g; polyunsaturated 1 g; monounsaturated 2 g; fiber 1 g; sodium 145 mg)

Cook's Tip

Chicken, flank steak, and eye-of-round roast are delicious with both the rub and the mop sauce. Try the mop sauce on its own over vegetable kebabs, beef, poultry, firm fish fillets, or shrimp.

Cook's Tip on Leftover Meat

If you have any leftover meat, such as part of this pork tenderloin, or if you cook "planned-overs" to use in other meals, you can use them to make French bread sandwiches, top salads with them, toss them with cooked pasta, wrap them in tortillas with grilled vegetables, or add them to soup with yolk-free noodles.

Marinated Pork Tenderloin

Serves 5

Steamed rice and snow peas go well with this Asian-flavored pork.

MARINADE

1 small onion, grated or minced (1/3 cup)

1/4 cup light soy sauce

1 tablespoon toasted sesame oil

2 teaspoons grated gingerroot or 3/4 teaspoon ground ginger

2 medium cloves garlic, crushed, or 1 teaspoon bottled minced garlic

1 teaspoon grated lemon zest

1 pound pork tenderloin, all visible fat removed

Vegetable oil spray

1/4 cup dry white wine (regular or nonalcoholic)

1/4 cup honey

1 tablespoon dark brown sugar

In an airtight plastic bag, combine marinade ingredients.

Add pork to marinade and turn to coat. Seal and refrigerate for about 8 hours.

Preheat oven to 375° F. Spray a shallow nonstick baking pan with vegetable oil spray.

Remove pork from marinade; drain well, discarding marinade. Put pork in baking pan.

In a small bowl, whisk together remaining ingredients. Pour over pork, coating all sides.

Bake for 25 to 30 minutes, or until internal temperature reaches 170° F.

Remove from oven and let rest for 5 minutes. Slice and serve.

Calories 178
Protein 19 g
Carbohydrates 16 g
Cholesterol 54 mg
Total Fat 3 g
Saturated 1 g
Polyunsaturated 0 g
Monounsaturated 1 g
Fiber 0 g
Sodium 189 mg

Cook's Tip on Toasted Sesame Oil

Widely used in Asian and Indian cuisines, this oil is also called Asian sesame oil and fragrant toasted sesame oil. Toasted sesame oil is darker and stronger in flavor than "plain" sesame oil. Since toasted sesame oil is polyunsaturated, it is an acceptable oil.

Orange Pork Medallions

Serves 4

An unusual combination of flavors enhances this dish. It's very good served with Couscous with Vegetables (see page 424).

SAUCE

Juice of 2 medium oranges (⅔ cup)

2½ tablespoons fresh lemon juice (1 medium lemon)

2 tablespoons orange marmalade

2 tablespoons minced fresh parsley

1 tablespoon cornstarch

2 teaspoons toasted sesame oil

¾ teaspoon prepared horseradish

½ teaspoon ground cinnamon

½ teaspoon dried rosemary, crushed

¼ teaspoon pepper

1 pound pork tenderloin, all visible fat removed, cut into ½-inch slices

Vegetable oil spray

4 green onions (green and white parts), thinly sliced (½ cup)

11-ounce can mandarin orange slices, canned in light syrup, drained (optional)

4 large sprigs of fresh parsley (optional)

In a small bowl, whisk together sauce ingredients. Set aside.

Put pork slices between sheets of plastic wrap. Flatten slightly with flat side of meat mallet, rolling pin, hamburger press, or tortilla press.

Spray a large nonstick skillet with vegetable oil spray. Heat over medium-high heat. Add pork and brown quickly, about 2 minutes per side.

Add green onions and sauté until tender, about 1 minute.

Add sauce and cook until thickened, 2 to 3 minutes, stirring constantly.

To serve, place medallions and sauce on serving platter and garnish with mandarin orange slices and parsley.

Calories 219
Protein 25 g
Carbohydrates 15 g
Cholesterol 67 mg
Total Fat 7 g
Saturated 2 g
Polyunsaturated 1 g
Monounsaturated 3 g
Fiber 1 g
Sodium 58 mg

Pork with Spiced Sauerkraut

Serves 8

This traditional holiday combination is a winning entrée for Christmas Eve or New Year's Day.

Vegetable oil spray

1 teaspoon acceptable vegetable oil

½ cup chopped onion (1 medium)

2 pounds sauerkraut, rinsed, drained, and squeezed dry

2 cups cold water

1 tablespoon sugar

2 large potatoes, peeled and grated (1⅓ cups)

6 whole peppercorns

5 whole dried juniper berries

2 bay leaves

¼ teaspoon caraway seeds

1 whole allspice

Vegetable oil spray

1½ pounds pork tenderloin, all visible fat removed, cut into ½-inch slices

Preheat oven to 325° F. Spray an 11 × 17-inch casserole dish with vegetable oil spray.

Pour oil into a large skillet over medium-high heat. Add onion and brown lightly, 4 to 5 minutes, stirring frequently.

Add sauerkraut, water, and sugar. Toss with a fork until sauerkraut is well separated.

Stir in potato. Cook for 5 minutes, stirring occasionally.

Put peppercorns, juniper berries, bay leaves, caraway seeds, and allspice in a piece of cheesecloth and tie with kitchen twine.

Put sauerkraut mixture in casserole dish. Make a well in center of sauerkraut; put cheesecloth bag in well.

Lightly spray a large skillet with vegetable oil spray. Brown pork over medium-high heat for 2 minutes per side. Place pork on sauerkraut.

Bake, covered, for about 1 hour, or until pork is no longer pink in center.

Uncover and bake for 30 minutes to allow meat to brown. Remove cheesecloth bag before serving casserole.

Time-Saver: Using a covered broilerproof dish, bake the casserole for about 1 hour, uncover, and put the dish about 6 inches from a preheated broiler. Broil for 3 to 4 minutes to brown the pork.

Calories 177
Protein 20 g
Carbohydrates 16 g
Cholesterol 50 mg
Total Fat 4 g
Saturated 1 g
Polyunsaturated 1 g
Monounsaturated 1 g
Fiber 4 g
Sodium 489 mg

Sweet-and-Sour Pork

Serves 4

You don't even need a wok to create this classic at home.

SWEET-AND-SOUR SAUCE

½ cup pineapple juice

2 teaspoons rice vinegar or cider vinegar

1 teaspoon dry sherry

½ teaspoon light soy sauce

Dash of hot-pepper oil

Dash of ground ginger

Dash of ground allspice

1 teaspoon cornstarch

2 tablespoons water

Vegetable oil spray

12 ounces pork tenderloin, all visible fat removed, cut into strips ¼ inch thick

2 tablespoons minced leeks, onion, green onions, or any combination

¼ cup sliced green bell pepper

¼ cup sliced onion

2 teaspoons snipped fresh parsley

¼ teaspoon pepper

In a small saucepan, combine pineapple juice, vinegar, sherry, soy sauce, hot-pepper oil, ginger, and allspice. Cook over medium-high heat for 2 to 3 minutes, or until sauce comes just to a boil.

Meanwhile, put cornstarch in a cup or small bowl. Add water, whisking to dissolve.

When pineapple juice mixture is hot, whisk in dissolved cornstarch. Cook over medium heat, whisking constantly, until sauce begins to thicken, 1 to 2 minutes. Remove from heat.

Spray a large nonstick skillet or wok with vegetable oil spray. Heat over medium-high heat and sauté pork until no longer pink, 3 to 4 minutes. Remove from skillet.

Reduce heat to medium. Put leeks, bell pepper, and onion in skillet. Put pork on vegetables and sprinkle with parsley and pepper. Cook for 4 to 5 minutes, stirring occasionally. Add sauce and heat through.

Calories 134
Protein 18 g
Carbohydrates 6 g
Cholesterol 50 mg
Total Fat 3 g
    Saturated 1 g
    Polyunsaturated 0 g
    Monounsaturated 1 g
Fiber 0 g
Sodium 59 mg

Scaloppine al Limone

Serves 6

This Italian dish is very good over spaghetti or fettuccine. It also goes well with Asparagus par Excellence (see page 355) or Tomato-Basil Salad with Balsamic Dressing (see page 84).

¼ cup plus 1 tablespoon all-purpose flour

½ teaspoon coarsely ground black pepper

¼ teaspoon salt

1½ pounds veal scallops, pounded to ¼-inch thickness

Olive oil spray

2 teaspoons olive oil

Olive oil spray (if needed)

1¾ cups Chicken Broth (see page 40 or use commercial low-sodium variety)

¼ cup fresh lemon juice (1 to 2 medium lemons)

¼ cup dry white wine (regular or nonalcoholic)

1 tablespoon finely snipped fresh parsley

6 thin lemon slices (optional)

Combine flour, pepper, and salt in a plastic or paper bag. Add veal and shake to coat evenly. Shake off excess flour.

Lightly spray a large nonstick skillet with olive oil spray. Add 1 teaspoon oil and heat over medium-high heat. Add half the veal pieces and brown lightly on both sides, 2 to 3 minutes. Repeat process. If veal pieces stick to skillet, remove it from heat and spray lightly with olive oil spray. Transfer veal to a plate.

Pour broth, lemon juice, and wine into skillet. Cook over medium-high heat, stirring to remove brown bits from bottom of skillet, until sauce reduces by about one third, 3 to 4 minutes.

Return veal to skillet and bring to a simmer over medium heat. Simmer for 5 to 7 minutes, or until sauce is slightly thickened, stirring occasionally. Using a slotted spoon or pancake turner, transfer veal to serving platter.

Stir parsley into sauce in skillet and pour over veal. Garnish with lemon slices.

Calories 305
Protein 27 g
Carbohydrates 6 g
Cholesterol 104 mg
Total Fat 17 g
  Saturated 6 g
  Polyunsaturated 1 g
  Monounsaturated 7 g
Fiber 0 g
Sodium 172 mg

Chicken Scallops al Limone

Replace veal cutlets with 1½ pounds boneless, skinless chicken breasts, flattened to ¼-inch thickness. (calories 175; protein 24 g; carbohydrates 6 g; cholesterol 63 mg; total fat 4 g; saturated 1 g; polyunsaturated 1 g; monounsaturated 2 g; fiber 0 g; sodium 156 mg)

Veal Stufino

Serves 6

The taste of veal chunks slowly oven-braised in a tomato-rich sauce with vegetables is delicious enough. We go one more step and serve it all on a bed of tricolor pasta.

1 tablespoon all-purpose flour
½ teaspoon salt
¼ teaspoon freshly ground pepper, or to taste
1½ pounds boneless lean veal stew meat, all visible fat removed, cut into large cubes
Olive oil spray
1 teaspoon olive oil
½ cup dry white wine (regular or nonalcoholic)
2 medium carrots, finely chopped (1½ cups)
2 ribs celery, finely chopped (1 cup)
1 medium onion, finely chopped (½ cup)
1 or 2 medium cloves garlic, minced, or ½ to 1 teaspoon bottled minced garlic
14½-ounce can no-salt-added stewed tomatoes, crushed
4½ cups dried tricolor pasta shells (about 1 pound)
¼ cup snipped fresh parsley

Preheat oven to 300° F.

Combine flour, salt, and pepper in a plastic or paper bag. Add veal and shake to coat. Shake off excess flour.

Spray a heavy ovenproof skillet with olive oil spray. Heat over medium-high heat. Add olive oil and swirl to coat bottom of skillet. Add veal and brown quickly on all sides.

Add wine, scraping pan and stirring.

Add carrots, celery, onion, and garlic. Cook for 2 to 3 minutes, stirring occasionally.

Add undrained tomatoes and bring to a boil.

Bake, covered, for 1 hour. Baste. If veal isn't tender, return to oven. Bake for 5 to 30 minutes, or until tender.

Meanwhile, cook pasta using package directions, omitting salt and margarine. Drain.

To serve, put pasta in a serving bowl, then top with veal mixture and parsley.

Calories 545
Protein 41 g
Carbohydrates 67 g
Cholesterol 111 mg
Total Fat 10 g
Saturated 3 g
Polyunsaturated 1 g
Monounsaturated 4 g
Fiber 4 g
Sodium 310 mg

Chicken Stufino

Replace veal with 1½ pounds boneless, skinless chicken breasts, cut into large chunks. (calories 467; protein 34 g; carbohydrates 67 g; cholesterol 63 mg; total fat 5 g; saturated 1 g; polyunsaturated 1 g; monounsaturated 2 g; fiber 4 g; sodium 290 mg)

Cook's Tip

If your skillet isn't ovenproof, transfer the mixture to a 1½-quart covered casserole dish before baking.

Osso Buco

Serves 5

Our version of this Italian dish contains most of the ingredients usually found in this classic—veal shanks, olive oil, white wine, tomatoes, and lemon zest. We've cut the fat by using less oil and cut the sodium by leaving out the anchovies.

Olive oil vegetable spray
4 1-inch veal shanks (about 2¾ pounds)
1 teaspoon olive oil
1 large onion, finely chopped (1¼ cups)
2 ribs celery, chopped (1 cup)
1 medium carrot, grated (¾ cup)
2 medium cloves garlic, minced, or 1 teaspoon bottled minced garlic
14½-ounce can whole no-salt-added tomatoes, crushed
1 cup Beef Broth (see page 39 or use commercial low-sodium variety)
½ cup dry white wine (regular or nonalcoholic)
½ cup water
2 strips fresh lemon zest, about 1½ inches long and ½ inch wide
2 bay leaves
4 sprigs of fresh thyme or ½ teaspoon dried, crumbled
1 teaspoon salt-free dried Italian herb seasoning, crumbled
¼ teaspoon salt
Pepper to taste
10 ounces dried angel hair pasta (about 2½ cups)
3 tablespoons snipped fresh parsley

Calories 587
Protein 65 g
Carbohydrates 54 g
Cholesterol 207 mg
Total Fat 9 g
Saturated 3 g
Polyunsaturated 1 g
Monounsaturated 3 g
Fiber 6 g
Sodium 291 mg

Preheat broiler. Spray broiler pan with olive oil spray.

Tie veal meat to bone with kitchen twine and put in broiler pan. Broil about 6 inches from heat for 8 to 10 minutes on each side, or until evenly browned. Set aside.

Preheat oven to 350° F.

Heat a large skillet over medium-high heat. Add oil and swirl to coat bottom of skillet. Sauté onion, celery, carrot, and garlic, stirring occasionally, until wilted, 3 to 4 minutes.

Put carrot mixture, then veal shanks, in a large, heavy casserole dish. Pour undrained tomatoes evenly over all. Add broth, wine, water, lemon zest, bay leaves, thyme, Italian herb seasoning, salt, and pepper.

Bake, covered, for 1½ to 2 hours, turning veal shanks three or four times, until veal is tender and sauce is thickened. Add water during cooking to maintain sauce around veal if needed.

Remove shanks from sauce; reserve sauce. Remove meat from bone and cut into bite-size pieces, discarding fat and marrow. Skim fat from sauce; discard fat.

Heat defatted sauce and veal in a large saucepan over medium heat until heated through, 3 to 4 minutes. Remove bay leaves.

Meanwhile, cook pasta using package directions, omitting salt and oil. Drain.

To serve, arrange pasta on platter, top with meat mixture, and sprinkle with parsley.

Cook's Tip on Gravy Skimmer

A gravy skimmer (also known as a gravy or fat separator) is a handy gadget for removing fat from gravy, soup, or sauce, as in this recipe. Pour the hot liquid into the cup portion of the skimmer. When the fat has risen to the top, slowly pour the fat-free liquid from the spout end. *Voilà*—the fat stays in the cup and spout.

Veal with Bell Peppers and Mushrooms

Serves 6

Veal scallops cook quickly, making this a perfect dish for the cook on the run.

⅓ cup flour

¼ teaspoon pepper

¼ teaspoon salt

1½ pounds veal scallops, pounded to ¼-inch thickness

Olive oil spray

2 teaspoons olive oil

1½ cups red bell pepper strips (1 to 2 medium)

8 ounces medium fresh mushrooms, quartered (3 cups)

3 medium cloves garlic, minced, or 1½ teaspoons bottled minced garlic

1½ cups Chicken Broth (see page 40 or use commercial low-sodium variety)

⅓ cup white wine (regular or nonalcoholic)

2 tablespoons fresh lemon juice

½ cup sliced green onions (4 to 5)

Snipped fresh parsley

Calories 328
Protein 29 g
Carbohydrates 11 g
Cholesterol 104 mg
Total Fat 17 g
Saturated 6 g
Polyunsaturated 1 g
Monounsaturated 7 g
Fiber 2 g
Sodium 174 mg

Combine flour, pepper, and salt in a plastic or paper bag. Add veal pieces and shake to coat evenly. Shake off excess flour.

Spray a large nonstick skillet with olive oil spray. Heat over medium-high heat. Add 1 teaspoon olive oil and swirl to spread over bottom of skillet. Add half the veal and brown lightly on both sides, 2 to 3 minutes. Transfer to a plate. Repeat process.

Add bell pepper, mushrooms, and garlic to skillet. Cook, covered, over medium-low heat for 7 to 9 minutes, stirring occasionally.

Pour broth, wine, and lemon juice into skillet and add veal. Cook over medium heat for 10 minutes, or until sauce thickens slightly, stirring occasionally.

Stir in green onions and cook for 1 minute.

To serve, sprinkle with parsley.

Chicken with Bell Peppers and Mushrooms

Replace veal with 1½ pounds boneless, skinless chicken breasts, pounded to ¼-inch thickness. (calories 198; protein 25 g; carbohydrates 11 g; cholesterol 63 mg; total fat 5 g; saturated 1 g; polyunsaturated 1 g; monounsaturated 2 g; fiber 2 g; sodium 158 mg)

Venison Stew

Serves 8

If you have venison from a hunting trip, whether to the woods or a specialty grocery store, this simple recipe is the answer.

Vegetable oil spray
2 pounds breast or shoulder venison, all visible fat removed, cut into 1-inch cubes
2 tablespoons all-purpose flour
6 cups water or Beef Broth (see page 39 or use commercial low-sodium variety)
½ teaspoon pepper
4 medium potatoes, peeled and diced (about 4 cups)
4 medium carrots, diced (3 cups)
4 medium onions, diced (2 cups)
2 medium turnips, diced (about 1 cup)

Preheat broiler.

Lightly spray a broiler pan and rack with vegetable oil spray. Broil venison about 6 inches from heat for 15 to 20 minutes, or until meat is brown on all sides, turning occasionally.

Put meat in a large, heavy nonstick skillet. Add flour and cook over medium-high heat for 2 minutes, stirring constantly.

Add water and pepper and bring to a boil, stirring constantly. Reduce heat and simmer, covered, for 1½ to 2 hours, or until meat is just tender.

Add diced vegetables and simmer, covered, for 30 minutes, or until meat and vegetables are tender.

Calories 241
Protein 28 g
Carbohydrates 25 g
Cholesterol 95 mg
Total Fat 3 g
Saturated 1 g
Polyunsaturated 1 g
Monounsaturated 1 g
Fiber 4 g
Sodium 93 mg

Lamb Chops Dijon

Serves 4

For an elegant meal, serve this dish with Mushrooms with White Wine and Shallots and French Peas (see pages 383 and 395).

RUB

3 tablespoons finely snipped fresh parsley

1 tablespoon finely chopped fresh rosemary or 1 teaspoon dried, crushed

3 medium cloves garlic, finely minced, or 1½ teaspoons bottled minced garlic

1½ teaspoons Dijon mustard

1 teaspoon olive oil

Pepper to taste

4 loin or shoulder arm lamb chops, ¾ inch thick (about 1 pound), all visible fat removed

Vegetable oil spray

In a small bowl, blend rub ingredients into a paste.

Spread evenly on both sides of lamb. Put on a platter in a single layer. Cover loosely with plastic wrap or aluminum foil and refrigerate for 45 minutes.

Meanwhile, preheat grill on medium-high or preheat broiler. If using broiler, spray broiler pan and rack with vegetable oil spray.

Grill lamb or broil about 6 inches from heat for 7 to 9 minutes, turn, and cook for 5 to 6 minutes, or until done to taste.

Calories 104
Protein 13 g
Carbohydrates 1 g
Cholesterol 49 mg
Total Fat 5 g
Saturated 2 g
Polyunsaturated 0 g
Monounsaturated 2 g
Fiber 0 g
Sodium 73 mg

Lamb Kebabs

Serves 6

Serve with a bed of wild rice and Mandarin Spinach Salad with Sesame Garlic Topping *(see page 75).*

MARINADE

½ cup cider vinegar

½ cup finely chopped onion (1 medium)

3 tablespoons finely chopped fresh rosemary or 1 tablespoon dried, crushed

3 tablespoons honey

2 tablespoons chopped fresh mint or 2 teaspoons dried, crumbled

3 medium cloves garlic, minced, or 1½ teaspoons bottled minced garlic

1 teaspoon olive oil

¼ teaspoon salt

¼ teaspoon pepper, or to taste

1½ pounds leg of lamb (after boning and trimming), cut into 24 cubes

1 medium red onion, cut into 12 wedges

2 9-ounce packages frozen no-salt-added artichoke hearts, thawed

24 cherry tomatoes

In an airtight plastic bag, combine marinade ingredients. Add lamb and turn to coat. Seal and refrigerate for 1 to 4 hours, turning occasionally.

Soak six long bamboo skewers in cold water for at least 10 minutes.

Drain lamb and put marinade in a small saucepan. Bring to a boil over medium-high heat and boil, covered, for at least 5 minutes.

Preheat grill on medium-high.

Separate each red onion wedge vertically into two parts, making 24 wedges. Separate artichoke hearts into 24 pieces.

For each kebab, thread a skewer as follows: 1 piece onion, 1 meat cube, 1 piece artichoke, 1 tomato. Repeat three times for each skewer.

Grill for 12 to 15 minutes, or until lamb is done to taste. Baste with hot marinade for last 5 minutes of cooking time.

Calories 271
Protein 27 g
Carbohydrates 27 g
Cholesterol 84 mg
Total Fat 7 g
- Saturated 3 g
- Polyunsaturated 1 g
- Monounsaturated 3 g

Fiber 6 g
Sodium 225 mg

Armenian Lamb Casserole

Serves 4

Tender chunks of lamb, cubes of vegetables, and lots of seasoning make this Middle Eastern dish a real winner.

Vegetable oil spray

1 teaspoon acceptable vegetable oil

1 pound lean lamb from loin or shoulder arm chop, all visible fat removed, cut into cubes

1 medium onion, sliced (½ cup)

1 medium clove garlic, minced, or ½ teaspoon bottled minced garlic

1 cup canned no-salt-added tomatoes, undrained

1 medium eggplant, cut into cubes

1 medium green bell pepper, coarsely chopped (1 cup)

2 medium carrots, sliced (1½ cups)

2 small zucchini, cut into cubes (1½ cups)

½ cup okra, sliced (optional) (6 to 7 small pods)

3 slices lemon

½ teaspoon paprika

⅛ teaspoon ground cumin

⅛ teaspoon pepper, or to taste

Spray a stockpot, Dutch oven, or large, deep skillet with vegetable oil spray. Add oil and heat over medium-high heat. Add lamb cubes and brown thoroughly on all sides, about 10 minutes, turning occasionally.

Add onion and garlic and brown slightly, 3 to 4 minutes.

Add undrained tomatoes and reduce heat to low. Cook, covered, for 1 hour, stirring occasionally and adding a small amount of water if necessary.

Preheat oven to 350° F.

Add remaining ingredients to stockpot and bring to a boil. Transfer mixture to a 3-quart ovenproof ceramic or glass casserole dish. (Don't use plain cast iron. It will discolor the vegetables.)

Bake, covered, for 1 hour, or until vegetables are tender.

Calories 272
Protein 28 g
Carbohydrates 22 g
Cholesterol 97 mg
Total Fat 9 g
 Saturated 4 g
 Polyunsaturated 1 g
 Monounsaturated 3 g
Fiber 7 g
Sodium 82 mg

Lamb Stew

Serves 12

You may want to freeze half of this wonderful stew for another meal.

Olive oil spray

1 teaspoon olive oil

1½ cups finely chopped onion (about 3 medium)

4 large cloves garlic, minced, or 2 to 3 teaspoons bottled minced garlic

2 pounds lean lamb from loin or shoulder arm roast, all visible fat removed, cut into cubes

4 cups water

½ cup dry white wine (regular or nonalcoholic)

2 pounds potatoes (about 6 medium)

5 medium carrots

1 pound fresh mushrooms

14½-ounce can diced no-salt-added tomatoes

6-ounce can no-salt-added tomato paste

1½ teaspoons coarsely ground black pepper

1 teaspoon salt

2 tablespoons finely chopped fresh rosemary or 2 teaspoons dried, crushed

2 tablespoons finely chopped fresh mint or 2 teaspoons dried, crumbled

Spray a large Dutch oven or stockpot with vegetable oil spray. Heat over medium-high heat. Add oil and swirl. Sauté onions until translucent, 2 to 3 minutes. Add garlic and sauté for 2 minutes. Add lamb and cook for 10 minutes, or until brown on all sides.

Add water and wine. Bring to a boil over medium-high heat. Reduce heat and simmer, covered, for 1 hour.

Meanwhile, peel potatoes and cut into chunks, peel carrots and cut into sticks, and cut mushrooms into quarters. Add to lamb mixture with undrained tomatoes, tomato paste, pepper, and salt. Stir well. Cook, covered, over medium-low heat for 30 minutes, or until vegetables are tender when pierced with tip of a knife.

Add rosemary and mint, and simmer for 2 minutes.

Calories 227
Protein 20 g
Carbohydrates 24 g
Cholesterol 65 mg
Total Fat 6 g
    Saturated 2 g
    Polyunsaturated 0 g
    Monounsaturated 2 g
Fiber 4 g
Sodium 267 mg

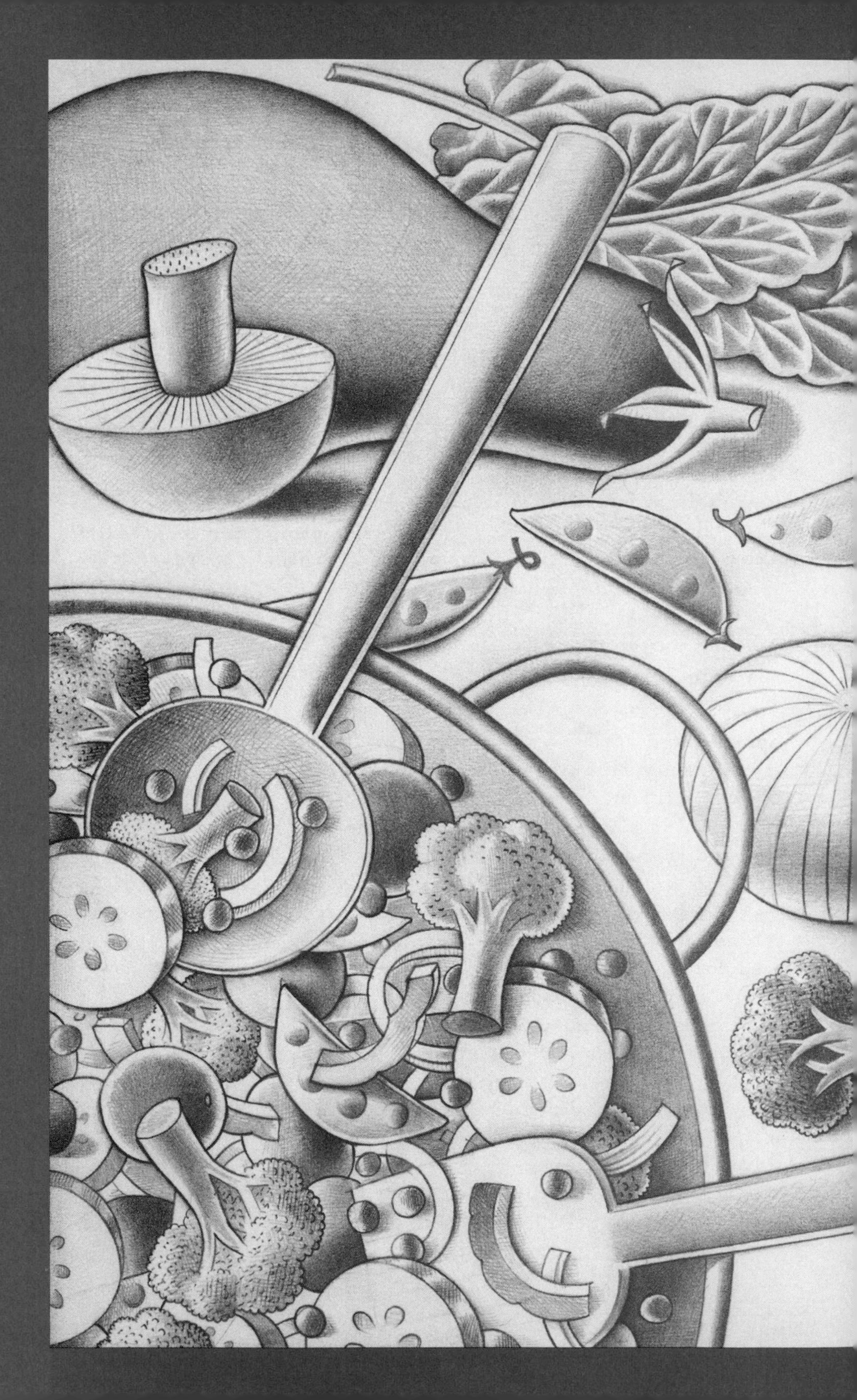

VEGETARIAN ENTRÉES

Artichoke-Tomato Pizza Bagels
Pasta Primavera
Spaghetti with Zesty Marinara Sauce
Spaghetti Cheese Amandine
Spaghetti with Perfect Pesto
Spaghetti with Lentil Sauce
Vegetarian Stir-Fry
Rice Sticks with Asian Vegetables (Pad Thai)
Sesame-Peanut Pasta
Curried Vegetable Wrap
Portobello Mushroom Wrap with Yogurt Curry Sauce
Spinach and Brown Rice Casserole
Stuffed Peppers
Portobello Mushroom Ragout with Sun-Dried Tomato Polenta
Hoppin' John
Artichoke and Chick-Pea Pilaf
Mediterranean Lentils and Rice
Old-Fashioned Baked Beans

Cuban Black Beans
Cheesy Stuffed Potatoes
Broccoli Rabe and Chick-Peas over Parmesan Toasts
Meatless Moussaka
Enchilada Bake
Curried Cauliflower and Tofu with Basmati Rice
Broiled Eggplant, Italian Style
Eggplant Parmesan
Eggplant Zucchini Casserole
Italian-Style Zucchini
Stuffed Zucchini
Spaghetti Squash Casserole
Spinach Artichoke Gratin
Spinach Soufflé
Spinach Roll with Alfredo Sauce
Spinach Ricotta Swirls
Steamed Veggies with Herbed Cheese
Tomato Quiche in Couscous Crust

Artichoke-Tomato Pizza Bagels

Serves 8

Artichokes and balsamic vinegar give a gourmet update to these pizza bagels.

2 Italian plum tomatoes, chopped
½ cup frozen artichoke hearts, thawed, drained, and chopped (about 6 ounces)
½ cup thinly sliced red onion
2 teaspoons olive oil
1 teaspoon balsamic vinegar
1 medium clove garlic, minced, or ½ teaspoon bottled minced garlic
½ teaspoon salt-free dried Italian herb seasoning, crumbled
4 ounces nonfat or part-skim mozzarella cheese, or fat-free mozzarella-flavor soy cheese, shredded (1 cup)
2 tablespoons grated Romano cheese
4 bagels, split and lightly toasted

Preheat broiler. Line a broilerproof pan with aluminum foil.

In a medium bowl, combine tomatoes, artichokes, onion, oil, vinegar, garlic, and Italian herb seasoning, stirring well.

In a small bowl, combine mozzarella and Romano.

Spread artichoke mixture on bagel halves and sprinkle with cheese mixture. Place bagels on broiler pan.

Broil about 6 inches from heat until bubbly, 2 to 3 minutes.

Cook's Tip on Italian Plum Tomatoes

Also called Roma tomatoes, Italian plum tomatoes are shaped more like pears or eggs than plums. They are often tastier and less expensive than "regular" tomatoes.

Calories 150
Protein 9 g
Carbohydrates 23 g
Cholesterol 3 mg
Total Fat 2 g
Saturated 1 g
Polyunsaturated 0 g
Monounsaturated 1 g
Fiber 2 g
Sodium 348 mg

Pasta Primavera

Serves 4

The vegetable possibilities for this dish range from A for asparagus to Z for zucchini. As your favorites come into season, substitute them for some of the vegetables here.

1 cup nonfat or low-fat cottage cheese

1 tablespoon fresh lemon juice

8 ounces dried thin spaghetti (2 cups)

1 teaspoon acceptable vegetable oil

½ cup chopped onion (1 medium)

¼ cup chopped green onions (2 to 3 medium)

1 medium clove garlic, minced, or ½ teaspoon bottled minced garlic

¼ teaspoon pepper, or to taste

2 cups sliced fresh mushrooms (about 8 ounces)

1½ cups sliced carrots (2 medium)

10-ounce package frozen no-salt-added broccoli, steamed

1 cup sliced bell pepper, any color (1 medium)

Calories 337
Protein 18 g
Carbohydrates 61 g
Cholesterol 5 mg
Total Fat 3 g
Saturated 0 g
Polyunsaturated 1 g
Monounsaturated 0 g
Fiber 9 g
Sodium 275 mg

Drain cottage cheese, discarding liquid. In a small bowl, combine cottage cheese and lemon juice. Set aside.

Cook spaghetti using package directions, omitting salt and margarine. Drain thoroughly.

Meanwhile, heat oil in a large skillet over medium-high heat, swirling to coat bottom. Sauté onion, green onions, garlic, and pepper for 1 minute.

Stir in mushrooms and cook for 1 minute, stirring occasionally.

Stir in remaining ingredients and cook for 3 to 4 minutes, stirring constantly.

In a large bowl, combine spaghetti and cottage cheese mixture. Top with sautéed vegetables.

Cook's Tip on Fresh Pasta

If you prefer to make your own pasta or buy fresh pasta, a rule of thumb is to substitute 3 ounces of fresh for 2 ounces of dried.

Spaghetti with Zesty Marinara Sauce

Serves 8

This aromatic sauce turns any meal into an Italian feast. It freezes well for up to six months, so make extra for another time.

ZESTY MARINARA SAUCE

1 teaspoon olive oil

1 large onion, finely chopped (½ cup)

2 large cloves garlic, crushed, or 1½ teaspoons bottled minced garlic

6-ounce can no-salt-added tomato paste

2 tablespoons minced fresh parsley

2 teaspoons sugar

1¼ teaspoons salt-free dried Italian herb seasoning, crumbled

½ teaspoon dried basil, crumbled

⅛ teaspoon salt

⅛ teaspoon crushed red pepper flakes, or to taste

¼ teaspoon pepper, or to taste

16-ounce can no-salt-added tomatoes, crushed, with liquid

1 cup water

8-ounce can no-salt-added tomato sauce

¼ cup dry red wine (regular or nonalcoholic)

1 bay leaf

16 ounces dried spaghetti (4 cups)

½ cup grated Parmesan cheese

In a medium saucepan, heat oil over medium-high heat, swirling to coat bottom. Sauté onion and garlic until onion is translucent, 2 to 3 minutes, stirring occasionally.

Whisk in tomato paste, parsley, sugar, herb seasoning, basil, salt, red peppers, and black pepper. Reduce heat to medium-low and cook for 3 to 4 minutes, stirring often.

Stir in remaining sauce ingredients and bring to a boil over high heat. Reduce heat and simmer, partially covered, for 1 to 1½ hours. Remove bay leaf.

Cook spaghetti using package directions, omitting salt and margarine. Drain; stir in Parmesan.

To serve, spoon sauce over spaghetti.

Calories 311
Protein 12 g
Carbohydrates 57 g
Cholesterol 5 mg
Total Fat 4 g
Saturated 2 g
Polyunsaturated 1 g
Monounsaturated 1 g
Fiber 6 g
Sodium 186 mg

Spaghetti Cheese Amandine

Serves 5

A textured sauce of cottage cheese, green peas, green onions, and Parmesan cheese tops bite-size pieces of spaghetti. Serve with sliced tomatoes, tossed salad, or fresh fruit.

8 ounces dried spaghetti, broken into small pieces (2 cups)

1 cup frozen green peas, thawed

1 cup nonfat or low-fat cottage cheese

¼ cup sliced green onions (2 to 3 medium)

2 tablespoons grated Parmesan cheese

2 tablespoons fat-free milk

½ teaspoon salt-free dried Italian herb seasoning, crumbled

1 tablespoon light margarine

Pepper to taste

½ cup slivered almonds, dry-roasted (about 2 ounces)

Cook spaghetti using package directions, omitting salt and margarine. Drain.

Meanwhile, in a medium bowl, combine peas, cottage cheese, green onions, Parmesan, milk, and herb seasoning, stirring well.

In a large skillet, melt margarine over medium-low heat. Stir in spaghetti.

When spaghetti is warm, add cottage cheese mixture. Cook until heated through, 3 to 4 minutes, stirring occasionally.

To serve, stir in pepper and sprinkle with almonds.

Calories 318
Protein 17 g
Carbohydrates 45 g
Cholesterol 6 mg
Total Fat 8 g
Saturated 1 g
Polyunsaturated 2 g
Monounsaturated 4 g
Fiber 6 g
Sodium 266 mg

Spaghetti with Perfect Pesto

Serves 6

This sauce is delicious—the mix of herbs is perfect!

PESTO SAUCE

2 cups firmly packed fresh spinach leaves, stems removed (3 to 4 ounces)

½ cup firmly packed fresh basil leaves, stems removed

½ cup firmly packed fresh parsley, stems removed

¼ cup Vegetable Broth (see page 41 or use commercial low-sodium variety)

2 tablespoons pine nuts, dry-roasted

2 tablespoons grated Romano cheese

2 tablespoons grated Parmesan cheese

1 tablespoon olive oil

2 medium cloves garlic or 1 teaspoon bottled minced garlic

Pepper to taste

1 to 2 tablespoons water (if needed)

12 ounces dried thin spaghetti (3 cups)

For sauce, process ingredients in a food processor or blender until almost pureed. If mixture is too thick, add water.

Cook spaghetti using package directions, omitting salt and margarine. Drain. Combine with sauce.

Cook's Tip on Pine Nuts

Native to many parts of the world, pine nuts are the nuts found in different varieties of pinecone. The difficulty in harvesting makes them rather expensive, but you use them in small quantities. Pine nuts—or *pignoli*—are traditionally used in pesto sauce. Also called piñons, they are very popular in southwestern cuisine. Store them covered in the refrigerator or freezer to keep them from turning rancid.

Calories 317
Protein 13 g
Carbohydrates 51 g
Cholesterol 4 mg
Total Fat 6 g
- Saturated 1 g
- Polyunsaturated 1 g
- Monounsaturated 3 g

Fiber 9 g
Sodium 87 mg

Spaghetti with Lentil Sauce

Serves 12

A medley of steamed vegetables, such as broccoli and baby carrots, would taste good with this dish.

LENTIL SAUCE

1 teaspoon acceptable vegetable oil

1 medium onion, chopped (½ cup)

1 medium clove garlic, minced, or ½ teaspoon bottled minced garlic

4 cups homemade Vegetable Broth (see page 41 or use commercial low-sodium variety)

1½ cups dried lentils, sorted for stones and rinsed (12 ounces)

1 dried hot red pepper, crumbled, or ¼ teaspoon crushed red pepper flakes or ⅛ teaspoon cayenne

¼ teaspoon black pepper, or to taste

15-ounce can no-salt-added tomatoes

6-ounce can no-salt-added tomato paste

1 tablespoon cider vinegar

¼ teaspoon dried basil, crumbled

¼ teaspoon dried oregano, crumbled

24 ounces dried spaghetti (6 cups)

For sauce, put oil in a Dutch oven, stockpot, or large skillet. Sauté onion and garlic over medium-high heat for 2 to 3 minutes, or until onion is translucent.

Stir in broth, lentils, red pepper, and black pepper. Bring to a boil, then reduce heat and simmer, covered, for 30 minutes.

Add remaining sauce ingredients. Simmer, uncovered, for 30 to 40 minutes, stirring occasionally.

Meanwhile, cook spaghetti using package directions, omitting salt and margarine. Drain. Combine with lentil sauce.

Calories 322
Protein 14 g
Carbohydrates 63 g
Cholesterol 0 mg
Total Fat 2 g
Saturated 0 g
Polyunsaturated 1 g
Monounsaturated 0 g
Fiber 11 g
Sodium 23 mg

Cook's Tip on Lentils

A member of the pea family, lentils are a staple of many vegetarian diets. Quicker cooking than other dried peas and beans, lentils don't need to be soaked.

Vegetarian Stir-Fry

Serves 4

Add some fresh vegetables, bamboo shoots, and seasonings to an already-prepared, already-tasty rice dish, and dinner is served.

3 tablespoons light soy sauce

2½ teaspoons sugar

1 teaspoon very low sodium or low-sodium Worcestershire sauce

4 cups shredded cabbage (about 8 ounces)

1 cup chopped onion (2 medium)

½ cup shredded carrot

8-ounce can bamboo shoots, drained

2 medium cloves garlic, minced, or 1 teaspoon bottled minced garlic

1 teaspoon grated gingerroot

Vegetable oil spray

1 tablespoon acceptable vegetable oil

3 cups reserved Water Chestnut and Bell Pepper Rice (see page 268)

In a small bowl, combine soy sauce, sugar, and Worcestershire sauce, stirring well.

In a large bowl, combine cabbage, onion, carrot, bamboo shoots, garlic, and gingerroot.

Spray a nonstick wok or skillet with vegetable oil spray and swirl to coat bottom. Pour in oil. Put wok over high heat for 1 minute, or until oil is very hot but not smoking. Cook cabbage mixture for 2 minutes, stirring constantly.

Add rice mixture and cook for 2 minutes, stirring constantly. Remove from heat.

Stir in soy sauce mixture.

Calories 260
Protein 7 g
Carbohydrates 50 g
Cholesterol 0 mg
Total Fat 4 g
Saturated 1 g
Polyunsaturated 2 g
Monounsaturated 1 g
Fiber 5 g
Sodium 411 mg

Rice Sticks with Asian Vegetables (Pad Thai)

Serves 6

An exciting blend of taste, color, texture, and aroma comes together in pad thai, a popular dish from Thailand. This dish is fun to eat with chopsticks.

8 ounces dried flat rice sticks (rice-flour noodles)

2 tablespoons fresh lime juice (1 to 2 medium limes)

1 tablespoon sugar

2 teaspoons fish sauce or 2 teaspoons light soy sauce

Vegetable oil spray

10.5-ounce package light tofu (firm), diced

1 teaspoon acceptable vegetable oil

½ teaspoon crushed red pepper flakes

2 medium cloves garlic, minced, or 1 teaspoon bottled minced garlic

4 stalks bok choy, stems and leaves thinly sliced (3 cups)

1 cup sugar snap peas, ends trimmed (4 ounces)

½ cup canned whole baby corn, drained

1 large carrot, cut into matchstick-size strips

1 tablespoon dry sherry (optional)

1 cup bean sprouts (optional)

2 green onions, thinly sliced (optional)

2 tablespoons chopped peanuts (optional)

Lime wedges (optional)

Sprigs of fresh cilantro (optional)

Calories 207
Protein 8 g
Carbohydrates 40 g
Cholesterol 0 mg
Total Fat 2 g
Saturated 0 g
Polyunsaturated 1 g
Monounsaturated 0 g
Fiber 4 g
Sodium 227 mg

Put noodles in a large bowl with enough hot tap water to cover by 1 inch. Cover with plastic wrap and let soak for 15 to 20 minutes.

Meanwhile, combine lime juice, sugar, and fish sauce. Set aside.

Heat a large nonstick skillet on medium-high heat. Remove pan from heat and spray with vegetable oil spray. Cook tofu for 2 to 3 minutes, or until warmed through, stirring occasionally. Remove from skillet and set aside.

Pour oil into skillet and swirl to coat bottom. Cook pepper flakes and garlic for 10 seconds.

Add bok choy, peas, corn, and carrot. Cook

for 1 to 2 minutes, or until tender-crisp, stirring occasionally.

Drain noodles, discarding water. Add noodles, tofu, lime juice mixture, and sherry to skillet. Cook for 2 to 3 minutes, or until noodles are warmed through, stirring occasionally (noodles get mushy if overcooked).

To serve, arrange noodle mixture on a serving platter and garnish with remaining ingredients.

Cook's Tip on Rice Sticks

Asian markets and some grocery and health food stores carry rice sticks, noodles made of rice flour and water. You can buy round or flat rice sticks in a variety of widths and even in some flavors. If you can't find the width you want, substitute a comparable pasta.

Sesame-Peanut Pasta

Serves 4

This is soooo good—and quick, too! Serve it either hot or cold.

2 medium green onions, thinly sliced (about 1/4 cup)
1/4 cup Vegetable Broth (see page 41 or use commercial low-sodium variety)
2 tablespoons reduced-fat peanut butter
1 tablespoon plus 1 teaspoon cider vinegar or rice vinegar
1 teaspoon toasted sesame oil
1/4 teaspoon cayenne, or to taste
4 cups hot cooked spaghetti (2 cups dried, uncooked)

In a medium bowl, combine all ingredients except spaghetti. Stir into hot spaghetti.

Serve immediately for a hot entrée, or cover and refrigerate for a cold entrée.

Calories 253
Protein 9 g
Carbohydrates 43 g
Cholesterol 0 mg
Total Fat 5 g
Saturated 1 g
Polyunsaturated 2 g
Monounsaturated 2 g
Fiber 4 g
Sodium 48 mg

Curried Vegetable Wrap

Serves 4

Americans have turned ancient flatbreads into an ultramodern way to serve a meal. Using tortillas, pita bread, and other pliable flat disks, we wrap everything from smoked salmon to leftovers. In this dish, the filling is fabulous curried vegetables and rice.

1 cup uncooked long-grain, medium-grain, basmati, or brown rice

1 medium onion

3 medium zucchini (about 1 pound)

2 or 3 medium green bell peppers, to taste

Vegetable oil spray

1 teaspoon acceptable vegetable oil

3 medium tomatoes, peeled and chopped, or 14.5-ounce can no-salt-added diced tomatoes, drained

¼ cup dried currants or raisins (optional)

2 teaspoons curry powder

1 teaspoon ground cumin

¾ teaspoon red hot-pepper sauce, or to taste

8 10-inch nonfat or low-fat flour tortillas (see Cook's Tip, page 27)

Calories 431
Protein 13 g
Carbohydrates 19 g
Cholesterol 0 mg
Total Fat 3 g
Saturated 0 g
Polyunsaturated 1 g
Monounsaturated 1 g
Fiber 9 g
Sodium 481 mg

Prepare rice using package directions, omitting salt and margarine.

Meanwhile, cut onion in half lengthwise, then in thin half-moon slices; cut zucchini into ½-inch cubes; and cut bell peppers into ½-inch squares.

Spray a large nonstick skillet with vegetable oil spray. Add oil and heat over high heat, swirling to coat. Sauté onion for 2 to 3 minutes, or until it starts to soften, stirring occasionally.

Reduce heat to medium. Add zucchini and bell peppers. Cook for about 10 minutes, or until vegetables are soft.

Stir in remaining ingredients except tortillas.

Place ¼ cup rice and ½ cup vegetables in center of a tortilla, spreading them horizontally to about 2 inches from each side. Fold one side of tortilla over filling (fold to where filling stops). Fold bottom up and top down to form a package that's open on one end. Place seam side down on a serving plate. Repeat with remaining tortillas.

Cook's Tip on Currants and Raisins

The currants add piquancy to this dish without being noticeably fruity. If you're using raisins, they'll be just as subtle if you cut them into small pieces. Spray your knife or kitchen shears with vegetable oil spray to make the task easy.

Portobello Mushroom Wrap with Yogurt Curry Sauce

Serves 8

What do you get when you wrap meaty grilled portobello mushrooms, aromatic rice, and slender asparagus in a tortilla and enhance it all with a creamy curry sauce? A heart-healthy meal to go!

YOGURT CURRY SAUCE

½ cup nonfat or low-fat plain yogurt

½ teaspoon curry powder

1 teaspoon fresh lemon juice

½ teaspoon sugar

2 medium portobello mushrooms (about 6 ounces)

2 tablespoons balsamic vinegar

1 tablespoon olive oil

2 medium cloves garlic, minced, or 1 teaspoon bottled minced garlic

2 cups cooked jasmine, basmati, brown, or wild rice

2 green onions, thinly sliced (¼ cup)

¼ cup shredded fat-free or part-skim mozzarella cheese or fat-free mozzarella-style soy cheese (about 1 ounce)

1 Italian plum tomato, diced

1 teaspoon light brown sugar

1 teaspoon rice vinegar

8 6-inch nonfat or low-fat flour tortillas (see Cook's Tip, page 27), Spinach Tortillas, or Tomato Tortillas (see pages 518 and 519)

16 asparagus spears, cooked until tender-crisp

For sauce, combine ingredients in a small bowl. Cover and refrigerate for 30 minutes to 2 days.

Meanwhile, cut each mushroom into 8 slices. Put in an airtight plastic bag.

In a small bowl, combine vinegar, olive oil, and garlic. Pour over mushrooms and turn bag to coat. Seal and marinate at room temperature for 10 to 15 minutes.

In a medium bowl, combine rice, green onions, mozzarella, tomato, brown sugar, and vinegar.

Preheat grill on medium-high.

Grill undrained mushrooms for 1 to 2 minutes on each side, or until tender.

Calories 188
Protein 7 g
Carbohydrates 36 g
Cholesterol 1 mg
Total Fat 2 g
Saturated 0 g
Polyunsaturated 0 g
Monounsaturated 1 g
Fiber 4 g
Sodium 273 mg

To assemble, put a tortilla on a microwave-safe plate. Put 2 slices grilled mushroom in center of tortilla. Top with 2 asparagus spears. Spoon ¼ cup rice mixture over asparagus. Microwave on 100 percent power (high) for 30 seconds. Roll tortilla jelly-roll style over filling, securing with a toothpick if desired. Repeat with remaining ingredients. Serve with sauce.

Spinach and Brown Rice Casserole

Serves 8

This casserole is a good way to use up leftover brown rice. Create a fruit parfait of bananas, mandarin oranges, and kiwifruit to serve with the casserole.

Vegetable oil spray

10 ounces fresh spinach or 10-ounce package frozen no-salt-added chopped spinach, thawed

3 cups cooked brown rice (about 1 cup uncooked)

2 cups nonfat or low-fat cottage cheese

Egg substitute equivalent to 1 egg, or 1 egg

1 tablespoon all-purpose flour

1 tablespoon grated Parmesan cheese

½ teaspoon dried thyme, crumbled

Pepper to taste

1 teaspoon light margarine

1½ cups chopped onion (3 medium)

3 medium cloves garlic, minced, or 1½ teaspoons bottled minced garlic

8 ounces fresh mushrooms, sliced (2 to 2½ cups)

3 tablespoons grated Parmesan cheese

2 tablespoons sunflower seeds

Preheat oven to 375° F. Lightly spray a 13 × 9 × 2-inch pan with vegetable oil spray.

If using fresh spinach, remove large stems and tear leaves into bite-size pieces. If using frozen spinach, squeeze out moisture. Set aside.

In a large bowl, combine rice, cottage cheese, egg substitute, flour, 1 tablespoon Parmesan, thyme, and pepper. Set aside.

In a large saucepan, melt margarine over medium-high heat. Sauté onions and garlic until onion is translucent, 2 to 3 minutes.

Reduce heat to low and add spinach and mushrooms. Cook, covered, for 3 to 5 minutes.

Add cottage cheese mixture and blend well. Spoon mixture into pan and sprinkle with 3 tablespoons Parmesan and sunflower seeds.

Bake, uncovered, for 25 to 30 minutes.

Calories 182
Protein 13 g
Carbohydrates 25 g
Cholesterol 8 mg
Total Fat 3 g
  Saturated 1 g
  Polyunsaturated 1 g
  Monounsaturated 1 g
Fiber 3 g
Sodium 319 mg

Stuffed Peppers

Serves 8

Stuff bell pepper halves with a refreshing, crunchy combination of vegetables, rice, and water chestnuts. Experiment with different bell peppers—red, yellow, purple, orange, or white.

4 large bell peppers, any color or combination

1 teaspoon olive oil

2 medium tomatoes, chopped (about 1½ cups)

1 medium crookneck squash, diced (about 2 cups)

1 medium zucchini, diced (about 2 cups)

½ cup diced onion (1 medium)

2 medium cloves garlic, minced, or 1 teaspoon bottled minced garlic

2 cups cooked brown rice (½ to ⅔ cup uncooked)

½ cup grated fat-free or low-fat Cheddar cheese (2 ounces)

¼ cup sliced water chestnuts (2 ounces)

1 cup no-salt-added tomato juice

Preheat oven to 375° F.

Cut peppers in half lengthwise, removing stems, ribs, and seeds.

Heat oil in a large skillet over medium heat, swirling to coat bottom. Sauté tomatoes, crookneck squash, zucchini, onion, and garlic until zucchini is tender-crisp, 3 to 4 minutes. Don't overcook.

In a medium bowl, combine rice, cheese, and water chestnuts. Gently stir into skillet. Stuff pepper halves with vegetable mixture. Place in 9-inch round or square casserole dish, then carefully pour tomato juice around peppers.

Bake, uncovered, for 30 minutes.

Calories 119
Protein 5 g
Carbohydrates 23 g
Cholesterol 1 mg
Total Fat 1 g
Saturated 0 g
Polyunsaturated 0 g
Monounsaturated 1 g
Fiber 3 g
Sodium 68 mg

Portobello Mushroom Ragout with Sun-Dried Tomato Polenta

Serves 6

Enjoy the rich, meaty flavor of giant portobello mushrooms over polenta, Italy's counterpart to our grits.

RAGOUT

1 tablespoon plus 2 teaspoons extra-virgin olive oil

3 portobello mushrooms, cut into ½-inch slices

2 medium sweet onions, such as Texas Sweet, cut into ¼-inch rings

2 large cloves garlic, thickly sliced

¼ cup coarsely chopped fresh Italian (flat-leaf) parsley

¼ cup firmly packed fresh basil leaves, coarsely chopped

2 teaspoons balsamic vinegar

¼ teaspoon salt

Pepper to taste

POLENTA

2½ cups water

12-ounce can fat-free evaporated milk

1 tablespoon no-salt-added tomato paste

5 dry-packed sun-dried tomatoes, thinly sliced

1 cup cornmeal (coarsely ground, finely ground, or combination)

2 tablespoons grated Parmesan cheese

Pepper to taste

Calories 217
Protein 12 g
Carbohydrates 34 g
Cholesterol 4 mg
Total Fat 5 g
Saturated 1 g
Polyunsaturated 1 g
Monounsaturated 3 g
Fiber 7 g
Sodium 264 mg

For ragout, heat a Dutch oven or large skillet over medium heat. Add oil and swirl to coat bottom. When oil is hot, add mushrooms, onions, and garlic. Cook, covered, for 10 to 20 minutes, or until mushrooms release their liquids, stirring occasionally.

Stir in parsley, basil, vinegar, salt, and pepper. Cook, covered, for 5 minutes, or until onions are tender, stirring occasionally. Set aside.

For polenta, combine water, milk, and tomato paste in a 4-quart pot or stockpot. Bring to a boil over high heat.

Stir in tomatoes.

Reduce heat to medium. Using a long-handled whisk, carefully stir mixture to create a swirl. Slowly pour cornmeal in a steady stream into mixture, whisking constantly. After adding all cornmeal, hold pot steady and continue whisking for 1 to 2 minutes, or until polenta is desired consistency.

To serve, pour polenta into a large, deep serving platter or bowl. Spoon mushroom ragout and liquids over polenta. Sprinkle with Parmesan and pepper. Serve immediately.

Cook's Tip on Sweet Onions

Growing conditions make onions sweet, and the locale where they grow is usually reflected in the name. Some examples are Maui from Hawaii, Vidalia from Georgia, and Walla Walla from Washington. You might also want to try Oso Sweet from Chile and Rio Sweet from Mexico.

When the ones you like are in season, you may want to freeze a big batch to have on hand for cooking. Chop the onions, put them on a baking sheet, and freeze them. Then seal the frozen onions in an airtight plastic freezer bag.

Hoppin' John

Serves 4

The certainty is that Hoppin' John always combines black-eyed peas with rice, onion, and herbs. The uncertainties are the history of the name and whether eating Hoppin' John on New Year's Day brings good luck throughout the year. Your family will definitely feel lucky when you serve this traditional dish.

1 cup uncooked rice
1 teaspoon acceptable vegetable oil
½ cup diced celery
⅓ cup sliced onion
2½ cups canned no-salt-added tomatoes
1 teaspoon chopped fresh basil or ¼ teaspoon dried, crumbled
½ teaspoon dried rosemary, crushed
Pepper to taste
16-ounce can black-eyed peas, drained and rinsed

Cook rice using package directions, omitting salt and margarine.

Heat oil over medium heat, swirling to coat bottom. sauté celery and onion until onion is translucent, 2 to 3 minutes, stirring frequently.

Stir in remaining ingredients except peas. Reduce heat and simmer, uncovered, for 20 minutes, stirring occasionally.

Add peas and cook, covered over low heat for 5 minutes, or until thoroughly heated. Serve peas over rice.

Calories 324
Protein 11 g
Carbohydrates 61 g
Cholesterol 0 mg
Total Fat 2 g
  Saturated 1 g
  Polyunsaturated 1 g
  Monounsaturated 1 g
Fiber 4 g
Sodium 244 mg

Cook's Tip on Mortar and Pestle

The mortar is a heavy bowl, and the pestle is the grinding tool—a handle with a large knob on the business end. They are wonderful for grinding spices. Put spices, such as caraway seeds, or herbs, such as rosemary, in the mortar and mash them against the bottom and sides with the pestle until they are as fine as you want.

Artichoke and Chick-Pea Pilaf

Serves 6

This pilaf is more artichoke hearts and chick-peas than quinoa. Feel free to double the amount of quinoa if you want to feed more people.

½ cup sun-dried tomatoes (dry-packed)

1 cup boiling water

1 cup uncooked quinoa

9-ounce package frozen no-salt-added artichoke hearts, thawed

1 teaspoon olive oil

1 medium clove garlic, minced, or ½ teaspoon bottled minced garlic

1 teaspoon dried oregano, crumbled

½ teaspoon crushed red pepper flakes

15.5-ounce can no-salt-added chick-peas (garbanzo beans), drained

3 ounces feta cheese, rinsed

Put tomatoes in a small bowl and add boiling water. Set aside for about 10 minutes to soften.

Drain tomatoes, saving liquid in a 2-cup measuring cup. Chop tomatoes and set aside.

Add enough water to tomato liquid to equal 2 cups. Pour into a medium saucepan.

Rinse quinoa under cold water; drain. Stir into saucepan. Bring to a boil over high heat. Reduce heat and simmer, covered, until all liquid is absorbed, about 15 minutes.

Meanwhile, chop artichokes.

Heat a large nonstick skillet over medium heat. Add oil and swirl to coat bottom. When oil is hot, add artichokes, garlic, oregano, and red pepper flakes. Cook for about 2 minutes, stirring occasionally. Stir in chick-peas and heat through, about 5 minutes.

Combine tomatoes, quinoa, and chick-pea mixture. Spoon onto a large serving platter. Crumble feta on top.

Calories 250
Protein 12 g
Carbohydrates 37 g
Cholesterol 13 mg
Total Fat 7 g
- Saturated 3 g
- Polyunsaturated 1 g
- Monounsaturated 2 g

Fiber 7 g
Sodium 219 mg

Mediterranean Lentils and Rice

Serves 4

Middle Eastern cuisine often combines sweet ingredients, such as cinnamon and currants, with more-savory ingredients, such as cumin and onion. That sweet and savory pairing "makes" this dish. Although the currants are so small that they aren't readily apparent, they add a depth and richness that's important.

Vegetable oil spray
1 medium onion, minced (½ cup)
2 teaspoons ground cumin
2 teaspoons ground cinnamon
½ teaspoon cayenne
¾ cup dried lentils
2 cups Vegetable Broth (see page 41 or use commercial low-sodium variety) or water
14.5-ounce can no-salt-added crushed tomatoes
2 cups Vegetable Broth (see page 41 or use commercial low-sodium variety) or water
1 cup uncooked rice
½ cup water
⅓ cup dried currants
¼ cup crumbled feta cheese, rinsed

Spray a large nonstick skillet with vegetable oil spray. Add onion, cumin, cinnamon, and cayenne. Cook over medium heat until onion is soft, about 10 minutes.

Stir in lentils and 2 cups broth. Bring to a boil over medium-high heat. Reduce heat and simmer, covered, for 20 minutes.

Add remaining ingredients except feta. Bring to a boil over medium-high heat, then reduce heat and simmer, covered, for 20 minutes, or until rice and lentils are tender.

To serve, sprinkle with feta.

Calories 394
Protein 16 g
Carbohydrates 77 g
Cholesterol 8 mg
Total Fat 3 g
Saturated 2 g
Polyunsaturated 1 g
Monounsaturated 1 g
Fiber 12 g
Sodium 90 mg

Old-Fashioned Baked Beans

Serves 8

What's a cookout without baked beans? This healthful version omits the meat but retains the flavor.

3 cups dried navy beans, sorted for stones and rinsed (1 pound 6 ounces)
2 medium onions, thinly sliced (2 cups)
¾ cup chili sauce
½ cup dark molasses
1½ teaspoons cider vinegar
¾ teaspoon dry mustard

Soak beans using package directions; drain beans and discard water.

Preheat oven to 300° F.

In an ovenproof crock or casserole dish, combine beans and remaining ingredients.

Bake, covered, for 5 hours. Add water if beans begin to dry out.

Calories 311
Protein 15 g
Carbohydrates 64 g
Cholesterol 0 mg
Total Fat 1 g
Saturated 0 g
Polyunsaturated 0 g
Monounsaturated 0 g
Fiber 11 g
Sodium 354 mg

Cuban Black Beans

Serves 8

It's the green onions and vinegar that give this dish its Cuban flavor. Serve with a crisp green salad and crunchy rolls for a colorful meatless meal.

2 cups dried black beans, sorted for stones and rinsed (about 1 pound)

1 teaspoon light margarine

1 cup chopped onion (2 medium)

¼ cup diced celery

½ medium lemon, cut into quarters

1 tablespoon fresh savory or 1 teaspoon dried, crumbled

2 medium cloves garlic, minced, or 1 teaspoon bottled minced garlic

1 bay leaf

Pinch of ground ginger

1½ cups uncooked rice

½ cup chopped green onions (green and white parts) (4 to 5 medium) (optional)

3 tablespoons red wine vinegar (optional)

2 medium oranges, sliced (optional)

Calories 308
Protein 14 g
Carbohydrates 61 g
Cholesterol 0 mg
Total Fat 1 g
Saturated 0 g
Polyunsaturated 0 g
Monounsaturated 0 g
Fiber 12 g
Sodium 9 mg

Soak beans using package directions; drain beans and discard water.

In a small nonstick skillet, melt margarine over medium-high heat. Sauté onions and celery until onions are translucent, 2 to 3 minutes. Put in a stockpot.

Add beans, lemon, savory, garlic, bay leaf, and ginger to stockpot. Add water to cover by 2 inches. Stir well. Bring to a boil over high heat. Reduce heat and simmer, covered, for 1 to 1½ hours, or until beans are tender. Remove bay leaf and lemon.

Meanwhile, cook rice using package directions, omitting salt and margarine.

To serve, spoon rice into individual bowls and top with beans. Add green onions and vinegar to taste, or garnish with orange slices.

Cheesy Stuffed Potatoes

Serves 3

When you need a filling entrée, these potatoes are sure to please.

3 medium baking potatoes (about 1 pound)

1 cup nonfat or low-fat cottage cheese

½ cup shredded nonfat or reduced-fat Cheddar cheese

½ cup thinly sliced green onions (4 to 5 medium)

½ teaspoon garlic powder

¼ teaspoon white pepper

Dash of paprika

Preheat oven to 400° F.

Pierce potatoes with a fork and bake for 1 hour. Remove from oven and reduce temperature to 375° F.

To prepare as an entrée, cut a lengthwise "lid" about a half-inch from top of each potato. Scoop out pulp and put in a large bowl. Set potato shells aside and discard lids. Mash potato pulp with a potato masher or fork.

Add cheeses, green onions, garlic powder, and pepper, stirring well. Fill potato shells with mixture, and dust with paprika.

Bake for 25 minutes.

To prepare as a side dish, cut potatoes in half lengthwise and fill as above.

Calories 224
Protein 19 g
Carbohydrates 37 g
Cholesterol 8 mg
Total Fat 0 g
Saturated 0 g
Polyunsaturated 0 g
Monounsaturated 0 g
Fiber 3 g
Sodium 453 mg

Broccoli Rabe and Chick-Peas over Parmesan Toasts

Serves 6

You can serve this interesting combination of broccoli rabe and chick-peas (also called garbanzo beans) over penne pasta instead of toast for a nice change.

1 pound dried chick-peas, sorted for stones or shriveled beans, or 4 16-ounce cans no-salt-added chick-peas, drained

2 medium bunches broccoli rabe

1 tablespoon plus 2 teaspoons extra-virgin olive oil

3 large cloves garlic, coarsely chopped, or 2¼ teaspoons bottled minced garlic

1 teaspoon fennel seeds

¼ teaspoon crushed red pepper flakes

¼ teaspoon salt

Pepper to taste

6 slices Italian or French bread, ½ inch thick

1 tablespoon plus 1½ teaspoons grated Parmesan cheese

Calories 409
Protein 21 g
Carbohydrates 64 g
Cholesterol 1 mg
Total Fat 9 g
 Saturated 2 g
 Polyunsaturated 3 g
 Monounsaturated 4 g
Fiber 13 g
Sodium 339 mg

Prepare dried chick-peas using package directions, omitting salt; drain and set aside.

Meanwhile, remove and discard bottom 4 inches of broccoli rabe. Coarsely chop remaining stems, leaves, and buds.

Steam broccoli rabe for about 10 minutes. (If you don't have a two-tiered steamer, you'll need to do this in batches.)

Heat a stockpot over medium-low heat. Add oil and swirl to cover bottom. When oil is hot, stir in broccoli rabe, garlic, fennel seeds, red pepper flakes, salt, and pepper. Cook, covered, for 12 to 15 minutes, or until broccoli rabe is desired tenderness, stirring occasionally.

Preheat broiler.

Stir chick-peas into broccoli rabe mixture. Cook, covered, for about 15 minutes, or until broccoli rabe is tender-soft, stirring occasionally. Remove from heat and leave covered to keep warm.

Put bread slices on a broilerproof baking sheet. Sprinkle bread with Parmesan. Broil about 4 inches from heat for about 1 minute, or until bread is golden brown and cheese is melted.

To serve, arrange toasts on a large, deep serving platter. Spoon broccoli rabe mixture and juices evenly over toasts.

Cook's Tip on Broccoli Rabe

Known by several other names—broccoli raab, broccoli rape, and rapini—broccoli rabe (*rahb*) is a bitter vegetable with a lemon-pepper taste. Look for deep, dark green leaves and buds (which look like tiny broccoli buds) with no trace of yellow (a sign of age). Broccoli rabe is rich in vitamin A.

Meatless Moussaka

Serves 8

This variation of the traditional Greek dish boasts all the richness and flavor of the original even without the meat. Serve with whole-wheat pita bread and tossed salad.

Olive oil spray

2 pounds eggplant, peeled and thickly sliced

Olive oil spray

SAUCE

1 teaspoon olive oil

1 cup finely chopped onion (2 medium)

3 medium cloves garlic, minced, or 1½ teaspoons bottled minced garlic

14.5-ounce can diced no-salt-added tomatoes

1 cup water

6-ounce can no-salt-added tomato paste

2 teaspoons dried rosemary, crushed

2 tablespoons finely snipped fresh parsley

2 tablespoons finely snipped fresh mint

FILLING

1 pound nonfat or low-fat cottage cheese

Egg substitute equivalent to 2 eggs, or 2 eggs

2 tablespoons grated Parmesan cheese

1 teaspoon dried rosemary, crushed

½ teaspoon dried oregano, crumbled

½ teaspoon pepper, or to taste

¼ cup grated Parmesan cheese

Calories 143
Protein 13 g
Carbohydrates 18 g
Cholesterol 8 mg
Total Fat 3 g
Saturated 1 g
Polyunsaturated 1 g
Monounsaturated 1 g
Fiber 4 g
Sodium 346 mg

Preheat broiler. Lightly spray a 3½-quart oblong glass baking dish with olive oil spray.

Put eggplant slices on 2 large baking sheets. Lightly spray both sides of slices with olive oil spray. Brown about 6 inches from heat for 5 minutes on each side, or until eggplant is tender.

Set oven temperature to 375° F.

For sauce, heat 1 teaspoon olive oil in a large nonstick skillet over medium-high heat. Sauté onions and garlic for 2 to 3 minutes, or until onion is translucent.

Stir in undrained tomatoes, water, tomato paste,

and rosemary. Reduce heat and simmer for 10 minutes, stirring occasionally.

Stir in parsley and mint. Remove from heat.

For filling, combine ingredients in a medium bowl.

Spread half of sauce in baking dish. Arrange half of eggplant over sauce. Spread all filling over eggplant, then top with remaining eggplant and remaining sauce. Sprinkle with remaining Parmesan.

Cover casserole with aluminum foil.

Bake for 40 to 45 minutes. Uncover and bake for 10 minutes.

Enchilada Bake

Serves 6

Layers of vegetables, creamy sauce, beans, and tortillas make a tasty casserole that's even better the day after you prepare it. Try our Spinach Tortillas (see page 518) for a flavor boost.

SAUCE

1 teaspoon light margarine

½ cup chopped onion (about 1 medium)

½ cup chopped green bell pepper (about ½ medium)

8 ounces fresh mushrooms, quartered (8 to 10 medium)

1 or 2 medium cloves garlic, minced, or ½ to 1 teaspoon bottled minced garlic

2 cups cooked black or pinto beans or 2 cups canned, no-salt-added, drained

14.5-ounce can no-salt-added stewed tomatoes

½ cup dry red wine (regular or nonalcoholic)

2 to 3 teaspoons chili powder

1 to 2 teaspoons ground cumin

¼ teaspoon salt

¾ cup nonfat or low-fat ricotta cheese

½ cup nonfat or low-fat yogurt

Vegetable oil spray

6 5½- or 6-inch corn tortillas, quartered

½ cup grated nonfat or part-skim mozzarella cheese

6 medium black olives, sliced

For sauce, melt margarine in a large saucepan over medium-high heat. Sauté onion, bell pepper, mushrooms, and garlic until onion is translucent, 2 to 3 minutes.

Stir in remaining sauce ingredients. Reduce heat and simmer for about 30 minutes.

Preheat oven to 350° F.

In a small bowl, whisk together ricotta and yogurt.

Spray a 1½-quart casserole dish with vegetable oil spray. Layer 3 tortillas, half the sauce, half the mozzarella, and half the ricotta mixture. Repeat layers. Top with olives.

Bake, covered, for 15 to 20 minutes.

Calories 228
Protein 14 g
Carbohydrates 37 g
Cholesterol 1 mg
Total Fat 2 g
Saturated 0 g
Polyunsaturated 1 g
Monounsaturated 1 g
Fiber 8 g
Sodium 327 mg

Curried Cauliflower and Tofu with Basmati Rice

Serves 6

The curry flavor here is so light and delicate that it makes this dish the *introduction if your family hasn't tried curry. Serve it over basmati rice for a one-dish meal.*

1 tablespoon plus 2 teaspoons extra-virgin olive oil
1 small head cauliflower, coarsely chopped
12 stalks asparagus, trimmed, cut into 1-inch pieces
12 fresh green beans, cut into 1-inch pieces
2 large tomatoes, cut into 1-inch wedges
1 large sweet onion, such as Texas Sweet, coarsely chopped (1¼ cups)
¼ cup coarsely chopped fresh Italian (flat-leaf) parsley
1 tablespoon curry powder
⅛ teaspoon cayenne, or to taste
1 cup fat-free evaporated milk
1 apple (Fuji preferred), finely diced
2 tablespoons mango chutney or honey
¼ teaspoon salt
Pepper to taste
1 pound reduced-fat firm tofu, drained, cut into ½-inch cubes
1 cup frozen green peas
¼ cup coarsely snipped cilantro
3 cups cooked basmati rice, prepared without salt or margarine
2 tablespoons dry-roasted cashews

Heat a stockpot over medium-low heat. Add oil and swirl. When oil is hot, stir in cauliflower, asparagus, green beans, tomatoes, onion, parsley, curry, and cayenne. Cook, covered, for 15 minutes, or until vegetables release their liquids, stirring occasionally.

Stir evaporated milk, apple, chutney, salt, and pepper into vegetable mixture. Cook, covered, for 10 to 12 minutes, or until green beans are tender-crisp, stirring occasionally.

Gently stir in tofu, peas, and cilantro. Cook, uncovered, for 5 minutes.

To serve, spoon cauliflower mixture and liquids over rice, then sprinkle with nuts.

Calories 334
Protein 15 g
Carbohydrates 54 g
Cholesterol 2 mg
Total Fat 8 g
Saturated 1 g
Polyunsaturated 1 g
Monounsaturated 4 g
Fiber 6 g
Sodium 300 mg

Broiled Eggplant, Italian Style

Serves 4

Double the flavor—marinate eggplant, broil it, top it with tomato sauce and mozzarella, then broil it again. Serve with whole-wheat pita bread and steamed zucchini.

MARINADE

½ cup fat-free or low-fat Italian salad dressing

1 teaspoon dried rosemary, crushed

¼ teaspoon dried oregano, crumbled

1 large eggplant

8 ounces no-salt-added tomato sauce

½ teaspoon pepper, or to taste

2 ounces grated nonfat mozzarella cheese (½ cup)

Combine marinade ingredients in an airtight plastic bag.

Peel eggplant and cut crosswise into ¾-inch slices. Add to marinade; turn bag to coat evenly. Seal and refrigerate for 1 hour. Drain, discarding marinade.

Preheat broiler.

Arrange eggplant slices in one layer on a baking sheet. Broil about 6 inches from heat for about 5 minutes on each side, or until eggplant is tender and lightly browned.

Arrange alternate layers of eggplant and tomato sauce in a broilerproof, 8-inch square baking dish, lightly seasoning each layer with pepper. Top with mozzarella.

Broil for about 2 minutes, or until cheese is brown.

Calories 100
Protein 6 g
Carbohydrates 19 g
Cholesterol 1 mg
Total Fat 1 g
Saturated 0 g
Polyunsaturated 0 g
Monounsaturated 0 g
Fiber 6 g
Sodium 437 mg

Eggplant Parmesan

Serves 6

Cooking the liquid out of the seasoned mushrooms raises their flavor level to new heights.

Olive oil spray
1 eggplant (about 1½ pounds)
1 teaspoon olive oil
8 ounces fresh mushrooms, sliced (2 to 2½ cups)
1 cup chopped onions (2 medium)
3 or 4 medium cloves garlic, minced, or 1½ to 2 teaspoons bottled minced garlic
½ teaspoon salt-free dried Italian herb seasoning, crumbled
¼ teaspoon salt
Pepper to taste
8-ounce can no-salt-added tomato sauce
4 ounces fat-free or part-skim mozzarella cheese, shredded (1 cup)
1 ounce (¼ cup) grated or shredded Parmesan cheese

Preheat broiler. Spray a baking sheet, 13 × 9 × 2-inch baking pan, and 11 × 15-inch piece of aluminum foil with olive oil spray.

Peel eggplant and cut crosswise into ¼-inch slices. Put on baking sheet and broil 6 inches from heat for 2 to 3 minutes on each side. Remove from broiler and set oven to 375° F.

Heat oil in a large nonstick skillet over medium heat, swirling to coat bottom. Add mushrooms, onions, garlic, herb seasoning, and salt. Cook, covered, for 7 to 9 minutes, stirring occasionally. Increase heat to high and cook, uncovered, for 2 to 3 minutes, or until pan juices have evaporated, stirring frequently.

Spread 1 cup mushroom mixture in baking pan. Cover with half of eggplant slices. Sprinkle with pepper. Top with ½ cup tomato sauce and half the mozzarella. Repeat layers except cheese. Cover with prepared foil.

Bake for 1 hour. Top with remaining mozzarella and all the Parmesan. Bake, uncovered, for 5 to 8 minutes, or until cheese is melted. Cool for at least 10 minutes before cutting.

Calories 118
Protein 10 g
Carbohydrates 15 g
Cholesterol 5 mg
Total Fat 3 g
Saturated 1 g
Polyunsaturated 0 g
Monounsaturated 1 g
Fiber 5 g
Sodium 372 mg

Eggplant Zucchini Casserole

Serves 8

Put uncooked spaghetti right in the casserole. Everything bakes together—no spaghetti pot to wash!

Vegetable oil spray

SAUCE

2 8-ounce cans no-salt-added tomato sauce

2 medium cloves garlic, crushed, or 1 teaspoon bottled minced garlic

2 teaspoons very low sodium or low-sodium Worcestershire sauce

1 teaspoon dried oregano, crumbled

½ teaspoon dried basil, crumbled

½ teaspoon dried marjoram, crumbled

Pepper to taste

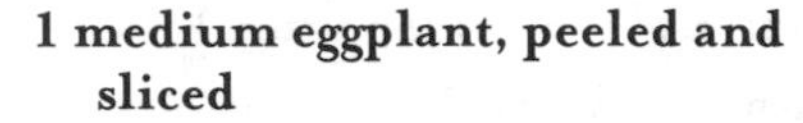

1 medium eggplant, peeled and sliced

2 medium zucchini, sliced

1 cup dried spaghetti, broken into pieces (4 ounces)

3 medium ribs celery, chopped (1½ cups)

1 medium onion, chopped (½ cup)

1 medium green bell pepper, chopped (1 cup)

8 ounces nonfat or part-skim mozzarella cheese, cut into 18 small slices

Preheat oven to 350° F. Spray a 13 × 9 × 2-inch casserole dish with vegetable oil spray.

For sauce, in a medium bowl, combine ingredients, stirring well.

In casserole dish, arrange half the eggplant slices in a single layer. Top with half of each of the following: zucchini, spaghetti, celery, onion, bell pepper, mozzarella, and tomato sauce mixture. Repeat layers.

Bake, covered, for about 1 hour, or until vegetables are tender.

Calories 142
Protein 12 g
Carbohydrates 23 g
Cholesterol 2 mg
Total Fat 1 g
Saturated 0 g
Polyunsaturated 0 g
Monounsaturated 0 g
Fiber 5 g
Sodium 293 mg

Italian-Style Zucchini

Serves 6

When summer squash are at the peak of their season, try this layered casserole. Serve with juicy sliced nectarines and Marinated White Beans and Cucumbers with Basil *(see page 97).*

Vegetable oil spray

6 medium zucchini or crookneck squash, thinly sliced (about 6 cups)

1 teaspoon olive oil

¾ cup sliced onion (1½ medium)

2 large tomatoes or 4 Italian plum tomatoes, thinly sliced

1¼ teaspoons dried basil, crumbled

1 teaspoon salt-free all-purpose seasoning

¾ teaspoon dried oregano, crumbled

4 ounces nonfat or part-skim mozzarella, shredded (1 cup)

⅓ cup grated Parmesan cheese

2 tablespoons finely snipped fresh parsley

Preheat oven to 375° F. Lightly spray a 2-quart casserole dish with vegetable oil spray.

Put zucchini in a saucepan with water to cover by ½ inch. Bring to a boil over high heat. Reduce heat and simmer for 4 to 5 minutes, or until tender. Drain. Transfer to a large bowl.

Heat olive oil in a small skillet over medium-high heat. Sauté onions until translucent, 2 to 3 minutes.

Add onions, tomatoes, basil, all-purpose seasoning, and oregano to zucchini, stirring well.

Spoon half the zucchini mixture into casserole dish. Sprinkle with mozzarella. Add remaining zucchini mixture. Sprinkle with Parmesan.

Bake, uncovered, for 25 to 30 minutes. Sprinkle with parsley.

Calories 110
Protein 10 g
Carbohydrates 13 g
Cholesterol 6 mg
Total Fat 3 g
  Saturated 1 g
  Polyunsaturated 0 g
  Monounsaturated 1 g
Fiber 3 g
Sodium 291 mg

Stuffed Zucchini

Serves 4

Brown rice flecked with color is used to stuff zucchini and transform it from its usual side dish status to main dish prominence.

4 small to medium zucchini

STUFFING

2 teaspoons extra-virgin olive oil

1 medium red onion, finely chopped (1/2 cup)

1 large clove garlic, coarsely chopped, or 3/4 teaspoon bottled minced garlic

1 chipotle pepper canned in adobo sauce, stemmed and finely chopped (see Cook's Tip, page 339)

1 medium tomato, finely chopped (2/3 cup)

1/4 teaspoon salt

2 cups coarsely chopped fresh spinach

4 large pimiento-stuffed green olives, coarsely chopped

2 tablespoons coarsely snipped cilantro

2 tablespoons white wine vinegar

3/4 teaspoon dried oregano, crumbled

1/4 teaspoon ground cumin

2 cups cooked brown rice

1 cup water

Cut zucchini in half lengthwise. Using a teaspoon, scrape out seeds and just enough flesh to make a cavity for stuffing.

Preheat oven to 400° F.

For stuffing, heat oil in a large, deep skillet over medium-low heat, swirling to coat bottom. Cook onion, garlic, chipotle pepper (no need to wipe off sauce), tomato, and salt for 5 to 7 minutes, or until the onion has softened, stirring occasionally.

Stir in remaining stuffing ingredients. Cook for 3 to 4 minutes, or until spinach is wilted, stirring frequently.

Stuff zucchini with spinach mixture. Place zucchini in a single layer in a large baking pan. Carefully pour water around—not on—zucchini. Cover pan tightly with aluminum foil.

Calories 192
Protein 5 g
Carbohydrates 34 g
Cholesterol 0 mg
Total Fat 4 g
  Saturated 1 g
  Polyunsaturated 1 g
  Monounsaturated 2 g
Fiber 5 g
Sodium 373 mg

Bake for 35 to 40 minutes, or until zucchini is tender when tested with a fork inserted into center.

Time-Saver: Instead of fresh spinach, use a 10-ounce package of frozen no-salt-added chopped spinach. Thaw, drain, and squeeze out moisture. Use as you would the fresh spinach.

Cook's Tip on Chipotle Peppers

Chipotle peppers are smoked jalapeños, so expect (and enjoy) a little heat! Buy them dried or packed in cans with flavorful adobo sauce in the produce or ethnic section of your supermarket. (The sauce is made of chiles, herbs, and vinegar.) Leftover canned chipotle peppers can be refrigerated in a jar with a tight-fitting lid for several months.

Spaghetti Squash Casserole

Serves 6

This casserole contains a colorful medley of ingredients. You can prepare it ahead and refrigerate it for up to two days before baking. Serve it with whole-wheat pita bread and grapefruit slices.

1 small spaghetti squash (about 2 pounds)
Vegetable oil spray
¼ teaspoon salt
¼ teaspoon pepper
15-ounce can no-salt-added kidney beans, drained
14.5-ounce can no-salt-added stewed tomatoes
1 cup no-salt-added frozen mixed vegetables, thawed
4 ounces frozen vegetarian ham substitute, thawed and diced, or 5 ounces frozen precooked soy burger, thawed and diced
½ cup fat-free shredded mozzarella-style soy cheese or fat-free shredded mozzarella

Preheat oven to 350° F.

Prick squash with a fork. Put squash in a baking pan and bake for 1 hour 20 minutes, or put on a microwave-safe plate and microwave on 100 percent power (high) for 12 to 14 minutes, or until squash yields to gentle pressure. Let cool for at least 30 minutes.

Lightly spray a 9-inch round cake pan with vegetable oil spray. Cut squash in half lengthwise and scrape out seeds with a spoon. Using a fork, scrape squash strands from shell into cake pan.

Sprinkle squash with salt and pepper. Top with kidney beans, then stewed tomatoes, mixed vegetables, and ham substitute. Cover pan with aluminum foil.

Bake for 30 to 40 minutes, or until mixture is warmed through. Uncover and sprinkle with soy cheese. Bake for 5 minutes, or until cheese is melted.

Here are three quick, inexpensive ideas for using spaghetti squash to serve four people:

Calories 164
Protein 10 g
Carbohydrates 27 g
Cholesterol 0 mg
Total Fat 3 g
- Saturated 1 g
- Polyunsaturated 1 g
- Monounsaturated 0 g

Fiber 9 g
Sodium 332 mg

Spaghetti Squash Spaghetti

Combine 2 tablespoons chopped fresh basil with 2 cups of low-fat, low-sodium spaghetti sauce. Toss with 4 cups of cooked spaghetti squash. (calories 95; protein 3 g; carbohydrates 21 g; cholesterol 0 mg; total fat 0 g; saturated 0 g; polyunsaturated 0 g; monounsaturated 0 g; fiber 4 g; sodium 418 mg)

"Pasta" Salad

Combine ¼ cup fat-free or low-fat bottled salad dressing (any variety) with 4 cups chilled, cooked spaghetti squash and 1 cup chopped vegetables (such as broccoli, carrots, and tomatoes) for a quick salad. (calories 60; protein 1 g; carbohydrates 13 g; cholesterol 0 mg; total fat 1 g; saturated 0 g; polyunsaturated 0 g; monounsaturated 0 g; fiber 3 g; sodium 180 mg)

Spaghetti Soup

Add 2 cups cooked spaghetti squash to 1 quart of your favorite soup, such as Vegetable Broth, Minestrone, or Lentil Soup (see pages 41, 55, and 62), for the last 5 minutes of cooking time. (calories 72; protein 2 g; carbohydrates 15 g; cholesterol 0 mg; total fat 1 g; saturated 0 g; polyunsaturated 1 g; monounsaturated 0 g; fiber 3 g; sodium 387 mg)

Spinach Artichoke Gratin

Serves 6

Spinach, artichokes, and cheese—a perfect combination of flavors. As they bake to bubbly richness, prepare steamed carrots and tossed salad with one of our salad dressings (see pages 119–25*) to complete your meal.*

Vegetable oil spray
16 ounces nonfat or low-fat cottage cheese
Egg substitute equivalent to 2 eggs, or 2 eggs
3 tablespoons grated Parmesan cheese
1 tablespoon fresh lemon juice
⅛ teaspoon white pepper
⅛ teaspoon ground nutmeg
2 10-ounce packages frozen no-salt-added chopped spinach, thawed
⅓ cup thinly sliced green onions (green part only) (6 medium)
10-ounce package frozen no-salt-added artichoke hearts, thawed
1½ tablespoons grated Parmesan cheese

Calories 130
Protein 17 g
Carbohydrates 12 g
Cholesterol 10 mg
Total Fat 3 g
Saturated 1 g
Polyunsaturated 1 g
Monounsaturated 1 g
Fiber 5 g
Sodium 473 mg

Preheat oven to 375° F. Spray a 1½-quart baking dish with vegetable oil spray.

In a food processor or blender, process cottage cheese, egg substitute, 3 tablespoons Parmesan, lemon juice, pepper, and nutmeg until smooth.

Squeeze moisture from spinach. In a large bowl, combine spinach, cottage cheese mixture, and green onions. Spread half in baking dish.

Cut artichoke hearts in half and pat dry with paper towels. Place in a single layer on spinach mixture. Sprinkle with 2 tablespoons Parmesan. Cover with remaining spinach mixture.

Bake, covered, for 25 minutes.

Spinach Soufflé

Serves 4

Complement this airy soufflé with brilliantly colored Harvard Beets (see page 365) and snow-white Parsnip Salad with Jícama and Apple (see page 89).

Vegetable oil spray
2 tablespoons light margarine
2 tablespoons whole-wheat flour
½ cup fat-free milk
5 ounces frozen no-salt-added chopped spinach, cooked and squeezed dry
1 tablespoon finely chopped onion
¼ teaspoon ground nutmeg
¼ teaspoon pepper, or to taste
Whites of 6 medium eggs (see Cook's Tip, page 345)
3 tablespoons grated Parmesan cheese

Preheat oven to 350° F. Spray a 1¾-quart casserole dish with vegetable oil spray. Set aside.

In a small, heavy saucepan, melt margarine over medium-high heat. Whisk in flour. Cook until mixture is smooth and bubbly, about 1 minute, whisking constantly.

Remove from heat and gradually whisk in milk. Return to heat and bring mixture to a boil over medium-high heat, stirring constantly. Reduce heat to low and cook for 1 minute, stirring occasionally. Remove from heat.

In a large bowl, combine spinach, onion, nutmeg, and pepper. Add milk mixture, stirring well.

Beat egg whites until stiff peaks form. Using a rubber scraper, fold gently into spinach mixture.

Pour into casserole dish. Sprinkle with Parmesan.

Bake for 35 minutes, or until center is set. Serve immediately.

Calories 101
Protein 10 g
Carbohydrates 7 g
Cholesterol 4 mg
Total Fat 4 g
  Saturated 2 g
  Polyunsaturated 1 g
  Monounsaturated 1 g
Fiber 1 g
Sodium 318 mg

Spinach Roll with Alfredo Sauce

Serves 3

This dish begins with a soufflé that's substantial enough to roll. Then it gets a rich and delicious Alfredo sauce. Even people who think they don't like spinach will love this dish. Serve this spinach roll as a meatless entrée, or try it with Lemon-Herb Roast Chicken (see page 171*).*

Vegetable oil spray

SOUFFLÉ

Egg substitute equivalent to 2 eggs, or 2 eggs

10-ounce package frozen no-salt-added chopped spinach, thawed and squeezed dry

2 tablespoons light margarine, melted

1 tablespoon fresh lemon juice

⅛ teaspoon pepper

⅛ teaspoon ground nutmeg, or to taste

Whites of 3 large eggs, stiffly beaten (see Cook's Tip, page 345)

FAT-FREE ALFREDO SAUCE

5-ounce can fat-free evaporated milk

½ medium clove garlic, crushed

2 tablespoons grated Parmesan cheese

¼ teaspoon salt-free Italian seasoning

⅛ teaspoon pepper, or to taste

4 medium fresh mushrooms, sliced

½ teaspoon light margarine

½ teaspoon fresh lemon juice

Calories 171
Protein 17 g
Carbohydrates 13 g
Cholesterol 5 mg
Total Fat 6 g
Saturated 2 g
Polyunsaturated 2 g
Monounsaturated 2 g
Fiber 3 g
Sodium 428 mg

Preheat oven to 350° F.

Line an 8-inch square baking pan with cooking parchment or wax paper; spray with vegetable oil spray.

For soufflé, in a large mixing bowl, beat egg substitute until foamy.

Add spinach, 2 tablespoons margarine, 1 tablespoon lemon juice, pepper, and nutmeg, stirring well.

Add one fourth of the egg whites, stirring well. Gently fold in remaining egg whites, being careful not to deflate them. Spoon mixture into baking pan.

Bake for 10 to 12 minutes, or until soufflé

springs back when lightly touched. Let cool for 10 minutes.

Meanwhile, prepare sauce. In a medium nonstick skillet, combine milk and garlic. Bring to a boil over medium-high heat, stirring frequently.

Stir in remaining sauce ingredients. Reduce heat to low and cook for 10 to 15 minutes, or until the cheese has melted, stirring frequently.

Invert baking pan to remove soufflé. Roll up, gently peeling away parchment while rolling. Place seam side down on a serving platter.

In a small skillet over medium heat, sauté mushrooms in ½ teaspoon margarine and ½ teaspoon lemon juice.

To serve, spoon mushroom mixture over spinach roll. Serve with Alfredo sauce on the side.

Cook's Tip on Egg Whites

Even a single drop of egg yolk will prevent egg whites from forming peaks when beaten, so separate eggs very carefully. Crack the egg and drain the white into a small bowl. Pour the yolk into a separate bowl. Pour the white into the mixing bowl. That way you won't spoil the whole bowl of whites if a yolk breaks. If you do get a speck of yolk in the white, you can blot the yolk up with the corner of a paper towel.

Spinach Ricotta Swirls

Serves 4

This dish will be a showstopper at your next dinner party.

8 dried lasagna noodles

Olive oil spray or vegetable oil spray

SAUCE

1 teaspoon olive oil

½ cup finely chopped onion

2 large cloves garlic, minced, or 1½ teaspoons bottled minced garlic

2 cups Vegetable Broth (see page 41 or use commercial low-sodium variety)

6-ounce can no-salt-added tomato paste

1 teaspoon salt-free dried Italian herb seasoning, crumbled

¼ teaspoon salt

FILLING

2 10-ounce packages frozen no-salt-added chopped spinach, thawed

1 cup nonfat or low-fat ricotta cheese (8 ounces)

2 tablespoons grated Parmesan cheese

¼ teaspoon white pepper

⅛ teaspoon ground nutmeg

Cook noodles using package directions, omitting salt and oil. Drain and set aside on wax paper.

Preheat oven to 350° F. Lightly spray an 8-inch square baking dish with vegetable oil spray.

For sauce, heat olive oil in a small nonstick saucepan over medium-high heat. Sauté onion and garlic until onion is translucent, 2 to 3 minutes, stirring occasionally.

Stir in remaining sauce ingredients. Simmer for 5 minutes, or until slightly thickened, stirring occasionally. Remove from heat. Set aside.

For filling, squeeze moisture out of spinach. Put in a large bowl. Add remaining filling ingredients to spinach, stirring well.

Spread scant ⅓ cup filling lengthwise down each noodle. Roll each noodle and place it on its side in baking dish. (Rolled noodles shouldn't touch each other.) Pour sauce over noodles.

Bake, covered, for 25 to 30 minutes, or until thoroughly heated.

Calories 287
Protein 16 g
Carbohydrates 48 g
Cholesterol 2 mg
Total Fat 3 g
  Saturated 1 g
  Polyunsaturated 1 g
  Monounsaturated 1 g
Fiber 7 g
Sodium 379 mg

Steamed Veggies with Herbed Cheese

Serves 4

Tender vegetables served with a rich cheese sauce can stand alone as an entrée, or serve them as a side dish with almost anything—seafood, poultry, or meat.

1 cup half-round sliced carrots (1 large)

1 cup broccoli florets (about 4 ounces)

1 cup cauliflower florets (about 4 ounces)

1 cup half-round sliced zucchini (about 1 medium)

1 cup half-round sliced crookneck squash (about 1 medium)

SAUCE

2 tablespoons Vegetable Broth (see page 41 or use commercial low-sodium variety)

2 shallots, finely chopped (2 tablespoons)

1 cup fat-free milk

2 tablespoons all-purpose flour

1/8 teaspoon white pepper

2 ounces grated fat-free sharp Cheddar cheese

2 tablespoons grated Parmesan cheese

1 tablespoon finely chopped fresh basil

1/2 teaspoon finely chopped fresh rosemary

In a large pot, steam carrots over medium-high heat for 5 minutes.

Add broccoli, cauliflower, zucchini, and crookneck squash. Steam for 10 minutes. Drain vegetables and pat dry with paper towels.

Arrange on a serving plate and cover with aluminum foil to keep warm.

For sauce, heat broth in a medium saucepan over medium heat. Cook shallots for 2 to 3 minutes, stirring occasionally. Whisk in milk, flour, and pepper. Bring to a boil over medium-high heat and cook until mixture thickens, 3 to 4 minutes, stirring occasionally.

Reduce heat to low and add remaining ingredients, stirring until Cheddar melts, 1 to 2 minutes. Pour over vegetables.

Calories 113
Protein 9 g
Carbohydrates 17 g
Cholesterol 5 mg
Total Fat 1 g
  Saturated 1 g
  Polyunsaturated 0 g
  Monounsaturated 0 g
Fiber 3 g
Sodium 340 mg

Tomato Quiche in Couscous Crust

Serves 8

Serve a wedge of this dill-flavored quiche with Asian Coleslaw (see page 87) and fresh strawberries.

CRUST

Vegetable oil spray

½ cup Vegetable Broth (see page 41 or use commercial low-sodium variety)

½ cup water

½ cup couscous

⅛ teaspoon powdered turmeric

White of 1 medium egg

FILLING

1 teaspoon olive oil

1 cup coarsely chopped fresh mushrooms (about 4 ounces)

¾ cup chopped green onions (6 to 7 medium)

2 medium cloves garlic, minced, or 1 teaspoon bottled minced garlic

6 Italian plum tomatoes or other fresh tomatoes, thickly sliced

2 tablespoons grated Parmesan cheese

Egg substitute equivalent to 3 eggs

5-ounce can fat-free evaporated milk (⅔ cup)

1 tablespoon fresh dillweed or 1 teaspoon dried, crumbled

¼ teaspoon pepper

Preheat oven to 400° F.

For crust, spray a 9-inch pie pan with vegetable oil spray.

In a medium saucepan, bring broth and water to a boil over medium-high heat. Stir in couscous and turmeric. Remove from heat and let stand, covered, for 5 minutes.

Stir egg white into couscous. Press mixture into bottom and up side of pie pan to form crust.

Bake for 10 minutes. Remove crust from oven; lower oven temperature to 350° F. Let crust cool completely, about 30 minutes.

For filling, heat oil in a medium nonstick skillet over medium-high heat, swirling to coat bottom. Sauté mushrooms, green onions, and garlic for 2 to 3 minutes, or until tender.

Arrange tomato slices on crust, cover with mushroom mixture, and sprinkle with Parmesan.

Calories 103
Protein 7 g
Carbohydrates 14 g
Cholesterol 2 mg
Total Fat 2 g
  Saturated 1 g
  Polyunsaturated 1 g
  Monounsaturated 1 g
Fiber 1 g
Sodium 138 mg

In a medium bowl, whisk together remaining ingredients. Pour over vegetables.

Bake for 40 to 45 minutes, or until a knife inserted in center comes out clean.

Tomato Quiche in Piecrust

Substitute a low-fat frozen crust for the couscous crust. Bake the empty crust for 5 minutes at 400° F, then let it cool for 10 minutes before filling as directed. (calories 138; protein 6 g; carbohydrates 13 g; cholesterol 2 mg; total fat 7 g; saturated 1 g; polyunsaturated 2 g; monounsaturated 3 g; fiber 1 g; sodium 191 mg)

Cook's Tip

An egg white is used as a binding agent in this couscous crust. Since color isn't a factor, you can use 2 tablespoons of egg substitute in place of 1 medium egg white.

VEGETABLES AND SIDE DISHES

Artichoke Hearts Riviera

Asparagus par Excellence

Asparagus with Garlic and Parmesan Bread Crumbs

Fresh Green Beans with Water Chestnuts

Dilled Green Beans

French-Style Green Beans with Pimiento and Dill Seeds

Green Beans and Rice with Hazelnuts

Louisiana Beans Oregano

Mediterranean Lima Beans

Barbecued Lima Beans

Deviled Beets

Harvard Beets

Crunchy Broccoli Casserole

Cabbage with Mustard-Caraway Sauce

Sweet-and-Sour Red Cabbage

Spiced Red Cabbage

Brussels Sprouts and Pecans

Tangy Carrots

Honeyed Carrots

Gingered Carrots

Baked Grated Carrots with Sherry

Creole Celery and Peas

Cauliflower and Roasted Corn with Chili Powder and Lime

Swiss Chard, Southern Style

Southwestern Creamy Corn

Cajun Corn

Grits Casserole with Cheese and Chiles

Creamy Kale with Red Bell Pepper

Mushrooms with White Wine and Shallots

Kohlrabi Gratin

Crispy Baked Onion Flower

Caramelized Onions

Two-Cheese Sour Cream Noodles

Parmesan Parsnip Puree with Leeks and Carrots

Three-Cheese Macaroni

Black-Eyed Peas with Canadian Bacon

Savory Peas

French Peas

Basil Roasted Peppers

Scalloped Potatoes

Potatoes with Leeks and Fresh Herbs

Rustic Potato Patties

Baked Fries with Creole Seasoning

Baked Sweet Potato Chips

Pineapple Sweet Potatoes

Orange Sweet Potatoes

Middle Eastern Brown Rice

Risotto Milanese

Risotto with Broccoli and Leeks

Mexican Fried Rice

Rice Pilaf

Wild Rice with Mushrooms

Rice Italiano

Savory Spinach

Acorn Squash Stuffed with Cranberries and Walnuts

Gingered Acorn Squash

Creole Squash

Pattypan Squash with Apple-Walnut Stuffing

Scalloped Squash

Squash Ruffles

Italian Vegetable Bake

Vegetable Medley with Lemon Sauce

Vegetable Stir-Fry

Southwestern Ratatouille

Triple Vegetable Bake

Couscous with Vegetables

Corn Bread Dressing

Celery Dressing

Apple Dressing

Cranberry Chutney

Baked Curried Fruit

Artichoke Hearts Riviera

Serves 6

This elegant side dish is ready in minutes. You can prepare the sauce while the artichoke hearts cook.

2 10-ounce packages frozen no-salt-added artichoke hearts

SAUCE

½ cup dry vermouth, dry white wine, or nonalcoholic white wine

2 tablespoons light margarine

1 tablespoon snipped fresh parsley

1 tablespoon fresh lemon juice

1 medium clove garlic, crushed, or ½ teaspoon bottled minced garlic

½ teaspoon dry mustard

½ teaspoon dried tarragon, crumbled

White pepper to taste

Snipped fresh parsley (optional)

Cook artichoke hearts using package directions, omitting salt and margarine. Drain.

Meanwhile, in a small saucepan, combine sauce ingredients. Bring to a boil over medium-high heat. Reduce heat and simmer, covered, for 5 minutes.

To serve, pour sauce over cooked artichoke hearts and sprinkle with parsley.

Calories 85
Protein 3 g
Carbohydrates 11 g
Cholesterol 0 mg
Total Fat 2 g
Saturated 0 g
Polyunsaturated 1 g
Monounsaturated 0 g
Fiber 4 g
Sodium 77 mg

Asparagus par Excellence

Serves 6

Excellent indeed, this side dish not only tastes good with turkey and dressing but also looks festive, with its sprinkling of red pimiento and green parsley and tarragon.

½ cup water

¼ cup diced onion

½ medium green bell pepper, chopped (½ cup)

Pepper to taste

2 10-ounce packages frozen no-salt-added asparagus spears

2 teaspoons finely snipped fresh parsley

2 teaspoons diced pimiento

½ teaspoon dried tarragon, crumbled

In a large skillet, bring water, onion, bell pepper, and pepper to a boil over medium-high heat. Reduce heat and simmer, covered, for 5 minutes.

Add asparagus and cook, covered, for 5 minutes, or until tender-crisp.

To serve, drain and discard liquid from skillet. Place asparagus mixture on a serving plate and sprinkle with remaining ingredients.

Calories 30
Protein 3 g
Carbohydrates 5 g
Cholesterol 0 mg
Total Fat 0 g
Saturated 0 g
Polyunsaturated 0 g
Monounsaturated 0 g
Fiber 2 g
Sodium 5 mg

Asparagus with Garlic and Parmesan Bread Crumbs

Serves 6

Seasoned bread crumbs blanket steamed asparagus spears in this easy side dish.

BREAD CRUMBS

2 slices bread, torn into 1-inch pieces

Olive oil spray

1 tablespoon light margarine

2 medium cloves garlic, minced, or 1 teaspoon bottled minced garlic

1½ teaspoons dried oregano, crumbled

2 tablespoons shredded, not grated, Parmesan cheese

1¼ pounds asparagus spears, trimmed

⅛ teaspoon salt

Put bread in a food processor or blender and pulse until texture of commercial bread crumbs.

Spray a large nonstick skillet with olive oil spray. Melt margarine over medium-high heat and swirl to coat bottom. Add garlic and cook for 10 seconds, stirring constantly.

Add bread crumbs and oregano. Cook for 5 minutes, or until crumbs are golden brown, stirring frequently. Remove from heat and stir in Parmesan. Set aside.

Steam asparagus for 3 minutes, or until just tender-crisp.

To serve, arrange asparagus on a serving platter. Sprinkle with salt and top with crumb mixture.

Calories 61
Protein 3 g
Carbohydrates 8 g
Cholesterol 2 mg
Total Fat 2 g
Saturated 1 g
Polyunsaturated 0 g
Monounsaturated 0 g
Fiber 1 g
Sodium 120 mg

Mixed Squash with Garlic and Lemon Bread Crumbs

Substitute 10 ounces thinly sliced crookneck squash and 10 ounces thinly sliced zucchini for asparagus, and 1 tablespoon lemon zest for Parmesan cheese. (calories 55; protein 2 g; carbohydrates 10 g; cholesterol 0 mg; total fat 1 g; saturated 0 g; polyunsaturated 0 g; monounsaturated 0 g; fiber 2 g; sodium 116 mg)

Fresh Green Beans with Water Chestnuts

Serves 6

Wondering what to serve with an Asian entrée besides steamed rice? Here's your answer.

1½ pounds fresh green beans, trimmed (about 5 cups)
2 teaspoons acceptable vegetable oil
1 teaspoon hot-pepper oil
8-ounce can sliced water chestnuts, drained
2 tablespoons sesame seeds, dry-roasted
½ teaspoon salt

In a large saucepan over high heat, bring to a boil enough water to cover beans. Meanwhile, cut beans diagonally into 1½-inch pieces. Boil beans for 4 minutes. Drain and plunge into ice water to halt cooking. Drain.

In a large skillet, heat oils over high heat, swirling to coat bottom. Stir-fry water chestnuts for 1 minute.

Add sesame seeds, beans, and salt. Cook until thoroughly heated, stirring constantly.

Cook's Tip on Water Chestnuts

Grown in water and frequently used in Chinese cooking, water chestnuts are underground stems of a marsh plant. Fresh and unpeeled, they do resemble chestnuts. You can find the fresh ones in Chinese markets. Peel them and use either raw or cooked to add crunch to salads or stir-fry dishes. Water chestnuts are also available whole or sliced in cans.

Calories 114
Protein 3 g
Carbohydrates 17 g
Cholesterol 0 mg
Total Fat 4 g
- Saturated 1 g
- Polyunsaturated 2 g
- Monounsaturated 1 g

Fiber 5 g
Sodium 203 mg

Dilled Green Beans

Serves 6

The secret's in the broth. The green beans absorb the vegetable broth, infused with bell pepper, onion, and dill seeds, which have a more intense flavor than dillweed.

1 cup Vegetable Broth (see page 41 or use commercial low-sodium variety)

¼ cup chopped green bell pepper

2 tablespoons chopped onion

½ teaspoon dill seeds

2 9-ounce packages frozen no-salt-added cut green beans

In a large saucepan over medium heat, cook all ingredients except green beans for 3 to 4 minutes, or until thoroughly heated.

Stir in beans. Cook, covered, for 5 to 8 minutes, or until beans are tender-crisp. Serve hot or refrigerate and serve chilled.

Cook's Tip

This recipe not only is quick and easy but is versatile as well. Experiment with different herbs and seeds to find out just how adaptable it is. Substitute any of the following for the dill seeds: caraway, fennel, mustard, or coriander seeds; dried marjoram or oregano, crumbled; or dried rosemary, crushed.

Calories 32
Protein 1 g
Carbohydrates 7 g
Cholesterol 0 mg
Total Fat 0 g
Saturated 0 g
Polyunsaturated 0 g
Monounsaturated 0 g
Fiber 3 g
Sodium 69 mg

French-Style Green Beans with Pimiento and Dill Seeds

Serves 4

A touch of cider vinegar and dill seeds, plus a trio of chopped vegetables, adds sparkle to this side dish.

1 tablespoon light margarine
1 tablespoon water
9-ounce package frozen no-salt-added French-style green beans
½ cup finely chopped celery (1 medium rib)
¼ cup finely chopped onion
2 tablespoons chopped pimiento
1 tablespoon cider vinegar
¼ teaspoon dill seeds
Pepper to taste

In a medium saucepan, heat margarine and water over medium heat until margarine melts, swirling to coat bottom.

Add beans and cook for 1 to 2 minutes, separating them with a fork. Reduce heat to low and cook, covered, for 5 to 6 minutes, or until beans are crisp-tender.

Stir in remaining ingredients and heat thoroughly. (Celery and onion should remain crisp.)

Calories 35
Protein 1 g
Carbohydrates 6 g
Cholesterol 0 mg
Total Fat 1 g
Saturated 0 g
Polyunsaturated 0 g
Monounsaturated 0 g
Fiber 2 g
Sodium 36 mg

Green Beans and Rice with Hazelnuts

Serves 8

Green onions and lemon enhance fluffy rice and green beans. Then chopped hazelnuts and red pimiento provide the crowning touch.

9-ounce package frozen no-salt-added French-style green beans or 16-ounce can no-salt-added French-style green beans

2 tablespoons light margarine

2 cups cooked rice (about ¾ cup uncooked)

3 tablespoons sliced green onions

½ to 1 teaspoon fresh lemon juice

Pepper to taste

¼ cup chopped or sliced hazelnuts, dry-roasted

¼ cup chopped pimiento

Cook frozen green beans using package directions, omitting salt and margarine, or heat canned beans. Drain.

In a large saucepan, melt margarine over medium heat. Stir in beans, rice, green onions, lemon juice, and pepper. Cook until heated thoroughly, stirring occasionally.

To serve, sprinkle with nuts and pimiento.

Cook's Tip on Hazelnuts, or Filberts

Traditionally used in many European dishes, hazelnuts, or filberts, are now produced in Washington and Oregon. They have a bitter brown skin that you'll want to remove. Put the nuts in a single layer on a baking pan and bake in a preheated 350° F oven for about 10 minutes. Let them cool for 1 to 2 minutes. While the hazelnuts are warm, put a handful in a dish towel and rub to remove the skin. Chop the nuts with a knife or in a food processor, if desired.

Calories 96
Protein 2 g
Carbohydrates 15 g
Cholesterol 0 mg
Total Fat 3 g
  Saturated 0 g
  Polyunsaturated 1 g
  Monounsaturated 2 g
Fiber 1 g
Sodium 22 mg

Louisiana Beans Oregano

Serves 4

Try these green beans with blackened redfish or roast chicken.

1 cup peeled and diced tomato (about 1½ medium)
½ cup diced celery (1 medium rib)
⅓ cup water
¼ cup diced green bell pepper
2 tablespoons chopped onion
½ teaspoon garlic powder
½ teaspoon onion powder
½ teaspoon dried oregano, crumbled
⅛ teaspoon white pepper
⅛ teaspoon salt
9-ounce package frozen no-salt-added Italian green beans

In a medium saucepan, combine all ingredients except green beans. Bring to a boil over high heat. Reduce heat and simmer, covered, for 10 minutes.

Increase heat to medium. Add beans and separate them with a fork. Cook, uncovered, for 5 to 8 minutes, or until beans are tender-crisp, stirring occasionally.

Calories 37
Protein 2 g
Carbohydrates 8 g
Cholesterol 0 mg
Total Fat 0 g
  Saturated 0 g
  Polyunsaturated 0 g
  Monounsaturated 0 g
Fiber 3 g
Sodium 96 mg

Mediterranean Lima Beans

Serves 4

Many typical ingredients of Mediterranean cooking—garlic, tomatoes, onion, and mint—flavor this dish. It tastes so authentic that you'll think you're basking in the sun by the Mediterranean Sea.

10-ounce package frozen no-salt-added lima beans

1 teaspoon light margarine

¼ cup chopped onion

1 medium clove garlic, crushed, or ½ teaspoon bottled minced garlic

1 cup canned no-salt-added tomatoes, undrained

½ teaspoon dried mint, crumbled

Cook lima beans using package directions, omitting salt and margarine. Drain.

In a medium skillet, melt margarine over medium-high heat. Sauté onion and garlic for 2 to 3 minutes, or until onion is translucent.

Stir in lima beans, tomatoes, and mint. Heat thoroughly.

Calories 98
Protein 6 g
Carbohydrates 18 g
Cholesterol 0 mg
Total Fat 1 g
Saturated 0 g
Polyunsaturated 0 g
Monounsaturated 0 g
Fiber 5 g
Sodium 34 mg

Barbecued Lima Beans

Serves 8

Serve this sweet-and-sour bean dish, reminiscent of baked beans, as a side dish at a cookout, on a vegetarian buffet, or as a main dish over rice.

1 pound dried baby lima beans, sorted for stones or shriveled beans and rinsed

4 cups Chicken Broth, Vegetable Broth (see pages 40 and 41 or use commercial low-sodium variety), or water

1 small onion

Vegetable oil spray

3 tablespoons light brown sugar

2 tablespoons very low sodium or low-sodium Worcestershire sauce

1 teaspoon chili powder

1 teaspoon pepper

1 teaspoon dry mustard

8-ounce can no-salt-added tomato sauce

2 tablespoons vinegar

Put beans in a stockpot or Dutch oven. Add water to cover by several inches. Bring to a boil over high heat. Remove from heat, cover, and set aside for 1 hour. Drain beans and return to stockpot.

Add broth to just cover beans (add water if needed). Bring to a boil over high heat. Reduce heat and simmer, covered, about 1¼ hours, or until tender, adding water if needed to keep beans just covered. When beans start to simmer, mince onion. Spray a large skillet with vegetable oil spray and sauté onion over medium-high heat until softened and browning, about 5 minutes. Add onion, brown sugar, Worcestershire sauce, chili powder, pepper, and mustard to beans. Leave beans uncovered for remainder of their 1¼-hour cooking time.

When beans are tender, stir in tomato sauce and vinegar.

Calories 116
Protein 5 g
Carbohydrates 21 g
Cholesterol 0 mg
Total Fat 1 g
Saturated 0 g
Polyunsaturated 0 g
Monounsaturated 0 g
Fiber 5 g
Sodium 22 mg

Deviled Beets

Serves 6

Are you looking for safe, fun ways to get your children involved in cooking? Letting them skin the beets may be the answer. The kids might even decide to eat the fruits of their labor.

3 pounds fresh beets or 3 15-ounce cans beets, drained
2 tablespoons rice wine vinegar
1 tablespoon light brown sugar
1 tablespoon light margarine
1 teaspoon very low sodium or low-sodium Worcestershire sauce
½ teaspoon paprika
¼ teaspoon dry mustard
¼ teaspoon ground cloves

Calories 107
Protein 4 g
Carbohydrates 23 g
Cholesterol 0 mg
Total Fat 1 g
Saturated 0 g
Polyunsaturated 0 g
Monounsaturated 0 g
Fiber 4 g
Sodium 175 mg

Cut all but 1 to 2 inches of stems from beets. Don't cut off root end.

Put fresh beets in a large saucepan, cover with water, and bring to a boil over medium-high heat. Reduce heat and simmer, covered, for 30 to 40 minutes, or until a knife easily pierces beets. Drain beets and let cool slightly. Slip skins off. Dice beets.

Combine remaining ingredients in a large saucepan over medium heat. After margarine melts, add beets and stir gently. Cook until heated through.

Microwave Method

Cook and dice beets as directed. Combine remaining ingredients in a 4-cup microwave-safe bowl. Heat on 100 percent power (high) for 2 minutes, stirring halfway through. Add beets and stir gently. Cook on 100 percent power (high) for 2 minutes.

Cook's Tip on Beets

Cooking time for whole beets depends on their size. If they are very large, they may have to cook for up to an hour.

Harvard Beets

Serves 4

Vibrant purple beets in a sweet-and-sour sauce is a classic. Try this version with lean pork or chicken and add your favorite green vegetable.

2 pounds fresh beets or 2 15-ounce cans beets, drained

SAUCE

⅓ cup fresh orange juice
2 tablespoons cider vinegar
½ teaspoon grated lemon zest
2 tablespoons fresh lemon juice
1½ tablespoons sugar
1 teaspoon cornstarch
⅛ teaspoon garlic powder
⅛ teaspoon salt

Cut all but 1 to 2 inches of stems from beets. Don't cut off root end.

Put beets in a large saucepan, cover with water, and bring to a boil over medium-high heat. Reduce heat and simmer, covered, for 30 to 40 minutes, or until a knife easily pierces beets. Drain beets and let cool slightly. Slip skins off and dice beets.

In a large saucepan, whisk together sauce ingredients. Bring to a boil over medium-high heat, whisking occasionally until thickened, 3 to 5 minutes. Stir in beets and cook for 2 minutes, or until heated through.

Microwave Method

Cook and dice beets as directed. Whisk together sauce ingredients except lemon zest in a microwave-safe bowl. Cook on 100 percent power (high) for 3 to 3½ minutes, or until sauce bubbles and is thick. Stir in lemon zest and beets. Cook on 100 percent power (high) for 2 minutes.

Calories 125
Protein 4 g
Carbohydrates 29 g
Cholesterol 0 mg
Total Fat 0 g
Saturated 0 g
Polyunsaturated 0 g
Monounsaturated 0 g
Fiber 4 g
Sodium 234 mg

Crunchy Broccoli Casserole

Serves 8

Put this attractive casserole together ahead of time, refrigerate, then bake just in time for your dinner guests to enjoy.

Vegetable oil spray

1 bunch fresh broccoli (about 1¾ pounds)

SAUCE

2 tablespoons Chicken Broth (see page 40 or use commercial low-sodium variety)

1 cup finely chopped onion (2 medium)

½ cup diced red bell pepper

4 tablespoons all-purpose flour

1 cup fat-free milk

2 cups Chicken Broth (see page 40 or use commercial low-sodium variety)

¼ cup grated Romano or Parmesan cheese

1 tablespoon finely chopped fresh basil or 1 teaspoon dried, crumbled

¼ teaspoon salt

⅛ teaspoon ground nutmeg

⅛ teaspoon white pepper

1 cup unsalted croutons, coarsely crushed

2 tablespoons finely chopped walnuts, dry-roasted

Preheat oven to 400° F. Lightly spray a 13 × 9 × 2-inch baking dish with vegetable oil spray.

Peel any broccoli stems that seem tough. Cut broccoli into 4-inch pieces. Steam for 4 minutes. Arrange in two lengthwise rows in baking dish. Set aside.

For sauce, in a medium saucepan, heat 2 tablespoons broth over medium-high heat. Cook onions and bell pepper until onions are translucent, 2 to 3 minutes.

In a small bowl, whisk together flour and milk. Whisk milk mixture and 2 cups broth into onion mixture. Reduce heat to medium and cook, whisking constantly, until thickened.

Whisk in remaining sauce ingredients. Pour over broccoli.

Calories 104
Protein 6 g
Carbohydrates 14 g
Cholesterol 4 mg
Total Fat 3 g
Saturated 1 g
Polyunsaturated 1 g
Monounsaturated 1 g
Fiber 3 g
Sodium 180 mg

In a small bowl, combine croutons and walnuts. Sprinkle over broccoli and sauce.

Bake for 20 to 25 minutes, or until sauce is bubbly.

Microwave Method

Trim and steam broccoli as directed. Arrange in two lengthwise rows in a 13 × 9 × 2-inch microwave-safe baking dish. Set aside. Cook 2 tablespoons broth, onion, and bell pepper on 100 percent power (high) for 2 to 3 minutes. Combine flour and milk. Stir into onion mixture with 2 cups broth and cook on 100 percent power (high) for 5 to 7 minutes. Stir in remaining sauce ingredients. Pour over broccoli and sprinkle with combined croutons and walnuts. Cover with vented plastic wrap and cook on 50 percent power (medium) for about 15 minutes, or until heated through. Let stand, covered, for 5 minutes before serving.

Cabbage with Mustard-Caraway Sauce

Serves 8

The distinctive flavor of caraway combines with spicy mustard and tangy yogurt in a sauce that goes nicely with both cabbage and brussels sprouts (see variation). Poached fish or chicken is a nice contrast to this robust dish.

8 cups coarsely shredded cabbage (about 2-pound head or 1-pound bag shredded cabbage)

MUSTARD-CARAWAY SAUCE

2 cups Chicken Broth (see page 40 or use commercial low-sodium variety)

1 tablespoon plus 1 teaspoon spicy brown mustard

1 tablespoon cornstarch

½ teaspoon caraway seeds, crushed

⅓ cup plain nonfat or low-fat yogurt

½ teaspoon grated lemon zest

¼ teaspoon salt

¼ teaspoon pepper

Steam cabbage for 5 minutes, or until tender-crisp. Remove from heat, drain, and set aside.

Meanwhile, in a large saucepan, whisk together broth, mustard, cornstarch, and caraway seeds. Bring to a boil over medium-high heat, stirring occasionally. Cook until thickened, 1 to 2 minutes.

Stir in remaining sauce ingredients, reduce heat to low, and cook for 2 to 3 minutes.

Add cabbage and stir until well coated. Cook until heated through, 2 to 3 minutes; don't overcook.

Calories 35
Protein 1 g
Carbohydrates 6 g
Cholesterol 0 mg
Total Fat 1 g
Saturated 0 g
Polyunsaturated 0 g
Monounsaturated 0 g
Fiber 2 g
Sodium 121 mg

Brussels Sprouts with Mustard-Caraway Sauce

Cook two 10-ounce packages frozen no-salt-added brussels sprouts using package directions, omitting salt and margarine, or steam 1½ pounds fresh brussels sprouts for 6 to 8 minutes, or until tender. Uncover fresh sprouts briefly after 2 to 3 minutes (to release odor). Drain and set aside. Prepare sauce as directed, increasing cornstarch to 2 tablespoons. Add sprouts to sauce and warm thoroughly, 1 to 2 minutes. (calories 49; protein 3 g; carbohydrates 8 g; cholesterol 0 mg; total fat 1 g; saturated 0 g; polyunsaturated 0 g; monounsaturated 0 g; fiber 3 g; sodium 130 mg)

Cook's Tip on Caraway Seeds

The fruit of an herb in the carrot family, caraway seeds are very popular in German, Austrian, and Hungarian foods. To release their flavor, crush them in a mortar and pestle. In many recipes, you can substitute other seeds, such as fennel, cumin, or dill.

Sweet-and-Sour Red Cabbage

Serves 8

This apple-flavored cabbage dish is a good accompaniment for game and poultry.

1 teaspoon acceptable vegetable oil
1⅓ cups diced carrots (2 medium)
1 cup finely chopped onion (2 medium)
1 cup diced red bell pepper (1 medium)
½ cup diced celery (1 medium rib)
3 cups shredded red cabbage (about 12 ounces)
1½ cups unsweetened apple juice
½ cup cider vinegar
¼ cup firmly packed light brown sugar
3 tablespoons cornstarch
2 tablespoons Dijon mustard
¼ teaspoon salt

In a large nonstick skillet, heat oil over medium-high heat, swirling to coat bottom. Sauté carrots, onions, bell pepper, and celery until onion is translucent, 2 to 3 minutes.

Reduce heat to low, stir in cabbage, and cook, covered, for 5 minutes.

In a small bowl, combine remaining ingredients. Stir into cabbage mixture. Increase heat to medium-high and cook until sauce is thick and clear, 2 to 3 minutes, stirring occasionally.

Calories 111
Protein 1 g
Carbohydrates 23 g
Cholesterol 0 mg
Total Fat 2 g
Saturated 0 g
Polyunsaturated 1 g
Monounsaturated 1 g
Fiber 2 g
Sodium 196 mg

Spiced Red Cabbage

Serves 6

Celebrate Oktoberfest or any other winter occasion with this festive dish of red cabbage, apple, and spices. Try it with one of our pork recipes, beginning on page 284.

4 cups shredded red cabbage (about 1 pound)
½ cup water (plus more as needed)
¼ cup cider vinegar
¼ teaspoon ground allspice
¼ teaspoon ground cinnamon
⅛ teaspoon ground nutmeg
2 medium tart apples, peeled, cored, and diced (about 2 cups)
1 tablespoon sugar

In a large saucepan, combine cabbage, water, vinegar, allspice, cinnamon, and nutmeg. Cook, covered, over low heat for 15 minutes, stirring occasionally and adding 2 to 3 tablespoons water if needed during cooking.

Stir in apples. Cook, covered, for 5 minutes. If necessary, uncover and cook until all moisture has cooked away.

Stir in sugar.

Cook's Tip on Tart Apples

Tart apples include Granny Smith and Gravenstein. Among the varieties that are tart but have a hint of sweetness are Braeburn, Jonathan, McIntosh, pippin (or Newton pippin), and Winesap.

Calories 52
Protein 1 g
Carbohydrates 13 g
Cholesterol 0 mg
Total Fat 0 g
  Saturated 0 g
  Polyunsaturated 0 g
  Monounsaturated 0 g
Fiber 3 g
Sodium 9 mg

Brussels Sprouts and Pecans

Serves 8

Tender brussels sprouts swim in a creamy sauce in this change-of-pace dish.

Vegetable oil spray

2 10-ounce packages frozen no-salt-added brussels sprouts or 1½ pounds fresh brussels sprouts

SAUCE

1 cup Chicken Broth (see page 40 or use commercial low-sodium variety)

⅔ cup fat-free evaporated milk

¼ cup all-purpose flour

¼ teaspoon salt

⅛ teaspoon pepper

2 tablespoons chopped pecans, dry-roasted

2 teaspoons chopped fresh sage or ½ teaspoon dried

½ cup plain dry bread crumbs

Vegetable oil spray

Preheat oven to 400° F. Lightly spray a 1½-quart casserole dish with vegetable oil spray.

Cook brussels sprouts using package directions, omitting salt and margarine, or steam fresh sprouts for 6 to 8 minutes, or until tender. Uncover fresh sprouts briefly after 2 to 3 minutes (to release odor). Drain and put in casserole dish.

In a medium saucepan, whisk together all sauce ingredients except pecans. Cook over medium-high heat until sauce comes to a boil and thickens, 3 to 4 minutes, stirring occasionally. Remove from heat and stir in pecans. Pour over brussels sprouts, then sprinkle with sage and bread crumbs. Lightly spray with vegetable oil spray.

Bake for 10 minutes, or until topping is lightly browned.

Calories 102
Protein 6 g
Carbohydrates 16 g
Cholesterol 1 mg
Total Fat 2 g
  Saturated 0 g
  Polyunsaturated 1 g
  Monounsaturated 1 g
Fiber 3 g
Sodium 173 mg

Tangy Carrots

Serves 6

The sharp flavors of mustard and pepper meet the tang of lime juice in this unusual side dish.

1 pound baby carrots
1 large shallot, very thinly sliced

SAUCE
1 tablespoon light margarine
1 tablespoon coarsely ground mustard
2 teaspoons fresh lime juice
Generous sprinkle of pepper
2 tablespoons minced fresh parsley

Steam carrots and shallot for 8 to 10 minutes, or until tender. Set aside.

For sauce, melt margarine in a small skillet over medium heat. Add remaining sauce ingredients except parsley. Cook until thoroughly heated, stirring constantly.

Transfer sauce to a medium bowl. Stir in parsley and carrot mixture. Serve hot or cover and refrigerate to serve chilled.

Microwave Method

Put carrots and shallot in a microwave steamer with 2 tablespoons water. Cook on 100 percent power (high) for 6 to 7 minutes, or until tender. Remove from microwave and set aside. Put remaining ingredients except parsley in a microwave-safe dish. Cook on 100 percent power (high) just until hot, 10 to 15 seconds. In a medium bowl, combine parsley, carrots, shallot, and sauce, stirring well.

Cook's Tip on Shallots

Shallots combine the flavor of onions and garlic but are milder than either. You can substitute 1 tablespoon minced onion for 1 large shallot.

Calories 58
Protein 2 g
Carbohydrates 10 g
Cholesterol 0 mg
Total Fat 2 g
Saturated 0 g
Polyunsaturated 0 g
Monounsaturated 1 g
Fiber 3 g
Sodium 59 mg

Honeyed Carrots

Serves 4

A tantalizing glaze of honey and brown sugar coats tender carrots.

2 cups water

10 to 12 small carrots (about 12 ounces)

2 tablespoons light margarine

1 tablespoon light brown sugar

1 tablespoon honey

2 tablespoons finely snipped fresh parsley or fresh mint

Calories 109
Protein 2 g
Carbohydrates 22 g
Cholesterol 0 mg
Total Fat 2 g
Saturated 1 g
Polyunsaturated 1 g
Monounsaturated 1 g
Fiber 5 g
Sodium 127 mg

In a large saucepan, bring water to a boil over medium-high heat. Add carrots and cook for 15 minutes, or until tender. Drain.

Dry pan. Add margarine and melt over medium heat. Stir in brown sugar, honey, and carrots. Reduce heat to low and cook until carrots are well glazed, 2 to 3 minutes, stirring frequently. Sprinkle with parsley.

Gingered Carrots

Serves 5

These peppy carrots are delicious with Chicken Philippine Style (see page 181).

1 pound carrots, peeled and cut into ¼-inch slices

2 teaspoons light margarine

2 teaspoons sugar

1 teaspoon grated fresh gingerroot

2 tablespoons finely snipped fresh parsley

Steam carrots for about 15 minutes, or until barely tender.

In a large skillet over medium heat, melt margarine until it bubbles. Stir in carrots, then sprinkle with sugar and gingerroot. Stir again to coat carrots. Cook for 1 to 2 minutes, or until carrots are lightly glazed. Sprinkle with parsley.

Calories 51
Protein 1 g
Carbohydrates 11 g
Cholesterol 0 mg
Total Fat 1 g
Saturated 0 g
Polyunsaturated 0 g
Monounsaturated 0 g
Fiber 3 g
Sodium 65 mg

Baked Grated Carrots with Sherry

Serves 6

Pop this casserole into the oven while you roast a chicken. Fix a salad while they cook, and an easy meal is ready.

3 cups grated carrots (3 large)
2 tablespoons light margarine, melted
2 tablespoons dry sherry
1 tablespoon fresh lemon juice
1 tablespoon chopped chives

Preheat oven to 350° F.

Combine all ingredients except chives, stirring well.

Put in a 1-quart casserole dish and sprinkle with chives.

Bake, covered, for 30 minutes.

Calories 42
Protein 1 g
Carbohydrates 6 g
Cholesterol 0 mg
Total Fat 1 g
Saturated 0 g
Polyunsaturated 1 g
Monounsaturated 0 g
Fiber 2 g
Sodium 57 mg

Creole Celery and Peas

Serves 10

When celery is on special at the grocery, this recipe will help you stretch your food budget.

16-ounce can no-salt-added tomatoes
1 teaspoon light margarine
1 medium onion, chopped (½ cup)
½ teaspoon red hot-pepper sauce
¼ teaspoon dried thyme, crumbled
4 cups diagonally cut celery (8 medium ribs)
10-ounce package frozen green peas

Drain tomatoes, reserving liquid. Set aside.

In a large skillet, melt margarine over medium-high heat. Sauté onion until translucent, 2 to 3 minutes.

Stir in liquid from tomatoes, hot-pepper sauce, and thyme. Bring to a boil over medium-high heat.

Stir in celery and peas. Reduce heat and simmer, covered, for 10 minutes, or until celery is barely tender.

Stir in tomatoes and heat through.

Calories 44
Protein 2 g
Carbohydrates 9 g
Cholesterol 0 mg
Total Fat 0 g
Saturated 0 g
Polyunsaturated 0 g
Monounsaturated 0 g
Fiber 3 g
Sodium 54 mg

Cauliflower and Roasted Corn with Chili Powder and Lime

Serves 8

Roasting or grilling gives corn an intense flavor. Serve this unusual combination with Turkey Loaf (see page 234).

2 ears of corn (about 1 pound), husks and silks removed
4 cups cauliflower florets (about ½ medium head)
¼ cup Chicken Broth (see page 40 or use commercial low-sodium variety)
2-ounce jar diced pimientos, drained
1 tablespoon fresh lime juice
1 tablespoon light margarine
¼ teaspoon chili powder
¼ teaspoon salt
⅛ teaspoon pepper

Preheat oven to 400° F.

Put corn on a baking sheet and roast, uncovered, for 15 minutes. Let cool on cooling rack for 5 to 10 minutes. Slice corn off cob and set aside.

In a large saucepan, bring cauliflower and broth to a boil over medium-high heat. Reduce heat to medium-low and cook, covered, for 10 to 15 minutes, or until cauliflower is tender.

Meanwhile, combine remaining ingredients in a small bowl.

Add pimiento mixture and roasted corn to cauliflower, stirring well. Cook, uncovered, over medium-low heat for 1 to 2 minutes, or until warmed through, stirring occasionally.

Calories 41
Protein 2 g
Carbohydrates 8 g
Cholesterol 0 mg
Total Fat 1 g
- Saturated 0 g
- Polyunsaturated 0 g
- Monounsaturated 0 g

Fiber 2 g
Sodium 94 mg

Swiss Chard, Southern Style

Serves 5

This peppery Swiss chard dish is rich in vitamins A and C, as well as iron. And it tastes good, too!

2 bunches Swiss chard (about 8 ounces each)

1 teaspoon acceptable vegetable oil

1 cup finely chopped onion (2 medium)

¼ cup water

1 teaspoon liquid smoke seasoning

¼ to ½ teaspoon crushed red pepper flakes

1 tablespoon imitation bacon bits

Remove stems from chard. Stack several leaves and cut into ½-inch slices. Repeat with remaining leaves.

In a large saucepan, heat oil over medium-high heat, swirling to coat bottom. Sauté onions until tender, 2 to 3 minutes.

Stir in chard and remaining ingredients except bacon bits. Cook, covered, for 5 to 7 minutes, or until chard is wilted and tender.

Stir in bacon bits.

Cook's Tip on Swiss Chard

When you want a serving of one of those famous leafy green vegetables, Swiss chard fills the bill. It has dark green leaves with silvery or red stalks. Select fresh-looking, crisp greens and cook them within 3 days. Wash thoroughly to remove dirt and sand, and use as you would spinach. For a fancy presentation, roll each leaf into a tube and cut into ½-inch slices.

Calories 38
Protein 2 g
Carbohydrates 6 g
Cholesterol 0 mg
Total Fat 1 g
Saturated 0 g
Polyunsaturated 1 g
Monounsaturated 0 g
Fiber 2 g
Sodium 163 mg

Southwestern Creamy Corn

Serves 6

Try this creamy side dish, flecked with color, with Beef Tostadas (see page 275).

1 teaspoon light margarine
½ cup finely chopped onion
½ cup diced red bell pepper
4 ounces nonfat or low-fat cream cheese
¼ cup diced green chiles
¼ cup fat-free milk
½ teaspoon pepper
½ teaspoon chili powder
2 cups frozen no-salt-added whole-kernel corn (11 to 12 ounces)
2 teaspoons finely snipped fresh cilantro

In a large nonstick skillet, melt margarine over medium-high heat. Sauté onion and bell pepper until onion is translucent, 2 to 3 minutes.

Reduce heat to low and add cream cheese, chiles, milk, pepper, and chili powder. Cook until mixture is smooth, 2 to 3 minutes, stirring constantly.

Stir in corn. Cook just until corn is warmed through, 2 to 3 minutes.

To serve, stir in cilantro.

Calories 75
Protein 5 g
Carbohydrates 14 g
Cholesterol 2 mg
Total Fat 1 g
Saturated 0 g
Polyunsaturated 0 g
Monounsaturated 0 g
Fiber 2 g
Sodium 106 mg

Cajun Corn

Serves 4

Richly browned onions are simmered with sweet yellow corn and served with a colorful "butter" compound of Cajun seasonings.

1½ tablespoons light margarine
¼ teaspoon dried thyme, crumbled
½ teaspoon paprika
⅛ teaspoon black pepper
⅛ teaspoon cayenne
⅛ teaspoon salt

Vegetable oil spray
1½ cups chopped yellow onion (3 medium)
¼ teaspoon sugar
3 cups frozen no-salt-added whole-kernel corn, thawed (17 ounces)

In a small bowl, combine margarine, thyme, paprika, pepper, cayenne, and salt, stirring well. Set aside.

Spray a large skillet, preferably cast iron, with vegetable oil spray. Heat over high heat for 1 minute. Cook onions for 2 minutes, stirring constantly. Reduce heat to medium.

Stir in sugar and cook for 3 minutes, or until golden brown, stirring frequently.

Add corn and cook for 3 minutes, stirring occasionally. Remove from heat.

Stir in margarine mixture.

Southwestern Corn

Substitute dried oregano, crumbled, for thyme, and add ¼ teaspoon ground cumin to margarine mixture. Add 2 seeded and finely chopped jalapeño peppers (see Cook's Tip, page 115) when adding corn to skillet. (calories 136; protein 4 g; carbohydrates 29 g; cholesterol 0 mg; total fat 2 g; saturated 0 g; polyunsaturated 1 g; monounsaturated 1 g; fiber 4 g; sodium 107 mg)

Calories 130
Protein 4 g
Carbohydrates 28 g
Cholesterol 0 mg
Total Fat 2 g
  Saturated 0 g
  Polyunsaturated 1 g
  Monounsaturated 1 g
Fiber 4 g
Sodium 106 mg

Grits Casserole with Cheese and Chiles

Serves 8

When simply prepared, grits are perfect for breakfast. This filling dish dresses them up so you can serve them for dinner as well. Grill pork tenderloins and a medley of fresh vegetables, and you'll have an easy dinner for eight.

Vegetable oil spray

2 cups Chicken Broth (see page 40 or use commercial low-sodium variety)

2 cups water

1 cup uncooked grits

½ cup fat-free milk

¼ cup grated Parmesan cheese

2 slices fat-free pasteurized process Swiss cheese, diced (2 ounces)

2 tablespoons canned chopped green chiles, rinsed and drained (2 ounces)

1 tablespoon light margarine

2 medium cloves garlic, minced, or 1 teaspoon bottled minced garlic

¼ teaspoon salt

⅛ teaspoon pepper

Egg substitute equivalent to 2 eggs, or 2 eggs

½ teaspoon chili powder

Preheat oven to 375° F. Lightly spray a 13 × 9 × 2-inch baking pan with vegetable oil spray. Set aside.

In a large saucepan, bring broth and water to a boil over medium-high heat. Gradually whisk in grits. Reduce heat to low and cook, covered, for 5 minutes, whisking occasionally.

Remove saucepan from heat. Stir in milk, Parmesan and Swiss cheeses, chiles, margarine, garlic, salt, and pepper.

Stir some hot grits mixture into egg substitute. Add egg substitute to saucepan, stirring well. Pour into baking pan, smoothing top with a spatula. Sprinkle with chili powder.

Bake, uncovered, for 45 minutes. Remove from oven and let cool for 5 to 10 minutes before serving.

Calories 127
Protein 6 g
Carbohydrates 19 g
Cholesterol 3 mg
Total Fat 2 g
  Saturated 1 g
  Polyunsaturated 1 g
  Monounsaturated 1 g
Fiber 0 g
Sodium 232 mg

Creamy Kale with Red Bell Pepper

Serves 4

The creamy sauce in this dish complements the mild cabbage flavor of kale. Like other cabbage, kale goes well with pork, or try it with braised eye-of-round roast.

1 bunch kale (about 1½ pounds)
1 cup diced red bell pepper
2 tablespoons water
2 tablespoons light margarine
2 tablespoons all-purpose flour
1 cup fat-free milk
¼ teaspoon salt
⅛ teaspoon pepper
½ teaspoon sugar

Tear kale leaves into small pieces and discard stalks. Put kale and bell pepper in a large saucepan over medium-high heat.

Add water. Reduce heat to low and cook, covered, for 5 to 6 minutes, or until leaves are wilted.

In a large saucepan, melt margarine over medium-high heat. Whisk in flour and cook for 1 minute, stirring constantly.

Whisk in remaining ingredients except sugar. Cook until mixture boils, stirring constantly.

Remove from heat and stir in kale mixture and sugar.

Cook's Tip on Kale

Kale has deep green frilly leaves, usually tinged with blue or purple. In small amounts, this mild, cabbagy-tasting vegetable is good in tossed salad. Prepare it as you would spinach. The best kale is available in the winter. It's a good source of vitamins A and C, folic acid, calcium, and iron.

Calories 124
Protein 6 g
Carbohydrates 19 g
Cholesterol 1 mg
Total Fat 3 g
  Saturated 1 g
  Polyunsaturated 1 g
  Monounsaturated 1 g
Fiber 3 g
Sodium 254 mg

Mushrooms with White Wine and Shallots

Serves 4

Cook succulent mushrooms with shallots and wine, then reduce the juices to intensify the flavor. Serve as a side dish or spoon the mushrooms over broiled sirloin steak.

2 tablespoons light margarine
½ cup finely chopped shallots (8 large)
1 pound fresh mushrooms, quartered (about 6 cups)
½ cup dry white wine (regular or nonalcoholic)
1 tablespoon finely snipped fresh parsley
Pepper to taste

In a large nonstick skillet, melt margarine over medium-high heat. Sauté shallots for 2 to 3 minutes, stirring constantly.

Add mushrooms and wine. Reduce heat to medium and cook, covered, for 7 to 9 minutes. Uncover and increase heat to high. Cook for 5 to 6 minutes, or until juices have evaporated.

To serve, stir in parsley and pepper.

Calories 80
Protein 2 g
Carbohydrates 9 g
Cholesterol 0 mg
Total Fat 2 g
Saturated 1 g
Polyunsaturated 1 g
Monounsaturated 1 g
Fiber 2 g
Sodium 41 mg

Kohlrabi Gratin

Serves 4

If you like scalloped potatoes, we think you'll enjoy kohlrabi prepared the same way. Although a member of the same family as turnips, kohlrabi is milder and sweeter.

Vegetable oil spray

2 medium kohlrabi bulbs (about 1¼ pounds)

1 cup water

SAUCE

1 teaspoon olive oil

2 large shallots, finely chopped (2 tablespoons)

1 cup Chicken Broth (see page 40 or use commercial low-sodium variety)

½ cup fat-free evaporated milk

1½ tablespoons all-purpose flour

¼ teaspoon salt

¼ teaspoon pepper

1 tablespoon snipped fresh dillweed or 1 teaspoon dried, crumbled

2 tablespoons grated Parmesan cheese

¼ cup plain dry bread crumbs

Preheat oven to 350° F. Spray a 1½-quart casserole dish with vegetable oil spray. Set aside.

With a sharp knife, peel kohlrabi and cut into ¼-inch slices. In a medium saucepan, bring kohlrabi and water to a boil over high heat. Reduce heat to medium-low and cook, covered, for 5 minutes, or until tender-crisp. Drain and set aside.

For sauce, heat a medium saucepan over medium-low heat. Add oil and swirl to coat bottom. When oil is hot, sauté shallots for 1 to 2 minutes, stirring occasionally.

In a medium bowl, whisk together broth, milk, flour, salt, and pepper. Add to shallots and bring mixture to a boil over medium-high heat, stirring occasionally. Reduce heat to medium and cook for 1 to 2 minutes, or until mixture thickens, stirring occasionally.

Stir in dillweed and Parmesan; remove from heat.

Calories 114
Protein 6 g
Carbohydrates 16 g
Cholesterol 4 mg
Total Fat 3 g
Saturated 1 g
Polyunsaturated 0 g
Monounsaturated 1 g
Fiber 3 g
Sodium 317 mg

Arrange half the kohlrabi in casserole dish. Spoon on half the sauce. Repeat. Cover dish with aluminum foil.

Bake for 20 to 25 minutes, or until kohlrabi is tender. Sprinkle with bread crumbs and bake for 10 minutes.

Cook's Tip on Kohlrabi

When you buy kohlrabi, look for crisp leaves with no yellow ends. Use the bulbs in recipes such as the one above, then stack the leaves, roll them jelly-roll style, and slice crosswise into thin strips. Cook about 4 cups of sliced leaves with ¼ cup Chicken Broth (see page 40 or use commercial low-sodium variety) or water, covered, over medium-low heat for 2 to 3 minutes, or until tender. Season with pepper. Uncooked kohlrabi strips are also good in soups. Add them for the last 2 to 3 minutes of cooking.

Crispy Baked Onion Flower

Serves 4

If you like onion rings, you will have fun making and eating this spectacular onion flower. Serve it with a lean grilled hamburger or chicken breast.

1 large yellow onion (about 1¼ pounds) or 2 medium yellow onions (about 10 ounces each)

4 cups water

Vegetable oil spray

¼ cup all-purpose flour

1½ teaspoons salt-free all-purpose seasoning

3 tablespoons egg substitute

½ cup cornflake crumbs (1½ cups cornflakes)

Trim root end of onion. Peel onion and put it root end down on a cutting board. With a long, sharp knife, leaving onion intact, cut it in quarters almost to root stem end. Still leaving onion intact, carefully cut it in eighths, then in sixteenths.

Pour water into a medium saucepan and bring to a boil over high heat. Reduce heat to medium-high. Add onion and cook for 7 minutes (5 minutes for medium onions), turning over halfway through cooking time. Remove onion with a slotted spoon and drain in a colander.

Put onion in a bowl with enough ice-cold water to cover by 1 inch. Refrigerate for at least 2 hours.

Preheat oven to 350° F. Lightly spray a baking sheet with vegetable oil spray.

Drain onion cut side down in colander and blot with paper towel.

Combine flour and all-purpose seasoning in an airtight plastic bag.

Put onion in bag and seal. Carefully shake and move bag around and upside down to coat onion. You may have to slightly open onion through bag to coat middle.

Pour egg substitute into bag and repeat process to coat onion. Remove onion from bag and place on a cutting board or large platter.

Calories 141
Protein 5 g
Carbohydrates 31 g
Cholesterol 0 mg
Total Fat 1 g
  Saturated 0 g
  Polyunsaturated 0 g
  Monounsaturated 0 g
Fiber 2 g
Sodium 176 mg

Sprinkle cornflake crumbs evenly over onion; slightly open onion to coat middle. Place onion on baking sheet.

Bake large onion for 1 hour 20 minutes, medium onions for 1 hour. Place on a serving plate and serve warm with low-sodium ketchup. If desired, have a pair of kitchen scissors handy so you can easily remove the crispy onion petals.

Cook's Tip

To keep from cutting all the way through the onion, insert a metal skewer horizontally through the onion, just below where you want to finish cutting. As you cut the onion, the skewer will stop your knife.

Caramelized Onions

Serves 4

Sweet onions are spiked with cloves, seasoned with Worcestershire and soy sauce, and broiled or grilled to a rich mahogany color.

Vegetable oil spray

2 yellow onions, about 8 ounces each, peeled and halved

20 whole cloves

1 tablespoon plus 1½ teaspoons very low sodium or low-sodium Worcestershire sauce

1 tablespoon sugar

1 tablespoon light soy sauce

2 teaspoons toasted sesame oil or acceptable vegetable oil

Spray grill or broiler pan and rack with vegetable oil spray. Preheat grill to medium-high heat or preheat broiler.

Cut a thin slice off round part of each onion half so onions will lie flat. Pierce each onion half with 5 cloves.

In a small bowl, whisk together remaining ingredients until sugar has dissolved. Using a pastry brush, lightly coat onions.

Put onions on grill or broiler rack. If using broiler, put rack at least 5 inches from heat. Cook onions until caramelized and tender-crisp, 15 to 18 minutes, basting frequently.

Cook's Tip on Broiler Pans

For easy cleanup, line broiler pans with aluminum foil.

Calories 58
Protein 1 g
Carbohydrates 9 g
Cholesterol 0 mg
Total Fat 2 g
 Saturated 0 g
 Polyunsaturated 1 g
 Monounsaturated 1 g
Fiber 1 g
Sodium 135 mg

Two-Cheese Sour Cream Noodles

Serves 4

You'll need to save the empty containers to prove you didn't use high-fat ingredients to make this rich side dish. By adding cooked ground beef or steamed shrimp, you can turn it into an entrée.

Vegetable oil spray
4 ounces dried yolk-free noodles (1½ to 2 cups)
¾ cup nonfat or light sour cream
½ cup fat-free or low-fat dry curd cottage cheese
¼ cup fat-free milk
1 medium clove garlic, minced, or ½ teaspoon bottled minced garlic
½ teaspoon very low sodium or low-sodium Worcestershire sauce
2 tablespoons grated Parmesan cheese

Preheat oven to 350° F. Spray a 1-quart casserole dish with vegetable oil spray.

Prepare noodles using package directions, omitting salt and oil. Drain well.

Meanwhile, in a large bowl, combine remaining ingredients except Parmesan, stirring well.

Stir in noodles. Spoon into casserole dish.

Bake, uncovered, for 15 minutes. Sprinkle with Parmesan. Bake for 5 minutes.

Calories 205
Protein 13 g
Carbohydrates 34 g
Cholesterol 5 mg
Total Fat 2 g
Saturated 1 g
Polyunsaturated 0 g
Monounsaturated 0 g
Fiber 1 g
Sodium 118 mg

Parmesan Parsnip Puree with Leeks and Carrots

Serves 6

Parsnips have a sweet, slightly peppery taste. Puree them with carrots, leeks, and Parmesan cheese for a pale gold side dish similar in texture to mashed potatoes.

1 pound parsnips, peeled and cut crosswise into ½-inch pieces (1½ cups)

2 small carrots, peeled and cut crosswise into ½-inch pieces (1¼ cups)

2 leeks, white part only, thinly sliced crosswise (2 cups)

½ cup Chicken Broth (see page 40 or use commercial low-sodium variety)

2 tablespoons grated Parmesan cheese

1 tablespoon light margarine

¼ teaspoon salt

½ cup Chicken Broth (see page 40 or use commercial low-sodium variety)

2 tablespoons thinly sliced almonds

In a large saucepan, bring parsnips, carrots, leeks, and ½ cup broth to a boil over high heat. Reduce heat to medium-low and cook, covered, for 10 minutes, or until tender. Remove from heat and let cool for 5 minutes.

Put parsnip mixture and remaining ingredients except almonds in a food processor or blender and puree.

To serve, spoon into a serving dish and sprinkle with almonds.

Microwave Method

Put parsnips, carrots, leeks, and broth in a 1-quart microwave-safe dish. Cover with plastic wrap. Microwave on 100 percent power (high) for 5 to 6 minutes, or until tender. Let cool for 5 minutes, then proceed as directed above.

Calories 117
Protein 3 g
Carbohydrates 21 g
Cholesterol 2 mg
Total Fat 3 g
  Saturated 1 g
  Polyunsaturated 1 g
  Monounsaturated 1 g
Fiber 4 g
Sodium 172 mg

Cook's Tip on Parsnips

Parsnips look like pale carrots and are in the same family. Whether you bake, sauté, roast, steam, or boil them, parsnips are sweet and aromatic. They turn mushy quickly, though, so don't overcook them. Look for firm parsnips without pitting. Don't worry if they're large—bigger size doesn't mean parsnips won't be tender. Wrapped in plastic wrap and refrigerated, parsnips will keep for several weeks to several months.

Here are four easy ideas for using parsnips:

1. Peel parsnips and cut into pieces to add to soups or stews for the last 10 minutes of cooking time.
2. Toss cooked parsnip slices with fresh herbs, such as rosemary or chives, for a side dish.
3. Add cooked parsnip slices to pasta salad.
4. Substitute them for carrots in almost any recipe.

Three-Cheese Macaroni

Serves 8

This jazzed-up version of an old favorite is easy to put together. You don't even have to cook the macaroni before adding it to the casserole.

Vegetable oil spray
16-ounce can no-salt-added tomato puree
1 cup water
2 teaspoons salt-free dried Italian herb seasoning, crumbled
2 medium cloves garlic, minced, or 1 teaspoon bottled minced garlic
24 ounces nonfat or low-fat cottage cheese
1 large shallot, finely chopped (about 1 tablespoon)
1 medium clove garlic, minced, or ½ teaspoon bottled minced garlic
8 ounces dried elbow macaroni (about 2 cups)
2 tablespoons grated Parmesan cheese
2 ounces fat-free or part-skim mozzarella cheese, sliced

Preheat oven to 350° F. Lightly spray a 9-inch square casserole dish with vegetable oil spray.

In a medium bowl, combine tomato puree, water, herb seasoning, and 2 cloves garlic.

In another medium bowl, combine cottage cheese, shallot, and 1 clove garlic.

Spoon one third of tomato mixture into casserole dish. In order, layer half the macaroni, all the cottage cheese mixture, one third of tomato mixture, all the Parmesan, remaining macaroni, and remaining tomato mixture.

Bake, covered, for 1 hour. Uncover and top with mozzarella. Bake, uncovered, for 5 minutes, or until cheese is melted.

Let casserole stand for 10 minutes before serving.

Calories 201
Protein 17 g
Carbohydrates 31 g
Cholesterol 9 mg
Total Fat 1 g
Saturated 0 g
Polyunsaturated 0 g
Monounsaturated 0 g
Fiber 2 g
Sodium 418 mg

Black-Eyed Peas with Canadian Bacon

Serves 16

In the South, black-eyed peas are traditionally served on New Year's Day to bring good luck throughout the coming year. This tasty version will bring you compliments no matter when you serve it.

1 pound dried black-eyed peas, sorted for stones and rinsed
4 ounces Canadian bacon
2 medium onions
2 ribs celery
6-ounce can no-salt-added tomato paste
1 small bay leaf
1 medium clove garlic, chopped, or ½ teaspoon bottled minced garlic
¼ teaspoon cayenne
Pepper to taste

Put peas in a large saucepan and add water to cover. Soak for 45 minutes.

Meanwhile, dice Canadian bacon and chop onions and celery.

Drain peas and return them to saucepan. Add just enough fresh water to cover.

Add all other ingredients. Bring to a boil over medium-high heat. Reduce heat and simmer, covered, for 3 hours, or until tender.

Cook's Tip on Canadian Bacon

Canadian bacon is really more like ham than like bacon. It has much less fat than bacon. Fully cooked when you buy it, Canadian bacon can be sliced and used as you would cooked ham.

Calories 105
Protein 7 g
Carbohydrates 18 g
Cholesterol 3 mg
Total Fat 1 g
Saturated 0 g
Polyunsaturated 0 g
Monounsaturated 0 g
Fiber 3 g
Sodium 86 mg

Savory Peas

Serves 6

Enliven the flavor of peas with bacon, Italian herbs, and fresh nutmeg. Serve with mashed potatoes and Smothered Steak with Sangría Sauce (see page 249).

3 pounds fresh green peas in shells or 16-ounce package frozen green peas
2 strips lower-sodium bacon or 3 tablespoons imitation bacon bits
1 teaspoon light margarine
6 medium green onions, finely chopped (green and white parts) (⅔ cup)
1 teaspoon salt-free Italian herb seasoning
¼ teaspoon freshly ground nutmeg, or to taste

Shell peas if using fresh. Put peas in a medium saucepan with enough water to cover by about ½ inch. Bring to a boil over high heat. Reduce heat and simmer, covered, until peas are tender-crisp, 5 to 8 minutes. If using frozen peas, follow package directions, omitting salt and margarine.

Meanwhile, cook bacon until crisp. Drain well, pat dry with paper towels, and dice.

In a large skillet, melt margarine over medium-high heat. Sauté green onions until soft, 1 to 2 minutes.

Reduce heat to low, add all ingredients, and heat through.

Calories 85
Protein 5 g
Carbohydrates 14 g
Cholesterol 2 mg
Total Fat 1 g
Saturated 0 g
Polyunsaturated 0 g
Monounsaturated 0 g
Fiber 5 g
Sodium 37 mg

Cook's Tip on Grinding Nutmeg

Freshly ground nutmeg is stronger and spicier than bottled ground nutmeg and makes a great difference in a recipe. It's best to use a nutmeg grater or nutmeg grinder, similar to a pepper mill, but you can use a knife. Frequently sprinkled on (low-fat) eggnog, nutmeg can also spice up tomato sauce or soup, mashed potatoes, cheese dishes, spinach dishes, and sweet breads and other baked goods.

French Peas

Serves 6

Tender peas, wilted lettuce, and crunchy water chestnuts provide a variety of textures in this side dish. For a quick trip to Paris, serve this with French-Style Braised Fish Fillets (see page 138).

10-ounce package frozen green peas
1 tablespoon acceptable vegetable oil
1 cup finely shredded lettuce
2 medium green onions, diced (¼ cup)
3 tablespoons Chicken Broth (see page 40), commercial low-sodium chicken broth, or water
1 teaspoon all-purpose flour
8-ounce can sliced water chestnuts, drained
Pepper to taste

Cook peas using package directions, omitting salt and margarine. Drain and set aside.

In a large saucepan, heat oil over low heat, swirling to coat bottom. Cook lettuce and green onions for 1 to 2 minutes, stirring occasionally.

In a small bowl, whisk together broth and flour. Add to lettuce mixture. Increase heat to medium and cook until thickened, 2 to 3 minutes, stirring occasionally.

Stir in peas, water chestnuts, and pepper. Heat through.

Calories 102
Protein 3 g
Carbohydrates 17 g
Cholesterol 0 mg
Total Fat 2 g
  Saturated 0 g
  Polyunsaturated 1 g
  Monounsaturated 1 g
Fiber 4 g
Sodium 8 mg

Basil Roasted Peppers

Serves 8

You'll find many uses for these roasted peppers in your cooking, or serve them cold as a garnish.

Vegetable oil spray
6 firm red bell peppers
¼ cup plus 1 tablespoon olive oil
¼ cup red wine vinegar
2 tablespoons finely chopped fresh basil
3 or 4 medium cloves garlic, minced, or 1½ to 2 teaspoons bottled minced garlic
½ teaspoon pepper, or to taste
¼ teaspoon salt

Preheat broiler. Spray a broiling pan and rack with vegetable oil spray.

Broil peppers about 2 inches from heat on broiling rack for 1 to 2 minutes on each side, or until lightly charred. Seal in an airtight plastic bag or put in a large bowl and cover with plastic wrap. Let cool for 5 to 10 minutes. Remove and discard skin, core, ribs, and seeds. Rinse peppers under cold water and pat dry with paper towels. Cut into strips ½ inch wide.

In a medium bowl, combine remaining ingredients. Stir in peppers. Cover and refrigerate for 30 minutes to 8 hours. Drain and discard marinade. Store drained peppers in an airtight container in the refrigerator for up to 5 days or in the freezer for up to 4 months.

Calories 35
Protein 1 g
Carbohydrates 4 g
Cholesterol 0 mg
Total Fat 2 g
- Saturated 0 g
- Polyunsaturated 0 g
- Monounsaturated 1 g

Fiber 1 g
Sodium 75 mg

Scalloped Potatoes

Serves 6

Serve these comforting potatoes with lean grilled pork chops and Asparagus par Excellence *(see page* 355*).*

Vegetable oil spray

SAUCE

5 tablespoons light margarine

1 cup finely chopped onion (2 medium)

¼ cup plus 1 tablespoon all-purpose flour

2½ cups fat-free milk

3 tablespoons finely snipped fresh parsley

1½ teaspoons grated lemon zest

⅛ teaspoon salt

⅛ teaspoon white pepper

2 pounds potatoes, peeled and thinly sliced (5 to 6 cups)

⅛ teaspoon salt

⅛ teaspoon white pepper

2 tablespoons grated Romano or Parmesan cheese

Preheat oven to 325° F. Lightly spray an 8-inch square baking dish with vegetable oil spray and set aside.

For sauce, heat margarine in a medium saucepan over medium-high heat, swirling to coat bottom. Sauté onions until translucent, 2 to 3 minutes.

Whisk in flour and cook for 1 minute, then whisk in milk. Cook until sauce is thickened, 3 to 4 minutes, stirring constantly.

Whisk in remaining sauce ingredients. Remove from heat.

Arrange potatoes in baking dish. Sprinkle with ⅛ teaspoon salt and ⅛ teaspoon pepper.

Pour sauce over potatoes and sprinkle with Romano.

Bake, uncovered, for 1½ hours.

Calories 228
Protein 7 g
Carbohydrates 40 g
Cholesterol 4 mg
Total Fat 4 g
Saturated 1 g
Polyunsaturated 2 g
Monounsaturated 1 g
Fiber 3 g
Sodium 241 mg

Potatoes with Leeks and Fresh Herbs

Serves 8

While this one-skillet side dish simmers, it will fill your kitchen with a tantalizing aroma. And the dish tastes even better than it smells.

Olive oil spray

2 medium leeks, white part only, sliced (about 2 cups)

2 medium cloves garlic, crushed, or 1 teaspoon bottled minced garlic

1 cup Chicken Broth (see page 40 or use commercial low-sodium variety)

½ cup snipped fresh parsley

¼ cup dry white wine (regular or nonalcoholic) (optional)

2-ounce jar diced pimientos, rinsed and drained (about ¼ cup)

2 tablespoons snipped fresh dillweed

1 tablespoon chopped fresh sage or thyme

2 teaspoons grated lemon zest

Pepper to taste

6 medium potatoes (about 2 pounds)

Spray a large skillet with olive oil spray. Put over medium heat. Sauté leeks and garlic until soft, 2 to 3 minutes, stirring occasionally.

Stir in remaining ingredients except potatoes. Remove from heat.

Peel and thinly slice potatoes. Arrange on leek mixture.

Bring potato mixture to a boil over medium-high heat. Reduce heat and simmer, covered, for 20 minutes, or until potatoes are tender.

Calories 102
Protein 2 g
Carbohydrates 23 g
Cholesterol 0 mg
Total Fat 0 g
Saturated 0 g
Polyunsaturated 0 g
Monounsaturated 0 g
Fiber 2 g
Sodium 11 mg

Cook's Tip

If you have any potatoes left over, combine them with sautéed fresh mushrooms and egg substitute or egg whites to make a wonderful frittata or omelet for breakfast, brunch, lunch, or dinner.

Rustic Potato Patties

Serves 4; 2 patties per serving

Black pepper and cayenne heat up these potato patties, which get their texture from the skins.

Vegetable oil spray
4 cups water
1 pound red potatoes, diced (3 medium)
½ cup minced onion
¼ cup plus 2 tablespoons fat-free evaporated milk
White of 1 large egg
½ teaspoon salt
⅛ teaspoon black pepper
⅛ teaspoon cayenne
¼ cup all-purpose flour
1 tablespoon acceptable vegetable oil, divided use

Preheat oven to warm or 140° F. Spray a large nonstick skillet with vegetable oil spray. Set aside.

In a medium saucepan, bring water to a boil over high heat. Add potatoes and return to a boil. Reduce heat and simmer, uncovered, for 7 to 8 minutes, or until tender but not mushy. Drain well. Return potatoes to pan or put in a large bowl; beat until no lumps remain.

Add onion, milk, egg white, salt, black pepper, and cayenne and beat until well blended.

Beat in flour.

Pour 1½ teaspoons oil into skillet; swirl to coat bottom. Heat over medium-high heat for about 2 minutes, or until hot. Spoon 4 rounded ⅓-cup mounds of potato mixture into skillet. Using back of a fork, flatten slightly until about ½ inch thick. Cook for 5 minutes on each side. Put patties on an ovenproof platter and set in oven. Repeat process, heating oil over medium-high heat for 30 seconds.

Time-Saver: Since you'll beat the cooked potatoes, you may wonder, why dice them first? It doesn't take long to dice them in the food processor, and using small pieces saves cooking time.

Calories 187
Protein 6 g
Carbohydrates 33 g
Cholesterol 1 mg
Total Fat 4 g
Saturated 1 g
Polyunsaturated 2 g
Monounsaturated 1 g
Fiber 3 g
Sodium 360 mg

Baked Fries with Creole Seasoning

Serves 4

The crispy, spice-flecked appearance of these fries is enough to make your mouth water. Serve them with a lean grilled hamburger and a thick slice of onion on a toasted whole-wheat bun.

4 medium unpeeled russet potatoes (1¼ to 1½ pounds)

CREOLE SEASONING
½ teaspoon chili powder
½ teaspoon ground cumin
½ teaspoon onion powder
½ teaspoon garlic powder
½ teaspoon paprika
½ teaspoon black pepper
¼ teaspoon salt
⅛ teaspoon cayenne (optional)

Vegetable oil spray

Cut potatoes into long strips about ½ inch wide. In a large bowl, soak for 15 minutes in enough cold water to cover by 1 inch.

Meanwhile, combine seasoning ingredients in a small bowl. Set aside.

Preheat oven to 450° F. Lightly spray a large baking sheet with vegetable oil spray.

Drain potatoes and pat dry with paper towels. Spread potatoes in a single layer on baking sheet. Lightly spray tops with vegetable oil spray. Sprinkle with seasoning mixture.

Bake for 30 to 35 minutes, or until crispy.

Cook's Tip on Creole Seasoning

To save time in the future, double or triple the seasoning mixture in this recipe and keep it in a container with a shaker top. This seasoning is excellent on seafood, chicken, beef, vegetables, or garlic toast (made with light margarine, of course!).

Calories 143
Protein 3 g
Carbohydrates 33 g
Cholesterol 0 mg
Total Fat 0 g
- Saturated 0 g
- Polyunsaturated 0 g
- Monounsaturated 0 g

Fiber 3 g
Sodium 159 mg

Baked Sweet Potato Chips

Serves 4

When you want to add a bit of flair to your meal, these sweet potato chips do it in a colorful, nutritious way. They're a great side dish for glazed ham with cranberries or roasted chicken with sugar snap peas.

Vegetable oil spray

SEASONING
1 teaspoon dried rosemary, crushed
1 teaspoon dried parsley, crumbled
½ teaspoon dry mustard
¼ teaspoon paprika
¼ teaspoon salt
¼ teaspoon pepper

2 medium unpeeled sweet potatoes (about 12 ounces)
Vegetable oil spray

Preheat oven to 450° F. Lightly spray a baking sheet with vegetable oil spray.

In a small bowl, combine seasoning ingredients.

Cut potatoes crosswise into ⅛-inch slices. Put in a single layer on baking sheet. Spray tops with vegetable oil spray. Sprinkle with seasoning mixture.

Bake for 25 minutes, or until tender-crisp.

Calories 68
Protein 1 g
Carbohydrates 15 g
Cholesterol 0 mg
Total Fat 0 g
Saturated 0 g
Polyunsaturated 0 g
Monounsaturated 0 g
Fiber 2 g
Sodium 272 mg

Pineapple Sweet Potatoes

Serves 6

Sweet potatoes flavored with pineapple are whipped to a creamy consistency, then drizzled with molasses. Serve with roast turkey.

4 medium sweet potatoes, unpeeled (about 1 pound), or 2 16-ounce cans, drained
Vegetable oil spray
¼ cup pineapple juice
2 tablespoons light margarine
1 tablespoon drained crushed pineapple, canned in its own juice
Pinch of ground cinnamon
Pinch of ground nutmeg
Pinch of ground allspice
1 tablespoon molasses or 2 tablespoons light brown sugar
1 teaspoon light margarine

In a stockpot with water just to cover, boil sweet potatoes until tender, about 30 minutes. Remove and discard skins.

Preheat oven to 425° F. Lightly spray a 1-quart casserole dish with vegetable oil spray.

In a large mixing bowl, mash sweet potatoes.

Add pineapple juice and 2 tablespoons margarine and beat until fluffy.

Stir in pineapple, cinnamon, nutmeg, and allspice. Spread mixture in casserole dish.

Drizzle molasses over sweet potato mixture and dot with margarine.

Bake, uncovered, for 15 minutes, or until thoroughly heated.

Calories 113
Protein 1 g
Carbohydrates 24 g
Cholesterol 0 mg
Total Fat 2 g
Saturated 0 g
Polyunsaturated 1 g
Monounsaturated 0 g
Fiber 2 g
Sodium 36 mg

Cook's Tip on Allspice

The Mayans and other Native Americans had used it for centuries, but Spanish explorers found allspice in the West Indies and soon created a market for it in Europe. Allspice looks like black peppercorns and tastes like a combination of cinnamon, nutmeg, and cloves.

Orange Sweet Potatoes

Serves 6

High in nutrition and smart for your heart, these sweet potatoes go well with lean pork or poultry. Add a dark green vegetable for color contrast and even more nutrients.

4 medium sweet potatoes, unpeeled (about 1 pound), or 2 16-ounce cans, drained
Vegetable oil spray
½ cup fresh orange juice
2 tablespoons light brown sugar
¼ to ½ teaspoon grated orange zest
¼ teaspoon ground cinnamon
2 dashes of bitters (optional)

In a stockpot with water just to cover, boil sweet potatoes until tender, about 30 minutes. Remove and discard skins.

Preheat oven to 350° F. Lightly spray a 1-quart casserole dish with vegetable oil spray.

In a large mixing bowl, mash sweet potatoes. Add remaining ingredients and beat until fluffy. Spread mixture in casserole dish.

Bake, covered, for 25 minutes, or until thoroughly heated.

Cook's Tips on Bitters

Developed in South America as a tonic and digestive aid, bitters are an alcoholic mix of aromatic plant products. Although many recipes call for small amounts of bitters, most people think of using them in mixed drinks, such as Manhattans or old-fashioneds. The name describes the flavor.

Calories 99
Protein 1 g
Carbohydrates 24 g
Cholesterol 0 mg
Total Fat 0 g
Saturated 0 g
Polyunsaturated 0 g
Monounsaturated 0 g
Fiber 2 g
Sodium 9 mg

Middle Eastern Brown Rice

Serves 8

Oranges and raisins add an interesting twist to wholesome brown rice.

1 tablespoon light margarine
1 large onion, minced (⅔ cup)
2 ribs celery, minced (1 cup)
2 cups uncooked brown rice
3 cups water
2 cups Chicken Broth (see page 40 or use commercial low-sodium variety)
⅔ cup golden raisins
Zest of 1 medium orange, minced (1 to 2 tablespoons)
2 medium oranges, peeled and cut into small pieces (1 cup)
⅛ teaspoon ground cloves
Sprigs of fresh mint (optional)

In a large saucepan, melt margarine over medium-high heat. Sauté onion and celery for 3 minutes.

Add rice and sauté for 2 minutes.

Add water, broth, raisins, and orange zest. Bring to a boil, then reduce heat and simmer, covered, for 30 to 40 minutes.

Stir in oranges and cloves and garnish with mint.

Calories 246
Protein 5 g
Carbohydrates 52 g
Cholesterol 0 mg
Total Fat 2 g
Saturated 0 g
Polyunsaturated 1 g
Monounsaturated 1 g
Fiber 5 g
Sodium 32 mg

Cook's Tip on Raisins

Seedless raisins are made from seedless grapes. Golden raisins and dark raisins are made from the same grape but dried differently. The golden ones are dried by artificial heat, and dark raisins are left in the sun for several weeks to achieve their deep color. This means that golden raisins are moister. If you need to chop raisins, freeze them first. They'll be easier to cut. If you're baking with raisins, coat them with some of the flour before adding to the batter. This will keep them from sinking to the bottom.

Risotto Milanese

Serves 8

The key ingredient in any risotto is arborio rice. This delectable rice releases its starch, giving risotto and other dishes a creaminess that no other rice provides. Saffron traditionally flavors Risotto Milanese.

2 tablespoons light margarine

1½ cups uncooked arborio rice

3 green onions, finely chopped (about ⅓ cup)

¼ cup dry white wine (regular or nonalcoholic)

4 cups Chicken Broth (see page 40 or use commercial low-sodium variety)

½ cup chopped fresh mushrooms (about 2 ounces)

⅛ teaspoon saffron or ½ teaspoon powdered turmeric

1 tablespoon grated Parmesan cheese

In a large, heavy saucepan, melt margarine over medium heat. Add rice and green onions. Cook slowly until rice is milky, 2 to 3 minutes, stirring constantly with a wooden spoon.

Add wine and continue to cook until wine is absorbed, 2 to 3 minutes, stirring constantly.

Stir in remaining ingredients except Parmesan. Bring to a boil over medium-high heat, stirring occasionally. Reduce heat to low and cook, covered, for 20 minutes, or until liquid is absorbed. Sprinkle with Parmesan.

Cook's Tip on Saffron

The world's most expensive spice, saffron comes from the pistil of a certain crocus. Each flower has 3 threads called stigmas, and it takes more than 14,000 stigmas to make 1 ounce of saffron. You can buy saffron in powder form or in threads. The threads are fresher and more flavorful. Crush them just before you use them.

Calories 154
Protein 3 g
Carbohydrates 28 g
Cholesterol 1 mg
Total Fat 1 g
Saturated 0 g
Polyunsaturated 1 g
Monounsaturated 0 g
Fiber 0 g
Sodium 39 mg

Risotto with Broccoli and Leeks

Serves 8

Three basics for a creamy risotto are using arborio rice, gradually adding the liquid as you cook, and doing plenty of stirring. If you can't find arborio rice, you can use medium-grain rice, but your finished dish won't be as creamy. Transform this side dish into a main dish by adding leftover cooked chicken, turkey, or ham with the broccoli and cheese.

2 leeks

3½ cups Chicken Broth (see page 40 or use commercial low-sodium variety)

½ cup dry white wine (regular or nonalcoholic) or Chicken Broth (see page 40 or use commercial low-sodium variety)

2 teaspoons chopped fresh thyme or ½ teaspoon dried, crumbled

¼ teaspoon salt

⅛ teaspoon pepper

1 teaspoon olive oil

3 medium cloves garlic, minced, or 1½ teaspoons bottled minced garlic

1 cup uncooked arborio rice

2 cups cooked broccoli florets (1 pound fresh or 13 to 14 ounces frozen no-salt-added broccoli)

¼ cup grated Romano cheese (1 ounce)

Calories 140
Protein 4 g
Carbohydrates 23 g
Cholesterol 3 mg
Total Fat 2 g
Saturated 1 g
Polyunsaturated 0 g
Monounsaturated 1 g
Fiber 1 g
Sodium 129 mg

Trim root ends off leeks. Cut a 2- to 3-inch section of white part from each leek (see Cook's Tip on Leeks, below). Cut sections in half lengthwise, then cut crosswise into thin slices. Put leeks in a small colander and rinse well under cold water. Drain.

Combine broth, wine, thyme, salt, and pepper in a large liquid measuring cup or other container with a handle and pouring spout; set aside.

Heat a deep skillet over medium-high heat. Add olive oil, leeks, and garlic and sauté for 2 to 3 minutes, or until leeks are tender, stirring occasionally.

Add rice and cook for 1 to 2 minutes or until lightly toasted, stirring constantly.

Pour about ½ cup broth mixture into skillet. Cook, uncovered, until liquid is absorbed, stirring occasionally. Repeat procedure until you've used all liquid (process takes 20 to 30 minutes). Reduce heat to medium if rice sticks excessively to skillet.

Stir in broccoli and Romano. Cook over medium heat for 1 to 2 minutes, or until broccoli is warmed through, stirring occasionally.

Mexican Fried Rice

Serves 6

Slightly brown the rice before cooking it to impart a mildly toasted flavor. Serve with fat-free refried beans and Chicken Fajitas (see page 213) for a Tex-Mex feast.

1 teaspoon acceptable vegetable oil

1 cup uncooked long-grain rice

2 cups Chicken Broth (see page 40 or use commercial low-sodium variety)

⅔ cup canned chopped green chiles, rinsed and drained

½ cup finely sliced green onions (4 to 5 medium)

½ cup diced tomatoes

1 medium clove garlic, minced, or ½ teaspoon bottled minced garlic

In a large, heavy nonstick skillet, heat oil over medium-high heat, swirling to coat bottom. Sauté rice until golden brown, 2 to 3 minutes, stirring constantly.

Stir in remaining ingredients. Reduce heat and simmer, covered, for 30 minutes, or until rice is tender and liquid is absorbed. Fluff with a fork.

Calories 147
Protein 3 g
Carbohydrates 29 g
Cholesterol 0 mg
Total Fat 1 g
 Saturated 0 g
 Polyunsaturated 1 g
 Monounsaturated 0 g
Fiber 1 g
Sodium 113 mg

Rice Pilaf

Serves 6

Perfect for a buffet dinner, this dish can be made ahead and reheated.

1 teaspoon light margarine
½ cup chopped onion
½ cup chopped green or red bell pepper
¼ cup chopped celery
2 cups Chicken Broth (see page 40), commercial low-sodium chicken broth, or water
1 cup uncooked long-grain rice
½ cup sliced fresh mushrooms (about 2 ounces)
2 tablespoons snipped fresh parsley
¾ teaspoon pepper, or to taste

In a small skillet, melt margarine over medium-high heat. Sauté onion, bell pepper, and celery for 3 minutes.

Put broth and rice in a large saucepan. Stir in onion mixture and mushrooms. Bring to a boil over medium-high heat. Reduce heat and simmer, covered, for 30 to 40 minutes, or until rice is tender and liquid is absorbed.

Stir in parsley and pepper. Fluff with a fork before serving.

Microwave Method

In a large microwave-safe dish, combine margarine, onion, bell pepper, and celery. Cook, covered, on 100 percent power (high) for 3 to 5 minutes. Stir in broth, rice, and mushrooms. Cook, covered, on 100 percent power (high) for 5 minutes, then on 50 percent power (medium) for 10 minutes. Let stand, covered, for 5 minutes. Add parsley and pepper. Fluff with a fork before serving.

Calories 142
Protein 3 g
Carbohydrates 29 g
Cholesterol 0 mg
Total Fat 1 g
Saturated 0 g
Polyunsaturated 0 g
Monounsaturated 0 g
Fiber 1 g
Sodium 14 mg

Wild Rice with Mushrooms

Serves 6

The nutty flavor of wild rice pairs nicely with earthy mushrooms. Serve this dish with lean venison or Cornish game hens.

1¼ cups uncooked wild rice (4 ounces)

¼ teaspoon salt

2 tablespoons light margarine

8 ounces fresh mushrooms, quartered (about 3 cups)

¼ cup dry white wine or nonalcoholic white wine

¼ teaspoon salt

⅔ cup sliced green onions (5 to 6 medium)

2 tablespoons white wine Worcestershire sauce

1 tablespoon finely chopped fresh sage

Cook rice using package directions, decreasing salt to ¼ teaspoon and omitting margarine.

In a large nonstick skillet, melt margarine over medium heat. Add mushrooms, wine, and ¼ teaspoon salt. Cook, covered, for 5 to 7 minutes. Uncover and increase temperature to high. Cook until juices evaporate, 2 to 3 minutes.

Reduce heat to medium. Stir in green onions and sauté for 2 minutes, stirring occasionally.

Stir in rice and remaining ingredients.

Calories 168
Protein 6 g
Carbohydrates 32 g
Cholesterol 0 mg
Total Fat 2 g
 Saturated 0 g
 Polyunsaturated 1 g
 Monounsaturated 0 g
Fiber 3 g
Sodium 231 mg

Rice Italiano

Serves 6

Here's a twist on spaghetti with tomato sauce that's less messy. The rice absorbs the sauce, making it dripless but retaining all the flavor of Italy.

1 tablespoon light margarine

4 ounces fresh mushrooms, sliced (1 to 1¼ cups)

½ cup chopped onion

¼ cup chopped green bell pepper

16-ounce can no-salt-added tomatoes

½ cup water

1 cup uncooked long-grain rice

2 tablespoons snipped fresh parsley

¼ teaspoon dried basil, crumbled

¼ teaspoon dried oregano, crumbled

Pepper to taste

In a large, deep skillet, melt margarine over medium heat. Sauté mushrooms, onion, and bell pepper until onion is tender and lightly browned, 3 to 4 minutes.

Add undrained tomatoes and water. Bring to a boil over medium-high heat.

Stir in remaining ingredients. Reduce heat and simmer, covered, for 30 minutes, or until rice is tender and liquid is absorbed.

Calories 154
Protein 4 g
Carbohydrates 32 g
Cholesterol 0 mg
Total Fat 1 g
Saturated 0 g
Polyunsaturated 0 g
Monounsaturated 0 g
Fiber 2 g
Sodium 22 mg

Savory Spinach

Serves 4

This zesty dish will stand up to the most succulent pork tenderloin, glazed ham, or meat loaf.

10-ounce package frozen no-salt-added leaf spinach
2 green onions, thinly sliced (green and white parts)
2 tablespoons chopped Canadian bacon
1 tablespoon prepared horseradish
1 teaspoon rice vinegar
1 teaspoon light soy sauce

Cook spinach using package directions, omitting salt and margarine.

Drain spinach well and stir in remaining ingredients.

Cook's Tip

If you have wasabi (Japanese horseradish) on hand, you can mix ½ teaspoon of the powder with 2 tablespoons of low-sodium chicken broth, let the mixture stand for about 5 minutes, and use the zesty combination in place of the horseradish.

Calories 28
Protein 3 g
Carbohydrates 4 g
Cholesterol 3 mg
Total Fat 1 g
 Saturated 0 g
 Polyunsaturated 0 g
 Monounsaturated 0 g
Fiber 2 g
Sodium 162 mg

Acorn Squash Stuffed with Cranberries and Walnuts

Serves 6

A bounty of ingredients, including wine-red dried cranberries, fills mellow squash for an elegant dish.

3 small acorn squash (about 4 inches in diameter)

STUFFING

1 cup cooked brown rice (about ⅓ cup uncooked)

1 cup unseasoned toasted croutons

½ cup finely chopped onion (1 medium)

½ cup Chicken Broth (see page 40 or use commercial low-sodium variety)

¼ cup dried cranberries

2 tablespoons chopped walnuts, dry-roasted

2 tablespoons light margarine

1 teaspoon dried sage

½ teaspoon dried thyme, crumbled

¼ teaspoon dried oregano, crumbled

¼ teaspoon salt

¼ teaspoon pepper

¼ cup water

Preheat oven to 400° F.

Cut each squash in half and remove seeds.

In a large bowl, combine stuffing ingredients. Fill squash halves loosely with mixture.

Pour water into a 13 × 9 × 2-inch casserole dish. Place squash halves in dish. Cover with aluminum foil.

Bake for 1 to 1¼ hours, or until squash is tender when pierced with tip of knife.

Calories 164
Protein 3 g
Carbohydrates 31 g
Cholesterol 0 mg
Total Fat 4 g
Saturated 1 g
Polyunsaturated 2 g
Monounsaturated 1 g
Fiber 6 g
Sodium 162 mg

Microwave Method

Put acorn squash halves (unstuffed) cut side down in a microwave-safe dish. Add ¼ cup water. Cover with plastic wrap and cook on 100 percent power (high) for 5 minutes. Carefully remove plastic wrap (steam from pan is hot). Remove squash from dish, leaving water in dish. Fill squash halves loosely with stuffing mixture. Return to dish and cover with plastic wrap. Cook on 100 percent power (high) for 10 to 12 minutes, or until squash is tender when pierced with tip of knife.

Time-Saver for Acorn Squash: To make acorn squash easier to cut, pierce it in several places with the tip of a knife. Put the squash on a paper towel in the microwave and cook on 100 percent power (high) for about 5 minutes. Handle carefully. Cut into halves and remove seeds with a spoon. Reduce baking time to 50 to 60 minutes, or proceed with stuffing squash using Microwave Method and cooking for 8 to 10 minutes.

Gingered Acorn Squash

Serves 4

You could almost serve this luscious vegetable dish for dessert!

Vegetable oil spray
2 acorn squash (about ¾ pound each)
8-ounce can pineapple tidbits in their own juice, drained
3 tablespoons raisins (optional)
2 tablespoons light brown sugar
1 tablespoon light margarine, melted
1 teaspoon freshly grated gingerroot

Preheat oven to 400° F. Lightly spray a 13 × 9 × 2-inch baking dish with vegetable oil spray.

Cut squash in half. Scoop out and discard seeds. Put squash halves cut side up in baking dish.

In a small bowl, combine remaining ingredients. Spoon mixture into each squash cavity. Carefully pour a small amount of water around squash.

Bake, covered, for 45 minutes.

Calories 120
Protein 1 g
Carbohydrates 29 g
Cholesterol 0 mg
Total Fat 1 g
Saturated 0 g
Polyunsaturated 1 g
Monounsaturated 0 g
Fiber 5 g
Sodium 24 mg

Creole Squash

Serves 10

This layered vegetable casserole would be super with Baked Catfish (see page 142).

SAUCE

¼ cup sliced fresh mushrooms (about 1 ounce)

2 tablespoons chopped onion

2 tablespoons chopped green bell pepper

1 teaspoon light margarine

2 cups canned no-salt-added stewed tomatoes or chopped fresh tomatoes (about 3 medium)

Pepper to taste

6 medium crookneck squash, cubed (about 2 pounds)

Vegetable oil spray

½ cup plain dry bread crumbs

1 tablespoon light margarine

For sauce, in a medium saucepan, cook mushrooms, onion, bell pepper, and margarine over low heat for 5 minutes, stirring occasionally.

Add tomatoes and pepper. Simmer, uncovered, for 30 minutes, or until sauce is thick, stirring occasionally.

Meanwhile, in a medium saucepan, boil squash in a small amount of water over medium-high heat for 10 minutes, or just until tender. Drain.

Preheat oven to 350° F. Lightly spray an 11 × 17-inch casserole dish with vegetable oil spray.

Alternate layers of squash and sauce in casserole dish, starting with squash and ending with sauce.

Sprinkle with bread crumbs and dot with margarine. Bake 30 minutes, or until bubbling.

Calories 52
Protein 2 g
Carbohydrates 10 g
Cholesterol 0 mg
Total Fat 1 g
Saturated 0 g
Polyunsaturated 0 g
Monounsaturated 0 g
Fiber 1 g
Sodium 65 mg

Creole Eggplant

Substitute about 1½ pounds of eggplant, sliced or cubed, for squash and proceed as above. (calories 56; protein 2 g; carbohydrates 11 g; cholesterol 0 mg; total fat 1 g; saturated 0 g; polyunsaturated 0 g; monounsaturated 0 g; fiber 2 g; sodium 66 mg)

Pattypan Squash with Apple-Walnut Stuffing

Serves 4

Here's a summertime version of stuffed squash. Like its wintertime counterpart, stuffed acorn squash, it goes well with poultry and pork.

4 medium pattypan squash
2 medium baking apples, such as Rome Beauty, chopped (2 cups)
¼ cup chopped walnuts
¼ cup dried currants or dried cranberries
2½ tablespoons light brown sugar
1½ tablespoons light margarine, melted

Preheat oven to 350° F.

Cut squash horizontally into halves. Scoop out and discard seeds. Put squash cut side down in a 13 × 9 × 2-inch glass baking dish.

Bake for 30 minutes.

Meanwhile, in a small bowl, combine remaining ingredients except margarine, stirring well. Spoon into squash halves, then drizzle with margarine.

Bake for 30 minutes, or until tender.

Cook's Tip on Pattypan Squash

A white summer squash, pattypan looks something like a scalloped flying saucer with a stem. You don't need to peel it. Use as you would crookneck or zucchini; its unique shape makes it perfect for stuffing.

Calories 165
Protein 2 g
Carbohydrates 27 g
Cholesterol 0 mg
Total Fat 7 g
Saturated 1 g
Polyunsaturated 4 g
Monounsaturated 1 g
Fiber 4 g
Sodium 31 mg

Scalloped Squash

Serves 6

Serve this herb-flecked dish with Lamb Chops Dijon (see page 298) and fresh green beans.

1 teaspoon light margarine

1 cup finely chopped onion (2 medium)

1½ pounds crookneck squash, sliced (4 to 5 medium)

⅔ cup Chicken Broth (see page 40 or use commercial low-sodium variety)

1 teaspoon dried basil, crumbled

1 teaspoon dried thyme, crumbled

1 teaspoon dried marjoram, crumbled

¼ teaspoon salt

2⅓ cups (4 ounces) seasoned croutons

¼ cup snipped fresh chives

In a large saucepan, melt margarine over medium-high heat. Sauté onion until translucent, 2 to 3 minutes.

Add squash, broth, basil, thyme, marjoram, and salt. Reduce heat to medium. Cook, covered, for 10 minutes, or until squash is tender.

Meanwhile, put croutons in a plastic bag and crush with a mallet or rolling pin. Stir into squash mixture. If mixture is too dry, stir in a small amount of hot water.

Stir in chives.

Calories 82
Protein 3 g
Carbohydrates 15 g
Cholesterol 0 mg
Total Fat 1 g
Saturated 0 g
Polyunsaturated 0 g
Monounsaturated 0 g
Fiber 3 g
Sodium 185 mg

Squash Ruffles

Serves 4

Red and yellow alternate to give this squash dish visual, as well as taste, appeal.

1/4 cup dry white wine (regular or nonalcoholic)
1 tablespoon chopped fresh basil or 1 teaspoon dried, crumbled
1 1/2 teaspoons extra-virgin olive oil
1/2 teaspoon pepper
1/4 teaspoon minced garlic
4 medium crookneck squash (about 1 1/4 pounds)
2 medium Italian plum tomatoes

Preheat oven to 350° F.

In a small bowl, whisk together wine, basil, olive oil, pepper, and garlic.

Cutting to within 1 inch of the stem end of each squash, make long vertical slices at 1/4-inch intervals.

Cut tomatoes into enough thin slices to have 1 slice for each slit in squash. Place 1 tomato slice in each slit.

Place squash in a 13 × 9 × 2-inch glass baking dish. Pour wine mixture evenly over squash. Cover loosely with aluminum foil.

Bake for 30 to 35 minutes, or until tender.

Cook's Tip

For a different flavor, grill the stuffed squash over medium-hot coals for 15 to 20 minutes, or until tender.

Calories 70
Protein 2 g
Carbohydrates 10 g
Cholesterol 0 mg
Total Fat 2 g
Saturated 0 g
Polyunsaturated 0 g
Monounsaturated 1 g
Fiber 4 g
Sodium 6 mg

Italian Vegetable Bake

Serves 4

Try different kinds of mushroom and vary the herbs and vegetables to "invent" different side dishes from this basic recipe.

Olive oil spray

3 cups sliced fresh mushrooms, any variety or combination (8 to 10 ounces)

1 small zucchini, thinly sliced

4 medium Italian plum tomatoes, sliced

2 small green onions, thinly sliced (about ¼ cup)

3 tablespoons fat-free or low-fat Italian salad dressing

2 teaspoons chopped fresh basil or ½ teaspoon dried, crumbled

2 teaspoons chopped fresh oregano or ½ teaspoon dried, crumbled

½ medium clove garlic, minced, or ¼ teaspoon bottled minced garlic

Preheat oven to 350° F. Spray an 8-inch square baking dish with olive oil spray.

Layer mushrooms, zucchini, tomatoes, and green onions in baking dish.

In a small bowl, combine remaining ingredients. Drizzle over vegetables.

Cover with aluminum foil and bake for 25 minutes, or until vegetables are tender.

To serve, use a slotted spoon to remove vegetables from liquid.

Calories 38
Protein 2 g
Carbohydrates 8 g
Cholesterol 0 mg
Total Fat 0 g
Saturated 0 g
Polyunsaturated 0 g
Monounsaturated 0 g
Fiber 2 g
Sodium 118 mg

Vegetable Medley with Lemon Sauce

Serves 8

*With its lemony sauce, this trio of veggies is sure to please. Serve with Turkey Loaf (**see page 234**) and pears.*

1 pound broccoli
1 small head cauliflower
9-ounce package frozen no-salt-added artichoke hearts

LEMON SAUCE
2 tablespoons light margarine
2 tablespoons finely chopped onion
3 tablespoons fresh lemon juice
¼ teaspoon paprika

1 pimiento, diced

Cut florets from broccoli; cut stems into 1½-inch pieces. Repeat with cauliflower. Keeping the vegetables in separate piles, steam broccoli, cauliflower, and artichoke hearts until tender-crisp, 6 to 8 minutes.

For sauce, in a small skillet or saucepan, melt margarine over medium-high heat. Sauté onion until translucent, 2 to 3 minutes.

Remove from heat and stir in lemon juice and paprika.

Arrange vegetables in groups on serving platter. Drizzle sauce over all. Sprinkle pimiento over artichoke hearts.

Calories 56
Protein 4 g
Carbohydrates 9 g
Cholesterol 0 mg
Total Fat 2 g
Saturated 0 g
Polyunsaturated 1 g
Monounsaturated 0 g
Fiber 5 g
Sodium 56 mg

Vegetable Stir-Fry

Serves 8

It's easy to master the technique of stir-frying. Then you can prepare this dish and many others for quick meals.

1 pound fresh broccoli
1 teaspoon acceptable margarine
1 teaspoon acceptable vegetable oil
1 pound carrots, peeled and thinly sliced
12 ounces fresh mushrooms, thinly sliced (3½ to 4 cups)
2 to 3 medium green onions, thinly sliced (about ⅓ cup)
2 tablespoons dry sherry
1 tablespoon fresh lemon juice
1 teaspoon ground nutmeg
1 teaspoon dried thyme, crumbled
Pepper to taste

Separate broccoli florets so they are of small, uniform size. Peel tough stems; cut stems into 2-inch pieces.

In a large skillet or wok, heat margarine and oil over medium heat, swirling to coat bottom. Stir-fry broccoli, carrots, mushrooms, and green onions for 5 minutes, or until vegetables are tender-crisp, stirring constantly.

Stir in remaining ingredients.

Calories 65
Protein 3 g
Carbohydrates 11 g
Cholesterol 0 mg
Total Fat 2 g
  Saturated 0 g
  Polyunsaturated 1 g
  Monounsaturated 0 g
Fiber 4 g
Sodium 57 mg

Southwestern Ratatouille

Serves 8

Southwestern spices combine with traditional Provençal vegetables in this version of ratatouille.

1 medium eggplant, peeled and diced

¼ teaspoon salt

1 teaspoon olive oil

1 medium onion, finely chopped (½ cup)

1 medium red or green bell pepper, cut into thin strips (1 cup)

2 tablespoons minced garlic

2 teaspoons dried oregano, crumbled

2 teaspoons chili powder

2 teaspoons ground cumin

3 sprigs of fresh thyme, leaves removed and crushed, or ½ teaspoon dried, crumbled

¼ teaspoon crushed red pepper flakes

4 large tomatoes, peeled, seeded, and chopped (2½ cups)

2 medium zucchini, sliced (about 2 cups)

2 tablespoons minced fresh parsley

1½ tablespoons grated Parmesan cheese

Put eggplant in a colander and sprinkle with salt. Let stand for 30 minutes. Rinse well and pat dry with paper towels.

In a large skillet, heat oil over medium-high heat, swirling to coat bottom. Sauté onion, bell pepper, and garlic until tender-crisp, 2 to 3 minutes.

Stir in oregano, chili powder, cumin, thyme, and red pepper flakes, then add tomatoes. Reduce heat and simmer for 4 to 5 minutes.

Add eggplant and zucchini. Simmer, covered, for 20 minutes.

To serve, stir in parsley and Parmesan, or cover and refrigerate to serve chilled.

Calories 77
Protein 3 g
Carbohydrates 15 g
Cholesterol 1 mg
Total Fat 2 g
Saturated 0 g
Polyunsaturated 0 g
Monounsaturated 1 g
Fiber 4 g
Sodium 114 mg

Cook's Tip on Eggplant

Salting eggplant and letting it stand awhile before rinsing helps draw out the bitterness and excess moisture. Then you can cook the eggplant without it soaking up lots of oil.

Triple Vegetable Bake

Serves 6

One bite and you'll be hooked on this rich, creamy casserole with its pretty broccoli border.

Vegetable oil spray

SAUCE

1 teaspoon olive oil

1 cup finely chopped onion (2 medium)

8 ounces fresh mushrooms, such as shiitake or button, quartered (2½ to 3 cups)

6 whole cloves garlic

¼ cup all-purpose flour

1½ cups fat-free milk

1 cup Chicken Broth (see page 40 or use commercial low-sodium variety)

⅓ cup dry white wine (regular or nonalcoholic)

2 tablespoons finely snipped fresh parsley

¼ teaspoon white pepper

¼ teaspoon salt

2 pounds potatoes, peeled and cubed (about 6 cups)

8 ounces fresh broccoli florets (about 2 cups)

Preheat oven to 325° F. Lightly spray an 8-inch-square baking dish with vegetable oil spray.

For sauce, heat oil in a large nonstick skillet over medium heat, swirling to coat bottom. Cook onions, mushrooms, and garlic, covered, for 5 minutes. Increase heat to medium-high and cook, uncovered, for 3 to 5 minutes, or until juices have evaporated, stirring occasionally.

Meanwhile, put flour in a small bowl. Whisk in milk. When thoroughly combined, pour into skillet.

Whisk in remaining sauce ingredients. Cook for 3 to 4 minutes, or until thickened, stirring constantly.

Arrange half of potatoes in baking dish. Cover with half of sauce. Repeat.

Bake, uncovered, for 1½ hours.

Meanwhile, steam broccoli until tender-crisp, 5 to 6 minutes.

Calories 211
Protein 7 g
Carbohydrates 41 g
Cholesterol 1 mg
Total Fat 1 g
  Saturated 0 g
  Polyunsaturated 0 g
  Monounsaturated 1 g
Fiber 4 g
Sodium 157 mg

To serve, arrange broccoli in a border around potatoes.

Microwave Method

In a large microwave-safe dish, cook olive oil and garlic on 100 percent power (high) for about 15 seconds. Add onions, cover with vented plastic wrap, and cook on 100 percent power (high) for 2 to 3 minutes. Add mushrooms and cook, covered, on 50 percent power (medium) for 2 to 3 minutes. Uncover and cook on 100 percent power (high) for 3 to 5 minutes to evaporate juices. Combine flour and milk. Whisk in milk mixture and remaining sauce ingredients. Cook on 100 percent power (high) for 4 to 6 minutes. Proceed as directed above.

Triple Vegetable Bake with Turkey and Ham

Add 1 cup (about 4 ounces) diced cooked skinless turkey or chicken breast and ½ cup (about 2 ounces) diced low-fat, low-sodium ham. Put half of meat on top of first layer of potatoes. Then layer sauce, potatoes, meat, and sauce. (calories 247; protein 15 g; carbohydrates 41 g; cholesterol 21 mg; total fat 2 g; saturated 0 g; polyunsaturated 0 g; monounsaturated 1 g; fiber 4 g; sodium 245 mg)

Couscous with Vegetables

Serves 5

Vivid green peas, velvety mushrooms, and fresh parsley are a terrific combination in this quick dish.

5 ounces frozen green peas, thawed and drained, or any other quick-cooking vegetable (1 cup)

½ cup minced onion

½ cup thinly sliced fresh mushrooms (about 2 ounces)

2 tablespoons dry white wine (regular or nonalcoholic)

½ teaspoon crushed garlic or ¼ teaspoon garlic powder

2 tablespoons finely snipped fresh parsley

½ teaspoon dried basil, crumbled

⅛ teaspoon pepper

½ cup uncooked couscous

In a medium nonstick saucepan, sauté peas, onion, mushrooms, wine, and garlic over medium-high heat for 3 to 5 minutes, stirring often.

Stir in parsley, basil, and pepper. Remove from heat.

Meanwhile, prepare couscous using package directions.

Stir together all ingredients in a large serving bowl.

Calories 84
Protein 4 g
Carbohydrates 16 g
Cholesterol 0 mg
Total Fat 0 g
  Saturated 0 g
  Polyunsaturated 0 g
  Monounsaturated 0 g
Fiber 2 g
Sodium 5 mg

Corn Bread Dressing

Serves 8

No one can resist this southern side dish. You'll get lots of flavor but very little fat in each golden spoonful.

Vegetable oil spray

3 cups crumbled Southern-Style Corn Bread (see page 498)

2 cups Chicken Broth (see page 40 or use commercial low-sodium variety)

1 cup fat-free, no-salt-added cracker crumbs

3 ribs celery, finely chopped (1½ cups)

1 large onion, finely chopped (⅔ cup)

Whites of 2 medium eggs or egg substitute equivalent to 1 egg

½ teaspoon pepper, or to taste

½ teaspoon dried sage or poultry seasoning

Preheat oven to 350° F. Lightly spray a 9-inch round or square baking dish with vegetable oil spray.

In a large bowl, combine remaining ingredients, stirring well. Pour into baking dish.

Bake, covered, for 45 minutes.

Optional Cooking Method

Stuff dressing loosely in cavity of 10- to 12-pound turkey just before roasting.

Cook's Tip on Poultry Seasoning

You can buy this salt-free herb mixture in the spice area of the supermarket or make your own. Experiment with proportions of dried sage, marjoram, thyme, and parsley, with perhaps some dried savory and pepper.

Calories 178
Protein 6 g
Carbohydrates 28 g
Cholesterol 9 mg
Total Fat 4 g
  Saturated 1 g
  Polyunsaturated 2 g
  Monounsaturated 1 g
Fiber 2 g
Sodium 367 mg

Celery Dressing

Serves 16

Celery adds traditional flavor and texture to this popular dish. Don't forget the cranberry sauce!

Vegetable oil spray
1½ cups diced celery, including leaves (3 medium ribs)
1 cup Chicken Broth (see page 40 or use commercial low-sodium variety)
½ cup chopped onion
3 cups fat-free milk
8-ounce package poultry dressing mix
2 cups no-salt-added toasted croutons

Preheat oven to 350° F. Lightly spray a 9-inch round or square baking pan with vegetable oil spray.

In a large saucepan, combine celery, chicken broth, and onion. Bring to a boil over medium-high heat. Reduce heat and simmer for 10 minutes, or until vegetables are tender.

Increase heat to medium-high. Add milk and bring almost to a boil.

Put dressing mix in a large bowl. Add milk mixture and stir until well moistened. If too dry, add a little boiling water. Transfer to baking pan.

Bake, covered, for 20 minutes.

Optional Cooking Method

Stuff dressing loosely in cavity of 10- to 12-pound turkey just before roasting.

Calories 104
Protein 4 g
Carbohydrates 18 g
Cholesterol 1 mg
Total Fat 2 g
Saturated 0 g
Polyunsaturated 0 g
Monounsaturated 0 g
Fiber 1 g
Sodium 348 mg

Apple Dressing

Serves 12

For a warming fall or winter meal, serve this apple-sage dressing with Orange Sweet Potatoes (see page 403) and a roast turkey breast or pork tenderloin.

Vegetable oil spray
1 teaspoon light margarine
¼ cup chopped onion
¼ cup chopped celery
4 cups toasted bread cubes or 6 cups fresh bread cubes
1 cup diced unpeeled apple
½ teaspoon poultry seasoning
½ teaspoon dried sage
Pepper to taste
½ cup Chicken Broth (see page 40 or use commercial low-sodium variety)

Preheat oven to 350° F. Lightly spray a 13 × 9 × 2-inch baking dish with vegetable oil spray.

In a small skillet, melt margarine over medium-high heat. Sauté onion and celery for 5 minutes, or until tender. Transfer to a large bowl.

Stir in remaining ingredients except broth, then lightly stir in broth. Transfer to baking dish.

Bake, covered, for 45 minutes.

Dressing with Mixed Dried Fruits

Omit diced apple. In a small saucepan, combine 1 cup chopped dried fruits, such as apricots, prunes, or peaches, or a combination, with ½ cup dried cranberries or raisins. Add water to cover. Simmer, covered, for 20 minutes. Drain and let cool slightly. Proceed as directed. (calories 90; protein 2 g; carbohydrates 20 g; cholesterol 0 mg; total fat 1 g; saturated 0 g; polyunsaturated 0 g; monounsaturated 0 g; fiber 2 g; sodium 76 mg)

Calories 52
Protein 1 g
Carbohydrates 10 g
Cholesterol 0 mg
Total Fat 1 g
Saturated 0 g
Polyunsaturated 0 g
Monounsaturated 0 g
Fiber 1 g
Sodium 74 mg

Cranberry Chutney

Serves 16

Especially good with curried meat dishes, this chutney also pairs well with turkey and chicken. The serving size is more for a condiment than for a true side dish.

16 ounces whole fresh cranberries (4 cups)
8 ounces dates, chopped
1¼ cups water
1 cup sugar
1 cup golden raisins
¾ cup cider vinegar
¼ cup fresh orange juice
1 tablespoon grated lemon zest
½ teaspoon salt
½ teaspoon ground cinnamon
½ teaspoon ground ginger
¼ teaspoon ground allspice
⅛ teaspoon ground cloves

In a large saucepan, combine all ingredients and bring to a boil over medium-high heat. Reduce heat and simmer, covered, for 15 minutes, stirring occasionally.

Transfer to a glass jar with a tight-fitting lid and refrigerate. Use within 2 weeks.

For a longer shelf life, spoon mixture into hot sterilized jars. Follow jar manufacturer's directions for sealing jars. Process for 10 minutes in a boiling water bath (water should cover jars by 2 inches). Remove jars from water and let cool for at least 12 hours at room temperature. Then check to be sure seal is tight (there should be no air pocket when you press middle of lid).

Calories 133
Protein 1 g
Carbohydrates 35 g
Cholesterol 0 mg
Total Fat 0 g
Saturated 0 g
Polyunsaturated 0 g
Monounsaturated 0 g
Fiber 3 g
Sodium 75 mg

Baked Curried Fruit

Serves 16

When the weather turns cold, serve this spicy fruit for brunch or instead of salad at dinner. It's excellent with baked ham or pork tenderloin.

20-ounce can peaches in fruit juice
20-ounce can Bing cherries in heavy syrup
20-ounce can pineapple chunks in their own juice
2 11-ounce cans mandarin oranges in light syrup
Vegetable oil spray
⅔ cup firmly packed light brown sugar
2 teaspoons curry powder
Juice of 1 medium lemon (3 tablespoons)
2 tablespoons light margarine

Put a colander in a large bowl to collect liquid that will drain out. (Make sure colander will not sit in drained juices.) Pour peaches, cherries, pineapple, and mandarin oranges into colander, cover, and refrigerate for 1 to 2 hours, or until all juice has drained.

Preheat oven to 300° F. Lightly spray a shallow 12 × 8-inch casserole dish with vegetable oil spray. Spoon fruit into dish.

In a small bowl, combine brown sugar and curry powder. Sprinkle over fruit.

Sprinkle fruit with lemon juice and dot with margarine.

Bake, covered, for 1 hour.

Calories 132
Protein 1 g
Carbohydrates 33 g
Cholesterol 0 mg
Total Fat 1 g
Saturated 0 g
Polyunsaturated 0 g
Monounsaturated 0 g
Fiber 2 g
Sodium 18 mg

SAUCES AND GRAVIES

Basic Gravy
Creamy Chicken Gravy
Basic White Sauce
Basic Mayonnaise Sauce
Sour Cream Sauce with Dill
Yogurt Sauce
Fresh Herb Sauce
Creamy Dijon-Lime Sauce
Red Bell Pepper Hollandaise
Mock Hollandaise Sauce
Mock Béarnaise Sauce
Quick Madeira Sauce
Lemon Parsley Sauce
Lemon Chablis Sauce
Tomato Sauce
Salsa Cruda
Tomatillo-Cilantro Salsa with Lime
Sweet-and-Sour Sauce
Chocolate Sauce
Fresh Fruit Sauce
Easy Jubilee Sauce
Orange Sauce
Hard Sauce

Basic Gravy

Serves 8; 2 tablespoons per serving

Adjust the amount of flour according to whether you want thin, medium, or thick gravy. This recipe doubles or triples well.

2 to 4 tablespoons flour

1 cup Chicken Broth or Beef Broth (see pages 40 and 39 or use commercial low-sodium variety), defatted meat drippings, or a combination

Gravy coloring (optional)

Spread flour in a medium skillet and cook over medium-high heat, 5 to 6 minutes, stirring occasionally, until lightly colored.

Pour half the liquid into a jar with a tight-fitting lid and add flour. Cover tightly and shake until mixture is smooth.

Pour mixture into a small saucepan and add remaining liquid. Bring to a simmer over medium heat. Cook until desired consistency, whisking constantly.

Stir in gravy coloring.

Mushroom Gravy

In a small skillet over medium heat, sauté ¼ cup sliced fresh mushrooms (about 1 ounce) in 2 tablespoons same liquid as used in gravy. Stir into cooked gravy. (calories 14; protein 0 g; carbohydrates 2 g; cholesterol 0 mg; total fat 0 g; saturated 0 g; polyunsaturated 0 g; monounsaturated 0 g; fiber 0 g; sodium 2 mg)

Calories 14
Protein 0 g
Carbohydrates 2 g
Cholesterol 0 mg
Total Fat 0 g
Saturated 0 g
Polyunsaturated 0 g
Monounsaturated 0 g
Fiber 0 g
Sodium 2 mg

Creamy Chicken Gravy

Serves 8; 2 tablespoons per serving

Everyone needs a recipe for basic chicken gravy. This one is low in fat and easy to make.

1 cup Chicken Broth (see page 40 or use commercial low-sodium variety) or defatted chicken drippings

¼ cup fat-free milk

2 tablespoons all-purpose flour

½ teaspoon pepper, or to taste

Warm broth in a medium saucepan over medium heat.

Put remaining ingredients in a small bowl and whisk until smooth, or put in a jar with a tight-fitting lid and shake until smooth. Gradually stir into chicken broth. Cook over medium heat for 3 to 5 minutes, or until thickened, stirring constantly.

Calories 13
Protein 0 g
Carbohydrates 2 g
Cholesterol 0 g
Total Fat 0 g
Saturated 0 g
Polyunsaturated 0 g
Monounsaturated 0 g
Fiber 0 g
Sodium 5 mg

Basic White Sauce

Serves 8; 2 tablespoons per serving

Here's an easy, fat-free version of classic white sauce. For the basic sauce, use 2 tablespoons of flour; for a thick sauce, use 3 to 4 tablespoons.

1 cup fat-free milk
2 to 4 tablespoons all-purpose flour
¼ teaspoon salt
Dash of white pepper, or to taste

In a small saucepan, whisk together all ingredients. Bring just to the boiling point over medium-high heat, stirring occasionally. Reduce heat to medium and cook for 1 to 2 minutes, or until thickened, stirring occasionally.

Cook's Tip

For a different flavor, add a hint of curry, dillweed, or nutmeg.

Calories 18
Protein 1 g
Carbohydrates 3 g
Cholesterol 1 mg
Total Fat 0 g
- Saturated 0 g
- Polyunsaturated 0 g
- Monounsaturated 0 g

Fiber 0 g
Sodium 89 mg

Basic Mayonnaise Sauce

Serves 8; 2 tablespoons per serving

You'll find many uses for this versatile recipe in your heart-healthy kitchen. Make it at least several hours ahead if you can, so the flavors will mingle.

½ cup fat-free, cholesterol-free or light, reduced-calorie mayonnaise dressing

½ cup plain nonfat or low-fat yogurt (8-ounce container)

In a medium bowl, whisk together mayonnaise and yogurt. Cover and refrigerate.

For each variation, add the listed ingredients to the above before refrigerating.

Tartar Sauce

Serves 10; 2 tablespoons per serving

¼ cup drained pickle relish
1 tablespoon minced onion
1 tablespoon finely snipped fresh parsley

(calories 22; protein 0 g; carbohydrates 5 g; cholesterol 0 mg; total fat 0 g; saturated 0 g; polyunsaturated 0 g; monounsaturated 0 g; fiber 0 g; sodium 141 mg)

Seafood Sauce

Serves 12; 2 tablespoons per serving

3 tablespoons chili sauce
¼ cup pressed-dry prepared horseradish
1 tablespoon finely snipped fresh parsley

(calories 17; protein 1 g; carbohydrates 3 g; cholesterol 0 mg; total fat 0 g; saturated 0 g; polyunsaturated 0 g; monounsaturated 0 g; fiber 0 g; sodium 138 mg)

Calories 16
Protein 1 g
Carbohydrates 3 g
Cholesterol 0 mg
Total Fat 0 g
Saturated 0 g
Polyunsaturated 0 g
Monounsaturated 0 g
Fiber 0 g
Sodium 114 mg

Mustard and Green Onion Sauce

Serves 10; 2 *tablespoons per serving*

3 tablespoons minced green onions
1 tablespoon Dijon mustard
1 teaspoon dry mustard
1/8 teaspoon garlic powder

(calories 15; protein 1 g; carbohydrates 3 g; cholesterol 0 mg; total fat 0 g; saturated 0 g; polyunsaturated 0 g; monounsaturated 0 g; fiber 0 g; sodium 130 mg)

Herb Sauce

Serves 8; 2 *tablespoons per serving*

1 tablespoon snipped fresh dillweed
1 tablespoon snipped fresh parsley

(calories 16; protein 1 g; carbohydrates 3 g; cholesterol 0 mg; total fat 0 g; saturated 0 g; polyunsaturated 0 g; monounsaturated 0 g; fiber 0 g; sodium 115 mg)

Sour Cream Sauce with Dill

Serves 8; 2 tablespoons per serving

Enjoy this sauce three ways. Try the dill sauce over grilled or poached salmon, the blue cheese version over steamed broccoli, and the garlic variation over boiled red potatoes.

8 ounces nonfat or light sour cream
1 tablespoon snipped fresh dillweed
1 tablespoon minced green onion
½ teaspoon pepper
2 to 3 tablespoons fat-free milk (optional)

In a medium bowl, whisk together all ingredients except milk. Thin mixture with milk, if desired. Cover and refrigerate.

For each variation, add the listed ingredients to the above before refrigerating.

Sour Cream Sauce with Blue Cheese

Serves 10; 2 tablespoons per serving

3 tablespoons crumbled blue cheese
1 tablespoon minced green onion
¼ teaspoon very low sodium or low-sodium Worcestershire sauce

(calories 34; protein 2 g; carbohydrates 4 g; cholesterol 2 mg; total fat 1 g; saturated 0 g; polyunsaturated 0 g; monounsaturated 0 g; fiber 0 g; sodium 53 mg)

Sour Cream Sauce with Garlic

Serves 8; 2 tablespoons per serving

1 tablespoon minced onion
1 tablespoon finely snipped fresh parsley
¼ teaspoon garlic powder
Dash of red hot-pepper sauce

(calories 33; protein 2 g; carbohydrates 6 g; cholesterol 0 mg; total fat 0 g; saturated 0 g; polyunsaturated 0 g; monounsaturated 0 g; fiber 0 g; sodium 24 mg)

Calories 32
Protein 2 g
Carbohydrates 5 g
Cholesterol 0 mg
Total Fat 0 g
Saturated 0 g
Polyunsaturated 0 g
Monounsaturated 0 g
Fiber 0 g
Sodium 23 mg

Yogurt Sauce

Serves 10; 2 tablespoons per serving

Try this dill-icious sauce over poultry, fish, or vegetables.

3/4 cup Chicken Broth (see page 40 or use commercial low-sodium variety)

2 tablespoons all-purpose flour

8-ounce container plain nonfat or low-fat yogurt

1/4 cup dry white wine (regular or nonalcoholic)

1 tablespoon snipped fresh dillweed or 1 teaspoon dried, crumbled

2 teaspoons grated lemon zest

1 teaspoon fresh lemon juice

1/4 teaspoon pepper, or to taste

In a medium saucepan, whisk together chicken broth and flour. Bring to a simmer over medium-high heat. Simmer until mixture thickens, 2 to 3 minutes, whisking occasionally. Reduce heat to low and cook for 1 to 2 minutes, whisking occasionally.

Whisk in remaining ingredients. Cook for 1 to 2 minutes, whisking occasionally. Serve hot or cover and refrigerate to serve cold.

Cook's Tip on Zest

Zest is the colored part of the lemon (or other citrus fruit) peel and carries the fruit's richest flavor and aroma. Remove the zest before you cut the fruit to squeeze out the juice. If you use citrus zest often, you may want to buy a special inexpensive tool called a zester, which removes the zest in thin strips. You also can grate the zest on a flat grater with small holes or peel it off with a paring knife or vegetable peeler. Try not to get any of the bitter white part (pith).

Calories 19
Protein 1 g
Carbohydrates 2 g
Cholesterol 0 mg
Total Fat 0 g
  Saturated 0 g
  Polyunsaturated 0 g
  Monounsaturated 0 g
Fiber 0 g
Sodium 13 mg

Fresh Herb Sauce

Serves 16; 2 tablespoons per serving

This sauce is especially good on baked, broiled, or grilled fish.

1½ cups fat-free milk
½ cup nonfat or low-fat cottage cheese
2 tablespoons light margarine
3 tablespoons all-purpose flour
1 tablespoon finely snipped fresh dillweed
1 tablespoon finely chopped fresh basil
1 tablespoon finely snipped fresh chives or green onion (green part only)
1 tablespoon finely snipped fresh parsley
Dash of pepper

Combine milk and cottage cheese in a food processor or blender. Process until smooth.

In a medium saucepan, melt margarine over medium heat. Whisk in flour and cook for 1 minute.

Whisk in milk mixture. Increase heat to medium-high and bring to a boil, stirring constantly. Cook until thickened, 3 to 4 minutes.

Remove pan from heat and whisk in herbs and pepper.

Microwave Method

Process milk and cottage cheese as directed. In a 4-cup microwave-safe bowl, melt margarine at 100 percent power (high) for 10 seconds. Whisk in flour and cook at 100 percent power (high) for 15 seconds. Whisk in milk mixture. Cook at 100 percent power (high) for 3 to 4 minutes, or until thickened. Whisk in remaining ingredients.

Calories 24
Protein 2 g
Carbohydrates 3 g
Cholesterol 1 mg
Total Fat 1 g
Saturated 0 g
Polyunsaturated 0 g
Monounsaturated 0 g
Fiber 0 g
Sodium 44 mg

Creamy Dijon-Lime Sauce

Serves 6; 2 tablespoons per serving

Serve this terrifically quick sauce at room temperature over chilled vegetables, such as fresh tomato slices or slightly steamed and chilled asparagus, or heat it to serve over steamed vegetables. Some possibilities are broccoli, cauliflower, lima beans, green beans, or carrots.

⅓ cup nonfat or low-fat plain yogurt
1 tablespoon plus 1 teaspoon Dijon mustard
1 teaspoon fresh lime juice
⅛ teaspoon salt
1 tablespoon plus 1 teaspoon extra-virgin olive oil

In a small bowl, whisk together all ingredients except oil until smooth.

If using over chilled vegetables, stir in oil. If using over hot cooked vegetables, put sauce in a small saucepan over medium-low heat and heat through; don't allow to boil. Remove from heat and stir in oil.

Cook's Tip

You'll get a more pronounced flavor from the olive oil by adding it after you take the sauce off the heat.

Calories 36
Protein 1 g
Carbohydrates 1 g
Cholesterol 0 mg
Total Fat 3 g
- Saturated 0 g
- Polyunsaturated 0 g
- Monounsaturated 2 g

Fiber 0 g
Sodium 141 mg

Red Bell Pepper Hollandaise

Serves 10; 2 tablespoons per serving

This sauce is excellent on cauliflower, asparagus, or broccoli. Add some chopped fresh herbs, such as parsley, basil, or lemon thyme, and serve it with seafood or chicken.

1 large red bell pepper
Egg substitute equivalent to 2 eggs, or 2 eggs
¼ cup light margarine, melted
3 tablespoons fresh lemon juice
¼ cup Chicken Broth (see page 40 or use commercial low-sodium variety)
1 tablespoon cornstarch
1 teaspoon chili powder
⅛ teaspoon cayenne

Preheat broiler. Broil bell pepper on broiler pan about 4 inches from heat, turning until pepper is charred all over. Put bell pepper in a plastic or paper bag, close the bag, and set aside for 5 to 20 minutes. Rinse bell pepper with cold water, removing and discarding skin, core, seeds, and stem. Blot dry with paper towel.

Warm egg substitute in a microwave on 20 percent power (low) for 1 minute, or put carton in 1 inch of warm water for 2 to 3 minutes. If using eggs, put in bowl of warm tap water for 2 to 3 minutes; crack and pour into a clean bowl.

Pour warm egg substitute into a food processor or blender. With motor running, add margarine in a thin stream.

Add bell pepper and lemon juice. Process on high for 1 minute, or until mixture is smooth.

In a small saucepan, whisk together broth, cornstarch, chili powder, and cayenne.

Add egg mixture and bring to a boil over medium-high heat, whisking occasionally. When mixture starts to thicken, whisk constantly. Remove from heat when thickened. Serve warm or cover and refrigerate to serve cold.

Calories 37
Protein 2 g
Carbohydrates 3 g
Cholesterol 0 mg
Total Fat 2 g
 Saturated 1 g
 Polyunsaturated 1 g
 Monounsaturated 1 g
Fiber 0 g
Sodium 54 mg

Mock Hollandaise Sauce

Serves 8; 2 tablespoons per serving

By using chicken broth and a small amount of oil instead of lots of butter, you can prepare a much lower fat hollandaise sauce that will dress up many dishes in your repertoire.

1 tablespoon cornstarch
1 tablespoon acceptable vegetable oil
¾ cup Chicken Broth (see page 40 or use commercial low-sodium variety)
2 tablespoons egg substitute or 1 egg yolk, lightly beaten
1 to 2 tablespoons fresh lemon juice

In a small saucepan, whisk together cornstarch and oil. Cook over low heat until mixture is smooth, about 1 minute, whisking constantly.

Add broth and increase heat to medium-high. Cook until mixture thickens, 3 to 4 minutes, whisking constantly. Remove from heat.

Stir a small amount of sauce into egg substitute. Slowly pour egg mixture into remaining sauce. Cook over low heat for 1 minute, whisking constantly. Remove from heat. Stir in lemon juice.

Cook's Tip on Juicing Lemons

Before you cut a lemon, let it reach room temperature if it's been refrigerated. Then roll it on the counter while pressing down hard with your hand. The lemon will release more of its juice.

Calories 25
Protein 0 g
Carbohydrates 1 g
Cholesterol 26 mg
Total Fat 2 g
  Saturated 0 g
  Polyunsaturated 1 g
  Monounsaturated 0 g
Fiber 0 g
Sodium 8 mg

Mock Béarnaise Sauce

Serves 8; 2 tablespoons per serving

Turn poached fish or steamed vegetables into something special with this elegant sauce.

¼ cup white wine vinegar

¼ cup dry white wine, dry vermouth, or nonalcoholic white wine

1 tablespoon minced shallots or green onion

1 tablespoon minced fresh tarragon or 1 teaspoon dried, crumbled

⅛ teaspoon white pepper

1 tablespoon cornstarch

1 tablespoon acceptable vegetable oil

¾ cup Chicken Broth (see page 40 or use commercial low-sodium variety)

2 tablespoons egg substitute or 1 egg yolk, lightly beaten

In a small saucepan, combine vinegar, wine, shallots, tarragon, and pepper. Bring to a boil over medium-high heat, whisking constantly. Cook until liquid is reduced to about 2 tablespoons, 4 to 5 minutes. Set aside.

In a small saucepan, whisk together cornstarch and oil. Cook over low heat until mixture is smooth, about 1 minute, whisking constantly.

Add broth and increase heat to medium-high. Cook until mixture thickens, 3 to 4 minutes, whisking constantly.

Remove from heat. Whisk a small amount of sauce into egg yolk. Whisk egg mixture slowly into remaining sauce. Cook over low heat for 1 minute, whisking constantly. Remove from heat.

Whisk vinegar mixture into sauce.

Calories 33
Protein 1 g
Carbohydrates 1 g
Cholesterol 0 mg
Total Fat 2 g
Saturated 0 g
Polyunsaturated 1 g
Monounsaturated 0 g
Fiber 0 g
Sodium 9 mg

Quick Madeira Sauce

Serves 8; 2 tablespoons per serving

Serve this flavorful sauce with pheasant or other game.

1¼ cups Chicken Broth (see page 40 or use commercial low-sodium variety)

⅓ cup Madeira or port

2 teaspoons cornstarch

1 tablespoon Madeira or port

Combine broth and ⅓ cup Madeira in a small saucepan. Bring to a boil over high heat and reduce rapidly to 1 cup, 3 to 4 minutes (stirring not necessary).

Put cornstarch in a cup or small bowl. Add 1 tablespoon Madeira, whisking to dissolve. Whisk mixture into sauce. Cook over medium heat until thickened, 1 to 2 minutes, whisking constantly.

Cook's Tip on Madeira and Port

Either Madeira or port will make this a rich-tasting sauce. Madcira varies from very dry to very sweet; port is sweet. You may want to experiment with different types to see which you like best.

Calories 24
Protein 0 g
Carbohydrates 2 g
Cholesterol 0 mg
Total Fat 0 g
Saturated 0 g
Polyunsaturated 0 g
Monounsaturated 0 g
Fiber 0 g
Sodium 3 mg

Lemon Parsley Sauce

Serves 6; 2 tablespoons per serving

Parsley provides the fresh taste, and lemon provides the burst of flavor in this sauce. It's delish over fish.

¼ cup fat-free margarine
¼ cup light margarine
1 teaspoon grated lemon zest
Juice of 1 large lemon (about 3 tablespoons)
1 tablespoon snipped fresh parsley

In a small saucepan, melt margarine over medium-high heat. Stir in remaining ingredients.

Calories 36
Protein 0 g
Carbohydrates 2 g
Cholesterol 0 mg
Total Fat 3 g
Saturated 1 g
Polyunsaturated 1 g
Monounsaturated 1 g
Fiber 0 g
Sodium 107 mg

Lemon Chablis Sauce

Serves 10; 2 tablespoons per serving

Pretty and flavorful, this light sauce complements baked, broiled, or poached fish.

1 tablespoon cornstarch
1 cup Chablis, other dry white wine, or nonalcoholic white wine
1½ tablespoons light margarine
1 teaspoon lemon zest
1½ tablespoons fresh lemon juice
½ medium lemon, thinly sliced

Put cornstarch in a small bowl. Pour in wine and whisk together until smooth.

In a small saucepan, melt margarine over medium heat. Whisk in wine mixture and cook until sauce is clear and slightly thickened, 3 to 4 minutes, whisking constantly.

Stir in remaining ingredients.

Calories 28
Protein 0 g
Carbohydrates 2 g
Cholesterol 0 mg
Total Fat 1 g
Saturated 0 g
Polyunsaturated 0 g
Monounsaturated 0 g
Fiber 1 g
Sodium 12 mg

Tomato Sauce

Serves 16; ¼ cup per serving

Serve this easy sauce over stuffed bell peppers, meat loaf, or stuffed cabbage.

28-ounce can no-salt-added Italian plum tomatoes
1 cup diced onion (about 2 medium)
3 tablespoons no-salt-added tomato paste
2 medium cloves garlic, minced, or 1 teaspoon bottled minced garlic
½ teaspoon pepper, or to taste
½ teaspoon dried oregano, crumbled
½ teaspoon dried basil, crumbled

Combine all ingredients in a heavy saucepan. Bring to a boil over medium-high heat. Reduce heat and simmer, covered, for 20 minutes.

Creole Sauce

Add 1 diced medium green bell pepper, ½ cup sliced fresh mushrooms (about 2 ounces), and ½ cup chopped celery, and cook as directed. (calories 18; protein 1 g; carbohydrates 4 g; cholesterol 0 mg; total fat 0 g; saturated 0 g; polyunsaturated 0 g; monounsaturated 0 g; fiber 1 g; sodium 11 mg)

Calories 16
Protein 1 g
Carbohydrates 4 g
Cholesterol 0 mg
Total Fat 0 g
  Saturated 0 g
  Polyunsaturated 0 g
  Monounsaturated 0 g
Fiber 1 g
Sodium 8 mg

Salsa Cruda

Serves 6; 2 tablespoons per serving

To serve this zippy salsa as a dip for your next party, simply double or triple the quantities listed. It also works as a terrific topping for many Mexican dishes, such as Beef Tostadas (see page 275).

1 large ripe tomato, cored, peeled, seeded, and diced
2 tablespoons finely chopped onion
1 teaspoon chopped fresh jalapeño pepper, ribs and seeds removed (see Cook's Tip, page 115)
1 teaspoon finely snipped fresh cilantro, or to taste
1 to 2 teaspoons fresh lime juice
⅛ teaspoon salt

Combine all ingredients in a medium bowl, stirring well. Cover and refrigerate.

Cook's Tip

For a different texture, combine all the ingredients in a food processor and process until fairly smooth.

Calories 8
Protein 0 g
Carbohydrates 2 g
Cholesterol 0 mg
Total Fat 0 g
Saturated 0 g
Polyunsaturated 0 g
Monounsaturated 0 g
Fiber 0 g
Sodium 51 mg

Tomatillo-Cilantro Salsa with Lime

Serves 4; ¼ cup per serving

Small green tomatoes known as tomatillos (tohm-ah-TEE-ohs) *join fresh cilantro, lime juice, and a bit of jalapeño for this winning salsa. Serve it as a dip for baked tortillas or with food from the grill, such as fish fillets or pork cutlets.*

8 ounces tomatillos, papery skin removed (5 or 6 medium)
½ cup snipped fresh cilantro
2 tablespoons chopped green onion
1 fresh jalapeño pepper, ribs and seeds removed, quartered (see Cook's Tip, page 115)
1 tablespoon fresh lime juice
⅛ teaspoon salt
1 tablespoon extra-virgin olive oil

In a food processor or blender, puree all ingredients except oil.

Pour into a serving bowl and stir in oil. Serve or cover and refrigerate for up to 2 days for a stronger flavor.

Variation

Replace tomatillos with 8 ounces finely chopped tomatoes and replace lime juice with 2 tablespoons cider vinegar. Don't use a food processor or blender with this variation; the color will be less brilliant if you do. Just chop the jalapeño and stir all ingredients together. (calories 53; protein 1 g; carbohydrates 4 g; cholesterol 0 mg; total fat 4 g; saturated 0 g; polyunsaturated 1 g; monounsaturated 3 g; fiber 1 g; sodium 75 mg)

Cook's Tip on Tomatillos

Choose firm tomatillos with close-fitting papery skin. Remove the brown skin and thoroughly rinse the tomatillos before cooking.

Calories 47
Protein 1 g
Carbohydrates 4 g
Cholesterol 0 mg
Total Fat 4 g
  Saturated 0 g
  Polyunsaturated 0 g
  Monounsaturated 3 g
Fiber 1 g
Sodium 79 mg

Sweet-and-Sour Sauce

Serves 24; 2 tablespoons per serving

Velvety-smooth sweet-and-sour sauce teams up well with broiled meatballs or grilled chicken breasts. For a different presentation, spoon some sauce onto each dinner plate, swirl to coat the plates, and arrange the breasts on the sauce.

1 tablespoon acceptable vegetable oil
¼ cup diced green bell pepper
¼ cup diced red bell pepper
¼ cup finely chopped onion
1¼ cups water
⅔ cup pineapple juice
2 tablespoons cornstarch
2 tablespoons light brown sugar
6-ounce can no-salt-added tomato paste
½ cup pineapple tidbits, canned in their own juice
¼ teaspoon salt
Dash of red hot-pepper sauce

In a small nonstick skillet, heat oil over medium-high heat. Sauté green and red bell peppers and onion until onion is translucent, 2 to 3 minutes. Set aside.

In a medium saucepan, whisk together water, pineapple juice, cornstarch, and brown sugar. Bring to a boil over medium-high heat, whisking constantly.

Whisk in tomato paste.

Stir in bell pepper mixture and remaining ingredients. Heat through.

Microwave Method

In a deep casserole dish, combine oil, green and red bell peppers, and onion. Microwave on 100 percent power (high) for 5 minutes. In a small bowl, whisk together water, pineapple juice, cornstarch, and brown sugar. Add to casserole dish and cook on 100 percent power (high) for 5 to 6 minutes, stirring twice. Whisk in tomato paste; stir in remaining ingredients.

Calories 24
Protein 0 g
Carbohydrates 5 g
Cholesterol 0 mg
Total Fat 1 g
 Saturated 0 g
 Polyunsaturated 0 g
 Monounsaturated 0 g
Fiber 0 g
Sodium 32 mg

Chocolate Sauce

Serves 8; 2 tablespoons per serving

Need a chocolate fix? Serve this sauce warm or cold over just about any flavor of nonfat frozen yogurt.

2 tablespoons light margarine
2 tablespoons unsweetened cocoa powder
½ cup sugar
2 tablespoons white corn syrup
¼ cup fat-free evaporated milk
1 teaspoon vanilla extract

In a small saucepan, melt margarine over medium-high heat. Whisk in cocoa powder, sugar, and corn syrup.

Add milk and bring to a boil, whisking constantly until smooth.

Remove from heat. Whisk in vanilla.

Cook's Tip on Cocoa Powder

Cocoa powder has much less fat than chocolate, which contains mostly saturated fat. To substitute cocoa for chocolate in baking, use 3 tablespoons of cocoa powder plus 1 tablespoon of acceptable vegetable oil for 1 ounce of unsweetened baking chocolate. You'll cut the total fat by about 50 percent.

Calories 85
Protein 1 g
Carbohydrates 19 g
Cholesterol 0 mg
Total Fat 1 g
Saturated 0 g
Polyunsaturated 1 g
Monounsaturated 0 g
Fiber 0 g
Sodium 33 mg

Fresh Fruit Sauce

Serves 20; 2 tablespoons per serving

Strawberries, raspberries, mangoes, peaches, blueberries—most of your favorite fruits—work well individually or combined in this dessert sauce. Spoon it over nonfat ice cream or cake (angel food is a deliciously healthy choice).

2 tablespoons cornstarch
½ cup sugar
½ cup water
2 cups coarsely chopped fresh fruit

In a medium saucepan, bring cornstarch, sugar, and water to a boil over medium-high heat, whisking constantly.

Stir in 1 cup fruit. Bring to a boil, immediately remove pan from heat, and add remaining fruit. Don't cook last addition of fruit.

Calories 26
Protein 0 g
Carbohydrates 7 g
Cholesterol 0 mg
Total Fat 0 g
Saturated 0 g
Polyunsaturated 0 g
Monounsaturated 0 g
Fiber 0 g
Sodium 1 mg

Easy Jubilee Sauce

Serves 13; 2 tablespoons per serving

This sauce is so easy to put together. Keep the ingredients with some nonfat ice cream on hand for unexpected company.

16-ounce jar dark cherry all-fruit preserves
¼ cup port
½ teaspoon almond extract

Calories 85
Protein 0 g
Carbohydrates 20 g
Cholesterol 0 mg
Total Fat 0 g
Saturated 0 g
Polyunsaturated 0 g
Monounsaturated 0 g
Fiber 0 g
Sodium 0 mg

Combine all ingredients in a small bowl, stirring well. Serve immediately, or cover and refrigerate to serve cold.

Cook's Tip

This sauce is named for the classic cherries jubilee, which is flambéed and served over ice cream. This one is quicker, and there's no fire to put out.

Orange Sauce

Serves 8; 2 tablespoons per serving

This sauce is scrumptious over Gingerbread, Easy Apple Cake (see pages 604 and 539), angel food cake, or rice pudding.

2 cups fresh orange juice (about 2 pounds or 6 medium oranges)
1 tablespoon cornstarch
1 tablespoon water
1 tablespoon sugar
1 tablespoon fresh lemon juice
2 teaspoons light margarine
½ teaspoon grated orange zest

In a small saucepan, cook orange juice over medium heat until reduced by half.

Put cornstarch in a cup or small bowl. Add water, whisking to dissolve.

Whisk in a little orange juice, then pour cornstarch mixture into remaining juice.

Whisk in sugar and cook for 1 to 2 minutes, or until thick.

Remove from heat. Whisk in remaining ingredients.

Calories 42
Protein 0 g
Carbohydrates 9 g
Cholesterol 0 mg
Total Fat 0 g
Saturated 0 g
Polyunsaturated 0 g
Monounsaturated 0 g
Fiber 0 g
Sodium 7 mg

Hard Sauce

Serves 12; 2 tablespoons per serving

The next time you serve bread pudding, top it with this super-simple sauce.

2 cups sifted confectioners' sugar (about 8 ounces)
½ cup light margarine
1 tablespoon sherry, brandy, or fruit juice

Cream sugar and margarine in a mixing bowl until fluffy.

Beat in liquid.

Cook's Tip

If you have leftover sauce, be sure to refrigerate it. Keep it in a covered container, and use it within 2 weeks.

Calories 96
Protein 0 g
Carbohydrates 18 g
Cholesterol 0 mg
Total Fat 3 g
Saturated 1 g
Polyunsaturated 1 g
Monounsaturated 1 g
Fiber 0 g
Sodium 47 mg

BREADS AND BREAKFAST DISHES

Whole-Wheat French Bread
Whole-Wheat Bread
Basic Bread
Multigrain Bread
Pumpernickel Bread
Anadama Bread
Oatmeal Bread
Herb Cheese Bread
Dilly Bread
Oatmeal Cinnamon Breakfast Bread
Cornmeal Bread
Candied Fruit Loaf
Focaccia
Boston "Light" Brown Bread
Irish Soda Bread
Peppercorn-Dill Flatbread
Nutmeg Bread
Savory Walnut Bread
Velvet Pumpkin Bread
Bananas Foster Bread
Whole-Wheat Apricot Bread
Orange Wheat Bread
Cranberry Bread
Applesauce Raisin Bread with Streusel Topping
Apple Coffee Cake
Banana Raisin Coffee Cake with Citrus Glaze
Quick Orange Streusel Cake
Orange Pull-Apart Breakfast Bread

Savory Bread
Southern-Style Corn Bread
Corn Bread with Kernels
Easy Refrigerator Rolls
Yogurt Dinner Rolls
Cold-Oven Popovers
Herb Twists
Southern Raised Biscuits
Drop Biscuits
Flaky Biscuits
Bagels
Fluffy Cottage Cheese Blintzes
Poppy Seed Scones with Dried Cranberries
Muffins
Whole-Wheat Muffins
Buttermilk Bran Muffins
Corn Bread Applesauce Muffins
Oat Bran Fruit Muffins
Blueberry Banana Muffins
Crepes
Whole-Wheat Crepes
Country-Style Breakfast Casserole
Spinach Tortillas
Apple Oatmeal Pancake
Cinnamon Orange Pancakes
Cinnamon French Toast
Cottage Cheese and Cinnamon Toasty
Breakfast Pizzas

Whole-Wheat French Bread

2 slices per serving

You'll love the versatility of this nutty-flavored, chewy bread. Make a standard loaf in your bread machine, or use the dough cycle and shape the dough into baguettes to bake in your oven.

	1-pound machine (12 servings)	**1½-pound machine** (18 servings)	**2-pound machine** (24 servings)
Water	¾ cup	1¼ cups	1½ cups
Whole-wheat flour	1¼ cups	2 cups	2½ cups
All-purpose flour	¾ cup	1 cup	1½ cups
Honey	¾ teaspoon	1 teaspoon	1½ teaspoons
Salt	¼ teaspoon	½ teaspoon	½ teaspoon
Active dry yeast	2 teaspoons	1 tablespoon	1 tablespoon

Put all ingredients in bread machine container in order given or using manufacturer's directions. When adding yeast, use a small spoon to make a well in dry ingredients; put yeast in well.

Select basic/white bread cycle. Proceed as directed. When bread is done, let cool on cooling rack.

Calories 74
Protein 3 g
Carbohydrates 16 g
Cholesterol 0 mg
Total Fat 0 g
Saturated 0 g
Polyunsaturated 0 g
Monounsaturated 0 g
Fiber 2 g
Sodium 66 mg

Whole-Wheat Bread

Serves 48; 1 slice per serving

Make this bread on Saturday or Sunday so you can enjoy its wholesome goodness throughout the week.

2½ cups lukewarm water (105° F to 115° F)
2 ¼-ounce packages active dry yeast
2 tablespoons honey
Egg substitute equivalent to 2 eggs, or 2 eggs
2 tablespoons acceptable vegetable oil
1 teaspoon salt
3½ cups all-purpose flour or bread flour (plus more as needed)
3 cups whole-wheat flour
¾ cup nonfat dry milk
½ cup soy flour, bread flour, or all-purpose flour
2 tablespoons gluten flour (optional)
1½ tablespoons wheat germ
Flour for kneading
Vegetable oil spray
Light margarine (optional)

Calories 78
Protein 3 g
Carbohydrates 14 g
Cholesterol 0 mg
Total Fat 1 g
Saturated 0 g
Polyunsaturated 0 g
Monounsaturated 0 g
Fiber 1 g
Sodium 60 mg

Pour water into a large mixing bowl. Add yeast and stir to dissolve. Stir in honey. Let stand for 5 minutes, or until mixture bubbles or foams.

Stir egg substitute, oil, and salt into yeast mixture.

In a large bowl, combine all-purpose flour, whole-wheat flour, dry milk, soy flour, gluten flour, and wheat germ. Gradually stir about three fourths of flour mixture into yeast mixture. Beat with mixer or sturdy spoon for 2 minutes.

Gradually add some of remaining flour mixture, beating after each addition, until dough starts to pull away from side of bowl. Add more flour if necessary to make dough stiff enough to handle.

Lightly flour a flat surface; turn out dough. Gradually knead in enough of remaining flour until dough is smooth and elastic, 6 to 8 minutes. (Dough shouldn't be dry or stick to surface. You may not need all the flour, or you may need up to ½ cup more if dough is too sticky. See Cook's Tip on Breadmaking, page 463.)

Lightly spray a large bowl with vegetable oil spray. Turn dough to coat all sides. Cover bowl with damp dish towel and let dough rise in a warm, draft-free place (about 85° F) until doubled in bulk, 1 to 1½ hours.

Punch down dough. Divide into thirds and shape into loaves. Lightly spray three 8½ × 4½ × 2½-inch loaf pans with vegetable oil spray. Put dough into loaf pans. Cover each with a damp dish towel and let dough rise in a warm, draft-free place (about 85° F) until doubled in bulk, about 30 minutes.

Preheat oven to 350° F.

Bake loaves for 50 to 60 minutes, or until bread registers 190° F on an instant-read thermometer or sounds hollow when rapped with knuckles. Turn bread onto cooling racks. Let cool for 15 to 20 minutes before cutting. If a softer crust is desired, brush tops with margarine while hot.

Cook's Tip

If you don't want to use dry milk, substitute 1½ cups warm water and 1½ cups lukewarm fat-free milk for 3 cups warm water and ¾ cup fat-free dry milk. Dissolve the yeast in the water. Then add the milk with the oil, egg substitute, and salt.

Cook's Tip on Soy Flour

Easy to find in health food stores, soy flour is made from soybeans. It looks like cornmeal and provides a super nutrition boost because it's high in protein. Store it in your refrigerator to preserve freshness.

Basic Bread

Serves 32; 1 slice per serving

Sharpen your culinary skills with this step-by-step bread recipe. You'll even get a bit of exercise from lively kneading.

¼ cup lukewarm water (105° F to 115° F)

2 ¼-ounce packages active dry yeast

1¾ cups fat-free milk

2½ tablespoons sugar

2 tablespoons acceptable vegetable oil

4 cups all-purpose flour

1 teaspoon salt

2 cups all-purpose flour (plus more as needed)

Vegetable oil spray

Calories 96
Protein 3 g
Carbohydrates 18 g
Cholesterol 0 mg
Total Fat 1 g
Saturated 0 g
Polyunsaturated 1 g
Monounsaturated 0 g
Fiber 1 g
Sodium 80 mg

Pour water into a large mixing bowl. Add yeast and stir to dissolve. Let stand for 5 minutes.

Stir milk, sugar, and oil into yeast mixture.

Gradually stir 4 cups flour and salt into yeast mixture. Beat with mixer or sturdy spoon for about 30 seconds, or until smooth.

Gradually add some of remaining flour, beating after each addition, until dough starts to pull away from side of bowl. Add more flour if necessary to make dough stiff enough to handle.

Lightly flour a flat surface; turn out dough. Gradually knead in enough of remaining flour until dough is smooth and elastic, 6 to 8 minutes. (Dough shouldn't be dry or stick to surface. You may not need all the flour, or you may need up to ½ cup more if dough is too sticky.)

Lightly spray a large bowl with vegetable oil spray. Turn dough to coat all sides. Cover bowl with damp dish towel and let dough rise in a warm, draft-free place (about 85° F) until doubled in bulk, about 1 hour.

Punch down dough. Divide in half and shape into loaves. Lightly spray two 10 × 5 × 3-inch loaf pans with vegetable oil spray. Put dough into loaf pans. Cover each with damp dish towel and let dough rise in a warm, draft-free place (about 85° F) until doubled in bulk, about 30 minutes.

Preheat oven to 425° F.

Bake loaves for 15 minutes. Reduce heat to 375° F and bake for 30 minutes, or until bread registers 190° F on an instant-read thermometer or sounds hollow when rapped with knuckles. Turn bread onto cooling racks. Let cool for 15 to 20 minutes before cutting.

Herb Bread

Just before kneading, add to dough 2 teaspoons caraway seeds; ½ teaspoon ground nutmeg; ½ teaspoon dried rosemary, crushed; and ¼ teaspoon dried thyme, crumbled. Proceed as directed.

Cook's Tip on Breadmaking

The more you practice, the easier it will be to develop a feel for when the dough has the proper consistency. If you knead in too much flour or overknead the dough, it will feel dry and stiff, and the resulting loaf can be heavy. If you use too little flour or don't knead the dough enough, your loaf won't retain its shape during baking.

Resist the urge to knead the dough completely flat against your counter or board. This can cause your dough to become sticky.

For basic kneading, fold the dough toward you. Using the heels of one or both hands, push the dough forward and slightly down in almost a rocking motion. Rotate the dough a quarter-turn and repeat. Follow this procedure until the dough is smooth and elastic. Add small amounts of flour when the dough starts to stick to the counter. Make note of the time you start, and knead for the amount of time called for in your recipe.

Multigrain Bread

This bread machine recipe yields a bread that works well for both sandwiches and toast.

	1-pound machine (12 servings)	**1½-pound machine** (18 servings)	**2-pound machine** (24 servings)
Fat-free milk	¾ cup plus 2 tablespoons	1¼ cups	1¾ cups
Vegetable oil	2½ teaspoons	1 tablespoon plus 1 teaspoon	1 tablespoon plus 2 teaspoons
Bread flour	¾ cup	1¼ cups	1⅔ cups
Whole-wheat flour	⅔ cup	1 cup	1⅓ cups
Quick-cooking oatmeal (uncooked)	½ cup	¾ cup	1 cup
Rye flour	⅓ cup	½ cup	⅔ cup
Gluten flour	2 tablespoons	3 tablespoons	¼ cup
Light brown sugar	2 tablespoons	3 tablespoons	¼ cup
Wheat germ (optional)	1½ tablespoons	2 tablespoons	3 tablespoons
Salt	½ teaspoon	¾ teaspoon	1 teaspoon
Quick-rising yeast or bread machine yeast	1 teaspoon	1 teaspoon	2 teaspoons
Quick-cooking oatmeal (uncooked) (for top) (optional)	½ tablespoon	1 tablespoon	1½ tablespoons

Put all ingredients except optional oatmeal in bread machine container in order given or using manufacturer's directions. When adding yeast, use a small spoon to make a well in dry ingredients; put yeast in well.

Select whole-grain cycle or basic/white bread cycle. Proceed as directed; if desired, sprinkle optional oatmeal over dough when baking starts.

When bread is done, let cool on cooling rack.

Calories 107
Protein 4 g
Carbohydrates 19 g
Cholesterol 0 mg
Total Fat 2 g
  Saturated 0 g
  Polyunsaturated 1 g
  Monounsaturated 0 g
Fiber 2 g
Sodium 107 mg

Cook's Tip

For a home-style round loaf, remove dough from bread machine before last rising. Let dough rest for 5 minutes. Spray a baking sheet with vegetable oil spray. Shape dough into a round (about 6 inches for a 1½-pound loaf) on baking sheet. With a sharp knife, make one or two slashes (forming an *X*) about ¼ inch deep and 3 inches long on top of dough. Let dough rise in a warm, draft-free place (about 85° F) for 25 minutes. Preheat oven to 350° F. Brush dough lightly with water and sprinkle with 1 tablespoon optional oatmeal. Bake for 30 to 35 minutes, or until done.

Cook's Tip on Bread Machines

It's especially important to measure flour accurately when using a bread machine. Stir flour and lightly spoon it into the measuring cup. Level the flour with a straight edge, such as a knife blade.

Pumpernickel Bread

Serves 32; 1 slice per serving

With or without the sourdough flavoring, this bread is excellent.

3 tablespoons caraway seeds, crushed
½ cup hot black coffee
1½ cups lukewarm water (105° F to 115° F)
2 ¼-ounce packages active dry yeast
½ cup molasses
2 tablespoons light margarine, softened
3 cups rye flour
3 cups all-purpose or bread flour (plus more as needed)
½ cup nonfat dry milk
¼ cup powdered instant sourdough flavoring (optional)
2 tablespoons gluten flour (optional)
½ teaspoon salt
Flour for kneading
Vegetable oil spray

Calories 100
Protein 3 g
Carbohydrates 21 g
Cholesterol 0 mg
Total Fat 1 g
Saturated 0 g
Polyunsaturated 0 g
Monounsaturated 0 g
Fiber 2 g
Sodium 50 mg

Put caraway seeds in a large bowl, then pour coffee over them. Let cool for 10 to 15 minutes.

Pour water into a small bowl. Add yeast and stir to dissolve. Let stand for 5 minutes.

Stir yeast mixture, molasses, and margarine into caraway mixture.

In another large bowl, combine rye flour and all-purpose flour. Gradually stir into caraway mixture 4 cups of flour mixture, dry milk, sourdough flavoring, gluten flour, and salt. Beat with mixer or sturdy spoon for about 30 seconds, or until smooth.

Gradually add some of remaining flour mixture, beating after each addition, until dough starts to pull away from side of bowl. Add more flour if necessary to make dough stiff enough to handle.

Lightly flour a flat surface; turn out dough. Gradually knead in enough of remaining flour mixture until dough is smooth and elastic, 8 to 10 minutes. (Dough shouldn't be dry or stick to surface. You may not need all the flour, or you may need up to ½ cup more if dough is too sticky. See Cook's Tip on Breadmaking, page 463.)

Lightly spray same bowl with vegetable oil spray. Turn dough to coat on all sides. Cover bowl with a damp dish towel and let dough rise in a warm, draft-free place (about 85° F) until doubled in bulk, about 1 hour.

Punch down dough. Divide in half and shape into loaves. Lightly spray two 9 × 5 × 3-inch loaf pans with vegetable oil spray. Put dough into loaf pans. Cover each with damp dish towel and let dough rise in a warm, draft-free place (about 85° F) until doubled in bulk, 30 to 45 minutes.

Preheat oven to 350° F.

Bake for 50 minutes, or until bread registers 190° F on instant-read thermometer or sounds hollow when rapped with knuckles. Turn bread onto cooling racks. Let cool for 15 to 20 minutes before cutting.

Optional Cooking Method

After first rise, shape into 2 round loaves and put on a baking sheet that has been sprinkled with cornmeal. Proceed as directed.

Cook's Tip on Instant-Read Thermometers

An instant-read thermometer is one of the handiest helpers you can have when you're baking bread. It will tell you when water is the proper temperature for dissolving yeast, as well as let you know when your loaf of bread is baked to perfection. You can also use your instant-read thermometer in candymaking and roasting meat and poultry.

Anadama Bread

Serves 32; 1 slice per serving

This traditional New England bread will be a family favorite. Slightly sweet with a velvety texture, it could almost be dessert.

2 cups boiling water
½ cup yellow cornmeal
2 tablespoons light margarine
½ teaspoon salt
½ cup lukewarm water (105° F to 115° F)
¼-ounce package active dry yeast
¾ cup molasses
3½ cups all-purpose flour or bread flour
½ cup soy or all-purpose flour
⅓ cup nonfat dry milk
2 tablespoons wheat germ
3 to 3½ cups all-purpose flour or bread flour (plus more as needed)
Vegetable oil spray

Calories 137
Protein 4 g
Carbohydrates 28 g
Cholesterol 0 mg
Total Fat 1 g
Saturated 0 g
Polyunsaturated 0 g
Monounsaturated 0 g
Fiber 1 g
Sodium 49 mg

In a large bowl, combine 2 cups water, cornmeal, margarine, and salt, stirring well. Let cool to lukewarm.

Meanwhile, pour ½ cup water into a small bowl. Add yeast and stir to dissolve. Let stand for 5 minutes.

Add yeast and molasses to *cooled* cornmeal mixture. Stir until well mixed.

In another large bowl, combine 3½ cups all-purpose flour, soy flour, dry milk, and wheat germ. Add to cornmeal mixture about 1 cup at a time, beating well with mixer or sturdy spoon after each addition. Gradually add some of the remaining 3 to 3½ cups flour about 1 cup at a time, stirring after each addition, until dough starts to pull away from side of bowl.

Lightly flour a flat surface; turn out dough. Gradually knead in enough of remaining flour until dough is smooth and elastic, 8 to 10 minutes. (Dough shouldn't be dry or stick to surface. You may not need all the flour, or you may need up to ½ cup more if dough is too sticky. See Cook's Tip on Breadmaking, page 463.)

Lightly spray a large bowl with vegetable oil spray. Turn dough to coat all sides. Cover bowl with damp dish towel and let dough rise in a warm, draft-free place (about 85° F) until doubled in bulk, 1 to 1½ hours.

Punch down dough. Divide into thirds and shape into loaves. Lightly spray three 8½ × 4½ × 2½-inch loaf pans with vegetable oil spray. Put dough into loaf pans. Cover each with a damp dish towel and let dough rise in a warm, draft-free place (about 85° F) until doubled in bulk, 30 to 45 minutes.

Preheat oven to 350° F.

Bake loaves for 40 to 50 minutes, or until bread registers 190° F on instant-read thermometer or sounds hollow when rapped with knuckles. Turn bread onto cooling racks. Let cool for 15 to 20 minutes before cutting.

Cook's Tip

A good place to let dough rise is in a corner on the kitchen counter where drafts won't blow on it. Another good place is in a cool oven. Even an oven with the pilot light on is fine.

Oatmeal Bread

Serves 16; 1 slice per serving

Oatmeal gives bread a nice texture. With this loaf, you can enjoy the heart-healthy benefits of oatmeal at breakfast, lunch, or dinner.

1 cup uncooked oatmeal
1 teaspoon salt
1½ cups boiling water
¼ cup lukewarm water (105° F to 115° F)
¼-ounce package active dry yeast
⅓ cup light molasses
1½ tablespoons acceptable vegetable oil
4 to 4½ cups all-purpose flour (plus more as needed)
Flour for kneading
Vegetable oil spray

Put oatmeal and salt in a large bowl. Pour in boiling water; stir well. Let cool to lukewarm.

Pour lukewarm water into a small bowl. Add yeast and stir to dissolve. Let stand for 5 minutes. Pour mixture into cooled oatmeal mixture.

Stir in molasses and oil.

Gradually add some flour, beating well with mixer or sturdy spoon after each addition, until dough starts to pull away from side of bowl. Add more flour if necessary to make dough stiff enough to handle.

Lightly flour a flat surface; turn out dough. Gradually knead in enough of remaining flour until dough is smooth and elastic, about 5 minutes. (Dough shouldn't be dry or stick to surface. You may not need all the flour, or you may need up to ½ cup more if dough is too sticky. See Cook's Tip on Breadmaking, page 463.)

Lightly spray a large bowl with vegetable oil spray. Turn dough to coat all sides. Cover bowl with damp dish towel and let dough rise in a warm, draft-free place (about 85° F) until doubled in bulk, about 1 hour.

Punch down dough. Shape into a loaf. Lightly spray a 9 × 5 × 3-inch loaf pan with vegetable oil

Calories 160
Protein 4 g
Carbohydrates 31 g
Cholesterol 0 mg
Total Fat 2 g
  Saturated 0 g
  Polyunsaturated 1 g
  Monounsaturated 0 g
Fiber 1 g
Sodium 148 mg

spray. Put dough into loaf pan. Cover with damp dish towel and let dough rise in a warm, draft-free place (about 85° F) until doubled in bulk, about 1 hour.

Preheat oven to 375° F.

Bake for 50 minutes, or until bread registers 190° F on instant-read thermometer or sounds hollow when rapped with knuckles. Remove bread from pan and let cool on cooling rack for 15 to 20 minutes before cutting.

Raisin Oatmeal Bread

Add ½ cup raisins to dough before kneading. (calories 174; protein 40 g; carbohydrates 35 g; cholesterol 0 mg; total fat 2 g; saturated 0 g; polyunsaturated 1 g; monounsaturated 0 g; fiber 2 g; sodium 149 mg)

Herb Cheese Bread

Serves 24; 1 slice per serving

All the herb flavor bakes into this bread, making every morsel delectable. No margarine needed here!

½ cup lukewarm water (105° F to 115° F)
¼-ounce package active dry yeast
2 tablespoons sugar
½ cup plain nonfat or low-fat yogurt
½ cup fat-free milk
¼ cup finely chopped green onions (2 to 3 medium)
2 tablespoons olive oil
¼ cup grated Parmesan cheese
1 tablespoon finely chopped fresh rosemary or 1 teaspoon dried, crushed
1 tablespoon finely snipped fresh dillweed or 1 teaspoon dried, crumbled
1 tablespoon finely chopped fresh basil or 1 teaspoon dried, crumbled
¾ teaspoon pepper
¼ teaspoon salt
4 cups all-purpose flour (plus more as needed)
Vegetable oil spray

(OVEN METHOD)
Calories 100
Protein 3 g
Carbohydrates 18 g
Cholesterol 1 mg
Total Fat 2 g
Saturated 0 g
Polyunsaturated 0 g
Monounsaturated 1 g
Fiber 1 g
Sodium 50 mg

Pour water into a large bowl. Add yeast and sugar, and stir to dissolve. Let stand for 5 minutes, or until mixture bubbles or foams.

Add yogurt, milk, green onions, oil, Parmesan, rosemary, dillweed, basil, pepper, and salt to yeast mixture, stirring well.

Gradually add some flour, beating after each addition, until dough starts to pull away from side of bowl. Add more flour if necessary to make dough stiff enough to handle.

Lightly flour a flat surface; turn out dough. Gradually knead in enough of remaining flour until dough is smooth and elastic, 8 to 10 minutes. (Dough shouldn't be dry or stick to surface. You may not need all the flour, or you may need up to ½ cup more if dough is too sticky. See Cook's Tip on Breadmaking, page 463.)

Lightly spray a large bowl with vegetable oil spray. Turn dough to coat all sides. Cover bowl with damp dish towel and let dough rise in a warm, draft-free place (about 85° F) until doubled in bulk, about 1 hour.

Punch down dough and shape into loaf. Lightly spray a 9 × 5 × 3-inch loaf pan with vegetable oil spray. Put dough into loaf pan. Cover with damp dish towel and let rise in a warm, draft-free place (about 85° F) until sides of loaf nearly reach top edges of pan, about 30 minutes.

Preheat oven to 350° F.

Bake for 50 minutes, or until bread registers 190° F on instant-read thermometer or sounds hollow when rapped with knuckles. Turn onto cooling rack. Let cool for 15 to 20 minutes before cutting.

(BREAD MACHINE METHOD)
Calories 108
Protein 4 g
Carbohydrates 19 g
Cholesterol 1 mg
Total Fat 2 g
- Saturated 0 g
- Polyunsaturated 0 g
- Monounsaturated 1 g

Fiber 1 g
Sodium 59 mg

Bread Machine Instructions

Follow manufacturer's instructions for the regular baking cycle.

	1-pound machine (12 servings)	1½-pound machine (18 servings)	2-pound machine (24 servings)
Fat-free milk	⅓ cup	½ cup	⅔ cup
Water	⅓ cup	½ cup	⅔ cup
Plain nonfat or low-fat yogurt	¼ cup	⅓ cup	½ cup
Bread flour	2 cups	3 cups	4 cups
Parmesan cheese	2 tablespoons	3 tablespoons	3 tablespoons
Green onions	2 tablespoons	3 tablespoons	4 tablespoons
Olive oil	1 tablespoon	1½ tablespoons	2 tablespoons
Sugar	1 tablespoon	1½ tablespoons	2 tablespoons
Rosemary	1½ teaspoons fresh or ½ teaspoon dried	2¼ teaspoons fresh or ¾ teaspoon dried	1 tablespoon fresh or 1 teaspoon dried
Dillweed	1½ teaspoons fresh or ½ teaspoon dried	2¼ teaspoons fresh or ¾ teaspoon dried	1 tablespoon fresh or 1 teaspoon dried
Basil	1½ teaspoons fresh or ½ teaspoon dried	2¼ teaspoons fresh or ¾ teaspoon dried	1 tablespoon fresh or 1 teaspoon dried
Salt	⅛ teaspoon	¼ teaspoon	¼ teaspoon
Pepper	¼ teaspoon	½ teaspoon	¾ teaspoon
Active dry yeast	2 teaspoons	1 tablespoon	1 tablespoon

Dilly Bread

Serves 16; 1 slice per serving

Serve this bread with Vegetable Rice Salad (see page 102) and Cucumber Watercress Soup (see page 46). Or slice it and spray both sides with vegetable oil spray, then grill it and serve with poultry or seafood.

¼ cup lukewarm water (105° F to 115° F)

¼-ounce package active dry yeast

1 cup fat-free or low-fat cottage cheese, heated to lukewarm

2 tablespoons sugar

1 tablespoon light margarine

1 tablespoon minced onion

2 teaspoons dill seeds

1 teaspoon salt

¼ teaspoon baking soda

2½ cups all-purpose flour

Vegetable oil spray

Pour water into a large mixing bowl. Add yeast and stir to dissolve. Let stand for 5 minutes.

Stir cottage cheese, sugar, margarine, onion, dill seeds, salt, and baking soda into yeast mixture.

Gradually beat in flour with a mixer or sturdy spoon for 2 to 3 minutes, or until smooth. Cover dough with a damp dish towel and let rise in a warm, draft-free place (about 85° F) until doubled in bulk, about 1 hour.

Lightly spray a 2-quart round casserole dish or 9 × 5 × 3-inch loaf pan with vegetable oil spray. Punch down dough and put in casserole dish. Cover dish with damp dish towel and let dough rise in a warm, draft-free place (about 85° F) for 40 minutes.

Preheat oven to 350° F.

Bake for 40 to 50 minutes, or until bread registers 190° F on instant-read thermometer or sounds hollow when rapped with knuckles. Put on cooling rack. Let cool for 5 minutes, then remove from pan. Let cool for 10 to 15 minutes before cutting.

(OVEN METHOD)
Calories 93
Protein 4 g
Carbohydrates 18 g
Cholesterol 1 mg
Total Fat 1 g
  Saturated 0 g
  Polyunsaturated 0 g
  Monounsaturated 0 g
Fiber 1 g
Sodium 225 mg

Bread Machine Variation

Follow manufacturer's instructions for the regular baking cycle.

(BREAD MACHINE METHOD)
Calories 93
Protein 4 g
Carbohydrates 18 g
Cholesterol 1 mg
Total Fat 1 g
Saturated 0 g
Polyunsaturated 0 g
Monounsaturated 0 g
Fiber 1 g
Sodium 60 mg

	1-pound machine (12 servings)	1½-pound machine (18 servings)	2-pound machine (24 servings)
Water	½ cup	¾ cup	1¼ cup
Fat-free cottage cheese	¼ cup	½ cup	¾ cup
Flour	2 cups	3 cups	4 cups
Light margarine	1 tablespoon	1½ tablespoons	2 tablespoons
Sugar	1½ tablespoons	2 tablespoons	3 tablespoons
Minced onion	1 tablespoon	1½ tablespoons	2 tablespoons
Dill seeds	1½ teaspoons	2½ teaspoons	1 tablespoon
Salt	⅛ teaspoon	¼ teaspoon	¼ teaspoon
Active dry yeast	2 teaspoons	1 tablespoon	1 tablespoon

Oatmeal Cinnamon Breakfast Bread

Serves 32; 1 slice per serving

An alluring swirl of cinnamon is revealed when you slice this bread.

1/3 cup lukewarm water (105° F to 115° F)
1/4-ounce package active dry yeast
1/2 cup sugar
1 1/2 cups warm fat-free milk
1/4 cup acceptable margarine
1 teaspoon salt
2 cups whole-wheat flour
1 1/2 cups uncooked oatmeal
Egg substitute equivalent to 2 eggs or 2 eggs, well beaten
3 to 3 1/2 cups all-purpose flour (plus more as needed)
Vegetable oil spray

FILLING
1/3 cup sugar
2 teaspoons cinnamon

Vegetable oil spray
2 tablespoons acceptable margarine, melted, divided use

Calories 134
Protein 4 g
Carbohydrates 24 g
Cholesterol 0 mg
Total Fat 3 g
Saturated 1 g
Polyunsaturated 1 g
Monounsaturated 1 g
Fiber 2 g
Sodium 112 mg

Pour water into a small bowl. Add yeast and stir to dissolve. Add a pinch of the sugar. Let stand for 5 minutes, or until mixture bubbles.

In a small bowl, combine remaining sugar, milk, margarine, and salt. Let cool to lukewarm.

Put whole-wheat flour into a large bowl. Stir in oatmeal and egg substitute. Add *cooled* milk mixture and yeast mixture. Beat with electric mixer for 2 minutes at medium speed (high speed with hand mixer).

Gradually add some of all-purpose flour, beating after each addition, until dough starts to pull away from side of bowl. Add more flour if necessary to make dough stiff enough to handle.

Lightly flour a flat surface; turn out dough. Gradually knead in enough of remaining flour until dough is smooth and elastic, 6 to 8 minutes. (Dough shouldn't be dry or stick to surface. You may not need all flour, or you may need up to 1/2 cup more if dough is too sticky. See Cook's Tip on Breadmaking, page 463.)

Lightly spray a large bowl with vegetable oil spray.

Turn dough to coat on all sides. Cover bowl with damp dish towel and let dough rise in a warm, draft-free place (about 85° F) until doubled in bulk, about 1 hour.

Punch down dough. Let rest for 10 minutes.

For filling, in a small bowl, combine sugar and cinnamon.

Spray two 10 × 5 × 3-inch loaf pans with vegetable oil spray. Divide dough in half. Roll out half of dough into a 15 × 8-inch rectangle. Brush with 1 tablespoon melted margarine and sprinkle with half the filling mixture. Beginning at short side, roll up tightly (like a jelly roll). Pinch seam to seal. Place seam side down in loaf pan. Repeat with second half of dough.

Let dough rise in a warm, draft-free place (about 85° F) until doubled in bulk, about 30 minutes.

Preheat oven to 375° F. Bake for 30 to 35 minutes, or until bread registers 190° F on instant-read thermometer or sounds hollow when rapped with knuckles. Turn pans on their sides on cooling racks and let cool for 15 minutes; turn out. Cool bread completely before cutting.

Oatmeal Cinnamon French Toast

Serves 2

In a shallow bowl, whisk together egg substitute equivalent to 1 egg and ½ cup fat-free milk. Spray a nonstick griddle with butter-flavor vegetable oil spray and put over medium-high heat. Dip both sides of 4 slices bread in mixture. Cook for 2 to 3 minutes per side, or until golden brown. (calories 316; protein 14 g; carbohydrates 51 g; cholesterol 2 mg; total fat 7 g; saturated 1 g; polyunsaturated 2 g; monounsaturated 3 g; fiber 4 g; sodium 312 mg)

Cornmeal Bread

1 slice per serving

Here's a bread machine version of Grandma's old-fashioned corn bread.

	1-pound machine (12 servings)	**1½-pound machine** (18 servings)	**2-pound machine** (24 servings)
Fat-free milk	¾ cup	1 cup	1½ cups
Vegetable oil	¾ tablespoon	1 tablespoon	1½ tablespoons
Egg substitute	¼ cup	¼ cup	⅓ cup
Bread flour	1½ cups	2 cups	3 cups
Yellow cornmeal	¾ cup	1¼ cups	1½ cup
Sugar	3 tablespoons	¼ cup	⅓ cup
Gluten flour	1½ tablespoons	2 tablespoons	2½ tablespoons
Salt	½ teaspoon	1 teaspoon	1½ teaspoons
Cayenne (optional)	⅛ teaspoon	¼ teaspoon	¼ teaspoon
Quick-rising yeast or bread machine yeast	1½ teaspoons	1½ teaspoons	1 tablespoon

Put all ingredients in bread machine container in order given or using manufacturer's directions. When adding yeast, use a small spoon to make a well in dry ingredients; put yeast in well.

Select whole-grain cycle or basic/white bread cycle. Proceed as directed.

When bread is done, let cool on cooling rack.

Calories 109
Protein 4 g
Carbohydrates 20 g
Cholesterol 0 mg
Total Fat 1 g
- Saturated 0 g
- Polyunsaturated 1 g
- Monounsaturated 0 g

Fiber 1 g
Sodium 146 mg

Cook's Tip on Gluten Flour

An extract of wheat flour, gluten flour is treated to increase its protein content. To produce lighter bread, gluten flour often is added to bread dough when low-gluten products, such as rye flour, cornmeal, or oats, are used. Store gluten flour in your refrigerator or freezer.

Candied Fruit Loaf

Serves 32; 1 slice per serving

Serve this festive bread for a holiday brunch.

BREAD

1 recipe Basic Bread (see page 462), unbaked

½ cup raisins

½ cup chopped walnuts, dry-roasted

¼ cup chopped candied orange peel

¼ cup chopped candied cherries

Vegetable oil spray

GLAZE

¼ cup sifted confectioners' sugar

1 tablespoon warm water

1 or 2 drops almond or vanilla extract

Make dough for Basic Bread. Cover with damp dish towel and let dough rise in a warm, draft-free place (about 85° F) until doubled in bulk, about 1 hour.

Meanwhile, in a small bowl, combine remaining bread ingredients.

After dough has risen, add raisin mixture and knead until well mixed, about 1 minute. Punch down dough.

Lightly spray two 9-inch round pans or ring molds with vegetable oil spray. Divide dough in half and put into pans. Cover each with a damp dish towel and let dough rise in a warm, draft-free place (about 85° F) until doubled in bulk, about 30 minutes.

Preheat oven to 350° F.

Bake loaves for 1¼ hours, or until bread registers 190° F on instant-read thermometer or sounds hollow when rapped with knuckles. Turn bread onto cooling racks.

While loaves are cooling, whisk together glaze ingredients in a small bowl. Spread on bread while loaves are still warm.

Calories 129
Protein 3 g
Carbohydrates 24 g
Cholesterol 0 mg
Total Fat 2 g
- Saturated 0 g
- Polyunsaturated 1 g
- Monounsaturated 1 g

Fiber 1 g
Sodium 81 mg

Focaccia

Serves 16

Delicious on its own, useful for getting that last bite of spaghetti sauce, and even a double for a pizza crust, this popular flatbread from Italy serves many purposes.

1½ cups bread flour or all-purpose flour

¼ cup semolina flour or all-purpose flour

¼ cup soy flour or all-purpose flour

1 package quick-rise yeast

1 tablespoon olive oil

2 teaspoons salt-free dried Italian seasoning, crumbled

1 teaspoon garlic powder

¼ teaspoon salt

1¼ cups warm water (120° F to 130° F)

1 cup bread flour or all-purpose flour

Flour for kneading and rolling dough

Olive oil spray

1 tablespoon pine nuts (optional)

1 teaspoon dried rosemary, crushed

In a large bowl, combine 1½ cups bread flour, semolina flour, soy flour, yeast, olive oil, Italian seasoning, garlic powder, and salt, stirring well. Add water and stir with a sturdy spoon for 30 seconds.

Gradually add some of remaining 1 cup bread flour, beating after each addition, until dough starts to pull away from side of bowl. Add more flour if necessary to make dough stiff enough to handle.

Lightly flour a flat surface; turn out dough. Gradually knead in enough of remaining flour until dough is smooth and elastic, 6 to 8 minutes. (Dough shouldn't be dry or stick to surface. You may not need all the flour, or you may need up to ½ cup more if dough is too sticky. See Cook's Tip on Breadmaking, page 463.) Cover dough with a dish towel and let rest for 10 minutes.

Lightly spray a 14-inch pizza pan with olive oil spray. Press dough to edges with fingers. Lightly spray with olive oil spray. Press in pine nuts; sprinkle with rosemary. Cover with a dish towel; let rise for 30 minutes.

Preheat oven to 375° F.

(OVEN METHOD)
Calories 102
Protein 4 g
Carbohydrates 18 g
Cholesterol 0 mg
Total Fat 2 g
Saturated 0 g
Polyunsaturated 0 g
Monounsaturated 1 g
Fiber 1 g
Sodium 38 mg

Bake for 20 to 25 minutes, or until golden brown. Let cool on a cooling rack for at least 10 minutes.

Bread Machine Instructions

Follow manufacturer's instructions for the regular baking cycle.

For a flat loaf, use the bread machine only to mix the dough, following manufacturer's directions for the dough cycle. Remove dough when it is ready, shape it, sprinkle with pine nuts and rosemary, and bake as directed above. For a regular loaf, add pine nuts and rosemary with other ingredients.

Focaccia Sandwich Loaves

Lightly spray two baking sheets with olive oil spray. Let dough rest for 10 minutes; divide into 8 pieces. Shape into disks, sprinkle with pine nuts and rosemary, and put on baking sheets. Cover with a dish towel and let rise for 30 minutes. Bake as directed for 15 to 20 minutes, or until golden brown. Let cool, then slice in half horizontally.

(BREAD MACHINE METHOD)

Calories 93
Protein 3 g
Carbohydrates 16 g
Cholesterol 0 mg
Total Fat 1 g
- Saturated 0 g
- Polyunsaturated 0 g
- Monounsaturated 1 g

Fiber 1 g
Sodium 34 mg

	1-pound machine (12 servings)	1½-pound machine (18 servings)	2-pound machine (24 servings)
Water	¾ cup	1¼ cups	1½ cups
Bread flour or all-purpose flour	1⅔ cups	2½ cups	3⅓ cups
Semolina flour or all-purpose flour	3 tablespoons	¼ cup	⅓ cup
Soy flour or all-purpose flour	3 tablespoons	¼ cup	⅓ cup
Active dry yeast	2 teaspoons	2½ teaspoons	1 tablespoon
Olive oil	2¼ teaspoons	1 tablespoon	1½ tablespoons
Salt-free dried Italian seasoning, crumbled	1½ teaspoons	2 teaspoons	1 tablespoon
Garlic powder	¾ teaspoon	1 teaspoon	1½ teaspoons
Salt	⅛ teaspoon	¼ teaspoon	½ teaspoon
Pine nuts (optional)	1½ teaspoons	1 tablespoon	1½ tablespoons
Dried rosemary, crushed	½ teaspoon	1 teaspoon	1 teaspoon

Boston "Light" Brown Bread

Serves 48; 1 slice per serving

See the Cook's Tip below for a fun way to prepare this dish.

Vegetable oil spray
3 cups raisins (1 pound)
2 cups nonfat or low-fat buttermilk
1½ cups unsweetened applesauce
¾ cup firmly packed light brown sugar
Egg substitute equivalent to 2 eggs, or 2 eggs
¼ cup acceptable margarine, melted and cooled
1 tablespoon grated orange zest
1 tablespoon vanilla extract
2½ cups all-purpose flour
2½ cups whole-wheat flour
1 tablespoon plus 1 teaspoon baking soda
1½ teaspoons salt

Lightly spray four 7⅜ × 3⅝ × 2½-inch loaf pans with vegetable oil spray. Preheat oven to 350° F.

Put raisins in a medium bowl. Add boiling water to cover. Set aside.

In a large bowl, whisk together buttermilk, applesauce, brown sugar, egg substitute, margarine, orange zest, and vanilla. In another large bowl, sift together remaining ingredients.

Drain raisins. Add raisins and half of flour mixture to buttermilk mixture. Whisk just until mixture is combined. Repeat with remaining flour mixture. Don't overmix. Divide batter evenly among loaf pans.

Bake for 25 to 30 minutes, or until cake tester or toothpick inserted in center comes out clean. Remove bread from pans and let cool on cooling racks.

Calories 104
Protein 3 g
Carbohydrates 21 g
Cholesterol 0 mg
Total Fat 1 g
Saturated 0 g
Polyunsaturated 0 g
Monounsaturated 1 g
Fiber 1 g
Sodium 207 mg

Cook's Tip

For an authentic Boston brown bread shape, spray four 1-pound coffee cans with vegetable oil spray, divide dough among them, and bake for 40 to 50 minutes at 350° F.

Irish Soda Bread

Serves 20; 1 slice per serving

This currant-flecked bread gets its lift from a duo of leaveners (baking soda and baking powder). No wonder it's so popular—there's only fifteen seconds of kneading and no rising time.

Vegetable oil spray
3 cups all-purpose flour
¼ cup sugar
1 teaspoon baking soda
¾ teaspoon salt
½ teaspoon baking powder
¼ teaspoon cream of tartar
⅓ cup acceptable margarine
1⅓ cups nonfat or low-fat buttermilk
⅓ cup dried currants

Preheat oven to 350° F. Lightly spray a baking sheet with vegetable oil spray. Set aside.

In a large bowl, sift together flour, sugar, baking soda, salt, baking powder, and cream of tartar.

Cut in margarine with a pastry blender until mixture is crumbly.

Add buttermilk and stir only until moistened.

Gently stir in currants.

Shape dough into a ball and knead for about 15 seconds. Put dough on baking sheet. With the palm of your hand, flatten dough into a circle about 7 inches in diameter and 1½ inches thick. With a sharp knife, on top of bread cut an *X* about ¼ inch deep and 5 inches long, to prevent cracking during baking.

Bake for 40 to 45 minutes. Remove from pan and let cool on cooling rack.

Calories 108
Protein 2 g
Carbohydrates 17 g
Cholesterol 1 mg
Total Fat 3 g
Saturated 1 g
Polyunsaturated 1 g
Monounsaturated 1 g
Fiber 1 g
Sodium 225 mg

Peppercorn-Dill Flatbread

Serves 15; 4 pieces per serving

Enjoy flatbread as a snack by itself or with a heart-healthy dip or spread, such as Roasted Pepper Hummus (see page 28).

1½ cups all-purpose flour
1 cup whole-wheat flour
½ cup soy flour or all-purpose flour
1 tablespoon olive oil
2 teaspoons celery seeds
2 teaspoons dried dillweed, crumbled
2 teaspoons baking powder
1 teaspoon coarsely ground pepper
1 teaspoon sugar
½ teaspoon baking soda
¼ teaspoon salt
1¼ cups nonfat or low-fat buttermilk
Flour for rolling out dough
Vegetable oil spray

Calories 105
Protein 4 g
Carbohydrates 18 g
Cholesterol 1 mg
Total Fat 2 g
Saturated 0 g
Polyunsaturated 0 g
Monounsaturated 1 g
Fiber 2 g
Sodium 169 mg

In a large mixing bowl, stir together flours, olive oil, celery seeds, dillweed, baking powder, pepper, sugar, baking soda, and salt.

Make a well in center and pour buttermilk into well. Stir until mixture forms a ball.

Lightly flour a flat surface; turn dough out and knead for 2 minutes. Set floured surface aside. Return dough to mixing bowl, cover dough with a dry dish towel, and let dough rest for 10 to 15 minutes.

Preheat oven to 400° F. Lightly spray two large baking sheets with vegetable oil spray.

Lightly flour flat surface again if needed. Roll out dough to ⅛-inch thickness. Using a pizza cutter or sharp knife, cut dough into strips about 1½ inches wide by 4 inches long (you should get about 60). Place strips on baking sheets. Prick each strip with a fork.

Bake for 15 minutes, or until crispy. Put baking sheets on cooling racks and let cool for 15 to 20 minutes. Store flatbread in an airtight container for up to 7 days.

Nutmeg Bread

Serves 16; 1 slice per serving

This bread freezes well and makes a great gift.

Vegetable oil spray
¾ cup sugar
¼ cup acceptable margarine
Egg substitute equivalent to 1 egg or 1 egg, well beaten
¼ cup unsweetened applesauce
2 cups sifted all-purpose flour
1 tablespoon freshly grated nutmeg or 1 teaspoon ground
½ teaspoon baking powder
½ teaspoon baking soda
1 cup nonfat or low-fat buttermilk

Preheat oven to 350° F. Lightly spray a 9 × 5 × 3-inch loaf pan with vegetable oil spray.

In a large mixing bowl, cream sugar and margarine.

Add egg substitute and applesauce and beat well.

Put remaining ingredients except buttermilk in a medium bowl. Sift together twice.

Alternately add flour mixture and buttermilk to sugar mixture, beginning and ending with flour, stirring after each addition. Pour batter into loaf pan.

Bake for 45 to 60 minutes, or until cake tester or toothpick inserted in center comes out clean. Let cool in pan for 10 minutes, then turn bread onto cooling rack.

Calories 126
Protein 3 g
Carbohydrates 22 g
Cholesterol 1 mg
Total Fat 3 g
Saturated 1 g
Polyunsaturated 1 g
Monounsaturated 1 g
Fiber 0 g
Sodium 111 mg

Savory Walnut Bread

Serves 16; 1 slice per serving

Here's a simple way to celebrate the robust flavor of walnuts.

Vegetable oil spray
2 cups all-purpose flour
2 teaspoons baking powder
½ cup firmly packed light brown sugar
½ teaspoon salt
¼ teaspoon baking soda
1 cup fat-free milk
Egg substitute equivalent to 1 egg, or 1 egg, beaten until slightly thickened and light yellow
½ cup finely chopped walnuts, dry-roasted

Preheat oven to 350° F. Lightly spray an 8½ × 4½ × 2½-inch loaf pan with vegetable oil spray. Set aside.

In a large bowl, sift together flour, baking powder, brown sugar, salt, and baking soda.

In another large bowl, whisk together milk and egg substitute.

Add flour mixture and walnuts to milk mixture, stirring until just moistened. Pour into loaf pan.

Bake for 40 minutes, or until a cake tester or toothpick inserted in center comes out clean. Loosen loaf from sides of pan with metal spatula. Remove bread from pan and let cool right side up on cooling rack.

Calories 111
Protein 3 g
Carbohydrates 19 g
Cholesterol 0 mg
Total Fat 3 g
Saturated 0 g
Polyunsaturated 2 g
Monounsaturated 1 g
Fiber 1 g
Sodium 172 mg

Cook's Tip on Baking Powder and Baking Soda

Baking powder usually is mixed in with other dry ingredients. It reacts and leavens when heated. It also reacts and leavens when liquid is added. Baking soda is also a leavener. If the two are combined, the baking powder helps leaven in the mixing and baking stage, and the baking soda helps neutralize acidic ingredients, such as fruit juices, molasses, and cranberries, so they don't interfere with the baking powder.

Velvet Pumpkin Bread

Serves 16; 1 slice per serving

The name says it all—this bread has a wonderful texture, and just wait till you smell it baking!

Vegetable oil spray
1 cup canned pumpkin
Egg substitute equivalent to 2 eggs, or 2 eggs, slightly beaten
1/3 cup fat-free milk
2 tablespoons light margarine
1 tablespoon acceptable vegetable oil
2 cups all-purpose flour
2 teaspoons baking powder
1 teaspoon ground cinnamon
1/2 teaspoon ground ginger
1/4 teaspoon ground nutmeg
1/4 teaspoon salt
1/2 cup chopped pecans, dry-roasted
1/2 cup sugar
1/2 cup firmly packed light brown sugar

Preheat oven to 350° F. Lightly spray a 10 × 5 × 3-inch loaf pan with vegetable oil spray. Set aside.

In a medium bowl, combine pumpkin, egg substitute, milk, margarine, and oil, stirring well.

In a large bowl, sift together flour, baking powder, cinnamon, ginger, nutmeg, and salt.

Stir in remaining ingredients, mixing well.

Make a well in center of flour mixture. Pour pumpkin mixture all at once into well. Stir until just moistened. Don't overmix. Pour batter into loaf pan.

Bake for 1 hour, or until cake tester or toothpick inserted in center comes out clean. Remove from pan and let cool on cooling rack.

Calories 159
Protein 3 g
Carbohydrates 28 g
Cholesterol 0 mg
Total Fat 4 g
 Saturated 1 g
 Polyunsaturated 2 g
 Monounsaturated 2 g
Fiber 2 g
Sodium 127 mg

Bananas Foster Bread

Serves 16; 1 slice per serving

The taste and texture of this bread are great—and it's moist, moist, moist! You'll love how it captures the flavor of bananas Foster.

Vegetable oil spray
1½ cups all-purpose flour
½ cup sugar
2 teaspoons baking powder
1 teaspoon baking soda
¼ teaspoon salt
3 medium very ripe bananas, mashed (about 1½ cups)
Whites of 4 large eggs
½ cup wheat germ
¼ cup nonfat or low-fat buttermilk
¼ cup unsweetened applesauce
1 tablespoon acceptable vegetable oil
1 teaspoon rum extract
½ teaspoon ground cinnamon
½ teaspoon imitation butter flavoring
¼ cup firmly packed light brown sugar

Preheat oven to 350° F. Lightly spray an 8½ × 4½ × 2½-inch loaf pan with vegetable oil spray.

In a large bowl, sift together flour, sugar, baking powder, baking soda, and salt.

Add remaining ingredients except brown sugar and stir until just combined. Don't overmix. Pour into loaf pan and sprinkle evenly with brown sugar.

Bake for 1 hour, or until cake tester or toothpick inserted in center comes out clean. Let cool in pan for at least 10 minutes; turn onto rack.

Calories 125
Protein 3 g
Carbohydrates 26 g
Cholesterol 0 mg
Total Fat 1 g
Saturated 0 g
Polyunsaturated 1 g
Monounsaturated 0 g
Fiber 1 g
Sodium 211 mg

Whole-Wheat Apricot Bread

Serves 16; 1 slice per serving

Plump, juicy bits of dried apricot flavor each bite of this quick bread. You may be tempted to dunk your slice in hot tea or flavored coffee.

Vegetable oil spray

1 cup chopped dried apricots (5 to 6 ounces)

⅔ cup boiling water

1 tablespoon acceptable vegetable oil

1 cup whole-wheat flour

1 cup all-purpose flour

½ cup sugar

2 teaspoons baking powder

¼ teaspoon baking soda

½ cup finely chopped walnuts, dry-roasted

½ cup fat-free evaporated milk

Egg substitute equivalent to 1 egg or 1 egg, slightly beaten

¼ cup unsweetened applesauce

Preheat oven to 350° F. Lightly spray a 10 × 5 × 3-inch loaf pan with vegetable oil spray.

Put apricots in a large shallow bowl. Add water and oil. Let cool for about 20 minutes, stirring occasionally.

In a large bowl, stir together whole-wheat flour, all-purpose flour, sugar, baking powder, baking soda, and nuts.

In a small bowl, whisk together remaining ingredients. Add to apricot mixture and stir until well blended.

Add apricot mixture all at once to flour mixture. Stir until dry ingredients are just moistened, then stir 10 strokes. Pour into loaf pan.

Bake for 1 hour, or until cake tester or toothpick inserted in center comes out clean. Remove from pan and let cool thoroughly on cooling rack (about 1 hour) before slicing.

Calories 142
Protein 4 g
Carbohydrates 25 g
Cholesterol 0 mg
Total Fat 4 g
  Saturated 0 g
  Polyunsaturated 2 g
  Monounsaturated 1 g
Fiber 2 g
Sodium 99 mg

Orange Wheat Bread

Serves 16; 1 slice per serving

The orange zest makes this bread smell wonderful as it bakes.

Vegetable oil spray
2 cups all-purpose flour
½ cup whole-wheat flour
½ cup wheat germ
½ cup sugar
¼ cup chopped, unsalted walnuts, dry-roasted
1 tablespoon baking powder
½ teaspoon baking soda
2 tablespoons grated orange zest
1 cup fresh orange juice (3 medium oranges)
⅓ cup unsweetened applesauce
Egg substitute equivalent to 1 egg, or 1 egg, beaten
1 tablespoon acceptable vegetable oil

Preheat oven to 350° F. Lightly spray a 9 × 5 × 3-inch loaf pan with vegetable oil spray.

In a large bowl, combine all-purpose flour, whole-wheat flour, wheat germ, sugar, walnuts, baking powder, and baking soda.

Add remaining ingredients, stirring just until blended. Don't overmix. Pour into loaf pan.

Bake for 55 minutes, or until cake tester or toothpick inserted in center comes out clean. Remove from pan immediately. Serve warm, or let cool completely and wrap tightly in aluminum foil or plastic wrap. Refrigerate for up to 4 days.

Calories 135
Protein 4 g
Carbohydrates 26 g
Cholesterol 0 mg
Total Fat 2 g
  Saturated 0 g
  Polyunsaturated 1 g
  Monounsaturated 1 g
Fiber 1 g
Sodium 139 mg

Cranberry Bread

Serves 16; 1 slice per serving

Slow down the kids with a slice of this bread and a glass of orange juice on their way to see what Santa brought.

Vegetable oil spray
2 cups all-purpose flour
⅔ cup firmly packed light brown sugar
2 teaspoons baking powder
½ teaspoon baking soda
¼ teaspoon salt
¼ teaspoon ground allspice
1 cup fresh cranberries, chopped
2 teaspoons grated orange zest
¾ cup fresh orange juice (2 medium oranges)
Egg substitute equivalent to 1 egg, or 1 egg
1 tablespoon acceptable vegetable oil
2 teaspoons vanilla extract

Preheat oven to 350° F. Lightly spray an 8½ × 4½ × 2½-inch loaf pan with vegetable oil spray.

In a large bowl, combine flour, brown sugar, baking powder, baking soda, salt, and allspice, stirring well.

In a medium bowl, combine remaining ingredients, stirring well.

Make a well in center of flour mixture. Pour cranberry mixture into well. Stir just until blended. Don't overmix. Pour into loaf pan.

Bake for 50 to 60 minutes, or until cake tester or toothpick inserted in center comes out clean. Remove from pan and let cool on cooling rack.

Cook's Tip on Cranberries

Look for fresh cranberries from October through December. Buy a few extra bags (they'll freeze for up to 12 months) so you can enjoy the berries throughout the year.

Calories 113
Protein 2 g
Carbohydrates 23 g
Cholesterol 0 mg
Total Fat 1 g
Saturated 0 g
Polyunsaturated 1 g
Monounsaturated 0 g
Fiber 1 g
Sodium 148 mg

Applesauce Raisin Bread with Streusel Topping

Serves 16; 1 slice per serving

Serve a warm slice of this bread with a steaming cup of orange tea and a cinnamon stick stirrer.

Vegetable oil spray

BREAD

1 cup unsweetened applesauce

½ cup sugar

¼ cup firmly packed light brown sugar

Egg substitute equivalent to 1 egg, or 1 egg

2 tablespoons fat-free milk

1 tablespoon acceptable vegetable oil

2 cups all-purpose flour

2 teaspoons baking powder

1 teaspoon ground cinnamon

¼ teaspoon salt

¼ teaspoon ground nutmeg

⅛ teaspoon ground cloves

½ cup raisins

TOPPING

2 tablespoons brown sugar

2 tablespoons uncooked quick-cooking oatmeal

2 tablespoons chopped pecans, dry-roasted

1 tablespoon light margarine

½ teaspoon ground cinnamon

Calories 138
Protein 2 g
Carbohydrates 28 g
Cholesterol 0 mg
Total Fat 2 g
Saturated 0 g
Polyunsaturated 1 g
Monounsaturated 1 g
Fiber 1 g
Sodium 113 mg

Preheat oven to 350° F. Lightly spray a 9 × 5 × 3-inch loaf pan with vegetable oil spray.

In a large mixing bowl, whisk together applesauce, sugars, egg substitute, milk, and oil.

In a medium bowl, sift together remaining bread ingredients except raisins. Stir in raisins. Pour into applesauce mixture and beat until well combined. Pour into loaf pan.

For topping, combine ingredients in a small bowl. Sprinkle evenly over batter.

Bake for 50 to 60 minutes, or until cake tester or toothpick inserted in center comes out clean. Remove from pan and let cool on cooling rack.

Apple Coffee Cake

Serves 9

You'll love the crisp crumb topping and moist center of this coffee cake.

Vegetable oil spray

TOPPING

⅓ cup firmly packed dark brown sugar

⅓ cup uncooked quick-cooking oatmeal

1 tablespoon plus 1½ teaspoons all-purpose flour

1 teaspoon ground cinnamon

1 tablespoon light margarine, melted

COFFEE CAKE

1½ cups all-purpose flour

½ cup sugar

2½ teaspoons baking powder

½ teaspoon ground cinnamon

¾ cup fat-free milk

1 Granny Smith apple, grated

¼ cup unsweetened applesauce

White of 1 large egg, beaten until frothy

¼ teaspoon vanilla extract

Preheat oven to 375° F. Lightly spray a 9-inch square baking pan with vegetable oil spray.

For topping, in a small bowl, combine ingredients except margarine. Stir in margarine, mixing well. Set aside.

In a large bowl, sift together flour, sugar, baking powder, and cinnamon.

In a small bowl, combine remaining coffee cake ingredients, stirring well. Add to flour mixture. Stir just until dry ingredients are moistened. Don't overmix. Pour into baking pan and sprinkle with topping.

Bake for 30 to 35 minutes. Let cool on cooling rack for about 30 minutes.

Calories 194
Protein 4 g
Carbohydrates 43 g
Cholesterol 0 mg
Total Fat 1 g
Saturated 0 g
Polyunsaturated 0 g
Monounsaturated 0 g
Fiber 2 g
Sodium 170 mg

Banana Raisin Coffee Cake with Citrus Glaze

Serves 12

This many-flavored coffee cake tastes best when eaten within a few hours of baking.

Vegetable oil spray
½ cup golden raisins
¼ cup unsweetened apple juice
½ cup nonfat or low-fat buttermilk
Whites of 2 large eggs
3 tablespoons honey
1 tablespoon acceptable vegetable oil
2 cups unbleached all-purpose flour or bread flour
1½ teaspoons baking powder
1 teaspoon baking soda
¼ cup firmly packed light brown sugar
½ teaspoon ground ginger
½ teaspoon ground cinnamon
2 medium bananas, mashed (about 1 cup)
1¼ cups confectioners' sugar, sifted
2 teaspoons fresh orange juice
2 teaspoons fresh lemon juice

Preheat oven to 350° F. Lightly spray a nonstick Bundt pan with vegetable oil spray.

In a small bowl, combine raisins and apple juice. Let stand for 5 minutes.

In a large bowl, whisk together buttermilk, egg whites, honey, and oil. Stir raisin mixture into buttermilk mixture.

Put flour, baking powder, and baking soda in a large bowl; sift.

Stir in brown sugar, ginger, and cinnamon. Add brown sugar mixture and bananas to raisin mixture and stir just until moistened. Spoon into Bundt pan.

Bake for 30 to 35 minutes, or until a cake tester or toothpick inserted in center comes out clean.

In a small bowl, whisk confectioners' sugar, orange juice, and lemon juice until smooth. Drizzle over warm coffee cake.

Calories 216
Protein 4 g
Carbohydrates 48 g
Cholesterol 0 mg
Total Fat 2 g
Saturated 0 g
Polyunsaturated 1 g
Monounsaturated 0 g
Fiber 1 g
Sodium 202 mg

Quick Orange Streusel Cake

Serves 9

This cake is scented with orange zest and juice—definitely worth waking up to!

Vegetable oil spray

TOPPING

¼ cup firmly packed light brown sugar

2 tablespoons all-purpose flour

1 tablespoon light margarine, melted

CAKE

2 cups all-purpose flour

⅓ cup sugar

2 teaspoons baking powder

¼ teaspoon baking soda

¼ teaspoon salt

½ cup fat-free milk

2 teaspoons grated orange zest

½ cup fresh orange juice (1 to 2 medium oranges)

⅓ cup unsweetened applesauce

Egg substitute equivalent to 1 egg, or 1 egg

1 tablespoon acceptable vegetable oil

1 teaspoon vanilla extract

Preheat oven to 375° F. Lightly spray an 8-inch square baking pan with vegetable oil spray.

For topping, combine ingredients in a small bowl. Set aside.

For cake, in a large bowl, sift flour, sugar, baking powder, baking soda, and salt together.

In a medium bowl, whisk together remaining cake ingredients.

Make well in center of flour mixture. Pour orange mixture into well and stir just to blend well. Don't overmix. Pour into baking pan and sprinkle with topping.

Bake for 30 to 35 minutes, or until cake tester or toothpick inserted in center comes out clean.

Calories 201
Protein 4 g
Carbohydrates 40 g
Cholesterol 0 mg
Total Fat 3 g
Saturated 0 g
Polyunsaturated 1 g
Monounsaturated 1 g
Fiber 1 g
Sodium 239 mg

Orange Pull-Apart Breakfast Bread

Serves 16

A traditional favorite, this bread is made with small pieces of buttermilk biscuits dipped in cinnamon sugar, layered, and baked with an orange-flavored brown sugar sauce. Use a Bundt pan if you want to make a spectacular presentation at your next brunch.

Vegetable oil spray
3 10-count cans refrigerator buttermilk biscuits
⅓ cup sugar
1 teaspoon ground cinnamon
¼ teaspoon ground nutmeg
¼ cup firmly packed light brown sugar
2 tablespoons light margarine
½ teaspoon ground cinnamon
1 teaspoon orange extract

Preheat oven to 350° F. Lightly spray a 10-inch Bundt pan or 9-inch round cake pan with vegetable oil spray.

Cut each biscuit into quarters with a sharp knife or kitchen scissors.

Combine sugar, 1 teaspoon cinnamon, and nutmeg in a small bowl. Coat biscuits. Layer in pan.

In a small saucepan, combine brown sugar, margarine, and ½ teaspoon cinnamon. Cook over low heat until margarine melts and sugar dissolves, 2 to 3 minutes, stirring occasionally.

Stir in orange extract. Pour over biscuits.

Bake for 30 to 35 minutes, or until biscuits are cooked through. Let bread cool in pan on cooling rack for 2 to 3 minutes. Invert onto a large serving plate and let cool for at least 10 minutes before slicing. Serve warm.

Calories 130
Protein 3 g
Carbohydrates 26 g
Cholesterol 0 mg
Total Fat 2 g
Saturated 0 g
Polyunsaturated 0 g
Monounsaturated 0 g
Fiber 0 g
Sodium 348 mg

Savory Bread

Serves 16

Here are several ideas for fast, tasty hot bread.

1-pound loaf French or Italian bread
5 tablespoons acceptable margarine, softened
1 tablespoon chopped fresh basil
¾ teaspoon salt-free lemon-pepper seasoning

Preheat oven to 375° F.

Cut bread into 16 slices.

In a small bowl, combine remaining ingredients, stirring well. Spread mixture evenly on each bread slice. Reassemble slices into loaf and wrap in aluminum foil. Put on baking sheet. Bake for 15 minutes.

Savory Bread with Chili or Green Onion Spread

For Chili Spread, omit the basil and lemon-pepper seasoning, and add the following to the margarine: 1 teaspoon chili powder; 1 teaspoon dried cilantro, crushed; dash of garlic powder; and dash of red hot-pepper sauce.

For Green Onion Spread, omit the basil, and add the following to the margarine and lemon-pepper seasoning: 2 tablespoons finely chopped green onion and 1 tablespoon finely chopped fresh parsley.

(FOR BREAD AND VARIATIONS)
Calories 109
Protein 3 g
Carbohydrates 15 g
Cholesterol 0 mg
Total Fat 4 g
- Saturated 1 g
- Polyunsaturated 1 g
- Monounsaturated 2 g

Fiber 1 g
Sodium 214 mg

Southern-Style Corn Bread

Serves 8

Buttermilk and all-purpose seasoning make this corn bread recipe stand out.

1 tablespoon acceptable vegetable oil
Egg substitute equivalent to 1 egg, or 1 egg
1 cup nonfat or low-fat buttermilk
1¼ cups yellow or white cornmeal
1 teaspoon baking powder
1 teaspoon sugar (optional)
¼ teaspoon baking soda
¼ teaspoon salt
¼ teaspoon salt-free all-purpose seasoning

Set oven at 400° F. Pour oil into heavy skillet with heatproof handle; heat in preheating oven. Don't forget it! (When oven temperature reaches 400° F is a good time to remove skillet.)

Meanwhile, in a small bowl, whisk together egg substitute and buttermilk.

In a large bowl, stir together remaining ingredients. Make well in cornmeal mixture. Pour egg mixture into well and whisk gently.

Whisk in hot oil from skillet. Pour mixture into hot skillet and bake for 20 minutes, or until top is golden brown and edges pull from pan.

Mexican-Style Corn Bread

Just before adding hot oil, add ½ cup grated onion; ⅓ cup fresh or no-salt-added frozen whole-kernel corn, thawed; ¼ cup grated nonfat or low-fat sharp Cheddar cheese; and ½ to 1 whole fresh jalapeño pepper, seeded and finely chopped (see Cook's Tip, page 115). (calories 120; protein 5 g; carbohydrates 19 g; cholesterol 1 mg; total fat 3 g; saturated 1 g; polyunsaturated 1 g; monounsaturated 1 g; fiber 2 g; sodium 255 mg)

Calories 104
Protein 4 g
Carbohydrates 16 g
Cholesterol 1 mg
Total Fat 3 g
 Saturated 1 g
 Polyunsaturated 1 g
 Monounsaturated 1 g
Fiber 1 g
Sodium 226 mg

Corn Bread with Kernels

Serves 8

This hearty corn bread is delicious served piping hot from the oven with Bayou Red Beans and Rice (see page 281).

1 cup frozen or canned no-salt-added whole-kernel corn
Vegetable oil spray
1 cup cornmeal
1 cup whole-wheat flour
¼ cup sugar
½ teaspoon baking soda
1½ cups nonfat or low-fat buttermilk
¼ cup acceptable vegetable oil
Egg substitute equivalent to 1 egg, or 1 egg, lightly beaten

Thaw corn if using frozen. Drain thawed or canned corn.

Preheat oven to 425° F. Lightly spray an 8-inch square baking dish with vegetable oil spray.

In a large bowl, blend cornmeal, flour, sugar, and baking soda.

In a medium bowl, whisk together remaining ingredients. Whisk into cornmeal mixture. Pour into baking dish.

Bake for 20 to 25 minutes, or until cake tester or toothpick inserted in center comes out clean.

Calories 232
Protein 6 g
Carbohydrates 35 g
Cholesterol 2 mg
Total Fat 8 g
  Saturated 1 g
  Polyunsaturated 5 g
  Monounsaturated 2 g
Fiber 4 g
Sodium 148 mg

Easy Refrigerator Rolls

Serves 36; 1 roll per serving

Enjoy these yeast rolls at your convenience. Mix and refrigerate the simple dough. When you want homemade rolls, shape them, let them rise, bake them, and enjoy!

¼ cup lukewarm water (105° F to 115° F)

¼-ounce package active dry yeast

Whites of 2 large eggs

¼ cup acceptable vegetable oil

½ cup sugar

1 teaspoon salt

1 cup lukewarm water (105° F to 115° F)

4 cups all-purpose or whole-wheat flour (plus more as needed)

Vegetable oil spray

Pour ¼ cup water into a small bowl. Add yeast and stir to dissolve. Let stand for 5 minutes.

Pour egg whites into a large bowl and whisk lightly.

Stir in oil, then sugar.

Stir in yeast mixture, then remaining ingredients in order given except vegetable oil spray. Cover and let stand at room temperature for 30 minutes. Refrigerate for at least 12 hours (up to 4 days).

Lightly spray a baking sheet with vegetable oil spray. Make 36 rolls in your favorite shape. Put rolls on baking sheet. Cover with a dry dish towel and let rolls rise in a warm, draft-free place (about 85° F) for 2 hours.

Preheat oven to 375° F.

Bake for 10 minutes.

Calories 76
Protein 2 g
Carbohydrates 13 g
Cholesterol 0 mg
Total Fat 2 g
Saturated 0 g
Polyunsaturated 1 g
Monounsaturated 0 g
Fiber 0 g
Sodium 71 mg

Yogurt Dinner Rolls

Serves 18; 1 roll per person

Tangy yogurt and fragrant herbs flavor these wheat-and-white rolls.

¼ cup lukewarm water (105° F to 115° F)
2 tablespoons sugar
¼-ounce package active dry yeast
1 cup plain nonfat or low-fat yogurt
Egg substitute equivalent to 1 egg, or 1 egg
2 tablespoons acceptable margarine, melted
2 tablespoons grated or minced onion
2 teaspoons dried basil, crumbled
1 teaspoon dried oregano, crumbled
¾ cup all-purpose flour
¾ cup whole-wheat flour
½ teaspoon salt
¾ cup whole-wheat flour
½ cup all-purpose flour
Vegetable oil spray
Flour for hands

Put water, sugar, and yeast, in a medium bowl and stir. Set aside for 5 minutes, or until mixture bubbles. Stir in yogurt, egg substitute, margarine, onion, basil, and oregano.

In a large mixing bowl, combine ¾ cup all-purpose flour, ¾ cup whole-wheat flour, and salt. Blend in yogurt mixture and beat with mixer on low for 30 seconds, then beat on high for 3 minutes. Stir in remaining flours. (Dough will be moist and sticky.)

Spray a large bowl with vegetable oil spray. Turn dough to coat evenly. Cover with damp dish towel and let rise in a warm, draft-free place (about 85° F) for 1½ hours. Punch down dough. Spray a 13 × 9 × 2-inch baking pan with vegetable oil spray. Lightly flour hands and form dough into 18 balls. Put on pan. Cover with dry dish towel and let rise in a warm, draft-free place (about 85° F) for 40 minutes.

Preheat oven to 400° F. Bake for 15 minutes.

Calories 92
Protein 3 g
Carbohydrates 16 g
Cholesterol 0 mg
Total Fat 2 g
Saturated 0 g
Polyunsaturated 1 g
Monounsaturated 1 g
Fiber 2 g
Sodium 95 mg

Cold-Oven Popovers

Serves 12; 1 large popover per serving

This recipe is really cheap entertainment! If your oven has a window and a light, you and your children will want to watch as the batter bubbles up. These popovers deserve a drizzle of honey when they come out of the oven, hot and crisp!

Vegetable oil spray
Whites of 6 large eggs
2 cups fat-free milk
2 tablespoons acceptable vegetable oil
1 tablespoon light margarine, melted
2 cups sifted all-purpose flour
¼ teaspoon salt

Lightly spray 12-cup popover pan with vegetable oil spray.

In a medium bowl, beat egg whites lightly with a fork.

Add milk, oil, and margarine, stirring well.

In a large mixing bowl, combine flour and salt. Gradually add milk mixture, beating with an electric mixer after each addition until well blended. Mix on high speed for 1 to 2 minutes.

Fill each popover cup half full of batter and put in *cold* oven. Set oven to 400° F and bake popovers for 45 to 60 minutes, or until a light golden color.

Cook's Tip

If you don't have a popover pan, substitute 12 large (about 9-ounce) or 18 medium (about 5-ounce) custard cups sprayed with vegetable oil spray. Muffin tins won't give you consistent results.

Calories 116
Protein 5 g
Carbohydrates 17 g
Cholesterol 1 mg
Total Fat 3 g
Saturated 0 g
Polyunsaturated 2 g
Monounsaturated 1 g
Fiber 1 g
Sodium 129 mg

Herb Twists

Serves 12; 1 roll per person

No need for margarine with these twists—they're terrific straight from the oven.

Vegetable oil spray
2 cups all-purpose flour
1 tablespoon baking powder
1 teaspoon sugar
½ teaspoon dried basil, crumbled
½ cup light margarine
8-ounce carton nonfat or low-fat sour cream dip with chives or onions
Flour for kneading

Preheat oven to 400° F. Spray a baking sheet with vegetable oil spray.

In a medium bowl, combine flour, baking powder, sugar, and basil.

Using a pastry blender, cut margarine into flour mixture until crumbly.

Stir in sour cream dip until well blended.

Lightly flour a flat surface and your hands; turn out dough. Knead about 10 strokes. Divide dough into 12 equal portions. Using your hands, roll one portion to a 12-inch length; fold in half and twist. Place on baking sheet. Repeat with remaining dough.

Bake for 10 to 14 minutes, or until starting to brown.

Calories 129
Protein 3 g
Carbohydrates 21 g
Cholesterol 0 mg
Total Fat 3 g
 Saturated 1 g
 Polyunsaturated 1 g
 Monounsaturated 1 g
Fiber 1 g
Sodium 184 mg

Southern Raised Biscuits

Serves 30; 1 biscuit per serving

Soak up some heart-healthy gravy with these full-flavored biscuits.

1 cup nonfat or low-fat buttermilk, slightly warmed
¼-ounce package active dry yeast
2½ cups all-purpose flour
¼ cup sugar
½ teaspoon baking soda
½ teaspoon salt
¼ cup acceptable vegetable oil
Flour for kneading
Vegetable oil spray

Calories 65
Protein 1 g
Carbohydrates 10 g
Cholesterol 0 mg
Total Fat 2 g
 Saturated 0 g
 Polyunsaturated 1 g
 Monounsaturated 0 g
Fiber 0 g
Sodium 73 mg

Pour buttermilk into a small bowl. Add yeast and stir to dissolve. Let rest for 5 minutes.

In a large bowl, combine 2½ cups flour, sugar, baking soda, and salt.

Add buttermilk mixture and oil to flour mixture. Stir gently and quickly until mixed.

Lightly flour a flat surface; turn out dough. Knead gently 20 to 30 times. Roll out or pat to ¼-inch thickness. With a floured 1-inch biscuit cutter, cut out 60 biscuits. Lightly spray each biscuit with vegetable oil spray.

Lightly spray a baking sheet. Put 30 biscuits on it. Put second biscuit on top of each. Cover with a dry dish towel and let dough rise in a warm, draft-free place (about 85° F) for 2 hours.

Preheat oven to 375° F. Bake 12 to 15 minutes.

Drop Biscuits

Serves 12; 1 biscuit per serving

Drop biscuits mean that even busy cooks and their families can have homemade goodness. These biscuits don't require rolling, cutting, or messy cleanup.

Vegetable oil spray
2 cups all-purpose flour
1 tablespoon baking powder
1 teaspoon salt
⅓ cup acceptable margarine
1 cup fat-free milk

Preheat oven to 450° F. Lightly spray a baking sheet with vegetable oil spray.

In a medium bowl, combine flour, baking powder, and salt. Using two knives or pastry blender, cut in margarine until margarine pieces are about pea size. Stir in milk.

Using a teaspoon, drop batter into 12 mounds, 1 inch apart, on baking sheet.

Bake 10 to 12 minutes.

Calories 128
Protein 3 g
Carbohydrates 17 g
Cholesterol 0 mg
Total Fat 5 g
Saturated 1 g
Polyunsaturated 2 g
Monounsaturated 2 g
Fiber 1 g
Sodium 385 mg

Herb Biscuits

Add herbs such as dried parsley, basil, tarragon, or aniseed to the dry ingredients.

Flaky Biscuits

Serves 16; 1 biscuit per serving

Biscuits, Savory Beef Stew (see page 258), and a cup of hot tea—comfort food at its best!

2 cups sifted all-purpose flour
1 tablespoon baking powder
½ teaspoon salt
⅔ cup fat-free milk
¼ cup acceptable vegetable oil
Flour for kneading

Preheat oven to 450° F.

In a large bowl, sift together flour, baking powder, and salt.

Pour milk and oil into a measuring cup but do not stir. Add all at once to flour mixture. Stir quickly with a fork until dough clings together.

Lightly flour a flat surface. Turn dough out and knead lightly about 10 times.

Put dough on a 12 × 16-inch piece of wax paper. Pat dough out until it is about ½ inch thick. Cut with an unfloured medium-size biscuit cutter. Put biscuits on ungreased baking sheet. Bake 12 to 15 minutes.

Calories 86
Protein 2 g
Carbohydrates 12 g
Cholesterol 0 mg
Total Fat 4 g
Saturated 0 g
Polyunsaturated 2 g
Monounsaturated 1 g
Fiber 0 g
Sodium 170 mg

Bagels

Serves 12

These are fun to make with the kids. Let each one choose his or her own topping (see Bagels with Toppings, below).

1¾ cups all-purpose flour
2 ¼-ounce packages active dry yeast
1½ cups lukewarm water (105° F to 115° F)
3 tablespoons sugar
1½ teaspoons salt
2¼ to 2¾ cups all-purpose flour (plus more as needed)
1 gallon water
1 teaspoon sugar

In a large mixing bowl, combine 1¾ cups flour and yeast.

Add 1½ cups water, 3 tablespoons sugar, and salt. Beat with mixer at low speed for 30 seconds, constantly scraping side of bowl. Increase speed to high and beat for 3 minutes.

Gradually stir in enough remaining flour, about 2 cups, so dough starts to pull away from side of bowl. Add more flour if necessary to make dough stiff enough to handle.

Lightly flour a flat surface; turn out dough. Gradually knead in enough of remaining flour until dough is smooth and elastic, 6 to 8 minutes. (Dough shouldn't be dry or stick to surface. You may not need all the flour, or you may need up to ½ cup more if dough is too sticky. See Cook's Tip on Breadmaking, page 463.) Cover with a damp dish towel and let rest for 15 minutes.

Punch down dough. Divide into 12 pieces. Shape each into a smooth ball. Flour index finger and punch a hole in center of each ball. Pull gently to enlarge hole, keeping uniform shape. Cover dough with damp dish towel and let rise for 20 minutes.

In a stockpot, combine 1 gallon water and 1 teaspoon sugar. Bring to a boil over medium-high heat. Reduce to simmer. Cook 4 bagels for 4 minutes, turning once about halfway through. Drain on

Calories 169
Protein 5 g
Carbohydrates 36 g
Cholesterol 0 mg
Total Fat 0 g
Saturated 0 g
Polyunsaturated 0 g
Monounsaturated 0 g
Fiber 1 g
Sodium 293 mg

paper towels. Repeat with remaining bagels, cooking 4 at a time.

Preheat oven to 375° F.

Bake on ungreased nonstick baking sheet for 35 to 40 minutes.

Whole-Wheat Bagels

Substitute whole-wheat flour for half the all-purpose flour. (calories 161; protein 5 g; carbohydrates 34 g; cholesterol 0 mg; total fat 1 g; saturated 0 g; polyunsaturated 0 g; monounsaturated 0 g; fiber 3 g; sodium 294 mg)

Bagels with Toppings

Before baking, sprinkle bagels with chopped onion, poppy seeds, sesame seeds, caraway seeds, or kosher salt.

Fluffy Cottage Cheese Blintzes

Serves 3; 2 blintzes per serving

Top these blintzes with fresh fruit or fat-free sour cream for a brunch treat.

Vegetable oil spray
2 tablespoons egg substitute
½ cup nonfat or low-fat cottage cheese
⅓ cup fat-free milk
¼ cup all-purpose flour
Whites of 3 large eggs

Lightly spray griddle with vegetable oil spray.

In a medium mixing bowl, beat egg substitute and cottage cheese until almost smooth.

Whisk in milk and flour.

In a small mixing bowl, beat egg whites until they form soft peaks. Fold into batter. Let stand for 5 minutes.

Preheat griddle over medium heat. Pour batter onto prepared griddle using ¼-cup measure. (You should have 6 pancakes.) Cook until tops are bubbly and edges are golden brown, 1 to 2 minutes. Turn and cook other side for 1 to 2 minutes.

Calories 99
Protein 12 g
Carbohydrates 11 g
Cholesterol 4 mg
Total Fat 0 g
Saturated 0 g
Polyunsaturated 0 g
Monounsaturated 0 g
Fiber 0 g
Sodium 261 mg

Poppy Seed Scones with Dried Cranberries

Serves 16

A cross between a cookie and a biscuit, a scone is perfect for teatime or with a piece of fruit after dinner. This porous Scottish classic is great for dunking in tea, coffee, or fat-free milk with a shot or two of fat-free chocolate syrup.

Vegetable oil spray
2 cups all-purpose flour
½ cup uncooked quick-cooking oatmeal
½ cup sugar
1 tablespoon poppy seeds
1 teaspoon baking powder
½ teaspoon baking soda
¼ teaspoon salt
2 tablespoons light margarine
½ cup dried cranberries
½ cup pineapple juice
Egg substitute equivalent to 1 egg, or 1 egg
Flour for hands

Preheat oven to 375° F. Lightly spray a baking sheet with vegetable oil spray.

In a large bowl, combine 2 cups flour, oatmeal, sugar, poppy seeds, baking powder, baking soda, and salt, stirring well.

Cut margarine into flour mixture with a fork or pastry blender until crumbly.

Stir in cranberries. Make a well in center of mixture.

Pour pineapple juice and egg substitute into well. Stir until just combined (don't overmix).

With floured hands, divide dough in half. Shape into 2 balls. Put 4 to 5 inches apart on baking sheet and flatten each into a 6-inch disk. Cut each into 8 wedges with a sharp knife or pizza cutter (don't separate wedges).

Bake for 15 to 20 minutes, or until edges are golden brown. Let cool for at least 5 minutes on a cooling rack. Separate wedges with a knife or pizza cutter.

Calories 121
Protein 3 g
Carbohydrates 24 g
Cholesterol 0 mg
Total Fat 1 g
  Saturated 0 g
  Polyunsaturated 1 g
  Monounsaturated 0 g
Fiber 1 g
Sodium 123 mg

Muffins

Serves 12

Muffins aren't just for breakfast and brunch. These taste almost like bread—with less work!

Vegetable oil spray
2 cups sifted all-purpose flour
2 tablespoons sugar
1 tablespoon baking powder
¼ teaspoon salt
1¼ cups fat-free milk
¼ cup unsweetened applesauce
Egg substitute equivalent to 1 egg, or 1 egg
1 tablespoon acceptable vegetable oil

Preheat oven to 425° F. Lightly spray a 12-cup muffin tin with vegetable oil spray.

In a large bowl, sift together flour, sugar, baking powder, and salt.

In a medium bowl, whisk together remaining ingredients.

Make well in center of flour mixture. Pour milk mixture into well. Stir just enough to moisten flour. Batter should be lumpy.

Fill muffin cups two-thirds full.

Bake for 20 to 25 minutes, or until toothpick inserted in center comes out clean.

Fruit Muffins

Add ½ cup fruit, such as blueberries, chopped dates, or raisins, to batter. (calories 107; protein 4 g; carbohydrates 20 g; cholesterol 1 mg; total fat 2 g; saturated 0 g; polyunsaturated 1 g; monounsaturated 0 g; fiber 1 g; sodium 194 mg)

Jelly Muffins

Fill muffin cups one-third full and put 1 teaspoon of all-fruit jam or jelly in the center of each. Cover with remaining batter. (calories 112; protein 4 g; carbohydrates 21 g; cholesterol 1 mg; total fat 2 g; saturated 0 g; polyunsaturated 1 g; monounsaturated 0 g; fiber 1 g; sodium 194 mg)

Calories 104
Protein 4 g
Carbohydrates 19 g
Cholesterol 1 mg
Total Fat 2 g
Saturated 0 g
Polyunsaturated 1 g
Monounsaturated 0 g
Fiber 1 g
Sodium 194 mg

Whole-Wheat Muffins

Serves 12

Serve these fragrant muffins fresh out of the oven with Curried Chicken Salad (see page 111) and apple or pear wedges.

Vegetable oil spray
1 cup whole-wheat flour
¾ cup all-purpose flour
¼ cup wheat germ
¼ cup sugar
2½ teaspoons baking powder
½ teaspoon ground cinnamon
¼ teaspoon salt
⅛ teaspoon ground cloves
1 cup fat-free milk
½ cup grated zucchini
⅓ cup unsweetened applesauce
Egg substitute equivalent to 1 egg, or 1 egg
1 tablespoon acceptable vegetable oil
1 teaspoon grated orange zest

Preheat oven to 375° F. Lightly spray 12-cup muffin tin with vegetable oil spray.

In a large bowl, combine flours, wheat germ, sugar, baking powder, cinnamon, salt, and cloves, stirring well.

In a medium bowl, whisk together remaining ingredients.

Make well in center of flour mixture. Pour milk mixture into well and stir just enough to moisten flour. Don't overmix. Batter should be lumpy. Pour batter evenly into muffin cups.

Bake for 20 to 25 minutes, or until muffins are firm.

Remove from oven and let muffins rest for a few minutes in pan before serving.

Time-Saver on Roasted Nuts: For dry-roasted nuts ready at a moment's notice, prepare extras for storing in an airtight container in the freezer. You don't even need to thaw them.

Calories 110
Protein 4 g
Carbohydrates 21 g
Cholesterol 0 mg
Total Fat 2 g
- Saturated 0 g
- Polyunsaturated 1 g
- Monounsaturated 0 g

Fiber 2 g
Sodium 171 mg

Whole-Wheat Nut Muffins

Add 3 tablespoons dry-roasted chopped walnuts to batter just before baking. (calories 122; protein 4 g; carbohydrates 21 g; cholesterol 0 mg; total fat 3 g; saturated 0 g; polyunsaturated 2 g; monounsaturated 1 g; fiber 2 g; sodium 171 mg)

Buttermilk Bran Muffins

Serves 12

Pack a muffin and fruit juice or fat-free milk for a snack at work or school. Save a few muffins for a later date. They'll keep in the freezer for up to four months.

1 cup nonfat or low-fat buttermilk
¾ cup bud-type bran cereal
½ cup raisins
½ cup shredded carrots
⅓ cup sugar
¼ cup unsweetened applesauce
Egg substitute equivalent to 1 egg, or 1 egg
1 tablespoon acceptable vegetable oil
½ teaspoon vanilla extract
1 cup all-purpose flour
½ cup oat bran flour
2 teaspoons baking powder
½ teaspoon ground cinnamon
¼ teaspoon ground nutmeg

Preheat oven to 375° F. Line 12-cup muffin tin with bake cups.

In a medium bowl, whisk together buttermilk, bran, raisins, carrots, sugar, applesauce, egg substitute, oil, and vanilla. Let stand for about 10 minutes.

In a large bowl, combine remaining ingredients. Make well in center and pour buttermilk mixture into well. Stir only enough to moisten flour. Don't overmix. Batter should be lumpy. Fill muffin cups two-thirds full of batter.

Bake for 20 to 25 minutes, or until cake tester or toothpick inserted in center comes out clean.

Calories 128
Protein 4 g
Carbohydrates 25 g
Cholesterol 1 mg
Total Fat 2 g
Saturated 0 g
Polyunsaturated 1 g
Monounsaturated 0 g
Fiber 3 g
Sodium 116 mg

Corn Bread Applesauce Muffins

Serves 8

If you have any left over, these muffins make great snacks. Toast leftovers in a toaster oven for breakfast.

Vegetable oil spray
½ cup all-purpose flour
½ cup coarse yellow cornmeal
1½ teaspoons baking powder
¼ teaspoon salt
½ cup fat-free milk
Egg substitute equivalent to 1 egg, or 1 egg
2 tablespoons honey
2 tablespoons unsweetened applesauce

Preheat oven to 425° F. Lightly spray eight muffin cups with vegetable oil spray.

Combine flour, cornmeal, baking powder, and salt in a large bowl, stirring well.

Beat remaining ingredients in a small bowl.

Make a well in cornmeal mixture. Pour milk mixture into well, stirring just until moistened. Fill muffin cups two-thirds full with batter.

Bake for 15 to 20 minutes, or until a cake tester or toothpick inserted in center of muffins comes out clean.

Cook's Tip on Muffin Cups

Put about 2 tablespoons of water in each muffin cup you aren't filling with batter. That will help prevent the pan from warping.

Calories 86
Protein 3 g
Carbohydrates 18 g
Cholesterol 0 mg
Total Fat 1 g
Saturated 0 g
Polyunsaturated 0 g
Monounsaturated 0 g
Fiber 1 g
Sodium 189 mg

Oat Bran Fruit Muffins

Serves 18

Do your heart a favor and start your day off right with a proper breakfast. One of these muffins, a cold glass of fat-free milk, and a bowl of sliced strawberries would fit the bill.

1½ cups high-fiber oat bran cereal
¾ cup all-purpose flour
¾ cup whole-wheat flour
½ cup raisins
½ cup chopped dates
½ cup chopped prunes
2 teaspoons baking powder
1 teaspoon baking soda
1 teaspoon ground cinnamon
1 cup nonfat or low-fat buttermilk
½ cup honey
¼ cup firmly packed dark brown sugar
Egg substitute equivalent to 2 eggs, or 2 eggs, well beaten
3 tablespoons acceptable vegetable oil

Preheat oven to 400° F. Line 12-cup and 6-cup muffin tins with bake cups.

In a large bowl, combine cereal, flours, raisins, dates, prunes, baking powder, baking soda, and cinnamon, stirring well.

In a medium bowl, whisk together remaining ingredients.

Make well in center of flour mixture. Pour buttermilk mixture into well and stir just enough to moisten flour. Don't overmix. Batter should be lumpy. Spoon into muffin cups.

Bake for 20 to 25 minutes, or until cake tester or toothpick inserted in center comes out clean.

Calories 151
Protein 3 g
Carbohydrates 30 g
Cholesterol 1 mg
Total Fat 3 g
Saturated 1 g
Polyunsaturated 2 g
Monounsaturated 1 g
Fiber 2 g
Sodium 167 mg

Blueberry Banana Muffins

Serves 12

A fruit lover's dream, these muffins combine blueberries, banana, orange juice, and applesauce.

Vegetable oil spray
1 cup all-purpose flour
½ cup whole-wheat flour
½ cup wheat germ
⅓ cup firmly packed light brown sugar
1 tablespoon baking powder
½ teaspoon salt
½ teaspoon ground cinnamon
⅛ teaspoon ground nutmeg
1 medium banana
½ cup fresh orange juice (1 to 2 medium oranges)
¼ cup unsweetened applesauce
Egg substitute equivalent to 1 egg, or 1 egg
1 tablespoon acceptable vegetable oil
1 cup fresh blueberries, stems removed

Preheat oven to 400° F. Lightly spray a 12-cup muffin tin with vegetable oil spray.

In a large bowl, combine flours, wheat germ, brown sugar, baking powder, salt, cinnamon, and nutmeg, stirring well.

In a small bowl, mash banana. Add remaining ingredients except blueberries. Whisk until well blended.

Make well in center of flour mixture. Pour banana mixture into well and stir just until moistened. Don't overmix. Mixture should be lumpy.

With rubber scraper, carefully fold blueberries into batter. Pour batter into muffin cups.

Bake for 15 minutes, or until cake tester or toothpick inserted in center comes out clean.

Calories 127
Protein 3 g
Carbohydrates 26 g
Cholesterol 0 mg
Total Fat 2 g
Saturated 0 g
Polyunsaturated 1 g
Monounsaturated 0 g
Fiber 2 g
Sodium 232 mg

Crepes

Serves 10; 2 crepes per serving

You can use this basic crepe recipe for everything from appetizers through dessert.

Egg substitute equivalent to 2 eggs, or 2 eggs, beaten

1 cup all-purpose flour

1 cup fat-free milk (plus more as needed)

1 tablespoon acceptable vegetable oil

Vegetable oil spray

Whisk together all ingredients except vegetable oil spray until batter is smooth and just thick enough to coat a spoon. If batter is too thick, add a little more milk. Cover and refrigerate for at least 1 hour.

Heat a 5- or 6-inch crepe pan or nonstick skillet over medium-high heat. When pan is hot, remove from burner and lightly spray with vegetable oil spray. Stir batter. With pan still off burner, pour in just enough batter (1½ to 2 tablespoons) to form a very thin layer, quickly swirling pan so batter spreads evenly. (If you haven't used enough batter and there are holes, pour on a small amount more. If you used too much, pour off excess.) Cook on one side for about 1 minute, or until edge turns golden brown; turn and brown on the other side for about 30 seconds. If crepes are cooking too quickly, reduce heat.

Repeat until all batter is used, stirring occasionally. As crepes are cooked, stack them alternating with a layer of wax paper. Keep warm if they are to be served immediately.

Calories 77
Protein 4 g
Carbohydrates 11 g
Cholesterol 1 mg
Total Fat 2 g
Saturated 0 g
Polyunsaturated 1 g
Monounsaturated 0 g
Fiber 0 g
Sodium 36 mg

Whole-Wheat Crepes

Serves 12; 1 crepe per serving

Use these crepes to dress up leftover chicken or turkey. Fill with Chicken Curry in a Hurry (see page 222). Or make Chicken à la King, omitting the rice (see page 216). Scrumptious!

1 cup fat-free milk
½ cup all-purpose flour
Egg substitute equivalent to 2 eggs, or 2 eggs
¼ cup whole-wheat flour
1 tablespoon acceptable vegetable oil
Vegetable oil spray

Put all ingredients except vegetable oil spray in a food processor or blender. Process until mixed thoroughly. Cover and refrigerate for at least 1 hour.

Heat a 6- to 8-inch nonstick skillet or crepe pan over medium-high heat. When pan is hot, remove from burner and lightly spray with vegetable oil spray. Stir batter. With pan still off burner, pour in about ¼ cup batter; quickly swirl pan so batter spreads evenly. (If you haven't used enough batter and there are holes, pour on a small amount more. If you used too much, pour off excess.) Cook on one side for about 1 minute, or until edge turns golden brown; turn and brown on the other side for about 30 seconds. If crepes are cooking too quickly, reduce heat.

When crepe edges start separating from pan, flip crepe. Brown slightly on the other side and remove to a plate.

Repeat until all batter is used. As crepes are cooked, stack them alternating with wax paper. Keep warm if they are to be served immediately.

Calories 54
Protein 3 g
Carbohydrates 7 g
Cholesterol 0 mg
Total Fat 2 g
  Saturated 0 g
  Polyunsaturated 1 g
  Monounsaturated 0 g
Fiber 0 g
Sodium 30 mg

Country-Style Breakfast Casserole

Serves 10

To have a special breakfast with no fuss, prepare this casserole of popular breakfast foods the night before.

Vegetable oil spray
8 ounces reduced-fat smoked link sausage
2 tablespoons maple syrup
2 pounds frozen country-style hash browns (no oil added)
2 cups fat-free milk
Egg substitute equivalent to 6 eggs
2 slices fat-free or low-fat American cheese, diced (2 ounces)
¼ cup grated Parmesan cheese
½ teaspoon dry mustard
¼ teaspoon pepper
2 tablespoons finely snipped green onion (green part only) (optional)

Preheat oven to 350° F. Lightly spray a 13 × 9 × 2-inch baking pan with vegetable oil spray.

Heat a medium skillet over medium-high heat. Sauté sausage for 3 to 4 minutes, or until browned, turning occasionally. Cut into bite-size pieces. Wipe skillet with a paper towel.

Add maple syrup and cook for 1 minute, stirring to coat sausage. Arrange in a single layer in baking pan, then top with hash browns.

In a medium bowl, whisk together remaining ingredients except green onion. Pour over hash browns.

Bake for 1 hour, or until center is set. Sprinkle with green onion and let cool for at least 10 minutes before cutting into squares.

Cook's Tip

If you prepare this casserole ahead of time, cover it with plastic and refrigerate. Put the cold casserole in a cold oven, set the thermostat to 350° F, and bake for 1 hour 10 minutes to 1 hour 15 minutes. Proceed as above.

Calories 184
Protein 14 g
Carbohydrates 25 g
Cholesterol 13 mg
Total Fat 3 g
Saturated 1 g
Polyunsaturated 1 g
Monounsaturated 1 g
Fiber 1 g
Sodium 463 mg

Spinach Tortillas

Serves 16; 1 tortilla per serving

Fun to make and eat, flavored tortillas add a colorful touch to any southwestern meal. Use them for dipping in salsa or for making quesadillas, enchiladas, or wraps, such as in Chipotle Chicken Wraps (see page 208).

¾ cup hot tap water
½ 10-ounce package no-salt-added frozen spinach, thawed, drained, and squeezed
1 cup all-purpose flour
1 cup masa harina (see Cook's Tip on Masa Harina, below)
1 tablespoon acceptable vegetable oil
¼ teaspoon salt
Flour for kneading and rolling dough

In a food processor or blender, puree water and spinach.

In a medium bowl, stir together flour, masa harina, oil, and salt. Make a well in center and pour spinach mixture into well. Stir with a sturdy spoon until mixture begins to form a ball.

Lightly flour a flat surface; turn out dough. Knead for 1 to 2 minutes. Return dough to bowl it was mixed in; cover bowl with plastic wrap. Let dough rest for 15 minutes.

Roll dough into a cylinder 16 inches long. Cut crosswise into 1-inch pieces. Using your hands, shape each piece into a ball.

Preheat a nonstick griddle over medium heat.

Lightly flour a flat surface. With a rolling pin, roll a dough ball into a 6-inch circle (don't worry if it isn't perfectly round). Cook on griddle for 1 to 2 minutes. Turn tortilla over and press it down for about 10 seconds with a spatula. Cook for 1 to 2 minutes. Remove tortilla and put on a cooling rack. Repeat with remaining dough balls. (Once you have mastered the technique, it will be easy to roll out a dough ball or two while other tortillas are

Calories 64
Protein 2 g
Carbohydrates 12 g
Cholesterol 0 mg
Total Fat 1 g
Saturated 0 g
Polyunsaturated 1 g
Monounsaturated 0 g
Fiber 1 g
Sodium 43 mg

cooking.) If griddle is big enough, cook several tortillas at a time.

Store tortillas in an airtight plastic bag in the refrigerator for up to 5 days or in the freezer for up to 4 months. To reheat, wrap tortillas in aluminum foil and heat in a 350° F oven for 5 minutes, or put tortillas in a microwave-safe tortilla warmer or wrap in damp paper towels and microwave at 100 percent power (high) for 1 minute.

Tomato Tortillas

Substitute 5 tablespoons no-salt-added tomato paste for spinach. Follow directions above, except whisk together tomato paste and water until smooth (no food processor or blender needed). When cooking these tortillas, watch them carefully. They tend to brown more quickly than spinach tortillas. (calories 66; protein 2 g; carbohydrates 12 g; cholesterol 0 mg; total fat 1 g; saturated 0 g; polyunsaturated 1 g; monounsaturated 0 g; fiber 1 g; sodium 42 mg)

Cook's Tip on Masa Harina

Masa harina is the flour traditionally used for making tortillas. It's made from dried corn kernels cooked in limewater. Look for masa harina in ethnic markets or with the other flours in your supermarket.

Apple Oatmeal Pancake

Serves 6

Here's a tasty breakfast dish for a cold Sunday morning.

Vegetable oil spray
1 tablespoon acceptable margarine
⅓ cup uncooked quick-cooking oatmeal
⅔ cup all-purpose flour
1 tablespoon light brown sugar
1 cup fat-free milk
Egg substitute equivalent to 6 eggs
1 tablespoon vanilla extract
1 teaspoon ground cinnamon
¼ teaspoon salt
2 tablespoons light brown sugar
½ teaspoon ground cinnamon
3 large Red Delicious apples (1½ pounds)
1 tablespoon light margarine
1 tablespoon fresh lemon juice

Preheat oven to 425° F. Spray a 13 × 9 × 2-inch pan with vegetable oil spray. Melt 1 tablespoon margarine in pan.

In a food processor or blender, process oatmeal, flour, and 1 tablespoon brown sugar until smooth. Add milk, egg substitute, vanilla, 1 teaspoon cinnamon, and salt. Process until smooth. Pour into hot pan. Bake for 25 minutes.

In a small bowl, combine 2 tablespoons brown sugar and ½ teaspoon cinnamon.

Peel, core, and slice apples.

Melt 1 tablespoon margarine in large nonstick skillet over medium heat. Add apples, stirring with rubber scraper to prevent breakage. Sprinkle with brown sugar mixture. Cook, covered, over medium heat for 7 to 8 minutes.

To serve, cut pancake into 6 pieces and place on individual plates. Stir lemon juice into apple mixture and spoon over each portion.

Calories 254
Protein 12 g
Carbohydrates 39 g
Cholesterol 1 mg
Total Fat 6 g
 Saturated 1 g
 Polyunsaturated 2 g
 Monounsaturated 2 g
Fiber 3 g
Sodium 269 mg

Cinnamon Orange Pancakes

Serves 6; 2 pancakes per serving

Serve hot with Orange Sauce (see page 454), light syrup, or cottage cheese topped with sliced bananas or strawberries.

1 cup whole-wheat flour
¾ cup all-purpose flour
2 tablespoons wheat germ
1 tablespoon sugar
2 teaspoons baking powder
1 teaspoon ground cinnamon
1 cup fat-free milk
1 teaspoon grated fresh orange zest
¾ cup fresh orange juice (2 medium oranges)
Egg substitute equivalent to 1 egg, or 1 egg
Vegetable oil spray

In a large mixing bowl, combine flours, wheat germ, sugar, baking powder, and cinnamon, stirring well.

In a small bowl, whisk together remaining ingredients except vegetable oil spray.

Pour milk mixture into flour mixture. Stir just until moistened. Don't overmix.

Preheat griddle or skillet over medium heat. Remove from burner and lightly spray with vegetable oil spray.

Pour batter onto griddle, using ¼-cup measure. (You should have 12 pancakes.) Cook until tops are bubbly and edges are dry, 2 to 3 minutes. Turn and cook other side for 2 to 3 minutes.

Calories 178
Protein 8 g
Carbohydrates 36 g
Cholesterol 1 mg
Total Fat 1 g
  Saturated 0 g
  Polyunsaturated 0 g
  Monounsaturated 0 g
Fiber 3 g
Sodium 204 mg

Cinnamon French Toast

Serves 3; 2 slices per serving

Serve with light syrup or all-fruit spread and Turkey Sausage Patties (see page 231).

Egg substitute equivalent to 2 eggs, or 2 eggs
¼ cup fat-free milk
1 teaspoon sugar
½ teaspoon vanilla extract
¼ teaspoon ground cinnamon
Dash of ground nutmeg
Vegetable oil spray
6 slices firm-textured thinly sliced white bread
Vegetable oil spray (butter flavor preferred)

Preheat oven to 200° F.

In a shallow bowl, whisk together egg substitute, milk, sugar, vanilla, cinnamon, and nutmeg.

Lightly spray a large nonstick griddle with vegetable oil spray and put over medium-high heat.

Dip both sides of bread slices in egg mixture (tongs work well for this). Cook until golden brown on one side, 2 to 3 minutes. Turn and brown on other side, 2 to 3 minutes. Put on an ovenproof plate and keep warm in oven.

Spray griddle with vegetable oil spray. Repeat with remaining bread slices.

Calories 211
Protein 10 g
Carbohydrates 29 g
Cholesterol 1 mg
Total Fat 4 g
Saturated 0 g
Polyunsaturated 1 g
Monounsaturated 1 g
Fiber 0 g
Sodium 357 mg

Cottage Cheese and Cinnamon Toasty

Serves 1

Cottage cheese adds protein and staying power to an old favorite.

1 slice bread
¼ cup nonfat or low-fat cottage cheese
½ teaspoon sugar
¼ teaspoon ground cinnamon

Preheat broiler if using.

Toast bread.

Spread with cottage cheese and sprinkle with sugar and cinnamon.

Put under broiler or in toaster oven until topping bubbles. Serve at once.

Cottage Cheese and Peach Toasty

Proceed as directed, substituting 1 fresh peach slice for sugar. (calories 139; protein 11 g; carbohydrates 21 g; cholesterol 6 mg; total fat 1 g; saturated 0 g; polyunsaturated 0 g; monounsaturated 0 g; fiber 1 g; sodium 348 mg)

Calories 140
Protein 10 g
Carbohydrates 21 g
Cholesterol 6 mg
Total Fat 1 g
Saturated 0 g
Polyunsaturated 0 g
Monounsaturated 0 g
Fiber 1 g
Sodium 348 mg

Breakfast Pizzas

Serves 4

Stack English muffins sky-high with scrambled eggs and veggies, crown them with tomato sauce and cheese, and serve them with a knife and fork.

Vegetable oil spray
8 ounces fresh mushrooms, sliced (2½ to 3 cups)
1 cup chopped green bell pepper
1 cup chopped yellow onion (2 medium)
Egg substitute equivalent to 3 eggs, or 2 large eggs and whites of 2 large eggs
¼ cup fat-free milk
½ cup no-salt-added tomato sauce
1 teaspoon salt-free dried Italian seasoning, crumbled
¼ teaspoon crushed red pepper flakes
2 English muffins, halved and toasted
2 tablespoons grated Parmesan cheese

Spray a large nonstick skillet with vegetable oil spray. Heat over medium-high heat for 1 minute. Sauté mushrooms for 4 minutes, or until soft.

Add bell pepper and onion. Sauté for 4 to 5 minutes, or until onion is translucent.

Meanwhile, in a small bowl, whisk together egg substitute and milk.

Reduce heat to medium and add egg mixture to vegetables. Cook until eggs are set, stirring occasionally with a rubber scraper. Remove from heat.

In a small bowl, combine tomato sauce, Italian seasoning, and red pepper flakes.

Spoon 2 tablespoons tomato mixture on each muffin half. Top with mushroom mixture and sprinkle with Parmesan.

Calories 177
Protein 12 g
Carbohydrates 26 g
Cholesterol 3 mg
Total Fat 3 g
Saturated 1 g
Polyunsaturated 1 g
Monounsaturated 1 g
Fiber 3 g
Sodium 292 mg

Mexican Breakfast Pizzas

Substitute 4 6-inch corn tortillas for English muffins; ½ teaspoon ground cumin for Italian seasoning; and 1 tablespoon chopped fresh cilantro and ¼ cup nonfat or low-fat sour cream for Parmesan. Put egg mixture on tortillas. Combine tomato sauce, cumin, and red pepper flakes. Spoon over egg mixture. Top with sour cream and sprinkle with cilantro. (calories 170; protein 11 g; carbohydrates 27 g; cholesterol 0 mg; total fat 3 g; saturated 0 g; polyunsaturated 1 g; monounsaturated 1 g; fiber 4 g; sodium 155 mg)

DESSERTS

Angel Food Truffle Torte with Fruit Sauce

Angel Food Layers with Chocolate Custard and Kiwifruit

Lemon Roll with Blueberries

Black Devil's Food Cake

Nutmeg Cake

Wacky Cake

Easy Apple Cake

Carrot Cake

Pineapple Upside-Down Cake

Pumpkin Spice Cupcakes with Nutmeg Cream Topping

Chocolate Swirl Cheesecake

Key Lime Cheesecake

Rum-Lime Pudding Cake

Seven-Minute Frosting

Confectioners' Glaze

Pumpkin Pie

Raspberry Chiffon Pie

Fresh Strawberry Pie

Deep-Dish Cobbler

Frozen Mocha Yogurt Pie

Baked Lemon Cheese Pie

Chocolate Chess Pie

Chocolate Mousse in Meringue Shells

Chocolate-Berry Pie

Berry-Filled Meringues

Crustless Apple Pie

Apple Raisin Crunch

Cherry Crisp

Deep-Dish Fruit Crisp

Sugar and Spice Peach Shortcake

Peach Clafouti

Cherry-Filled Phyllo Rollovers

Oat Crumb Piecrust

Gingersnap and Graham Cracker Crust

Meringue Shell

Chocolate Oatmeal Cookies

Chewy Chocolate Chip Cookies

Peanut Butter Cookies

Bourbon Balls

Sugar Cookies

Ginger Cookies

Fudgy Buttermilk Brownies

Butterscotch Brownies

Apricot Raisin Bars

Oatmeal Carrot Bar Cookies

Apricot-Almond Biscotti

Sherry Thins

Frozen Raspberry Cream

Fresh Strawberry Mousse

Cannoli Cream with Strawberries and Chocolate

Honey Almond Custards

Caramel Custard with Poached Pears

Chocolate Chip Custard with Caramelized Sugar Topping

Indian Pudding

Apple-Berry Dessert Couscous

Delicious Rice Pudding

Guiltless Banana Pudding

Fruit with Vanilla Cream and Wafer Wedges

Cinnamon-Apple Dessert Tamales with Kahlúa Custard Sauce

Berries in Rich Vanilla Cream

Dessert Crepes

Gingerbread

Spiced Skillet Bananas with Frozen Yogurt

Grapefruit Orange Palette

Claret-Spiced Oranges

Baked Ginger Pears

Golden Poached Pears

Special Baked Apples

Fall Fruit Medley

Mint Julep Fruit Cup

Kiwifruit Sundaes

Strawberries with Champagne Ice

Strawberry-Banana Sorbet with Star Fruit

Fresh Fruit Ice

Strawberry-Raspberry Ice

Tropical Breeze

Sunny Mango Sorbet

Chocolate Mocha Freeze

Tequila Lime Sherbet

Berry Peachy Frozen Yogurt

Hong Kong Sundae

Cardinal Sundae

Angel Food Truffle Torte with Fruit Sauce

Serves 12

Chocolate truffles are traditionally made with melted chocolate and cream. Our heart-healthy dessert incorporates layers of low-fat chocolate truffle filling between light layers of angel food cake. The cake nestles on a pool of marshmallow creme, strawberries, and passion fruit. Feel free to experiment with seasonal fruit for the sauce.

9-inch angel food cake

FILLING

½ cup reduced-fat chocolate chips

8 ounces fat-free or low-fat cream cheese, softened

¼ cup sifted confectioners' sugar

2 tablespoons cocoa powder (dark, European style preferred)

1 teaspoon vanilla extract

SAUCE

2 ripe passion fruit (1½ ounces each), ¼ cup passion fruit nectar, or ¼ cup passion fruit juice blend

1 cup marshmallow creme (4 ounces)

1 cup strawberries, stemmed

Calories 203
Protein 5 g
Carbohydrates 42 g
Cholesterol 1 mg
Total Fat 1 g
Saturated 1 g
Polyunsaturated 0 g
Monounsaturated 0 g
Fiber 1 g
Sodium 384 mg

With a long, serrated knife, cut cake horizontally into 4 equal layers.

For filling, in a small, heavy saucepan, melt chocolate chips over low heat, 1 to 2 minutes, stirring constantly. With a rubber scraper, scrape chocolate into a medium mixing bowl.

Add remaining filling ingredients. Beat with an electric hand mixer on medium-high speed for 2 minutes, or until smooth.

Place a layer of cake on a plate. Spread with one third of chocolate mixture. Repeat with remaining cake and filling, ending with cake. Cover with plastic wrap and refrigerate for at least 30 minutes.

For sauce, halve passion fruit and scoop out pulp with a spoon. Press pulp through a fine sieve to remove seeds; discard seeds.

In a food processor or blender, puree pulp, juice, marshmallow creme, and strawberries.

To serve, spoon 2 to 3 tablespoons of sauce onto dessert plate. Swirl to coat plate evenly. Cut cake into 12 slices. Place one slice on prepared plate. Repeat with remaining sauce and cake.

Cook's Tip

You can layer the cake slices and filling, cover the dessert with plastic wrap, and refrigerate it for up to 4 days before serving. Prepare the sauce up to 2 days ahead and refrigerate it separately.

Cook's Tip on Passion Fruit

Passion fruit is available from spring to the beginning of fall. Ripe passion fruit is soft and slightly wrinkled. Unripe passion fruit has a much smoother appearance. The fruit will ripen in 3 to 5 days on the counter or in a paper bag.

Angel Food Layers with Chocolate Custard and Kiwifruit

Serves 6

Dark chocolate custard and jade-green kiwifruit nestle between layers of angel food cake in this decadent dessert. But we're not finished—a ruby-red strawberry glaze and a dollop of whipped topping crown it all.

CHOCOLATE CUSTARD

1 cup fat-free milk

½ cup sugar

Egg substitute equivalent to 1 egg, or 1 egg

2 tablespoons unsweetened cocoa powder (dark, European style preferred)

2 tablespoons cornstarch

1 tablespoon all-purpose flour

½ teaspoon vanilla extract

½ 9-inch angel food cake

6 kiwifruit, peeled and thinly sliced

¾ cup strawberry glaze

½ cup frozen nonfat whipped topping, thawed

For chocolate custard, whisk together all ingredients except vanilla in top of a double boiler. Set over simmering water. Cook for 3 to 4 minutes, whisking occasionally until mixture starts to thicken. Whisk constantly until custard is thick and smooth, about 1 minute.

Add vanilla and cook for 1 minute, whisking occasionally. Remove top of double boiler and let custard cool for 10 to 15 minutes. Place plastic wrap directly on custard and refrigerate for up to four days.

To assemble, cut angel food cake into 6 slices; cut each slice in half crosswise. Put 1 piece of cake on a dessert plate. Arrange 3 slices of kiwifruit on cake. Spread about ¼ cup custard over kiwifruit. Cover

Calories 258
Protein 5 g
Carbohydrates 58 g
Cholesterol 1 mg
Total Fat 1 g
Saturated 0 g
Polyunsaturated 0 g
Monounsaturated 0 g
Fiber 4 g
Sodium 238 mg

with another piece of cake. Spread ¼ cup custard over cake. Top with 3 to 4 slices of kiwifruit. Drizzle with about 2 tablespoons strawberry glaze. Top with 1 tablespoon whipped topping. Repeat with remaining ingredients.

Time-Saver: The custard sauce takes only 6 to 8 minutes to make and is worth every rich and creamy spoonful. However, you can substitute a small package (3 to 4 ounces) of fat-free instant chocolate pudding prepared according to package directions but using fat-free milk.

Lemon Roll with Blueberries

Serves 16

Use angel food cake mix to create a sinfully delicious dessert? You bet! You won't believe this dessert until you try it.

22-ounce can lemon pie filling
16-ounce package angel food cake mix
1 tablespoon confectioners' sugar
2 cups fat-free frozen whipped topping, thawed
¼ teaspoon grated lemon zest
12 ounces fresh blueberries (1½ cups)

Preheat oven to 350° F. Line a 10 × 15-inch jelly-roll pan with wax paper.

In a large bowl, combine pie filling and cake mix. Beat on medium setting for 5 to 7 minutes. Spoon into pan.

Bake for 25 to 30 minutes, or until a toothpick inserted in center comes out clean.

Sprinkle a dish towel with confectioners' sugar. Invert cake onto towel. Peel away and discard wax paper. Neatly trim edges of cake roll. Starting from a short end, roll up cake in dish towel. Let cool on a cooling rack for 2 hours.

Put whipped topping in a small bowl. Stir in lemon zest.

Unroll cake and remove dish towel. Spread cake with whipped topping; reroll. Freeze until whipped topping is firm, about 2 hours.

To serve, cut into 16 slices. Sprinkle with blueberries.

Calories 273
Protein 5 g
Carbohydrates 57 g
Cholesterol 51 mg
Total Fat 3 g
Saturated 1 g
Polyunsaturated 1 g
Monounsaturated 1 g
Fiber 1 g
Sodium 314 mg

Black Devil's Food Cake

Serves 20

When the chocolate urge hits, try this rich, moist cake, which goes together as quickly as it disappears! Frost it with Seven-Minute Frosting (see page 549), dress it up with a dusting of confectioners' sugar, or enjoy it without any topping at all.

Vegetable oil spray
Flour for dusting pan
2 cups all-purpose flour
1¾ cups sugar
½ cup unsweetened cocoa powder
1 tablespoon baking soda
⅔ cup unsweetened applesauce
1 cup fat-free or low-fat buttermilk
2 tablespoons acceptable vegetable oil
1 cup strong coffee

Preheat oven to 350° F. Spray a 13 × 9 × 2-inch pan with vegetable oil spray. Dust with flour; shake off excess.

In a large mixing bowl, sift together flour, sugar, cocoa powder, and baking soda.

Whisk in remaining ingredients except coffee.

In a small saucepan, bring coffee to a boil over medium-high heat. Stir gently into batter; mixture will be soupy. Pour into pan.

Bake for 35 to 40 minutes, or until a toothpick inserted in center comes out clean. Serve warm or let cool completely.

Calories 140
Protein 2 g
Carbohydrates 30 g
Cholesterol 0 mg
Total Fat 2 g
Saturated 0 g
Polyunsaturated 1 g
Monounsaturated 0 g
Fiber 1 g
Sodium 202 mg

Nutmeg Cake

Serves 16

The tempting aroma of nutmeg will fill the air as this cake bakes. Cover and refrigerate any leftovers for up to five days.

Vegetable oil spray
Flour for dusting baking pan

CAKE
2 cups all-purpose flour
1 teaspoon baking powder
1 teaspoon baking soda
1 teaspoon freshly grated or ground nutmeg
1 cup sugar
½ cup unsweetened applesauce
Egg substitute equivalent to 2 eggs, or 2 eggs
1 tablespoon acceptable vegetable oil
1 teaspoon butter flavoring
1 cup fat-free or low-fat buttermilk, room temperature
½ teaspoon vanilla extract

TOPPING
⅔ cup uncooked quick-cooking oatmeal
⅓ cup firmly packed dark brown sugar
2 tablespoons finely chopped pecans, dry-roasted
½ teaspoon freshly grated or ground nutmeg
2 tablespoons light margarine, melted
3 tablespoons (about) fat-free milk

Calories 178
Protein 4 g
Carbohydrates 34 g
Cholesterol 1 mg
Total Fat 3 g
Saturated 1 g
Polyunsaturated 1 g
Monounsaturated 1 g
Fiber 1 g
Sodium 152 mg

Preheat oven to 350° F. Spray a 13 × 9 × 2-inch baking pan with vegetable oil spray. Dust pan with flour; shake off excess. Set aside.

For cake, in a medium bowl, sift together flour, baking powder, baking soda, and nutmeg.

In a large mixing bowl, beat sugar, applesauce, egg substitute, oil, and butter flavoring until smooth.

Gradually add flour mixture and buttermilk alternately, beginning and ending with flour; beat after each addition.

Stir in vanilla. Pour into baking pan.

Bake for 30 to 35 minutes, or until a toothpick inserted in center comes out clean.

Meanwhile, for topping, combine oatmeal, brown sugar, pecans, and nutmeg in a small bowl, stirring well.

Stir in margarine.

Slowly add milk, stirring constantly, until mixture is spreading consistency (some milk may remain). Spread on hot cake. Serve warm.

Cook's Tip

To heat leftovers, preheat broiler and broil pieces of cake about 6 inches from heat for 1 minute or until top of cake is slightly caramelized.

Wacky Cake

Serves 9

Children love to make this cake—and the cleanup is so easy.

Vegetable oil spray
1½ cups all-purpose flour
1 cup sugar
¼ cup unsweetened cocoa powder
1 teaspoon baking soda
1 teaspoon vanilla extract
1 teaspoon cider vinegar
2 tablespoons light margarine, melted
¼ cup unsweetened applesauce
1 cup water

Preheat oven to 350° F. Spray an 8-inch square cake pan with vegetable oil spray.

Sift together into pan the flour, sugar, cocoa powder, and baking soda.

Make three wells in flour mixture. Pour vanilla into the first well, vinegar into the second, and margarine into the third.

Put applesauce in a small bowl and gradually stir in water. Pour over batter and mix with a fork until entirely moist.

Bake for 30 minutes, or until a toothpick inserted in center comes out clean.

Calories 183
Protein 3 g
Carbohydrates 41 g
Cholesterol 0 mg
Total Fat 1 g
- Saturated 0 g
- Polyunsaturated 1 g
- Monounsaturated 0 g

Fiber 2 g
Sodium 157 mg

Easy Apple Cake

Serves 9

Double your pleasure with apples two ways in this moist cake. Serve it with Orange Sauce (see page 454) if desired.

Vegetable oil spray
2 cups diced apples (peeled or unpeeled) (2 to 3 medium)
¾ cup sugar
1½ cups unsifted all-purpose flour
½ cup raisins
1½ teaspoons pumpkin pie spice or apple pie spice
1 teaspoon baking powder
1 teaspoon baking soda
¼ teaspoon salt
⅓ cup unsweetened applesauce
Egg substitute equivalent to 1 egg, or 1 egg
1 tablespoon acceptable vegetable oil
1 teaspoon vanilla extract

Preheat oven to 350° F. Spray an 8-inch square cake pan with vegetable oil spray.

In a large bowl, combine apples and sugar. Set aside for about 10 minutes.

Meanwhile, in a medium bowl, combine flour, raisins, pumpkin pie spice, baking powder, baking soda, and salt, stirring well.

Stir remaining ingredients into apple mixture. Gradually stir flour mixture into apple mixture and stir again. Spread batter evenly in cake pan.

Bake for 35 to 40 minutes, or until a toothpick inserted in center comes out clean.

Cook's Tip on Pumpkin or Apple Pie Spice

To make your own spice mixture, start with four parts ground cinnamon, two parts each ground nutmeg and ground cloves, and one part each ground allspice and ground cardamom. Adjust the amounts to suit your own taste.

Calories 210
Protein 3 g
Carbohydrates 45 g
Cholesterol 0 mg
Total Fat 2 g
  Saturated 0 g
  Polyunsaturated 1 g
  Monounsaturated 0 g
Fiber 2 g
Sodium 274 mg

Carrot Cake

Serves 12

Enjoy a piece of this cake with hot tea, or pack one in your brown bag for a lunchtime treat.

Vegetable oil spray
Egg substitute equivalent to 2 eggs, or 2 eggs, beaten
½ cup sugar
½ cup unsweetened applesauce
½ cup plain nonfat or low-fat yogurt
¼ cup firmly packed light brown sugar
1 tablespoon acceptable vegetable oil
2 cups all-purpose flour
1½ cups grated carrots (2 medium)
½ cup raisins (optional)
¼ cup chopped walnuts, dry-roasted
1½ teaspoons ground cinnamon
1 teaspoon baking soda

Preheat oven to 350° F. Spray an 8-inch square cake pan with vegetable oil spray.

In a large bowl, whisk together egg substitute, sugar, applesauce, yogurt, brown sugar, and oil.

In another large bowl, whisk together remaining ingredients. Add to liquid mixture and whisk until just combined. Don't overmix. Pour batter into cake pan.

Bake for 30 to 35 minutes, or until a toothpick inserted in center comes out clean.

Calories 175
Protein 4 g
Carbohydrates 32 g
Cholesterol 0 mg
Total Fat 3 g
Saturated 0 g
Polyunsaturated 2 g
Monounsaturated 1 g
Fiber 1 g
Sodium 141 mg

Pineapple Upside-Down Cake

Serves 9

Luscious brown sugar and pineapple top this moist, light sponge cake.

2 tablespoons light margarine, melted
½ cup firmly packed light brown sugar
15¼-ounce can crushed pineapple in its own juice, drained (1½ cups)
1 cup cake flour
½ cup sugar
1½ teaspoons baking powder
½ cup fat-free milk
¼ cup unsweetened applesauce
1 tablespoon acceptable vegetable oil
½ teaspoon vanilla extract
Whites of 3 large eggs (see Cook's Tip, page 345)

Preheat oven to 350° F.

Pour margarine into an 8-inch square baking pan and sprinkle with brown sugar.

Spread pineapple evenly in pan. Set aside.

In a medium bowl, sift together flour, sugar, and baking powder. Stir in remaining ingredients except egg whites.

In a medium bowl, beat egg whites until they form stiff peaks. Using a rubber scraper, fold into flour mixture. Pour batter over pineapple.

Bake for 35 to 40 minutes, or until a toothpick inserted in center comes out clean.

Let cake cool slightly, then invert onto plate.

Cook's Tip on Cake Flour

Cake, or pastry, flour helps make baked goods tender and light. It is fine textured, with a high starch content. You can substitute 1 cup minus 2 tablespoons all-purpose flour for 1 cup cake flour.

Calories 207
Protein 3 g
Carbohydrates 44 g
Cholesterol 0 mg
Total Fat 3 g
  Saturated 0 g
  Polyunsaturated 1 g
  Monounsaturated 1 g
Fiber 1 g
Sodium 145 mg

Pumpkin Spice Cupcakes with Nutmeg Cream Topping

Serves 24; 1 cupcake per serving

Doubly moist, these tasty cupcakes abound with the flavors of autumn.

Vegetable oil spray

CUPCAKES

18.25-ounce box spice cake mix

1 cup canned pumpkin (not pumpkin pie filling)

1 cup unsweetened apple juice

Egg substitute equivalent to 2 large eggs, or 2 large eggs

Whites of 2 large eggs

1 teaspoon vanilla, butter, and nut flavoring or vanilla extract

NUTMEG CREAM TOPPING

8-ounce container frozen nonfat whipped topping, thawed

2 teaspoons ground nutmeg

Preheat oven to 350° F. Spray two 12-cup nonstick muffin tins with vegetable oil spray.

In a large mixing bowl, combine cupcake ingredients. Using electric mixer, beat on low speed for 30 seconds, scraping sides with rubber scraper. Increase to medium speed and beat for 2 minutes, scraping sides.

Fill muffin cups with equal amounts of batter.

Bake for 20 minutes, or until a toothpick inserted in center of muffins comes out clean.

Let cool on cooling racks for 15 minutes; remove cupcakes from muffin tins and let cool completely.

Meanwhile, put whipped topping in a medium bowl. Using a rubber scraper, gently fold nutmeg into whipped topping. Cover and refrigerate until ready to use.

When cupcakes are completely cool, frost with chilled topping.

Calories 124
Protein 2 g
Carbohydrates 21 g
Cholesterol 6 mg
Total Fat 3 g
- Saturated 1 g
- Polyunsaturated 0 g
- Monounsaturated 1 g

Fiber 1 g
Sodium 191 mg

Cook's Tip

You can make the cupcakes up to 24 hours in advance. Put them in an airtight container or cover with plastic wrap and refrigerate or keep at room temperature. You can also make the topping up to 24 hours in advance. Refrigerate it separately. Frost the cupcakes up to 8 hours in advance; cover and refrigerate.

Variation

Substitute a mixture of 2 teaspoons sugar and ½ teaspoon ground cinnamon for Nutmeg Cream Topping. Sprinkle on cupcakes. (calories 109; protein 2 g; carbohydrates 19 g; cholesterol 6 mg; total fat 3 g; saturated 1 g; polyunsaturated 0 g; monounsaturated 1 g; fiber 1 g; sodium 186 mg)

Banana Spice Cupcakes

Substitute 1 cup very ripe, well-mashed bananas (2 to 3 large) for pumpkin. Bake as directed above or make a sheet cake and bake at 325° F in a 13 × 9 × 2-inch nonstick baking pan for 45 minutes, or until cake tester or toothpick inserted in center comes out clean. Cool completely and top with Nutmeg Cream Topping or cinnamon sugar (see Variation). Cut into 24 squares. (Nutmeg Cream Topping: calories 130; protein 2 g; carbohydrates 23 g; cholesterol 6 mg; total fat 3 g; saturated 1 g; polyunsaturated 0 g; monounsaturated 1 g; fiber 0 g; sodium 191 mg) (Cinnamon Sugar Topping: calories 114; protein 2 g; carbohydrates 20 g; cholesterol 6 mg; total fat 3 g; saturated 1 g; polyunsaturated 0 g; monounsaturated 1 g; fiber 0 g; sodium 186 mg)

Chocolate Swirl Cheesecake

Serves 12

Swirl classic cheesecake batter with chocolate cheesecake batter, then add luscious caramel topping for good measure.

Vegetable oil spray
⅓ cup crushed chocolate graham cracker crumbs (about 9 small rectangles)
12 ounces fat-free cream cheese, softened
4 ounces reduced-fat cream cheese, softened
¾ cup sugar
Egg substitute equivalent to 3 eggs
8 ounces nonfat or light sour cream
1 teaspoon vanilla extract
⅓ cup unsweetened cocoa powder
¼ cup fat-free caramel apple dip

Calories 162
Protein 9 g
Carbohydrates 24 g
Cholesterol 7 mg
Total Fat 3 g
Saturated 1 g
Polyunsaturated 0 g
Monounsaturated 0 g
Fiber 1 g
Sodium 258 mg

Preheat oven to 325° F. Spray a 9-inch springform or 9-inch round cake pan with vegetable oil spray. If using cake pan, line bottom with cooking parchment or wax paper and spray again. Sprinkle graham cracker crumbs on bottom of pan. Set aside.

In a large mixing bowl, beat cream cheeses and sugar on medium-high setting until light and fluffy, about 3 minutes.

Add egg substitute and beat on medium setting until mixed in.

Add sour cream and vanilla. Beat on medium setting until smooth, about 30 seconds. Remove 1 cup batter and set aside.

Stir cocoa powder into remaining batter and beat on medium setting for 30 seconds, or until mixed in. Pour half the chocolate batter into springform pan (no need to spread over bottom of pan). Pour half the reserved white batter on chocolate batter. Spoon half the caramel apple dip onto white batter. Pour remaining chocolate batter into pan. Drop spoonfuls of remaining white batter onto chocolate batter. Spoon remaining caramel apple dip on top. Gently shake pan back and forth to distribute batter evenly. With a sharp knife, lightly swirl batter to create a marbled effect. (Don't overswirl or you'll have no pattern.)

Bake for 55 minutes, or until center is just set. Put pan on a cooling rack and let cool for 1 hour. Refrigerate for at least 3 hours. Run a knife along inside of pan. Release side of springform pan or invert cake pan onto a plate.

Cook's Tip on Slicing Cheesecake

To slice your cheesecake with ease, use a sharp knife dipped into hot water. Wipe the knife with a dish towel or paper towel after each slice; reheat the knife in hot water as needed.

Key Lime Cheesecake

Serves 10

Try this light, refreshing dessert the next time Key limes are available. You'll be glad you did!

4 cups fat-free or low-fat plain yogurt without gelatin

Vegetable oil spray

1 tablespoon light margarine

12 reduced-fat gingersnaps, finely crushed

1 tablespoon plus 1½ teaspoons grated Key lime zest (4 to 5 medium limes)

¼ cup Key lime juice

1 tablespoon plus 2 teaspoons cornstarch

1 teaspoon vanilla extract

Whites of 3 large eggs (see Cook's Tip, page 345)

½ cup sugar

½ cup plus 2 tablespoons nonfat or low-fat frozen whipped topping, thawed

10 Key lime slices (3 limes)

Put a double-thick layer of fine-mesh cheesecloth or paper coffee filters in a rustproof colander. Put colander in a bowl, leaving enough space for about 2 cups of whey (watery liquid) to drain out. Pour yogurt into colander and refrigerate for 8 to 10 hours.

After yogurt has drained completely, preheat oven to 375° F. Spray a 9-inch springform pan with vegetable oil spray.

Melt margarine. Put gingersnap crumbs in a small bowl; stir in margarine. Press mixture over bottom of pan.

Bake for 5 minutes. Let cool on cooling rack.

Reduce oven temperature to 325° F.

In a large bowl, whisk together drained yogurt, lime zest, lime juice, cornstarch, and vanilla.

In a medium mixing bowl, beat egg whites until foamy. Add sugar gradually, beating constantly until soft peaks form. Fold into yogurt mixture. Spoon into cooled crust.

Bake for 50 to 55 minutes, or until the center of the cheesecake springs back when lightly pressed. Let stand until cool, about 15 minutes. Refrigerate

Calories 121
Protein 5 g
Carbohydrates 24 g
Cholesterol 2 mg
Total Fat 1 g
Saturated 0 g
Polyunsaturated 0 g
Monounsaturated 0 g
Fiber 0 g
Sodium 163 mg

until serving time, at least 2 hours. To serve, cut the cheesecake into 10 wedges. Place on individual dessert plates. Spoon 1 tablespoon of whipped topping over each wedge and garnish with a lime slice.

Cook's Tip on Key Limes

If you don't live in Florida or a large city, you may have to go to a specialty market to get Key limes. Use fresh Key limes if you can, or substitute regular (Persian) limes.

Rum-Lime Pudding Cake

Serves 9

You'll feel as though you're in the Caribbean when you savor this dessert. Try serving it with glasses of pineapple-orange juice, decorated with paper umbrellas and slices of lime.

Vegetable oil spray
¼ cup plus 2 tablespoons egg substitute
1½ cups fat-free milk
⅔ cup sugar
¼ cup all-purpose flour
1 tablespoon grated lime zest
⅓ cup fresh lime juice (3 to 4 medium limes)
2 tablespoons acceptable margarine, melted and cooled
1 teaspoon rum extract
⅛ teaspoon salt
3 large egg whites
1 tablespoon sugar

Preheat oven to 350° F. Spray an 8-inch square baking pan with vegetable oil spray.

Put egg substitute, milk, sugar, flour, lime zest, lime juice, margarine, rum extract, and salt in a food processor or blender and process until smooth. Pour into a large bowl.

In a medium bowl, beat egg whites until soft peaks form. Add 1 tablespoon sugar and beat until whites are stiff. Stir about one third of whites into batter. Fold in remaining whites. Pour batter into baking pan. Set baking pan in a larger pan and add hot water to a depth of 2 inches.

Bake for 35 to 40 minutes, or until center is set (jiggle pan gently). Serve warm, or cover and refrigerate to serve chilled.

Calories 130
Protein 4 g
Carbohydrates 22 g
Cholesterol 1 mg
Total Fat 3 g
Saturated 1 g
Polyunsaturated 1 g
Monounsaturated 1 g
Fiber 0 g
Sodium 136 mg

Seven-Minute Frosting

Makes enough to frost two-layer cake

Fluffy and rich, this old favorite spreads easily over your cake. Try the delicious variations to jazz up a "plain" cake.

1½ cups sugar
⅓ cup water
Whites of 2 large eggs (see Cook's Tip, page 345)
¼ teaspoon cream of tartar or 1 tablespoon light corn syrup
1 teaspoon vanilla, rum, or sherry extract

Combine all ingredients except vanilla in top of double boiler. With electric mixer, beat on high speed for 1 minute. Put over boiling water (don't let water touch the top of double boiler) and beat on high speed for 7 minutes, or until stiff peaks form.

Remove top of double boiler from heat. Add vanilla. Beat on high speed for 2 minutes, or until spreading consistency.

Spread on completely cooled cake.

Lemon-Flavored Seven-Minute Frosting

Substitute 1 tablespoon fresh lemon juice for vanilla extract. Add ¼ teaspoon grated lemon zest during last minute of beating.

Seven-Minute Frosting with Fruit

Add 1 cup drained canned fruit, such as crushed pineapple, fruit cocktail, or mandarin oranges, to cooked frosting, or substitute fruit flavoring, such as orange extract, for vanilla extract. (calories 113; protein 1 g; carbohydrates 28 g; cholesterol 0 mg; total fat 0 g; saturated 0 g; polyunsaturated 0 g; monounsaturated 0 g; fiber 0 g; sodium 18 mg)

Calories 100
Protein 1 g
Carbohydrates 25 g
Cholesterol 0 mg
Total Fat 0 g
Saturated 0 g
Polyunsaturated 0 g
Monounsaturated 0 g
Fiber 0 g
Sodium 18 mg

Confectioners' Glaze

Serves 16; 1 tablespoon per serving

Use this versatile glaze to frost and decorate cupcakes, cakes, or cookies. You can even drizzle it on graham crackers or toast.

1 cup confectioners' sugar, sifted
½ teaspoon vanilla or rum extract
¼ cup fat-free milk

Put confectioners' sugar in a small bowl. Add vanilla, then gradually whisk in milk, whisking after each addition, until desired consistency.

Lemon or Orange Confectioners' Glaze

Replace milk with lemon or orange juice. (calories 31; protein 0 g; carbohydrates 8 g; cholesterol 0 mg; total fat 0 g; saturated 0 g; polyunsaturated 0 g; monounsaturated 0 g; fiber 0 g; sodium 0 mg)

Chocolate Confectioners' Glaze

Add 2 tablespoons unsweetened cocoa powder to confectioners' sugar and proceed as directed. (calories 32; protein 0 g; carbohydrates 8 g; cholesterol 0 mg; total fat 0 g; saturated 0 g; polyunsaturated 0 g; monounsaturated 0 g; fiber 0 g; sodium 2 mg)

Calories 31
Protein 0 g
Carbohydrates 8 g
Cholesterol 0 mg
Total Fat 0 g
Saturated 0 g
Polyunsaturated 0 g
Monounsaturated 0 g
Fiber 0 g
Sodium 2 mg

Pumpkin Pie

Serves 8

The whole family can enjoy this heart-healthy American tradition at Thanksgiving or any other time of the year.

FILLING
⅔ cup sugar
½ teaspoon ground cinnamon
½ teaspoon ground ginger
½ teaspoon ground nutmeg
Pinch of ground cloves
1½ cups canned pumpkin
1½ cups fat-free evaporated milk
¼ cup brandy
Whites of 3 large eggs, slightly beaten
1 teaspoon vanilla extract
½ teaspoon grated orange zest

9-inch low-fat pie shell, unbaked

Preheat oven to 450° F.

In a large bowl, combine sugar, cinnamon, ginger, nutmeg, and cloves.

Add pumpkin, evaporated milk, brandy, egg whites, vanilla, and orange zest. Beat until smooth. Pour into pie shell.

Bake for 10 minutes. Reduce heat to 325° F and bake for 45 minutes, or until a knife inserted in center comes out clean.

Cook's Tip on Pie Shells

Pie shells can be high in fat. When shopping, select the pie shell that has the lowest fat.

Calories 216
Protein 6 g
Carbohydrates 33 g
Cholesterol 2 mg
Total Fat 5 g
Saturated 1 g
Polyunsaturated 2 g
Monounsaturated 2 g
Fiber 2 g
Sodium 190 mg

Raspberry Chiffon Pie

Serves 8

A piece of this pie would be just the right treat for Valentine's Day. Sprinkle a small amount of cocoa powder on each dessert plate before you place the slice of pie on it.

FILLING

10-ounce package frozen sweetened raspberries (about 1½ cups), thawed

½ cup cold water

1 tablespoon unflavored gelatin

¼ cup sugar

1 tablespoon all-purpose flour

2 tablespoons fresh lemon juice

⅓ cup nonfat dry milk

⅓ cup ice water

1 tablespoon fresh lemon juice

2 tablespoons sugar

9-inch low-fat pie shell (see Cook's Tip, page 551), baked and cooled

Chill a small mixing bowl and beaters of electric mixer.

Drain raspberries, reserving juice. Reserve 6 firm berries for garnish.

Pour ½ cup water into cup or small bowl. Stir in gelatin to soften.

In a medium saucepan, combine ¼ cup sugar and flour.

Stir in raspberry juice and softened gelatin. Heat slowly over low heat until sugar is dissolved, stirring frequently.

Remove saucepan from heat and stir in 2 tablespoons lemon juice and berries. Let cool until thick and syrupy but not set, about 8 to 10 minutes.

In chilled bowl, combine milk and ⅓ cup ice water. Beat on medium-high with chilled beaters for 3 to 4 minutes, or until soft peaks form.

Add 1 tablespoon lemon juice and beat for 3 to 4 minutes, or until stiff.

Gradually add 2 tablespoons sugar and beat on medium-high for about 30 seconds. Fold into raspberry mixture.

Calories 191
Protein 3 g
Carbohydrates 37 g
Cholesterol 1 mg
Total Fat 3 g
    Saturated 1 g
    Polyunsaturated 0 g
    Monounsaturated 0 g
Fiber 2 g
Sodium 114 mg

Pour into pie shell. Cover and refrigerate until firm, about 2 hours. To serve, garnish with reserved raspberries.

Cook's Tip on Whipping Dry Milk

The keys to success in whipping nonfat dry milk are chilling the mixing bowl and beaters and beating lemon juice into the mixed powder and liquid.

Cook's Tip on Gelatin

Soften gelatin in a cold liquid so that it will dissolve more readily when heated. Never boil gelatin. Boiling destroys its jelling ability. One envelope of unflavored gelatin (1 tablespoon) is enough for about 2 cups of liquid.

Fresh Strawberry Pie

Serves 8

For an extra treat, serve each slice of pie with a dollop of thawed nonfat dairy topping.

FILLING

1 tablespoon cold water

1½ teaspoons unflavored gelatin

6 cups fresh strawberries, hulled (3 pints)

1 cup water

½ cup sugar

3 tablespoons cornstarch

1 teaspoon grated orange zest

⅛ teaspoon almond extract

Few drops of red food coloring

9-inch low-fat pie shell (see Cook's Tip, page 551), baked and cooled

In a cup or small bowl, combine 1 tablespoon water and gelatin (a fork works well). Set aside to let gelatin soften.

Measure 4 cups whole strawberries of uniform size. Place strawberries, points up, on pie shell.

In a medium bowl, crush remaining strawberries with a potato masher or fork. Pour into medium saucepan and stir in water, sugar, and cornstarch. Cook over medium-high heat until thick and clear, 3 to 4 minutes, stirring constantly.

Remove from heat and add gelatin. Let cool for about 10 minutes.

Stir zest, almond extract, and food coloring into strawberry mixture. Pour into pie shell, cover, and refrigerate for several hours before serving.

Calories 165
Protein 2 g
Carbohydrates 29 g
Cholesterol 0 mg
Total Fat 5 g
- Saturated 1 g
- Polyunsaturated 2 g
- Monounsaturated 2 g

Fiber 3 g
Sodium 95 mg

Deep-Dish Cobbler

Serves 8

Cobbler is the perfect "comfort food" dessert. Take advantage of whatever fruit is in season.

FILLING

6 cups fresh or frozen fruit (blueberries, cherries, peaches, blackberries, raspberries, apples, apricots, or any combination)

⅓ to ½ cup all-purpose flour (depends on juiciness of fruit)

½ cup sugar

1½ tablespoons lemon zest (2 medium lemons)

9-inch low-fat pie shell (see Cook's Tip, page 551), unbaked

Preheat oven to 425° F.

In a large bowl, combine filling ingredients, stirring well. Pour into a 9-inch deep-dish pie pan.

Place pie shell over fruit and pinch around edge of pan to seal. Cut slits in crust.

Bake for about 50 minutes, or until golden brown.

Cook's Tip

If the fruit seems very juicy, use about ½ cup flour; for fruit with very little juice, use about ⅓ cup.

Calories 206
Protein 2 g
Carbohydrates 40 g
Cholesterol 0 mg
Total Fat 5 g
Saturated 1 g
Polyunsaturated 2 g
Monounsaturated 2 g
Fiber 3 g
Sodium 99 mg

Frozen Mocha Yogurt Pie

Serves 8

Kids—of every age—will have fun using chocolate syrup to decorate the dessert plates for this rich pie.

Vegetable oil spray

¾ cup crushed chocolate graham crackers (about 5 rectangles)

FILLING

2 cups nonfat or low-fat frozen vanilla yogurt, slightly softened

2 cups nonfat or low-fat frozen coffee yogurt, slightly softened

2 cups nonfat or low-fat frozen chocolate yogurt, slightly softened

1 cup fat-free chocolate syrup

Spray a 9-inch pie pan with vegetable oil spray. Sprinkle with graham cracker crumbs.

Put vanilla yogurt on an 8-inch plate (such as a small dinner plate). Using a spoon or sturdy spatula, press yogurt down and out to sides of plate. (This will help when you put yogurt in pie plate.) Slip vanilla yogurt layer into pie plate; using spatula, carefully spread yogurt to edges.

Repeat with coffee yogurt, then with chocolate yogurt. Cover with double layer of plastic wrap and freeze for at least 2 hours.

To serve, cut pie into 8 wedges. Drizzle 2 tablespoons chocolate syrup in a decorative pattern on a pretty dessert plate. Place a pie wedge on syrup. Repeat with remaining syrup and pie.

Calories 318
Protein 6 g
Carbohydrates 70 g
Cholesterol 1 mg
Total Fat 1 g
Saturated 0 g
Polyunsaturated 0 g
Monounsaturated 0 g
Fiber 1 g
Sodium 256 mg

Cook's Tip on Cutting Frozen Desserts

Dipping a sharp knife into hot water makes cutting frozen desserts easier.

Baked Lemon Cheese Pie

Serves 8

Lemon lovers, rejoice! You'll almost swoon over this refreshing treat. Serve with sparkling water or iced tea garnished with lemon slices.

CRUST

1 cup reduced-fat graham cracker crumbs (15 crackers)

3 tablespoons light margarine, melted

1 teaspoon grated lemon zest

FILLING

1⅓ cups nonfat or low-fat cottage cheese, drained

⅔ cup Yogurt Cheese (see page 16)

Egg substitute equivalent to 2 eggs, or 2 eggs

½ cup sugar

⅓ cup fat-free milk

1 tablespoon grated lemon zest

5 tablespoons fresh lemon juice (2 medium lemons)

3 tablespoons all-purpose flour

¼ teaspoon vanilla extract

Preheat oven to 300° F.

In a small bowl, combine crust ingredients, stirring well. Remove 1 tablespoon of mixture and set aside. Press remaining mixture on bottom and up side of 9-inch pie pan.

Bake for 5 minutes. Remove from oven and let cool. Leave oven on.

For filling, in a food processor or blender, process cottage cheese and yogurt cheese until creamy.

Add egg substitute slowly, processing constantly.

Gradually add sugar and milk, processing well after each addition.

Add remaining filling ingredients, processing until smooth. Pour into cooled pie shell. Sprinkle with reserved crumbs.

Bake for 1½ hours, or until filling is set. Cover and refrigerate for several hours.

Calories 196
Protein 10 g
Carbohydrates 33 g
Cholesterol 5 mg
Total Fat 3 g
- Saturated 1 g
- Polyunsaturated 1 g
- Monounsaturated 1 g

Fiber 0 g
Sodium 333 mg

Chocolate Chess Pie

Serves 8

Chess pie is the original "transparent pie," a traditional southern dessert whose shimmering filling comes from loads of eggs, butter, and sugar. Add chocolate and reduce the fat, as we've done, and you have the best of all possible worlds. The gingersnap piecrust provides lots of flavor, yet doesn't dominate the chocolate.

GINGERSNAP PIECRUST

1½ cups crushed reduced-fat gingersnaps

2 tablespoons light margarine, softened

1 tablespoon honey

FILLING

½ cup plus 1 tablespoon unsweetened cocoa powder

⅓ cup firmly packed light brown sugar

1 ounce unsweetened chocolate, melted

Egg substitute equivalent to 4 eggs

1 cup dark corn syrup

2 tablespoons bourbon or coffee

1 teaspoon vanilla extract

Time-Saver: Use a commercial low-fat graham cracker piecrust.

Preheat oven to 350° F.

In a medium bowl, combine piecrust ingredients, stirring well. Press over bottom and up side of a 9-inch glass pie pan.

Bake for 10 minutes. Leave oven on.

Meanwhile, for filling, combine cocoa and brown sugar in a large bowl, stirring until smooth.

Stir in chocolate, then add remaining filling ingredients, whisking or beating until well combined. Pour into baked piecrust.

Bake for 35 minutes.

Cook's Tip

It isn't necessary for this crust to cool before you fill it.

Calories 295
Protein 6 g
Carbohydrates 57 g
Cholesterol 0 mg
Total Fat 5 g
Saturated 2 g
Polyunsaturated 1 g
Monounsaturated 1 g
Fiber 3 g
Sodium 264 mg

Chocolate Mousse in Meringue Shells

Serves 8

With its double dose of chocolate and pretty meringue "bowls," this chocolate mousse is as elegant and delicious as the French version.

1 envelope unflavored gelatin
1½ cups fat-free milk, divided use
⅓ cup sifted unsweetened cocoa powder
¼ cup sugar
½ teaspoon cornstarch
½ teaspoon vanilla extract
½ teaspoon almond extract
Whites of 3 large eggs (see Cook's Tip, page 345)
6 tablespoons sugar
1 tablespoon water
¼ teaspoon cream of tartar
8 individual Meringue Shells (see page 571)
2 tablespoons plus 2 teaspoons nonfat or low-fat chocolate syrup

In a medium saucepan, whisk together gelatin and ½ cup milk. Let stand for 1 minute. Cook over medium heat, whisking constantly, until gelatin is completely dissolved, about 3 minutes.

Whisk in 1 cup milk, cocoa powder, ¼ cup sugar, and cornstarch. Cook over medium heat for 5 to 7 minutes, or until slightly thickened, whisking constantly.

Whisk in vanilla and almond extracts. Transfer to a bowl and put plastic wrap directly on surface. Refrigerate for about 1 hour.

In top of a double boiler, beat egg whites, 6 tablespoons sugar, water, and cream of tartar. Beating constantly with a hand mixer, cook over low heat until mixture registers 160° F. Spoon into a large bowl and beat constantly until soft peaks form. Fold chocolate mixture into egg white mixture. Cover and refrigerate for 3 hours. Spoon into meringue shells and drizzle each with 1 teaspoon chocolate syrup.

Calories 169
Protein 5 g
Carbohydrates 38 g
Cholesterol 1 mg
Total Fat 1 g
Saturated 0 g
Polyunsaturated 0 g
Monounsaturated 0 g
Fiber 2 g
Sodium 114 mg

Chocolate-Berry Pie

Serves 8

A delicate, crunchy meringue crust balances beautifully with a rich chocolate layer and fresh berries.

Vegetable oil spray

MERINGUE CRUST

Whites of 2 large eggs, room temperature (see Cook's Tip, page 345)

½ teaspoon vanilla extract

¼ teaspoon cream of tartar

⅔ cup sugar

FILLING

Egg substitute equivalent to 1 egg, or 1 egg

⅓ cup unsweetened cocoa powder

2 tablespoons sugar

2 tablespoons cornstarch

14-ounce can fat-free sweetened condensed milk

1 cup water

½ teaspoon vanilla extract

TOPPING

¾ cup fresh raspberries or sliced fresh strawberries

Calories 249
Protein 7 g
Carbohydrates 55 g
Cholesterol 3 mg
Total Fat 1 g
Saturated 0 g
Polyunsaturated 0 g
Monounsaturated 0 g
Fiber 2 g
Sodium 95 mg

Preheat oven to 300° F. Spray a 9-inch pie pan with vegetable oil spray.

For crust, in a small mixer bowl, combine egg whites, vanilla, and cream of tartar. With electric mixer, beat on medium speed until soft peaks form. Add sugar, 1 tablespoon at a time, beating on high speed until stiff peaks form and sugar has almost dissolved. Spread mixture in pie pan, building up side slightly to form a shell.

Bake for 40 minutes. Turn off oven. Let meringue dry in oven, with door closed, for about 45 minutes. Remove meringue from oven and let cool on cooling rack.

Meanwhile, for filling, pour egg substitute into a small bowl. Set aside.

In a heavy medium saucepan, combine cocoa powder, sugar, and cornstarch, stirring to blend.

Whisk in milk and water. Cook over medium-high heat until mixture comes to a boil, about 4 minutes, whisking constantly. Reduce heat to medium. Boil gently, whisking constantly, until thickened, about 1 minute. Continue to cook for 2 minutes, whisking constantly.

Whisk a small amount of hot chocolate mixture into egg substitute; return all to saucepan. Cook for 1 minute, whisking constantly. Whisk in vanilla extract.

Pour filling into a medium bowl. Place plastic wrap directly on surface of filling and let cool at room temperature for 30 minutes. Pour into meringue shell, spreading evenly.

To serve, top with berries.

Cook's Tip on Freezing Raspberries

Rinse raspberries gently and quickly in a bowl of cold water. Drain the berries and put them on paper towels to absorb the excess water. Put the berries in a single layer on a baking sheet and freeze. Freeze the berries in airtight containers or plastic freezer bags for up to one year.

Berry-Filled Meringues

Serves 4

A crisp meringue shell with a thickened berry sauce makes a light, refreshing dessert. Experiment with strawberries, blueberries, and blackberries.

10-ounce package frozen unsweetened berries, thawed
1 tablespoon sugar
1½ teaspoons cornstarch
1 tablespoon fresh lemon juice
¼ teaspoon ground ginger
4 individual Meringue Shells (see page 571)

Calories 90
Protein 1 g
Carbohydrates 22 g
Cholesterol 0 mg
Total Fat 0 g
Saturated 0 g
Polyunsaturated 0 g
Monounsaturated 0 g
Fiber 2 g
Sodium 28 mg

Drain berries, reserving ½ cup juice.

In a medium saucepan, combine berry juice, sugar, and cornstarch. Cook over medium-high heat until thickened, 2 to 3 minutes, stirring constantly.

Stir in berries, lemon juice, and ginger. Spoon into meringue shells and serve.

Crustless Apple Pie

Serves 8

Moist and rich, this pie is also easy and tasty—it's a real winner! Serve it warm or chilled.

Vegetable oil spray
Whites of 2 large eggs, or egg substitute equivalent to 1 egg
¾ cup sugar
2 tablespoons light brown sugar
1 teaspoon baking powder
1 teaspoon vanilla extract
½ teaspoon ground cinnamon
½ teaspoon grated lemon zest
⅛ teaspoon ground nutmeg
½ cup all-purpose flour
1 cup diced peeled apples (1 to 1½ medium)
¼ cup chopped walnuts, dry-roasted

Preheat oven to 350° F. Spray an 8-inch pie pan with vegetable oil spray.

In a large mixing bowl, beat egg whites, sugars, baking powder, vanilla, cinnamon, lemon zest, and nutmeg until smooth and fluffy.

Beat in flour until smooth and well blended.

Stir in apples. Turn into pie pan and sprinkle with nuts.

Bake for 30 minutes, or until golden brown. Pie will puff up as it cooks, then collapse as it cools.

Calories 151
Protein 2 g
Carbohydrates 31 g
Cholesterol 0 mg
Total Fat 3 g
Saturated 0 g
Polyunsaturated 2 g
Monounsaturated 1 g
Fiber 1 g
Sodium 89 mg

Apple Raisin Crunch

Serves 6

Enjoy this versatile dessert as prepared or spoon it over fat-free ice cream or frozen yogurt.

Vegetable oil spray

FILLING

2 pounds Granny Smith apples, peeled, cored, and sliced (about 5½ cups) or 2 20-ounce cans unsweetened sliced apples

½ cup raisins

½ cup fresh orange juice (1 to 2 medium oranges)

⅓ cup sugar

¼ teaspoon ground nutmeg

TOPPING

¼ cup firmly packed dark brown sugar

¾ cup uncooked quick-cooking oatmeal

½ teaspoon ground cinnamon

2 tablespoons light margarine, melted

Preheat oven to 350° F. Spray an 8-inch square baking pan with vegetable oil spray.

For filling, combine ingredients except nutmeg in baking pan. Sprinkle with nutmeg.

In a small bowl, combine topping ingredients, stirring well. Sprinkle evenly over fruit.

Bake for 40 minutes. Let cool slightly before serving.

Calories 260
Protein 3 g
Carbohydrates 60 g
Cholesterol 0 mg
Total Fat 3 g
Saturated 1 g
Polyunsaturated 1 g
Monounsaturated 1 g
Fiber 4 g
Sodium 29 mg

Cherry Crisp

Serves 9

Sprinkle crunchy oatmeal topping over juicy red cherries for a luscious dessert.

Vegetable oil spray

TOPPING

¾ cup uncooked rolled oatmeal
⅓ cup all-purpose flour
2 tablespoons light margarine
¼ cup sugar
¼ cup firmly packed light brown sugar

FILLING

2 16-ounce cans pitted tart cherries in water
½ cup sugar
3 tablespoons cornstarch
1 tablespoon fresh lemon juice
¼ teaspoon ground cinnamon
¼ teaspoon ground nutmeg

Preheat oven to 350° F. Spray an 8-inch square baking pan with vegetable oil spray.

For topping, in a medium bowl, combine oatmeal and flour.

Cut in margarine with a fork or pastry blender until mixture is crumbly.

Add ¼ cup sugar and brown sugar, stirring well.

For filling, drain cherries, reserving juice. Set both aside.

In a medium saucepan, combine remaining ingredients and cherry juice. Cook over medium-high heat until sauce is thick and clear, 3 to 4 minutes, whisking occasionally.

Stir in cherries. Pour into baking pan and sprinkle with topping.

Bake for 30 minutes, or until golden brown.

Calories 188
Protein 2 g
Carbohydrates 43 g
Cholesterol 0 mg
Total Fat 1 g
Saturated 0 g
Polyunsaturated 1 g
Monounsaturated 0 g
Fiber 2 g
Sodium 26 mg

Cook's Tip on Canned Cherries

It's a good idea to check canned cherries carefully before using them. Occasionally, a pit is accidentally left in the can.

Deep-Dish Fruit Crisp

Serves 8

Take advantage of fresh fruits in season, but remember this recipe in the winter, too. The aroma of fruit and spices can help chase away those winter blahs.

FILLING

6 cups fresh or unsweetened frozen fruit (blueberries, blackberries, cherries, peaches, raspberries, apples, apricots, or any combination)

¼ cup all-purpose flour

¼ cup firmly packed light brown sugar

2 teaspoons lemon zest

TOPPING

½ cup uncooked quick-cooking oatmeal

¼ cup all-purpose flour

½ cup firmly packed light brown sugar

2 tablespoons light margarine

½ teaspoon ground cinnamon

¼ teaspoon ground nutmeg or mace

¼ teaspoon ground allspice

Preheat oven to 350° F.

In a large bowl, combine filling ingredients, stirring well. Pour into a 9-inch deep-dish pie pan.

Put topping ingredients in a small bowl. Mix with a fork, cutting margarine into other ingredients until slightly crumbly. Sprinkle over fruit.

Bake for 30 to 35 minutes, or until golden brown.

Calories 221
Protein 3 g
Carbohydrates 49 g
Cholesterol 0 mg
Total Fat 3 g
Saturated 1 g
Polyunsaturated 1 g
Monounsaturated 1 g
Fiber 3 g
Sodium 26 mg

Sugar and Spice Peach Shortcake

Serves 4

Less sweet and spicier than many other shortcakes, this one is perfect not only for dinner but for breakfast as well.

Vegetable oil spray
1 pound frozen unsweetened peach slices, thawed
3 tablespoons sugar
1 tablespoon cornstarch
1 teaspoon vanilla extract
½ teaspoon vanilla, butter, and nut flavoring or vanilla extract
1 teaspoon apple pie spice or pumpkin pie spice
½ cup plus 2 tablespoons all-purpose flour
2 tablespoons sugar
1 tablespoon acceptable margarine
½ teaspoon baking powder
⅛ teaspoon baking soda
⅓ cup nonfat or low-fat buttermilk or fat-free milk
⅛ teaspoon apple pie spice or pumpkin pie spice

Preheat oven to 450° F. Spray an 8-inch square nonstick baking pan with vegetable oil spray.

In a large bowl, combine peaches; 3 tablespoons sugar; cornstarch; vanilla extract; vanilla, butter, and nut flavoring; and 1 teaspoon apple pie spice, stirring well. Pour into baking pan.

In a food processor or blender, combine flour, 2 tablespoons sugar, margarine, baking powder, and baking soda. Pulse until well blended. Put in bowl that held peaches. Pour buttermilk into flour mixture. Stir with a rubber scraper, scraping bottom and sides until just blended.

Spoon mixture on top of peaches, making 4 mounds. Sprinkle with ⅛ teaspoon apple pie spice.

Bake for 25 minutes, or until shortcake begins to flake in center. Let cool on cooling rack for 10 minutes to set slightly.

Calories 228
Protein 4 g
Carbohydrates 43 g
Cholesterol 1 mg
Total Fat 4 g
Saturated 1 g
Polyunsaturated 1 g
Monounsaturated 1 g
Fiber 3 g
Sodium 156 mg

Lemony Blueberry Shortcake

Substitute slightly thawed frozen blueberries for peaches, and apple pie spice for vanilla, butter, and nut flavoring. Add 1½ teaspoons grated lemon zest. (calories 237; protein 3 g; carbohydrates 48 g; cholesterol 1 mg; total fat 4 g; saturated 1 g; polyunsaturated 1 g; monounsaturated 2 g; fiber 4 g; sodium 157 mg)

Peach Clafouti

Serves 8

A clafouti usually consists of a layer of batter topped with fresh fruit. Here, we've sandwiched the fruit between two layers of batter instead—a double treat.

Vegetable oil spray
1¼ cups fat-free milk
1 cup all-purpose flour
Egg substitute equivalent to 3 eggs
¼ cup firmly packed light brown sugar
1 tablespoon vanilla extract
1 teaspoon almond extract
½ teaspoon ground cinnamon
¼ teaspoon ground nutmeg or mace
¼ teaspoon salt
1½ pounds fresh peaches, peeled and sliced (about 3½ cups)

TOPPING

1½ teaspoons sugar
¼ teaspoon ground cinnamon
3 tablespoons pine nuts, dry-roasted

Preheat oven to 350° F. Spray a 9-inch square baking pan with vegetable oil spray.

In a food processor or blender, process milk, flour, egg substitute, brown sugar, vanilla, almond extract, ½ teaspoon cinnamon, nutmeg, and salt until smooth. Pour about ¼ cup batter into baking pan.

Bake for 5 to 10 minutes, or until set.

Evenly distribute peaches on cooked batter. Pour remaining batter on top.

Bake for 20 minutes.

Meanwhile, in a small bowl, combine sugar and ¼ teaspoon cinnamon. Sprinkle pine nuts, then sugar mixture, over clafouti.

Bake for 40 minutes, or until center is set. Serve warm.

Calories 172
Protein 7 g
Carbohydrates 30 g
Cholesterol 1 mg
Total Fat 3 g
Saturated 1 g
Polyunsaturated 1 g
Monounsaturated 1 g
Fiber 2 g
Sodium 139 mg

Cherry-Filled Phyllo Rollovers

Serves 4

You don't need chopsticks to enjoy these flaky dessert "egg rolls."

16-ounce can pitted tart red cherries in water, drained
¼ cup sugar
1 tablespoon cornstarch
1 teaspoon vanilla extract
½ teaspoon almond extract
4 sheets frozen phyllo dough, thawed
Butter-flavored vegetable oil spray
1 teaspoon acceptable margarine, melted
2 teaspoons sugar
⅛ teaspoon ground cinnamon
1 teaspoon acceptable margarine, melted

Preheat oven to 400° F.

In a small saucepan, combine cherries, ¼ cup sugar, and cornstarch, stirring to dissolve cornstarch. Bring to a boil over medium-high heat, then stir. Boil for 1 to 2 minutes, or until thickened, stirring occasionally.

Stir in vanilla and almond extracts.

Keeping unused phyllo covered with a damp dish towel, lightly spray 1 sheet of dough with vegetable oil spray. Working quickly, fold dough in half, bringing short ends together. Spoon one fourth of cherry mixture about 4 inches from one end; fold that end over cherry mixture. Fold sides over cherry mixture and roll up (should resemble an egg roll). Place seam side down on a nonstick baking sheet. Repeat with remaining phyllo and cherry mixture.

Brush tops of rollovers with 1 teaspoon melted margarine. Bake for 15 minutes.

Meanwhile, in a small bowl or cup, combine 2 teaspoons sugar with cinnamon.

Place rollovers on cooling rack. Brush with 1 teaspoon margarine and sprinkle with cinnamon sugar. Let cool for 15 minutes.

Calories 183
Protein 2 g
Carbohydrates 37 g
Cholesterol 0 mg
Total Fat 3 g
Saturated 1 g
Polyunsaturated 1 g
Monounsaturated 1 g
Fiber 2 g
Sodium 122 mg

Oat Crumb Piecrust

Serves 8

This crust smells so wonderful as it bakes that you'll want to eat it even before adding the filling!

Vegetable oil spray
1 cup graham cracker crumbs
⅓ cup uncooked quick-cooking oatmeal
2 tablespoons sugar
1 teaspoon freshly grated orange zest
½ teaspoon ground cinnamon
¼ to ½ teaspoon freshly grated lemon zest
2½ tablespoons light margarine, melted

Calories 106
Protein 2 g
Carbohydrates 18 g
Cholesterol 0 mg
Total Fat 3 g
Saturated 1 g
Polyunsaturated 1 g
Monounsaturated 1 g
Fiber 1 g
Sodium 113 mg

Preheat oven to 375° F. Spray a 9-inch pie pan with vegetable oil spray.

In a medium bowl, combine remaining ingredients except margarine, stirring well.

Stir in margarine. Put mixture in pie pan. Using back of fork, press on bottom and up side of pan to form a shell.

Bake for 8 to 10 minutes, or until lightly toasted. Cool before filling.

Gingersnap and Graham Cracker Crust

Serves 8

The flavorful pairing of gingersnaps and graham crackers makes this crust almost a dessert in itself! The corn syrup and apple juice bind the dough and make it easy to shape the piecrust.

¾ cup crushed low-fat graham crackers (about 9 squares)
¾ cup crushed low-fat gingersnaps (about 18 cookies)
2 tablespoons corn syrup
2 tablespoons unsweetened apple juice

In a medium bowl, mix all ingredients with a spoon. Using your fingers, press mixture evenly in a 9-inch pie pan.

The crust is ready to fill and bake. If you need a prebaked crust, bake it at 350° F for 10 minutes, then cool and fill.

Calories 99
Protein 1 g
Carbohydrates 22 g
Cholesterol 0 mg
Total Fat 1 g
  Saturated 0 g
  Polyunsaturated 0 g
  Monounsaturated 0 g
Fiber 0 g
Sodium 184 mg

Meringue Shell

Serves 8

Fill this meringue shell with juicy fruit fillings, nonfat frozen yogurt, or pudding.

Vegetable oil spray
Whites of 3 large eggs (see Cook's Tip, page 345)
¼ teaspoon cream of tartar
⅔ cup sugar
¼ teaspoon vanilla extract

Preheat oven to 275° F.

In a mixing bowl, combine egg whites and cream of tartar. Beat on medium until foamy.

Gradually add sugar, beating on medium-high until stiff, glossy peaks form. Add vanilla and beat for 1 minute.

To make one piecrust, spray a 9-inch pie pan with vegetable oil spray. Spread mixture in pie pan, building up so side is thicker than bottom.

To make individual piecrusts, put cooking parchment on baking sheet. Shape mixture into eight 5-inch-diameter circles. Make a depression in each with a spoon.

Bake for 1¼ hours, or until dry and a light creamy color. Let cool, then remove carefully from pan or baking sheet.

Calories 71
Protein 1 g
Carbohydrates 17 g
Cholesterol 0 mg
Total Fat 0 g
  Saturated 0 g
  Polyunsaturated 0 g
  Monounsaturated 0 g
Fiber 0 g
Sodium 40 mg

Chocolate Oatmeal Cookies

Serves 30; 2 cookies per serving

When your sweet tooth craves a nibble of chocolate, try these cookies.

1½ cups firmly packed light brown sugar
½ cup sifted unsweetened cocoa powder
½ cup fat-free milk
¼ cup light margarine, softened
¼ cup pureed prunes, unsweetened baby food prunes, or fat-free fruit-based oil and margarine replacement
2 teaspoons vanilla extract
1¾ cups all-purpose flour
2½ teaspoons baking powder
¼ teaspoon salt
1½ cups uncooked quick-cooking oatmeal

Preheat oven to 350° F.

In a large mixing bowl, cream brown sugar, cocoa powder, milk, margarine, prunes, and vanilla.

In a small bowl, sift together flour, baking powder, and salt. Beat into margarine mixture.

Stir in oatmeal.

Drop by teaspoonfuls onto ungreased baking sheets. (You should have about 60 cookies.)

Bake for 7 to 9 minutes, or until set in the center.

Calories 105
Protein 2 g
Carbohydrates 23 g
Cholesterol 0 mg
Total Fat 1 g
Saturated 0 g
Polyunsaturated 0 g
Monounsaturated 0 g
Fiber 1 g
Sodium 77 mg

Chewy Chocolate Chip Cookies

Serves 16; 3 cookies per serving

Soft, chewy, packed with chocolate—these cookies are delightful.

½ cup firmly packed light brown sugar
¼ cup sugar
1 large egg
3 tablespoons acceptable margarine, softened
1 teaspoon vanilla, butter, and nut flavoring or vanilla extract
¾ cup self-rising flour
⅓ cup chocolate mini morsels
Vegetable oil spray

Preheat oven to 350° F.

In a medium mixing bowl, combine sugars, egg, margarine, and flavoring. Using an electric mixer, beat until well blended.

Gradually add flour to batter, beating on low speed.

Using a rubber scraper, stir in chocolate morsels, scraping sides of bowl.

Liberally spray two nonstick baking sheets with vegetable oil spray. Spoon 12 slightly rounded teaspoons of dough onto one baking sheet. Bake for 9 minutes.

Meanwhile, on a second baking sheet, spoon out enough dough for 12 cookies.

When cookies have baked for 9 minutes (they may not appear done), put baking sheet on cooling rack for 1½ minutes. Don't leave cookies on baking sheet more than 2 minutes; they will harden and crumble. Put wax paper on counter. Using a flat, thin metal spatula (plastic is too thick), gently transfer first batch of cookies to wax paper. When cookies have cooled, place between layers of wax paper to keep them from sticking together.

Repeat baking until all dough is used.

Calories 110
Protein 1 g
Carbohydrates 18 g
Cholesterol 13 mg
Total Fat 4 g
Saturated 1 g
Polyunsaturated 1 g
Monounsaturated 1 g
Fiber 0 g
Sodium 106 mg

Peanut Butter Cookies

Serves 30; 2 cookies per serving

Enjoy these cookies fresh from the oven with a glass of ice-cold fat-free milk.

Vegetable oil spray
¼ cup light margarine, softened
¾ cup firmly packed light brown sugar
½ cup sugar
⅓ cup reduced-fat peanut butter
Egg substitute equivalent to 1 egg, or 1 egg
¼ cup unsweetened applesauce
½ teaspoon baking soda
2½ cups all-purpose flour
1 teaspoon vanilla extract

Preheat oven to 350° F. Spray baking sheets with vegetable oil spray.

In a large mixing bowl, cream margarine. Gradually add sugars, beating after each addition, until creamy.

Add peanut butter, egg substitute, applesauce, and baking soda; beat well.

Gradually add flour to batter, beating after each addition.

Stir in vanilla.

Roll dough into 60 balls about the size of a pecan or the bowl of a measuring teaspoon. Put on baking sheets. Flatten balls slightly with back of wet fork.

Bake for 12 to 15 minutes, or until light brown.

Calories 95
Protein 2 g
Carbohydrates 18 g
Cholesterol 0 mg
Total Fat 2 g
 Saturated 0 g
 Polyunsaturated 1 g
 Monounsaturated 1 g
Fiber 0 g
Sodium 52 mg

Cook's Tip on Cookie Dough

Cookies are easier to roll if you moisten your hands first with cold water. Also, dip your fork in cold water before flattening the cookies.

Bourbon Balls

Serves 24; 2 cookies per serving

These tasty morsels are great for holiday parties.

3 cups finely crushed reduced-fat vanilla wafers

1 cup confectioners' sugar, sifted

½ cup chopped pecans, dry-roasted

3 tablespoons light corn syrup

1½ tablespoons unsweetened cocoa powder

6 tablespoons bourbon (plus more as needed)

¼ cup sifted confectioners' sugar

In a large bowl, combine all ingredients except ¼ cup confectioners' sugar, stirring well.

Form dough into about 48 small balls. (If balls tend to crumble, stir in a few extra drops of bourbon.) Roll each in confectioners' sugar. Refrigerate in airtight container for about 1 week to mellow.

Calories 105
Protein 1 g
Carbohydrates 18 g
Cholesterol 0 mg
Total Fat 3 g
Saturated 0 g
Polyunsaturated 0 g
Monounsaturated 1 g
Fiber 1 g
Sodium 51 mg

Sugar Cookies

Serves 24; 2 cookies per serving

Make these cookies the next time you're home on a snowy day. For holidays, decorate them with Confectioners' Glaze (see page 550).

1 cup sugar
⅓ cup acceptable margarine, softened
Egg substitute equivalent to 1 egg, or 1 egg
2 tablespoons fat-free milk
1 teaspoon vanilla extract
2 cups all-purpose flour
2 teaspoons baking powder
½ teaspoon salt
⅛ teaspoon ground nutmeg
Vegetable oil spray

In a large bowl, cream sugar and margarine. Beat in egg substitute, milk, and vanilla.

In a medium bowl, sift together remaining ingredients except vegetable oil spray. Gradually beat into sugar mixture.

Cover and refrigerate dough until chilled thoroughly, about 2 hours.

Preheat oven to 375° F. Spray baking sheets with vegetable oil spray.

Form dough into about 48 balls 1 inch in diameter; put on baking sheets. Lightly press thumb in center of each cookie.

Bake for 8 minutes, or until light brown. Remove cookies from baking sheet and let cool on cooling rack.

Calories 96
Protein 1 g
Carbohydrates 17 g
Cholesterol 0 mg
Total Fat 3 g
  Saturated 0 g
  Polyunsaturated 1 g
  Monounsaturated 1 g
Fiber 0 g
Sodium 124 mg

Lemon Sugar Cookies

Substitute 2 tablespoons fresh lemon juice and 1 teaspoon grated lemon zest for milk and vanilla. (calories 95; protein 1 g; carbohydrates 17 g; cholesterol 0 mg; total fat 3 g; saturated 0 g; polyunsaturated 1 g; monounsaturated 1 g; fiber 0 g; sodium 123 mg)

Ginger Cookies

Serves 30; 2 cookies or 1 gingerbread man per serving

If you like a spicy, soft cookie, you'll love these.

1 cup sugar
½ cup unsweetened applesauce
¼ cup acceptable margarine
Egg substitute equivalent to 1 egg, or 1 egg, slightly beaten
¼ cup molasses
3 cups all-purpose flour
1 teaspoon baking soda
1 teaspoon ground cinnamon
1 teaspoon ground ginger
Vegetable oil spray

In a large mixing bowl, beat sugar, applesauce, and margarine with a sturdy spoon, then beat in egg substitute and molasses.

In another large bowl, sift together remaining ingredients except vegetable oil spray. Add to margarine mixture, stirring well. Cover and refrigerate dough until thoroughly chilled, about 2 hours.

Preheat oven to 350° F. Spray baking sheets with vegetable oil spray.

Using a teaspoon, drop mounds of dough onto baking sheets, about 1 inch apart. (You'll have about 60 cookies.)

Bake for 10 to 12 minutes.

Gingerbread Men

Prepare dough as directed, using 3½ cups flour. Lightly flour a flat surface and roll chilled dough to ¼-inch thickness. Cut out gingerbread men shapes with a 5-inch cookie cutter. Bake for 10 to 12 minutes at 350° F. Decorate with ½ cup Confectioners' Glaze (see page 550). Makes about 30 gingerbread men. (calories 110; protein 2 g; carbohydrates 22 g; cholesterol 0 mg; total fat 2 g; saturated 0 g; polyunsaturated 1 g; monounsaturated 1 g; fiber 0 g; sodium 65 mg)

Calories 96
Protein 2 g
Carbohydrates 19 g
Cholesterol 0 mg
Total Fat 2 g
Saturated 0 g
Polyunsaturated 1 g
Monounsaturated 1 g
Fiber 0 g
Sodium 65 mg

Fudgy Buttermilk Brownies

Serves 16; 1 brownie per serving

Here's a wonderfully moist brownie to serve alone or topped with nonfat frozen yogurt.

Vegetable oil spray

BROWNIES

1 cup all-purpose flour

1 cup firmly packed light brown sugar

⅓ cup unsweetened cocoa powder

½ teaspoon baking soda

¼ teaspoon salt

Whites of 2 large eggs, egg substitute equivalent to 1 egg, or 1 egg

½ cup fat-free fruit-based fat replacement or unsweetened applesauce

½ cup nonfat or low-fat buttermilk

2 teaspoons vanilla extract

FROSTING

1½ cups sifted confectioners' sugar

¼ cup unsweetened cocoa powder

1 teaspoon vanilla extract

2 to 3 tablespoons fat-free milk

Preheat oven to 350° F. Spray a 9 × 9-inch square baking pan with vegetable oil spray; set aside.

For brownies, in a medium bowl, combine flour, brown sugar, cocoa powder, baking soda, and salt, stirring well.

In a small bowl, lightly whisk egg whites. Whisk in remaining brownie ingredients. Whisk into flour mixture until well blended. Pour batter into baking pan.

Bake for 30 minutes. Let cool in pan on cooling rack.

For frosting, combine confectioners' sugar and cocoa powder in a small bowl, stirring well.

Stir in vanilla extract, then gradually stir in milk until frosting is spreading consistency. Spread over cooled brownies. Cut into 16 squares.

Calories 163
Protein 2 g
Carbohydrates 38 g
Cholesterol 0 mg
Total Fat 1 g
 Saturated 0 g
 Polyunsaturated 0 g
 Monounsaturated 0 g
Fiber 1 g
Sodium 112 mg

Butterscotch Brownies

Serves 16; 1 brownie per serving

Serve these brownies with a cup of hot cocoa made with fat-free milk (you can even add a marshmallow or two).

Vegetable oil spray
1 cup firmly packed dark brown sugar
2 tablespoons acceptable margarine
Egg substitute equivalent to 1 egg, or 1 egg
2 tablespoons unsweetened applesauce
½ teaspoon imitation butter flavoring
½ teaspoon vanilla extract
¾ cup sifted all-purpose flour
1 teaspoon baking powder

Preheat oven to 350° F. Spray an 8-inch square baking pan with vegetable oil spray.

In a large mixing bowl, cream brown sugar and margarine with electric hand mixer on medium-high.

Add egg substitute, applesauce, butter flavoring, and vanilla. Beat on medium until smooth.

In a small bowl, sift together flour and baking powder. Stir into brown sugar mixture. Spread evenly in baking pan.

Bake for 20 to 25 minutes. Let cool slightly and cut into 16 bars.

Cook's Tip on Brown Sugar

You can interchange equal amounts of light brown and dark brown sugar. If a recipe calls for dark brown sugar and you prefer a less butterscotchy flavor, use light brown sugar and vice versa. To "make" light brown sugar, use half dark brown sugar and half white sugar.

Calories 85
Protein 1 g
Carbohydrates 18 g
Cholesterol 0 mg
Total Fat 2 g
  Saturated 0 g
  Polyunsaturated 0 g
  Monounsaturated 0 g
Fiber 0 g
Sodium 60 mg

Apricot Raisin Bars

Serves 48; 1 cookie per serving

These bars make a welcome treat in lunch boxes or as an after-school snack.

6-ounce package dried apricots, chopped
1 cup golden or dark raisins
1¾ cups unsweetened apple juice, divided use
3 tablespoons cornstarch
1½ teaspoons grated lemon zest
Vegetable oil spray
1½ cups all-purpose flour
1 teaspoon baking powder
1¼ cups uncooked quick-cooking oatmeal
¾ cup firmly packed light brown sugar
¼ cup sugar
⅔ cup light margarine

In a medium saucepan, combine apricots, raisins, and 1½ cups apple juice. Cook over medium-low heat for 20 minutes, or until fruit is tender.

In a small bowl, whisk together ¼ cup apple juice, cornstarch, and zest. Whisk into apricot mixture. Cook over medium-high heat until mixture thickens, 2 to 3 minutes, stirring constantly. Remove from heat and let cool.

Preheat oven to 375° F. Spray a 13 × 9 × 2-inch pan with vegetable oil spray.

Sift flour and baking powder together into a large bowl.

Stir in oatmeal and sugars; with a pastry blender or fork, blend in margarine until mixture is crumbly. Press about two thirds of mixture in pan.

Spread fruit mixture over crust, then top with remaining oatmeal mixture.

Bake for 30 minutes, or until crust is lightly golden. Cut into 48 squares.

Calories 76
Protein 1 g
Carbohydrates 16 g
Cholesterol 0 mg
Total Fat 1 g
Saturated 0 g
Polyunsaturated 1 g
Monounsaturated 0 g
Fiber 1 g
Sodium 28 mg

Oatmeal Carrot Bar Cookies

Serves 24; 1 cookie per serving

Bursting with flavor, these cookies also boast the health benefits of oatmeal. Don't be surprised when you open the cookie jar and find only crumbs!

Vegetable oil spray
½ cup raisins
2 tablespoons light margarine, room temperature
½ cup firmly packed light brown sugar
¼ cup unsweetened applesauce
Egg substitute equivalent to 1 egg, or 1 egg
1¼ cups grated carrots (1 to 2 large)
½ teaspoon ground cinnamon
½ teaspoon grated lemon or orange zest
½ teaspoon vanilla extract
¼ teaspoon ground nutmeg
1 cup all-purpose flour
½ cup uncooked quick-cooking oatmeal
1 teaspoon baking powder
1 tablespoon sifted confectioners' sugar

Preheat oven to 350° F. Spray an 11½ × 7½ × 2-inch baking pan with vegetable oil spray.

Put raisins in a small bowl and cover with boiling water. Soak for 15 minutes. Drain and set aside.

Meanwhile, in a large mixing bowl, cream margarine and brown sugar until fluffy.

Add applesauce and egg substitute. Beat well.

Stir in carrots, cinnamon, lemon zest, vanilla, nutmeg, and raisins.

In a medium bowl, stir together flour, oatmeal, and baking powder. Add to margarine mixture, stirring well. Pour into baking pan.

Bake for 20 to 25 minutes, or until cookies are lightly golden. Let cool. Sprinkle lightly with confectioners' sugar. Cut into 24 bars.

Calories 62
Protein 1 g
Carbohydrates 13 g
Cholesterol 0 mg
Total Fat 1 g
Saturated 0 g
Polyunsaturated 0 g
Monounsaturated 0 g
Fiber 1 g
Sodium 37 mg

Apricot-Almond Biscotti

Serves 28; 1 cookie per serving

Biscotti are typically baked, sliced, and baked again, making them quite hard to bite into. They're perfect for dunking in hot coffee for a midmorning treat or as a light dessert.

Vegetable oil spray
2 cups all-purpose flour
⅔ cup sugar
2 teaspoons baking powder
¼ teaspoon salt
Egg substitute equivalent to 2 eggs, or 2 eggs
2 tablespoons acceptable vegetable oil
2 tablespoons unsweetened applesauce
1 teaspoon grated lemon zest
¼ teaspoon almond extract
¾ cup finely chopped dried apricots (4 ounces)
¼ cup chopped almonds, dry-roasted
Flour for kneading
¾ cup sifted confectioners' sugar
2 to 3 teaspoons water

Calories 92
Protein 2 g
Carbohydrates 18 g
Cholesterol 0 mg
Total Fat 2 g
Saturated 0 g
Polyunsaturated 1 g
Monounsaturated 1 g
Fiber 1 g
Sodium 65 mg

Preheat oven to 350° F. Spray a baking sheet with vegetable oil spray. Set aside.

In a medium bowl, combine flour, sugar, baking powder, and salt, stirring well.

In a small bowl, whisk together egg substitute, oil, applesauce, lemon zest, and almond extract.

Whisk apricots and almonds into egg mixture, then whisk egg mixture into flour mixture.

Lightly flour a flat surface; turn out dough. Knead just until blended, 10 to 12 strokes. Form into two 8-inch logs (slightly moistening your hands helps). Put logs on baking sheet; flatten slightly to 2½-inch width.

Bake for 25 minutes. Reduce oven temperature to 300° F. Let biscotti cool on cooling rack for 10 minutes.

Put confectioners' sugar into a small bowl. Gradually stir in water until desired consistency. Brush on logs. Cut into ½-inch slices and place cut side down on baking sheet.

Bake for 10 minutes. Turn slices over and bake for 10 minutes. Let cool on cooling rack.

CHOCOLATE-PECAN BISCOTTI

Prepare as above except replace ½ cup of the flour with ½ cup of unsweetened cocoa powder; sugar with ⅔ cup firmly packed light brown sugar; apricots and almonds with ½ cup finely chopped pecans, dry-roasted; and almond extract and lemon zest with 1 teaspoon vanilla extract. (calories 88; protein 2 g; carbohydrates 15 g; cholesterol 0 mg; total fat 3 g; saturated 0 g; polyunsaturated 1 g; monounsaturated 1 g; fiber 1 g; sodium 66 mg)

Sherry Thins

Serves 30; 2 cookies per serving

Flavored with the sweet richness of cream sherry, these cookies are great for the holidays.

1 cup sugar
¼ cup light margarine
Egg substitute equivalent to 1 egg, or 1 egg
1 teaspoon vanilla extract
3 cups sifted all-purpose flour
2 teaspoons baking powder
½ teaspoon salt
⅓ cup cream sherry
Vegetable oil spray
Flour for rolling dough

In a large mixing bowl, cream sugar and margarine until fluffy.

Add egg substitute and vanilla, beating well.

In a large bowl, sift together 3 cups flour, baking powder, and salt. Add to margarine mixture alternately with sherry, beating after each addition. Cover and refrigerate dough for at least 2 hours.

Preheat oven to 375° F. Spray baking sheets with vegetable oil spray.

Lightly flour flat surface. Roll out half of dough. Cut out shapes with small cookie cutters. Repeat with remaining dough. (You'll have about 60 cookies if using 2-inch round biscuit cutter.) Put on baking sheets.

Bake for 5 to 7 minutes, or until edges are light golden brown.

Calories 85
Protein 1 g
Carbohydrates 18 g
Cholesterol 0 mg
Total Fat 1 g
 Saturated 0 g
 Polyunsaturated 0 g
 Monounsaturated 0 g
Fiber 0 g
Sodium 84 mg

Frozen Raspberry Cream

Serves 8; ¾ cup per serving

Sweet, tart berries combine with whipped topping for a dream of a dessert.

Whites of 2 large eggs, room temperature (see Cook's Tip, page 345)
2 teaspoons water
⅛ teaspoon cream of tartar
¾ cup sugar
10-ounce package frozen raspberries or unsweetened strawberries, thawed
1 tablespoon fresh lemon juice
1 cup frozen nonfat whipped topping, thawed
8 fresh raspberries (optional)
8 fresh sprigs of mint (optional)

Combine egg whites, water, and cream of tartar in top of a double boiler; beat well. Cook over simmering water for 7 to 10 minutes, or until mixture registers 160° F on an instant-read or candy thermometer. Pour into a large bowl.

Add sugar 1 tablespoon at a time, beating constantly until smooth.

Stir in berries and lemon juice. Beat until soft peaks form.

Fold in whipped topping. Spoon into 8 goblets.

Freeze for 8 hours or longer.

To serve, place raspberry and mint sprig on each serving.

Time-Saver: Skip the freezing and just refrigerate the raspberry cream for 2 hours if you're pressed for time.

Calories 128
Protein 1 g
Carbohydrates 31 g
Cholesterol 0 mg
Total Fat 0 g
  Saturated 0 g
  Polyunsaturated 0 g
  Monounsaturated 0 g
Fiber 2 g
Sodium 32 mg

Fresh Strawberry Mousse

Serves 8; ½ cup per serving

Spoon this cool summertime treat into your favorite dessert dishes and garnish with mint leaves and fresh fruit slices. You'll have a dessert that looks as delectable as it tastes.

½ cup cold fresh orange juice
2 envelopes unflavored gelatin
4 cups strawberries, hulled (2 pints)
½ teaspoon grated orange zest
1 cup nonfat or low-fat cottage cheese
8-ounce container nonfat or low-fat strawberry yogurt or nonfat or low-fat vanilla yogurt
2 tablespoons sugar
2 cups nonfat or low-fat frozen dairy topping, thawed
6 drops red food coloring (optional)
½ cup sliced strawberries (optional)
4 orange slices, cut in half (optional)
8 sprigs of fresh mint (optional)

In a small saucepan, combine orange juice and unflavored gelatin (a fork works well). Let gelatin soften for 5 minutes.

Cook over low heat for 1½ to 2 minutes, or until gelatin dissolves, stirring constantly. Remove from heat and set aside to cool, about 10 minutes.

Meanwhile, in a food processor or blender, puree 4 cups strawberries and orange zest. Pour into a large bowl.

Stir cooled gelatin mixture into strawberry mixture. Cover and refrigerate until slightly thickened, about 20 minutes.

In a food processor or blender, puree cottage cheese, yogurt, and sugar until smooth.

Fold cottage cheese mixture, whipped topping, and food coloring into strawberry mixture. Cover and refrigerate for at least 1 hour.

To serve, garnish with strawberries, orange slices, and mint.

Calories 116
Protein 7 g
Carbohydrates 21 g
Cholesterol 3 mg
Total Fat 0 g
  Saturated 0 g
  Polyunsaturated 0 g
  Monounsaturated 0 g
Fiber 2 g
Sodium 142 mg

STRAWBERRY DESSERT SAUCE

Serves 16; ½ cup per serving

Follow the above instructions, omitting the gelatin and stirring the orange juice into the pureed strawberry mixture. Serve over angel food cake, Black Devil's Food Cake (see page 535), brownies, fresh fruit salad, or nonfat ice cream or frozen yogurt. (calories 55; protein 3 g; carbohydrates 10 g; cholesterol 1 mg; total fat 0 g; saturated 0 g; polyunsaturated 0 g; monounsaturated 0 g; fiber 1 g; sodium 69 mg)

Cannoli Cream with Strawberries and Chocolate

Serves 4; 1 cup per serving

Creamy and elegant, this make-ahead dessert is just the way to end a meal for company.

¼ cup cold fat-free milk

1 envelope unflavored gelatin

½ cup boiling fat-free milk

¾ cup fat-free or low-fat ricotta cheese

¾ cup fat-free or low-fat cottage cheese

½ cup sugar

1 teaspoon vanilla extract

8 to 10 unsweetened frozen strawberries, thawed, or fresh strawberries

3 tablespoons shaved sweet chocolate

Pour cold milk into a food processor or blender; sprinkle gelatin over milk. Let stand for 2 minutes.

Pour boiling milk into food processor or blender. Process until gelatin is completely dissolved, about 1 minute.

Add ricotta cheese, cottage cheese, sugar, and vanilla. Process for 2 minutes. Divide mixture evenly between two medium bowls.

Puree strawberries in food processor. Fold into one bowl of pudding. Stir chocolate into remaining bowl.

Alternate layers of strawberry pudding and chocolate pudding in stemmed dessert dishes or wineglasses until all ingredients are used. Refrigerate for 3 hours, or until set.

Calories 205
Protein 13 g
Carbohydrates 36 g
Cholesterol 5 mg
Total Fat 2 g
  Saturated 1 g
  Polyunsaturated 0 g
  Monounsaturated 0 g
Fiber 1 g
Sodium 231 mg

Honey Almond Custards

Serves 6; ½ cup per serving

After a highly seasoned entrée, serve these honey-sweetened custards to balance out the meal.

Vegetable oil spray
2 cups fat-free milk
Egg substitute equivalent to 3 eggs
¼ cup honey
2 teaspoons vanilla extract
¼ teaspoon almond extract
⅛ teaspoon salt

Preheat oven to 350° F. Spray six 6-ounce ovenproof custard cups with vegetable oil spray.

Heat milk in a small saucepan over medium-high heat until very hot but not boiling, stirring constantly. Remove from heat.

In a medium bowl, gently whisk together remaining ingredients, then gently whisk in milk (don't create foam). Pour mixture into custard cups.

Place cups in large baking pan and pour hot tap water into pan to a depth of 1 inch.

Bake, uncovered, for 30 to 40 minutes, or until knife inserted halfway between cup and center of custard comes out clean (center won't quite be firm).

Microwave Method

Prepare custard mixture as directed. Pour into microwave-safe custard cups sprayed with vegetable oil spray. Put cups in microwave-safe baking dish. Add water as directed. Microwave on 100 percent power (high) for 12 to 15 minutes, or until center is just set.

Calories 103
Protein 7 g
Carbohydrates 16 g
Cholesterol 2 mg
Total Fat 1 g
Saturated 0 g
Polyunsaturated 1 g
Monounsaturated 0 g
Fiber 0 g
Sodium 148 mg

Caramel Custard with Poached Pears

Serves 6

Caramel custard is delectable on its own, but when served on poached pears and topped with chopped hazelnuts, it is heavenly! You can serve this dish either warm or chilled. It's also good with apples instead of pears

3 medium pears
2 cups water
1 cup dry white wine (regular or nonalcoholic) or unsweetened fruit juice

CUSTARD
1 cup fat-free milk
½ cup sugar
Egg substitute equivalent to 1 egg, or 1 egg
2 tablespoons all-purpose flour
2 tablespoons cornstarch
1 teaspoon vanilla extract
¼ cup fat-free caramel apple dip

2 tablespoons chopped hazelnuts
Sprigs of fresh mint (optional)

Peel pears, cut them in half, and remove seeds and cores (a melon baller works well). Put pears in a large skillet; add water and wine. Bring to a simmer over medium-high heat. Reduce heat and simmer, covered, for 15 to 20 minutes, or until tender. Drain and discard liquid. Place pears on a plate, cover with plastic wrap, and refrigerate until ready to use.

For custard, bring water to a simmer in bottom of a double boiler. Combine milk, sugar, egg substitute, flour, and cornstarch in top of double boiler set over water. (Water shouldn't touch container.) Whisk together thoroughly. Cook for 3 to 4 minutes, whisking occasionally until mixture starts to thicken. Whisk constantly until custard is thick and smooth, 1 to 2 minutes.

Add vanilla and cook for 1 minute, whisking occasionally. Remove from heat and let mixture cool for 10 to 15 minutes.

Add caramel apple dip, stirring to mix well.

To assemble, place one pear half cut side up on dessert plate. Spoon some caramel custard over

Calories 203
Protein 4 g
Carbohydrates 37 g
Cholesterol 1 mg
Total Fat 2 g
 Saturated 0 g
 Polyunsaturated 0 g
 Monounsaturated 1 g
Fiber 2 g
Sodium 47 mg

pear. Sprinkle with chopped hazelnuts and garnish with mint. Repeat.

Cook's Tip on Caramel Apple Dip

Look for fat-free caramel apple dip in the produce section, near the apples.

Chocolate Chip Custard with Caramelized Sugar Topping

Serves 6; ½ cup per serving

You'll love this version of crème brûlée. Both the creamy custard base, enhanced with chocolate chips, and the caramelized topping can be prepared ahead.

2 cups fat-free milk
Egg substitute equivalent to 4 eggs
⅓ cup sugar
2 teaspoons vanilla extract
3 tablespoons reduced-fat chocolate chips
Vegetable oil spray
¼ cup firmly packed light brown sugar

Preheat oven to 325° F.

In a medium mixing bowl, whisk together milk, egg substitute, sugar, and vanilla extract.

Stir in chocolate chips.

Pour mixture into a shallow 1-quart casserole dish or 8-inch round cake pan. Place dish in a 12 × 17 × 1-inch jelly-roll pan or large baking pan. Fill jelly-roll pan half full with warm water, or add warm water to a depth of 1 inch in large baking pan.

Bake for 1 hour 10 minutes, or until center of custard is set. Cover and refrigerate for up to 2 days.

For topping, place a piece of aluminum foil shiny side up over custard pan. Press foil over top of pan and about 1 inch over side. Remove foil and place it shiny side down on a broilerproof pan. (The upturned side will help hold in the sugar.) Spray flat surface (not side) of foil with vegetable oil spray. Sprinkle brown sugar evenly over sprayed portion of foil.

Broil sugar about 6 inches from heat for 1½ to 2 minutes, or until melted and bubbly. (The sugar will burn quickly, so watch it closely. Be careful not to touch sugar until it has cooled completely.) Let sugar cool for 10 to 15 minutes, then invert foil over custard and carefully peel off foil (the topping may

Calories 176
Protein 8 g
Carbohydrates 30 g
Cholesterol 2 mg
Total Fat 3 g
  Saturated 1 g
  Polyunsaturated 1 g
  Monounsaturated 0 g
Fiber 0 g
Sodium 122 mg

break into pieces). Topping can be kept in an airtight container for 2 to 3 days.

Cook's Tip on Dessert Garnishes

Before placing your dessert on the plate, sprinkle the plate with a bit of colored sugar or a light sifting of confectioners' sugar, or cocoa powder. Try a light drizzle of fat-free chocolate or caramel syrup.

Indian Pudding

Serves 8; ½ cup per serving

Originally from New England, Indian pudding typically contains cornmeal, molasses, and spices. You can top it with nonfat ice cream or dairy topping.

2 cups fat-free milk
¼ cup cornmeal
¼ cup sugar
½ teaspoon ground ginger
½ teaspoon ground cinnamon
⅛ teaspoon baking soda
¼ cup molasses
1 cup cold fat-free milk
Ground nutmeg

Preheat oven to 275° F.

In a double boiler or medium saucepan, heat 2 cups milk over low heat.

Gradually add cornmeal, whisking constantly. Cook for 15 minutes, or until thick, whisking constantly. Remove from heat.

In a small bowl, combine sugar, ginger, cinnamon, and baking soda, stirring well. Whisk into cornmeal mixture.

Add molasses and 1 cup milk, whisking well. Pour into 1-quart casserole dish.

Bake for 2 hours, or until top is light golden brown.

Sprinkle with nutmeg and serve warm.

Calories 98
Protein 3 g
Carbohydrates 21 g
Cholesterol 2 mg
Total Fat 0 g
Saturated 0 g
Polyunsaturated 0 g
Monounsaturated 0 g
Fiber 0 g
Sodium 72 mg

Cook's Tip on Double Boilers

A double boiler provides gentle heat for heat-sensitive foods that contain milk, eggs, chocolate, etc. It has two pans. Bring a small amount of water in the bottom pan to a boil, then reduce it to a simmer. Add the food to the top and set it, covered, into the bottom. If you don't have a conventional double boiler, use a stainless steel bowl and saucepan. Whichever you use, don't let the hot water in the bottom touch the top pan or bowl.

Apple-Berry Dessert Couscous

Serves 6; 1 1/4 cups per serving

Enjoy this unusual dessert hot or at room temperature. To add a touch of elegance, serve it in wine goblets, alternating layers of couscous and fat-free frozen yogurt.

1 teaspoon acceptable vegetable oil
2 medium apples (such as Fuji, McIntosh, or Rome Beauty), cut into 1/2-inch pieces (2 cups)
1/4 cup dried cherries or cranberries
1/4 cup golden raisins
3 tablespoons dried currants
2 tablespoons light brown sugar
1 teaspoon ground cinnamon
2 cups unsweetened apple juice
1/2 cup water
1 teaspoon coarsely grated lime zest
3 tablespoons fresh lime juice (2 medium limes)
2 cups uncooked couscous

In a large saucepan, heat oil over low heat, swirling to coat bottom. Stir in apples, cherries, raisins, currants, brown sugar, and cinnamon. Cook, covered, for 10 minutes, or until apples have released some of their juices, stirring occasionally.

Add remaining ingredients except couscous. Bring to a boil, covered, over high heat.

Add couscous, stirring well. Cover pan and remove from heat. Let stand for 15 minutes. Fluff with a fork before serving.

Cook's Tip on Couscous

Couscous (*KOOS-koos*), which looks like tiny bits of pasta, is made from a coarse wheat flour called semolina. Couscous cooks in about 5 minutes, making it a boon when you're in a hurry. The name "couscous" also refers to a stew made of the grain, lamb or chicken, and vegetables.

Calories 303
Protein 7 g
Carbohydrates 67 g
Cholesterol 0 mg
Total Fat 1 g
Saturated 0 g
Polyunsaturated 1 g
Monounsaturated 0 g
Fiber 5 g
Sodium 14 mg

Delicious Rice Pudding

Serves 6; ½ cup per serving

Eat this traditional comfort food unadorned, or try Easy Jubilee Sauce (see page 454) as an interesting addition.

Vegetable oil spray
2 cups fat-free milk, heated
2 cups cooked rice
⅓ cup sugar
1½ teaspoons vanilla extract
¼ teaspoon ground nutmeg
½ teaspoon ground cinnamon
Egg substitute equivalent to 1 egg, or 1 egg

Preheat oven to 350° F.

Spray a 1-quart casserole dish with vegetable oil spray. Put ingredients in dish in order listed. Stir well and cover. Set dish in a large baking pan and pour hot tap water into pan to a depth of 1 inch.

Bake pudding for 1 hour, or until mixture is thick. Serve warm or cover and refrigerate to serve chilled.

Lemon Rice Pudding

Add 1½ teaspoons grated lemon zest and ½ teaspoon lemon extract.

Cook's Tip on Bain-Marie

A bain-marie (*bahn mah-REE*), or water bath, is a technique for cooking custards and some other fragile foods. The container holding the food is placed in a larger pan (also called a bain-marie) that holds a small amount of hot, not boiling, water. (If the water starts to boil, add a little cold water.) The technique keeps the food from separating or curdling.

Calories 153
Protein 6 g
Carbohydrates 30 g
Cholesterol 2 mg
Total Fat 1 g
 Saturated 0 g
 Polyunsaturated 0 g
 Monounsaturated 0 g
Fiber 0 g
Sodium 62 mg

Guiltless Banana Pudding

Serves 8; 1 cup per serving

It's so rich and creamy that you'll wonder how this revised favorite can be guiltless.

1 cup fat-free milk

Small package fat-free vanilla instant pudding mix (3 to 4 ounces)

8 ounces frozen nonfat whipped topping, thawed

⅔ cup fat-free sweetened condensed milk

2 tablespoons plus 1 teaspoon fresh lemon juice, or to taste

20 reduced-fat vanilla wafers, whole or crushed

2 medium bananas, sliced

In a large mixing bowl, whisk or beat milk and pudding mix until thickened.

Fold in whipped topping, condensed milk, and lemon juice. Layer half the vanilla wafers, half the bananas, and half the pudding mixture in an 8-inch square glass dish, glass serving dish, or individual bowls; repeat. Put plastic wrap directly on surface of pudding and refrigerate.

Guiltless Strawberry Pudding

Replace the vanilla wafers with reduced-fat gingersnaps, and replace the bananas with 1 cup sliced fresh strawberries. (calories 224; protein 4 g; carbohydrates 48 g; cholesterol 2 mg; total fat 1 g; saturated 0 g; polyunsaturated 0 g; monounsaturated 0 g; fiber 1 g; sodium 342 mg)

Calories 243
Protein 4 g
Carbohydrates 53 g
Cholesterol 2 mg
Total Fat 1 g
Saturated 0 g
Polyunsaturated 0 g
Monounsaturated 0 g
Fiber 1 g
Sodium 272 mg

Fruit with Vanilla Cream and Wafer Wedges

Serves 4

A thick, cheesecake-flavored topping covers fresh or frozen fruit to serve with easy-to-make cookies.

Vegetable oil spray

WAFER WEDGES

3 tablespoons firmly packed dark brown sugar

White of 1 large egg

1 tablespoon acceptable margarine, melted and slightly cooled

½ teaspoon vanilla, butter, and nut flavoring or 1 teaspoon vanilla extract

¼ cup all-purpose flour

¼ teaspoon ground cinnamon

¼ teaspoon ground nutmeg

8 ounces unsweetened frozen sliced peaches, slightly thawed, or peeled fresh peaches (2 cups)

VANILLA CREAM

½ cup nonfat or light sour cream

¼ cup sifted confectioners' sugar

2 teaspoons vanilla extract

¾ cup frozen nonfat whipped topping, thawed

8 slices unsweetened frozen peaches, slightly thawed, or peeled fresh peaches

Preheat oven to 375° F. Spray a 9-inch glass pie pan with vegetable oil spray.

For wafer wedges, in a small mixing bowl, whisk together brown sugar, egg white, margarine, and flavoring until smooth.

Add remaining wafer ingredients. Whisk until well blended. Pour into pie pan and smooth to cover bottom evenly.

Bake for 18 minutes, or until edges begin to brown slightly. Let cool on cooling rack for 10 minutes. Gently remove from pan (cookie will still be warm and slightly flexible). Cut into 12 wedges and let cool completely.

Meanwhile, dice 8 ounces peaches.

For vanilla cream, in small mixing bowl, whisk

Calories 221
Protein 4 g
Carbohydrates 40 g
Cholesterol 0 mg
Total Fat 4 g
- Saturated 1 g
- Polyunsaturated 1 g
- Monounsaturated 1 g

Fiber 2 g
Sodium 94 mg

together all ingredients except whipped topping until smooth. Gently fold in whipped topping.

Place diced peaches in decorative bowl or individual ramekins. Spoon vanilla cream over fruit; arrange peach slices on top.

Serve at room temperature or cover and refrigerate for up to 2 hours. At serving time, randomly spear wafers around outer edges of bowl or stick one wafer in each ramekin.

Variation

Replace peaches with strawberries, blueberries, raspberries, or a combination.

Cinnamon-Apple Dessert Tamales with Kahlúa Custard Sauce

Serves 12

Tamales for dessert? A savory favorite turns into a luscious dessert with apples and cinnamon. The tamales are easy to make with our step-by-step instructions.

24 dried cornhusks or 5-inch squares aluminum foil

4 dried cornhusks (optional)

Vegetable oil spray (if using aluminum foil)

FILLING

2 cups cornmeal

2 Granny Smith apples, peeled and diced (about 2 cups)

¾ cup firmly packed light brown sugar

¼ cup golden raisins

1 teaspoon ground cinnamon

1 cup mashed bananas (about 2)

¾ cup fat-free milk

KAHLÚA CUSTARD SAUCE

1 envelope (about 1 ounce) custard pudding dessert mix

2½ cups fat-free milk

3 tablespoons sugar

2 tablespoons Kahlúa or strong brewed coffee

Sprigs of fresh mint (optional)

Calories 218
Protein 4 g
Carbohydrates 48 g
Cholesterol 8 mg
Total Fat 1 g
Saturated 0 g
Polyunsaturated 0 g
Monounsaturated 0 g
Fiber 3 g
Sodium 63 mg

Place 24 cornhusks in enough cold water to cover. Let soak for 15 minutes. With your fingers, tear remaining 4 husks into 6 strips each. (Strips are used to tie tamales to hold them together.) If using aluminum foil, lay squares on a flat surface. Lightly spray one side of each with vegetable oil spray.

For filling, in a large bowl, combine cornmeal, apples, brown sugar, raisins, and cinnamon, stirring well.

Make a well in center of cornmeal mixture. Place bananas and milk in well and stir until just combined.

Shake excess water from 1 cornhusk. Place wide end closest to you, and the narrower, pointed end away from you. Spoon about 2 tablespoons filling onto center of cornhusk and spread toward wide end. Fold left side of husk over filling and roll to right to enclose. Fold pointed end toward open end of tamale. Tie cornhusk strip around tamale to secure; set aside. (Don't tie too tightly—leave room for tamale to expand.) If using aluminum foil, spoon filling onto center and fold foil in half, crimping edges to seal. Repeat with remaining filling.

Put a steamer basket in a large stockpot. Add water to just below basket. Bring to a simmer over high heat. Place tamales in basket, open end up if using husks. Water shouldn't touch tamales. Place a dish towel over tamales (this will keep water from dripping on them while cooking). Reduce heat to low and cook, covered, for 45 minutes.

Meanwhile, prepare custard sauce according to package directions (using mix, milk, and sugar). When sauce is cooked, stir in Kahlúa. Set aside.

Cool tamales for at least 5 minutes before serving. Unwrap 2 tamales and place on a dessert plate. Ladle ¼ cup sauce over tamales and garnish with mint. Repeat with remaining tamales, sauce, and mint.

Cook's Tip

To reheat, place wrapped tamales in a steamer basket over simmering water for 5 minutes, or microwave 6 at a time on a microwave-safe plate covered with plastic wrap on 100 percent power (high) for 30 to 60 seconds (leave in husks but remove foil).

Berries in Rich Vanilla Sauce

Serves 4

Summer fruits decoratively arranged on a bed of rich, thick, sweet vanilla cream sauce—what a beautiful way to end a meal.

VANILLA SAUCE

1 cup fat-free milk

3 tablespoons sugar

¼ cup fat-free milk

1 tablespoon plus 1 teaspoon cornstarch

1 tablespoon vanilla extract

6 ounces fresh blueberries (about 1 cup)

8 ounces fresh strawberries, halved

1 whole strawberry with stem (optional)

For sauce, in a small saucepan, whisk together 1 cup milk and sugar. Bring to a boil over medium-high heat, whisking occasionally.

Meanwhile, in a small bowl, whisk together ¼ cup milk and cornstarch until cornstarch has dissolved. Add to sugar mixture and cook for 2 to 3 minutes, or until thickened, whisking constantly.

Remove from heat and whisk in vanilla. Pour into a 10-inch quiche pan or onto a serving platter. Let cool for 20 minutes to set slightly.

Arrange blueberries in a mound in center of pan. Circle with strawberries. Place a whole strawberry or strawberry fan (see Cook's Tip on Strawberry Fans, below) on blueberries. Cover with plastic wrap and refrigerate for about 2 hours.

Calories 123
Protein 3 g
Carbohydrates 26 g
Cholesterol 1 mg
Total Fat 1 g
- Saturated 0 g
- Polyunsaturated 0 g
- Monounsaturated 0 g

Fiber 2 g
Sodium 43 mg

Cook's Tip on Strawberry Fans

To make a strawberry fan, thinly slice the strawberry up to the stem (4 to 6 slices), but *don't* detach the stem. Gently press down with fingertips to allow the slices to separate slightly to form a fan.

Dessert Crepes

Serves 6; 2 crepes per serving

Add a French flair to any meal with these delectable crepes. Serve with a demitasse of espresso.

1½ cups nonfat or low-fat cottage cheese
½ teaspoon vanilla extract
Whole-Wheat Crepes (see page 516)
1½ cups fresh or frozen fruit (strawberries, raspberries, blueberries, or other fruit)

In a food processor or blender, puree cottage cheese and vanilla.

Put 2 tablespoons whipped cottage cheese in center of each crepe. Fold in each side of crepes. Top each crepe with 2 tablespoons fruit.

Applesauce Crepes

Fill each crepe with 2 tablespoons unsweetened applesauce. Fold as directed. Add ½ teaspoon ground cinnamon to whipped cottage cheese. Top each crepe with 1 tablespoon cottage cheese mixture. (calories 173; protein 9 g; carbohydrates 23 g; cholesterol 25 mg; total fat 5 g; saturated 1 g; polyunsaturated 2 g; monounsaturated 2 g; fiber 2 g; sodium 189 mg)

Jubilee Crepes

Fill each crepe with whipped cottage cheese. Fold as directed. Top each with ¼ cup Easy Jubilee Sauce (see page 454). (calories 507; protein 12 g; carbohydrates 97 g; cholesterol 27 mg; total fat 5 g; saturated 1 g; polyunsaturated 2 g; monounsaturated 2 g; fiber 1 g; sodium 300 mg)

Calories 177
Protein 13 g
Carbohydrates 19 g
Cholesterol 27 mg
Total Fat 5 g
Saturated 1 g
Polyunsaturated 2 g
Monounsaturated 2 g
Fiber 2 g
Sodium 298 mg

Gingerbread

Serves 16

Delicious alone, this gingerbread may be even better with Confectioners' Glaze *(see page 550).*

Vegetable oil spray

3/4 cup firmly packed light brown sugar

2 2 1/2-ounce jars no-sugar-added baby food prunes, 1/2 cup pureed prunes, or 1/2 cup fat-free fruit-based oil and margarine replacement

1/2 cup dark molasses

1 tablespoon acceptable vegetable oil

1 teaspoon ground ginger

1/2 teaspoon ground cinnamon

1/2 teaspoon ground nutmeg

1/4 teaspoon ground cloves

1 cup boiling water

2 1/2 cups all-purpose flour

1 teaspoon baking soda

2 tablespoons hot water

Preheat oven to 350° F. Spray a 13 × 9 × 2-inch baking pan with vegetable oil spray.

In a large bowl, whisk together brown sugar, prunes, molasses, oil, ginger, cinnamon, nutmeg, and cloves.

Whisk in boiling water.

Whisk in flour until just combined. Don't overmix (batter will be lumpy).

In a small bowl, combine baking soda and hot water, whisking until baking soda has dissolved. Whisk into batter. Pour batter into baking pan.

Bake for 30 to 35 minutes, or until a toothpick inserted in center comes out clean. Let cool for at least 30 minutes before serving.

Calories 150
Protein 2 g
Carbohydrates 34 g
Cholesterol 0 mg
Total Fat 1 g
Saturated 0 g
Polyunsaturated 1 g
Monounsaturated 0 g
Fiber 1 g
Sodium 90 mg

Spiced Skillet Bananas with Frozen Yogurt

Serves 4

Sample a taste of the Deep South with these bananas in a brown sugar glaze.

Vegetable oil spray
1 tablespoon light margarine
2 tablespoons dark brown sugar
2 cups sliced bananas (3 to 4 medium)
½ teaspoon vanilla, butter, and nut flavoring or vanilla extract
2 cups frozen nonfat or low-fat vanilla yogurt

Coat a large nonstick skillet with vegetable oil spray. Melt margarine over medium-high heat. Add brown sugar, stirring until mixture is bubbly and sugar has dissolved.

Add bananas, gently stirring to coat evenly. Cook until just softened and beginning to glaze and turn golden, about 3 minutes. Don't overcook, or the bananas will break down.

Remove skillet from heat and gently stir in flavoring.

Spoon banana mixture over frozen yogurt. Serve immediately.

Spiced Skillet Apples with Frozen Yogurt

Replace bananas with thinly sliced peeled apples, such as Red Delicious, and vanilla, butter, and nut flavoring with apple pie spice. Cook for 6 to 8 minutes, or until apples are just tender. (calories 170; protein 3 g; carbohydrates 35 g; cholesterol 0 mg; total fat 1 g; saturated 0 g; polyunsaturated 1 g; monounsaturated 0 g; fiber 1 g; sodium 94 mg)

Calories 209
Protein 4 g
Carbohydrates 45 g
Cholesterol 0 mg
Total Fat 1 g
Saturated 0 g
Polyunsaturated 1 g
Monounsaturated 0 g
Fiber 2 g
Sodium 95 mg

Grapefruit Orange Palette

Serves 6

This is an artistic delight. Serve it as a late-night dessert or for Sunday brunch.

3 medium seedless oranges, peeled and chilled

12-ounce package frozen sweetened raspberries, thawed

2 tablespoons black currant jelly or crème de cassis (black currant liqueur)

¼ cup sifted confectioners' sugar

3 medium pink or ruby red grapefruit, peeled, sectioned, and chilled

6 sprigs of fresh mint

Slice each orange into 5 slices crosswise, then cut each slice in half. Set aside.

In a food processor or blender, puree raspberries. Using a fine-mesh strainer, remove seeds. Reserve pulp in a small bowl; discard seeds.

In a small microwave-safe bowl, microwave jelly on 100 percent power (high) for 30 seconds.

Stir jelly and sugar into raspberries.

For each serving, arrange one sixth of grapefruit sections and 5 orange pieces alternately in a circular pattern (like flower petals) on a dessert plate. Drizzle raspberry sauce in a circle over fruit and place sprig of mint in center. Repeat for each plate.

Cook's Tip

You can prepare the fruit and the sauce ahead of time. Cover and refrigerate grapefruit sections, orange pieces, and pureed raspberries separately. Assemble just before serving.

Calories 168
Protein 2 g
Carbohydrates 41 g
Cholesterol 0 mg
Total Fat 0 g
- Saturated 0 g
- Polyunsaturated 0 g
- Monounsaturated 0 g

Fiber 5 g
Sodium 1 mg

Claret-Spiced Oranges

Serves 6

Here's a light, elegant way to end a holiday meal.

4 medium oranges, peeled and sectioned
¾ cup claret, red wine, or nonalcoholic red wine
½ cup water
5 tablespoons sugar
3-inch cinnamon stick
1 tablespoon fresh lemon juice
2 whole cloves

Put orange sections in a medium bowl.

In a small saucepan, combine remaining ingredients. Bring to a boil over medium-high heat. Reduce heat and simmer for 5 minutes. Pour over orange sections.

Let mixture cool slightly, then cover and refrigerate for at least 4 hours.

To serve, remove cloves and cinnamon stick.

Calories 103
Protein 1 g
Carbohydrates 21 g
Cholesterol 0 mg
Total Fat 0 g
Saturated 0 g
Polyunsaturated 0 g
Monounsaturated 0 g
Fiber 2 g
Sodium 3 mg

Baked Ginger Pears

Serves 8

These Asian-influenced pears go nicely with a chicken or vegetable stir-fry.

8 canned pear halves in fruit juice (about 2 1-pound cans)
1/3 cup firmly packed light brown sugar
2 tablespoons chopped pecans, dry-roasted
1 teaspoon fresh lemon juice
1/4 teaspoon ground ginger or chopped crystallized ginger to taste
Crystallized ginger (optional)
8 maraschino cherries (optional)

Preheat oven to 350° F.

Drain pears, reserving juice. Arrange pears cut side up in a baking dish just large enough to hold them.

In a small bowl, combine brown sugar, pecans, lemon juice, and 1/4 teaspoon ginger, stirring well. Spoon into pear halves.

Pour reserved juice around pears.

Bake for 15 to 20 minutes.

Serve warm or cover and refrigerate to serve chilled. Garnish with bits of crystallized ginger and maraschino cherries.

Calories 69
Protein 0 g
Carbohydrates 15 g
Cholesterol 0 mg
Total Fat 1 g
Saturated 0 g
Polyunsaturated 0 g
Monounsaturated 1 g
Fiber 1 g
Sodium 5 mg

Microwave Variation

Drain juice from pears, reserving 1 cup. Arrange pear halves cut side up in a glass pie pan. Prepare as directed. Microwave, uncovered, on 100 percent power (high) for 5 minutes. Let cool for at least 10 minutes before serving. Garnish with ginger and cherries.

Cook's Tip on Crystallized Ginger

Crystallized ginger has been cooked in a sugar syrup and coated with sugar. Look for it in the spice section at your supermarket.

Golden Poached Pears

Serves 6

Serve these delicately poached pears with a sparkling flute of champagne or white grape juice. A great fall dessert!

6 Bartlett pears
1 tablespoon fresh lemon juice
2 12-ounce cans apricot nectar
½ cup sugar
1 teaspoon freshly grated lemon zest
¼ cup fresh lemon juice (2 medium lemons)
½ cup sherry (cream sherry preferred)
6 sprigs of fresh mint (optional)

Peel pears. (Leave cores and stems.) Sprinkle pears with 1 tablespoon lemon juice to prevent discoloration.

Combine apricot nectar, sugar, lemon zest, and ¼ cup lemon juice in a large, deep saucepan. Bring to a boil over medium-high heat, reduce heat, and simmer for 5 minutes.

Stir in sherry.

Simmer pears in syrup, basting and turning occasionally to cook evenly, for 20 to 25 minutes, or until just tender. (Cooking time may vary depending on size and firmness of pears.)

Transfer pears to a storage container. Continue simmering sauce until reduced by half. Pour sauce over pears, cover, and refrigerate.

To serve, spoon sauce over pears and garnish with fresh mint.

Cook's Tip on Pears

Pears are ripe when they yield to gentle pressure at the stem end. The body of the pear will still be firm. To ripen pears, put them in a paper bag and fold the top down. To ripen them faster, put an apple in the bag with them. A pear's skin toughens as it cooks, so always peel before cooking.

Calories 295
Protein 1 g
Carbohydrates 76 g
Cholesterol 0 mg
Total Fat 1 g
Saturated 0 g
Polyunsaturated 0 g
Monounsaturated 0 g
Fiber 5 g
Sodium 13 mg

Special Baked Apples

Serves 4

To help you reach your five-a-day fruits and vegetables, serve this fragrant dessert. It's luscious on a cold day, served warm in a pool of nonfat or low-fat vanilla yogurt.

4 medium Jonathan or Granny Smith apples

2 teaspoons fresh lemon juice

1 tablespoon plus 1 teaspoon golden raisins

1 tablespoon plus 1 teaspoon light brown sugar

2 teaspoons sugar

2 teaspoons ground cinnamon

2 teaspoons light margarine

1 tablespoon finely chopped pecans or walnuts, dry-roasted

½ cup rum or sherry

Preheat oven to 350° F.

Core apples but do not cut through bottoms. Cut ½-inch-wide strip of peel off top of each apple (to keep apples from bursting). Put apples in baking dish and sprinkle with lemon juice.

Fill centers with raisins and sugars, then sprinkle with cinnamon.

Dot apples with margarine and sprinkle with nuts.

Pour rum into baking dish.

Bake for 30 to 35 minutes, or until apples are tender, basting several times. Serve warm or chilled.

Microwave Method

Put filled apples in individual microwave-safe custard cups. Cover loosely with plastic wrap and cook on 100 percent power (high) for 3 to 4½ minutes. Let stand for 3 minutes and serve.

Calories 218
Protein 1 g
Carbohydrates 36 g
Cholesterol 0 mg
Total Fat 3 g
  Saturated 0 g
  Polyunsaturated 1 g
  Monounsaturated 1 g
Fiber 5 g
Sodium 14 mg

Fall Fruit Medley

Serves 6

This is a wonderful combination of seasonal fruits. Use the fruits listed or substitute whatever fruits are available.

2 apples
2 pears
1 Fuyu persimmon
5-ounce box frozen sweetened raspberries, thawed and drained
¼ cup fresh orange juice
¼ cup kirsch (optional)

Slice apples, pears, and persimmon. Put in a bowl; stir together.

Gently stir in raspberries.

Pour in orange juice and kirsch, stirring gently. Cover and refrigerate.

Cook's Tip on Persimmons

A Fuyu persimmon resembles a squatty tomato in shape. You can eat it, peel and all, like an apple. A Fuyu persimmon is firm when ripe. Larger and acorn shaped, the Hachiya persimmon is ripe when the flesh around the stem is very soft but not mushy. After it's picked, a Hachiya may take 2 to 3 weeks at room temperature to ripen. And be *sure* it's ripe, or you may have a permanent pucker! Scoop out the flesh with a spoon and discard the peel. A recipe calling for persimmons will usually specify which variety to use.

Calories 94
Protein 1 g
Carbohydrates 24 g
Cholesterol 0 mg
Total Fat 0 g
- Saturated 0 g
- Polyunsaturated 0 g
- Monounsaturated 0 g

Fiber 4 g
Sodium 0 mg

Mint Julep Fruit Cup

Serves 6

Make this for the Kentucky Derby instead of the traditional mint julep. You may substitute other fresh fruit, such as peaches or blueberries.

1 fresh medium pineapple, peeled and cubed (3 cups)
2 cups sliced fresh strawberries (1 to 1½ pints)
¼ cup crème de menthe or ¼ teaspoon mint extract
1½ cups lime sherbet
6 fresh mint leaves or 6 pieces crystallized mint leaves (optional)

Calories 165
Protein 1 g
Carbohydrates 33 g
Cholesterol 2 mg
Total Fat 2 g
  Saturated 1 g
  Polyunsaturated 0 g
  Monounsaturated 0 g
Fiber 2 g
Sodium 25 mg

Combine pineapple and strawberries; spoon into compotes or dessert bowls.

Sprinkle with crème de menthe. Serve with a scoop of sherbet and garnish with mint.

Cook's Tip on Crystallized Mint Leaves

You can buy crystallized mint leaves in a specialty shop or make your own. In a small saucepan, bring ¼ cup sugar and ¼ cup water to a simmer over medium heat. Simmer for 3 minutes. Let cool for 10 minutes. Dip mint stems with leaves attached (1 cup total) into syrup. Put ½ cup sugar on a plate and roll leaves in sugar. Place leaves on a baking sheet lined with aluminum foil and let sit at room temperature for 1 hour. Refrigerate in an airtight container for up to 4 days.

Kiwifruit Sundaes

Serves 4

For variety, spoon this pretty sauce over angel food cake or pudding instead of frozen yogurt.

4 kiwifruit, peeled
⅓ cup fresh orange juice
¼ cup honey
2 teaspoons cornstarch
1 teaspoon grated orange zest
2 tablespoons fresh orange juice or orange liqueur
⅛ teaspoon almond extract
2 cups fat-free or low-fat frozen yogurt or ice cream

Puree 2 kiwifruit in a food processor or blender. Slice remaining kiwifruit and set aside.

Combine puree, ⅓ cup orange juice, honey, and cornstarch in a microwave-safe bowl. Microwave on 100 percent power (high) for 3 minutes, stirring once.

Add orange zest, 2 tablespoons orange juice, and almond extract to kiwifruit mixture, stirring well.

To serve, spoon frozen yogurt into dessert bowls. Spoon sauce over yogurt and top with sliced kiwifruit.

Calories 240
Protein 4 g
Carbohydrates 55 g
Cholesterol 0 mg
Total Fat 0 g
Saturated 0 g
Polyunsaturated 0 g
Monounsaturated 0 g
Fiber 3 g
Sodium 80 mg

Strawberries with Champagne Ice

Serves 14; ½ cup per serving

The flavors of strawberries and champagne marry well in this cool, refreshing dessert.

2 medium oranges
1 medium lemon
1½ cups water
¾ cup sugar
3 tablespoons orange-flavored liqueur
2 cups champagne
2 cups fresh strawberries
1 cup champagne
1 tablespoon sugar

With a vegetable peeler, peel zest in strips from oranges and lemon. Squeeze juice from oranges and lemon.

In a large saucepan, combine water, ¾ cup sugar, and citrus zest. Bring mixture to a boil over medium-high heat; boil for 5 minutes. Remove from heat. Discard zest. Pour liquid into a large bowl and stir in orange and lemon juices and liqueur. Cover and refrigerate for 2 hours.

Stir 2 cups champagne into juice mixture. Pour into 8-inch square pan and freeze until slushy, 2½ to 3 hours.

Beat juice mixture in a mixing bowl or process in a food processor or blender until smooth. Pour back into pan and refreeze for 2 to 3 hours, stirring occasionally.

Meanwhile, hull strawberries and cut in half. Put in a medium bowl and stir in 1 cup champagne and 1 tablespoon sugar. Cover and refrigerate for at least 2 hours.

Place strawberries in goblets and fill with champagne ice.

Calories 99
Protein 0 g
Carbohydrates 15 g
Cholesterol 0 mg
Total Fat 0 g
  Saturated 0 g
  Polyunsaturated 0 g
  Monounsaturated 0 g
Fiber 0 g
Sodium 5 mg

Strawberry-Banana Sorbet with Star Fruit

Serves 5

Give your guests the star treatment by garnishing this light dessert with star fruit.

1 cup peach, apricot, or strawberry nectar or orange juice

¼ cup sugar

1 cup sliced fresh strawberries

1 cup sliced bananas (1½ to 2 medium)

2 tablespoons dry white wine (regular or nonalcoholic) or fresh orange juice

1 tablespoon fresh lemon juice

1 star fruit

Sprigs of fresh mint (optional)

Combine nectar and sugar in a small saucepan, stirring to dissolve sugar. Bring to a boil over medium-high heat. Reduce heat and simmer for 5 minutes, stirring occasionally. Pour into a medium bowl and refrigerate for 10 to 15 minutes.

Meanwhile, puree strawberries, bananas, wine, and lemon juice in a food processor or blender. Pour into nectar mixture, stirring well.

Pour mixture into an 8-inch square baking pan. Cover and put in freezer for 2 hours, stirring every 30 minutes. Freeze without stirring for 4 to 5 hours, or until completely frozen.

To serve, trim ends off star fruit. Cut crosswise into thin slices. Using an ice cream scoop, fill dessert dishes or wineglasses with sorbet. Garnish with star fruit and mint.

Calories 114
Protein 1 g
Carbohydrates 28 g
Cholesterol 0 mg
Total Fat 0 g
Saturated 0 g
Polyunsaturated 0 g
Monounsaturated 0 g
Fiber 2 g
Sodium 45 mg

Mango-Peach Sorbet with Star Fruit

Replace strawberries and bananas with 2 cups diced fresh mangoes (about 2 large) or 14-ounce can mangoes, drained and diced.

Fresh Fruit Ice

Serves 8; ½ cup per serving

When summer is in full swing, use your favorite fruit for this chilled delight.

1 envelope unflavored gelatin
½ cup cold water
1 cup strawberries, peaches, or other fresh fruit, sliced
3 bananas, mashed
1 cup fresh orange juice (3 medium oranges)
6 tablespoons fresh lemon juice (2 medium lemons)
¼ cup sugar

Calories 90
Protein 2 g
Carbohydrates 22 g
Cholesterol 0 mg
Total Fat 0 g
Saturated 0 g
Polyunsaturated 0 g
Monounsaturated 0 g
Fiber 2 g
Sodium 3 mg

In a large saucepan, combine gelatin and water (a fork works well). Let gelatin soften for 5 minutes. Cook over low heat, ½ to 2 minutes, until dissolved, stirring constantly.

Add remaining ingredients, stirring well. Pour into a medium bowl and freeze until almost set, 1 to 1½ hours. Beat until fluffy.

Cover and return to freezer until set, 3 to 4 hours.

Strawberry-Raspberry Ice

Serves 8

A refreshingly cool double dose of berries, this ice looks lovely in chilled wine or champagne glasses with sprigs of fresh mint.

6 ounces frozen white grape juice concentrate
1 cup water
1 tablespoon confectioners' sugar
8 ounces frozen unsweetened strawberries, slightly thawed
6 ounces frozen raspberries, slightly thawed
6 ice cubes (about 1 cup)
Sprigs of fresh mint (optional)

In a food processor or blender, combine all ingredients except mint in the order listed. Puree, stirring occasionally. Pour into a large airtight plastic bag and seal. Put bag on its side in freezer until mixture freezes solid, at least 2 hours.

About 15 minutes before serving, remove bag from freezer and allow ice to thaw slightly, mashing with fork if needed. Spoon into chilled glasses and garnish with mint. Serve immediately.

Calories 99
Protein 0 g
Carbohydrates 25 g
Cholesterol 0 mg
Total Fat 0 g
- Saturated 0 g
- Polyunsaturated 0 g
- Monounsaturated 0 g

Fiber 2 g
Sodium 10 mg

Tropical Breeze

Serves 4

You'll think you've had a quick trip to the islands when you drink this creamy blend of tropical flavors. It's best when served in glasses that have been chilled in the freezer.

½ cup pineapple juice
2 cups nonfat or low-fat vanilla yogurt
¾ cup very ripe mashed banana (about 1½ medium)
¼ cup confectioners' sugar
2 teaspoons vanilla extract
½ teaspoon coconut extract
8 ice cubes (about 1⅓ cups)
4 fresh pineapple spears (optional)

In a food processor or blender, combine all ingredients except pineapple spears in the order listed; puree. Pour into a large airtight plastic bag and seal. Put bag on its side in freezer until mixture is very thick, about 1 hour. Spoon into glasses and garnish with pineapple spears. If mixture is too frozen to pour or spoon into glasses, return it to processor or blender and process until slushy. Serve immediately.

Calories 205
Protein 7 g
Carbohydrates 43 g
Cholesterol 2 mg
Total Fat 0 g
- Saturated 0 g
- Polyunsaturated 0 g
- Monounsaturated 0 g

Fiber 1 g
Sodium 86 mg

Sunny Mango Sorbet

Serves 4

Thick, creamy, rich, tart, and sweet—this supersimple sorbet is all these and more. Serve it in wineglasses or decorative bowls.

4 cups coarsely chopped mangoes (about 5 medium)
½ cup fresh lime juice
2 tablespoons sugar

In a food processor or blender, puree all ingredients. Pour into a large airtight plastic bag and seal. Put bag on its side in freezer for about 2 hours, or until sorbet is thick. If mixture is frozen solid, put bag on counter for about 30 minutes, then stir before serving.

Cook's Tip

If you want a completely smooth sorbet, strain the processed mixture before freezing.

Calories 140
Protein 1 g
Carbohydrates 37 g
Cholesterol 0 mg
Total Fat 0 g
- Saturated 0 g
- Polyunsaturated 0 g
- Monounsaturated 0 g

Fiber 3 g
Sodium 4 mg

Chocolate Mocha Freeze

Serves 5

Luscious chocolate ice cream blended with the rich flavors of strong coffee and sweet vanilla—a coffeehouse treat to serve at home!

1 tablespoon plus ½ teaspoon instant coffee granules
¼ cup boiling water
¾ cup cold water
½ cup fat-free milk
½ cup confectioners' sugar
1 tablespoon vanilla extract
12 ice cubes (about 2 cups)
2 cups nonfat or low-fat chocolate ice cream

Put coffee granules in a cup or small bowl. Pour boiling water over granules, stirring to dissolve. Pour into a food processor or blender.

Add remaining ingredients except ice cream and process until smooth.

Add ice cream and process until smooth.

Put work bowl in freezer for 30 minutes to slightly freeze and thicken ice cream mixture.

Cook's Tip

You can freeze this dish for later use. Pour the mixture into a large airtight plastic bag and seal. Put the bag on its side in the freezer. To serve, put the bag on the counter to thaw slightly. Break the ice cream mixture into small pieces, put them in a food processor or blender, and process until smooth.

Calories 146
Protein 3 g
Carbohydrates 31 g
Cholesterol 0 mg
Total Fat 0 g
  Saturated 0 g
  Polyunsaturated 0 g
  Monounsaturated 0 g
Fiber 0 g
Sodium 56 mg

Tequila Lime Sherbet

Serves 6; ½ cup per serving

Tequila and lime make a refreshing combination. Serve this sherbet after a spicy Tex-Mex meal.

2 tablespoons cold water
1 envelope unflavored gelatin
1 cup water
¾ cup sugar
1 cup plain nonfat or low-fat yogurt
1 tablespoon grated lime zest
½ cup fresh lime juice (6 to 8 medium limes)
⅓ cup tequila

In a cup or small bowl, combine 2 tablespoons water and gelatin (a fork works well). Set aside to let gelatin soften.

In a medium saucepan, combine 1 cup water with sugar. Bring to a boil over medium-high heat; boil for 5 minutes, stirring occasionally.

Remove from heat. Whisk in gelatin mixture and remaining ingredients until smooth. Pour into 8-inch square pan and freeze until slushy, 2½ to 3 hours.

Process mixture in a food processor or blender until smooth. Return to pan and freeze, about 6 hours. Remove from freezer 15 minutes before serving.

Calories 150
Protein 2 g
Carbohydrates 29 g
Cholesterol 1 mg
Total Fat 0 g
Saturated 0 g
Polyunsaturated 0 g
Monounsaturated 0 g
Fiber 0 g
Sodium 29 mg

Berry Peachy Frozen Yogurt

Serves 6; ⅔ cup per serving

Sweet summer fruits keep you cool in a heart-healthy way.

2 cups plain nonfat or low-fat yogurt

2 tablespoons fresh lemon juice

½ teaspoon vanilla extract

2 cups diced fresh peaches or nectarines, mashed with a fork (about 4 medium)

2 cups sliced fresh strawberries (1 to 1½ pints) or bananas (4 to 5), mashed with a fork

½ cup sugar

In a large bowl, whisk together yogurt, lemon juice, and vanilla. Cover and refrigerate.

In another large bowl, combine fruit and sugar. Let stand for 10 minutes, or until sugar dissolves. Stir into yogurt mixture.

Freeze in ice cream freezer as directed by manufacturer.

Calories 136
Protein 3 g
Carbohydrates 31 g
Cholesterol 2 mg
Total Fat 0 g
Saturated 0 g
Polyunsaturated 0 g
Monounsaturated 0 g
Fiber 2 g
Sodium 51 mg

Hong Kong Sundae

Serves 4; ½ cup per serving

This is a great dessert to serve around Chinese New Year (the end of January or early February). You'll have lots of extra topping. Spoon some over angel food cake on another day.

TOPPING

11-ounce can mandarin oranges in light syrup

1 tablespoon cornstarch

8½-ounce can crushed pineapple in its own juice

½ cup orange marmalade

½ teaspoon ground ginger

2 to 4 tablespoons chopped crystallized ginger or ½ cup sliced preserved kumquats

2 cups nonfat or low-fat vanilla ice milk or frozen yogurt

Calories 148
Protein 3 g
Carbohydrates 34 g
Cholesterol 0 mg
Total Fat 0 g
Saturated 0 g
Polyunsaturated 0 g
Monounsaturated 0 g
Fiber 0 g
Sodium 56 m

For topping, drain oranges, reserving ¼ cup syrup. Set oranges aside.

In a medium saucepan, whisk together syrup and cornstarch.

Whisk in undrained pineapple, marmalade, and ginger. Cook over medium-high heat until mixture thickens and bubbles, 2 to 3 minutes, whisking constantly.

Stir in oranges and crystallized ginger.

To serve, put ice milk in individual bowls. Spoon 2 tablespoons of warm topping over each. Cover and refrigerate remaining topping. (Topping: calories 48; protein 0 g; carbohydrates 13 g; cholesterol 0 mg; total fat 0 g; saturated 0 g; polyunsaturated 0 g; monounsaturated 0 g; fiber 0 g; sodium 6 mg)

Cook's Tip on Kumquats

The kumquat is a tiny citrus fruit that looks much like an orange. Native to China, it is now grown in Florida, California, and Japan. The whole fruit is edible. The peel is sweet, and the flesh is tart and dry.

Cardinal Sundae

Serves 16

Frosty lime sherbet topped with a vibrant berry mixture makes a delicious treat with a beautiful color contrast.

TOPPING

½ cup frozen unsweetened strawberries, thawed

½ cup frozen sweetened raspberries, thawed

1 teaspoon cornstarch

¼ teaspoon fresh lemon juice

1 tablespoon currant jelly

8 cups lime sherbet

For topping, drain strawberries and raspberries, reserving juices. Set berries aside.

In a small saucepan, whisk together berry juices, cornstarch, and lemon juice. Bring to a boil over medium-high heat; cook for 1 minute, whisking constantly.

Add jelly and stir until it melts.

Remove sauce from heat and stir in berries. Pour into a small bowl, cover, and refrigerate.

To serve, put ½ cup sherbet in each bowl and top with 1 tablespoon sauce. Cover and refrigerate any remaining topping.

Calories 150
Protein 1 g
Carbohydrates 34 g
Cholesterol 5 mg
Total Fat 2 g
Saturated 1 g
Polyunsaturated 0 g
Monounsaturated 1 g
Fiber 1 g
Sodium 46 mg

SHOPPING FOR A HEALTHY HEART

The next time you're waiting in line at the supermarket, take a look at what's in the grocery carts around you. This is where healthful eating begins—or doesn't. One shopper's cart brims with fresh fruits and vegetables, whole-grain breads and rolls, low-fat dairy products, pasta and dried beans, skinless chicken, and seafood. A second shopper's cart is overflowing with high-fat snacks, sugary breakfast foods, rich desserts, rib-eye steaks, bacon, frozen French fries, and solid shortening.

The differences between the contents of these two carts are profound and far-reaching. For one thing, the first shopper will probably pay significantly less at the checkout than Shopper Number 2. Contrary to what many people think, lots of healthful foods are cheaper, pound for pound, than high-fat ones. More important, along with his or her groceries, Shopper Number 1 is taking home a week's worth of better health, increased energy, and improved odds of a longer life. Shopper Number 2 is taking home what might accurately be described as a cartful of trouble.

Shopper Number 1 has joined the growing ranks of ordinary Americans whose food-shopping habits reflect a new awareness of nutrition and a desire to apply it daily in their lives. Shopper Number 2 is still stuck in a sort of nutritional time warp. That person is clinging to ingrained buying and eating habits that were once typical in this country but now are known to be potentially harmful to your health.

Today, you don't have to go on buying foods that are high in total fat, saturated fat, cholesterol, and sodium. Now it's easy to find healthful alternatives that taste just as good. It's also easy to incorporate them into your daily diet.

THE FIRST STEP: READ THE LABELS

With fresh produce and other foods that reach the supermarket in their natural, unaltered state, you have total control over how much fat, salt, and calories you add in preparation. With packaged or prepared foods, however, the only way to be sure of what you're getting is to check the federally required nutrition label on each one. It tells you instantly how much fat and saturated fat a serving of the product contains; the number of calories per serving; the amount of cholesterol, sodium, and sugars; and the amount

Nutrition Facts			
Serving Size 1/2 cup (114g)			
Servings Per Container 4			
Amount Per Serving			
Calories 90		Calories from Fat 30	
		% Daily Value*	
Total Fat 3g		**5%**	
Saturated Fat 0g		**0%**	
Cholesterol 0mg		**0%**	
Sodium 300mg		**13%**	
Total Carbohydrate 13g		**4%**	
Dietary Fiber 3g		**12%**	
Sugars 3g			
Protein 3g			
Vitamin A 80% •		Vitamin C 60%	
Calcium 4% •		Iron 4%	

*Percent Daily Values are based on a 2,000 calorie diet. Your daily values may be higher or lower depending on your calorie needs:

	Calories	2,000	2,500
Total Fat	Less than	65g	80g
Sat Fat	Less than	20g	25g
Cholesterol	Less than	300mg	300mg
Sodium	Less than	2,400mg	2,400mg
Total Carbohydrate		300g	375g
Fiber		25g	30g

Calories per gram:
Fat 9 • Carbohydrate 4 • Protein 4

of total carbohydrates, dietary fiber, and protein. The content of all these nutrients is expressed in both weight (in grams or milligrams) and percentages of recommended daily amounts, based on a 2,000-calorie-per-day diet. The percentage of some vitamins and minerals is also shown.

Packaged foods must also carry a list of all ingredients they contain. This list usually appears directly below the nutrition label. It gives all the ingredients by weight, starting with the heaviest. Obviously, if beef fat, butter, or vegetable shortening is at the top of the list, you can assume that the product is extremely high in fat. This fact will be amply reflected in the "Calories from Fat" and "% (of) Daily Value" shown at the top of the nutrition label.

For example, the label on one popular national brand of margarine lists 70 total calories per 1-tablespoon serving and 70 calories from fat. This means that 100 percent of the calories are derived from fat. That same serving contains 7.7 grams of fat, 11 percent of the recommended daily value for a person consuming 2,000 calories a day.

The American Heart Association recommends a 1-teaspoon serving of margarine. This translates into 2.6 grams of fat, or 4 percent of the recommended daily value for 2,000 calories.

Dietary cholesterol comes only from animal sources. In the past, many brands of margarine, cooking oil, and vegetable shortening boasted of being "cholesterol free" if the product contained no animal fat. However, since the product could contain a high amount of saturated fat, which increases blood cholesterol, the AHA and other health agencies held that to be misleading. Under Food and Drug Administration (FDA) labeling regulations, a product labeled "cholesterol free" can contain no more than 2 grams of saturated fat per serving. That's so even if it contains no cholesterol itself.

YOU CAN TRUST THE LABEL

In addition to the Nutrition Facts label now required on most food products, the federal regulations that went into effect in 1994 also provided some dependable definitions. Once-confusing and frequently misused terms, such as "lite," "lean," and "low-fat," have been clearly defined. To qualify for these designations, food products must meet strict criteria established by the FDA.

Today, you can be sure that these key words and health claims on product labels really mean what they say. Here are some of the terms the FDA clarified, along with their government-approved definitions.

- Fat-free—less than 0.5 grams of fat per serving
- Low-fat—no more than 3 grams of fat per serving
- Lean (as applied to meats)—less than 10 grams of total fat, 4.5 grams of saturated fat, and 95 milligrams of cholesterol per serving
- Extra lean (as applied to meats)—less than 5 grams of fat, 2 grams of saturated fat, and 95 milligrams of cholesterol per serving
- Light or lite—one-third fewer calories or no more than half the fat of the regular version
- Low sodium—no more than half the sodium of the regular version
- Cholesterol-free—less than 2 milligrams of cholesterol and 2 grams or less of saturated fat per serving

FOOD CERTIFICATION PROGRAM

The AHA's Food Certification Program, featuring the heart-check mark on food packages, is designed as a tool for grocery shoppers. The heart-check indicates that the product meets the AHA food criteria for saturated fat and cholesterol. These criteria apply to healthy people over age two.

Heart-check products meet FDA criteria that let food manufacturers say on the package that the food may help reduce one's risk for heart disease.

WHICH TYPE OF FAT—AND HOW MUCH?

It's also important to note the amounts of fat, saturated fat, and cholesterol in a product, as shown on the Nutrition Facts label.

There are three kinds of fat in the foods we eat: saturated, polyunsaturated, and monounsaturated. Most foods contain all three, but in varying amounts. Only saturated fat and dietary cholesterol raise blood cholesterol. In the typical American diet, the main sources of saturated fat are foods from animals. Palm, palm kernel, and coconut oils are also high in saturated fat. The *only* dietary source of cholesterol is animal products.

Coconut and palm kernel oils were once used in dozens of processed food products. They have a bland, pleasant taste and very long shelf life. These so-called tropical oils are much more heavily saturated than even butter or lard. Therefore, they pose a much greater health hazard. Palm oil, another tropical oil, is similar to butter and lard in saturated fat content. For the sake of your heart and arteries, the AHA advises watching out for foods that include these oils in their ingredient lists.

Oils that stay liquid at room temperature are high in unsaturated fats. They include polyunsaturated and monounsaturated fats. The oils include corn, safflower, soybean, sunflower, sesame, olive, and canola (rapeseed). All are low in saturated fatty acids and can help lower cholesterol as part of a diet low in saturated fatty acids. Of all oils in general use, safflower is highest in polyunsaturates. Next in line are sunflower, corn, soybean, and sesame oils. Canola and olive oils are primarily monounsaturated. Peanut oil is also primarily monounsaturated but in animal studies has been shown to harm the artery wall. You should use it only occasionally.

MARGARINE

Margarines vary greatly in their fat composition. Avoid the ones with more than 2 grams of saturated fat per tablespoon. Margarines that list liquid oils as their first ingredient are invariably the lowest in saturated fat among the spreads that are 100 percent fat. Margarines listing partially hydrogenated oil as the first ingredient have more saturated fat. Also, the more liquid the margarine is, the less trans fatty acid it contains. Trans fatty acids can raise blood cholesterol but not as much as saturated fatty acids do.

Trans fatty acids are by-products created when the unsaturated fats in margarine are hydrogenated. Hydrogenation—adding hydrogen—converts liquid oils into a more stable form. This gives the product greater shelf life. It also makes the margarine harder and less likely to melt at room temperature.

At present, trans fatty acids aren't listed on the nutrition labels of food products. You can, however, tell a lot about how much trans fatty acid a margarine contains by seeing what form it's packaged in. The softer the spread, the lower it is in trans fatty acids. The harder it is, the more of these fats it contains. The AHA still recommends margarine over butter, and the rule when buying margarine is "the softer the better." This recommendation includes liquid spreads and sprays that are primarily water and/or fat-free milk. They contain so little liquid vegetable oil that they can be classified as fat free.

Here are cooking guidelines from the National Association of Margarine Manufacturers.

- Margarines containing 60 percent or more fat can be used almost anywhere butter or margarine is specified. However, they should not be used for baked goods such as pastry crust and spritz cookies that require precise amounts of fat and moisture.
- Margarines containing 50 to 59 percent fat also work well for cooking, such as in the preparation of side dishes and sautéing; they can also be used as a topping or spread.
- Margarines containing 49 percent or less fat should only be used for spreading, topping, and adding flavor to recipes that already contain a significant amount of moisture (e.g., pasta or rice). They are not designed for baking or frying.

SMALL CHANGES, BIG RESULTS

For many food shoppers, it's hard to break lifelong buying habits and eating patterns all at once. But making just a few minor changes can pay big health dividends by reducing fat, saturated fat, cholesterol, and calories in key food items.

Let's say you decide to make just two changes this week: Instead of whole milk, you try fat-free milk. And instead of butter, you try a fat-free spread. To find out what kind of "savings" you will see in calories, fat, and cholesterol, check the charts below. (All figures are based on the Nutrition Facts labels.)

NUTRITION INFORMATION

Per Serving	Whole Milk	Fat-Free Milk
Serving size	1 cup	1 cup
Calories	150	80
Total fat	8 g	0 g
Saturated fat	5 g	0 g
Cholesterol	33 mg	5 mg
Total carbohydrate	11 g	12 g
Protein	8 g	8 g

Per Serving	Butter	Margarine, Tub	Nonfat Spread
Serving size	1 tbsp	1 tbsp	1 tbsp
Calories	101	101	5
Total fat	11.4 g	11.4 g	0 g
Saturated fat	7.1 g	1.8 g	0 g
Polyunsaturated fat	0.4 g	3.9 g	0 g
Cholesterol	31 mg	0 mg	0 g
Total carbohydrate	0.1 g	0.1 g	1 g
Protein	0.1 g	0.1 g	0 g

It's easy to see that each time you replace a cup of whole milk with a cup of fat-free, you save 70 calories. You also save 8 grams of total fat, 5 grams of saturated fat, and 28 milligrams of cholesterol. Each time you use a tablespoon of fat-free spread instead of butter or tub margarine, you save 96 calories and 11.4 grams of total fat. Butter also has 7.1 grams more saturated fat than the fat-free spread and 31 milligrams more cholesterol than either the margarine or the fat-free spread.

If you drink two 8-ounce glasses of milk and use 1 tablespoon of butter every day, look at the savings you could make in only a month. By switching to fat-free milk and nonfat spread, you could save almost 5,000 calories; 582 grams of fat, including 363 grams of saturated fat; and almost 2,000 milligrams of cholesterol. You could lose almost a pound and a half each month without making any other changes in your diet or activity level!

If fat-free milk doesn't appeal to you, drink 2 percent milk for a couple of weeks. Then switch to fat free. After getting used to fat-free milk, many people find that even 2 percent milk seems too rich.

As for the fat-free and low-fat spreads, they lack some of the qualities of butter. It's difficult to use them for baking a cake, for instance. They work well, though, as a seasoning for cooked vegetables, topping for a baked potato, or coating for an ear of corn.

Once you've adjusted to a few changes in the way you shop for food, it will be easier to make other healthful changes and substitutions. You'll cook skinless chicken breasts instead of spareribs or brisket. You'll make nachos with baked tortilla chips and nonfat Cheddar cheese instead of regular chips and whole-milk cheese. You'll serve egg-substitute mushroom omelets instead of scrambled eggs and bacon. With each small innovation, you and your family will move a step closer to heart-healthy eating.

WHAT'S A SERVING? IT ALL DEPENDS

Serving size is the first item listed on the Nutrition Facts label. The number of servings per container follows. Sometimes serving sizes can be hard to calculate. For many vegetable oil cooking sprays, for example, the listed serving size is a "⅓-second spray." The most logical approach is not to time your spray with a stopwatch but to take an educated guess and go on. Remember, though, that fat-containing products such as cooking sprays can be labeled fat free only because their serving sizes are extremely small. If you spray for 10 seconds instead of one-third second, the spray is definitely *not* fat free.

Few of us weigh or measure the food we eat. Unless we're on a very exacting diet, it's just too much trouble. Most of us can, however, tell the difference between 1 cup and ½ cup. When we consume twice as much of a certain food as the listed serving size, we need to adjust the calories, fats, cholesterol, sodium, and other nutrients to match.

TWO KINDS OF SALT—OBVIOUS AND HIDDEN

You call it salt; the nutrition labels call it sodium. Either way, it can add up to high blood pressure in some people.

Many processed foods sold in America still contain far too much salt. Most of us get considerably more salt than we need. With foods such as pretzels, pickles, olives, snack crackers, cured meats, and salted nuts, the salt content is obvious. You can taste and sometimes even see the salt. In other cases, it may be less noticeable. It may be hidden among other flavors or even disguised under other names.

Ordinary table salt is about 40 percent sodium. Its chemical name is sodium chloride. A number of other chemical compounds also are high in sodium, and several of them are frequently used as food additives. The following are major sources of hidden salt that could be making your intake of sodium much higher than you realize.

- monosodium glutamate (MSG) (flavor enhancer)
- sodium bicarbonate (leavening agent)
- sodium nitrite (meat-curing agent)
- sodium benzoate (preservative)
- sodium propionate (mold inhibitor)
- sodium citrate (acidity controller)

If a product contains less than 5 milligrams of sodium per serving, it can be labeled "sodium free." If its sodium content is 35 milligrams or less per serving, it can be designated "very low sodium." If it has 140 milligrams or less per serving, it can be called "low sodium." "Reduced sodium" means that the product contains at least 75 percent less sodium than the amount in the food it replaces.

"Unsalted," "no salt added," and "without added salt" mean the product is made without the salt added to the regular version of the product. Be aware, though, that the unsalted product still contains whatever sodium may be a natural part of the food.

STARTING OFF ON THE RIGHT FOOT

Even before you leave for the supermarket, you can take a few tried-and-true steps to make your fresh approach to shopping a lot easier.

It's a good idea to plan your meals—at least the entrées—for the whole week. Write out a detailed list of what you'll need. This saves time at the store and helps you cut down on impulse buying. Variety is one of the keys to a healthful eating plan. As you map out the menus for a day, try to choose something from each of the major food groups. Then, for the next day, pick something a little different in each group.

You can simplify your job by keeping these principles of the Healthy Heart Food Pyramid firmly in mind as you design your menus.

- Use pasta; rice; starchy vegetables, such as potatoes; dried beans; or dried peas as a foundation for your meals.
- Limit the meat, seafood, or poultry you use each day to no more than 6 ounces (cooked) per person. That's the size of two decks of cards.

- Include whole-grain or enriched bread or cereal products for bulk.
- Include at least five servings of vegetables and fruits, including one serving of citrus fruit or a vegetable high in vitamin C and one serving of dark green, leafy vegetables or deep yellow vegetables.
- Plan on two to four daily servings of fat-free milk or nonfat or low-fat dairy products for adults, children, and adolescents.
- Use sweets sparingly.

Now you're ready to pick the right foods from the major food groups.

MEAT, POULTRY, AND SEAFOOD

Lean meat is an excellent protein choice. Look for USDA Select or Choice grades of lean cuts, such as round steak, sirloin tip, tenderloin, or flank steak. Avoid cuts such as T-bones and rib eyes. Avoid Prime grade. It's heavily marbled, so it's high in saturated fat. Here are some other tips.

- Choose lean or extra-lean ground beef. Or buy turkey or chicken ground without the skin. If none of the ground meats are low enough in fat, ask the butcher to remove all the visible fat from lean steak, roast, or stewing beef and grind the meat for you.
- When figuring serving sizes, remember that meat loses about 25 percent of its weight during cooking. (For example, 4 ounces of raw meat becomes about 3 ounces cooked.)
- Serve liver, brains, kidney, and sweetbreads only occasionally. They are high in cholesterol.
- Pork tenderloin, loin chops, center cut ham, and Canadian bacon are good choices for leanness. Prepackaged hams usually have only a fraction of the fat of whole hams and are labeled for fat content to eliminate guesswork.
- All cuts of veal are lean except veal cutlets (ground or cubed) and breast.
- The lean cuts of lamb are leg, arm, shank, and loin.
- Some wild game, such as venison and rabbit, is very lean. Some exotic "new" meats also low in fat are ostrich, emu, and buffalo.
- Processed meats should be eaten only if they contain no more than 10 percent fat or 3 grams of fat per ounce.

Lower in saturated fat than many cuts of red meat, poultry is popular and easy to prepare. These tips will guide you in buying poultry.

- Much of the fat in poultry is in the skin, so you need to remove the skin or buy skinless, boneless chicken and turkey.
- Skinless white chicken meat has half the fat of skinless dark meat.
- Goose, duck, and some poultry products are high in saturated fat.

- Some—but not all—commercial basting solutions in prebasted turkeys contain highly saturated fats. Even those that don't are usually high in sodium. You may prefer to baste your turkey with an unsalted broth.

Fresh fish is low in sodium, and it generally contains less saturated fat than red meat and about the same (or slightly less) cholesterol. That's why the AHA recommends that you eat fish at least two times a week. Here are some seafood facts.

- Some fish contain omega-3 fatty acids, which may be the element in fish that helps lower the risk of heart disease. Some fish high in omega-3 fatty acids are Atlantic and coho salmon, albacore tuna, mackerel, carp, lake whitefish, sweet smelt, and lake and brook trout.
- Fresh and frozen fish are good selections, as is tuna canned in distilled or spring water. Uncreamed or smoked herring and sardines, canned in tomato sauce or rinsed, are good choices. Generally, the whiter the fish, the lower the fat content.
- Shrimp, lobster, crab, crayfish, and most other shellfish are very low in fat. Shrimp and crayfish are higher in cholesterol than most other seafood, but lower in fat than most meats and poultry.

DAIRY PRODUCTS

Dairy products can play a major role in a prudent diet. Nonfat and low-fat versions of most dairy products except cheese are readily available. Most supermarkets carry reduced-fat cheeses, but fat-free cheeses are still limited. Look for cheese with 3 grams of fat or less per ounce. The hints below will help you choose dairy products.

- Although 2 percent milk is labeled "reduced-fat," it still contains almost half the fat of whole milk. Fat-free or ½ percent milk is much more suitable for a low-fat diet. Despite its name, most buttermilk is very low in fat.
- The most readily available types of nonfat cheese include Cheddar, mozzarella, American, and Swiss. Parmesan mixtures (called Italian topping or something similar), cottage cheese, and ricotta also come in fat-free versions. Creamy cheeses, such as Brie and processed cheese spreads, are high in saturated fat. Save them for rare occasions.
- You now have a wide selection of nonfat or low-fat dairy desserts: frozen and nonfrozen yogurt, ice cream, ice milk, and sherbet.
- Most nondairy coffee creamers and whipped toppings now come in nonfat or low-fat versions. Read labels carefully and avoid the products that are high in saturated fatty acids.

THE EGG AND YOU

One large egg yolk contains about 213 to 220 milligrams of cholesterol. That's two thirds of an entire day's allowance. It's a good idea to limit your egg yolk consumption, including egg yolks used in cooking. If you follow this suggestion, it will help you stay within the maximum of 300 milligrams of cholesterol a day.

On the other hand, egg whites contain no cholesterol and are an excellent, inexpensive source of protein. Simply discard the egg yolks, as you do the inedible parts of other natural foods, and use only the whites.

In many recipes, you can substitute egg whites for whole eggs. Use two egg whites for each whole egg called for. You can also use a commercial egg substitute.

It's never safe to eat raw eggs or egg whites.

FATS AND OILS

Polyunsaturated and monounsaturated oils are the kinds of fat you'll want to include in your daily diet. A reasonable total to aim for is 5 to 8 teaspoons of fat daily. This includes the hidden fat in baked and snack foods, as well as the fats used in cooking and the spreads you use on bread.

Pay close attention to the kinds of fat and oil in packaged foods. Look on the labels for the unsaturated oils that tend to lower blood cholesterol. The amount and the kinds of fat you consume are the major key to staying within AHA dietary guidelines and keeping your cholesterol low. (See pages 628–31 for a review.)

Selecting acceptable fats and oils is easy if you keep these things in mind.

- Buy margarine in place of butter. Always look for margarine with no more than 2 grams of saturated fat per tablespoon.
- Because diet or nonfat margarine contains water, it's often difficult to use for baking. However, it's very useful as a spread and in a number of cooking procedures.
- Select safflower, sunflower, corn, soybean, olive, or canola oil for your primary vegetable oil.
- Buy nonstick vegetable oil sprays to use in place of butter, margarine, or oil in cookware.
- Many commercial salad dressings contain large amounts of fat and salt. Try making your own salad dressings (see recipes pages 119–25), or use commercial nonfat or low-fat salad dressings.
- Because of their high fat content, most nuts and seeds, olives, peanut

butter, and avocado are listed in the category of fats. Because they are so high in calories, select them only occasionally.

- Chocolate, coconut, coconut oil, and palm kernel oil contain more saturated than unsaturated fat. When selecting commercial food items containing these ingredients, look for fatty acid information on the label. Select the foods with the lowest amounts of saturated fat, and use them in small quantities.

VEGETABLES AND FRUITS

Fresh vegetables and fruits have little or no fat, tend to be low in sodium, and, in most cases, are high in fiber and vitamins. By and large, you can eat them freely, with no concern about how they may affect your cholesterol.

The exceptions include coconut meat and avocados. Coconut meat is high in saturated fatty acids. Avocados are high in fat, although it's largely unsaturated. It's best to eat these foods in moderation.

In canning, packaging, and processing, however, many things can happen to fruits and vegetables. Not all of those changes are beneficial. When shopping, here are a few thoughts to keep in mind.

- Vegetables prepared with butter, cream, or whole-milk cheese can be high in fat.
- Fried vegetables have much more fat and many more calories than vegetables prepared without fat.
- Fruits that are fresh or canned in water are lower in calories than fruits canned in juice or in syrup. Drain fruits canned in syrup.
- Most calories in olives come from fat. Some brands of stuffed green olives are lower in fat than the plain ones. Green olives are high in sodium, and black olives are moderately high.
- Vegetables packed in brine, such as pickles and sauerkraut, are loaded with sodium. It helps to rinse them. Look for reduced-sodium pickles, too.

BREADS, CEREALS, PASTA, AND STARCHY VEGETABLES

One of the most encouraging facts about following a heart-healthy eating plan is that whole-grain or enriched breads, cereals, pastas, and starchy vegetables provide lots of nutrients, plenty of satisfying volume, and relatively few calories.

You can experiment enjoyably with different breads, such as whole or cracked wheat, rye, Italian, and pumpernickel. Although they contain some sodium and a small amount of fat, all are full of flavor and nutritive value.

Keep these tips in mind when shopping.

- Some commercially baked products (croissants, muffins, biscuits, and butter rolls) contain large amounts of saturated fat. It's much better to make your own.
- Check the labels on baked goods. If they're made with whole milk and dehydrated egg yolks, select them only occasionally.
- Some crackers are heavy in fats and oils, but stores also stock fat-free and reduced-fat varieties. Scandinavian-style rye crackers and other whole-grain crackers are often made without added fat or salt.
- For a low-sodium diet, use crackers with unsalted tops when recipes call for crackers or cracker crumbs. Nonfat saltines are also available.
- Cook brown rice, bulgur wheat, millet, or other whole grains in seasoned broth for a side dish or as part of an entrée. They're high in fiber, relatively low in calories, and economical.
- Substitute dried beans, peas, and lentils for meats in casseroles, stews, and soups. They're excellent, inexpensive protein sources.
- Hot cereals, rice, and pastas contain almost no sodium—if you cook them without salt.
- Most packaged dry cereals are low in saturated fat, but some contain salt. Check the nutrition label for calories and see whether the cereal contains a large quantity of sugar. (Sugar intake has not been directly linked to heart disease. However, the AHA recommends a diet moderate in sugar because the additional calories can lead to obesity, which is a risk factor.) In fact, always check the label and the ingredients list because some so-called natural cereals and granolas contain added salt, sugar, and saturated fat in the form of coconut or coconut oil.
- Look for reduced-salt versions of canned soups and canned vegetables.
- Look for canned or dehydrated varieties of soup with no more than 2 grams of fat per cup.

SNACKS

It's easier than ever before to indulge yourself with snacks occasionally and still stay within safe dietary limits. The best snacks are those that fit in with the Healthy Heart Food Pyramid (see page xvii).

A crisp red apple or a small dish of raspberry sorbet is refreshingly delicious. Sometimes, though, you just want a typical snack food. It's best to make it yourself, using acceptable oil or margarine. If you can't swing that, read the labels and select from the many good snack products in the supermarket. Here are a few other suggestions to keep in mind.

- Many nuts and seeds are available unsalted. They contain lots of fat, but it's mostly unsaturated. Still, the calorie count is high. If you're watching your weight, you may want to go easy on nuts and seeds.
- A growing number of prepared cookies and cakes are offered in reduced-fat versions. Some are actually fat free if you eat only one serving. Angel food cake is still fat free.
- You can make terrific sweets, using acceptable margarine or oil, nonfat milk, and egg substitute or egg whites.
- Some brands of baked tortilla chips have as little as 1 gram of fat per ounce (about nine chips), and many pretzels are fat free. Among fried chips, look for those with small amounts of saturated fat. It also helps to check the ingredients list for an acceptable vegetable oil listed first.

MISCELLANEOUS FOODS, FLAVORINGS, AND BEVERAGES

Lots of other foods can have more fat, calories, or sodium than you might expect. Again, read the labels and choose your foods carefully. Here are some helpful tips about miscellaneous foods.

- When your recipe calls for baking chocolate, substitute unsweetened cocoa powder and acceptable vegetable oil or margarine.
- Drink beverages that are low in sodium, fat, and cholesterol. Examples include fat-free milk and low-sodium fruit juices.
- If you're trying to lose weight, it won't help your cause to drink sugared carbonated sodas, syrupy fruit drinks, or beer, wine, or other alcoholic beverages. If you do drink alcohol, it's best to limit yourself to 1 to 2 ounces a day. Alcoholic drinks contain empty calories that can sabotage your healthy eating plan. Heavy alcohol consumption is associated with high blood pressure and other severe health problems. Alcohol can also relax your intent to control what you eat.
- If you're trying to cut down on salt, watch seasonings, condiments, and sauces that may contain a lot of sodium. These include soy sauce, steak sauce, ketchup, chili sauce, monosodium glutamate, meat tenderizer, relishes, flavored seasoning salts, bouillon cubes, and salad dressings. Many of these items are available in low-sodium versions.

COOKING FOR A HEALTHY HEART

Filling your grocery cart with healthful foods is just the beginning of the process. You want the low-fat foods you buy to stay that way until they reach your plate.

Some cooking methods add loads of fat to any food. Deep-fat frying is a good example. Other methods help retain vitamins and minerals and keep fat and calories low. These include roasting, baking, broiling, braising, poaching, sautéing, stir-frying, and microwaving.

The idea is to avoid cooking methods that add fat or let food cook in its own fat. Instead, look for techniques that enhance flavor and preserve nutrients. When adding fat and sodium, be miserly.

Here are some help-your-heart cooking techniques that will let you cook your favorite dishes so they'll give you the flavor without the fat.

ROASTING

A slow, dry-heat method of cooking, roasting creates a delicious product—and keeps fat to a minimum.

If you're preparing a roast, trim as much fat as you can, but leave a very thin covering of fat across the top. Simply season the meat, if desired, and cook it fat side up on a rack in an uncovered roasting pan. The rack keeps the meat from sitting in its own fat drippings. This method increases the fat drip-off. Some meats may require basting with a fat-free liquid, such as wine, tomato juice, or lemon juice. Remove the visible fat before eating the meat. (When roasting poultry, leave the skin on during cooking, then remove it.)

BAKING

Baking is another form of cooking that's excellent for poultry, seafood, and meat. It differs from roasting in two ways. You don't use a rack to allow juices to drain, and you sometimes use a covered container and add liquid before cooking. The liquid adds flavor and helps keep the meat moist.

BRAISING OR STEWING

Braising is great for tenderizing tougher cuts of meat. Brown the meat on all sides, using vegetable oil spray or a minimum of vegetable oil, or dredge the meat in seasoned flour. Add ¼ to ½ cup of liquid and whatever seasonings you wish, cover tightly, and simmer. For stewing, follow the same directions, but add water to cover.

The fat cooks out of the meat and into the liquid. It's a good idea to cook the meat a day ahead, then refrigerate it. This hardens the fat so you can remove it easily and lets the flavors intensify.

Braising is also an excellent way to cook vegetables.

POACHING

Poaching is cooking by immersing in simmering liquid. It works particularly well with chicken and seafood.

Place a single layer of food in a wide, shallow pan. Barely cover with liquid, such as water seasoned with spices and herbs, fat-free milk, low-sodium broth, or white wine. After cooking, you can reduce the liquid—lessen the volume by boiling the liquid rapidly—to intensify the flavor. You can thicken the reduced liquid to make a delicious sauce.

STEAMING

Food cooked in a basket over simmering water is just about perfect. It keeps its natural flavor, its color, and all its vitamins and minerals.

A steam cooker is ideal, but you can also use a steamer basket that fits into a pot with a tight-fitting lid. If you don't have a steamer rack, use a metal colander or anything else that will let the steam cook the food. Just be sure the water doesn't touch the food.

Steaming is great for vegetables and fish. Bring about an inch of water to a boil, then reduce the heat so the water simmers. Add herbs, spices, or broth to the water for extra flavor, put the food in the basket, and cover the pot. In just a few minutes, your food will be ready to eat. You can even use the liquid for soup stock.

SAUTÉING

Leave it to the French to invent a cooking method this wonderful! Just rub a little unsaturated oil on a sauté pan or skillet, use nonstick vegetable oil spray, or use a small amount of broth or wine. Add some herbs or spices to bring out the flavor. Cook meat, seafood, poultry, or vegetables, uncovered, over a medium to high temperature. Stir the food frequently to keep it from sticking. *Voilà!*

STIR-FRYING

This is the Asian version of sautéing. The idea is to cook food quickly in a minimum of oil or broth. The high temperature and the constant stirring keep the food from sticking and burning.

The key to successful stir-frying is to dice or slice each food into small pieces before you heat the oil in a wok or skillet. Use an oil that won't smoke at high temperatures. Peanut oil works best. Use only a small amount.

Because the hottest area is at the base of the wok, cook each food quickly there. Push that food up on the side of the wok while you cook the next one.

Stir-frying preserves the color, flavor, and crispness of vegetables. It also seals in the natural juices of meats and seafood.

When your recipe calls for soy sauce, use the low-sodium variety. This helps control the amount of sodium in your diet.

GRILLING OR BROILING

Placing food on a rack and cooking it over or under direct heat is an excellent way to help control the amount of fat in your diet. The fat drips away, either into the coals or into a broiling pan. Either way, much of the fat cooks out.

Skewered vegetables and chunks of meat taste great browned over a flame or under the broiler. Steaks, seafood, and poultry are ideal, too. For extra flavor, marinate these foods and then baste with the marinade during cooking. This keeps the food moist. But be careful: Always boil the marinade before using it for basting or as a sauce. Bacteria tend to grow in marinating meat mixtures, and boiling will kill the bacteria.

MICROWAVE COOKING

Microwaving is fast, easy, and so moisture-producing that it requires no added fats or oils. In fact, you can put some food between layers of paper towels so the fat drains as the food cooks.

You'll need to cook in glass, paper, dishwasher-safe plastic, china, or earthenware containers.

You can adapt conventional recipes for the microwave. Try to find a microwave recipe similar to the one you want to adapt. If you don't find one, cut the microwave cooking time to one fourth to one third of the conventional amount. Then, if the food isn't ready, continue cooking it for short periods. Refer to the manufacturer's instructions for guidance.

COOKING TIPS

Now that you know the basics of low-fat cooking, you're ready to specialize. We've compiled some specific fat-cutting techniques and some flavor-enhancing ideas you may want to try.

Meat Drippings

While meat is cooking, a rich essence drips into the roasting or broiler pan along with the fat. To keep the essence without the fat, refrigerate the contents of the pan—fat and all. The next day, you can easily remove the hardened fat, leaving only the flavorful juice. This juice adds zest to meat pies, soups, sauces, hash, or meat loaf.

Gravy

You don't have to add meat fat to have a wonderfully thick gravy. Try this one and see what we mean.

Pour ½ cup of clear, defatted broth into a jar with a tight-fitting lid. Add 1 tablespoon of cornstarch, 1 tablespoon of flour, or 1 to 2 tablespoons of browned flour. (Browned flour gives the sauce a rich mahogany color.) Shake until smooth. Heat an additional ½ cup broth in a saucepan. Shake and pour the cornstarch or flour mixture into the broth and simmer, adding seasonings as desired. Cook until the gravy is the consistency you want, whisking constantly.

Broth

Once you taste homemade broth, the canned or bouillon-cube varieties will seem tame by comparison. Just remember to make the broth a day ahead so you can remove the fat after it cools and hardens in the refrigerator. Use broth to make soups or stews, and be sure to defat the finished dish. If you do use canned broth, choose a low-sodium variety. You can refrigerate the can before opening, then remove the fat before using the broth.

Wine and Spirits

The wines and spirits you use for cooking don't have to be expensive, but they should be good to drink. Avoid using cooking wines, which are heavily laced with salt. Most alcohol evaporates during cooking, leaving the flavor and tenderizing qualities of the beverages.

Vinegar

Good wine vinegars and herb vinegars are delicious on salads. Vinegar also is flavorful in other recipes, even some desserts.

Whole-Grain Flour

Keep whole-grain flour in the refrigerator for freshness. You can substitute 1 cup of whole-wheat pastry flour for 1 cup of all-purpose flour, or 1 cup of whole-wheat flour for ⅞ cup of all-purpose flour.

Low-Fat Cooking Tips

Whether you want to lower your blood cholesterol level or lose weight, these cooking tips can make it easier.

- A nonstick skillet makes it possible to cook with vegetable oil spray or a minimum of oil. Be careful not to use spray near a heat source or open flame.
- Trim all visible fat from meat before cooking except when roasting.
- Buy only the leanest ground beef, pork, and turkey. After browning ground meat without other ingredients, put it in a colander and run hot water over it to get rid of some of the remaining fat.
- Ground meat is generally higher in fat than unground meat. To get the leanest ground beef possible, have the butcher grind a round steak for you. (Ask him or her to cut off the fat first and to clean the grinder to remove any fat from previous grindings.)
- Either buy skinless chicken parts or skin the chicken before cooking and remove all visible fat below the skin. Be sure to scrub the cutting surface and utensils well with hot, sudsy water after preparing poultry for cooking. You may roast a whole chicken or turkey with the skin on. Just be sure to remove skin before eating the poultry.
- Fresh fish should be cooked for about 10 minutes per inch of thickness. Add 5 minutes to the total figure if the fish is wrapped in foil. Frozen fish requires about 20 minutes per inch of thickness, plus 10 minutes if it's wrapped in foil. Cooking time may vary, depending on the cooking method used. Fish is done when the flesh is opaque and flakes easily when tested with a fork.
- Prepare scrambled eggs or omelets so that no more than 1 egg yolk per portion is used. Add extra egg whites to make more generous servings. Or use egg substitute.
- Drain and rinse canned salmon and sardines to remove oils or salty liquids.
- Cut down on cholesterol by using more vegetables and less poultry or meat in soups, stews, and casseroles. Finely chopped vegetables are great for stretching ground poultry or ground meat, too.

SAVOR THE FLAVOR!

Easy Flavor Enhancers

Look for easy, inexpensive (or free) ways to enhance the flavor of foods. Use your imagination to keep from feeling deprived. Here are some ideas to get you started.

- Seal natural juices into foods by wrapping the foods in aluminum foil before cooking. Or try wrapping foods in edible pouches made of steamed lettuce or cabbage leaves.

- Cook vegetables just until tender-crisp. Overcooked vegetables lose both flavor and important nutrients.
- Sweeten plain nonfat yogurt with pureed fruit, applesauce, or undiluted frozen orange juice. This will save you the extra sugar calories in some prepared fruit yogurts.

Spicing Up Low-Fat, Low-Sodium Cuisine

Just because you're cutting down on fat and salt doesn't mean your taste buds have to take a vacation. A creative cook can make low-fat, low-sodium cooking exciting, imaginative, and crowd-pleasing by experimenting with seasonings. Here are a few flavorful ideas to help spice up your everyday dishes as well as your treats for special occasions.

- Use fresh herbs whenever possible.
- Use fresh ginger and fresh horseradish for extra flavor. Grate fresh ginger with a flat, sheet-type grater. Use a food processor to grate fresh horseradish.
- Use citrus zest, the colored part of the peel without the pith. It holds the true flavor of the fruit. Remove it with a zester or a vegetable peeler or grate it.
- Toast seeds, nuts, and whole or ground spices to bring out their full flavor. Cook them in a dry skillet or bake them on a baking sheet.
- Roasting vegetables in a hot oven will caramelize their natural sugars and bring out their full flavor.
- Use vinegar or citrus juice as a wonderful flavor enhancer. Try vinegar on vegetables such as greens. Citrus juice works well on fruits such as melons. Either is great with fish.
- Use dry mustard for a zesty flavor in cooking, or mix it with water to make a very sharp condiment.
- Add fresh hot peppers for a little more "bite" in your dishes. (See Cook's Tip, page 115.)
- Some vegetables and fruits, such as mushrooms, tomatoes, chili peppers, cherries, cranberries, and currants, have a more intense flavor when dried than when fresh. Use them when you want a burst of flavor. As an added bonus, keep the flavored water they soaked in and use it for cooking.

HOW TO ADAPT RECIPES

We have filled this cookbook with recipes that are low in fat and high in flavor. Even with hundreds of new recipes to try, many of us still yearn to enjoy our favorite family recipes. What about Grandma's deep-dish peach cobbler, Aunt Mary's devil's food cake, or your own specialty of the house? What if they weren't exactly low in fat? Do you really have to give these up?

Absolutely not! The secret is learning to adapt them. Most dishes *can* be adapted to fit into a low-fat eating plan. This appendix will show you how.

It helps to use a three-step approach when adapting recipes. First, single out the "problem" ingredients—those high in total fat, saturated fat, cholesterol, or sodium. The next step is finding more healthful substitutes for these ingredients. Occasionally, an ingredient has to be left out. Other times, you can use less of the usual ingredient. Finally, you can change your method of food preparation. For example, if you're used to deep-fat frying, try broiling instead.

On the following pages we'll show you a sample recipe and the new low-fat version. We'll begin with Traditional Eggplant Parmesan and substitute fat-free or low-fat ingredients. The analysis for each recipe shows how dramatic the differences are in calories, total fat, and saturated fat.

ANALYSIS: HOW WE ADAPTED OUR RECIPE

Our first low-fat technique was simple. We reduced the huge amount of olive oil and omitted the butter. Then instead of frying the eggplant, we broiled it, using no fat. In the process, we also dropped the eggs.

Next we reduced the serving size to a reasonable amount.

We added a generous helping of fresh mushrooms to enrich the flavor. Fresh garlic also adds more interest. Finally, we used fat-free instead of whole-milk mozzarella and used less of both cheeses.

To reduce the sodium we cut the salt in half and dropped the garlic salt. We dropped the high-sodium bread crumbs and added salt-free Italian herb seasoning. We substituted no-salt-added tomato sauce for the high-sodium canned tomatoes.

Once you get the hang of adapting recipes, you'll see that it's easy. Also, there's always room for creativity. Ultimately, you'll have the best of all worlds: great food, wonderful taste, and a diet to help you stay well.

Traditional Eggplant Parmesan

Serves 6

¼ cup olive oil
1 cup chopped onions
1 clove garlic, minced
5 cups chopped canned tomatoes, drained
¼ teaspoon dried basil, crumbled
½ teaspoon salt
¼ teaspoon pepper
2 medium eggplants
2 large eggs, beaten
¼ teaspoon dried oregano, crumbled
¼ teaspoon garlic salt
4 cups Italian-style dry bread crumbs
1½ cups olive oil
Olive oil spray
6 ounces sliced mozzarella cheese
1 cup grated Parmesan cheese
1 tablespoon butter

In a large skillet, sauté onions and garlic in ¼ cup oil over medium-high heat. Stir in tomatoes, basil, salt, and pepper. Simmer, uncovered, 30 minutes, stirring occasionally.

Meanwhile, in a medium bowl, beat eggs with oregano and garlic salt. Put bread crumbs in a large plate. Peel eggplants and cut into ⅓-inch slices. Pat with paper towels to remove moisture. Dip into crumbs, egg mixture, and crumbs.

In a large skillet, heat 1½ cups oil over medium-high heat. Fry eggplant, turning once, until brown on both sides.

Meanwhile, preheat oven to 325° F. Spray a large baking dish with olive oil spray. Alternate layers of eggplant, tomato mixture, and cheeses; dot with butter. Bake for 30 minutes.

Calories 668
Protein 29 g
Carbohydrate 77 g
Cholesterol 111 mg
Total fat 29 g
 Saturated fat 10 g
 Polyunsaturated fat 2 g
 Monounsaturated fat 11 g
Fiber 9 g
Sodium 2,184 mg

In regard to the nutritional analysis, data is not available on how much oil the eggplant absorbs, so the analysis doesn't include the 1½ cups of oil used in frying. It includes only the amount of fat that we know is consumed. The actual total would be somewhat higher.

Eggplant Parmesan

Serves 6

Olive oil spray

1 eggplant (about 1½ pounds)

1 teaspoon olive oil

8 ounces fresh mushrooms, sliced (2 to 2½ cups)

1 cup chopped onions (2 medium)

3 or 4 medium cloves garlic, minced, or 1½ to 2 teaspoons bottled minced garlic

½ teaspoon salt-free dried Italian herb seasoning, crumbled

¼ teaspoon salt

Pepper to taste

8-ounce can no-salt-added tomato sauce

4 ounces fat-free or part-skim mozzarella cheese, shredded (1 cup)

1 ounce (¼ cup) grated or shredded Parmesan cheese

Preheat broiler. Spray a baking sheet, 13 × 9 × 2-inch baking pan, and 11 × 15-inch piece of aluminum foil with olive oil spray.

Peel eggplant and cut crosswise into ¼-inch slices. Put on baking sheet and broil 6 inches from heat for 2 to 3 minutes on each side. Remove from broiler and set oven to 375° F.

Heat oil in a large nonstick skillet over medium heat, swirling to coat bottom. Add mushrooms, onions, garlic, herb seasoning, and salt. Cook, covered, for 7 to 9 minutes, stirring occasionally. Increase heat to high and cook, uncovered, for 2 to 3 minutes, or until pan juices have evaporated, stirring frequently.

Spread 1 cup mushroom mixture in baking pan. Cover with half of eggplant slices. Sprinkle with pepper. Top with ½ cup tomato sauce and half the mozzarella. Repeat layers except cheese. Cover with prepared foil.

Bake for 1 hour. Top with remaining mozzarella and all the Parmesan. Bake, uncovered, for 5 to 8 minutes, or until cheese is melted. Cool for at least 10 minutes before cutting.

Calories 118
Protein 10 g
Carbohydrate 15 g
Cholesterol 5 mg
Total fat 3 g
  Saturated fat 1 g
  Polyunsaturated fat 0 g
  Monounsaturated fat 1 g
Fiber 5 g
Sodium 372 mg

MENUS FOR HOLIDAYS, SPECIAL OCCASIONS, AND EVERY DAY

Dishes served at holidays and celebrations are traditionally high in fat and calories. More people are tempted to overeat on these special occasions than at any other time.

The good news is that special-occasion food doesn't have to harm your health to be special. You can take control of your holiday fare. Set a table that's not only beautiful and taste-tempting but low in fat and calories, too. Mix attractive colors, blend flavors, and choose textures that create an appealing contrast. Since more people are opting for lighter cuisine, you'll find that your guests will appreciate your efforts.

We've developed the following menus to help you plan holiday and special-occasion meals, as well as "regular" meals, using recipes found in this cookbook. Feel free to mix and match these menus to suit your own taste. With a little creativity and skill, you can make each occasion an affair to remember.

NEW YEAR'S DAY BRUNCH

Country-Style Breakfast Casserole
Sliced Tomatoes*
Southern Raised Biscuits
Claret-Spiced Oranges

CHINESE NEW YEAR

Lemongrass-Lime Baked Chicken
Asian Coleslaw
Fresh Green Beans with Water Chestnuts
Baked Ginger Pears

APRÈS SKI DINNER

Chicken Stew with Cornmeal Dumplings
Steamed Broccoli*
Special Baked Apples

VALENTINE'S DINNER FOR TWO

Linguine with White Clam Sauce
Dilled Green Beans
Cold-Oven Popovers
Chocolate Swirl Cheesecake

* Recipes not included.

SNOWY-NIGHT DINNER

European Cabbage and White Bean Soup
Apple and Orange Slices*
Whole-Wheat French Bread
Pumpkin Spice Cupcakes with Nutmeg Cream Topping

LOW-FAT TUESDAY

Crispy Cajun Catfish Nibbles with Red Sauce
Steamed Green Beans*
Baked Fries with Creole Seasoning
Apple Raisin Crunch

ST. PATRICK'S DAY SUPPER

Lamb Stew
Tossed Salad Greens* with Creamy Chef's Dressing
Irish Soda Bread
Crustless Apple Pie

EASTER DINNER

Crumb-Crusted Mushrooms with Lemon
Lamb Chops Dijon
Hot and Spicy Watercress and Romaine Salad
Steamed Carrots*
Savory Peas
Yogurt Dinner Rolls
Angel Food Layers with Chocolate Custard and Kiwifruit

CINCO DE MAYO FIESTA

Beef Tostadas
Raw Vegetables* with Salsa Cruda
Zesty Corn Relish
Tequila Lime Sherbet

KENTUCKY DERBY DINNER

Crispy Baked Chicken
Parsley Potato Salad
Deviled Beets
Mint Julep Fruit Cup

MOTHER'S DAY BREAKFAST

Apple Oatmeal Pancake
Turkey Sausage Patties
Sparkling Cranberry Cooler

MEMORIAL DAY PICNIC

Southwestern Turkey Wraps
Tabbouleh
Assorted Chilled Melon Slices*
Fudgy Buttermilk Brownies

POST-TENNIS LUNCH

Cucumber Watercress Soup
Asian Chicken and Rice Salad
Fat-Free Wheat Crackers*
Strawberry-Banana Sorbet with Star Fruit

FATHER'S DAY DINNER

French-Style Braised Fish Fillets
Marinated Asparagus, Tomato, and Hearts of Palm Salad
Steamed Rice*
French Peas
Peach Clafouti

FOURTH OF JULY BARBECUE

Spicy Grilled Chicken
Tomato-Basil Salad with Balsamic Dressing
Grilled Zucchini*
Caramelized Onions
Sunny Mango Sorbet

* Recipes not included.

DINNER FOR A BUSY DAY

Island Chicken Salad with Fresh Mint
Chilled Asparagus Soup
Multigrain Rolls*

VEGETARIAN FEAST

Minted Cantaloupe Soup with Fresh Lime
Spinach Roll with Alfredo Sauce
Sliced Tomatoes, Carrots, and Cucumbers*
Muffins
Chocolate Chess Pie

SUMMER CELEBRATION

Red Snapper à l'Orange
Asparagus with Garlic and Parmesan Bread Crumbs
Celery Sticks and Cherry Tomatoes*
Chilled Melon Slices with Citrus Marinade

LABOR DAY PICNIC

Artichoke and Chick-Pea Pilaf
Spinach Salad with Kiwifruit and Raspberries
Peanut Butter Cookies

BACK-TO-SCHOOL BREAKFAST

Breakfast Pizzas
Assorted Fresh Fruit*

AFTER THE FOOTBALL GAME

Slow-Cooker White Chili
Confetti Coleslaw
Herb Cheese Bread
Fall Fruit Medley

HALLOWEEN SUPPER

Savory Beef Stew
Drop Biscuits
Easy Apple Cake

THANKSGIVING DINNER

Flavorful Tomato Bouillon
Roast Turkey*
Basic Gravy
Apple Dressing
Steamed Broccoli*
Cranberry Orange Salad
Easy Refrigerator Rolls
Pumpkin Pie

HANUKKAH DINNER

Carrot, Parsnip, and Potato Pancakes
Stuffed Cornish Hens with Orange-Brandy Sauce
Vegetable Medley with Lemon Sauce
Deep-Dish Fruit Crisp

CHRISTMAS BUFFET DINNER PARTY

Fillet of Beef with Herbes de Provence
Rice Pilaf
Crunchy Broccoli Casserole
Baked Curried Fruit
Chocolate Mousse in Meringue Shells

KWANZAA SUPPER

Savory Black-Eyed Peas and Pasta
Tangy Cucumbers
Swiss Chard, Southern Style
Cornmeal Bread
Guiltless Banana Pudding

* Recipes not included.

QUICK AND EASY FOODS

Sometimes the last thing you want to do on a busy day is cook. But you're determined to control the fat and calories that you're getting in food—and that usually means preparing food at home. We have some ideas for dealing with this dilemma.

One suggestion is to go grocery shopping only once a week. In addition to saving time, it will encourage you to at least roughly plan your daily menus instead of just grabbing whatever's handy. That way, you can have more control over what you eat—and you're at the mercy of the fast-food restaurant down the street less often.

Another suggestion is to try cooking in quantity. Instead of one casserole, make two. Enjoy one right away and freeze one to use later. Let the second one thaw overnight in the refrigerator, then reheat part of it for your own nutritious version of fast food during the week. Soups, spaghetti sauce, meat and poultry dishes, and breads also freeze well, so keep one of these "aces" in your freezer for those evenings when you just don't feel like cooking. Preparing a roast, chicken, or turkey is another way to provide several family meals, including some delicious lunchbox sandwiches.

Have a marathon session during the weekend to cook and freeze food for the entire week. That not only helps control the fat and calories you consume but also makes cooking for the rest of the week a breeze!

A little advance preparation can cut cooking time way down. For example, make rice in large quantities and serve it with stir-fried vegetables and meats several times during the week. Clean and store salad greens in a plastic container with a tight-fitting lid—they'll stay fresh and crisp for a week.

Here are more time-saving ideas. Work them into your routine and see how much you can cut down your cooking time!

- Organize your kitchen. Arrange foods, utensils, and equipment so you can cook quickly and efficiently.
- Make sure your pantry, refrigerator, and freezer are stocked with easy-to-fix foods, such as canned and frozen vegetables, lean ground beef, fish fillets, and chicken.
- Keep a running shopping list so you can jot down needed items as you think of them.

- Before cooking, think through the ingredients and preparation steps.
- Assemble equipment and ingredients before you begin cooking.
- Make one-dish meals to save cleanup time.
- If you're making a complex dish, prepare simple foods to go with it. For example, if your entrée needs a lot of attention, fix a simple salad. If your entrée is simple, create an interesting side dish.
- Enlist members of your family to help with the cooking, table setting, or cleaning up.
- Cook vegetables in the microwave. It usually saves time, retains nutrients, and maximizes flavor. Microwaving is also great for heating leftover vegetables.
- Try microwave or quick stovetop versions of dishes you usually bake.
- Use other labor-saving devices, such as a food processor, convection oven, pressure cooker, or slow cooker.
- Cut down on food-transfer and cleanup time by using cookware in which food can be cooked, served, and stored.

In this cookbook we've included lots of recipes you can put together quickly. They're nutritious, low in fat and calories, and packed with taste and texture. Some of these recipes are listed below. Using them and others in the cookbook, you can whip up nutritious meals in no time! Notice that you need to make some of these ahead of time for chilling, marinating, or blending of flavors.

APPETIZERS AND SNACKS

Want a quick snack or an appetizer for a party? Here are some ideas.

- Southwestern Turkey Wraps (see page 229)—These will bring you rave reviews.
- Cucumber and Yogurt Dip (see page 8)—It's low in calories but high in taste. Serve with a tray of raw vegetables.
- Pita Crisps (see page 32)—Make these healthful chips in quantity and store them in a plastic freezer bag. They're good with Cucumber and Yogurt Dip.
- Curry Yogurt Dip (see page 8)—It's as simple as mixing together Yogurt Cheese, fat-free mayonnaise, and curry powder. (Make the Yogurt Cheese [see page 16] ahead of time.)
- Fire-and-Ice Cream Cheese Spread (see page 12)—This is quick, but you need to make it ahead of time to chill the cheese and cool the sauce.

SOUPS

Soup is a year-round favorite. Team it with a fresh green salad, a nonfat or low-fat cheese, and fruit for dessert. Try these quick and easy favorites.

- Tomato Corn Soup (see page 52)—An herb mixture heightens the flavor in this combination of canned tomatoes and cream-style corn.
- Greek Egg Lemon Soup (see page 42)—This soup tastes very rich but actually is light. Fresh lemon juice adds zip.
- Any-Season Fruit Soup (see page 56)—Made with dried prunes, apricots, and raisins, this soup cooks quickly and is equally good hot or chilled.
- Spinach Pasta Soup (see page 49)—The tiny pasta in this soup cooks in about 5 minutes.
- Spicy Chick-Pea and Chayote Soup (see page 61)—If you have some leftover chicken or turkey, you can make this dish in no time at all.
- Gazpacho (see page 53)—Just put all the ingredients into a food processor or blender, and you have soup in seconds.
- Five-Minute Soup (see page 56)—It really is! This is a good dish for leftover chicken.
- Minted Cantaloupe Soup with Fresh Lime (see page 58)—A food processor special with a light, fresh taste.

SALADS AND SALAD DRESSINGS

Just about everyone loves a well-prepared salad. It's a quick side dish, and it's great when you're counting calories. Consider taking an extra 5 to 10 minutes to make your own salad dressing. The results are more than worth the small investment of time.

- Tangy Cucumbers (see page 86)—Sweet-and-sour cucumbers go together in a flash. They need to marinate for at least 1 hour.
- Hot and Spicy Watercress and Romaine Salad (see page 73)—An eclectic salad, this combines a decidedly Asian dressing with watercress, romaine, radishes, and Mexican jícama.
- Chilled Melon Slices with Citrus Marinade (see page 91)—As soon as cantaloupe comes into season, rush to try this so-easy salad.
- Cranberry Orange Salad (see page 93)—A gelatin salad with a tangy holiday taste, it looks festive on a bed of romaine or green leaf lettuce.
- Carrot Salad with Jícama and Pineapple (see page 90)—A new take on a classic.
- Tomato-Basil Salad with Balsamic Dressing (see page 84)—No other salad is easier!

- Zesty Tomato Dressing (see page 119)—Put all the ingredients in a jar, shake, and serve.

SEAFOOD

Tender, flaky fish and shellfish cook in less than 10 minutes—and preparation time is even shorter. Here are some sample recipes.

- Baked Catfish (see page 142)—Dip catfish into a mixture of buttermilk, whole-wheat crackers, and hot-pepper sauce, then bake it. Dinner's ready!
- Oven-Fried Scallops with Cilantro and Lime (see page 166)—Another buttermilk coating, this time with cilantro and lime.
- Ginger Broiled Fish (see page 129)—Fresh gingerroot, white wine, green onions, soy sauce, and horseradish make a very interesting sauce.
- Grilled Salmon Oriental (see page 151)—Allow time for the marinade to develop its exotic flavor.
- Red Snapper à l'Orange (see page 149)—Prepare a vegetable and a salad while the red snapper bakes.
- Tuna Salad (see page 161)—An easy way to add new life to tuna salad.

POULTRY

Hundreds of taste-tempting recipes call for poultry—and many of them are so easy. Here are some excellent examples.

- Lemon-Herb Roast Chicken (see page 171)—A year-round favorite. After minimal preparation time, let the chicken bake while you do other things. Cook a larger chicken than you need so you'll have enough for "planned-overs."
- Chicken Curry in a Hurry (see page 222)—Here's where you can use that leftover chicken. Put this dish together in about 15 minutes.
- Chicken Philippine Style (see page 181)—Cleanup is a snap.
- Burgundy Chicken with Mushrooms (see page 194)—This dish tastes "fancy," but it's easy to put together and cooks quickly in one skillet.
- Broiled Chicken with Hoisin-Barbecue Sauce (see page 198)—Skewered chicken in a spicy sauce is served with green peas and rice flavored with turmeric. There's also a variation with a curried sweet-and-sour sauce.
- Spicy Grilled Chicken (see page 202)—Allow 2 to 3 hours to marinate. Then pop it onto the grill at dinnertime. It'll be ready for your plate in about 15 minutes. This recipe makes enough to use for Chicken Fajitas for another meal.

- Chicken Fajitas (see page 213)—Once again, your great planning has paid off. Cook some onions and bell pepper, heat the chicken and the tortillas, and add toppings. Olé!
- Slow-Cooker White Chili (see page 224)—Put this together before you go to work, and dinner will be almost ready when you get home.

MEATS

Lean meats are easy to prepare, too. You'll find all sorts of simple recipes that will make mealtime a snap!

- Beef and Pasta Skillet (see page 267)—An old favorite reduced in fat and cholesterol but not in flavor.
- Beef Tostadas (see page 275)—Crispy tortillas with seasoned ground beef, salsa, cheese, lettuce, and tomatoes—all the usual ingredients but without the fat.
- Pepper-Coated Steak (see page 245)—This is as elegant as it is easy.
- Philadelphia-Style Cheese Steak Wrap (see page 262)—Strips of marinated eye of round are wrapped in flour tortillas with nonfat Cheddar cheese and sautéed onion and bell pepper.
- Portobello Mushrooms and Sirloin Strips over Spinach Pasta (see page 252)—Allow at least 30 minutes for marinating.
- Orange Pork Medallions (see page 287)—Try this taste-tempting sliced pork tenderloin in spicy orange sauce.
- Rosemary-Sage Steak (see page 246)—The preparation and broiling times are quick, but you'll need to marinate the meat for at least 1 hour.
- Veal with Bell Peppers and Mushrooms (see page 296)—Veal scallops cook on the stove with red bell pepper strips and mushroom pieces.

VEGETARIAN ENTREÉS

More people are turning to meatless meals—sometimes as often as several times a week. These recipes will prove that going meatless can be a great way to cut down on saturated fat and cholesterol.

- Pasta Primavera (see page 306)—This dish is full of tender, crisp vegetables. You'll have it ready in 20 minutes.
- Portobello Wrap with Yogurt Curry Sauce (see page 316)—Wrap grilled portobellos, aromatic rice, cheese, and asparagus in tortillas. Serve the wraps with creamy curry sauce. It's a yummy combination.
- Hoppin' John (see page 322)—Prepare seasoned black-eyed peas while the rice cooks.
- Stuffed Peppers (see page 319)—Filled with a taste-tempting combination of sautéed vegetables.

- Artichoke and Chick-Pea Pilaf (see page 323)—While the sun-dried tomatoes soak and the quinoa cooks, you'll have time to get all the other ingredients ready.
- Artichoke-Tomato Pizza Bagels (see page 305)—Quick and tasty pizza.
- Sesame-Peanut Pasta (see page 313)—Serve this Thai-flavored dish hot or cold.

VEGETABLES AND SIDE DISHES; SAUCES

We've come up with a host of delicious recipes whose fresh vegetables, spices, and herbs can be whipped together before you can spell "asparagus." You'll also find many easy sauces, one of which is listed below, to add sparkle to your vegetables.

- Scalloped Squash (see page 416)—Sautéed in a skillet with fresh herbs and broth, it's a side dish ready in minutes.
- Savory Peas (see page 394)—Flavor green peas with lower-sodium bacon and nutmeg.
- Tangy Carrots (see page 373)—Mustard and lime furnish the tang in this unusual recipe.
- Asparagus par Excellence (see page 355)—This attractive dish features frozen asparagus with bell pepper, pimiento, tarragon, and parsley.
- Cajun Corn (see page 380)—A spicy change from "plain" corn.
- Dilled Green Beans (see page 358)—Use frozen green beans for this dish. Give them lots of flavor with vegetable broth, dill seeds, bell pepper, and onion.
- Savory Spinach (see page 411)—Canadian bacon, horseradish, rice vinegar, and soy sauce provide frozen spinach with lots of zest.
- Mock Hollandaise Sauce (see page 443)—A great sauce for vegetables, it has all the taste of the real thing.

BREADS

If you think homemade bread always takes hours to prepare, think again. Some of our most delicious bread recipes can be put together quickly.

- Orange Pull-Apart Breakfast Bread (see page 496)—Cut refrigerator biscuits in pieces, add sugar and spices, then bake. You'll soon have a delicious layered treat.
- Nutmeg Bread (see page 485)—Ready in about an hour, it's a family favorite that also makes a great gift.
- Easy Refrigerator Rolls (see page 500)—You make the dough ahead of time and refrigerate it. Then, when you want homemade yeast rolls,

these cook in minutes. (They do have to rise for 2 hours before baking, however.)

- Savory Bread (see page 497)—Take your favorite French or Italian bread and season it according to our directions. Invest a few minutes, and you have a delicious hot bread.
- Southern-Style Corn Bread and its variation, Mexican-Style Corn Bread (see page 498)—They're low in fat, and like most other corn bread recipes, they're easy to make and quick to bake.
- Oat Bran Fruit Muffins (see page 513)—Make them ahead, and have some for breakfast or as an afternoon snack. It doesn't take long to prepare these treats.

DESSERTS

Not all desserts are fancy and time-consuming to make. Try these tempting dishes to see what we mean.

- Delicious Rice Pudding (see page 596)—Just combine all the ingredients in a casserole dish and bake for 1 hour.
- Honey Almond Custards (see page 589)—Made with fat-free milk, honey, and egg substitute, this simple dessert will be a favorite.
- Easy Apple Cake (see page 539)—A cake made from scratch that's almost as easy as using a mix. It's packed with apples and raisins.
- Wacky Cake (see page 538)—Mix the batter in the baking pan, pop it into the oven, and dessert is ready in no time.
- Cardinal Sundae (see page 623)—Combine frozen raspberries and strawberries for a tasty sauce to top lime sherbet.
- Chocolate Oatmeal Cookies (see page 572)—This classic lunchbox dessert is about as basic and easy as a recipe can get. The cookies are a hit with kids and adults alike.

BREAKFAST FOODS

Think you don't have time to make breakfast? Yes, you do!

- Cinnamon French Toast (see page 522)—It's not only easy, but it's also low in fat.
- Cottage Cheese and Cinnamon Toasty and its variation, Cottage Cheese and Peach Toasty (see page 523)—They don't take much longer than toast and supply part of your daily protein.

PLANNED-OVERS

When you prepare a dinner entrée, it's often just as easy to make extra. The suggestions that follow take that idea one more step. They use the "leftovers" in specific recipes designed around them, thus the name "planned-overs." When the week gets hectic, you'll really be glad you planned ahead.

- Triple-Pepper Chicken
- Cajun Chicken Salad

A spice rub of black pepper, lemon pepper, and cayenne, plus chili powder, lime, and other flavorful ingredients, heats up chicken breasts for one dinner. Save half the recipe for a speedy salad of mixed greens, roasted red bell peppers, mushrooms, and low-fat cheese to enjoy a few days later.

- Sweet-Spice Glazed Chicken
- Island Chicken Salad with Fresh Mint

First, have a meal of broiled chicken breasts with an incredible glaze of sweet-and-sour sauce. Then, in a flash, create a beautiful salad with mango and kiwifruit for a change of pace.

- Glazed Meatballs on Water Chestnut and Bell Pepper Rice
- Vegetarian Stir-Fry

Prepare glazed meatballs with orange zest and crushed red pepper flakes and serve them for one meal over rice flavored with bell peppers and water chestnuts. Transform the extra rice from this meat-based meal into a totally different entrée by adding fresh gingerroot and stir-fried cabbage, carrots, and bamboo shoots.

- Mexican Chicken and Vegetables with Chipotle Peppers
- Chipotle Chicken Wraps

Start with a stew of chicken, bell peppers, tomatoes, and chipotle peppers. The planned-overs entrée is the chicken mixture rolled in flour tortillas along with sour cream, cilantro, olives, and lime juice.

- Grilled Lemongrass Flank Steak
- Grilled Flank Steak Salad with Sweet-and-Sour Sesame Dressing

Marinate flank steak in a mixture of lemongrass, rice vinegar, and chili garlic sauce, and serve it hot off the grill. Plan to use part of the steak later in a salad of colorful vegetables, wild rice, and napa cabbage, topped with an Asian-inspired dressing.

CHOLESTEROL AND HEART DISEASE

High blood cholesterol is a major risk factor for coronary heart disease, most of which is caused by atherosclerosis. Atherosclerosis can also lead to stroke, peripheral artery disease (in the legs), and kidney disease.

Atherosclerosis is a slowly developing process in which fats and cholesterol, combined with other substances in the bloodstream, build up in the inner lining of the arteries. We once thought this happened only in older people, but now we know it often starts in childhood. Studies have detected the beginning of atherosclerotic changes in the arteries of people in their early 20s, sometimes even in their teens.

Over many years, this buildup forms plaque that damages the artery walls. It eventually begins to block the flow of blood and oxygen to the heart, brain, or other areas. An artery can close off completely if the plaque bursts or a blood clot stops up the narrowed passage. When this happens in a coronary artery supplying the heart muscle, it causes a heart attack. If it happens in an artery supplying the brain, it causes a stroke. A blockage in a leg artery can lead to gangrene, or the kidneys can shut down as a result of blocked blood vessels feeding those organs.

CHOLESTEROL AND HEART ATTACK

A high level of cholesterol in the blood is a powerful indicator of the risk of heart attack. Other major risk factors include high blood pressure, cigarette smoking, physical inactivity, obesity, and diabetes. What and how much you eat have a bearing on several of these, but no risk factor is more closely related to diet than high blood cholesterol.

Countless scientific studies have produced overwhelming evidence that high blood cholesterol increases the danger of heart and blood vessel disease. These studies also strongly suggest that reducing the blood cholesterol level will reduce the risk of heart attack. People with high cholesterol simply have more heart attacks and are more likely to die of heart disease than people with low cholesterol.

Men have a greater risk than women, and they develop heart disease earlier in life. In both sexes, the longer the atherosclerotic process caused by high blood cholesterol continues, the higher the risk. But heart attack doesn't affect only middle-aged or older men. It can also affect women, especially after menopause. After menopause, a woman who has a heart attack is less likely to survive than a man.

Heart attack risk is also greater in younger people with hereditary high cholesterol.

Even people with only mildly elevated blood cholesterol are at somewhat higher risk. And research now shows that people with a desirable blood cholesterol level also can benefit from lowering their cholesterol.

UNDERSTANDING THE RISK

Health authorities now agree that everyone age 20 and older should have his or her cholesterol checked. This is done by means of a simple blood test in which cholesterol is measured in milligrams per deciliter of blood (mg/dl). The table below classifies total blood cholesterol levels as they relate to the risk of heart disease, using guidelines established by the National Cholesterol Education Program of the National Heart, Lung, and Blood Institute.

CLASSIFICATION BASED ON TOTAL CHOLESTEROL

Cholesterol Level	Classification
Less than 200 mg/dl	Desirable
200 to 239 mg/dl	Borderline high
240 mg/dl or greater	High

Most heart attacks in middle age and later in life are linked to long-term high blood cholesterol levels. How do our blood cholesterol levels get too high? Genetic factors can certainly play a part. Most high blood cholesterol levels, however, result from our dietary habits.

We get blood cholesterol from two primary sources. One is the cholesterol in the foods we eat. The other is the body, which also manufactures cholesterol. When we eat saturated fat, the body increases its cholesterol production. Current evidence indicates that more of the harm within the arteries is done by cholesterol manufactured from saturated fat than by cholesterol in the diet.

The bottom line is this:

Eating foods high in cholesterol increases blood cholesterol levels.

Eating foods high in saturated fat increases blood cholesterol levels.

GOOD CHOLESTEROL VS. BAD

Total blood cholesterol is important, but scientists now know that assessing a person's relative risk involves other factors, too. Where is the cholesterol going? What is happening to it? Different types of particles carry cholesterol through the blood. Cholesterol is not soluble in water. To be carried through the bloodstream, it has to be encased in a water-soluble particle called a lipoprotein. Cholesterol attached to some lipoproteins appears to be a threat to our health, but some lipoproteins may actually help safeguard it.

Lipoproteins are tiny spheres with an outer coat of protein and triglycerides. Most fats are in the chemical form of triglycerides—both body fat and most of the fat we eat. Lipoproteins differ in density and the amounts of cholesterol, triglycerides, and protein they contain. They fall into four groups—chylomicrons, very low density lipoproteins (VLDLs), low-density lipoproteins (LDLs), and high-density lipoproteins (HDLs).

Chylomicrons and VLDLs mostly carry triglycerides. After the triglycerides are removed, the remaining lipoprotein parts are further broken down to produce LDLs. These LDLs are identified as "bad" because they carry the cholesterol that is likely to be laid down in the artery walls. Scientists now believe that when LDLs combine with oxygen (are oxidized), it is relatively easy for them to enter artery walls and build up atherosclerotic plaque there. Antioxidants in the blood, such as vitamins C and E, may prevent the oxidation of LDLs and thus prevent plaque from forming. Perhaps you have seen articles saying these vitamins may help prevent heart disease and stroke.

The AHA does not advocate the use of vitamin supplements. We do advocate taking in many natural antioxidants through consuming a variety of fruits, vegetables, and whole grains. Plants contain a variety of beneficial substances, many of which presumably have not yet been identified.

HDLs, meanwhile, carry one third to one fourth of the blood cholesterol. They are considered "good" because they seem to protect against heart attack by clearing fat from the bloodstream and removing excess cholesterol to the liver for disposal. A high level of LDL cholesterol in the total cholesterol reading increases the risk of heart attack, and a level of HDL cholesterol below 40 mg/dl may further add to the risk.

If you are interested in finding out more about the science related to atherosclerosis, coronary heart disease, and stroke, visit the AHA's website at http//www.americanheart.org.

b

C

h

p

S

V